# Psychological Dynamics of Sport and Exercise

## Second Edition

**Diane L. Gill, PhD**

**University of North Carolina, Greensboro**

Human Kinetics

**Library of Congress Cataloging-in-Publication Data**

Gill, Diane L., 1948-
    Psychological dynamics of sport and exercise / Diane L. Gill.--2nd ed.
        p. cm.
    Rev. Ed. of: Psychological dynamics of sport. c1986
    Includes bibliographical references (p.  ) and index.
    ISBN 0-87322-956-8
    1. Sports--Psychological aspects.   2. Exercise--Psychological aspects.   3. Motivation
(Psychology)   I. Gill, Diane L., 1948-  Psychological dynamics of sport.   II. Title.

GV706.4.G55 2000
796'.01--dc21

                                                            99-057712

ISBN: 0-87322-956-8

Copyright © 2000, 1986 by Diane L. Gill

This book is a revised edition of *Psychological Dynamics of Sport,* published in 1986 by Human Kinetics.

**Developmental Editor:** Lynn Hooper-Davenport; **Assistant Editors:** Derek Campbell, Melissa Feld, Susan Hagan, and Laurie Stokoe; **Copyeditor:** Joyce Sexton; **Proofreader:** Jim Burns; **Indexer:** Betty Frizzell; **Permission Manager:** Heather Munson; **Graphic Designer:** Stuart Cartwright; **Graphic Artist:** Kathleen Boudreau-Fuoss; **Photo Editor:** Clark Brooks; **Cover Designer:** Robert Reuther; **Photographer (interior):** Tom Roberts (except where otherwise noted); **Illustrators:** Tim Offenstein and Jennifer Delmotte; **Printer:** Versa Press; **Binder:** Dekker

Printed in the United States of America

10 9 8 7 6 5 4 3 2 1

**Human Kinetics**
Web site: http://www.humankinetics.com/

*United States:* Human Kinetics
P.O. Box 5076
Champaign, IL 61825-5076
1-800-747-4457
e-mail: humank@hkusa.com

*Canada:* Human Kinetics
475 Devonshire Road Unit 100
Windsor, ON N8Y 2L5
1-800-465-7301 (in Canada only)
e-mail: humank@hkcanada.com

*Europe:* Human Kinetics, P.O. Box IW14
Leeds LS16 6TR, United Kingdom
+44 (0)113-278 1708
e-mail: humank@hkeurope.com

57A Price Avenue
Lower Mitcham, South Australia 5062
(08) 82771555
e-mail: liahka@senet.com.au

*New Zealand:* Human Kinetics
P.O. Box 105-231, Auckland Central
09-523-3462
e-mail: humank@hknewz.com

To my family—
who always gave me
support, encouragement,
and acceptance.

# contents

# *acknowledgments*

Many people made important contributions to this text. First I must acknowledge the contributions of everyone at Human Kinetics. Rainer Martens is my former advisor, and my most helpful critic and colleague through my early career and the writing of the first edition of this text. Although he is now less directly involved in sport and exercise psychology, he continues to provide support and advice and serve as a professional model in many ways. Many other people at Human Kinetics have helped me as this revision has stretched over an extended time. I want to give special thanks to Lynn Hooper-Davenport. She has been incredibly helpful and patient in her work as developmental editor. Lynn has done great editing, and she probably deserves authorship for her extra work with chapter objectives and supplementary material, as well as the main content.

When the first edition of this text was published, I was just moving to my current position at the University of North Carolina at Greensboro. After 13 years at UNCG, I have many colleagues and graduate students to thank for their contributions to this text, and to all of my work. Dan Gould has been my friend and colleague since graduate school, and a colleague at UNCG for 12 years. Dan has been a source of information and support in many ways, as well as the source for some of the best material in this text. I have had the good fortune to work with many talented graduate students. Several have contributed directly through their sport and exercise psychology research or professional work, and all of them have contributed to my sport and exercise psychology understanding. Justine Reel deserves special recognition for many hours working on the references of this text.

Lavon Williams, who is listed as the author of several chapters in this text, has made contributions beyond authorship. I asked Lavon to work on this text because she understands and can communicate the material, and also because I knew she would help keep me on track with my writing. Lavon has done all that, and as a valued colleague and friend, she always challenges me to consider options and to think in new ways.

Last in position in this section, but first and always for me, I thank my family. As I noted in the dedication to the first edition, my parents and grandparents "always knew I could do it." From my grandparents through the next generations, my family has been a consistent source of encouragement, support, and acceptance. Now that I have lived away from my upstate New York roots for many years in many places, and learned more about others' lives and backgrounds, I now realize that I grew up in the *only* functional family in existence during the 1950s and 1960s. I thank my family, and I give a special thank-you to my Dad. In his steady, quiet way, he showed me that bald, white guys can be supportive.

# preface

Sport and exercise psychology is an exciting and dynamic scholarly area with potential applications that reach many people in many settings. In this book I have tried to provide a comprehensive view of sport and exercise psychology—the scientific study of human behavior in sport and exercise and the practical application of that knowledge in sport and exercise settings. The chapters cover a wide scope, with topics moving from personality to social diversity, and approaches ranging from individual psychological skills training to team building. The book is targeted to courses that provide a comprehensive overview of sport and exercise psychology at the upper undergraduate and graduate levels. I have included extensive references to provide information and support for the themes and guidelines in the text, and also to help readers go beyond the current information to move in new directions in research or practice.

This text reflects the tremendous growth and diversity of sport and exercise psychology. When I completed my graduate work and began my first academic position in the mid-1970s, sport and exercise psychology was limited to a few courses in a few institutions. Today students in many different programs take our courses, and both professionals and participants in varied health, educational, and social programs apply sport and exercise psychology knowledge.

When I wrote the first edition of this text in 1986, I noted the growth in the field in the 10 years I had been teaching sport psychology courses. Now, as we move into the new millennium, sport and exercise psychology has expanded its research in both traditional and new directions, and professionals have applied the knowledge in many different areas. Readers who are familiar with the 1986 edition may not recognize the current text. Several new chapters cover topics that were just emerging in 1986, and even those chapters with familiar titles contain largely new material.

Although much of the material is new, my approach to sport and exercise psychology is consistent. My training and professional life has been within exercise and sport science, and I have focused my efforts in academic sport and exercise psychology, with limited professional consulting activity. Note that I consider my work *applied*. In my scholarly work, and in writing this text, my goal is to develop "practical theory"—guidelines based on the best available knowledge that we can use to enhance sport and exercise experiences for all.

Throughout this text, I have tried to pull together the strongest research findings, consistent themes, and logical theories to provide those guidelines. Human behavior is complex, dynamic, and social, and you will not find simple, final answers. I hope that this text helps you recognize the complexities and raises questions, but also helps you find useful, practical theories.

The text is organized into five parts representing major topic areas in sport and exercise psychology. The text follows the organization that I typically use with a first graduate class in sport and exercise psychology, but others may re-order, add, or delete material to fit other purposes.

Part I provides an orientation to sport and exercise psychology, with an introductory overview chapter followed by chapters covering the history and approaches to theory, research, and practice in sport and exercise psychology. Part II focuses on the individual, with chapters on personality, attention and cognitive styles, and self-perceptions.

Part III covers the huge topic of motivation, beginning with a chapter on participation motivation. Lavon Williams, my coauthor for several chapters in this edition of the text, wrote chapters on motivational orientations and intrinsic motivation. Part III also includes chapters on the broad area of emotions and on the specific area of competitive anxiety.

Part IV includes three chapters on psychological interventions. Although this text is not focused on professional practice, the application of sport and exercise psychology through psychological skills training is a large part of our field and the literature has grown tremendously. Thus, this section has chapters on cognitive interventions and stress management, as well as a chapter on psychological skills training (PST) that provides information and guidelines on intervention programs.

Part V, on social processes, contains chapters on social development and aggression, with Lavon Williams as the primary author. Part V includes a chapter on one of my favorite topics, gender and social diversity. Finally, part V and the text conclude with three chapters on social influence and group dynamics.

In addition to the updates to the content in the chapters, we have included some additions in this edition to help the reader. Each chapter begins with objectives to help guide your reading. Chapter summaries follow each chapter, and you can test your understanding with the review questions that follow. Throughout the text I have included the most current and comprehensive references that I know to help the reader who wishes to explore the topic in more depth. For readers who find many references distracting or unnecessary, I have given key references at the end of each chapter. These references are my recommendations for further reading, but readers may well have other directions to pursue.

I hope this book helps you understand sport and exercise psychology. Perhaps you will find information that helps you become a more effective teacher or consultant, or information to guide your research, or information that you can use in your own sport and exercise activities and other areas of your life. I hope you find information you can use—not answers, but guidelines as you move through your sport and exercise psychology study and on to new directions.

# Overview of Sport and Exercise Psychology

Part I of this text presents our framework for the psychological dynamics of sport and exercise. In chapter 1, we will consider the focus and scope of sport and exercise psychology. This text follows my own orientation to the discipline as part of the multidisciplinary, applied field of exercise and sport science. We will also consider how sport and exercise psychology relates to other exercise and sport science subfields, as well as to psychology.

Chapter 2 reviews the history of sport and exercise psychology. We will explore its roots in both psychology and physical education, and also review its development from isolated studies to the discipline today, which is incredibly diverse in both research and practice.

In chapter 3 we will consider varying perspectives on science and knowledge, as well as the relation of our knowledge to professional practice. Many approaches have been used to address our questions. Sound, theoretically driven research provides some answers; in-depth, interpretive approaches offer fresh insights; and many questions require an educated, experienced professional to integrate many sources of knowledge.

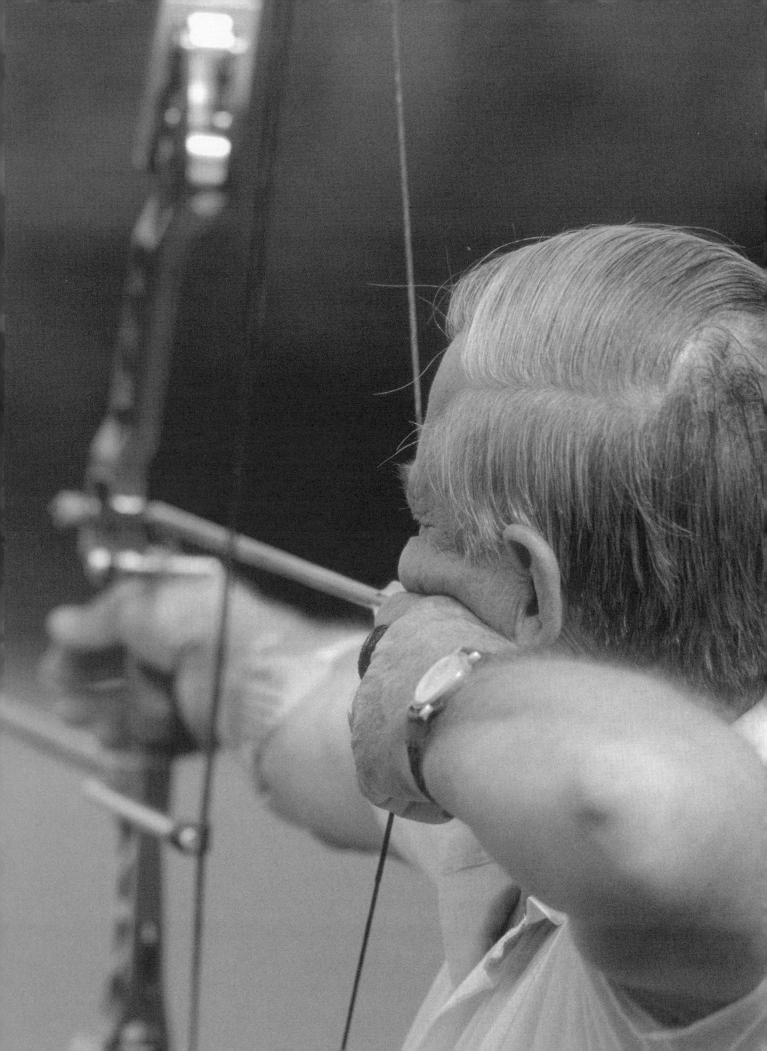

# chapter 1

# The Focus and Scope of Sport and Exercise Psychology

## CHAPTER OBJECTIVES

After studying this chapter, you should be able to

- understand the focus and scope of sport and exercise psychology and
- explain the relationship between sport and exercise psychology and other exercise and sport science subfields.

Sport and exercise psychology is the branch of sport and exercise science that seeks to provide answers to questions about human behavior in these areas. Teachers, coaches, fitness directors, sport psychology consultants, athletes, and exercisers must answer such questions every day. Because their actions depend on the answers, sport and exercise participants seek accurate, reliable information about the psychology of sport and exercise, just as they seek information about the physiological aspects of exercise and the biomechanical principles of movement.

To become acquainted with some of the issues in sport and exercise psychology, consider the following questions:

Are distance runners more introverted than soccer players?

Should a sport psychology consultant help a promising junior tennis player "psych up" for a championship match?

Will more children participate in an afterschool activity program if the middle school physical education teacher sets up a point system with awards for the top students?

Will the participants in the "Fit at Fifty-Plus" program exercise longer in a group than if they exercise alone?

Should youth sport coaches encourage aggressive play in their programs as a way to "let off steam"?

Is there an "I" in team?

At the end of this chapter we will return to these questions and their answers. Look for the "Putting It Into Practice" box on page 9 to see how your answers compare. Some answers may surprise you: many, based on the most recent sport and exercise psychology research, run counter to popular beliefs and practices. Also, you will note that answers are not simple or absolute. I might have discussed exceptions and variations, but for all the questions I have made the answers as straightforward as possible. Sport and exercise psychology is a relatively new field, and new findings often modify knowledge.

The remainder of this text will elaborate on these and other psychological issues in sport and exercise. Instead of simple yes and no answers, you will find information on how some individual characteristics affect some sport and exercise behaviors in some situations. Such information is never complete, but as the discipline advances, our understanding of human behavior in sport and exercise will gradually increase. First, though, let's consider the focus and scope of sport and exercise psychology, its place within exercise and sport science, and its relation to other subdisciplines and to psychology.

## EXERCISE AND SPORT SCIENCE: A MULTIDISCIPLINARY, APPLIED FIELD

As a branch of exercise and sport science, sport and exercise psychology is part of the overall study of human movement, also known as kinesiology. Exercise and sport science is multidisciplinary. In fact, it incorporates the entire range of sciences from the physical to the social sciences and even extends into scholarly areas, such as history, that are typically considered humanities rather than sciences. In my view, exercise and sport science is an applied field. That is, we try to integrate information from the various sciences to understand our field from a biopsychosocial perspective.

I prefer *exercise and sport science* as the term for the field that encompasses sport and exercise psychology, but academic programs go by many aliases, such as kinesiology, human movement, or, more traditionally, physical education. Kinesiology (the science of human movement) is the term preferred by those who focus on the basic discipline and science of the field. Departments of kinesiology often include no professional programs (e.g., teacher education, fitness management), and

People of all ages participate in sport and exercise activities.

typically extend the discipline to basic movements activities and mechanisms that cannot be called sport or exercise. Many departments of exercise and sport science or physical education also take that approach, but such programs are more likely to include a professional component and to emphasize sport and exercise activities rather than basic movements.

Exercise and sport science fits my emphasis on applying sport and exercise psychology in the real world. Still, I interpret sport and exercise broadly, and moreover, I consider sport and exercise overlapping labels for varied physical activities. Sport is not restricted to highly organized competition or highly skilled athletes. Sport and exercise activities range from aerobics classes to the Olympic Games, and participants include 8-year-olds in gymnastics classes and 72-year-olds in cardiac rehabilitation programs, as well as professional athletes. Sport and exercise psychology may also extend to skilled movements and physical activities that we do not consider "sports," such as movement with an artificial limb or exercise in space.

Because sport and exercise psychology is part of a multidisciplinary, applied field, and because it occupies the middle of the physical-to-social continuum, it has ties to all other subareas within exercise and sport science. The most prominent subareas are the following:

- *Biomechanics.* As the subarea closest to the physical science end, biomechanics applies principles and knowledge from physics to human movement.

- *Exercise physiology.* Exercise physiology is clearly aligned with biology, and draws upon anatomy and physiology to understand the biology of human movement and exercise activities.
- *Psychology of sport and exercise.* Sport and exercise psychology fits between, and overlaps with, biology and sociocultural studies; we will discuss our subarea in the next section.
- *Sociocultural sport studies.* Sociocultural sport studies include scholarly areas sometimes separated into sociology, history, and philosophy of sport.

Several subareas fall under the "umbrella" of exercise and sport science.

Each subarea within exercise and sport science incorporates information from the related discipline (e.g., physics, sociology) but draws from the disciplines selectively. Not all information in physiology and anatomy is equally applicable to exercise, nor are all aspects of psychology. Exercise and sport scientists apply selected theories, concepts, and methods from the basic disciplines to sport and exercise.

Borrowing of theories and information does not constitute a scholarly field of study. Exercise and sport science is multidisciplinary because we integrate information and develop our own theories, concepts, and methods to create unique knowledge. Many sport and exercise psychology scholars emphasize sport-specific theories and methods to address unique sport and exercise issues. Rainer Martens's work on competitive anxiety (see chapter 11) illustrates the value of sport-specific approaches. The psychology literature contains considerable research, theory, and varied anxiety measures, but Martens (1977) proposed that anxiety in sport has unique properties. The research of Martens and others confirmed that individuals who tend to become anxious in sport competition can be identified more effectively with a sport-specific measure than with a general anxiety measure—and provided a valid, sport-specific measure that many sport psychologists have used in research and practice.

Others have developed sport-specific constructs and measures providing insights and information about sport and exercise behavior that cannot be gleaned from more general psychology research. Sport and exercise psychology, then, borrows selected, relevant information from the associated discipline of psychology, and also develops theoretical models and approaches unique to sport and exercise.

Sport and exercise psychology also draws upon theories, constructs, and methods from the other exercise and sport sciences. Indeed, a thorough understanding of sport and exercise requires integration of information from all the subareas within exercise and sport science. For example, we will understand the psychological effects of distance running more fully if we also consider the physiological effects. Knowledge and techniques from biomechanics or sociocultural sport studies may provide further insights. Biomechanical approaches may be particularly useful when we study skilled movements, and sociocultural constructs are prominent in sport and exercise psychology research on social processes, such as gender relations and group cohesion.

## THE SUBDISCIPLINE OF SPORT AND EXERCISE PSYCHOLOGY

Now that we have considered the overall field of exercise and sport science, we will look at sport and exercise psychology as a distinct subdiscipline. Sport and exercise psychology is the branch of exercise and sport science that incorporates theories and approaches of psychology. In contrast to our wide-ranging interpretation of sport and exercise, we will take a more limited approach to psychology in this text. Psychology is a diverse field with many subareas. The American Psychological Association, the primary professional organization in psychology, lists 49 divisions, including the larger, more recognizable divisions such as clinical, developmental, experimental, and personality and social psychology; such divergent specialties as military psychology and psychopharmacology; and our own division of exercise and sport psychology.

## Relationships Among Motor Control, Motor Development, and Sport and Exercise Psychology

Given the wide scope of psychology, it is not surprising that sport and exercise psychology does not incorporate all aspects of the more general discipline. The North American Society for the Psychology of Sport and Physical Activity (NASPSPA), one of the main professional organizations for sport and exercise psychology, includes two other areas:

- *Motor learning and motor control.* Motor learning and control aligns most closely with the psychology areas of cognition and perception, and the experimental psychology of learning and performance. Motor learning and motor control specialists might focus on cognitive and perceptual processes involved in learning and performing motor skills, or the neuropsychological processes underlying controlled movements. Schmidt and Lee's (1999) text provides an overview of the motor learning and control area.

- *Motor development.* Motor development focuses on developmental psychology issues related to sport and motor performance. Much motor development content overlaps with motor learning and motor control under the more general rubric of motor behavior, and motor development specialists might investigate the development of motor patterns and skilled performance across the life span. Haywood (1993) provides an overview of the motor development area.

The three areas within NASPSPA reflect the typical division of psychological study within exercise and sport science in North America. Thus, in this text we separate sport and exercise psychology from the related motor behavior areas. Notably, European sport psychology—and most sport psychology around the world—includes cognition, perception, and other motor behavior topics. Moreover, international work on motor behavior topics is more applied and more directly related to sport and exercise than in North America.

Just as a thorough understanding of sport and exercise psychology often requires incorporating information from the other exercise and sport sciences, the subareas within the psychological study of sport and exercise have much to offer each other, and the borders are quite permeable. For example, the relationship between attention and performance is a prominent topic in both sport psychology and motor behavior. Thus, sport and exercise psychologists and motor behavior specialists share many theoretical models and methods, and each subarea provides insights that enrich the overall work on attention and sport. For example, educational programs for youth sport coaches might draw upon knowledge from motor development and motor learning, as well as sport psychology.

### Key Point

NASPSPA considers (1) motor control and learning and (2) motor development part of exercise and sport psychology. Because motor control and learning aligns most closely with the psychology areas of cognition and perception and because motor development focuses on developmental psychology issues related to sport and motor performance, we've chosen to define exercise and sport psychology more narrowly in this text.

## Special Emphases of Sport and Exercise Psychology

As noted earlier, sport and exercise psychology does not include all aspects of psychology. Sport and exercise psychology, as commonly interpreted and as used in this text, emphasizes certain subareas of psychology, particularly personality and social psychology. Like social psychology, our discipline focuses on meaningful social behavior rather than portions of behavior. Psychophysiology, cognition, and psychology areas that focus on portions of behavior contribute to our understanding of sport and exercise, but these issues are typically addressed within motor behavior.

Sport and exercise psychology is not, however, restricted to personality and social psychology. Whereas the social psychological aspects of sport dominated the field 10 years ago, that area is now overshadowed by applied sport psychology and exercise psychology. Some prominent scholars focus on psychophysiological or developmental aspects of sport and exercise, and applied sport psychology has introduced a number of counseling and clinical psychology theories and approaches.

## Sport and Exercise Psychology: An Updated Definition

In the first edition of this text (Gill, 1986), I defined sport psychology as the scientific study of human behavior in sport and exercise. Now, more than 10 years later, with the field having continued to change rapidly, that definition seems limited in several ways. First, the book's title and most current sources refer to the field as sport and exercise psychology to ensure that the exercise component is not overlooked and to counter the perception that sport = athletics. Many sport and exercise psychologists focus on health-oriented exercise, devoting research programs to such topics as exercise motivation or psychophysiological aspects of exercise and stress.

Second, "scientific study" seems to exclude many applied and professional concerns that most sport and exercise psychologists consider part of the field. Applied sport psychology has mushroomed into the most visible aspect of the field, and researchers are expanding the applied knowledge base. Thus, the definition of the field should include both the science and practice of sport and exercise psychology. Moreover, science is interpreted broadly to include alternative methods and sources of knowledge.

Finally, although I consider sport and exercise psychology a branch of exercise and sport science, that is not the only perspective today. Many sport psychologists have psychology backgrounds, consider sport psychology a branch of psychology, lack specific training in sport and exercise psychology, have no background in exercise science or physical education, and do not relate to the overall field of exercise and sport science.

So, in this text, sport and exercise psychology will be defined in the following way:

*Sport and exercise psychology is that branch of exercise and sport science that involves the scientific study of human behavior in sport and exercise, and the practical application of that knowledge in sport and exercise settings.*

### Key Point

Sport and exercise psychology is that branch of exercise and sport science that involves the scientific study of human behavior in sport and exercise, and the practical application of that knowledge in sport and exercise settings.

# THE COMPLEXITY OF SPORT AND EXERCISE BEHAVIOR

In sport and exercise psychology we try to understand meaningful behavior, and take what we might call a "wholistic" approach. We want to understand the behavior as it occurs in the real world so that we can apply the knowledge. This is no easy task. Human behavior in sport and exercise, as everywhere, is complex. We cannot find one

The relationships among the individual characteristics of a person (P), the social process and environment (E), and behavior (B) are dynamic, changing over time. Kurt Lewin (1935) stated this tenet in the equation B = f (P, E).

Children respond to constructive comments differently and it's important for teachers and coaches to be familiar with the level of instruction that each child is comfortable with.

clear source or "cause" of behavior. Even when we think we understand a behavior (e.g., why an athlete choked in the big game, or how to help a student learn a skill), we may find that our explanation does not hold up a week later.

In seeking to understand sport and exercise behavior, try to keep in mind one theme of this text: both individual characteristics and the social situation affect behavior. This premise reflects a basic tenet of social psychology set forth in a formal but simple way by Kurt Lewin (1935):

$$B = f (P, E)$$

That is, behavior is a function of the person and the environment. As you read this book you will move from an emphasis on individual characteristics (part II) and motivational orientations (part III) to an emphasis on the environment and social process (part V). In reality, we cannot shift from the person to the environment so easily. As Lewin emphasized, individual and environmental factors do not operate independently; they interact. Personal characteristics influence behavior in some situations and not others; situational factors (e.g., spectators, teachers' comments) affect different people differently; and perhaps most important, the person affects the situation just as the situation affects the person. Thus, the equation, or the relationships among person (P), environment (E), and behavior (B), are dynamic, changing over time.

For example, a 10-year-old baseball player may make a costly error. If the child is anxious about competition (P) and then hears critical comments (E), he or she likely will become even more anxious and make more errors, and that may lead to more tentative play and errors and change the situation for future games. Similarly, if the child were more confident and received constructive feedback, he or she might be more alert and ready in that situation the next time and develop stronger skills and confidence for the future.

Any behavior takes place within the context of many interacting personal and environmental factors, and all those factors along with their interactions or relationships change over time. The dynamic complexity of sport and exercise behavior makes precise prediction nearly impossible. Still, with greater understanding of individual and social processes and their relationships with behavior, we can make informed choices. We may not predict how one child will react to a particular teacher's comments, but we may help the physical education teacher, intercollegiate coach, fitness director, or sport psychology consultant relate to different individuals and enhance the sport and exercise experience for all participants.

With that caveat in mind, let's return to the questions posed at the beginning of the chapter.

**Are distance runners more introverted than soccer players?**

No. Although we hold many stereotypes about athletes' personalities, sport personality research has not uncovered consistent differences in general personality characteristics among sport participants. Athletes represent the entire range of personality characteristics and, as a group, do not differ consistently from nonathletes. Varying subgroups of sport and exercise participants (e.g., distance runners and soccer players) do not differ consistently in personality characteristics. Chapter 4 includes a discussion of research on personality profiles of athletes.

**Should a sport psychology consultant help a promising junior tennis player "psych up" for a championship match?**

No. (At least mostly no.) Again, many of us hold stereotyped beliefs about preparing for competition. We often believe that the best athletes increase arousal ("psych up"), and many precompetition coaching techniques aim to increase athletes' arousal levels. But many athletes, especially those who are young, need to calm down; and control of arousal seems to be a key psychological skill. Exceptions exist. Some top athletes, especially those in strength or endurance activities such as weight lifting, use psych-up or arousal-increasing strategies effectively to enhance performance. Still, emotional and arousal control methods should be used much more often, especially with younger, less experienced participants. For a discussion of arousal and performance, see chapter 11 on competitive anxiety; and see chapter 13 for some practical suggestions on stress management.

**Will more children participate in an afterschool activity program if the middle school physical education teacher sets up a point system with awards for the top students?**

Yes. But awards create problems. The chance to receive awards may act as an incentive to some children who would otherwise not participate. However, most children participate in sport and exercise activities for intrinsic reasons, such as fun and challenge. If most would participate anyway, using rewards accomplishes nothing and introduces many problems. Research indicates that extensive use of rewards encourages children to see themselves as participating to get the rewards, thus lowering their intrinsic interest. The more we emphasize extrinsic rewards, the more likely many children (and adults) will participate only under these circumstances. This issue is discussed in chapter 9.

**Will the participants in the "Fit at Fifty-Plus" program at the community center exercise longer in a group than if they exercise alone?**

Yes. Research on social influence indicates that people usually exercise longer and work harder when others are watching or doing the same thing, and social support often helps people stay with an exercise program. Many people find that they can run farther if they jog with others. The presence of others does not always improve performance. In general, it enhances the performance of simple or well-learned skills, especially speed and endurance tasks, whereas it usually interferes with the learning of more complex skills that require coordination and timing. Chapter 19 presents additional discussion of social influence.

**Should youth sport coaches encourage aggressive play in their programs as a way to "let off steam?"**

No. Many theories or explanations for aggression exist. Some propose that aggressive behavior is a natural, instinctive response and that we should channel those inevitable behaviors into nondestructive outlets, such as youth sports. The most accepted theories and most research, in contrast, suggest that aggression is a learned social behavior. Encouraging aggression in sport probably teaches and reinforces aggressive behavior and increases the likelihood of aggression elsewhere. Issues surrounding aggression and moral behavior in sport and exercise are reviewed in chapter 17.

### Is there an "I" in team?

Yes. The standard locker-room slogan, "There is no I in team" provides a spelling lesson, but unwise psychological advice. We use such slogans to imply that team members should forget about individual goals and focus only on team goals. Research indicates that we elicit the best performance from both individuals and groups when we explicitly recognize and reinforce individual contributions. When individual efforts are not recognized, individuals tend to slack off, which lowers overall group performance. Most successful coaches realize the importance of individual recognition and often take steps to ensure that individual goals are set and individual achievements reinforced. Chapter 20 includes more detailed explanations of group performance.

## Summary

Sport and exercise psychology is the branch of exercise and sport science that involves the scientific study of human behavior in sport and exercise, and the practical application of that information in sport and exercise settings. Like the other disciplines within exercise and sport science, sport and exercise psychology can be applied to varied skilled movements, physical activities, and health-oriented exercise programs as well as traditional physical education and competitive athletics.

Within North America, sport and exercise psychology is differentiated from the related psychological areas of motor learning/control and motor development. It emphasizes personality and social psychology, but draws upon many subareas of psychology to focus on the complex relationships among individual characteristics, the social situation, and human behavior in sport and exercise settings. It is a relatively young field, just beginning to answer some of our many questions. As you read this text, use the ideas and research findings to help you answer not only the questions posed here, but also future questions about human behavior in sport and exercise.

## Review Questions

1. Define exercise and sport psychology as it is used in this text.
2. Discuss motor control and learning, as well as motor development, and the relationship of exercise and sport psychology to these concepts.
3. Explain the dynamic relationships among the person, the environment, and the behavior.

## Recommended Reading

★ Lewin, K. (1935). *A dynamic theory of personality*. New York: McGraw-Hill

In *A Dynamic Theory of Personality*, Lewin presented the classic B = f (P, E), an elegant representation of the complexities of human behavior. As Lewin recognized, behavior depends on both the person and environment. Moreover, a rereading of Lewin reveals that he emphasized the complexities and dynamic nature of behavior. Behaviorism and simpler explanations dominated Lewin's time, but he was committed to the challenge of understanding behavior in the real, complex world. In his later works, *Resolving social conflicts* (1948) and *Field theory in social science* (1951), he moved on to larger social issues and "action research." These classics have been reissued (Lewin, 1997) and I urge readers who want to apply psychological science to complex, real-world problems to read Lewin—you may find some new insights.

If you're not ready to delve into Lewin and think about new directions in theory and research, that's fine. Most people who have been in sport and exercise psychology are not at that point either. If you want to get more information about sport and exercise psychology—who's involved, what do they do, what are the major topics and issues in research and practice—go to the most current sources. Check recent issues of the major journals in the field. Specifically, go to your university library and browse through these journals:

★ *Journal of Sport & Exercise Psychology (JSEP)* and *The Sport Psychologist (TSP)*

Both of these journals focus on sport and exercise psychology and both include current research by the major scholars. *JSEP* emphasizes theory-based research, whereas *TSP* has a more applied focus and includes articles on professional activities as well as applied research.

If you want even more current information, go to Web sites of the major sport and exercise psychology organizations. Specifically, both Division 47 (Exercise and Sport) of the American Psychological Association (APA) and the Association for the Advancement of Applied Sport Psychology (AAASP) have Web sites that include information on sport psychology conferences, contact people, resources, and issues, as well as information on the organization. Web site addresses often change. You can get to division 47 through the main APA Web site, and the publisher of this text, Human Kinetics, has links to many sport and exercise psychology sites through its homepage. The current Web sites are AAASP: **http://www.aaasp.online.org/** and APA-47: **http://www.psyc.unt.edu/apadiv47/**.

# History of Sport and Exercise Psychology

## CHAPTER OBJECTIVES

After studying this chapter, you should be able to

- trace the roots of sport and exercise psychology, beginning in psychology and physical education and
- identify the key stages of the development of sport and exercise psychology as an international discipline.

Sport and exercise psychology as a scholarly field is relatively young. In practice, it has existed as long as people have engaged in sport and exercise activities; and there are traces of sport and exercise psychology research in psychology and in exercise and sport science from the past. Throughout the history of psychology as a science, a few psychologists have addressed sport and exercise; and as long as scholars have studied exercise and sport science, some of those efforts have involved psychological issues.

## EARLY ROOTS: 1890-1920

Organizations and research in both psychology and physical education developed around the turn of the century; that early work includes evidence of sport and exercise psychology. Both Wiggins (1984) and Ryan (1981) cite an early psychological study of football by G.T.W. Patrick (1903) and note the words of G. Stanley Hall (1908), founding president of the American Psychological Association: "Physical education is for the sake of mental and moral culture and not an end in itself. It is to make the intellect, feelings and will more vigorous, sane, supple, and resourceful" (pp. 1015-1016).

The most widely recognized early contribution to sport psychology is Norman Triplett's (1898) lab study of social influence and performance, often considered the first social psychology experiment. Triplett's experiment is a benchmark for sport and exercise psychology because it originated in his observations of sport and involved a physical task (winding fishing reels). Triplett, a cycling enthusiast, noted that social influence (pacing machine, competition) seemed to motivate cyclists to better performance.

Along with Triplett, others from both psychology and physical education (often aligned with physical training and medical schools) espoused psychological benefits of physical education and conducted isolated studies of sport and exercise psychology issues. George W. Fitz (1895) of Harvard, operating from what may have been the first physical education research lab in North America, conducted experiments on the speed and accuracy of motor responses. Wiggins (1984) also cites turn-of-the-century work by William G. Anderson on mental practice; Walter Wells Davis's studies of transfer of training; Robert A. Cummins's investigation of the effects of basketball practice on motor reaction, attention, and suggestibility; and E.W. Scripture's study of character development and sport.

**Key Point**

The subdiscipline of sport and exercise psychology began by adding a social psychology aspect to motor learning.

## COLEMAN R. GRIFFITH'S SPORT PSYCHOLOGY WORK: 1920-1940

The first person to do systematic sport psychology research and practice was Coleman R. Griffith. Griffith began this work in 1918, as a doctoral student at the University of Illinois, with informal studies on psychological factors in basketball and football. Griffith's work caught the attention of George Huff, Director of Physical Welfare for Men at Illinois, who developed plans for Griffith's lab.

**Key Point**

Coleman Griffith was the first person to do systematic sport psychology research and practice. He focused on psychomotor skills, learning, and personality. He developed research measures and procedures in addition to working outside the lab.

Griffith was a prolific researcher who focused on psychomotor skills, learning, and personality and developed research measures and procedures. He taught sport psychology classes and published numerous articles, as well as two classic texts, *Psychology of Coaching* (1926) and *Psychology and Athletics* (1928). As many current sport and exercise psychologists advocate, Griffith did not stay in his lab, but ventured into the field to make observations and interview athletes. For example, he used an interview with Red Grange after the 1924 Michigan-Illinois football game, in which Grange noted that he could not recall a single detail of his remarkable performance, to illustrate that top athletes perform skills automatically. Griffith also corresponded with Knute Rockne on the psychology of coaching and motivation (see chapter 11 for details).

When financial constraints closed the Athletics Research Laboratory in 1932, Griffith continued as a professor of educational psychology, and eventually provost, at Illinois; but he did not abandon sport psychology. In 1938 he was hired by Philip Wrigley as sport psychologist for the Chicago Cubs. Griffith always maintained his scientific perspective while recognizing the expertise of coaches and athletes. A concern he expressed in 1925 still fits today:

> A great many people have the idea that the psychologist is a sort of magician who is ready, for a price, to sell his services to one individual or one group of men. Nothing could be further from the truth. Psychological facts are universal facts. They belong to whoever will read while he runs. There is another strange opinion about the psychologist. It is supposed that he is merely waiting until he can jump into an athletic field, tell the old-time successful coach that he is all wrong and begin, then, to expound his own magical and fanciful theories as to proper methods of coaching, the way to conquer overconfidence, the best forms of strategy, and so on. This, of course, is far from the truth, although certain things have appeared in the application of psychology to business and

*industry to lead to such an opinion. During the last few years and at the present time, there have been and are many men, short in psychological training and long in the use of the English language, who are doing psychology damage by advertising that they are ready to answer any and every question that comes up in any and every field. No sane psychologist is deceived by these self-styled apostles of a new day. Coaches and athletes have a right to be wary of such stuff. (pp. 193-194)*

Griffith's research, publications, and thoughtful insights make him one of the most significant figures in the history of sport psychology, and he is widely characterized as the father of sport psychology in North America. However, as Kroll and Lewis (1970) note, Griffith was a prophet without disciples, and "father" is really a misnomer. Sport psychology research and practice did not continue after Griffith's pioneering work. Parallel efforts in Germany by R.W. Schulte and in Russia by Peter Roudik and A.C. Puni continued, but did not influence North America.

## ISOLATED SPORT AND EXERCISE PSYCHOLOGY WORK: 1940-1965

From Griffith's time through the late 1960s when an identifiable sport and exercise psychology specialization emerged, sustained programs were nonexistent. As Ryan (1981) noted, most physical education texts of the time had sections on psychological aspects, and many physical education objectives were psychological, but research was sporadic. C.H. McCloy (1930) of Iowa examined character building through physical education, and Walter Miles (1928, 1931) of Stanford studied reaction time; but other work awaited the post-World War II extension of psychological research on learning and performance.

After World War II, several scholars developed research programs in motor behavior that incorporated some current sport psychology topics. Arthur Slater-Hammel at Indiana, Alfred (Fritz) Hubbard at Illinois, John Lawther at Penn State, and most notably Franklin Henry at Berkeley developed research programs focusing on motor learning and performance. In *The Psychology of Coaching*, Lawther (1951) extended his work into applied sport psychology as well as learning and performance principles. Warren Johnson's (1949) study of precontest emotion in football is a notable contribution of this time and a precursor to later studies of competitive emotion.

In the 1960s, more texts that covered psychology topics began to appear. Bryant Cratty published *Movement Behavior and Motor Learning* in 1964 and *Psychology and Physical Activity* in 1967, and continued into the 1990s as one of the most prolific authors of texts in sport psychology. In 1968 Robert Singer published the first edition of *Motor Learning and Human Performance*, a text that introduced many undergraduate and graduate physical education students to both motor learning and sport psychology. Bruce Ogilvie and Thomas Tutko published their controversial *Problem Athletes and How to Handle Them* in 1966. The clinical approach of that handbook, and the absence of a scientific framework or supporting evidence, led to a cold reception from motor behavior and physical education scholars. However, Ogilvie and Tutko's work was popular in the coaching community and foreshadowed the influx of similar applied sport psychology works in the 1980s.

## EMERGENCE OF SPORT AND EXERCISE PSYCHOLOGY AS A SUBDISCIPLINE: 1965-1975

Despite the innovative work during the first half of the 20th century, sport and exercise psychology did not emerge as an identifiable field until the late 1960s, when several individuals developed research programs and graduate courses and eventually channeled that interest into developing specialized organizations and publications. Simultaneously, many people became active sport psychologists in other countries, particularly in Europe, and sport psychology became an established area.

## International Organization

As individuals developed sport psychology interests, they began to organize. The International Society of Sport Psychology (ISSP) formed in 1965 and held the first International Congress of Sport Psychology in Rome. The ISSP holds meetings every four years and has become a forum for the international exchange of sport psychology information.

Reflecting on the development of ISSP, Miroslav Vanek (1993), a key figure in international sport psychology, noted that the use of psychology in sport was stimulated in the 1950s by the sovietization of top-level sport. Thus, international sport psychology traditionally has had a closer alignment with performance enhancement of elite athletes and has a clearer applied psychology foundation than the more exercise and sport science-oriented discipline in North America.

Several sport psychologists from Europe and the Soviet Union were instrumental in forming an international society, but Ferruccio Antonelli, founding president of ISSP and organizer of the first international congress in Rome in 1965, was the primary organizing force. The second international congress was held in Washington, DC, in 1968, and the proceedings of that congress (Kenyon & Grogg, 1970) provide a nice overview of sport psychology at that time. Antonelli remained ISSP president for several years, and in 1970 founded the *International Journal of Sport Psychology*, the first sport psychology research journal. Vanek (1985), who was president of ISSP from 1973 to 1985, described the field:

> *The psychology of sport has become an institutionalized discipline within the sport sciences in the later half of this century. . . . It is now possible to say that sport psychology has emerged as a distinctive subdiscipline and as a recognized member of the sport sciences. Our membership has grown, we have journals devoted to sport psychology, national and international societies, coursework and textbooks, specific courses for training in sport psychology, increasing research efforts, and so on. In fact, sport psychology has become a profession in many countries. (p. 1)*

The ISSP has continued to expand and serve as the primary international forum for the field since then.

**Key Point**

The formation of sport psychology organizations, including the ISSP's formation in 1965 and the official incorporation of NASPSPA in 1967, mark sport and exercise pychology's organization as a field of study.

## North American Society for the Psychology of Sport and Physical Activity

At the same time international sport psychology was organizing, North American scholars began to meet in conjunction with the American Association of Health, Physical Education, and Recreation (AAHPER; now American Alliance for Health, Physical Education, Recreation and Dance, AAHPERD) and developed plans for a sport psychology organization. John Loy, who described the early history of the North American Society for the Psychology of Sport and Physical Activity (NASPSPA) (Loy, 1974), reported that a small group who began to discuss forming a sport psychology organization met at the 1965 Dallas AAHPER conference, that discussions continued at the first ISSP congress, and that NASPSPA's first officers were elected at the 1966 Chicago AAHPER meetings (see table 2.1 for a list of NASPSPA presidents).

The first meeting of NASPSPA was held on March 8, 1967, at the AAHPER conference in Las Vegas; NASPSPA, officially incorporated just after that meeting, continued to meet in conjunction with the AAHPER conference until 1972.

At the 1972 meeting, NASPSPA members decided to hold the annual meeting separately, and Rainer Martens and colleagues hosted the first independent meeting

**Table 2.1   Presidents of Major Sport and Exercise Psychology Organizations**

| Year | NASPSPA | AAASP | ISSP | APA-47 |
|---|---|---|---|---|
| 1965–66 | | | Ferruccio Antonelli | |
| 1966–67 | | | | |
| 1967–68 | Arthur Slater-Hammel | | | |
| 1968–69 | | | | |
| 1969–70 | Bryant Cratty | | | |
| 1970–71 | | | | |
| 1971–72 | E. Dean Ryan | | | |
| 1972–73 | | | | |
| 1973–74 | Rainer Martens | | Miroslav Vanek | |
| 1974–75 | Dorothy Harris | | | |
| 1975–76 | Don Kirkendall | | | |
| 1976–77 | Waneen Spirduso | | | |
| 1977–78 | Richard Schmidt | | | |
| 1978–79 | Harriet Williams | | | |
| 1979–80 | Robert Christina | | | |
| 1980–81 | Ronald Marteniuk | | | |
| 1981–82 | Tara Scanlan | | | |
| 1982–83 | Glyn Roberts | | | |
| 1983–84 | Robert Schutz | | | |
| 1984–85 | Richard Magill | | | |
| 1985–86 | Daniel Landers | John Silva | Robert Singer | |
| 1986–87 | Mary Ann Roberton | | | William Morgan |
| 1987–88 | Michael Wade | Ronald Smith | | |
| 1988–89 | Craig Wrisberg | Robert Weinberg | | Dan Landers |
| 1989–90 | Diane Gill | Daniel Gould | | |
| 1990–91 | Jerry Thomas | Lawrence Brawley | | Steve Heyman |
| 1991–92 | Gil Reeve | Michael Sachs | | |
| 1992–93 | Jane Clark | Charles Hardy | | Dan Kirschenbaum |
| 1993–94 | Robert Weinberg | Jean Williams | Denis Glencross | |
| 1994–95 | Karl Newell | Tara Scanlan | | Robert Singer |
| 1995–96 | Stephen Wallace | Penny McCullagh | Atsushi Fujita (interim) | |
| 1996–97 | Howard Zelaznik | Maureen Weiss | | Shane Murphy |
| 1997–98 | Janet Starkes | Len Zaichowsky | Gershon Tenenbaum | |
| 1998–99 | Beverly Ulrich | Robin Vealey | | Diane Gill |
| 1999–2000 | Kathleen Haywood | Andrew Meyers | | |

of NASPSPA at Allerton Park, Illinois, on May 14-16, 1973. The proceedings of that conference were published (Wade & Martens, 1974), marking the start of Human Kinetics Publishers—and a milestone for sport psychology. Since then NASPSPA has continued to hold separate meetings each year, usually in early June; and NASPSPA continued as the major sport and exercise psychology organization through the 1970s and 1980s.

The organization of NASPSPA reflected the overlapping of sport psychology and motor behavior in the 1960s and 1970s. Many early sport psychology specialists branched out from motor learning, and NASPSPA included subareas of motor learning, motor development, and social psychology of physical activity (now the sport psychology area). Those three subareas remain in NASPSPA, although each has changed and grown more specialized since NASPSPA's foundation.

Although NASPSPA has a strong Canadian presence, a separate Canadian organization, the Canadian Society for Psychomotor Learning and Sport Psychology (CSPLSP; now using the French acronym SCAPPS for Societe Canadienne d'Apprentissage Psychomoteur et Psychologie du Sport) was founded in 1969 and became an independent society in 1977.

## Publications

Sport and exercise psychology emerged as individuals developed research interests and programs, then moved into organizations, and eventually began scholarly publications for the growing literature. Earlier studies appeared in a variety of psychology journals and in the *Research Quarterly*, later renamed *Research Quarterly for Exercise and Sport*, the primary research publication of AAHPERD. The latter has continued to publish sport and exercise psychology research, along with other exercise and sport science work; but as research expanded in the late 1960s and 1970s, sport psychologists developed specialized publications.

The *International Journal of Sport Psychology* began publishing in 1970, but has never served as the primary source or outlet for North American scholars. The *Journal of Motor Behavior* began publishing in 1969 and included some sport psychology research, particularly on social influence and motor behavior (e.g., lab research on social facilitation or social reinforcement with motor tasks).

Probably the most important publication outlet for sport and exercise psychology research during the 1970s was the NASPSPA proceedings. Proceedings of the 1973 (Wade & Martens, 1974) and 1975 (Landers, Harris, & Christina, 1975) conferences were published, and from 1976 to 1980 the conference proceedings were published by Human Kinetics as *Psychology of Motor Behavior and Sport*.

With the 1979 appearance of the *Journal of Sport Psychology* (JSP), NASPSPA stopped publishing full papers. This journal (*Journal of Sport and Exercise Psychology*, JSEP, since 1988) was immediately recognized, as it is today, as the leading publication outlet for sport and exercise psychology research (see table 2.2 for list of journals and editors).

# FURTHER DEVELOPMENT OF THE SUBDISCIPLINE: 1975-1995

From the 1970s through the 1990s, sport psychology scholars developed a research base separate from but related to motor behavior; they also established research labs and graduate programs, held successful annual conferences, developed a respected research journal, and gradually became the largest and most diverse of the three areas within NASPSPA.

Rainer Martens's (1975a) text, *Social Psychology and Physical Activity*, one of the first books used in sport and exercise psychology courses, reflects the content and orientation of those years. Major psychological theories (e.g., inverted-U hypothesis, Zajonc's social facilitation theory, Atkinson's achievement motivation theory) framed the content; most supporting research was from psychology; and the sport psychology work cited seldom involved *sport*, but more likely involved laboratory experiments with motor tasks such as the rotary pursuit and stabilometer.

**Table 2.2 Major Sport Psychology Journals, Publication Years, and Editors**

*International Journal of Sport Psychology*

| | |
|---|---|
| 1970–1989 | Ferruccio Antonelli |
| 1989–present | Alberto Cei & John Salmela |

*Journal of Sport Psychology* (became *Journal of Sport and Exercise Psychology*, 1988)

| | |
|---|---|
| 1979–1985 | Daniel M. Landers |
| 1986–1990 | Diane L. Gill |
| 1990–1994 | W. Jack Rejeski |
| 1995–1997 | Thelma S. Horn |
| 1998–present | Robert Brustad |

*The Sport Psychologist*

| | |
|---|---|
| 1987–1991 | Daniel Gould & Glyn C. Roberts |
| 1992–1995 | Robin S. Vealey |
| 1996–1997 | Graham Jones |
| 1997–present | Peter Crocker |

*Journal of Applied Sport Psychology*

| | |
|---|---|
| 1989–1991 | John M. Silva |
| 1992–1995 | Joan L. Duda |
| 1996–1997 | Albert V. Carron |
| 1998–present | Robert Weinberg |

By the mid-1980s, 10 years after the exciting beginning at Allerton, sport psychology had grown as promised, but also changed directions. While motor behavior continued to emphasize psychological theories and experimental research, sport psychology moved to more applied issues and approaches. Martens was a leading advocate for change, and his 1979 article in the second issue of *JSP*, which had been presented as "From Smocks to Jocks" at the 1978 CSPLSP conference in Toronto, led many sport psychologists to more applied research and practical concerns. For example, Ron Smith and Frank Smoll took a practical issue (effective coaching in youth sports), conducted systematic observations and field research, and developed coach education programs (e.g., Smoll & Smith, 1984; see chapter 15 for details).

**Key Point**

In the mid-1980s, motor behavior continued to emphasize psychological theories and experimental research. Sport psychology moved to more applied issues and approaches, and made a strong move to sport relevance as sport-specific models and measures were developed.

Through the 1980s, field research and applied issues moved to the forefront of sport and exercise psychology and captured the attention of students and the public. A few sport psychologists moved from research to focus on applied work with athletes. Before 1980, sport psychology application largely meant application to physical education; but with the 1980s, it came to imply psychological skills training with elite competitive athletes. This applied focus caught the attention of some psychologists who began to see sport and athletics as a setting for clinical and counseling applications.

With more diverse students and psychologists participating in sport psychology, the original NASPSPA structure no longer fit all interests. John Silva initiated an organizational meeting at Nags Head, North Carolina, in October 1985, that marked the beginning of the Association for the Advancement of Applied Sport Psychology (AAASP). As summarized in the first issue of the *AAASP Newsletter* (Winter, 1986), AAASP provides a forum for individuals interested in research, theory development, and application of psychological principles in sport and exercise.

The first AAASP conference took place at Jekyll Island, Georgia, October 9-12, 1986; annual conferences continue with the same three areas of intervention/

performance enhancement, health psychology, and social psychology that were set in 1985 (see table 2.1 for list of AAASP presidents).

Martens's keynote address at the first AAASP conference, like his "smocks and jocks" paper eight years earlier, advocated major changes in sport psychology. Martens suggested that academic sport psychology and practicing sport psychology had diverged because of an unjustified reliance on orthodox science as the only source of knowledge. Martens encouraged sport psychologists to accept more diverse sources of knowledge, to consider alternative approaches to science, and to develop truly useful knowledge.

That widely cited paper (Martens, 1987b), which has moved many sport psychology scholars to adopt alternative research strategies, was published in the inaugural issue of *The Sport Psychologist (TSP)*. The purpose of *TSP* was to focus on the emerging applied sport psychology literature and to complement the successful *JSP*.

## Key Point

In the early years, academic sport psychologists relied on orthodox science as the only source of knowledge. One key journal is the *Journal of Sport and Exercise Psychology*. Today, sport psychologists adopt alternative research strategies. *The Sport Psychologist* and AAASP's *Journal of Applied Sport Psychology* focus on applied research and professional issues.

Before 1980, sport psychology was applied primarily to physical education settings. The field has changed and grown notably during the past two decades.

With *TSP* focusing on applied research and professional issues, *JSP* received fewer of those submissions, concentrated more on strong sport psychology research, and in 1988, during my editorial term, added exercise to the title and more explicitly sought research on health-oriented exercise as well as sport. The two journals, *JSEP* and *TSP*, continue to complement each other. Also, in 1989, AAASP started its own journal, the *Journal of Applied Sport Psychology (JASP)*, with John Silva as editor. The *JASP* serves many of the same purposes as *TSP* and also provides AAASP information, publishes major addresses from the conference, and has developed informative theme issues.

The foundation and rapid rise to prominence of AAASP and *TSP* are the most visible markers of applied sport psychology growth in the 1980s, but some other organizations also contributed to this movement. As alluded to earlier, several individuals trained in traditional psychology programs moved into sport psychology during this time, and sport and exercise psychology began to appear in psychology literature. A few psychologists had done isolated applied sport psychology work earlier. Most notably, Bruce Ogilvie, whose earlier applied work had not been accepted in sport and exercise science in the 1960s, was recognized for those pioneering efforts when applied sport psychology organized in the 1980s.

The early work of Richard Suinn, clinical psychologist and active member of the American Psychological Association (APA), should also be noted. Suinn was one of the first psychologists to work with top athletes, and his work with Olympic skiers did much to bring sport psychology to public attention. Suinn and others, including Steve Heyman and William Morgan, organized a sport and exercise psychology presence within APA. After starting as an interest group, Division 47—Exercise and Sport Psychology—became a formal division of APA in 1986. Division 47 brought sport and exercise psychology to the attention of many psychologists who were otherwise unaware of the field, and also drew some sport and exercise science specialists into APA.

The organizations that most sport and exercise psychologists identify with are NASPSPA, AAASP, and Division 47, but sport psychology also has a presence in other exercise and sport science organizations: AAHPERD, which was the site of the initial organization of the subdiscipline, includes a Sport Psychology Academy; and many sport psychology scholars, especially those interested in applications to physical education, participate in that organization. The American College of Sports Medicine, a large and powerful organization dominated by exercise physiology and sports medicine, has expanded its psychology constituency and accommodated more sport and exercise psychology work in recent years.

Suinn's early work with skiers in the 1976 Olympics helped the U.S. Olympic Committee (USOC) recognize the potential role of sport psychology. Several other sport psychologists began to work with teams, and in 1983 the USOC established an official sport psychology committee and a registry with three categories—clinical, educational, and research sport psychology. Many sport psychologists have worked with athletes, coaches, and training programs through the USOC since then; in January 1987, the USOC hired Shane Murphy as the first permanent full-time sport psychologist at the training center in Colorado Springs.

As applied sport psychology organized and became known to students and the public, applied courses and psychological skills training workshops developed, creating a market for more literature. Few sport psychology texts existed when I wrote the first edition of this text (Gill, 1986), but by the late 1980s, sport psychology literature had expanded. Many applied sport psychology books appeared, including Robert Nideffer's (1976a) *The Inner Athlete* and (1985) *Athlete's Guide to Mental Training*; Dorothy Harris and Bette Harris's (1984) *The Athlete's Guide to Sport Psychology*; Terry Orlick's (1980) *In Pursuit of Excellence* (now in 2nd edition, 1990); Rainer Martens's (1987a) *Coaches Guide to Sport Psychology*; and Jean Williams's (1986) *Applied Sport Psychology* (now in 3rd edition, 1998).

## SPORT AND EXERCISE PSYCHOLOGY TODAY

As we enter the new millennium, sport and exercise psychology is much different from the subdiscipline that emerged in the 1960s. The field began by adding a social psychology aspect to motor learning and in the early stages relied heavily on experimental social psychology theories and research models. Sport and exercise psychology made a strong move to sport relevance about 10 years later, as research shifted to the field and scholars developed sport-specific models and measures. Shortly thereafter, with an influx of people from psychology and with more direct applied concerns, sport psychologists began to apply sport psychology information more directly in education and consulting work.

As applied interests continue to expand, academic and research interests also are expanding and changing. Sport and exercise psychology responded to the public concern for health and fitness with increased attention to health-oriented exercise. Also, research on both sport and exercise has widened beyond the social psychology perspective to include other psychological theories and perspectives such as developmental and psychophysiological approaches.

Sport and exercise psychology today is incredibly diverse in both research and practice. Some researchers emphasize theory-based basic research with tight controls and search for underlying physiological mechanisms, while others shun traditional research for interpretive approaches and seek experiential knowledge. Some do no research at all, but educate, consult with, or clinically treat sport and exercise participants.

## Benchmarks in the History of Sport and Exercise Psychology

**1898**

Norman Triplett conducts the first social psychology experiment, confirming his observations that people perform tasks faster in the presence of others.

**1925**

The Board of Trustees at the University of Illinois establishes the Athletics Research Laboratory with Coleman R. Griffith as director.

**1967**

The North American Society for the Psychology of Sport and Physical Activity (NASPSPA) is officially incorporated on March 13, 1967.

**1979**

The first issue of the *Journal of Sport Psychology* (*Journal of Sport and Exercise Psychology* since 1988) is published by Human Kinetics with Dan Landers as editor.

**1985**

The Association for the Advancement of Applied Sport Psychology is formed with John Silva as president.

**1987**

The first issue of *The Sport Psychologist* is published with Dan Gould and Glyn Roberts as coeditors.

## Summary

Although sport and exercise psychology is relatively young as an identifiable area, we can trace our roots back over 100 years. A review of that century of sport and exercise psychology history is presented in more detail elsewhere (Gill, 1997).

Retrospectively, we can identify several isolated studies from the 1890s to the 1960s as sport and exercise psychology; but generally the subdiscipline did not exist. One brief period of identifiable sport psychology work punctuated this time period, when Coleman R. Griffith directed the Athletics Research Laboratory at Illinois and conducted his sport psychology work.

Sport and exercise psychology organized as a field of study in the late 1960s when several scholars with sport and exercise psychology interests initiated research meetings and formal organizations. The clearest marker of this organizing was the official incorporation of NASPSPA in 1967.

Sport and exercise psychology has expanded rapidly, changed, and developed new directions since then. During the 1970s, graduate programs and research expanded, creating a knowledge base and a need for specialized publications. The 1979 publication of *JSP* (*JSEP* since 1988) marked this growth. During the 1980s, the most notable trend in sport and exercise psychology was a turn toward applied research and practice. This widespread trend is marked most clearly by the formation of AAASP in 1985 and the initial publication of *TSP* in 1987.

Today sport and exercise psychology includes researchers who emphasize controlled theory-based research on basic issues, scholars who use alternative methods and sources of knowledge, and practitioners who educate and consult in varied sport and exercise settings.

## Review Questions

1. Name the first person to do systematic sport psychology research, and discuss his work.

2. Discuss the early history of sport and exercise psychology.

3. Discuss the divergence of motor behavior and sport psychology.

4. Discuss the development of applied sport psychology.

## Recommended Reading

★ *The Sport Psychologist*, 1995, 4. "Sport Psychology: A Historical Perspective."

This special issue, edited by Penny McCullagh, contains several articles by scholars who clearly know their history and want to communicate that historical knowledge to others. I especially recommend Gould and Pick's (1995) article on the Griffith years, 1920-1940. You will learn a great deal more about Coleman Griffith's remarkable work than I could communicate in this chapter. Read any two other articles, depending on your particular interests, and you will have a much better understanding of sport and exercise psychology.

# *chapter* 3

# Approaches to Knowledge in Sport and Exercise Psychology

## CHAPTER OBJECTIVES

After studying this chapter, you should be able to

- explain the scientific method and how it is used in sport and exercise psychology research and
- identify theories and paradigms that have shaped the field of sport and exercise psychology.

This chapter addresses how we develop and use sport and exercise psychology knowledge. We will discuss the scientific method, progress in the research, and challenges and alternatives to our methods. As we look at the role of scientific research, we will also consider links between our research and practice. That is, how do we obtain knowledge that is not only scientifically sound, but also relevant and useful in professional practice?

## USING THEORY TO LINK RESEARCH AND PRACTICE

Theory is the critical link in the theory-research-practice triad. Traditional discussions of science have always emphasized research-practice connections; the real world offers research ideas, and research results are ultimately tested for usefulness in the real world. To enrich the picture, I will emphasize the links of theory to both research and practice.

Research ideas may stem from practical events, but theories are what guide research. Within traditional "normal" science, which we will discuss later, theory is both the guide and goal of research. Theory, typically described as a systematic explanation of a phenomenon based on sound scientific evidence, is our goal in that theory explains behavior. For example, catastrophe theory, discussed in chapter 11, is an explanation of the relationship between anxiety and performance. And, as you will discover, catastrophe theory is a good example of how theories incorporate multiple constructs in a complex network of interrelationships. Theories are never final, but are constantly developed and revised or replaced with new information. Thus, theory also serves as a source of questions and guide for research. As Forscher (1963) pointed out in "Chaos in the Brickyard," one of my favorite gems of scientific wisdom, theory is the key to useful research. Research without theory as a guide or blueprint gives us piles of bricks (facts) but no useful structures.

Theory is the critical link in the theory-research-practice triad. Theory is both the guide and goal of research—it serves as a source of questions to research and it explains behavior.

Later in this chapter we will consider theory in a larger sense as we look at "meta-theories"—the grand theories or frameworks that form our big picture of sport and exercise behavior. I will argue that sport and exercise psychology scholars have devoted too much time to debates on methodology and neglected the larger theoretical issues, which have the greater impact on the development and use of knowledge. More specifically, our grand theories have neglected the critical role of context; but we must focus on the *context* of sport and exercise if our research is to be valid and relevant.

I will also argue that theory—what I term "practical theory"— is the key to effective practice. Too often practitioners look for a "quick fix" to a problem rather than searching for common themes and unifying principles that apply in varying contexts.

In writing this chapter I have drawn upon the work of other scholars and blended their views with my own observations, interpretations, and reflections. As the sources may not be evident, I will acknowledge the major influences now: Rainer Martens's (1979, 1987b) influential calls for changes in our approaches to science and knowledge, Dewar and Horn's (1992) chapter, and Dzewaltowski's recent (1997) call for an ecological model focusing on context. Additionally I will cite Kurt Lewin's classic work, which I find more insightful with each rereading. I highly recommend the recent republication (Lewin, 1997) of Lewin's *Field Theory in Social Science* (1951) and *Resolving Social Conflicts* (1948). I always appreciate Michael Mahoney's provocative challenges to psychology's science and knowledge; his *Human Change Processes* (1991), calling for a more complex and dynamic approach to human behavior and change, is particularly relevant here. My approach blends many of these works, along with my naive interpretation of some of the chaos and complexity models that are challenging all of science. I do not claim to have the meta-theory for everyone, but my approach frames my thinking and presentation of sport and exercise psychology knowledge. I will refer to Lewin's $B = f(P, E)$ model, emphasize the person and behavior in context (as Lewin actually proposed), and strive to communicate "practical theory" to provide unifying principles and guidelines that both researchers and practitioners can apply within the ever-changing, dynamic context of sport and exercise.

## IDENTIFYING RESEARCH QUESTIONS

At a recent symposium I was asked to identify measurement, statistics, and design issues in sport and exercise psychology. That charge seems a formal way of asking, "How do we answer our questions?" Before addressing that issue, however, we must ask, "What are our questions?" My main point at the symposium, and a central theme in this chapter, is that identifying our research questions is the source of and solution for measurement, statistics, and design issues. When research has a clear purpose and conceptual framework, when constructs are clearly defined, and when clear and relevant questions are asked, we solve many problems.

My favorite research advice was originally published in 1865 in *Alice's Adventures in Wonderland* (Carroll, 1992). Alice (the searching researcher or graduate student) asks "Cheshire-Puss" (the resident expert) for advice: "Would you tell me, please, which way I ought to walk from here?" Cheshire-Puss returns the question (as do all expert advisors)—"That depends a good deal on where you want to get to." When Alice replies that she doesn't much care where, the sage responds, "Then, it doesn't matter which way you walk." If we cannot tell our advisors where we want to get to, we cannot expect them to tell us how to get there.

Before setting off, let's decide "where we want to get to"—a destination for sport and exercise psychology. As we saw in chapter 1, the destination is understanding behavior in sport and exercise settings. Our guide is Kurt Lewin's (1935) classic formula, $B = f(P, E)$: behavior (B) is a function of the person (P) and the environment (E). If we know we want to understand sport and exercise behavior, we can ask what methods will take us closer to our destination.

# UNDERSTANDING THE SCIENTIFIC METHOD IN SPORT AND EXERCISE PSYCHOLOGY

Sport and exercise psychology developed as a discipline by following psychology's lead with its reliance on traditional scientific methods. The scientific method has served us well, has helped us develop a knowledge base and gain credibility, and continues to dominate both psychology and exercise and sport science, as well as sport and exercise psychology. Traditional science with its related assumptions or meta-theories has its critics and is not the only accepted form of knowledge today. Before we consider challenges and alternatives we must first understand "normal science." Much has been written on the scientific method; this overview comes from Thomas and Nelson (1996).

## Nonscientific Sources of Knowledge

Nonscientific methods of knowing have always existed (Thomas & Nelson, 1996). We do not devise an experiment to answer all questions in life, or even in the sport and exercise worlds. Typically listed nonscientific sources of knowledge are the following:

- Tenacity—clinging to beliefs, such as superstitions
- Intuition—commonsense or self-evident truths
- Authority—accepting the authority's truth (e.g., that of teachers, experts, church doctrine)
- Rationalistic method—logic, for example, the classic syllogism: All men are mortal; Socrates is a man; therefore, Socrates is mortal
- Empirical method—experience and observation, data gathering

We might use any of these sources in our lives and in our sport and exercise psychology lives, although most are decidedly nonscientific. Both the rationalistic (logic) and empirical methods are part of the scientific method, and the most careful researcher might be wise to rely on intuition for some knowledge.

Adapted from Thomas & Nelson, 1996.

Science is a process, and the scientific method is a series of steps to solve problems. Steps vary depending on the specific reference (or authority); Thomas and Nelson outline the following:

- **Step 1: Developing the problem.** In the scientific method, the researcher must be very specific, typically identifying independent and dependent variables. The independent variable is manipulated to determine the effect on the dependent variable.
- **Step 2: Formulating the hypothesis.** The hypothesis is the prediction or expected result. The hypothesis must be *testable*.
- **Step 3: Gathering the data.** The researcher must first plan the methods to maximize internal and external validity, then make the observations to gather data. *Internal validity* means you are certain the results can be attributed to the treatment. For example, giving participants choice of exercises was what in-

creased adherence—you can rule out other alternatives. *External validity* refers to the generalizability of results. If choice increased adherence in the study, choice should increase adherence in other studies and settings.

- **Step 4: Analyzing and interpreting results.** Most studies involve statistical analyses, and the researcher must then interpret the results to support or refute the hypothesis and compare results with other research, theories, or other sources of information.

### Key Point

The traditional scientific method is a stepwise approach to solving problems. Thomas and Nelson (1996) outline four steps:

1. Developing the problem
2. Formulating the hypothesis
3. Gathering the data
4. Analyzing and interpreting the results

## REVIEWING PROGRESS IN SPORT AND EXERCISE PSYCHOLOGY RESEARCH

Sport and exercise psychology has made progress with the scientific method, and we have improved measurement, design, and analysis procedures. Although behavior (B) is central in our guiding model, and behavior is influenced by the environment (E), the research has emphasized personality (P) from the earliest sport psychology work using general personality measures. Coleman Griffith used personality measures and interviewed athletes in the 1930s and '40s, although he also used lab measures (e.g., reaction time, motor coordination, attention) and took a more scientific and broader view of sport behavior (Gould & Pick, 1995). As Heil and Henschen (1996) note, personality measures dominated early sport psychology, hitting a peak (or valley depending on the viewpoint) with the popular, but psychometrically unsound, Athletic Motivation Inventory (Tutko, Lyon, & Ogilvie, 1969). We have gradually moved from global personality measures to more specific measures (e.g., motivational orientation, perceptions, expectations, attentional style) in recent work.

### Sport-Specific Measures

One of the most important advances for sport psychology measurement was the move from general personality measures to sport-specific measures. Martens's (1975b) development of the Sport Competition Anxiety Test (SCAT) initiated that move, and others followed the example. Carron, Widmeyer, and Brawley (1985) developed the Group Environment Questionnaire to measure cohesion; I worked with colleagues to develop a sport-specific measure of competitive achievement orientation, the Sport Orientation Questionnaire (Gill & Deeter, 1988); and several more recent sport anxiety measures have improved upon the SCAT.

Many of the better measures are multidimensional. For example, anxiety is now conceptualized and examined as a multidimensional construct, usually with cognitive anxiety/worry and somatic anxiety/physiological arousal dimensions, and our measures have progressed from the unidimensional SCAT.

### Perceptions and Cognitions

In moving from global personality, sport and exercise psychology also shifted from personality dispositions (although not entirely) to more immediate perceptions and cognitions. This work reflects the strong social-cognitive movement in psychology

# Understanding the Scientific Method

**Step 1:** Developing the problem.

**Step 2:** Formulating the hypothesis.

**Step 3:** Gathering the data.

**Step 4:** Analyzing and interpreting the results.

through the 1980s, and sport and exercise psychology has adopted that approach with related models and measures. Within that general social-cognitive approach, sport and exercise psychologists have investigated and measured attributions, expectations, self-perceptions, and particularly self-efficacy. Because these perceptions are measured for the immediate situation, we do not have standard measures with established reliability and validity, which introduces some measurement issues.

For example, as discussed in chapter 6, self-efficacy—the belief that one has the capability to successfully perform a task or behavior—is particularly popular in research and practice. Bandura (1977a, 1986) offered guidelines for measures, and most measures are similar: respondents rate how confident they are that they can do a specific task (e.g., finish the 10K in 35 minutes) on a scale from 0% (not at all confident) to 100% (absolutely certain). However, the specific referent tasks are not standard, and researchers seldom pilot measures or check reliability or validity.

## MEASUREMENT ISSUES IN SPORT AND EXERCISE PSYCHOLOGY RESEARCH

Despite progress, sport and exercise psychologists continue to debate issues related to personality measures, as well as our methods. First, there are too many sport

psychology measures. In his first edition of the *Directory of Psychological Tests in the Sport and Exercise Sciences*, Ostrow (1990) listed nearly 200 measures, and the updated edition (Ostrow, 1996) nearly doubles that number. Very few of these measures meet even minimal psychometric standards of test development; most were simply developed and used for a particular study without preliminary item analyses or reliability or validity testing.

Even when some psychometric information is provided, statistical methods are weak, often involving misapplication, misunderstanding, or misinterpretation of some aspect of factor analysis (Schutz & Gessaroli, 1993). Developers of sport and exercise psychology measures seldom use multitrait-multimethod matrices, typically ignore (if even acknowledge) conceptual models by using exploratory methods rather than confirmatory analyses, and often combine subscores (developed from analyses yielding uncorrelated factors) into global scores without ever checking for second-order factors or hierarchical structures.

Besides these statistical shortcomings identified by Schutz and Gessaroli, I would add that most sport and exercise psychologists never consider important validity issues. If measures are to be useful, they must validly measure constructs rel-

Human behavior in sport is complex and multifaceted.

evant to sport and exercise behavior. Of course, we cannot assess validity if we do not know what we are trying to measure, and we return to the main message—conceptual clarity is the first step. Otherwise, measures may contain interrelated items yielding a score, but we have no justification for interpreting the score.

The availability of these measures prompts sport and exercise psychologists to focus on the "P" part of the Lewin model to the neglect of other components, processes, and a "wholistic" approach. For example, as discussed in chapter 8, readily available goal orientation measures such as the Task and Ego Orientation in Sport Questionnaire have prompted reliance on individual dispositions, but most theories and observations suggest that the immediate situation and larger social context have more influence on goal-directed behavior.

Despite the oversupply of measures, most were developed for competitive sport contexts and may not be relevant to exercise and health-related physical activity. Some motivational measures have been adapted for exercise settings, but the expanded research in this area calls for more diverse measures. In particular, health-related quality of life (QOL) (for a review see Rejeski, Brawley, & Shumaker, 1996) is a frequently used construct. The National Institutes of Health funding guidelines call for the inclusion of QOL measures along with typical health and medical outcome measures, and QOL or psychological well-being is a practical concern in exercise and health settings. However, the current QOL literature is a hodgepodge of varying combinations of selected depression, anxiety, and mood measures. So far, health psychologists and behavioral medicine researchers have not provided much guidance in delineating coherent constructs and developing sound measures of health-related QOL. Sport and exercise psychologists, along with measurement colleagues, could contribute to this effort and further advance research and practice concerning health-related physical activity.

## STATISTICS AND DESIGN ISSUES IN SPORT AND EXERCISE PSYCHOLOGY RESEARCH

Sport and exercise psychology has other issues related to statistics and design. At the 1993 conference of the International Society of Sport Psychology, Schutz (1993) listed a number of sport psychology methodological and measurement issues. (For a more detailed discussion, see Schutz, 1993; or Gill, 1997.) I'll highlight those that are particularly relevant, noting progress and continuing issues.

- Hypothesis testing versus heuristic research
- The null hypothesis as the research hypothesis
- The measurement and analysis of change
- Measuring the magnitude of an effect
- Statistical sophistication versus multivariate obfuscation
- The measurement of latent constructs
- The proliferation of scales and inventories
- Establishing the validity, reliability, and stability of factor structures

The last three issues relate to the measurement problems we just covered. The first issue is a big one for sport and exercise psychology, but in a larger sense than discussed by Schutz (1993).

### Hypothesis Testing Versus Heuristic Research

The issue in our discipline is not really hypothesis testing versus heuristic research. Theoretical research can and should have heuristic value, as Lewin (1951) states in his classic line, "There is nothing so practical as a good theory" (p. 169). The larger issue is dealing with the growing interest in "qualitative" research. Martens (1987b) called for more heuristic research and adoption of alternative methods, such as case studies and introspective reports. Since then, several sport and exercise psychologists have incorporated alternative, qualitative methods, and some have provided models (e.g., Scanlan's work on sport enjoyment and stress, discussed in chapter 10).

> **Key Point**
>
> Heuristic research and qualitative research must be balanced with careful planning and scientific rigor. Using *relevant* theory is key.

Unfortunately, others have taken Martens's call for alternative approaches as justification for abandoning all scientific rigor, measurement standards, hypotheses testing, and statistical analyses. The best qualitative research, from my perspective, is done by specialists with experience in traditional methods who see new possibilities, but not a cure-all, and who recognize limits of qualitative approaches and what one trades off by leaving traditional approaches. Good qualitative research—and note that qualitative research encompasses many methods and approaches (see Denzin & Lincoln's excellent 1994 handbook for further information)—demands careful planning and rigor. In fact, without the established guidelines of more traditional methods, it is even more critical to do careful planning, pilot testing, and attentive monitoring of measures, procedures, and analyses. The challenge for our discipline is to develop standards and guidelines for conducting and evaluating that research.

## The Null Hypothesis as the Research Hypothesis

The null hypothesis as a research hypothesis is nonsensical—I have no other insights on it. However, I would add that sport and exercise psychology research seldom presents clear, testable hypotheses, even when introductions to articles appear to hypothesize something. Many papers present results that "support" a model or theory; but scrutiny reveals no way that alternative results would have disproved the theory or led to any other conclusions. Sport and exercise psychology research is no model of Platt's (1964) "strong inference" approach, which Landers (1983) advocated for our area. Again, we come back to the main message—clear, relevant research questions are the first step.

> **Key Point**
>
> The null hypothesis is not a valid research hypothesis—a clear, relevant, and testable research question is needed.

## Measurement of Change and the Magnitude of Effects

Measurement of change and of the magnitude of our effects, also listed by Schutz (1993), is less central to current sport and exercise psychology research than other issues are. As Schutz pointed out, we still have far to go, and we can do more to *evaluate* effects. In a 1996 American College of Sports Medicine address, Rejeski, who has investigated physical activity and QOL, pointed out that *ecological* validity and clinical significance may well be more important than our typical psychometric tests. Researchers must develop measures of constructs and behaviors important to the health and well-being of our participants.

## Statistical Sophistication Versus Multivariate Obfuscation

The issue of statistical sophistication versus multivariate obfuscation is my personal favorite. Many papers offer multivariate obfuscation, often in misguided attempts to use the most complex techniques and computer programs. Give us a hammer, and everything looks like a nail. About 15 years ago, multivariate analyses (MANOVA) became commonplace, and many sport and exercise psychology reviewers and advisors told everyone to use MANOVA whenever possible. Today, structural modeling is the gateway to acceptability. MANOVA is not the automatic solution; if we do not have a multivariate question, a multivariate answer is not needed, and probably not desirable.

Structural equation modeling (SEM) can help answer sport and exercise psychology questions, and confirmatory analyses are appropriate to test or confirm a model. However, SEM is no substitute for careful conceptualization and design. Many overinterpret SEM and forget that it's a statistical technique. Although confirmatory analyses are appropriate for testing a model, exploratory techniques may be more appropriate to delineate constructs and refine models. For example, multidimensional scaling (MDS) techniques are seldom used in sport and exercise psychology, but MDS may be a promising approach for delineating and refining our constructs, models, and measures. Most of all, any statistical technique that dominates our research literature tends to limit research. We must plan and design studies to fit our questions, not to fit the standard measures and hot techniques.

### Key Point

The research question at hand, not a standard measure or a hot technique, must determine how a study is planned and designed.

## PARADIGMS AND META-THEORIES

We have progressed with the scientific method, but according to some sport and exercise psychology scholars we have exhausted its possibilities and should move to other alternatives. Most often critics have pointed the finger at normal science and promoted more subjective forms of knowledge in real-world settings. I applaud moves to the real world and welcome alternative methods, but the scientific method is not our downfall. The fault, dear reader, is not in our methods, but in our questions. As Dewar and Horn (1992) suggested and Dzewaltowski (1997) explicitly advocated, we must question our paradigms and meta-theories. The most often cited challenges to our paradigms are Martens's (1979, 1987b) influential papers, but most have interpreted Martens's work only in terms of the methodological critiques.

### Martens's Paradigm Challenges

In his influential "smocks and jocks" paper, as noted earlier, Martens (1979) criticized sport psychology research for its lack of relevance to the real world and called for more relevant research in the field. Although many interpreted that call as an excuse to abandon scientific rigor and theory, Landers (1983)—a strong advocate of theory testing—pointed out that Martens did not call for abandoning theory, but for using relevant theory.

### Key Point

Martens (1979) called for using relevant theory—research relevant to the real world.

Martens's 1987b paper on science and knowledge in sport psychology was even more influential, prompting many sport and exercise psychologists not only to move to the field, but also to abandon other aspects of normal science in favor of more subjective forms of knowing. As Dewar and Horn (1992) noted, Martens's concern was not simply methodological, but a broader concern about what it means to know in sport psychology.

## Dewar and Horn's Postmodern and Feminist Critiques

Dewar and Horn (1992) offered a different critique of existing sport and exercise psychology science and knowledge, based on postmodern and feminist critiques of science. They echoed many of Martens's concerns, but added a much stronger plea for contextualizing knowledge. Science is not neutral, and more to the point, sport and exercise psychology reflects the dominant culture in its values and interpretations. Dewar and Horn made three specific recommendations. First, we must question how knowledge is developed and incorporate alternative ways of knowing. Second, we must recognize that human behavior in sport is complex and multifaceted. These first two recommendations support what Martens said, but Dewar and Horn's final point is a welcome addition: that we must interpret our results in ways that are sensitive to the social and political contexts to develop a more inclusive knowledge.

### Key Point

Dewar and Horn (1992) recommended that knowledge be contextualized. The social and economic environments have a powerful influence on sport and exercise behavior.

## Dzewaltowski's Ecological Meta-Theory

Dzewaltowski (1997) has moved beyond critique to propose an ecological meta-theory as an alternative to previous dominant frameworks. First Dzewaltowski describes and contrasts the existing meta-theories that guide our work:

- **Biological-dispositional.** These approaches emphasize person characteristics or physiological mechanisms as the source of behavior and regulation, and are closely tied to rational objective and normal science methods.

- **Cognitive-behavioral.** These approaches focus on the social and physical environment as a source of behavioral regulation and also rely on natural science, but they stress cognition rather than individual characteristics.

- **Cognitive-phenomenological.** These approaches are similar to the cognitive-behavioral, but follow the Gestalt tradition to focus more on the "whole" than on isolated behaviors.

- **Social constructionist.** These approaches are the farthest removed from the scientific method and consider all knowledge as socially constructed and subjective.

Dzewaltowski offers the ecological model as an alternative to all the others. The ecological model, which does not totally reject the notion of objective reality, incorporates varied methods. The key is the focus on the environment, specifically the person-in-environment. The approach focuses on the relationship between people and their environment and uses varied descriptive, exploratory, and experimental methods. The environment is not static; the person transforms the environment (note that this is not the same as the view that the person constructs the environment) just as the environment transforms the person. Dzewaltowski's model stresses behavior and people in context, with greater emphasis on the specific sport or exercise environment. That emphasis seems critical if we are to answer questions about sport and exercise behavior.

### Key Point

Dzewaltowski's (1997) ecological meta-theory focuses on the person-in-environment and uses varied descriptive, exploratory, and experimental methods.

## Toward a Dynamic Model of Complexity

I would extend the ecological model somewhat by incorporating some aspects of complexity notions and emphasizing the dynamic complexity of the sport and exercise environment. Some aspects of chaos and complexity seem particularly relevant to a sport and exercise psychology framework. First, complexity models are nondeterministic. We cannot specify all conditions or sources of behaviors, and we cannot predict behavior no matter how much we improve our measures. The best we can do is to develop guidelines and general descriptive patterns. Human behavior is far more complex than most of the phenomena that fit complexity models. We will not identify a pattern that fits all behavior, or even all behavior in a very limited setting. And not only is behavior complex, it is dynamic: conditions constantly change, and initial, seemingly trivial conditions can have tremendous later impact, as in the classic example of the butterfly flapping its wings to affect distant storm patterns. For a more relevant example, one hurried comment from an elementary physical education teacher affects the activity patterns of the adult. Moreover, that one comment is part of a limitless set of comments and events. Each precise combination is unique, and even with identical circumstances, individuals interact with their circumstances in unique ways.

Behavior—like a cross country race—is dynamic. Conditions constantly change and initial, seemingly trivial conditions can have tremendous later impact.

One response to my dynamic approach might be to give up, assume we cannot predict anything, and therefore say we have nothing to learn from any sport and exercise psychology work. That is not at all what I suggest. I do argue that we cannot find one specific answer to such questions as "How do I stick to an exercise program?" or "How can I help a soccer player maintain an optimal emotional state?"

I suggest that we stop trying to find such elusive answers, but look to the literature and other sources of knowledge to find guidelines and patterns. Researchers can help develop and specify those unifying principles. Practitioners can adapt those guidelines in light of their experience and the immediate situation. With these approaches, we will move toward *practical theory*.

## Practical Theory

In my view, practical theory is not an oxymoron. Rather, practical theory is theory, that is, guidelines rather than facts, and practical, that is, relevant to the real world. Lewin's (1951) statement, "There is nothing so practical as a good theory," reflects this view. Practitioners must look for theories rather than facts: facts continually change in the real world.

Lewin's line comes from a larger statement (1951) addressed to researchers:

> *This can be accomplished . . . if the theorist does not look toward applied problems with highbrow aversion or with a fear of social problems, and if the applied psychologist realizes that there is nothing so practical as a good theory. (p. 169)*

Boyer (1990), whose work on higher academic scholarship is influential in higher education, made the same point in noting that the scholarship of application is not a one-way street:

> *It would be misleading to suggest knowledge is first discovered and then applied . . . the process is far more dynamic. . . . New understandings can arise out of the very act of application—whether in medical diagnosis, serving clients, shaping public policy or working with the public schools. In activities such as these, theory and practice vitally interact, and one renews the other. (p. 23)*

Scholars must ask real-world questions with an eye on the person-in-context. Researchers as well as practitioners must stop searching for the facts and aim for practical theory.

## Summary

Sport and exercise psychology theory, research, and practice have progressed since the late 1960s. Understanding the links in the theory-research-practice triad and the key role of theory is critical to our continuing progress. We have emphasized personality measures and individual differences, and we have advanced largely by using the methods of traditional, "normal" science. The traditional scientific method has been criticized for its shortcomings and inability to guide us in developing relevant knowledge. To increase relevance of our research and provide practical theory to guide professional practice, we must continually reconsider the paradigms and meta-theories that guide knowledge development. The most promising routes to relevant, useful knowledge recognize the powerful influence of the social environment, focus on people-in-context, and stay mindful of the complex dynamics of sport and exercise behavior.

## Review Questions

1. Describe the functions of theory and explain why it is the critical link in the theory-research-practice triad.

2. Recognize and explain nonscientific sources of knowledge.

3. Explain the scientific method and its steps.

4. Discuss the issues related to the development and use of personality measures.

5. Explain issues to keep in mind when evaluating or designing research methods and measures.

6. List and explain three alternative approaches to knowledge development.

## Recommended Reading

★ Martens, R. (1987b). Science, knowledge and sport psychology. *The Sport Psychologist, 1*, 29-55.

> Martens's 1987 article is one of our most influential works. Martens was an active researcher through the 1970s and 1980s, but gradually moved from his early experimental lab research to sport-relevant issues. In this paper, he urges more dramatic changes and suggests that we not only make research more relevant, but that we reconsider our sources of knowledge and the relationship of our academic work to practicing sport psychology. The issues Martens raised over 10 years ago remain. Several rereadings of Martens's article and continual reconsideration of the issues will help you understand and contribute to ongoing debates.

★ Schutz, R.W., & Gessaroli, M.E. (1993). Use, misuse, and disuse of psychometrics in sport psychology research. In R.N. Singer, M. Murphey, & L.K. Tennant (Eds.), *Handbook of research on sport psychology* (pp. 901-917). New York: Macmillan.

> Schutz is a leading scholar in the area of measurement in exercise and sport science, and one with a strong understanding of psychology and motor behavior. In this chapter, he and his coauthor outline important statistical, measurement, and design issues. Those who wish to conduct valid research and develop sound measures should read this chapter carefully.

★ Forscher, B.K. (1963). Chaos in the brickyard. *Science, 142*, 3590.

> Forscher's *Science* article is short and entertaining, and I consider it a classic must-read for any graduate student. It reads like a fable, and like most fables, it has a clear message. Using the analogy of bricks and buildings, Forscher makes the point that *theory* (the blueprint) is the key difference between a useful building and a pile of bricks.

# Individual Characteristics Influencing Sport and Exercise Behavior

Sport and exercise psychology focuses on individual behavior, and thus we begin our exploration of the discipline by reviewing the literature on individual characteristics that influence sport and exercise behavior. That is, we focus on the person in the classic formula (chapter 1) defining behavior (B) as a function of the person (P) and the environment (E). In chapter 4, we will emphasize enduring personality dispositions and review the literature on personality and its application in sport and exercise psychology. As chapter 4 reveals, general personality models and measures have been widely used, but not very usefully, in our discipline. Sport and exercise psychologists have moved to more sport-specific individual characteristics and psychological skills.

In chapter 5 we will address individual differences in attention and cognitive styles that have been applied specifically to sport and exercise. Later, in chapter 12, we will consider cognitive strategies and skills, including imagery. In chapter 6 we will cover self-perceptions. We'll start with self-concept, including recent work on multidimensional, physical self-perceptions. Finally, we will look at self-confidence and the extensive sport and exercise psychology work on self-efficacy.

# *c h a p t e r* 4

# Personality

## CHAPTER OBJECTIVES

After studying this chapter, you should be able to

- explain several general personality theories and measures and
- trace the sport and exercise psychology research on personality characteristics and behavior.

Individual differences are obvious. One youth soccer player relishes center stage while a teammate shuns the limelight; one person goes on long, daily runs while a neighbor socializes and exercises at the fitness center; one gymnast rises to the challenge of competition, but another chokes and performs far below expectations. Such individual differences reflect personality. Not only do we recognize individual differences, but we often assess personality when we "size up" opponents, consider how different students might react to feedback, or evaluate our own strengths and weaknesses. Those personality assessments in turn affect our behaviors. A diver poised on deck before the first dive might ponder, "Can I maintain my poise and concentration through this competition?" The diver who answers, "Yes! I'm confident and ready to hit that first dive," likely will feel differently and perform differently than one who answers hesitantly or worries about mistakes. We also use personality judgments when interacting with others. Instructors do not make the same comments to the student they consider fragile or sensitive as to the student they judge mentally tough.

The goal of personality research in sport and exercise psychology is to provide accurate and reliable information about individual differences and the relationships of such differences to sport and exercise behaviors. In this chapter we will consider general personality theories and measures and then focus on the sport and exercise psychology research on personality characteristics and behavior.

## PERSONALITY DEFINED

Personality is the individual's unique psychological makeup or, more formally, "the underlying, relatively stable, psychological structures and processes that organize human experience and shape a person's actions and reactions to the environment" (Lazarus & Monat, 1979, p. 1). Thus defined, personality denotes characteristic or consistent individual differences in behavior. The personality characteristic of aggressiveness is attributed to an individual who consistently displays aggressive behavior (e.g., often argues, easily angers, initiates fights). One can describe personality as the sum total or overall pattern of such characteristics and tendencies. We commonly

Social behavior is just one aspect of personality; perceptual and cognitive characteristics are other aspects of personality.

think of personality as including social characteristics, such as introversion or aggressiveness; but personality also includes perceptual and cognitive characteristics, such as the ability to concentrate.

**Key Point**

Personality is the overall pattern of psychological characteristics that make each person unique.

## BIOLOGICAL THEORIES OF PERSONALITY

No doubt individual differences have been obvious as long as people have interacted, and explanations can be found as far back as there are records. Personality theories range from primitive, commonsense explanations to elaborate, sophisticated models and vary from the purely biological to purely environmental. Traditionally, personality theories are categorized as psychodynamic/organismic, trait, and social learning theories.

### Early Theories

As far back as the ancient Greeks and Romans we find theories to explain individual differences in personality and behavior. The early Greeks believed that all persons had four basic body fluids or "humors." Varying individual temperaments or personalities were due to differing relative proportions of these humors. Blood was associated with a "sanguine" or cheerful temperament; yellow bile, with "choleric" or irritable behavior; black bile, with a "melancholic" or sad temperament; and phlegm, with a "phlegmatic" temperament, or indifferent, apathetic behavior.

Today's theorists do not refer to the four body fluids, but we can find some "humor" in current personality research. Many biological explanations of individual differences have considerable credibility, but even proponents of biological explanations do not claim a biological basis for all behaviors. Moyer (1973), discussing the physiological basis of aggression, emphasized that no physiological characteristic or process explains all aggressive behavior; and he further acknowledged the crucial role of learning and situational factors. For example, as we will see in chapter 17, heightened physiological arousal (a biological factor) may increase the likelihood of aggressive behavior, but situational factors play a greater role in whether aggression actually occurs.

## Sheldon's Constitutional Theory

One biological explanation of personality from the 1940s attracted the attention of exercise and sport science scholars: Sheldon's constitutional theory (Sheldon & Stevens, 1942). Sheldon developed the system of *somatotyping* to rate a person's physique along the three dimensions of endomorphy (roundness), ectomorphy (linearity), and mesomorphy (muscularity). By further suggesting that each dimension is associated with a distinct set of personality characteristics, Sheldon proposed a biological personality theory. Endomorphy is characterized by affection, sociability, and relaxation (Santa Claus is the prototypic endomorph in both body type and personality). Ectomorphy is characterized by tenseness, introversion, and a preponderance of artistic and intellectual characteristics. The mesomorph, with the typical athletic build, has the stereotypical personality of aggressiveness, dominance, and risk taking. Although Sheldon offered correlational evidence, subsequent studies failed to confirm the theory, which is not prominent today.

## Current Biological Theories

Exercise and sport psychologists recognize the role of biology in sport and exercise behavior, and some advocate a combination of biological characteristics, learning, and other individual characteristics to explain sport and exercise behavior. Dishman (1982, 1984) proposed a psychobiological model of exercise adherence that includes biological factors (such as body composition) and psychological factors (particularly self-motivation) as influences on adherence. Theories of exercise adherence have been modified and refined, as we will discuss in chapter 7; and the incorporation of both biological and psychological components is common.

Two current lines of research on biology and temperament merit discussion. First, Jerome Kagan's work on the genetic aspects of temperament, specifically shyness versus outgoingness, is widely respected and has considerable support. Similarly, Marvin Zuckerman's work on sensation-seeking emphasizes biological factors and has relevance to sport and exercise behavior.

Kagan (1995) titled his recent book *Galen's Prophecy*, reflecting ties to the ideas of Hippocrates and the later views of Galen, a second-century physician. Like Hippocrates and Galen, Kagan defines temperament as "any moderately stable, differentiating emotional or behavioral quality whose appearance in childhood is influenced by an inherited biology, including differences in brain neurochemistry" (p. xvii). Kagan has focused on the *inhibited-uninhibited* or shy-bold temperament, and along with colleagues has amassed considerable evidence supporting a biological and genetic basis for this temperament. However, he also makes it clear that temperamental phenomena cannot be reduced to biology; instead, a temperamental profile is an emergent phenomenon that requires both biological and experiential conditions acting together over time (1995, p. xxi). If we look for a biological base or an experiential one, we can find it, but attempts at separating the complex interdependent relationships are ill-advised. Instead, we will understand personality and behavior better if we investigate these complexities.

Zuckerman (1994) raises similar issues in his text on sensation seeking, and devotes a chapter to risk taking in sport. For Zuckerman, sensation seeking is part of a broader impulsive-sensation-seeking trait, which represents the optimistic tendency to approach novel stimuli and explore the environment (p. 385). Sensation seeking has a high biological or genetic basis; monoamine neurotransmitter and gonadal hormones may be the underlying factors. But like Kagan, Zuckerman does not argue for a purely biological basis. Instead, he advocates incorporating biological and experiential factors in a psychobiological context.

Although most current personality theorists do not explore biological factors, most would agree with the main themes of Kagan and Zuckerman. Personality is determined by multiple, interdependent factors, and we are not likely to identify simple biological or experiential sources.

## PSYCHOLOGY MODELS OF PERSONALITY STRUCTURE

Much current personality work focuses on personality structure and on identifying the dimensions or categories that define one's personality. This work includes various trait theories (personality is a collection of traits), as well as more current approaches that do not rely totally on traits as predictors of behavior. Before discussing these models, we'll note two other traditional approaches to personality: psychodynamic/organismic theories and social learning theories.

### Psychodynamic and Organismic Theories

Clinically oriented theories, including psychodynamic and organismic theories, are particularly prominent in therapeutic and counseling settings. Psychodynamic approaches reflect the influence of Freud and psychoanalytic theory: personality develops through the resolution of conflicts as the ego arbitrates between the unconscious drives of the id and the conscience of the superego. Psychodynamic theories stem from clinical observations and intuition, focus on psychopathology, and offer few testable predictions, especially about healthy personalities.

Organismic theories, such as Maslow's (1954) self-actualization theory, are more optimistic and humanistic than Freudian approaches. Organismic theories view personality as shaped by an overall field of forces and posit self-change or growth as a central feature. Although applied sport and exercise psychologists who consult with individuals may find the more "wholistic" approach useful in helping people develop healthy lifestyles, these theories offer few testable predictions and have little impact on our research and practice.

### Social Learning Theories

Social learning theories might be considered antipersonality theories. In relation to personality and behavior, these are reactions to the extreme trait theories, which assume that traits predict behavior. In reality, traits are notoriously poor predictors of behavior. In an often cited critique, Mischel (1968) pointed out that even the most psychometrically sound trait measures predict only a small proportion of behavior. The assertive basketball player does not display assertive behavior in every contest and every situation, and may be very nonassertive in other settings. The inability of trait measures to predict behavior led many psychologists to renounce trait theories; many adopted a social learning approach, which downplays the role of personality traits and focuses on the situation and learned behaviors. Referring to a social learning view, Bandura (1977b) stated, "Psychological functioning is explained in terms of a continuous reciprocal interaction of personal and environmental determinants" (pp. 11-12). An extreme view such as B.F. Skinner's behaviorism discounts personality altogether. A basketball player exhibits assertive behavior because the situation calls for it and because it has been reinforced in the past; any person in the same situation would display the same behavior.

The same individual may be aggressive and confident in some settings, such as sports, but tentative and less confident in other settings, such as class discussions.

## Personality Traits or Dispositions

Most personality research and most commonly used personality measures (e.g., Cattell 16PF, Minnesota Multiphasic Personality Inventory [MMPI]) are based on trait approaches. Traits are relatively stable, highly consistent attributes that exert widely generalized causal effects on behavior (Mischel, 1973). Trait theories imply consistency and generalizability of behavior; the person with a high level of shyness consistently displays shy behavior in varied situations, such as classes, team meetings, and activities. These theories assume that once we identify traits, we can predict behavior. Thus, many have worked on developing psychometrically sound personality measures.

## Interactionist Approaches

Modern personality psychology has moved from the more extreme trait theories toward social learning theories. Today, most personality psychologists prefer an interactionist approach that considers the interrelated roles of personality factors and situational factors as codeterminants of behavior. Certain personality characteristics predict behavior in certain, but not all, situations. A tennis player might consistently become anxious when facing competition but not when facing other challenges, such as academic tests or verbal presentations.

### Key Point

Most personality psychologists today prefer an interactionist approach, which can be represented by the simple equation B = f (P, E). The approach does not provide simple predictions because any behavior is the function of a seemingly limitless number of personality, environmental, and situational factors.

B = f (P, E), the formula presented in chapter 1, is a simple representation of the interactionist approach, but the interactionist approach is not simple. Any behavior, such as aggressive behavior in ice hockey, is the function of a seemingly limitless number of personality and environmental factors. Selected personality characteristics may have considerable influence at one time but little effect in a later situation.

An opponent's insult may provoke an aggressive response from a player in one situation but not from another in the same situation, and perhaps not even in the same player in a slightly different situation (e.g., perhaps a lack of sleep or problems outside sport facilitated the aggressive response).

An interactionist approach does not make simple, absolute predictions. Instead, it depends on considerable research to identify personality characteristics that influence specific behaviors in varying situations and to determine how these characteristics interact with varying situational factors. Moreover, insight and experience help coaches, instructors, or consultants transfer those research implications into real situations with sport and exercise participants. The interactionist approach is more complex, but also more realistic, than the extreme trait and situational approaches. As noted in chapter 1, we should not expect simple answers to human behavior questions.

## The "Big Five" Model of Personality

Psychologists continue to explore and debate the structure of personality, but the literature suggests consensus. Most personality psychologists accept the "Big Five" model with its five major dimensions (see figure 4.1):

1. Neuroticism

2. Extraversion

3. Openness to experience (Culture or Intellect in some versions)

4. Agreeableness

5. Conscientiousness

Most models of personality, from that of Hippocrates and the four-humor model to more modern trait conceptualizations, reflect some aspects of the Big Five. Today's theorists (e.g., Goldberg, 1993; John, 1990; McCrae & Costa, 1987) cite Sir Francis Galton's (1883) attempts to categorize all the many descriptive terms for individuals as one of the first dimensional models. In the 20th century, scholars had the advantage of statistical analyses, and Cattell in particular used factor analysis to develop his model of personality and the widely used 16PF measure of 16 key personality factors. Eysenck (1991), on the other hand, continues to argue for fewer dimensions. Ironically, his early three-factor model of Psychoticism-Extraversion-Neuroticism served as the basis for much five-factor work. Although debate continues on the specific labels and components of the five-factor model, the general structure is accepted, and corresponding measures have been developed. Specifically, the Neuroticism-Extraversion-Openness Personality Inventory (Costa & McCrae, 1985) is widely used today.

**Figure 4.1**
Personality dimensions: the big five.

1. **(N) Neuroticism**
   Nervousness, anxiety, depression, anger versus emotional stability.

2. **(E) Extraversion**
   Enthusiasm, sociability, assertiveness, high activity level versus introversion.

3. **(O) Openness to experience**
   Originality, need for variety, curiosity, artistic sensitivity.

4. **(A) Agreeableness**
   Amiability, altruism, modesty, trust versus egocentrism, narcissism, skepticism.

5. **(C) Conscientiousness**
   Constraint, achievement striving, self-discipline.

**Key Point**

The general structure of the five-factor model is accepted, and corresponding measures have been developed. Most models of personality reflect some aspect of the Big Five model's dimensions—extraversion, agreeableness, conscientiousness, neuroticism, and openness to experience.

## PERSONALITY MEASURES

Personality assessment in sport and exercise psychology usually involves personality inventories, but can also take the form of life histories, projective measures, or behavioral observations. Clinicians are especially likely to use projective measures, in-depth interviews, or case histories to assess the whole person. Projective measures such as the Rorschach inkblot test or the Thematic Apperception Test, used to assess achievement motivation, present vague stimuli (e.g., inkblots, pictures) and allow people to project their personalities by telling a story.

Objective personality inventories, the most common measures, involve structured responses (e.g., multiple-choice or true/false items) and are easily administered and scored; their wide use permits comparisons with norms and other samples. Several of the most common personality measures, such as the Cattell 16PF, MMPI, and Eysenck's EPI (Eysenck Personality Inventory), have been used with sport and exercise participants. Other personality measures assessing single traits or characteristics, such as Spielberger's (1966) Trait Anxiety Inventory and Rotter's (1966) Internal-External Locus of Control Scale, have also been used in sport and exercise psychology and will be discussed in later chapters.

One of the most popular personality measures, the Myers-Briggs Type Indicator (MBTI), has not been used very much in our research but is gaining popularity in sport psychology consultation. The MBTI (available from Consulting Psychologists Press), which may be interpreted from a five-factor perspective (McCrae & Costa, 1989), reports preferences on four scales.

Extraversion (E)—Introversion (I)

Sensing (S)—Intuition (N)

Thinking (T)—Feeling (F)

Judging (J)—Perceiving (P)

You can use the MBTI to classify yourself on each dimension and determine your overall personality type. For example, an ISTJ (introverted, sensing, thinking, judging type) tends to be serious and quiet and to succeed through concentration and thoroughness; to be practical, orderly, matter-of-fact, logical, realistic, and dependable; to be well organized; to take responsibility; and to make up his or her own mind about goals and work toward them steadily, regardless of obstacles. Similar descriptions are available in reports on various forms of the MBTI, including popular versions available in bookstores. The MBTI is probably the most widely used personality measure, particularly in training and educational settings and in counseling. But many personality theorists express reservations. The dichotomous classifications encourage stereotypes and labels. The accompanying descriptions reflect "normal" (vs. clinical or pathological) samples, which certainly has some advantages; but the descriptions tend to be intuitively obvious and recognizable. The MBTI may be a useful icebreaker for discussion, including discussion of interpersonal styles and interactions, but relationships to specific sport and exercise behaviors are elusive.

## PERSONALITY RESEARCH IN SPORT AND EXERCISE PSYCHOLOGY

Personality is a consistently popular topic in sport and exercise psychology. Perhaps the apparent, unique physical characteristics of athletes prompt a search for analogous psychological profiles. Most of the research involves certain types of questions: Is there an "athletic personality?" Are runners more introverted than volleyball players? Can we predict success from personality information?

Some have posed the questions in reverse: "How do sport and exercise affect personality?" We often claim effects to justify programs: we might claim that sport fosters leadership, moral development, or teamwork. More recently, exercise has been promoted as an avenue to improved mental health. So far, claims of general personality changes have not been supported, but research on specific relationships between sport behaviors and moral development, and exercise effects on specific self-perceptions and emotions, is providing provocative information (such work will be discussed in later chapters).

## Personality Profiles of Athletes

As part of his pioneering sport psychology work, Coleman Griffith (1926, 1928) examined the personality profiles of successful athletes. Through observations of and interviews with college and professional athletes, Griffith identified the following "characteristics of great athletes": ruggedness, courage, intelligence, exuberance, buoyance, emotional adjustment, optimism, conscientiousness, alertness, loyalty, and respect for authority. Griffith did not do empirical research, and you may notice that his list reflects the all-American boy image that characterized the athletes of his day.

Many athletes have filled out many personality inventories between Griffith's time and the present, and some reviewers have seen some consistency. On the basis of the sport personality literature, Ogilvie (1968) concluded that certain traits are associated with successful athletes. With colleagues, he developed the Athletic Motivation Inventory (Tutko, Lyon, & Ogilvie, 1969) to measure those traits (figure 4.2). You may notice the similarity between the AMI list and Griffith's list, which is also shown in the figure.

## Mental Health Model

With his "mental health model" of success in athletics, Morgan (1978, 1980) offers the most systematic work. The model suggests that positive mental health and athletic success are directly related whereas psychopathology and success are inversely related. In studies with college and Olympic wrestlers, national-team rowers, and elite distance runners, Morgan demonstrated that successful athletes possessed more positive mental health characteristics and fewer negative mental health characteristics than the general population. The pattern emerging from Morgan's research,

**Figure 4.2**
Personality traits associated with superior athletes.

| Coleman Griffith list | AMI traits (Tutko, Lyon, & Ogilvie) |
| --- | --- |
| Ruggedness | Drive |
| Courage | Determination |
| Intelligence | Leadership |
| Exuberance | Aggressiveness |
| Buoyance | Guilt proneness |
| Emotional adjustment | Emotional control |
| Optimism | Self-confidence |
| Conscientiousness | Conscientiousness |
| Alertness | Mental toughness |
| Loyalty | Trust |
| Respect for authority | Coachability |

**Figure 4.3**

Profile of Mood States (POMS) summaries for elite wrestlers, distance runners, and rowers.

From W.P. Morgan and M.L. Pollock, 1977, "Psychological characterization of the elite distance runner," *Annals of the New York Academy of Sciences, 301,* 387. Copyright 1977 by the New York Academy of Sciences. Reprinted with permission.

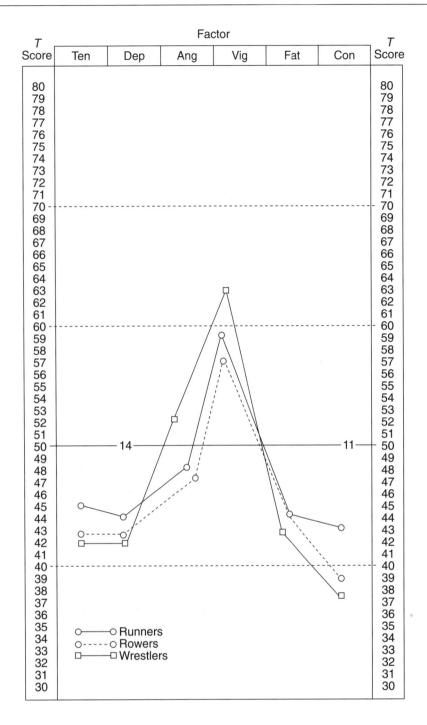

depicted in figure 4.3, has been termed the "iceberg profile." On the Profile of Mood States (POMS; McNair, Lorr, & Droppleman, 1971), successful athletes typically score above the waterline (population norm) on vigor, but below on the negative moods of tension, depression, anger, fatigue, and confusion.

Although Morgan's model is widely cited and the iceberg profile has been replicated with other athlete samples, cautions are in order. The model is general; not every successful athlete has the iceberg profile, and many less-than-successful athletes do match the profile. It is not surprising that psychopathology is negatively related to success in athletics; quite likely psychopathology is negatively related to success in most endeavors. Furthermore, the iceberg profiles of athletes do not necessarily imply that positive mental health (personality) leads to success; success in sport may lead to more positive mood profiles and enhanced mental health.

Notably, Morgan's clearest results are with the POMS, a measure of moods, rather than with global personality inventories. Recently, Rowley, Landers, Kyllo, and Etnier (1995) conducted a meta-analysis of POMS research and raised questions about the model. Although athletes tended to show the iceberg profile, the effect size was a meager 0.15, accounting for less than 1% of the variance. Rowley et al. concluded that successful athletes possess a mood profile slightly more positive than less successful athletes but that the small, nonrobust effect raises questions about the utility of POMS in predicting athletic success.

**Key Point**

Morgan's Profile of Mood States (POMS), from which the "iceberg profile" of athletes emerges, is a measure of moods, not a global personality profile. Morgan and colleagues (1987) used POMS to track mood changes in athletes over a competitive season. They found that, generally, variations in the iceberg profile reflect overtraining.

Even so, an offshoot of POMS research offers more promise. The POMS assesses mood, and mood varies over time and situations. Morgan and colleagues (e.g., Morgan, Brown, Raglin, O'Conner, & Ellickson, 1987) used POMS to track mood changes in athletes over a competitive season, and Raglin (1993) summarized that research. Generally, variations in the iceberg profile reflect overtraining: the iceberg profile of swimmers flattens in the midseason overtraining period, reflecting greater mood disturbance. The mood disturbances, which may be useful for tracking athletes, may reflect parallel physiological changes; but Raglin reported that physiological monitoring of cardiovascular, metabolic, or hormonal measures has not pinpointed clear mechanisms. Indeed, many questions remain open, but the relationships of mood (personality), physiological measures and processes, and performance are certainly worthy of further research.

## Problems With Sport Personality Research

Despite Morgan's work, most scholars see little value in global personality measures. Fisher, Ryan, and Martens (1976) concluded that global personality traits relate slightly if at all to sport participation or performance; this skeptical view holds today. The findings are as varied as the studies; different studies show different traits that characterize athletes, and some findings are contradictory. For every study indicating that runners are more introverted than volleyball players, another shows no difference. Little evidence supports a general athletic personality type, a personality profile that separates elite athletes from the rest of us, or specific personality profiles associated with specific activities. Given the diversity and unreliability of findings, personality information cannot predict meaningful sport and exercise behaviors or help participants much.

With such vast quantities of sport personality research yielding such meager information, we might ask whether personality relates to sport and exercise behavior at all. Although the literature to date tells us little, individual differences play a crucial role in human behavior in sport and exercise. Unfortunately, many studies were undertaken because they were easy to conduct rather than to answer meaningful questions.

**Key Point**

There are conceptual, methodological, and interpretive problems with sport psychology research. Sound research must address meaningful questions within a theoretical framework and use appropriate samples and measures. Results must not be overgeneralized.

If sport and exercise psychologists address relevant issues about personality and behavior, and do quality research, personality information can have value. First, we might consider and remedy problems with the previous research. Martens (1975a) classified problems with the early sport personality research into three general categories: conceptual, methodological, and interpretive problems.

### Conceptual Problems

The major conceptual problem in sport personality research is that many studies were done without a good reason. As discussed in chapter 3, research should address meaningful questions within a theoretical framework. Unfortunately, sport personality studies have seldom been carefully planned. Instead, as Ryan (1968) stated:

> The research in this area has largely been of the "shot gun" variety. By this I mean the investigators grabbed the nearest and most convenient personality test, and the closest sport group, and with little or no theoretical basis for their selection fired into the air to see what they could bring down. It isn't surprising that firing into the air at different times and at different places, and using different ammunition, should result in different findings. In fact, it would be surprising if the results weren't contradictory and somewhat contrary. (p. 71)

A sound conceptual basis is critical. Without meaningful questions, research cannot provide meaningful answers.

### Methodological Problems

Once they identify meaningful questions, researchers must follow sound methodology. Too often, sport personality researchers have used inappropriate samples (such as a single basketball team to represent all basketball players) or inappropriate measures (such as the MMPI, which was designed for clinical diagnoses, to assess nonclinical athlete samples).

### Interpretive Problems

Even if research is conceptually and methodologically sound, we must be cautious in interpreting findings. The most common interpretive error is overgeneralization—trying to make too much of the findings. Relationships found with one sample of athletes may not generalize to others.

When interpreting results, we cannot infer that a characteristic caused success, or a specific behavior; and we must be cautious about such generalizations. For example, suppose someone conducted a sound study and found that intercollegiate volleyball players were more independent than the norm. Should we assume that players scoring high on independence are better volleyball players? Should we use independence scores to select players? No! First, we cannot assume that independence makes a person a better volleyball player; the data are correlational. Correlations indicate a relationship, but not necessarily a cause-effect relationship. Perhaps the experience of playing volleyball leads to higher independence scores, or some other factor influences both independence scores and volleyball participation. From a practical perspective, why would a coach want high independence scores? What does high independence mean in terms of actual performance or behavior in volleyball? Are high scores on independence (or any other personality factor) likely to override the influence of coaching, strategies, training, or team norms?

## Use of Personality Measures to Screen Athletes

Although some personality characteristics may relate to important behaviors in sport and exercise, even the best measures are weak predictors. Present knowledge does not justify using personality measures to select participants. Unfortunately, some personality measures have been used for this purpose.

One of the earliest sport personality measures, the AMI (Tutko et al., 1969), is especially likely to be misinterpreted and misused. The AMI presumably assesses personality traits relevant to success in athletics. Supporting data are meager at best, but the marketing of the AMI, primarily to coaches, allows for considerable misinterpretation. Even with the best intentions, a coach might expect certain behaviors, key on particular actions, and alter the coach-athlete or intrateam relationships. At worst, an athlete might be slotted into certain roles or dropped. Such actions are unjustified and unfair to the athlete and coach and are detrimental to sport and exercise psychology.

Even if the AMI traits predicted certain behaviors, that would not justify dropping athletes. Height is related to success in volleyball; no doubt, the relationship between height and volleyball success is stronger and more reliable than that between any personality trait and success. Also, the relationship has a logical basis. But even given this strong, logical relationship, most coaches would not automatically select one starter over another simply because of a one-inch height difference. Selection on the basis of personality measures, when reliable relationships are not established, is indefensible. After much criticism, as well as advances in sport and exercise psychology, the AMI no longer is widely used. Sport and exercise psychologists must be similarly cautious about using and interpreting more current and reliable measures.

## SPORT-SPECIFIC PSYCHOLOGICAL SKILLS MEASURES

In the last 15 years, researchers have created more valid and useful personality measures focusing on sport-specific psychological skills and characteristics. Current applied sport psychology consultation emphasizes an initial assessment to provide a guide for development and maintenance of psychological skills for performance enhancement and overall development. Thus, consultants seldom use global personality measures, but focus on sport-specific skills and characteristics.

In one of the first attempts to assess psychological skills of elite athletes, psychologist Michael Mahoney and collaborator Marshall Avener used interviews, surveys, and observations with participants at the tryouts for the 1976 U.S. Olympic gymnastics team. Their study (1977), comparing Olympic qualifiers and nonqualifiers, showed that qualifiers were more self-confident, were more likely to think and dream about gymnastics, were more likely to use self-talk and internal mental imagery, and were able to control worry and concentrate on the task at the time of performance. Others replicated many of these findings, especially the higher confidence of more successful athletes (Gould, Weiss, & Weinberg, 1981; Highlen & Bennett, 1979; Meyers, Cooke, Cullen, & Liles, 1979); and, as chapter 11 will relate, the ability to control anxiety seems to characterize successful performers.

These studies involved limited samples; the measures lacked reliability and validity, and causality was not established. Nevertheless, the initial, exploratory findings encouraged similar investigations and set a direction for sport personality research. The initial work did not establish a personality profile for elite athletes, and that was not the purpose. Mahoney and colleagues continued their investigations of psychological skills and eventually used the results to develop a measure for research and practice (Mahoney, Gabriel, & Perkins, 1987). The Psychological Skills Inventory for Sports (PSIS) parallels the skills identified in the earlier work, with subscales for concentration, anxiety control, confidence, mental preparation, motivation, and team emphasis. Mahoney et al. (1987) assessed several groups of elite (national/international teams), preelite (junior national teams), and nonelite (intercollegiate teams) athletes, and also asked several sport psychologists to describe the "ideal athlete" on the PSIS measure. As expected (and providing some validity evidence for the PSIS), elite athletes reported stronger psychological skills than did the pre-elite and non-elite athletes. Specifically, elite athletes

- experienced fewer problems with anxiety,
- were more successful at deploying their concentration,
- were more self-confident,
- relied more on internally referenced and kinesthetic mental preparation,

- were more focused on their own performance than that of the team, and

- were more highly motivated to do well in their sport.

Still, the elite athletes' self-reports were not quite up to the profiles provided by the sport psychologists, whose ideal athlete was more confident, motivated, and team focused; had fewer anxiety and concentration problems; and used more internal mental preparation. It is not surprising that even elite athletes are not perfect. And the results have practical implications in suggesting that even top athletes have varying psychological strengths and limits, and can benefit by continued work on the mental aspects of their activities.

Although the PSIS and initial comparisons provide information and a measure for applied sport psychology, considerable caution is in order to avoid the problems associated with earlier sport personality work. Notably, the initial sample of athletes presented several confounds (e.g., elite athletes were older; different activities were represented at the three levels), and Mahoney et al. cautioned readers not to draw solid conclusions from preliminary results with measures lacking psychometric testing. Subsequent work with the PSIS by Chartrand, Jowdy, and Danish (1992) revealed problems with the PSIS and confirmed these cautions. Most of the PSIS subscales do not have satisfactory internal consistency (i.e., all items do not measure the same thing), although the confidence subscale was relatively consistent (Chartrand et al., 1992). For example, mental preparation had very low reliability, indicating that its items are not related to each other or to any single "mental preparation" construct—that is, we don't know what the scores mean.

Recently, Smith, Schutz, Smoll, and Ptacek (1995) developed and validated a multidimensional measure of sport-specific psychological skills, the Athletic Coping Skills Inventory-28 (ACSI). The ACSI assesses psychological skills similar to those assessed with the PSIS but has superior psychometric properties. The ACSI was originally developed as part of a project on coping with athletic injury. The refined 28-item ACSI contains seven subscales:

- Coping with adversity

- Peaking under pressure

- Goal setting/Mental preparation

- Concentration

- Freedom from worry

- Confidence and achievement motivation

- Coachability

With confirmatory factor analyses, Smith et al. (1995) demonstrated the factorial validity of the seven ACSI subscales for male and female athletes. The seven subscales can be summed to yield a personal coping resources score; and Smith et al. have provided preliminary evidence for validity of the ACSI in measuring personal coping resources as a multifaceted construct with seven underlying coping skill facets.

Applied sport psychologists continue to work on assessment, and further efforts may yield a sounder PSIS, confirm the value of the ACSI in applied work, or lead to the development of alternative measures. Some personality comparisons identified by Mahoney and colleagues have been confirmed in other research. Self-confidence, in particular, clearly relates to success in athletics and to successful performance of many sport and exercise behaviors. We will explore self-confidence in greater detail in chapter 6. Similarly, concentration, anxiety control, and mental preparation (e.g., imagery, goal setting) are consistently identified as important psychological skills for sport and exercise participants. When we cover those topics in later chapters, we'll include the critical role of individual differences. For now, we note that the PSIS may be helpful but is not an established, sound measure of such individual differences in research or practice.

Vanden Auweele, De Cuyper, Van Mele, and Rzewnicki (1993) provided a nice review of the work on elite performance and personality. As we have here, they noted the limited information from earlier sport personality research. For example, a meta-analysis of 25 studies on introversion/extraversion of athletes showed an overall effect size of –0.100, indicating no difference between athletes and the norm. Discussing work on psychological skills, Vanden Auweele et al. (1993) offered three specific directions or shifts that hold promise for personality research:

- A shift from traditional personality assessment to behavioral assessment
- A shift from interindividual to intraindividual (e.g., idiographic, case, "wholistic") research
- Abandoning deterministic models for probabilistic models (e.g., we cannot perfectly predict behavior because we cannot expect to identify all antecedents)

## EFFECTS OF SPORT AND EXERCISE ON PERSONALITY

Although most sport and exercise personality work explores how personality influences participation and behavior, research on the reverse relationship—how sport and exercise experiences influence the individual—is increasing. Organizers of activity programs often claim that sport builds character or values, but the research seldom supports such claims. In fact, some of the stronger work suggests that sport participation may decrease individuals' emphasis on ethical behaviors and values such as fair play (see chapters 16 and 17 for discussion of social development, moral behavior, and sport).

Although no evidence supports claims that sport and exercise programs affect overall personality, the rapidly expanding research on health-oriented exercise suggests that physical activity may promote both physical and mental health. However, that research focuses on mood (as with POMS), emotion, or psychological states such as anxiety and depression rather than more global and stable personality traits. At present, the testimony about psychological benefits of programs like jogging for anxiety reduction, aerobic dance for confidence, and survival training for enhanced self-esteem seems stronger than the empirical evidence; but rapidly expanding research suggests that there may be some basis for these claims. In fact, in chapter 6 we'll consider these issues in detail.

## Summary

Personality is the overall pattern of psychological characteristics that make each person unique. Individual differences are obvious in sport and exercise settings, and personality plays a key role in nearly all sport and exercise behaviors. The vast research on personality, conducted throughout the history of sport and exercise psychology, has yielded little useful information. Global personality measures are poor predictors of specific sport and exercise behaviors. This summary has changed little since the 1986 edition of this text. However, sport and exercise psychology has advanced greatly in the understanding of individual differences. Those advances involve more specific characteristics and psychological skills, sport-specific measures, and more clearly delineated relationships among individual differences, situational factors, and specific behaviors. We will look at many of these advances and insights in later chapters.

## Review Questions

1. Define personality.
2. Describe two current lines of research on biology and temperament, and state a commonality between them.

3. Describe the approach most personality psychologists prefer today, and explain why the representation of that approach is simple, but the approach is not.

4. Discuss five-factor models of personality, and list the dimensions of the Big Five Model.

5. List three types of problems with sport psychology research and discuss guidelines for avoiding these pitfalls and conducting sound research.

## *Recommended Reading*

★ Goldberg, L.R. (1993). The structure of phenotypic personality traits. *American Psychologist, 48,* 26-34.

> The "Big Five" model dominates in personality psychology. Goldberg is one of the key researchers in personality psychology, and his *American Psychologist* article provides a nice overview of the current research and continuing debates on personality structure and measures.

★ Smith, R.E., Schutz, R.W, Smoll, F.L., & Ptacek, J.T. (1995). Development and validation of a multidimensional measure of sport-specific psychological skills: The Athletic Coping Skills Inventory-28. *Journal of Sport & Exercise Psychology, 17,* 379-398.

> Those who work directly with athletes find sport-specific measures much more helpful than global personality measures. Mahoney and his colleagues did some of the early work and developed a psychological skills inventory for sport. Smith and his colleagues have moved beyond that work to develop a stronger measure of sport-specific skills. This article describes their work in developing the Athletic Coping Skills Inventory.

★ Rowley, A.J., Landers, D., Kyllo, L.B., & Etnier, J.L. (1995). Does the Iceberg Profile discriminate between successful and less successful athletes? A meta analysis. *Journal of Sport & Exercise Psychology, 17* (2), 185-199.

> Morgan's provocative research and description of the "iceberg profile," which suggests highly successful athletes are high on positive mental health or mood and low on negative moods, prompted considerable research. Rowley and colleagues conducted a meta-analysis of that work, and this article presents their findings and interpretations.

# chapter 5

# Attention and Cognitive Styles

## CHAPTER OBJECTIVES

After studying this chapter, you should be able to

- understand the sport and exercise psychology research relating to individual differences in attention and

- identify the most prominent research done in the area of individual differences in imagery ability, including widely used imagery tests.

Attention and cognitive styles are key psychological skills, and sport psychology consultants devote considerable time to concentration exercises and imagery rehearsal. We will discuss specific psychological skill interventions in chapter 12. In this chapter we'll focus on attention and cognitive style as individual differences and part of personality.

We need not look to elite athletes to recognize the role of attention and cognitive skills. We can hear the instructions "Concentrate" and "Pay attention" in the fitness club and the elementary physical education class. We can listen to a coach tell a 10-year-old "Keep your eye on the ball," or watch an Olympic diver "do" the dive while standing on the platform mentally rehearsing.

Furthermore, individual differences in attention and cognitive skills are obvious. Some 10-year-olds are better than others at keeping their eye on the ball. Diver Greg Louganis reported that imagery helped him perform, but other athletes find imagery more trouble than benefit. Some soccer players quickly take in the whole field and find the open player for the pass, but others can't see three feet beyond the ball. Some exercisers use mirrors as monitors or prompts, but others find them distracting.

Individual differences in attention and cognitive styles reflect personality, and some early sport personality work involved cognitive skills. For example, some researchers investigated Witkin's (1973) field independence-dependence—the degree to which a person relies on an internal frame of reference versus an external reference. As Pargman's (1993) review suggests, the research on field independence-dependence in relation to gender and sport participation had most of the flaws of the early sport personality research and did not yield much information.

The cognitive characteristics most prominent in our discipline are attention and imagery, which we'll stress in this chapter. Cognitive skills, such as the ability to focus and maintain attention, have clear implications for performance and behavior. To date, interest in cognitive interventions has far outpaced the related research, but the initial work offers directions for addressing many questions about the role of attention and cognition in sport and exercise behavior.

# ATTENTIONAL STYLE

As Abernethy (1993) notes, interest in attention is at least as old as experimental psychology itself. In *The Principles of Psychology*, William James (1890) described attention as follows:

> *Everyone knows what attention is. It is taking possession by the mind, in clear and vivid form, of one out of what seems several simultaneously possible objects or trains of thought. Focalization, concentration or consciousness are its essence. It implies withdrawal from some things in order to deal effectively with others, and is a condition which has a real opposite in the confused, dazed, scatterbrained state which in French is called distraction, and Zerstreutheit in German. (pp. 403-404)*

We still understand attention much as James described it, but modern cognitive psychologists have more to say about attentional processes. Cognitive psychologists and motor behavior scholars typically take an information-processing approach in considering attention, learning, and memory for motor skills.

## Key Point

Attention is "taking possession by the mind, in clear and vivid form, of one out of what seems several simultaneously possible objects or trains of thought" (James 1890).

Boutcher (1993) categorized the attention-performance literature into three perspectives—information processing, social psychological, and psychophysiological—but concluded by advocating a synthesis of the three perspectives as a guide for research and practice. As Boutcher noted, research on attention in sport is underdeveloped. Most of the limited work, done by motor behavior researchers, has taken the information-processing perspective (for discussions see Keele, 1973; Schmidt, 1988). Information-processing models typically provide frameworks for examining processes of perception, memory, decision making, and attention. Attention is a key process in taking in information, and we have considerable work on attentional selectivity, capacity, and alertness.

## Attentional Selectivity

James recognized the importance of selective attention, and we understand that the ability to selectively attend to cues, events, or thoughts while disregarding others is a key to successful performance. One distinction particularly relevant to athletes is control versus automatic processing. Control processing, which the individual does deliberately (as when a golfer decides which club to use), is slow and effortful. Automatic processing, which typically occurs with well-learned skills, is fast and effortless and not under conscious control. As Coleman Griffith observed in his interview with football star Red Grange (see chapter 2), elite athletes often report that they make moves without thinking. Indeed, events or instructions that make the athletes think about what they're doing disrupt automatic processing and impair performance.

## Key Point

Attentional selectivity is the ability to selectively attend to certain cues, events, or thoughts while disregarding others. Control processing, which the individual does deliberately, is slow and effortful. Automatic processing is fast and effortless and not under conscious control. It does not require attention.

We can't look at two things or think two different thoughts at the same time. *Attentional capacity* refers to the limits in the amount of information we can process at one time.

## Attentional Capacity

Attentional capacity refers to limits in the amount of information that one can process at one time. We can't look at two things or think two different thoughts at exactly the same time. Control processing is particularly vulnerable to structural and central limits on attentional capacity. Structural interference occurs when two tasks require the same receptor or effector systems. For example, listening for both the starter's gun and a coach's command could provoke structural interference. Cognitive psychology offers several theories and considerable research on central-capacity limits. Fixed-capacity theories (e.g., Keele, 1973) assume that capacity is fixed and the same for different tasks. Theories of undifferentiated capacity (e.g., Kahneman, 1973) view attention as a resource that can be channeled to varying processes. Multiple-resource theory (Wickens, 1984), a variation on the undifferentiated view, suggests that attention consists of pools of resources and that parallel processing of more than one stimulus is possible. The ability to simultaneously process multiple information sources depends on the importance and difficulty of the task and structural factors.

Although control processing requires great attention, effort, and awareness, automatic processing does not, and is not so limited by attentional capacity. Skilled performers do complex tasks that would be impossible if they had to pay attention to and consciously process all information. Control processing eventually gives way to automatic processing and effortless skill performance. Those working with individuals who are learning skills, and performers themselves, must consider the implications of the capacity limits on control processing to advance to more automatic skilled performance.

### Key Point

Attentional capacity refers to limits in the amount of information that one can process at one time. Control processing is particularly vulnerable to structural and central limits on attentional capacity. Automatic processing is not limited by attentional capacity.

## Attentional Alertness

Attentional alertness is related to information-processing research on arousal and attention. We'll discuss other work on arousal in chapters 10 and 11 on emotion and anxiety. In relation to attention, we'll focus on Easterbrook's (1959) cue utilization model, which proposes that increases in emotional arousal result in narrowing of the attentional field. Several sport and exercise psychology scholars (e.g., Landers, 1980) have applied the Easterbrook model to explain the arousal-performance relationship. As arousal increases, some attentional narrowing enhances performance, but further increases and narrowing impair performance as important cues are lost.

More recently, Landers and others have taken a psychophysiological perspective and focused on the role of brain activity and electroencephalogram measures. Hatfield, Landers, and Ray (1984) assessed right- and left-brain electroencephalogram activity of elite rifle shooters and found systematic patterns suggesting that these performers reduced unnecessary conscious mental activity of the left hemisphere at the time of the shot. Using a different psychophysiological measure, Landers, Christina, Hatfield, Doyle, and Daniels (1980) found heart rate deceleration in elite shooters just prior to the shot, and subsequent studies showed similar deceleration on a golf putting task (Boutcher & Zinsser, 1990; Crews & Landers, 1991).

Although a few sport and exercise psychologists have continued to pursue psychophysiological perspectives, and others have crossed into motor behavior with information-processing perspectives, most who study attention take what Boutcher (1993) termed a social psychological perspective. Actually, most of the work is not very "social" but rather focuses on individual differences in attentional style, as we'll discuss in the next section. But first we'll consider Boutcher's call for an integrated perspective synthesizing the information-processing, psychophysiological, and social psychology work on attention.

Boutcher (1993) advocates an interaction model similar to the interaction approaches advocated in the personality literature. Boutcher calls for incorporating questionnaire, observational, performance, and psychophysiological measures in a multilevel, multifaceted model in which enduring dispositions, demands of the activity, and environmental factors interactively determine initial arousal. During performance, arousal may be channeled into control or automatic processing to reach optimal attention. The model is complex, with feedback loops and multiple interconnections; specific hypotheses and practical implications are not obvious, and few aspects of the model have been tested. Still, Boutcher's preliminary framework, considering the individual, the environment, and behavior in continual, dynamic interaction, reflects the general approach to sport and exercise behavior described in part I.

## Nideffer's Attentional Model

Attentional style came to the "attention" of sport and exercise psychology largely through the work of Robert Nideffer. Nideffer (1976a) proposed a model of attention with two dimensions, width and direction (figure 5.1). Width ranges from narrow to broad; narrow and broad attention focus on a limited and a wide range of cues, respectively. Direction shifts on a continuum from an internal focus on one's own thoughts and feelings to an external focus on objects and events outside the body.

### Key Point

Nideffer's (1976a) model of attention has two dimensions, width and direction. These dimensions describe the range of cues attended to (narrow or broad) and the focus of attention (within oneself [internal] or outside oneself [external]).

Nideffer posited that varying combinations of attentional width and direction are appropriate for varying activities, and that use of the appropriate attentional focus can enhance performance. A broad-internal focus is an analytical style useful for planning strategies or analyzing previous performances; coaches often need a broad-internal style. Many sports, especially highly interactive team sports, call for a broad-external attentional style, which involves taking in a great deal of informa-

**Figure 5.1**
Nideffer's model of attentional focus.

From R. Nideffer, 1976, *The inner athlete* (New York: Crowell), 49. Copyright 1976 by Robert Nideffer. Adapted with permission.

tion. A quarterback trying to pick out primary and secondary receivers, or a soccer goalie facing the offense, could use a broad-external focus. A narrow-external focus is useful for activities requiring concentration on a ball or target, such as bowling, archery, and golf. A narrow-internal focus is appropriate for mentally rehearsing a task, and focusing internally may be helpful for distance running or weight lifting.

Although all attentional focuses are useful, problems arise when an individual relies too heavily on one style or uses a style inappropriately. Most activities require shifting of attention. For example, the soccer goalie might use a broad-external focus in preparing for a shot, shift to a narrow-external focus to make the save, and perhaps use some broad-internal analysis to set up the shift to the offense. People differ in how well they use the various focuses and how efficiently they shift. A performer using a broad-internal style might become preoccupied with analysis and miss the action. And although a broad-external focus allows one to take in important information, taking in too much irrelevant information may lead to confusion or overreaction. On the other hand, an inappropriate narrow-internal focus could lead a performer to miss relevant external information, as with an outfielder who makes a good catch but then misses the throw to the base. Finally, an extreme narrow-internal focus could imply concentrating on negative thoughts such as past errors and thus inattention to important external cues.

## MEASURES OF ATTENTIONAL STYLE

Because individuals differ in attentional style and in the ability to use varying styles effectively, attentional style is a personality variable. Nideffer (1976b) developed the Test of Attentional and Interpersonal Style (TAIS) to assess individual tendencies to use broad and narrow attention to internal and external information appropriately. The specific attentional subscales of the TAIS, along with sample items, are shown in figure 5.2.

Nideffer (1976b) provided preliminary information on the reliability and validity of the TAIS, and some initial work suggested that attentional styles influence sport performance and behavior. However, continuing work also indicates that the validity of the TAIS and its ability to predict sport and exercise behaviors are limited. Nideffer (1976b) reported that swimmers categorized by coaches as inconsistent in performance were overloaded with internal (OIT) and external (OET) stimuli, and

**Figure 5.2**

TAIS attentional subscale definitions and sample items. Responses are on a Likert scale with the following anchors: Never, Rarely, Sometimes, Frequently, All the time.

Modified from R. Nideffer, 1976, *The inner athlete* (New York: Crowell), 116-118. Copyright 1976 by Robert Nideffer. Reprinted with permission.

---

**BET (Broad-External)**

The higher the score, the more the individual's answers indicate that he or she deals effectively with a large number of external stimuli. The individual has a broad-external focus that is effective.

1. I am good at quickly analyzing a complex situation such as how a play is developing in football or which of four or five kids started a fight.
2. In a room filled with children or on a playing field, I know what everyone is doing.

**OET (External Overload)**

The higher the score, the more the individual's answers indicate that he or she makes mistakes because he or she is overloaded and distracted by external stimuli. He or she has difficulty narrowing attention when he or she needs to.

1. When people talk to me, I find myself distracted by the sights and sounds around me.
2. I get confused trying to watch activities such as a football game or circus where many things are happening at the same time.

**BIT (Broad-Internal)**

The higher the score, the more the individual indicates that he or she is able to think about several things at once when it is appropriate to do so. He or she has a broad-internal focus.

1. All I need is a little information and I can come up with a large number of ideas.
2. It is easy for me to bring together ideas from a number of different areas.

**OIT (Internal Overload)**

The higher the score, the more the individual indicates that he or she makes mistakes because he or she thinks about too many things at once. He or she is interfered with by his or her own thoughts and feelings.

1. When people talk to me, I find myself distracted by my own thoughts and ideas.
2. I have so many things on my mind that I become confused and forgetful.

**NAR (Narrow Effective Focus)**

High scorers indicate that they are able to narrow attention effectively when the situation calls for it.

1. It is easy for me to keep thoughts from interfering with something I am watching or listening to.
2. It is easy for me to keep sights and sounds from interfering with my thoughts.

**RED (Errors of Underinclusion)**

High scorers have chronically narrowed attention. They make mistakes because they cannot broaden attention when they need to.

1. I have difficulty clearing my mind of a single thought or idea.
2. In games I make mistakes because I am watching what one person does and I forget about the others.

---

Landers and Courtet (1979) found that rifle and pistol shooters who had an effective broad-internal focus (BIT) performed more accurately. Otherwise, support for the predictive validity of the TAIS attentional scales was weak, and continued research and applied work has produced further challenges.

Van Schoyck and Grasha (1981), reasoning that a sport-specific measure might be more reliable and valid than the general TAIS, developed a tennis-specific version (T-TAIS). The T-TAIS did produce higher test-retest reliability and internal consistency; and more importantly, the T-TAIS was more consistently related to tennis ability and match scores than was the TAIS. Albrecht and Feltz (1985) followed similar procedures and developed a sport-specific attentional measure for baseball/softball (B-TAIS). As with the tennis studies, they found that B-TAIS scores, but not TAIS scores, related to batting performance. Dewey, Brawley, and Allard (1989) reported that TAIS subscores did not relate to behavioral tests of attention as expected, casting further doubt on the measure's validity.

Sport-specific measures of attentional style are superior to general measures.

These studies not only demonstrated the superiority of sport-specific measures of attentional style but also raised questions about Nideffer's two-dimensional model of attention. Van Schoyck and Grasha's (1981) factor analysis supported the width (narrow-broad), but not the direction (internal-external) dimension. Instead, the authors described a bandwidth dimension with two components, scanning and focusing. Martens (1987a), in his coaches' guide, similarly suggested that while attentional width does seem to vary along a continuum from very narrow to very broad, internal-external direction seems to be a dichotomous category rather than a continuum. Albrecht and Feltz (1985) also failed to confirm Nideffer's model. Their analysis revealed two factors, an effective attentional style (NAR, BET, BIT) and an ineffective style (RED, OET, OIT), which mixes Nideffer's dimensions.

After reviewing the literature on attentional styles and measures in sport, Landers (1981, 1985) concluded that the TAIS does not differentiate attentional direction, is a poor predictor of sport and motor performance, and has limited value in sport. The TAIS may be useful for examining the breadth or bandwidth of attention, but Landers advocated less reliance on questionnaires and greater use of behavioral and psychophysiological indicators. Along with the growing psychophysiological research, some innovative studies conducted from an information-processing perspective, discussed in the next section, provide more insight into the relationship of attentional styles and processes to sport performance.

## ATTENTION AND SPORT EXPERTISE

Operating from an information-processing perspective and using a paradigm from studies of chess experts (Chase & Simon, 1973), Allard, Starkes, and colleagues (Allard & Starkes, 1980; Allard & Burnett, 1985; Allard, Graham, & Paarsalu, 1980; Starkes, 1987; Starkes & Allard, 1983) examined individual differences in attention and perception in various sports. Allard et al. (1980) tested the ability of basketball players and nonplayers to recall slides, which depicted structured situations of basketball plays and unstructured situations, after a four-second view. Basketball players were better than nonplayers at remembering slides from structured, but not unstructured, situations—confirming chess findings that experts have better recall accuracy for specific game situations. Subsequent studies revealed that field hockey experts were also better at recalling positions and that volleyball experts were faster than nonexperts at detecting volleyballs in game slides.

Experts—individuals who regularly play a particular game—have better recall accuracy for specific game situations than do nonplayers.

Studies using occlusion techniques with varied sport tasks (Abernethy, 1993; Abernethy & Russell, 1987) indicate that advance cues (e.g., racquet position) in fast ball sports can help predict ball flight, that experts are better at picking up this advance information, and that differences relate to selective attention. See Abernethy (1993) for more detailed discussion of related research on attention and sport.

## ASSOCIATION, DISSOCIATION, AND PERFORMANCE

One of the most widely cited works on attentional style and performance is Morgan and Pollock's (1977) study of marathon runners. Many runners use a dissociative

A quarterback trying to pick out primary and secondary receivers would likely use a broad-external focus; that is, he'd take in a great deal of external information before throwing the football.

© iPhotoNews.com

attentional style highlighted by distraction; that is, we focus on external objects or thoughts, perhaps replaying the day's events or playing songs in our minds, or on anything other than running and internal sensations. One innovative runner interviewed by Morgan and Pollock imagined stepping on the faces of disliked coworkers as she ran. Surprisingly, elite marathoners did not use dissociation but instead reported using an associative strategy; they focused on their breathing, paid attention to the feelings in their leg muscles, adopted an internal attentional focus, and monitored their bodily sensations. Morgan and Pollock's observations were widely cited to support the claim that an associative or narrow-internal focus is desirable for endurance events. However, Morgan and Pollock did not claim that association is advantageous for all runners at all times. Other evidence argues against such a blanket conclusion.

A study from our laboratory at Iowa (Gill & Strom, 1985) illustrates that a narrow-internal focus is not necessarily best for endurance activities. Female athletes performed an endurance task (on the quadriceps machine of the Universal gym) for as many repetitions as possible using either a narrow-internal focus on feelings in their legs or a narrow-external focus on a collage of pictures. Not only did the external focus lead to more repetitions, but nearly all participants preferred that style.

Our study is not unique. Pennebaker and Lightner (1980) demonstrated that distraction led to superior performance in two experiments. First, individuals exercising on a treadmill reported less fatigue when distracted than when listening to their own breathing. In another experiment, individuals ran faster on a cross-country course, where they were more likely to focus on external cues, than when running laps on a circular track.

Weinberg, Smith, Jackson, and Gould (1984) compared association, dissociation, and positive self-talk strategies on an aerobic task (30-minute run) and an anaerobic task (leg lift). They observed no differences for the run, but people using dissociation or self-talk performed longer on the leg lift than did those using association.

Morgan's own research (Morgan, 1981b; Morgan, Horstman, Cymerman, & Stokes, 1983) revealed that dissociation resulted in superior performance on a treadmill task, and that even elite marathoners sometimes use dissociation while running. Dissociation may reduce perceptions of pain or fatigue and help a performer keep going and maintain performance. With jogging and tasks such as the quadriceps machine, maintaining performance may be the primary goal, and dissociation may help. However, elite runners usually have goals (time or place) beyond simply maintaining performance. The runners in Morgan and Pollock's study apparently monitored bodily sensations to pace themselves and achieve performance goals.

### Key Point

Dissociation may be useful for some tasks, and association more effective for others. How one uses association may be critical. Individual preferences may determine the effectiveness of differing cognitive strategies.

In an innovative study, Schomer (1987) had runners use two-way radios to report during their runs. Content analysis confirmed that runners use both association and dissociation, with considerable variation during the run. Silva and Applebaum (1989) reported similar results based on retrospective reports of Olympic trial marathoners.

Smith, Gill, Crews, Hopewell, and Morgan (1995), reasoning that experienced runners might use association as a relaxation strategy to improve performance, assessed attentional strategies and running economy of experienced distance runners. The most economical runners reported less use of dissociation and more use of relaxation than the least economical runners, but there were no differences in use of association. The results suggest that although relaxation strategies may benefit runners, association per se is not the source of the benefits.

Dissociation may be useful for some tasks, and association more effective for others; and as Smith et al. suggest, how one uses association may be critical. Individual preferences may determine the effectiveness of differing cognitive strategies. Weinberg et al. (1984) suggested that the experienced runners in their study may have developed preferred attentional styles that interfered with the manipulations and led to the lack of strategy effects. Similarly, most individuals in our lab study preferred dissociation, but a few specifically stated that they focused on the feelings in their legs to concentrate and push themselves. Through continuing investigations of attention, we may discover how varying individual attentional styles interact with task characteristics and situational factors to influence attentional processes and performance—and whether such individual differences are stable or are readily changed through instructions, training, or experiences.

## INDIVIDUAL DIFFERENCES IN IMAGERY ABILITY

We have just seen that individual differences are prominent in the work on attentional styles. Individual differences have received much less attention in relation to imagery. Instead, sport and exercise psychology work focuses on the use of imagery techniques to prepare for performance and competition. We'll consider imagery for anxiety management and mental rehearsal in chapter 12 on psychological interventions.

Although sport and exercise psychologists' enthusiasm for imagery is recent, psychologists have been investigating imagery for some time. As early as 1883, Sir Francis Galton discussed imagery extensively and reported that he had given a questionnaire on imaging ability to a diverse sample. Thus, Galton probably was the first to examine individual differences in imagery ability. Many books on imagery have been written, and the *Journal of Mental Imagery* has been published for some time. Individual differences in imagery abilities and the role of such differences in imagery processes are prominent in the literature. For example, in a review, Marks (1977) emphasized individual differences in perceptual, encoding, and retrieval mechanisms related to imagery.

Many psychologists have investigated individual differences in imagery, and there are many measures (Sheehan, Ashton, & White, 1983). Some investigators use objective, performance-based assessments in which one infers imagery ability from performance on sample items or selected tasks. Imagery researchers have used the spatial relations subtest of Thurstone's (1938) Test of Primary Mental Abilities, a performance measure. As Sheehan et al. note, most measures are self-report questionnaires. Some of the most widely used imagery tests include the following:

- **Betts's Questionnaire Upon Mental Imagery (QMI).** The shortened version (Sheehan, 1967) of Betts's (1909) original QMI measures imagery vividness in seven sensory modalities.

- **Gordon's Test of Imagery Control.** Gordon's (1949) test assesses how well individuals can control or transform images.

- **Vividness of Visual Imagery Questionnaire (VVIQ).** Marks's (1973) VVIQ is an extended version of the QMI visual imagery subscale.

- **Individual Differences Questionnaire (IDQ).** The IDQ (Paivio, 1971) and its abbreviated form, the Verbalizer-Visualizer Questionnaire developed by Richardson (1977), assess the degree to which an individual uses imaginal and verbal thinking modes.

Although imagery vividness as measured by the Betts QMI was positively related to improvement in a physical skill with the use of mental practice (White, Ashton, & Lewis, 1979), few of these measures have been used to investigate imagery in sport and exercise settings. That may not be a failing, as even in the psychology literature, the self-report measures do not consistently predict much about imagery or performance.

Sheehan et al. (1983) suggest that experience-based measures, such as thought sampling, might offer new insights, especially into motivational and emotional processes associated with imagery. Researchers also advocate varied assessments, including psychophysiological measures, to help probe individual differences. Kosslyn (1983) proposed a computer metaphor theory of imagery and emphasized the shortcomings of single self-report scales. Kosslyn suggests that individuals have not one, but several, imagery abilities. A person might be very adept at picking out specific aspects of an image (e.g., seeing the position of a bat during a swing) but may develop "grainy" images rather than sharp, detailed images. Thus, multidimensional measures are needed to assess and investigate individual differences in imagery abilities.

In any case, sport and exercise psychologists seldom use measures of imagery ability and have not developed measures to match imagery use in applied work and consultation. Many sport psychology consultants use some form of imagery assessment. For example, in a helpful chapter on imagery training, Vealey and Walter (1993; updated in Vealey & Greenleaf, 1998) present a Sport Imagery Questionnaire that may be useful for self-assessment or for consultants working with athletes. However, the questionnaire was not developed within any theoretical framework and has no established reliability or validity. Craig Hall and colleagues (Hall, Pongrac, & Buckolz, 1985) developed the Movement Imagery Questionnaire to assess imagery abilities in athletes, and later the Imagery Use Questionnaire (Hall, Rodgers, & Barr, 1990). Hall et al. (1990) assessed athletes' use of imagery, but employed the measure descriptively rather than to relate imagery abilities to sport and exercise behavior or to examine the effectiveness of varied imagery techniques. In addition to the lack of sound imagery measures in sport and exercise psychology, there are no conceptual models. We advocate imagery (chapter 12 will examine the literature on imagery interventions), but we have not developed the models and measures to provide a knowledge base for such interventions.

**Key Point**

Although many imagery tests have been developed, sport and exercise psychologists seldom use measures of imagery ability and have not developed measures to match imagery use in applied work and consultation.

## RESEARCH EVIDENCE FOR IMAGERY USE

Much of the support for imagery interventions comes from early work comparing mental practice with physical practice, without considering individual differences or imagery processes. In reviewing that literature, Richardson (1967a, 1967b) concluded that mental practice improved motor performance. Corbin (1972) more cautiously suggested that the findings were inconclusive and that varying tasks and characteristics of the studies yielded varying results. In any case, the findings provided little insight into mental rehearsal processes.

Feltz and Landers (1983) provided the most thorough review of the mental practice literature. Using meta-analysis, they reached several conclusions:

- *Mental practice effects are primarily associated with cognitive-symbolic rather than motor elements of the task.* Mental practice seems especially useful for tasks involving movement sequences, timing, or cognitive problem solving.

- *Mental practice effects are not limited to early learning—they are found in early and later stages of learning and may be task specific.* There are imagery effects both in early learning and with more familiar tasks; mental rehearsal may operate differently at different stages of learning.

- *It is doubtful that mental practice effects are produced by low-gain innervation of muscles to be used during actual performance.* Although Suinn (1983) and others report electromyogram patterns during imagery, Feltz and Landers found no evidence for the claim that low-gain neuromuscular activity accounts for mental rehearsal effects. Instead, imagery appears to elicit general muscle innervation.

- *Mental practice functions to assist the performer in psychologically preparing for the skill to be performed.* The general muscle innervation might set appropriate tension levels and attentional focus.

**Key Point**

Feltz and Landers' (1983) meta-analysis of the mental research literature led to several conclusions, including the conclusion that mental practice primarily affects cognitive-symbolic elements of the task and the effects are not limited to early learning.

Other research, done since the Feltz and Landers review, provides few new insights. Recent research has generally been more descriptive in reporting athletes' imagery use—or more applied, incorporating imagery into psychological skills interventions. As we will discuss in chapter 12, imagery is prominent in psychological skills programs, but we have far to go with our research to provide a stronger base for that applied work.

## IMAGERY THEORIES

Although limited research evidence offers few insights, several theories may provide guidance and direction. Prior to the Feltz and Landers (1983) review, the psychoneuromuscular theory and the symbolic learning theory were dominant. Since then, several sport and exercise psychologists have adopted Lang's (1979) bioinformational theory or have focused on psychological or mental states (Gould & Damarjian, 1996; Vealey & Greenleaf, 1998).

- **Psychoneuromuscular theory.** Psychoneuromuscular theory, alluded to in Feltz and Landers's third conclusion, is also referred to as *muscle memory*. Jacobson (1931) first reported that imaginary movements produced muscle innervation similar to those produced in the actual movement. Suinn (1983), in his work with Olympic skiers, observed electromyogram patterns during imagery that paralleled those during a ski run. Although researchers continue to explore psychophysiological aspects of imagery, we still do not have any strong support for the psychoneuromuscular theory.

- **Symbolic learning theory.** According to symbolic learning theory, imagery works like a mental blueprint: we use it to develop a mental code for movements. Much sport and exercise psychology research on imagery is consistent with symbolic learning, but we have no convincing tests of the theory.

- **Bioinformational theory.** Lang's (1977, 1979) psychophysiological information-processing theory assumes that an image is a functionally organized set of propositions. When imaging, we activate stimulus propositions that describe the content of the image, as well as response propositions that describe our responses in that situation. If imagery is to affect performance, both stimulus and response propositions must be activated. This implies that imagery training should include not only conditions of the situation (e.g., the setting), but also the behavioral, psychological, and physiological responses in that situation. Thus, we might think of response sets (Vealey & Greenleaf, 1998) or response scenarios (Gould & Damarjian, 1996) rather than simple responses. Ahsen's (1984) triple code theory is similar to Lang's theory, but Ahsen adds that the meanings of particular images are individual and should be incorporated in the process.

- **Psychological states.** Psychological states or mental sets do not refer to a specific theory, but explain imagery effects by referring to optimal arousal or attentional states. As we will discuss in later chapters, imagery may be effective for controlling emotions to maintain an optimal psychological state, but that does not explain how imagery might affect performance and cannot be considered a theory of imagery.

### Key Point

Among the theories that may provide guidance and direction for imagery research and practice are the psychoneuromuscular theory, the symbolic learning theory, and the bioinformational theory.

Despite the prominence of imagery in the sport and exercise psychology literature, considerable research, and several credible theories, we can draw few conclusions about how imagery works. Generally, imagery seems to be one way to facilitate skill learning and performance, but we can offer few specific guidelines with any confidence. Many sport and exercise participants find imagery effective, and the accumulating work on imagery interventions in applied psychological skills training suggests that sport and exercise psychology researchers could contribute greatly by continuing to investigate imagery processes.

## Summary

Attention and cognitive skills are prominent in sport and exercise psychology. Consultants advocate cognitive interventions and the development of attention and imagery skills, but our research and measures lag far behind. Nideffer (1976a) offered an initial model and measure of attention. Subsequent research has exposed limits of both, but we have little to offer as replacements. Some work by cognitive psychologists and motor behavior scholars on attention and information processing offers more promise. Similarly, the expanding research from a psychophysiological perspective may greatly amplify our understanding of cognitive processes relevant to sport and exercise behavior. By following Boutcher's (1993) suggestions and taking a more integrative approach to attention and cognitive processes, we may provide sound knowledge to guide practice.

## Review Questions

1. Define attention.

2. Define attentional selectivity and attentional capacity, and explain how each of these concepts is related to control processing and automatic processing.

3. Discuss the two dimensions of Nideffer's attentional model.

4. Comment on general versus sport-specific measures of attentional style.

5. Explain how attention and sport expertise are related.

6. Explain the relationships among association, dissociation, and performance, and explain factors affecting the effectiveness of these strategies.

7. Discuss imagery tests and their use by sport and exercise psychologists.

8. Discuss the most thorough review of the motor research literature (Feltz and Landers, 1983).

9. List and explain several theories that may provide guidance and direction for sport and exercise imagery research and practice.

## Recommended Reading

★ Abernethy, B. (1993). Attention. In R.N. Singer, M. Murphey, & L.K. Tennant (Eds.), *Handbook of research on sport psychology* (pp. 127-170). New York: Macmillan.

> Abernethy has conducted considerable research on the role of attention in sport and cognitive strategies of elite performers. This chapter summarizes work by scholars of motor behavior and sport psychology, and it provides a solid review with suggestions for continuing work.

★ Suinn, R. (1993). Imagery: In R.N. Singer, M. Murphey, & L.K. Tennant (Eds.), *Handbook of research on sports psychology* (pp. 492-510). New York: Macmillan.

> Suinn was one of the first established clinical psychologists to work with athletes. Much of his work focused on visuo-motor behavior rehearsal, which combines relaxation techniques with imagery. In this chapter, Suinn reviews the research on imagery and sport and provides the background information for more applied work.

★ Vealey, R.S., & Greenleaf, C.A. (1998). Seeing is believing: Understanding and using imagery in sport. In J.M. Williams (Ed.), *Applied sport psychology: Personal growth to peak performance* (3rd ed., pp. 237-269). Mountain View, CA: Mayfield.

> In the third edition of Williams' applied sport psychology book, Vealey collaborates with Greenleaf to update her earlier chapters on imagery and sport. The chapter provides a good overview of research and current theories and provides helpful guidelines for imagery training.

# Self-Perceptions

## CHAPTER OBJECTIVES

After studying this chapter, you should be able to

- understand multidimensional views of the self and the related sport and exercise psychology work on physical self-concept and

- trace the development of self-efficacy theories, including Bandura's original model and other, more recent variations.

We turn now to the self. The study of the self and self-perceptions has taken some exciting new directions recently, but the area is not new in psychology. Issues related to the self were central early on in psychology, and self-concept is the core of traditional views of personality.

In his classic texts, William James (1890, 1892) discussed the development of a sense of global self-worth from more specific self-judgments. C.H. Cooley (1902) proposed that self-concept was formed through social interaction, and he introduced the notion of reflected appraisal and the term "looking glass self." The notion of self and self-identity has always been central in writings on psychodynamic personality, including Erikson's (1968) on identity, Horney's (1950) and Sullivan's (1953) on self-acceptance, and the widely recognized self-actualization models of Rogers (1951) and Maslow (1954).

More recently, psychologists in nonclinical areas have sparked a resurgence of interest in the self. Bem's (1967) work on self-perception, Duval and Wicklund's (1972) on self-awareness, and Jones's (1964) on self-presentation and self-handicapping (Berglas & Jones, 1978) have led to continuing research and to more specific lines of research on self-regulation, self-monitoring, and impression management (Baumeister, 1986; Carver & Scheier, 1990; Leary, 1992; Snyder, 1987). Sport and exercise psychologists have adapted several "self" concepts, and in this chapter we will focus on two general "self" areas that play a large role in sport and exercise psychology.

First we will look at multidimensional views of the self and the related sport and exercise psychology work on physical self-concept. Next we will turn to a particular form of self-perception: self-confidence—more specifically, self-efficacy. Self-efficacy, which is a self-perception of capabilities for performing specific tasks or behaviors (e.g., making a golf putt, completing a cardiac rehabilitation program), is a major theoretical framework for much of psychology, and one that has been particularly useful for sport and exercise psychology. We will cover Bandura's (1977a) original self-efficacy model as well as more recent variations and self-confidence work.

# MULTIDIMENSIONAL SELF-CONCEPT

Researchers investigating the influence of activity on psychological factors, and practitioners promoting sport and exercise programs, often focus on self-concept or self-esteem. Typically, *self-concept* is the overall perception of the self, whereas *self-esteem* is the evaluative component. In reality, self-concept and self-esteem are difficult to separate; researchers use both the terms and the measures interchangeably, and the evaluative component usually is the key for study of the self.

Early self-concept constructs and measures emphasized a unidimensional, global view of the self. For example, Coopersmith (1967) viewed self-concept as unidimensional, and his widely used measure combines items reflecting self-evaluations across many content areas. Others (e.g., Harter, 1983; Rosenberg, 1979; Wylie, 1979) have criticized this approach, arguing that individuals do not value all areas equally and that they make evaluative distinctions about their competence in different domains of their lives.

## Harter's Model of Perceived Competence

Susan Harter's (1983, 1985, 1990) developmental approach to self-perceptions has been particularly influential in our discipline. Harter not only advocates a multidimensional approach; she has also looked at developmental changes in self-evaluations. Harter (1990) reports that children as young as 4-7 years make reliable judgments about four domains: cognitive competence, physical competence, social acceptance, and behavioral conduct. However, at these ages the four domains are not yet clearly differentiated, and children are not capable of making overall judgments of their global self-worth. During middle childhood (age 8-12), children clearly differentiate five domains and form an overall judgment of self-worth. Harter's (1985) Self-Perception Profile for Children, widely used in sport and exercise psychology and in developmental and educational settings, assesses five specific domains as well as global self-worth:

- Scholastic competence
- Social acceptance
- Athletic competence
- Physical appearance
- Behavioral conduct

Harter (1990) suggests further developmental changes in self-perceptions, adding close friendship, romantic appeal, and job competence domains for adolescents. According to Harter, college students make clear differentiations among scholastic competence, intellectual ability, and creativity; but for slightly older adults, a single dimension of intelligence suffices. Harter's work suggests that developmental changes in self-evaluations continue into middle age and older adulthood, and multidimensional models let us investigate such variations.

### Key Point

Harter's approach is both developmental and multidimensional. Her influential work suggests that developmental changes in self-evaluations continue from early childhood through older adulthood, and multidimensional models let us investigate such variations.

## Hierarchical Models of Self-Concept

Harter did not specify a structure for perceived competence, but others have proposed hierarchical models of self-esteem that serve as the basis for sport-specific

**GLOBAL
SELF-CONCEPT**

| **Academic self-concept** | **Social self-concept** | **Emotional self-concept** | **Physical self-concept** |
|---|---|---|---|

Math   English   Science   History

Physical appearance   Physical ability

A hierarchical model of self-esteem.

measures. Shavelson, Hubner, and Stanton (1976) proposed a multifaceted, hierarchical model with global self-concept at the top level. At the next level, academic self-concept and three nonacademic components—social self-concept, emotional self-concept, and physical self-concept—form the basis of the global self-concept. Each of these four components, in turn, includes subareas based on evaluations of behavior in specific situations. For example, academic self-concept includes subareas of English, history, math, and science, and the physical self-concept includes physical ability and physical appearance. Marsh (1990, 1992, 1993) has researched multidimensional self-concept following the Shavelson et al. approach and has developed several self-description questionnaires, including physical self-description measures particularly relevant to sport and exercise psychology.

> ### Key Point
>
> Hierarchical models of self-concept are multifaceted and multilevel. The broad term being analyzed, such as global self-esteem or global self-concept, is at the top level. Each lower level includes components or subareas of the level above it.

Several sport and exercise researchers have adapted multidimensional models that highlight physical self-concept. Sonstroem (1978) was among the first to develop sport-specific constructs and measures with his Physical Estimation and Attraction Scales. Ken Fox (1990; Fox & Corbin, 1989) closely followed the Shavelson et al. (1976) model to develop his Physical Self-Perception Profile (PSPP). In Fox's three-tier hierarchical model, global self-esteem is at the top level. Physical self-worth, at the next level, is based on the four subdomains of sports competence, attractive body, physical strength, and physical condition. The PSPP matches this model and includes these subscales:

- **Sports Competence (SPORT):** Perceptions of sport and athletic ability, ability to learn sport skills, and confidence in the sport environment
- **Physical Condition (CONDITION):** Perceptions of level of physical condition, stamina, and fitness; ability to maintain exercise; and confidence in the exercise and fitness setting
- **Body Attractiveness (BODY):** Perceived attractiveness of figure or physique, ability to maintain an attractive body, and confidence in appearance
- **Physical Strength (STRENGTH):** Perceived strength, muscle development, and confidence in situations requiring strength

- **Physical Self-Worth (PSW):** General feelings of happiness, satisfaction, pride, respect, and confidence in the physical self

Fox and Corbin (1989) provided evidence for the sensitivity, reliability, and stability of the subscales; confirmed the subscale factor structure; and reported associations of the subscales with physical activity involvement to provide initial validity support. Sonstroem, Speliotis, and Fava (1992) subsequently found that the PSPP showed strong internal consistency, separated exercisers from nonexercisers, and predicted degree of exercise involvement among adults; they recommended its continued use.

Sonstroem and Morgan (1989) proposed a model similar to the hierarchical models of Fox (1990) and Marsh (1990) with three associated hypotheses:

1. Physical fitness is more highly related to physical self-efficacy than to physical competence, physical acceptance, and global self-esteem.

2. Physical self-efficacy is more highly related to physical competence than to physical acceptance or global self-esteem.

3. Physical competence is more highly related to global self-esteem than is physical self-efficacy or physical fitness.

More recently, Herbert Marsh (Marsh, Richards, Johnson, Roche, & Tremayne, 1994; Marsh, 1996) used psychometric techniques to develop the Physical Self-Description Questionnaire (PSDQ), a multidimensional physical self-concept measure with 11 scales: Strength, Body fat, Activity, Endurance/Fitness, Sports competence, Coordination, Health, Appearance, Flexibility, Global physical, and Global esteem. Marsh and colleagues provided good psychometric support for the measure; they confirmed its validity by correlating PSDQ subscales with external criterion measures of body composition, physical activity, endurance, strength, and flexibility.

These conceptually based physical self-perception measures are valuable for examining claims about physical activity. Earlier reviews of research on psychological benefits of physical activity (Folkins & Sime, 1981; Hughes, 1984; Morgan, 1985) concluded that sport participation did not affect personality, but suggested that vigorous exercise and enhanced fitness might positively affect mood and self-concept.

## Body Image

Perceptions of the physical body are part of self-concept; body perceptions are particularly relevant to physical self-concept, and both Fox (1990) and Marsh (1990, 1996) include body image constructs in their models. Moreover, body image is particularly relevant to sport and exercise psychology work on eating disorders and related issues with athletes and for all females.

Body perceptions and body image measures have been associated with self-concept for some time. Secord and Jourard (1953), who developed the Body Cathexis Scale to assess body satisfaction, found that body cathexis scores were related to self-concept, particularly for women. Rosen and Ross (1968) similarly reported a relationship between body satisfaction and self-concept with college undergraduates. Franzoi and Shields (1984), using their Body Esteem Scale, found that women's sense of attractiveness was related to perceived sexuality, feelings about specific body parts, and physical characteristics such as stamina, strength, and conditioning.

Hart, Leary, and Rejeski (1989), drawing on self-presentation and self-esteem literature, developed the Social Physique Anxiety Scale (SPAS) to assess anxiety associated with others' evaluation of one's physique. They provided evidence that the SPAS demonstrates good internal consistency, test-retest reliability, and correlations with other body image and body esteem measures and public self-con-

Athletes face extraordinary pressures to maintain an "ideal" body.

sciousness; they also found that women scoring high on SPAS reported being less comfortable and having more negative thoughts during physical evaluations than did women scoring low on SPAS. The SPAS may be useful for research on exercise settings and for developing programs to fit individual needs, as well as for further investigations of body image and eating disorders.

In a review, Rodin and Larson (1992) concluded that cultural and social factors emphasize unrealistic body shapes and that thinness is joined by fitness within body shape ideal. Developmental factors conspire against females as physical maturation conflicts with the prevailing cultural imperative. Of particular interest to our discipline, Rodin and Larson further concluded that athletes face extraordinary pressures, culturally and psychologically, to maintain an ideal body and that such pressures may lead to eating and weight problems. In "The Real Swimsuit Issue," Barbara Ehrenreich (1996) discussed body image and self-concept for women, saying, "Where is the FDA when you need it? There should be warning labels on every suit: this product may be hazardous to your self-esteem" (p. 68).

Relationships between body image and eating behaviors were the focus of a study by Reel and Gill (1996) of high school and college cheerleaders, who might be at risk for problems with body image and eating disorders. The cheerleaders completed the SPAS and Garner's (1984) Eating Disorders Inventory, which includes a subscale for body dissatisfaction as well as measures of anorexia and bulimia. There were strong relationships between both SPAS and body dissatisfaction and eating behavior, suggesting body image as an important predictor.

## Sport and Exercise Psychology Research on Physical Self-Concept

The recent multidimensional self-perception measures allow consideration of more specific relationships among self-perceptions and physical activity, and may be especially useful with the growing interest in health-oriented exercise and the psychological benefits of physical activity. As Berger (1994; Berger & McInman, 1993) notes, the research on exercise and quality of life (psychological well-being, self-esteem) is not conclusive, at least partly due to inadequate measures.

Initial studies on the relationship between self-concept and exercise suggest promising directions. Cross-sectional studies, comparing exercisers and nonexercisers or correlating physical fitness and self-esteem measures, indicate a positive relationship (Albinson, 1974; Adame, Johnson, Cole, Matthiasson, & Abbas, 1990; Heinzelmann & Bagley, 1970; Tucker, 1987; Young, 1985). However, results are mixed, and also vary with measures. For example, body esteem shows stronger relationships to fitness than does global self-concept, and physical strength and body fat percentage are two physical measures that particularly relate to self-concept. Berger and McInman (1993) report that longitudinal or intervention studies with exercise are more mixed, with less than half showing significant improvements in self-concept. Again, results are stronger for body concept, and characteristics of the program may be relevant. For example, studies of weight training (Brone & Reznikoff, 1989; Brown & Harrison, 1986; Trujillo, 1983; Tucker, 1983, 1987) and outdoor adventure programs (Marsh, Richards, & Barnes, 1986a, 1986b) have shown improvements. Several of these studies used specific body-concept measures, and the

Marsh et al. research on outdoor adventure programs used Marsh's multidimensional Self Description Questionnaire (SDQ) measures.

Overall, sport, exercise, and physical activity programs do not have strong effects on global self-worth, and we would not expect such effects. As noted in previous chapters, general personality is not likely to change with short-term programs. However, activity programs may well influence specific perceptions of physical competence or body concept, and the multidimensional measures may help us investigate such effects. More specific perceptions of self-efficacy for specific tasks are even more amenable to change; we will consider those self-perceptions later in this chapter. Also, issues related to quality of life and psychological well-being encompass mood and emotion, as well as personality and self-concept, and we will consider emotion in more depth in chapter 10.

# MARKUS'S DYNAMIC SELF

Before turning to self-confidence and self-efficacy, we will consider Hazel Markus's work on the self, which fits the social dynamics approach of this text and offers exciting possibilities for sport and exercise psychology work on the self. Markus's (1977) initial work on self-schema reflects a social-cognitive approach to self-concept. Markus defines self-schema as cognitive representations of the self, related to specific domains (e.g., athlete). Schema are active, dynamic representations, derived from past experiences, that organize and direct behaviors. We not only must have capabilities, we must perceive these capabilities.

More recently, Markus and Wurf (1987) proposed a more active, dynamic view of the self: Markus's dynamic self continually interacts with ongoing behavior. Illustrating the dynamic self is like trying to illustrate a basketball game with a single snapshot: one picture misses the action, the shifts, the reactions, and everything that really makes it a game. Similarly, shifts and reactions are the essence of the dynamic self, and we cannot show that in a figure. Instead, we will highlight the main features of Markus's model. Specifically, the self is *multifaceted*, *dynamic*, and *social*. These three features overlap, and all are important for study of the self.

> **Key Point**
>
> Markus's dynamic self continually interacts with ongoing behavior. Shifts and reactions are the essence of the dynamic self, which is multifaceted, dynamic, and social.

In Markus's view, the self is *multifaceted*: it is not one self, but many selves. We have many self-schema, or self-representations, and they work together in a self-system. Some self-representations are more salient than others. For example, the athlete schema is highly salient and is the dominant influence for some athletes but not for others. Less salient and less elaborate schema have less influence. Selves may be positive or negative (competent or incompetent) and may be in the past, present, or future. Markus discusses possible selves (selves we see as possibilities) as important motivators and bridges from the present to the future. For example, a golfer who sees a possible self as a professional may develop a more elaborate golfer schema, a sense of mastery and confidence, and specific goals and strategies. Markus sees imagery as use of an elaborate, possible self to develop competence; imagery helps when it is specific, or detailed, and we can see ourselves doing it—it's possible.

The working self is particularly important in Markus's model. At any given time, only a subset of the self is active, and that working self varies. For example, the working self may be quite different at soccer practice, in class, and at home.

The self is *dynamic*; this is the most intriguing aspect of Markus's model. The working self continually changes as it regulates behavior (controls and directs actions) in a reciprocal interaction process. Self affects behavior; behavior affects self.

The self also is *social* rather than isolated or introspective. The immediate social situation affects the self, and social groups or culture affects the self. Recently Markus discussed two views of the self that differ across cultures—independent and interdependent. The independent view (e.g., individual achievement, self-focused, private, direct) dominates our North American culture, including our sport culture. Other cultures, such as most in Asia, take an interdependent view and see the self in relation to others (e.g., linked, relational, indirect, cooperative). In this country our typical athlete and exerciser schema fit the independent view. We see athletes as independent, competitive, individual achievers, and if that does not fit with your gender or cultural identity you may not easily see yourself as athlete—it's not a possible self. Our exerciser schema may not be competitive; but it is independent as well as white and middle class, and exercise may be seen as self-indulgent to cultures with more community identity.

## Athlete Identity

Recently researchers have adopted Markus's views to focus on self-identity as an athlete or exerciser. Brewer, Van Raalte, and Linder (1993) defined athletic identity as the degree to which an individual identifies with the athletic role and looks to others for acknowledgement of that role. An individual with a strong athletic identity has an athlete self-schema and processes information from an athletic perspective. For example, individuals with strong athletic identities might think about how their eating and sleeping habits affect performance. Brewer et al. developed the Athletic Identity Measurement Scale (AIMS); initial findings suggested that individuals establish strong athletic identities through the development of skills, confidence, and social interactions during sport. However, a strong, exclusive athletic identity may predispose athletes to emotional difficulties when they cannot participate. Brewer and colleagues have continued to work with the AIMS, and Martin and colleagues (Martin, Adams-Mushett, & Eklund, 1994; Martin, Adams-Mushett, & Smith, 1995) have extended the work on athletic identity to adolescent swimmers with disabilities. This continuing research suggests that the AIMS may be multidimensional, inclusive of (a) social identity—the strength with which athletes identify with the athletic role, which may be further subdivided into self-identity (views of the self as athletes) and social identity (others' views of them as athletes in samples of athletes with disabilities); (b) exclusivity—the degree to which athletes rely solely on the athletic setting for identity; and (c) negative affectivity—negative emotional responses to not being able to train or compete.

## Exerciser Identity

Just as Brewer and colleagues applied Markus's self-schema approach to athletic identity, Kendzierski (1994) has used the approach to study exercise schema and exercise behaviors. In initial studies Kendzierski classified individuals as exerciser schematics (they identified as exercisers), nonexerciser schematics (they identified as nonexercisers), or aschematics (no relevant identity), and found that exerciser schematics process information differently. Subsequent studies showed that exerciser schematics exercised more frequently, performed more exercise activities, were more likely to report exercising three times per week, and were more likely to start an exercise program than were nonexerciser schematics and aschematics. Exerciser and athlete schema, our overall self-identities, influence our sport and exercise behaviors.

## SELF-CONFIDENCE AND SELF-EFFICACY

Self-confidence and self-efficacy may be the most critical self-perceptions in sport and exercise psychology. Many top athletes exude confidence. Muhammad Ali and Joe Namath were known for their colorful and convincing boasts. Before the Los

Angeles Olympic Games, eventual gold medal winner Mary Lou Retton said, "The competition is worried about me this time around. I welcome the added pressure. It makes me fight even more" (Callahan, 1984b, p. 63). Flamboyant two-time Olympic decathlon champion Daley Thompson once fantasized about meeting Jim Thorpe, Bob Mathias, Bruce Jenner, and other champions in an all-time decathlon contest: "Then we'd see who's best. I know, of course, but it would be great fun" (Leo, 1984a, p. 65). Athletes recognize the value of a positive attitude, and we tell performers to "think like a winner" or "believe in yourself." As noted in chapter 4, the most consistent difference between elite and less successful athletes is that elite athletes possess greater self-confidence (e.g., Gould, Weiss, & Weinberg, 1981; Mahoney & Avener, 1977).

Is self-confidence really that important? If so, can we enhance an athlete's confidence? If confidence increases, will individuals perform better, enjoy the activity more, or experience other benefits? Sport and exercise psychologists have applied Bandura's self-efficacy model and social-cognitive theory to address these issues, and the work continues to advance in many directions.

## Bandura's Self-Efficacy Theory

Albert Bandura (1977b, 1982, 1986) proposed an elegant model of self-efficacy and behavior. Here *self-efficacy* is a situation-specific form of self-confidence, or the belief that one is competent and can do whatever is necessary in a specific situation. *Self-confidence* is a more global and stable personality characteristic. Self-efficacy may fluctuate greatly. A high school wrestler in a tournament might feel very confident or efficacious going into the first match. If he goes into the final period behind on points and feeling tired, and sees the opponent looking fresh and eager, he may quickly feel much less confident.

### Key Point

Self-efficacy is a situation-specific form of self-confidence, or the belief that one is competent and can do whatever is necessary in a specific situation. Self-confidence is a more global and stable personality characteristic, whereas self-efficacy may fluctuate greatly.

For Bandura, self-efficacy predicts actual performance when necessary skills and appropriate incentives are present. He suggests that efficacy expectations are the primary determinants of choice of activity, level of effort, and degree of persistence. High-efficacious people seek challenges, try hard, and persist, whereas low-efficacious people tend to avoid challenges, give up, and become more anxious or depressed when faced with adversity. Self-efficacy theory implies that various strategies used by coaches, instructors, and performers affect performance and behavior because they affect self-efficacy—the critical mediating variable. Efficacy expectations develop and undergo change through four major types of information: performance accomplishments, vicarious experiences, verbal persuasion, and emotional arousal. Changes in self-efficacy, in turn, influence actual behavior. Figure 6.1 diagrams the role of self-efficacy in athletic performance. For more information about research on these four sources of self-efficacy, see pages 79-80.

So far we have considered self-efficacy as an individual characteristic, but Bandura has also suggested the possibility of a collective form of efficacy. Such a notion seems particularly applicable to sport teams. Feltz and colleagues (1979) have conducted exploratory studies indicating that beliefs in group capabilities influence performance. Spink (1990), examining the relationship between collective efficacy and team cohesion, reported positive relationships for elite but not recreational-level volleyball teams. At present, research and measures of collective efficacy are exploratory, but promising.

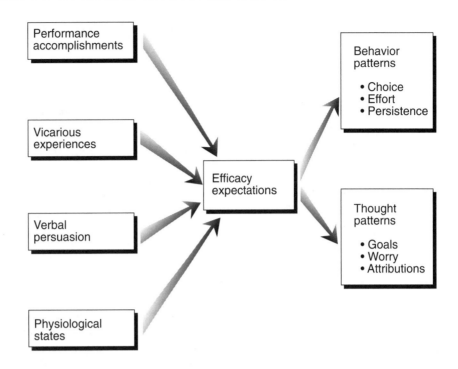

**Figure 6.1**

Relationship between major sources of efficacy information, efficacy expectations, and behavior and thought patterns as predicted by Bandura's theory.

From D.L. Feltz, 1988, "Self-confidence and sports performance." In *Exercise and Sport Sciences Reviews* (Vol. 16), edited by K.B. Pandolf. Copyright 1988 American College of Sports Medicine. Adapted with permission of Lippincott Williams & Wilkins.

## Research on the Sources of Self-Efficacy

Most sport and exercise psychology research on confidence and self-efficacy follows Bandura's original model and uses typical efficacy strength measures. Because the original model stressed sources of efficacy, much initial work focused on its four sources—performance accomplishment, vicarious experience, verbal persuasion, and emotional arousal—and the relationship of efficacy expectations to performance.

### Performance Accomplishments

Performance accomplishments, or mastery experiences, provide the most dependable information and have the most powerful effects on self-efficacy. If you are learning the topspin serve, practicing and performing the correct serve is more likely to lead you to believe you can perform the serve than the instructor's statements. In sport and exercise settings, we use many tactics to help people get the experience of successful performance. We might have a football team walk slowly through an offensive play, physically guide a gymnast through a complex move, or have young basketball players use a smaller ball and lower basket.

Studies have demonstrated the effectiveness of techniques to increase efficacy and improve performance (Feltz, Landers, & Raeder, 1979; McAuley, 1985). Feltz and colleagues compared participant modeling (demonstration plus guided performance), live modeling, and videotaped modeling presenting the back dive. McAuley used participant modeling, live modeling, and a control condition to teach participants a dive roll mount onto the balance beam. Both studies showed that participant modeling was the most effective in increasing self-efficacy, reducing anxiety, and improving performance. Further analyses with both studies (Feltz, 1982; McAuley, 1985) supported Bandura's causal predictions: modeling treatments affected self-efficacy, and self-efficacy affected performance.

### Vicarious Experience

Self-efficacy can also be increased through vicarious experience, or watching someone else accomplish the skill. We often use demonstrations when teaching sport skills, and watching another student do a task may reduce worry and enhance confidence— for example, seeing one student in a beginning swimming class go underwater, or watching one member of the gymnastics club do a scary move. Although vicarious experience is not as effective as actual experience, several studies confirm that modeling enhances self-efficacy (Gould & Weiss, 1981; McAuley, 1985; Weinberg, Gould, & Jackson, 1979).

### Verbal Persuasion

Verbal persuasion is less powerful than experience, but teachers and coaches often encourage performers with statements such as "You've got the talent; I know you can do it." Sometimes we even resort to deception. Ness and Patton (1979) compared the weight-lifting performance of individuals who thought the weight was greater than it actually was, those who thought it was less, and those who were unaware of the weight. Performers lifted more weight when they believed it was less than it actually was. However, Mahoney (1979) could not replicate those findings. Moreover, using deception with students or athletes may undermine your credibility and trustworthiness.

### Emotional Arousal

The role of the fourth source of efficacy information, emotional arousal, is less clear. Bandura suggests that arousal, or more precisely, perceptions of arousal, affect behavior through efficacy expectations. If you notice your heart pounding and your knees shaking just before a match, you likely will feel less confident. Relaxation training or arousal control strategies may enhance self-efficacy, but the individual's interpretation of arousal is the key.

Feltz (1982) failed to confirm a relationship between self-efficacy and arousal, as measured by heart rate, but a subsequent study (Feltz & Mugno, 1983) revealed a negative relationship between self-efficacy and perceived arousal. Feltz (1984b) proposed that if an athlete's interpretation of arousal as fear or anxiety can be changed to arousal as a state of being psyched up or prepared, self-efficacy should be enhanced. However, in our study (Lan & Gill, 1984), we were unable to change competitors' perceived anxiety or self-efficacy by telling them that arousal is a typical response that benefits good competitors. Such findings suggest that stronger tactics are needed to change perceptions of arousal and self-efficacy.

## Research on Exercise and Self-Efficacy

Over the last 10 years, self-efficacy theory has been applied more widely in exercise activities and sport and athletic settings. Self-efficacy theory has been useful in behavioral medicine and health psychology (O'Leary, 1985), and researchers interested in health-related physical activities have adopted similar approaches. Ewart, Taylor, Reese, and DeBusk (1983) reported that postmyocardial infarction (PMI) patients who were more efficacious about their physical capabilities exerted more effort, recovered faster, and returned to normal activities more quickly. Ewart et al. (1986) also demonstrated that PMI patients' efficacy predicted exercise compliance, whereas physical capabilities did not. Taylor, Bandura, Ewart, Miller, and DeBusk (1985) reported that not only patients' efficacy, but also their spouses' efficacy, predicted cardiac function.

Several studies support strong links between self-efficacy and physical activity or exercise. McAuley and his colleagues have conducted several leading studies in this area, and his reviews (McAuley, 1992c, 1993) summarize that work. Self-efficacy predicted exercise behavior in college undergraduates (Dzewaltowski, 1989; Dzewaltowski, Noble, & Shaw, 1990); self-efficacy predicted exercise adherence for middle-aged adults (McAuley, 1992b); and efficacy related to physical activity in a community sample (Sallis et al., 1986). These studies suggest that self-efficacy theory may contribute substantially to our understanding of exercise behavior in both asymptomatic and diseased populations (McAuley, 1993). The range of applications for self-efficacy and physical activity offers exciting possibilities for sport and exercise psychology, which we are just beginning to tap. McAuley advocates longitudinal studies considering efficacy and exercise behavior. Social-cognitive theory (Bandura, 1986) with its dynamic interrelationships

**Figure 6.2**
The relationships between the three major classes of determinants in triadic reciprocal causation. B represents behavior; P the internal personal factors in the form of cognitive, affective, and biological events; and E the external environment.

From *Social Foundations of Thought and Action* by Bandura, © 1986. Reprinted by permission of Prentice-Hall, Inc., Upper Saddle River, N.J.

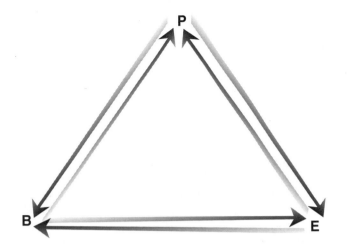

proposes continual reciprocal influences among efficacy cognitions, the environment, and behavior, and we must continue with innovative methodologies to explore the possibilities.

## Bandura's Social-Cognitive Theory

Bandura (1986) also developed a social-cognitive theory positing reciprocal interrelationships among cognitions (self-efficacy), the environment, and behavior. The model (figure 6.2) encompasses the earlier self-efficacy research, but also offers a more dynamic and social approach. Although most self-efficacy research focuses on the relationships of figure 6.1, social-cognitive theory offers many more possibilities.

## Self-Efficacy Measures

No matter how we study or apply social-cognitive theory, we must assess self-efficacy. Unlike personality measures discussed in earlier chapters, self-efficacy by definition is unstable and situation specific. Bandura (1977a, 1986) argued (and most researchers agree) that self-efficacy measures should be microanalytic, assessing efficacy along three dimensions: level, strength, and generality.

- **Level** reflects the expected performance attainment or number of tasks that can be completed. For example, in the Feltz (1984a) diving studies, performing the back dive from the board was the highest level, whereas jumping feetfirst from the side of the pool was a lower level. Components of a complex skill, or lead-up activities, might reflect levels.

- **Strength** represents the certainty with which the individual expects to successfully attain each level. Typically, strength of efficacy is measured on a percentage scale with 100% reflecting absolute certainty. On the diving task, a person might be 100% certain of jumping off the side of the pool, but only 20% certain of successfully completing the back dive from the board.

- **Generality** refers to the number of domains in which individuals consider themselves efficacious. For example, gymnastics efficacy might generalize from efficacy for floor exercise to efficacy for the balance beam and uneven parallel bars.

Because self-efficacy measures refer to specific tasks and situations, they vary widely across studies. Strength is usually the key measure, and most studies use the percentage format. Levels are also common, but not as critical as strength. For example, Feltz (1984a) focused on the strength of efficacy for the ultimate task (back dive from the board) for her main tests of self-efficacy theory. Generality is even rarer in self-efficacy measures and research.

Bandura (1977, 1986) argued that self-efficacy measures should assess efficacy along three dimensions: level, strength, and generality.

Although self-efficacy seems to preclude standard measures, some have approached self-confidence as a more stable disposition and developed sport-specific measures of physical self-efficacy or sport confidence. Ryckman, Robbins, Thornton, and Cantrell (1982) developed the Physical Self-Efficacy Scale to assess perceived physical confidence. Two subscales assess (a) the individual's perceived physical ability and (b) physical self-presentation confidence. Together they assess efficacy expectations across a variety of physical abilities (e.g., speed, strength, reaction time). Although the scale has been applied with physical tasks (Gayton, Matthews, & Burchstead, 1986; McAuley & Gill, 1983; Ryckman et al., 1982), this physical efficacy measure is a weaker predictor of skilled performance than more specific self-efficacy measures (McAuley & Gill, 1983).

## Vealey's Sport-Confidence Inventories

Robin Vealey (1986) has drawn on self-efficacy theory and other self-perception work, as well as the sport personality research, to develop two separate, related measures of trait and state sport confidence. The Trait Sport-Confidence Inventory (TSCI) assesses sport confidence as the belief or degree of certainty individuals usually possess about their ability to be successful in sport, and the State Sport-Confidence Inventory (SSCI) assesses the degree of certainty at one particular moment. Vealey collected data over a five-phase project and demonstrated adequate item discrimination, internal consistency, test-retest reliability, and content and concurrent validity. She also examined construct validity and found support for several predictions based on her conceptual model. These measures may be useful in both research and practice, but they are not self-efficacy measures. The TSCI is a personality measure, and may be useful as a sport-specific measure of confidence. The SSCI taps a state, which is changeable and situation specific, but the SSCI items reflect sport in general and do not measure specific efficacy expectations. Sport confidence, as a more stable disposition, might influence self-efficacy for sport tasks. Deeter (1989) considered this possibility and used structural modeling to examine achievement behavior in physical activity classes. Deeter found that sport confidence (TSCI) and perceived competence influenced self-efficacy, and that self-efficacy in turn mediated performance and instructor influence.

## *Summary*

Self-perception is among the most active research areas in sport and exercise psychology today. Although the self is not a new topic for psychology, most of the promising work on physical self-perceptions and dynamic approaches to efficacy expectations and behavior were just emerging when the earlier edition of this text was written. The work on physical self-concept had adopted the multidimensional and sport-specific frameworks that have advanced other areas of personality and individual differences. That approach provides stronger conceptual frameworks and sounder measures that allow us to investigate multifaceted relationships among self-perceptions and sport and exercise behaviors. Self-efficacy theory has been useful in the investigation of many behaviors, and sport and exercise psychology has moved from self-efficacy work with sport to a wide range of exercise and activity settings. Moreover, self-efficacy theories and research findings offer practical suggestions for enhancing performance and exercise as well as maintaining health-related activities. Continuing exploration of the dynamic reciprocal relationships not only advances our understanding of self-perceptions, but also has implications for understanding motivation and emotion, as we will discuss in several subsequent chapters, and even for interpersonal and group dynamics in sport and exercise.

## Review Questions

1. Explain the significance of Harter's Model of Perceived Competence.

2. Describe hierarchical models of self-concept, and provide examples.

3. Discuss Markus's work on the dynamic self, and list characteristics of the self.

4. Define and contrast self-efficacy and self-confidence.

5. List and describe the three dimensions along which self-efficacy should be analyzed.

## Recommended Reading

★ Fox, K.R., & Corbin, C.B. (1989). The Physical Self-Perception Profile: Development and preliminary validation. *Journal of Sport & Exercise Psychology, 11,* 408-430.

> This article is the source for the conceptual framework and information on the development and psychometric properties of the Physical Self-Perception Profile, one of our most useful measures of physical self-perceptions. For more current information and other views, go to Fox's (1997) edited book, *The Physical Self,* which includes chapters by Sonstroem and Marsh, two of the leading scholars of physical self-perceptions, as well as chapters on more specific populations and practice.

★ Kendzierski, D. (1994). Schema theory: An information processing focus. In R.K. Dishman (Ed.), *Advances in exercise adherence* (pp. 137-159). Champaign, IL: Human Kinetics.

> Deb Kendzierski has been doing excellent work on identity and self-perceptions from a social psychology perspective for some time. This chapter highlights her work on schema theory and exercise behavior. Her work is solid, and she offers fresh perspectives and new directions for sport and exercise psychology.

★ Bandura, A. (1986). *Social foundations of thought and action: A social cognitive theory.* Englewood Cliffs, NJ: Prentice-Hall.

> Bandura is my favorite psychology scholar (I'll present my biases). His work is scientifically sound and his theories are not only carefully developed, but also useful. Self-efficacy theory is particularly elegant and applicable to sport and exercise behavior. Bandura continues to research, write, and take new directions, but his 1986 book on social cognitive theory, with extensive research review and insightful applications and new directions, is the first one I recommend.

# Motivation

In part III we turn to motivation, a broad and pervasive topic that defies definition. In general terms, motivation refers to the intensity and direction of behavior. Motivation essentially addresses why people behave as they do—and that is the essence of sport and exercise psychology. As seen in other chapters, behavior is determined (or motivated) by both the individual and the environment.

In part III we focus on motivational processes and cover the major theories applicable to sport and exercise motivation. We will first address research on participation motivation. This work is largely descriptive, but current researchers are beginning to incorporate motivational theory. We will discuss achievement and competitiveness in chapter 8; this sport and exercise psychology work is based on prominent achievement orientation theories and models. In chapter 9 we will address intrinsic motivation and the social-cognitive models dominating that research. In chapter 10, we will turn to the intensity dimension and focus on emotion. Part III concludes with a chapter on competitive anxiety, a pervasive research and applied issue, and one that incorporates much from other motivational perspectives.

# chapter 7

# Participation Motivation

## CHAPTER OBJECTIVES

After studying this chapter, you should be able to

- trace the sport and exercise psychology research relating to youth participation motivation and recreational participation motivation and
- understand the relationships between motivation and exercise initiation and maintenance.

This chapter concentrates on participation motivation, or why people become and stay involved in sport and exercise activities. Because everyone does not participate, and many who start do not continue, we also consider nonparticipation. Much research on participation motivation is descriptive, presenting reasons participants give for engaging in physical activity programs. Most studies involve either participation in youth sports or recreational activities, or exercise initiation and maintenance, and we will emphasize these two areas.

### Key Point

Participation motivation refers to the basic motivational issue of why people participate in sport and exercise.

## PARTICIPATION MOTIVATION IN YOUTH SPORTS

In the 1970s and 1980s, youth sport captured the interest of sport and exercise science scholars, including many sport psychologists. Sport psychologists focused on reasons for participating and factors related to enjoying the activity, given the large drop-off at older age levels. Sapp and Haubenstricker (1978) were the first to study participation and discontinuation motives with youth sport participants, and scholars at Michigan State University have continued to focus on youth sport issues. Gould, summarizing the research in 1982, reported that both practitioners and researchers regarded why young athletes participate, and why they stop participating, as important psychological issues.

At that time I began to investigate participation motivation in youth sports. On the basis of literature surveys, discussions with colleagues, and pilot projects addressing reasons for participation in youth sports, we developed the Participation Motivation Questionnaire (Gill, Gross, & Huddleston, 1983). We then used that questionnaire to assess participation motivation with a large sample of youth sport participants in

Studies have shown that American youth are not as physically active as they need to be to enjoy the health benefits of physical activity.

Reprinted from U.S. Department of Health and Human Services, Public Health Service, Centers for Disease Control and Prevention, National Center for Chronic Disease Prevention and Health Promotion, Division of Nutrition and Physical Activity, 1999, *Promoting Physical Activity: A Guide for Community Action* (Champaign, IL: Human Kinetics), 203. Data from Kann et al. 1998.

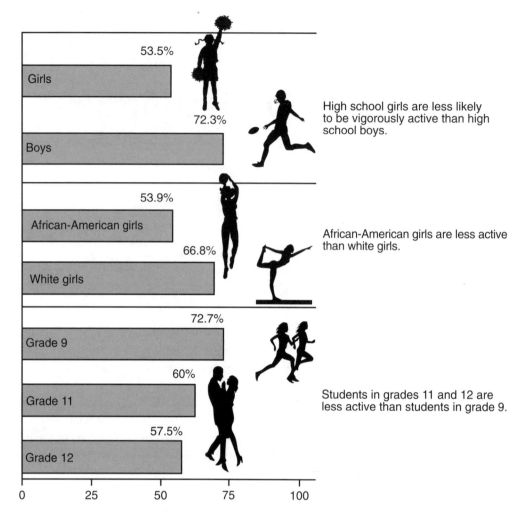

High school girls are less likely to be vigorously active than high school boys.

African-American girls are less active than white girls.

Students in grades 11 and 12 are less active than students in grade 9.

Iowa. Although the questionnaire has not undergone further psychometric testing and refinement, it has been widely referenced and used to assess participation motivation. Respondents check a list of 30 reasons for participating to indicate the importance of each reason for them (figure 7.1).

### Key Point

The Participation Motivation Questionnaire, or a modification of it, has been used in several studies of motives for participation in youth sports.

That initial study showed that the most important reasons for participating were to improve skills, to have fun, to learn new skills, to be challenged, and to be physically fit. Although we did not conduct extensive psychometric analyses, we used factor analyses that yielded the following dimensions:

- Achievement/Status
- Team
- Fitness
- Energy release

- Situational factors
- Skill development
- Friendship
- Fun

Several others used this measure, or a modification, with other youth sport samples (Gould, Feltz, & Weiss, 1985; Klint & Weiss, 1986; Passer, 1988; Wankel & Kreisel, 1985), and results are consistent in several ways. Summarizing this literature, Weiss and Chaumeton (1992) cited three common threads. First, several different

Below are some reasons that people give for participating in sports. Read each item carefully and decide if that item describes a reason why you participate in your sport. Mark an "X" to indicate if that reason is very important, somewhat important, or not at all important for you.

| | Very important | Somewhat important | Not at all important |
|---|---|---|---|
| 1. I want to improve my skills. | ❑ | ❑ | ❑ |
| 2. I want to be with my friends. | ❑ | ❑ | ❑ |
| 3. I like to win. | ❑ | ❑ | ❑ |
| 4. I want to get rid of energy. | ❑ | ❑ | ❑ |
| 5. I like to travel. | ❑ | ❑ | ❑ |
| 6. I want to stay in shape. | ❑ | ❑ | ❑ |
| 7. I like the excitement. | ❑ | ❑ | ❑ |
| 8. I like the teamwork. | ❑ | ❑ | ❑ |
| 9. My parents or close friends want me to play. | ❑ | ❑ | ❑ |
| 10. I want to learn new skills. | ❑ | ❑ | ❑ |
| 11. I like to meet new friends. | ❑ | ❑ | ❑ |
| 12. I like to do something I'm good at. | ❑ | ❑ | ❑ |
| 13. I want to release tension. | ❑ | ❑ | ❑ |
| 14. I like the rewards. | ❑ | ❑ | ❑ |
| 15. I like to get exercise. | ❑ | ❑ | ❑ |
| 16. I like to have something to do. | ❑ | ❑ | ❑ |
| 17. I like the action. | ❑ | ❑ | ❑ |
| 18. I like the team spirit. | ❑ | ❑ | ❑ |
| 19. I like to get out of the house. | ❑ | ❑ | ❑ |
| 20. I like to compete. | ❑ | ❑ | ❑ |
| 21. I like to feel important. | ❑ | ❑ | ❑ |
| 22. I like being on a team. | ❑ | ❑ | ❑ |
| 23. I want to go on to a higher level. | ❑ | ❑ | ❑ |
| 24. I want to be physically fit. | ❑ | ❑ | ❑ |
| 25. I want to be popular. | ❑ | ❑ | ❑ |
| 26. I like the challenge. | ❑ | ❑ | ❑ |
| 27. I like the coaches or instructors. | ❑ | ❑ | ❑ |
| 28. I want to gain status or recognition. | ❑ | ❑ | ❑ |
| 29. I like to have fun. | ❑ | ❑ | ❑ |
| 30. I like to use the equipment or facilities. | ❑ | ❑ | ❑ |

factor analyses yielded consistent factors, including competence, fitness, affiliation, team aspects, competition, and fun. Second, children and adolescents typically indicated that several motives were important. Third, there were minimal age, gender, experience, or sport activity differences.

### Key Point

Several descriptive studies have yielded consistent results. Children participate in sports for many different reasons, which fall into common dimensions. Skill development, competence demonstration, and particularly excitement, challenge, and fun are important motives.

Studies of participation motivation have extended to college-age and adult participants and to participants in other countries. Although some variations have emerged, the general pattern of factors and important reasons is consistent. Regarding youth sport samples in England (White & Coakley, 1986), Canada (Wankel & Kreisel, 1985), Australia (Longhurst & Spink, 1987), and Israel (Weingarten, Furst, Tenenbaum, & Schaefer, 1984), Weiss and Chaumeton (1992) noted that the culture's social context likely affects participation motivation. Weingarten and colleagues (1984) found that motives such as achievement/competitiveness, affiliation, competence, future success orientation, and family/social expectations were more important to city children than kibbutz children, suggesting a sociocultural basis for participation motivation. Weiss and Chaumeton further suggested that investigations with more diverse youth samples might yield more variations.

More recently, participation motivation research has extended to non-English-speaking countries. Buonamano, Cei, and Mussino (1995) surveyed a large sample of Italian youth sport participants using the Participation Motivation Questionnaire with a modified seven-point response scale. Generally, their factor analyses and other results were consistent with the results for Anglophone samples. However, they also found some differences related to gender, age, parents' education, and geographic region, and suggested that the relevance of motivational dimensions varies according to sociocultural and geographic factors.

Others have used the Participation Motivation Questionnaire with college-age samples. Dwyer (1992) sampled university students using a five-point response format to examine the measure's internal structure. His resulting six-factor structure (team orientation, achievement/status, fitness, friendship, skill development, fun/excitement/challenge) was similar to the results with youth samples, and all subscales were internally consistent. The most important motives for participating were to (a) maintain fitness, (b) experience fun, excitement, and challenge, and (c) acquire and improve skills—findings consistent with the youth literature (Gill et al., 1983; Gould et al., 1985; Klint & Weiss, 1987). The least important reasons were friendship, achievement/status, and team factors; these do vary from the results with youth.

### Key Point

Adults and children are motivated to participate in sports for similar reasons, although health concerns are more important and skill development and competence are less relevant for adults in exercise settings than for children.

## Dropouts and Discontinuation Motives

Fewer studies have been done on discontinuation, which involves concern about dropouts. Orlick (1974) sparked this concern when his interviews of young former sport participants in Canada revealed that most who did not plan to continue cited negative experiences such as lack of playing time, competitive emphasis, and dislike for the coach. Sapp and Haubenstricker (1978) in their Michigan Youth Sports Institute survey also found a large number (37% of 11-18-year-olds, 24% of 6-10-year-olds) who did not plan to continue, but the negative experiences reported by Orlick were cited only 15% of the time. More often the potential dropouts cited "other interests" as the reason. Other studies suggest that "dropouts" may not really be dropouts. In a study by Klint and Weiss (1986), 95% of former competitive gymnasts were participating in another sport or in gymnastics at a less competitive level. Gould, Feltz, Horn, and Weiss (1982) found that 68% of the youth who withdrew from competitive swimming were active in other sports, and most planned to reenter swimming. Similarly, White and Coakley (1986) concluded that "dropout" and "nonparticipant" were inappropriate descriptors and that discontinuation of a sport often was a good decision from a developmental perspective.

Dishman (1986) suggested similar issues for exercise participation and adherence. Specifically, when considering individuals who "drop out" we must look beyond organized exercise programs to unstructured exercise activities. Exercisers who drop out from one program might be compliers in another. Moreover, 100% compliance is not a realistic or even desirable exercise standard. Weiss and Chaumeton (1992) noted similarities between the youth dropout and exercise dropout issues, and there are other areas of overlap with the exercise motivation literature. However, the exercise and health-promotion area has unique issues and a developing research base that addresses some of these issues. The exercise motivation literature relies more on theoretical models than on purely descriptive studies; we will discuss some of these studies later.

## Theory-Based Participation Motivation Studies

Some more recent work on youth sport participation does stem from theory, particularly social-cognitive models. Substantial research goes beyond participation to consider achievement and specific behaviors; we will look at that work in later chapters on motivation orientation and intrinsic motivation. As Weiss and Chaumeton (1992) note, within the area of participation motivation, Harter's (1978, 1981a) competence motivation theory (discussed in chapter 6) has been the most useful. Weiss and colleagues have conducted much of this research with youth sport participants, and Weiss (1993) continues to set the standard for developmental sport psychology research. For example, Klint and Weiss (1987) found that children high in perceived physical competence were more motivated by skill-development factors, whereas gymnasts high in perceived social competence were more motivated by affiliation factors. Thus, children were motivated to demonstrate competence in those areas in which they perceived themselves to have abilities.

## Butt's Competence Motivation Model

Susan Butt (1995) has incorporated competence motivation literature in her more psychodynamic motivational model and has developed accompanying motivational scales. Butt's model specifies four levels of sport motivation:

1. **Biological motivations:** The first major source of sport motivation; the life force or energy; the struggle for survival and the will to win.

2. **Psychological motivations:** *Aggression* (the aggressive individual is energetic, eager, active, and impulsive); *conflict* (the conflict-ridden individual is unhappy, under pressure, prone to complain and make excuses); and *competence* (the competence-oriented individual has maturity and self-insight, and finds joy and challenge in sport).

3. **Social motivations:** *Competition,* which evolves from aggression and conflict; and *cooperation,* which evolves from competence.

4. **Secondary reinforcements as motivations:** Competitive as well as cooperatively motivated individuals are influenced by secondary reinforcers. Com-

petitively motivated individuals tend to be motivated by external reinforcers such as recognition, attention, prizes, money, position, and status, whereas cooperatively motivated individuals are reinforced by internal feelings of well-being, self-esteem, confidence, and identity.

Butt (1995) has developed 10-item scales for the three psychological motivations (aggression, conflict, and competence) and the two social motivations (competition and cooperation). Although Butt's model and measures have not been used as widely in sport and exercise psychology as those based on social-cognitive theory, she offers information on the measure and suggests possible uses related to health and well-being with older adults as well as younger sport participants.

> **Key Point**
>
> Butt (1995) incorporated competence motivation literature into her more psychodynamic motivational model, which specifies four levels of sport motivation: biological motivations, psychological motivations, social motivations, and secondary reinforcements as motivations.

## CAREER TRANSITIONS AND CHANGES IN PARTICIPATION

As already noted, dropping out of youth sports may be part of a developmental transition. Many developmental transitions occur in relation to sport and exercise participation across the life span, and researchers are beginning to address related issues.

Career transitions have particularly profound implications for sport psychology consultation with elite athletes. At this point, applied sport psychologists have discussed issues, reviewed literature, and offered workshops and programs for athletes, but the research is sparse.

After reviewing the literature on career transitions in sport, Baillie and Danish (1992) offered suggestions for research and practice. The process of identifying as an athlete begins early; and the associated activity, teamwork, and competition have implications for social, physical, and personal development. The transitions athletes experience as they move through high school and college athletics have profound implications for further development and later life adjustment. Kennedy and Dimick (1987) reported that although only 2% of college student-athletes were likely to play professional sports, 48% expected to do so. Several studies (Blann, 1985; Kennedy & Dimick, 1987; Greendorfer & Blinde, 1985) suggest that college athletes are heavily invested in the role of athlete, to the potential detriment of their career development. College athletes who overly identify with the role may limit future options and increase the likelihood of psychological difficulties when the athlete role ends; those who move into professional or other elite levels may encounter similar transition difficulties later.

*Athletes may encounter psychological difficulties when the role of athlete ends, whether due to injury or other factors.*

In one of the few studies on transitions, Werthner and Orlick (1986) interviewed Canadian Olympians, and while acknowledging individual differences, cited seven common factors:

1. **A new focus:** An alternative to sport participation allowed redirection of energy.

2. **A sense of accomplishment:** The feeling that goals had been reached tended to facilitate transition.

3. **Coaches:** Difficulties with coaches led to bitterness; a close relationship with a coach was linked with achieving goals and enjoying success.

4. **Injuries/health problems:** Premature termination due to injury predicted negative transition experiences.

5. **Politics/sport-association problems:** The Canadian system and decision not to attend the 1980 Olympics had a negative impact on transitions.

6. **Finances:** Lack of funds and cost of continuing often led to retirement and bitterness.

7. **Support of family and friends:** Support was a positive factor in transitions.

Most athletes had positive memories of athletics but experienced difficulty in the transition from international athlete to ordinary citizen (Werthner & Orlick, 1986). The authors suggested that models of coping with important losses might be useful for sport retirement.

Others have discussed sport transitions using models from literature on disability and death, such as Kubler-Ross's (1969) *On Death and Dying*. This work suggests that those experiencing loss go through stages of shock and denial, anxiety or guilt, depression, and finally adjustment or acceptance. Blinde and Greendorfer (1985) argued that applying gerontological or thanatological models to sport retirement may limit our perspective. Sport retirement occurs within an overall life history, including specialization into the role of athlete, disengagement, and movement into new roles (Baillie & Danish, 1992). Theories and models that include these developmental elements may be more appropriate.

## Scanlan's Sport Commitment Model

The Sport Commitment Model of Tara Scanlan and colleagues (Scanlan, Carpenter, Schmidt, Simons, & Keeler, 1993; Scanlan, Simons, Carpenter, Schmidt, & Keeler, 1993), which Baillie and Danish (1992) advocate, offers a framework for understanding participation and transitions. The model is based on theoretical concepts of commitment in social and organizational psychology. Scanlan, Carpenter, et al. (1993) define sport commitment as "a psychological construct representing the desire and resolve to continue sport participation" (p. 6). The model further defines five factors that influence sport commitment:

1. **Sport enjoyment:** A positive affective response to the sport experience that reflects generalized feelings such as pleasure, liking, and fun

2. **Involvement alternatives:** The attractiveness of the most preferred alternative(s) to continued participation in the current endeavor

3. **Personal investments:** Resources invested in the activity that cannot be recovered if participation is discontinued

4. **Social constraints:** Social expectations or norms that create feelings of obligation to continue the activity

5. **Involvement opportunities:** Valued opportunities that are present only with continued involvement

### Key Point

The more athletes enjoy playing, the more they have invested in their sports, the more opportunities involvement offers, the more constrained they feel to continue playing, the less attractive their alternatives, and the greater their commitment.

In initial investigations, sport enjoyment was the strongest predictor of commitment for youth participants, with personal investment also adding to the prediction. Scanlan, Simons, et al. (1993), continuing to develop survey measures to assess the model's constructs, reported that the measures were reliable with their youth sport samples.

As Scanlan (Scanlan, Carpenter, Schmidt, et al., 1993) stated in introducing the model, "While we have taken a significant step in the process of model development, we obviously expect the Sport Commitment Model to undergo change. With further testing, we will better understand which model components work in diverse sport contexts, and what modifications and additions to the model and measures are required" (p. 2). Scanlan and colleagues continue to extend their work from the youth samples and survey measures by using in-depth interviews and diverse methods with elite athletes from around the world. With the publication of these and other results, we will develop our conceptual models and measures and continue to learn more about sport participation and transitions.

## Extending Participation Motivation to Activity Settings

Brodkin and Weiss's (1990) study with swimmers of varied ages extended participation work beyond youth sports. The focus was a competitive sport, and motives used with younger participants likely are applicable. However, in more health-oriented settings, these may not be adequate. Duda and Tappe (1988, 1989) developed a participation motivation measure that retains the wide range of options of the participation motivation measures (e.g., Gill et al., 1983) but places them within the framework of personal investment theory. Also, Duda and Tappe designed their measure to assess motives for participation in exercise activities and included motives that should apply to a wide range of participants.

Duda and Tappe's (1989) Personal Incentives for Exercise Questionnaire (PIEQ) is a 48-item inventory with 10 subscales: Appearance, Competition, Mental benefits, Affiliation, Social Recognition, Mastery, Flexibility/agility, Health benefits, Weight management, and Fitness. We (Gill, Dowd, Williams, Beaudoin, & Martin, 1997) used the PIEQ with older and more diverse samples than in earlier research. We gave the PIEQ to adults in a running club, at a fitness club, and in a cardiac rehabilitation program and used a shorter version with senior games participants. Overall, all four groups were similar to each other and to previous samples, but they varied on specific motives. Females rated fitness, flexibility, affiliation, and appearance higher than males did. Generally, participants were diverse in motives and positive about participation.

# EXERCISE PARTICIPATION MOTIVATION

Much interest in exercise participation stems from the public's increasing recognition of the health benefits of exercise coupled with the fact that most people do not act on that recognition. According to one estimate, 89% of adults know they should exercise three times a week for good health, but only 27% actually do so ("Vital Statistics", 1996). The U.S. Centers for Disease Control and Prevention (USCDCP) and the American College of Sports Medicine (ACSM) (Pate et al., 1995) recommend at least 30 minutes of moderate physical activity on most, if not all, days of the week. Yet data from the Behavioral Risk Factor Surveillance System showed that 58% of the U.S. population are sedentary (USCDCP, 1993). Sedentary behavior is related to being older, African-American, female, poorly educated, and overweight and to having a history of being physically inactive (Blair et al., 1993). After adolescence and early adulthood, participation decreases (Gartside, Khoury, & Glueck, 1984; Schoenborn, 1986) with progressively larger proportions of older adults reporting no leisure physical activity (Caspersen & DiPietro, 1991; Caspersen, Merritt, Heath, & Yeager, 1990). Moreover, 50% of the adults who start to exercise drop out within six months (Dishman, 1990; Sallis et al., 1986). Sport and exercise psychology has addressed this public health issue through research on exercise motivation.

Unlike the largely descriptive research on youth sport motivation, the work on exercise motivation is largely theory based. Bess Marcus, a major contributor in this area, and her colleagues (Marcus, Bock, Pinto, & Clark, 1996) have provided an excellent review of that research and of theoretical models that have been applied to exercise behavior.

## Health Belief Model

The Health Belief Model (Janz & Becker, 1984), developed by Rosenstock, (1966) includes four major components: (a) perceived susceptibility, or the assessment of risk for the particular health threat; (b) perceived severity of the health threat; (c) perceived benefits of taking action to reduce the threat; and (d) perceived barriers to or costs of the action. The Health Belief Model has considerable support in relation to health behaviors and medical compliance, but limited application to exercise. The strongest support has been found for components related to other theories. Perceived barriers, which relates to self-efficacy, has stronger support than other components. Recent research suggests social support, which relates to social norms, as an added component (Kelly, Zyzanski, & Alemagno, 1991; Zimmerman & Conner, 1989); and a self-efficacy component has been added to the model (Rosenstock, Strecher, & Becker, 1988).

## Theories of Reasoned Action and Planned Behavior

The attitude-based theories of reasoned action (Fishbein & Ajzen, 1975) and planned behavior (Ajzen, 1985) have received more attention. Both propose that *intentions* are the main determinants of behavior. That is, to predict whether people will exercise, ask them what they intend to do. Behavioral intentions, in turn, are determined by *attitudes* toward the behavior, along with *social norms.* The planned-behavior theory moves beyond reasoned action by adding the notion of *perceived behavioral control.* Perceived behavioral control is similar to self-efficacy (as discussed in chapter 6); it involves perceptions that one has the resources and opportunities to carry out the behavior or attain the goal. Early studies with the planned-behavior model measured perceived control as barriers, similar to those in the Health Belief Model; and researchers continue to debate these issues. One strength of these theories is their emphasis on measures specific to the behavior, context, and goal in question (Maddux, 1993). Moreover, several sport and exercise psychologists have applied reasoned action or planned behavior to understand and predict exercise behavior (Brawley & Rodgers, 1992; Godin, 1993; McAuley & Courneya, 1993).

Work site exercise facilities serve to break down perceived barriers to physical activity. When work site attitudes about physical activity are positive, employees may feel more comfortable starting a new exercise program.

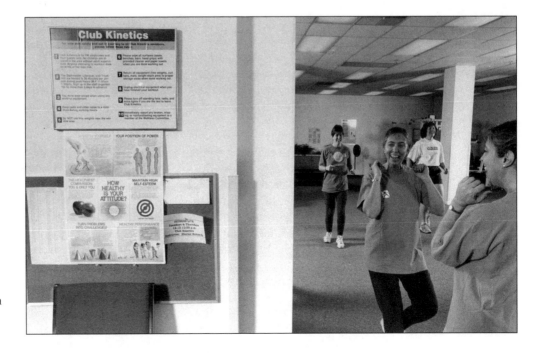

## Social-Cognitive Theory

Self-efficacy, and the more recent social-cognitive theory (Bandura, 1986; discussed in chapter 6), have been applied to many health behaviors, including exercise behavior. On the basis of earlier work with other health behaviors (e.g., weight management, smoking cessation), Marcus, Selby, Niaura, and Rossi (1992) developed a five-item self-efficacy measure for exercise that includes as situational factors negative affect, resisting relapse, and making time for exercise. As discussed in chapter 6, considerable literature (McAuley, 1992c) supports self-efficacy and social-cognitive theory in relation to exercise participation. Dzewaltowski (1989; Dzewaltowski, Noble, & Shaw, 1990) compared self-efficacy theory with the attitudinal models of reasoned action and planned behavior. They found that self-efficacy was a significant predictor of exercise behavior whereas neither reasoned action nor planned behavior added to the prediction.

## Decision Theory

Decision theory (Janis & Mann, 1977) entails the perception and evaluation of relative costs and benefits. In applied settings, individuals might generate lists of short- and long-term consequences of an exercise program and then weigh them. Decision theory has been applied successfully with smoking behavior (Marlatt & Gordon, 1985), and these decision-balancing procedures have been adopted and applied to exercise behavior (Marcus, Rakowski, & Rossi, 1992; Wankel, 1984). Decision balancing procedures may increase awareness of exercise benefits and promote participation.

## Transtheoretical Model

Several researchers have advocated some integration of the many available theoretical approaches. Maddux (1993) proposed an integrated model with the planned-behavior model as a base. At this time, the most productive approach to determining exercising behavior is the transtheoretical model, advocated by Marcus and colleagues, in which individuals progress through a series of stages of change:

- Precontemplation
- Contemplation
- Preparation
- Action
- Maintenance

### Key Point

According to the transtheoretical model, individuals progress through a series of stages of change: precontemplation, contemplation, preparation, action, and maintenance.

Precontemplators do not exercise and do not intend to do so within the next six months. Contemplators do not exercise, but intend to start within six months. Preparers are exercising, but not regularly (three or more times per week for 20 minutes or longer, or accumulating 30 minutes or more per day five or more days per week, as recommended by ACSM, 1990; Pate et al., 1995). Individuals at the action stage exercise regularly, but have done so for less than six months, whereas those at the maintenance stage have been exercising regularly for over six months (Marcus, Rossi, Selby, Niaura, & Abrams, 1992).

The transtheoretical model implies that intervention programs should match the stage of change. Although most programs are designed for people in the action stage, most people are not in the action stage. For example, of over 1000 participants in a work site health-promotion project, Marcus, Rossi, et al. (1992) found 24.4% in

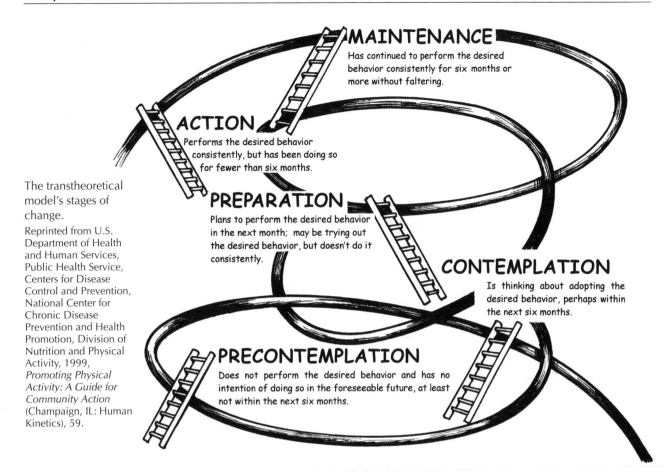

**MAINTENANCE**
Has continued to perform the desired behavior consistently for six months or more without faltering.

**ACTION**
Performs the desired behavior consistently, but has been doing so for fewer than six months.

**PREPARATION**
Plans to perform the desired behavior in the next month; may be trying out the desired behavior, but doesn't do it consistently.

**CONTEMPLATION**
Is thinking about adopting the desired behavior, perhaps within the next six months.

**PRECONTEMPLATION**
Does not perform the desired behavior and has no intention of doing so in the foreseeable future, at least not within the next six months.

The transtheoretical model's stages of change.

Reprinted from U.S. Department of Health and Human Services, Public Health Service, Centers for Disease Control and Prevention, National Center for Chronic Disease Prevention and Health Promotion, Division of Nutrition and Physical Activity, 1999, *Promoting Physical Activity: A Guide for Community Action* (Champaign, IL: Human Kinetics), 59.

precontemplation, 33.4% in contemplation, 9.5% in preparation, 10.6% in action, and 22% in maintenance. According to the model, when stages and interventions are a mismatch, attrition is high; therefore, matching intervention strategies to the individual's stage should improve adherence. In addition to describing stages of change, Marcus, Rossi, et al. (1992) proposed processes of change related to the stages. Processes are either (a) cognitive, including consciousness raising, dramatic relief, environmental reevaluation, self-evaluation, and social liberation; or (b) behavioral, including counterconditioning, helping relationships, reinforcement management, self-liberation, and stimulus control. Use of cognitive processes peaks in the preparation stage, whereas behavioral processes peak in the action stage. Generally, the transtheoretical model helps us understand the relationship between individual readiness and actual exercise behavior, and provides guidance to those offering intervention programs aimed at increasing exercise.

Marcus also relates the decisional balance and self-efficacy constructs to stages of change. In relation to stages, the decisional balance typically favors the costs in the precontemplation and contemplation stages, crosses over in the preparation stage, and favors benefits over costs in the action and maintenance stages (Marcus, Rakowski, et al. 1992; Prochaska et al., 1994). Over several studies (Marcus & Owen, 1992; Marcus, Pinto, Simkin, Audrain, & Taylor, 1994; Marcus, Selby, et al. 1992; Marcus, Eaton, Rossi, & Harlow, 1994), Marcus and colleagues have found a positive relationship between enhanced self-efficacy and higher levels of readiness for change.

**Key Point**

According to the transtheoretical model, matching intervention strategies to an individual's stage should improve adherence, and this hypothesis has been supported by research (Marcus, Emmons, et al., 1994).

## Using the Transtheoretical Model to Change Behavior

The transtheoretical model incorporates many aspects of the other theories, with the underlying theme that people are at different readiness levels and require different interventions using different strategies to change exercise behavior. Marcus and colleagues have carried out interventions based on the model. In the "Imagine Action" campaign, 610 adults enrolled through work sites in response to community announcements and received a six-week intervention consisting of stage-matched self-help materials, resource manual, weekly fun walks, and activity nights. The manual for contemplators was titled "What's in It for You," as this is the critical question at that stage; the preparation manual was "Ready for Action;" and the manual for those in action was "Keeping It Going."

After the intervention, 30% of those in contemplation and 61% of those in preparation progressed to action, and an additional 31% of those in contemplation progressed to preparation, whereas only 4% of those in preparation and 9% in action regressed. A subsequent controlled, randomized-design investigation of a stage-matched intervention at the workplace followed (Marcus, Emmons, et al., 1994). The intervention was successful with more subjects in the stage-matched group, demonstrating stage progression at the three-month follow-up; more subjects in the standard-care group displayed stage stability or regression.

## Relapse-Prevention Model

Regardless of how one starts exercising, relapse is a problem, as for most health behaviors (Brownell, Marlatt, Lichtenstein, & Wilson, 1986). As noted earlier, about 50% of exercise program participants typically drop out within six months. Sallis et al. (1990) found that 40% of exercisers experienced relapse (stopped exercising for at least three months) and that 20% had three or more relapses. The principles of relapse prevention include (a) identifying high-risk situations (e.g., change in work hours) and (b) problem-solving for those high-risk situations (e.g., when it starts to snow, move inside the mall to walk).

When individuals experience a relapse they must deal with the abstinence violation effect (AVE): the belief that one slip means doom (one cookie ruins the diet). Brownell (1989) differentiates between lapse (slip), relapse (string of lapses), and collapse (giving up and returning to past behaviors) and recommends helping people become aware of AVE and of these distinctions in order to reduce recidivism. Marcus and Stanton (1993) have found this model helpful when exercise is not possible (e.g., medical problems), but they have not found a planned relapse, advocated by some researchers, beneficial in exercise settings.

## EXCESSIVE PARTICIPATION: EXERCISE ADDICTION

So far, we have focused on encouraging participation and adherence, but exercise addiction suggests that participation can be excessive and problematic. Running addiction has been discussed in popular as well as sport psychology literature, and more recently the discussion has broadened to exercise addiction.

Whether or not "addiction" is an appropriate term is questionable. The phenomenon of excessive exercise has been termed "compulsion," "dependence," and "obsession" but might also be characterized as commitment or a healthy habit. Sachs (1981) defined running addiction as a psychological and/or physiological addiction to regular running that is characterized by withdrawal symptoms after 24 to 36 hours without running. To characterize negative addiction, Morgan (1979) suggested that (a) addicted runners believe they need to exercise and cannot live without running daily; (b) if deprived of exercise, these runners experience withdrawal symptoms including anxiety, restlessness, guilt, irritability, tension, and discomfort, as well as apathy, sluggishness, lack of appetite, sleeplessness, and headaches.

When Michael Jordan retired from the NBA, it allowed him more time to participate in other physical activities he enjoys.

Several studies suggest that many regular runners fit the addiction criteria. Kagan and Squires (1985) found that college students who exercised regularly tended to fit an addictive personality, and Robbins and Joseph (1985) reported that over 50% of a large sample of runners experienced deprivation sensations when unable to run.

According to William Glasser's (1976) popular book, running may be a *positive addiction* as identified by the following criteria:

- The activity must be something one chooses to do.

- It must have some value to the person.

- It must be something the person can become proficient in and can do on his or her own.

- The activity must have sufficient worth for a person to devote about an hour a day to it.

- The activity must have an inherent value in order for the person to persevere long enough to become positively addicted.

Some authors have proposed classifying commitment rather than simply using the addiction label. Joseph and Robbins (1981) proposed four levels of running commitment. At the highest level, Type I, running is the most important commitment; at the other three levels (Types II through IV), it is a crucial commitment, a hobby, and an occasional activity, respectively. Thompson and Blanton (1987) proposed a physiological explanation, hypothesizing that exercise dependence relates to sympathetic arousal. They suggest that exercise dependence is mediated by adaptive reductions in sympathetic output during exercise, which is the result of increased efficiency of energy use with exercise training.

Not only has excessive exercise been discussed as a problem in itself; some reports have linked excessive exercise with anorexia nervosa and bulimia. Yates, Leehey, and Shisslak (1983) interviewed 60 obligatory runners and in a preliminary report noted that character, style, and background were similar to those of anorexia nervosa patients. They did note two major differences: most people with anorexia were women and most obligatory runners men, and most anorexia cases began in adolescence whereas obligatory running began at ages 30-50. Blumenthal, O'Toole, and Chang (1984), testing the suggestions of Yates et al., found that obligatory runners generally fell within the normal range of behavior while persons with anorexia did not. In a follow-up article, Blumenthal, Rose, and Chang (1985) argued against a psychopathological or disease model of habitual running. Other research confirms the point in showing no support for the Yates et al. hypotheses (Knight, Schocken, Powers, Feld, & Smith, 1987; Weight & Noakes, 1987; Wheeler, Wall, Belcastro, Conger, & Cumming, 1986). However, habitual runners or excessive exercisers may well display unhealthy behaviors, and professionals should be alert for signs of impaired health as well as disruption of normal occupational and social functioning resulting from exercise (Willis & Campbell, 1992).

© Chuck Rydlewski/SportsChrome-USA

**Key Point**

Excessive exercise participation, sometimes termed an "addiction," a "dependence," or a "commitment," has been discussed as a problem in itself. Some reports have also linked excessive exercise with eating disorders.

## Summary

Participation motivation refers to the basic motivational issue—why do people participate in sport and exercise? Answers are many and varied. Much sport and exercise psychology research on participation motivation is descriptive, starting with studies of motives for participating in youth sports. But several descriptive studies have yielded consistent findings. Children participate for many different reasons, and those reasons fall into common dimensions, with skill development, competence demonstration, and particularly excitement, challenge, and fun appearing as important motives. Similar reasons have emerged with adult participants, although health concerns become more prominent and skill development and competence less relevant in exercise settings.

More recently, participation motivation work has incorporated more theoretical models. Several theories have been applied to issues of exercise participation and maintenance. At present, models incorporating features of several theories seem most useful. Motivational theories have been applied extensively in sport and exercise psychology research that moves beyond participation to investigate sport and exercise behaviors, particularly achievement behaviors. We will cover that research in the remaining chapters in part III.

## Review Questions

1. Define participation motivation.
2. Discuss several descriptive studies of participation motivation and their findings.
3. Compare and contrast the factors that motivate adults and children to participate in sports.
4. Describe Butt's competence motivation model, and list her four levels of sport motivation.
5. Discuss factors that influence sport commitment, including factors that affect transitions in sport and exercise participation.
6. List and explain the stages that form the basis of the transtheoretical model.
7. Discuss the relationship between an individual's stage of readiness and the potential success of an intervention.
8. Explain the ways in which excessive exercise participation can be a problem.

## *Recommended Reading*

★ Scanlan, T.K., Carpenter, P.J., Schmidt, G.W., Simons, J.P., & Keeler, B. (1993). An introduction to the Sport Commitment Model. *Journal of Sport & Exercise Psychology, 15,* 1-15.

★ Scanlan, T.K., Simons, J.P., Carpenter, P.J., Schmidt, G.W., & Keeler, B. (1993). The Sport Commitment Model: Measurement development for the youth-sport domain. *Journal of Sport & Exercise Psychology, 15,* 16-38.

These two articles provide an overview of the initial work of Tara Scanlan and her colleagues on enjoyment and commitment in sport. The articles not only provide information on leading work on the positive side of emotions, but also provide a good model for the development of a research line. The first article presents the guiding model for the research and the second article presents their initial research testing and refining the model. Scanlan continues to do fine work using multiple approaches to address important issues. I'm sure you will enjoy reading the work of this committed sport and exercise psychology scholar.

★ Marcus, B.H., Bock, B.C., Pinto, B.M., & Clark, M.M. (1996). Exercise initiation, adoption, and maintenance. In J.L. Van Raalte & B.W. Brewer (Eds.), *Exploring sport and exercise psychology* (pp. 133-158). Washington, DC: American Psychological Association.

Bess Marcus and her colleagues have done considerable research on exercise motivation, focusing on applying the transtheoretical model to enhance exercise participation in different populations. This chapter summarizes her work and provides an overview of the different perspectives that have been applied to encourage everyone to be physically active.

# Motivational Orientations: Achievement and Competitiveness

**Lavon Williams, PhD**
*Northern Illinois University*
**Diane L. Gill, PhD**
*University of North Carolina–Greensboro*

## CHAPTER OBJECTIVES

After studying this chapter, you should be able to

- understand the sport and exercise psychology research relating to the desire to compete, the desire to win, and the desire to attain goals and
- explain the relationship between individual motivation characteristics and environmental conditions.

Most people in sport and exercise are interested in achievement. For example, we may wonder why some people take on challenges, work hard, and persist whereas others avoid challenge, exert little effort, and give up easily. We may also question why some athletes appear devastated by a loss and others take it in stride, or why some people eagerly approach competition and others avoid it. Achievement behavior is central to sport and exercise endeavors, and understanding individual differences in motivational orientations is a key to understanding achievement.

## ATKINSON'S THEORY OF ACHIEVEMENT MOTIVATION

Many explanations for individual differences in achievement behavior exist. Some emphasize personality and others stress perceptions and interpretations, but nearly all stem from the classic work of Atkinson. Atkinson's (1964, 1974) theory of achievement motivation is an interaction model that specifies personality and situational factors as determinants of achievement behavior in precise, formal terms.

### Personality Factors

Murray (1938) first discussed achievement motivation as a personality factor, defining the need to achieve as the desire

> to accomplish something difficult. To master, manipulate or organize physical objects, human beings, or ideas. To do this as rapidly and as independently as possible. To overcome obstacles and attain a high standard. To excel one's self. To rival and surpass others. To increase self-regard by the successful exercise of talent. (p. 164)

Atkinson, extending Murray's work, delineated achievement motivation as a combination of two personality constructs: the *motive to approach success* (or the capacity to experience pride in accomplishment) and the *motive to avoid failure* (or the capacity to experience shame in failure). Everyone has both; we all feel good when we accomplish something and bad when we fail.

But we do not all have the two motives to the same degree, and the personality factor is the key to the difference or balance between the two motives. We commonly refer to persons as "high" or "low" achievers. Individuals with a high motive to approach success and low motive to avoid failure are the high achievers who seek out challenging achievement situations without worrying about possible failures. Low achievers worry about failure a great deal and avoid achievement situations. For people in between, that is, those who have equal levels of the two motives, predictions according to Atkinson's theory are not very clear.

### Key Point

The key personality factor affecting achievement motivation is the balance between the two motives Atkinson delineated: the motive to approach success and the motive to avoid failure.

## Situational Factors

Atkinson's theory does not predict solely on the basis of the motives but incorporates situational factors also. The main situational factor is task difficulty, or the *probability of success*, which ranges from 0 (no chance at all) to 1.00 (certain success). Another situational factor is the *incentive value* of success. The lower the chances of success, the greater the incentive value. An average tennis player has a very slim chance against top pro player Martina Hingis, but would be elated to win a game; the incentive value is high. At the other extreme, the average player would not be very inspired by the prospect of playing a beginner.

### Key Point

Situational factors affecting achievement behavior include task difficulty—or the probability of success—and the incentive value of success.

Individuals we commonly refer to as "high achievers" routinely seek out challenging situations without worrying about possible failures.

© Paul Souders

## Behavioral Tendencies Related to Achievement

According to Atkinson, the behavioral tendency to approach success is a function of the person's motive to approach success as well as the situational factors. Similarly, individuals with a strong motive to avoid failure are not likely to approach achievement situations but have a strong tendency to avoid them. Situations in which we are matched with an opponent of equal ability, or in which our chances of success are very uncertain, bring out the strongest achievement behaviors, and the difference between the high and low achiever is greatest in the most challenging situations because those situations bring out the strongest behavioral tendencies.

### Cognitive Approaches to Achievement Motivation

Many contemporary theorists have built on Atkinson's foundation by developing multidimensional approaches that consider personality, development, and environment. Over the last 25 years, cognitive approaches have dominated achievement research. Bernard Weiner (1974) sparked a dramatic change in the study of motivation when he proposed that high and low achievers think differently and therefore act differently. Since then, several multidimensional, goal perspective approaches have emerged to explain achievement behaviors such as task choice, behavioral intensity, and persistence (Dweck & Elliott, 1983; Dweck & Leggett, 1988; Maehr, 1984; Maehr & Braskamp, 1986; Maehr & Nicholls, 1980; Nicholls, 1989; Spence & Helmreich, 1983). Although each theorist has a distinct perspective, they all contend that individuals use goals to evaluate an experience as a success or failure. In achievement settings, people experience feelings of success when they demonstrate high ability (i.e., their goal) and failure when they do not. Therefore, success is subjective. It depends on how one defines ability, which in turn depends on personal, developmental, and situational factors.

### Key Point

Although each theorist has a distinct perspective, they all contend that individuals use goals to evaluate an experience as a success or a failure.

## GOAL PERSPECTIVE THEORY

Sport and exercise psychology research has relied heavily on Nicholls's (1989) goal perspective theory adapted by Glyn Roberts and Joan Duda to investigate achievement behaviors, cognitions, and affect in sport and exercise settings. Also, Tom Martinek (Martinek & Griffith, 1994; Martinek & Williams, 1997) applied Dweck's theory of achievement motivation to study learned helplessness in physical education classes, and Diane Gill (Gill & Deeter, 1988) used the theoretical concepts of Spence and Helmreich (1978, 1983) to ground her work on competitiveness.

According to Nicholls (1989), achievement behaviors are related to the individual's definition of ability. Very young children construe ability in a self-referenced manner and do not differentiate between effort and ability. With an undifferentiated conception of ability, children see those who try harder as more able. Around age 8 or 9 years, children begin to rely on normative criteria, and ability begins to depend on how many other people can do a task. At this time, children partially differentiate effort and ability, and understand that an individual who does not exert much effort to succeed at a task must be more skilled.

By 11 or 12 years, children can completely differentiate ability and effort. Ability is stable, and ability limits the impact of effort. Children at this age understand that when two players perform equally well on a task, the player who exerts the least effort is the most able. An individual's cognitive development, as well as the conception of ability, is partly a function of relatively stable personal orientations. The undifferentiated conception of ability is associated with a *task goal orientation;* that is, goals are based on learning or task mastery. Individuals who set self-referenced goals that are focused on improvement and greater mastery are task oriented. The differentiated conception of ability is associated with *ego goal orientation.* Individuals who tend to set norm-referenced goals that focus on outperforming others, or performing equally with less effort, are ego oriented.

### Key Point

Both the task goal orientation, in which goals are based on learning or task mastery, and the ego goal orientation, in which goals focus on outperforming others or on performing equally with less effort, are relatively stable personal orientations.

For Nicholls (1989), task and ego orientation are independent constructs; individuals could be equally ego and task oriented, or higher in one than in the other. Both dispositional goal orientation and the situation affect achievement goals. Situations involving competition are more ego-inducing than situations that emphasize skill mastery (Ames, 1992; Dweck & Leggett, 1988; Nicholls, 1989). Suppose, for example, that Katie is predominantly task oriented: she defines ability as learning, improving, and trying hard and feels successful when she demonstrates these characteristics. However, if we put Katie into a competitive junior tennis program that emphasizes winning and rankings, she is likely to adopt an ego-involving perspective in which ability can be demonstrated and success experienced only by outperforming others.

## Benefits of Task Goal Perspective

There is wisdom in using an undifferentiated conception of ability or a task goal perspective (Nicholls, 1989). With a task goal perspective, feelings of competence are not constrained by the performances of others. Everyone can demonstrate ability through effort and improvement. A task goal perspective should relate to increased persistence, effort, and interest in challenging tasks regardless of one's perceptions of competence (Nicholls, 1989; Nicholls & Miller, 1984).

Conversely, the differentiated conception of ability or ego goal perspective mandates that only one person can be the best (Duda, 1992; Nicholls, 1989; Nicholls & Miller, 1984). Individuals with a strong task and weak ego perspective are not constrained by the performances of others, and they are more likely than highly ego-oriented individuals to persist in difficult situations (Nicholls, 1989; Nicholls & Miller, 1984). Individuals with a strong ego and weak task perspective who question their competence level are apt to give up in the face of failure, choose either simple or very difficult tasks, or lose interest (Nicholls & Miller, 1984). These relationships underscore the importance of fostering a task goal perspective in children in achievement settings (Duda, 1992; Dweck, 1986; Nicholls, 1989).

### Key Point

Unlike the task goal perspective, in which feelings are not constrained by the performance of others, the ego goal perspective maintains that only one person can be the best.

Goal perspective research, which began in academic classroom settings, has been extended to sport over the last 15 years. Before discussing the sport-specific research, we should consider how goal perspectives are measured.

## Goal Perspective Measures

Currently, goal perspective researchers rely upon specific inventories to assess goal orientations, including the Task and Ego Orientation in Sport Questionnaire (TEOSQ; Nicholls, 1992; Duda, 1992) and Perception of Sport Questionnaire (POSQ; Roberts & Balague, 1991; Roberts, Treasure, & Balague, 1998). Both are valid and reliable inventories that assess the degree to which individuals identify with task and ego orientation. The TEOSQ was adapted from the measure of Nicholls, Patashnick, and Nolen (1985) for use in sport settings by John Nicholls and Joan Duda. For measuring goal orientations, individuals think about a time when they felt most successful in sport. The stem phrase "I feel most successful in sport when" is followed by 13 response items with which individuals indicate their level of agreement on a scale ranging from "Strongly agree" to "Strongly disagree." Figure 8.1 shows sample questions.

**Key Point**

TEOSQ and POSQ are inventories used to assess goal orientation.

The adult and children's versions of the POSQ were developed by Glyn Roberts and Gloria Balague (1991) using extensive scale construction procedures. When completing the POSQ, which is similar in construction to the TEOSQ, individuals think about what sport means to them in responding to the stem phrase "When playing sport, I feel most successful when." Sample questions are in figure 8.2.

**Figure 8.1**
Task and Ego Orientation in Sport Questionnaire (TEOSQ) sample.

|  | Strongly disagree | Disagree | Neutral | Agree | Strongly agree |
|---|---|---|---|---|---|
| **Examples of TEOSQ task items:** I feel most successful in sport when: |  |  |  |  |  |
| I learn something that is fun to do. | 1 | 2 | 3 | 4 | 5 |
| I work really hard. | 1 | 2 | 3 | 4 | 5 |
| **Examples of TEOSQ ego items:** I feel most successful in sport when: |  |  |  |  |  |
| I can do better than my friends. | 1 | 2 | 3 | 4 | 5 |
| The others can't do as well as me. | 1 | 2 | 3 | 4 | 5 |

**Figure 8.2**
Perception of Sport Questionnaire (POSQ) (adult version) sample.

|  | Strongly disagree | Disagree | Neutral | Agree | Strongly agree |
|---|---|---|---|---|---|
| **Examples of POSQ task orientation items:** When playing sport, I feel most successful when: |  |  |  |  |  |
| I work hard. | A | B | C | D | E |
| I overcome difficulties. | A | B | C | D | E |
| **Examples of POSQ ego orientation items:** When playing sport, I feel most successful when: |  |  |  |  |  |
| I beat other people. | A | B | C | D | E |
| I am the best. | A | B | C | D | E |

Research with these measures supports Nicholls's contentions that individuals high in ego goal orientation believe they are good athletes when they outperform others while exerting less effort, whereas individuals high in task goal orientation believe they are good athletes when they work hard, learn, and improve.

## Goal Perspective Research in Sport

Studies show that sport participants set both task- and ego-oriented goals and that perceptions of success and failure relate to perceptions of demonstrated ability (Burton, 1989; Duda, 1981, 1985, 1986b; Kimiecik, Allison, & Duda, 1986; Roberts & Duda, 1984; Spink & Roberts, 1980). For example, Spink and Roberts (1980) found that perceptions of success and failure were not synonymous with winning and losing. They identified four categories of racquetball players: satisfied winners, satisfied losers, unsatisfied winners, and unsatisfied losers. Perceptions of ability and quality of performance were better predictors of feelings of success than actually winning or losing.

Goal perspective researchers have continued to examine relationships among goal perspectives, self-perceptions, and behavior, finding positive relationships with task orientation and negative associations with ego goal orientation. Specifically, task goal orientation is positively related to effort (Duda, 1988; Duda, Newton, & Chi, 1990), persistence (Duda, 1988), satisfaction (Duda, Fox, Biddle, & Armstrong, 1992), intrinsic motivation (Duda et al., 1990; Duda et al., 1995; Seifriz et al., 1991), perceived competence (Duda & Nicholls, 1992; Seifriz et al., 1991), and the belief that success in sport is a function of trying hard and cooperating (Duda, 1989a, 1989c; Treasure & Roberts, 1994). Conversely, ego orientation is associated with the belief that external factors (e.g., proper dress, gaining favor with coach) and innate talent are major causes of success (Duda et al., 1992), with work avoidance and the use of deceptive tactics (Duda et al., 1992), with belief in the legitimacy of injurious acts (Duda, Olson, & Templin, 1991), and with trait anxiety (Newton & Duda, 1992). Lochbaum and Roberts (1993) recently concluded that task-oriented athletes endorse effort and persistence as a means to success, whereas ego-oriented athletes cite chance and social approval as contributors to success. In sum, the results support the contention that task goal orientation relates to adaptive self-perceptions and motivated behaviors, whereas ego goal orientation relates to maladaptive perceptions and behaviors.

Given the findings, it is not surprising that scholars promote task goal orientation (Ames, 1984, 1992; Burton, 1989; Duda, 1992; Dweck, 1986; Nicholls, 1989; Roberts, 1992). But despite this endorsement, we know little about how to foster a task goal orientation, perhaps because we know little about the determinants of goal orientations.

## DETERMINANTS OF GOAL ORIENTATIONS

Although Nicholls's theory is developmental, age differences in goal orientations have not been substantiated in sport (Treasure & Roberts, 1994; Williams, 1994a, 1994b). Most studies involve student-athletes who would have the cognitive maturity level for a differentiated conception of ability; socialization factors may be more salient than age in how they define ability (Maehr & Nicholls, 1980; Nicholls, 1984, 1989).

Gender reflects socialization, and most agree that boys and girls (and men and women) are treated differently. Interestingly, though, goal perspective research has produced equivocal gender difference results. Some studies find males more ego oriented and females more task oriented (Duda, 1985, 1988, 1989a, 1989c; Duda et al., 1994, 1992; White & Duda, 1994), but others fail to support gender differences (Duda et al., 1994; Duda & Hom, 1993; White, Duda, & Keller, 1993; Williams, 1994a, 1994b). Like age, gender may not be an adequate indicator of individuals' social experiences.

We can also look at environmental influences such as ethnicity, personal sport history, and team climate. Duda (1985) found that Anglo males preferred to be an athlete who was successful in sport because of ability and who failed because of a lack of effort, whereas females and Mexican-American males were more likely to emphasize effort-based success over ability-based success. Duda (1986) also found that white males were the most ego oriented.

Sport and exercise psychology research has demonstrated that goal orientations are related to years of sport experience (Duda, 1988), level of sport involvement (Duda, 1989a; White & Duda, 1994), and motivational climate. In general, individuals who have played longer tend to be more task oriented (Duda, 1988). White and Duda (1994) found that intercollegiate athletes were more ego oriented than younger and recreational athletes, and interestingly, high school male and recreational participants scored the lowest in task orientation.

One current line of inquiry focuses on the specific sport environment and shows that students and athletes recognize the dominant goal perspective in a classroom or athletic team. Researchers have investigated environmental influences on goal perspectives in sport through the study of reward structures and motivational climate.

# ENVIRONMENTAL FACTORS: REWARD STRUCTURES AND MOTIVATIONAL CLIMATE

The study of reward structures and goal perspectives examines the question: What is the meaning of success and failure (goal orientations) to individuals within different situations? Carol Ames identifies two types of situations or, more specifically, reward structures related to goal orientations: competitive and individualistic. *Competitive reward structures* encourage individuals to compare their performance to that of others, fostering ego involvement. Over time, a competitive reward structure promotes an ego goal orientation (Ames, 1984; Nicholls, 1989). In contrast, *individualistic reward structures* focus on personal improvement and learning through effort, and over time promote a task goal orientation (Ames, 1984; Nicholls, 1989).

## Key Point

Competitive reward structures encourage individuals to compare their performance to that of others, while individualistic reward structures focus on personal improvement and learning through effort.

Studies in both the academic and sport contexts have demonstrated a relationship between goal perspectives and reward structures (Ames, 1984; Ames & Ames. 1981; Williams, 1998). Ames and her colleagues demonstrated that in competitive academic situations, students displayed greater ego involvement by making more ability attributions, while in individualistic settings they made more effort attributions and were more task involved.

Williams (1998), assessing goal perspectives in both a competitive and a more individualistic setting, found that middle school female softball athletes were more task involved and less anxious in practice than in game situations. Interestingly, athletes were not less ego involved in practices than in games.

Because studies of reward structures ignore the individual's interpretation of the environment, some researchers advocate the study of motivational climate. Motivational climate refers to individuals' perceptions of the goal structure and is a function of group goals, underlying reward system, interactions among group members, and individual interpretation of the specific social structure (Ames & Archer, 1988). A *mastery-based climate* reflects an individualistic reward structure and is characterized by effort-based goals. Individuals in mastery climates are rewarded for effort, learning, and improvement. A *performance-based climate* emphasizes social comparison and rewards individuals for outperforming others.

Motivational climate refers to individuals' perceptions of the goal structure. The climate can be mastery-based, which promotes an individualist reward structure, or performance-based, which emphasizes social comparison and outperforming others.

Research in the academic setting has shown that mastery climates are positively related to task orientation and negatively related to ego orientation, whereas performance climates are positively related to ego orientation and negatively related to task orientation. Similar results have been found in the sport setting (Ebbeck & Becker, 1994; Seifriz et al., 1992; Walling, Duda, & Chi, 1993). For example, Seifriz et al. (1992) reported that individuals who perceived their team as more mastery based felt that all players had an important role on the team and that their coaches emphasized improvement and learning, rewarded effort, encouraged players, and allowed most athletes to play in games. In contrast, those who perceived a more performance-based climate felt that outplaying teammates was important, that players were punished for mistakes, and that the coach favored the "star" players.

Walling et al. (1993) obtained similar results, but Ebbeck and Becker (1994) found support only for the relationship between mastery climate and task goal orientation. Williams (1998), examining motivational climate and changes in goal orientations over the course of a competitive softball season, found that athletes' increases in task orientation over the season were related to both performance and mastery climate, while increases in ego orientation were positively related to performance climate only. Collectively, these studies are encouraging, as they suggest that environments emphasizing effort, learning, and improvement foster a task goal perspective, which in turn provides greater opportunity for athletes to feel successful and develop adaptive achievement behaviors and self-perceptions. Unfortunately, such a happy ending does not always occur.

## COMPETITIVE ORIENTATION IN SPORT

The work of Diane Gill and her colleagues (Gill, 1988; Gill & Deeter, 1988; Gill & Dzewaltowski, 1988) examines achievement behavior in competitive sport using the theoretical underpinnings advanced by Spence and Helmreich (1978, 1983). Spence and Helmreich conceptualize achievement motivation as multidimensional, with mastery, work, and competitiveness dimensions, implying that some people approach achievement situations with the desire to strive for excellence, others emphasize hard work, and still others desire to outperform other people.

Gill (1993) suggests that individuals' achievement orientation toward sport may differ from their orientation in other achievement settings. To illustrate, how would you rate yourself on the motive to approach success and the motive to avoid failure in competitive sport and academics? First, do you consider yourself higher or lower than the average student on the motive to approach success in sport? Is success in sport very important to you? Do you seek challenges? Does intense competition bring out your best performance? Next, do you consider yourself high or low on the motive to avoid failure in sport competition? For example, do you become tense and anxious in close competitions? Do you worry about how you will perform? Do you make more errors in highly competitive contests?

Now rate yourself in the same way for academic achievement. Are you higher or lower than the average student on your motive to approach success in academics? For example, is success in school very important to you? Do academic challenges bring out your best? Finally, do you consider yourself high or low in the motive to avoid failure in academics? Do you choke before important tests or presentations? Do you worry about poor grades?

Individuals are motivated to succeed based on their environment. Some people are highly motivated in academic settings but don't feel the same sense of motivation in sport settings, for example.

How do your motives toward sport and academics compare? Usually about half of the students in a typical class find themselves in different classifications for these two areas. Even if you classify yourself the same for both, you may find that your motives and reactions are more intense or differ in some other way from one setting to the other. If we extend the illustration further, perhaps to social achievement or artistic achievement, you might find even greater diversity in your motives.

The point is that most models and measures of achievement motivation were not developed for sport or exercise, and their value in explaining competitive behavior may be quite limited. In her study of competitive orientation in sport, Gill has blended Spence and Helmreich's framework with Martens's work on competitive anxiety (Martens, Vealey, & Burton, 1990). According to Martens (1976b), competition is a social process; he offers the following definition:

> Competition is a process in which the comparison of an individual's performance is made with some standard in the presence of at least one other person who is aware of the criterion for comparison and can evaluate the comparison process. (p. 14)

As we will see in chapter 11, this definition captures most competitive activities in sport. Most sporting events occur in the presence of others, and in most cases others know of and evaluate the attainment of performance goals.

Martens's model of the competitive process starts with the objective competitive situation. The subjective competitive situation involves the interplay between individual differences and the objective competitive situation. Individuals who are highly competitive will interpret the sport situation differently than those who are not very competitive, and their perceptions will influence their behaviors in competitive situations.

To examine the antecedents of competitiveness, Scanlan (1978, 1988) adopted Martens's model of competition and incorporated two other approaches: White's (1959) effectance motivation theory and Veroff's (1969) developmental model of achievement motivation.

As seen by White (1959), the effectance motive is the basic motive to be competent and effective. We are born with competence motivation. Even infants strive to explore, try tasks, cause outcomes, and otherwise accomplish something. Competence motivation develops into achievement motivation when the child begins to set goals and to direct effort toward reaching those goals. As soon as the child is mature enough to set a goal and maintain efforts to reach that goal, achievement motivation may begin to develop.

According to Veroff (1969), achievement motivation develops through three stages: autonomous competence, social comparison, and integrated achievement motivation. The first stage, autonomous competence, involves internal standards. A child might decide to set up a row of blocks and try to knock them over with a ball. The child sets the goal, attempts to reach it, and decides whether the performance was successful. The child's autonomous evaluation of achievement is critical; other people have little to do with setting the goals or evaluating success, and competition is not involved. This stage could be likened to establishing a personal sense of competence.

### Key Point

According to White (1959), the effectance motive is the basic motive to be competent and effective. According to Veroff (1969), achievement motivation develops through three stages: autonomous competence, social comparison, and integrated achievement motivation.

A child who has some success in the autonomous stage may advance into the social comparison stage, usually during the early school years. Social comparison obviously entails social standards, or competition. The individual who succeeds in social comparisons may advance to the final stage of integrated achievement motivation. The integrated stage involves both autonomous competence and social comparison. An individual uses either autonomous internal standards or social standards, depending on which are appropriate for the situation. A golfer, for example, might set personal goals and work toward those goals in practice rounds and informal play but attend to competitive standards in a match play round.

Not everyone progresses through the three stages, and some individuals never master the autonomous stage. Those persons are low achievers who do not attempt any achievement tasks, either competitive or noncompetitive. People who successfully master the autonomous stage but are unsuccessful in social comparison will not be very competitive. They might be high achievers when personal goals are involved, but they probably would avoid competition. Persons who are successful at social comparison and advance to the integrated stage will be comfortable in competitive situations, but they might also work hard toward personal, noncompetitive goals.

According to Veroff, a person must use social comparison for informative purposes to evaluate skills and abilities in order to advance into the integrated stage of achievement motivation. A person who uses social comparison for what Veroff terms normative purposes focuses on winning and uses competition as an ego boost. That

An example of autonomous competence: first a child sets a goal of building a tower of blocks and then knocking them down. Then the child evaluates—internally—whether they've successfully met the goal. The child's standards are the only ones that matter.

person cannot be satisfied with autonomous achievement and will not advance to the integrated stage. Such persons may be supercompetitors who turn every situation into competition.

Scanlan identifies those in the social comparison or integrated stages as competitive. Those in the social comparison stage would strive for success only in competitive settings, and would compete to win. Those in the integrated stage would strive for success in competitive situations, but might also strive for mastery goals. Scanlan's initial work provided a general framework for the study of competitiveness as a sport-specific achievement construct (Gill, 1993).

## A Measure of Competitive Orientations

Diane Gill used Martens's (1976b; 1977) sport-specific framework and the multidimensional achievement perspective of Spence and Helmreich (1978, 1983) to develop the sport-specific construct of competitiveness and a measure of competitive orientation. Gill and colleagues developed a 25-item questionnaire that assesses sport-specific achievement orientation, or more specifically competitiveness, called the Sport Orientation Questionnaire (SOQ; Gill & Deeter, 1988). The SOQ measures three orientations. Competitiveness, the dominant factor, reflects enjoyment of competition and the desire to strive for success in competitive situations. Win orientation reflects an emphasis on interpersonal comparison and winning, whereas goal orientation emphasizes personal performance standards. The validity and reliability of the SOQ have been established through a series of studies (Gill, 1993). Figure 8.3 shows sample questions.

**Figure 8.3**
Sport Orientation Questionnaire (SOQ) sample.

| | Strongly disagree | Disagree more than agree | Disagree | Neither agree nor disagree | Agree more than disagree |
|---|---|---|---|---|---|
| **Examples of SOQ competitive items:** | | | | | |
| I am a competitive person. | 1 | 2 | 3 | 4 | 5 |
| I enjoy competing against others. | 1 | 2 | 3 | 4 | 5 |
| **Examples of SOQ win orientation items:** | | | | | |
| Winning is important. | 1 | 2 | 3 | 4 | 5 |
| I hate to lose. | 1 | 2 | 3 | 4 | 5 |
| **Examples of SOQ goal orientation items:** | | | | | |
| I set goals for myself when I compete. | 1 | 2 | 3 | 4 | 5 |
| Performing to the best of my ability is very important to me. | 1 | 2 | 3 | 4 | 5 |

## Competitive-Orientation Research

In several samples, athletes were more competitive than nonathletes on all SOQ measures, and the competitiveness score was the primary discriminator between athletes and nonathletes. We further explored competitiveness with other measures that force a choice between winning and goals (outcome and performance) and found that athletes were more likely than nonathletes to endorse performance goals and less likely to emphasize winning outcomes. That particular finding—surprising to many—confirms current sport psychology practice, which emphasizes a mastery orientation and focuses on performance goals.

In initial studies by Gill and her associates with university and high school samples, males scored higher on competitiveness and win orientation than females, whereas females scored higher on goal orientation than males (see Gill, 1993). However, closer examination revealed that the gender differences in competitiveness were primarily related to competitive experience rather than to interest in sport or to general achievement motivation.

Research exploring competitive orientations among athletes revealed some interesting findings (Acevedo, Gill, & Dzewaltowski, 1987; Gill & Dzewaltowski, 1988; Kang, Gill, Acevedo, & Deeter, 1990). Gill and Dzewaltowski sampled women and men athletes from a highly competitive intercollegiate program, as well as men and women enrolled in physical activity classes in the same university. Statistical analyses revealed both gender and athletic team differences. Gender differences paralleled those found in previous SOQ research, with males scoring higher than females on competitiveness and win orientation and lower on goal orientation. However, the strongest differences were between athletes and nonathletes, with athletes scoring higher on all three SOQ subscales: competitiveness, win orientation, and goal orientation. It is important to note that competitiveness was the primary factor discriminating athletes and nonathletes. Collecting data at a Taiwanese university, Kang et al. (1990) found that international athletes scored the highest on all three SOQ subscales, followed by university athletes and then nonathletes; there were no significant gender differences.

In another study, Acevedo et al. (1987) used the SOQ to survey Western States 100 ultramarathon race finishers and nonfinishers. Runners encounter rough terrain, extreme temperatures, and altitude changes as they trek across 100 miles in California. No differences were found for gender or finishing status. The most interesting aspects of the results were comparisons to other studies. The competitiveness scores of the ultramarathoners were high and were similar to those of other athletes; and although the ultramarathoners' goal scores were high, their win scores were lower than those of both athlete and nonathlete university samples.

Gill (1993) concluded that although athletes generally score higher on both general and sport-specific achievement motivation, the orientation that best distinguishes between athletes and nonathletes is sport-specific competitiveness. Interestingly, athletes do not uniformly emphasize a win orientation; they put greater emphasis on performance than on outcome. Athletes are competitive, but winning isn't the only thing. Lastly, although athletes generally differ from nonathletes, there also is substantial variation among athletes.

## Summary

To understand achievement behavior we must consider individual differences. Cognitive motivation theorists focus on individuals' perceptions in achievement settings. Many approaches involve individuals' competitive orientations, or their desire to engage in competitive situations (competitiveness), to win (win orientation), and to attain goals (goal orientation). Several approaches incorporate individuals' definitions of success and failure. Some individuals focus on winning and outperforming others (ego orientation), while others focus on task mastery (task orientation).

Over the last decade, sport-specific measures of goal perspectives (TEOSQ and POSQ) and competitiveness (SOQ) have been developed and used to advance our knowledge of individual differences. Recently, sport and exercise psychology researchers have also begun to examine the relationship between these individual characteristics and environmental conditions. In general, this research indicates that a task or goal orientation leads to greater motivation, achievement, and positive self-perceptions than an ego or win orientation. Continued research may provide a greater understanding of the role of individual differences and contextual factors in individuals' motivation in sport and exercise settings.

# Review Questions

1. Explain Atkinson's theory of achievement motivation, and describe the personality and situational factors that interact to determine achievement behavior.

2. Explain one key tenet held by several multidimensional, goal perspective approaches to achievement motivation.

3. Define, compare, and contrast the task goal orientation and the ego goal orientation.

4. Identify two common goal perspective measures.

5. Compare and contrast competitive reward structures and individualistic reward structures.

6. Define motivational climate.

7. Explain Martens's definition of competition.

8. Explain White's (1959) effectance motivation theory and Veroff's (1969) developmental model of achievement motivation.

9. Identify the three orientations measured by Gill and Deeter's (1988) SOQ.

10. Explain the research findings of several SOQ studies.

# Recommended Reading

★ Duda, J.L. (1992). Motivation in sport settings: A goal perspective approach. In G.C. Roberts (Ed.), *Motivation in sport and exercise* (pp. 57-91). Champaign, IL: Human Kinetics.

> Duda began collaborating with Nicholls on his goal orientations work, and she has since led the development of a line of research on goal orientations in sport. This chapter summarizes the goal orientation model and research and presents the popular Task and Ego Orientation in Sport Questionnaire (TEOSQ), which is widely used in research on sport goal orientations.

★ Gill, D.L. (1993). Competitiveness and competitive orientation in sport. In R.A. Singer, M. Murphey, & L.K. Tennant (Eds.), *Handbook of research on sport psychology* (pp. 314-327). New York: Macmillan.

> Gill's work on competitiveness overlaps the goal orientation work in some ways, but she approached sport orientation using a multidimensional achievement model. This chapter presents work on the Sport Orientation Questionnaire, which assesses competitiveness, win and goal orientation, and related research on competitiveness and sport orientation.

★ Ames, C. (1992). Achievement goals, motivational climate, and motivational processes. In G.C. Roberts (Ed.), *Motivation in sport and exercise* (pp. 161-176). Champaign, IL: Human Kinetics.

> Ames presents yet another approach to achievement orientation. Like other theorists, she emphasizes mastery. She specifically emphasizes the role of the educational environment, and advocates moving from competition to individualistic performance-based structures to promote the development of mastery orientation. This chapter summarizes her views and gives you a great target with helpful guidelines for practice.

## chapter 9

# Cognitive Approaches to Motivation

**Lavon Williams, PhD**
*Northern Illinois University*
**Diane L. Gill, PhD**
*University of North Carolina–Greensboro*

## CHAPTER OBJECTIVES

After studying this chapter, you should be able to

- describe the relationship between extrinsic rewards and intrinsic motivation,
- trace the development of theories concerning expectations and self-confidence, and
- understand attribution theory in relation to achievement behavior in sport and exercise.

Behavioral approaches assume that all behavior is determined by past reinforcements and present contingencies. In cognitive approaches, in contrast, the individual is an active perceiver and interpreter of information, and cognitive processes are the key to understanding motivation and behavior.

Cognitive theories hold that the primary source of motivation is not extrinsic reinforcers but intrinsic motivation. According to Deci (1975), "Intrinsically motivated behaviors are behaviors which a person engages in to feel competent and self-determining" (p. 61). Seeking out challenges and striving to meet them are the primary intrinsically motivated behaviors. The absence of extrinsic rewards is often the measure of intrinsic motivation; the more a person engages in an activity that involves no extrinsic rewards, the higher the intrinsic motivation for that activity.

Extrinsic rewards are common in sport and exercise, but if asked why they participate, most people will give intrinsic reasons such as excitement, challenge, or sense of accomplishment. The flow experience, discussed in chapter 10, is sometimes considered the definitive intrinsic reason for participation in an activity. The flow state described by Csikszentmihalyi (1990) and Jackson (1995), with control and competence as key characteristics, is a state of intrinsic motivation as defined by Deci (Deci, 1975; Deci & Ryan, 1985). This focus on feelings of competence and self-determination is central to most cognitive approaches. The cognitive theories and research discussed here cover a wide range, but all emphasize cognitive processes, intrinsic motivation, and a sense of perceived control and competence. In this chapter we will examine extrinsic rewards and intrinsic motivation, theories concerning expectations and self-confidence, and attribution theory in relation to achievement behavior in sport and exercise.

**Key Point**

Considerable research indicates that perceptions and interpretations—cognitive processes—are critical to understanding participation and behavior.

## COMBINING INTRINSIC MOTIVATION AND EXTRINSIC REWARDS

Most people participate in physical activity for intrinsic reasons. They enjoy the competition, they like the action, they feel good when they perform well, and they just have fun. Extrinsic rewards, such as trophies, T-shirts, and scholarships, are also common. The practical question concerns what happens when we combine extrinsic rewards and intrinsic motivation. At first glance, the answer is the more motivation the better. Extrinsic rewards can be powerfully motivating. If we add extrinsic rewards to an activity that is already intrinsically motivating (e.g., giving special awards to all children who compete in an intramural track meet), those rewards should increase the total motivation. We assume that at worst, extrinsic rewards would have no effect and that they certainly could do no harm. Such conventional wisdom held until the mid-1970s, when researchers shocked the psychological community with studies on rewards and intrinsic motivation (Greene & Lepper, 1974; Lepper & Greene, 1975; Lepper, Greene, & Nisbett, 1973). In one study subtitled "Turning Play Into Work," Lepper and Greene (1975) demonstrated that extrinsic rewards can actually undermine intrinsic motivation. To test their ideas, they selected an activity that was intrinsically motivating for nursery school children: drawing with felt pens. They observed the amount of free time the children spent using the pens over a baseline period and then introduced a reward manipulation.

Each child was asked to draw with the felt pens under one of three reward conditions. In the expected-reward condition, an experimenter promised the child a "Good Player" certificate for drawing with the pens and gave the certificate to the child after the session. In the unexpected-reward condition, children did not learn about the certificates before drawing, but later received them. In the no-reward condition, the children were not promised rewards and did not receive certificates. One week later, as predicted, the children who had used the felt pens for the expected rewards showed a drop in intrinsic motivation, whereas the other two groups continued to draw just as much as they had before the experiment.

**Key Point**

Though extrinsic rewards are common, most people participate in physical activities for intrinsic reasons, and intrinsic motivation is a key influence on sport and exercise behavior.

Many other studies confirm that extrinsic rewards can undermine intrinsic motivation. Deci and Ryan's (1985) research has demonstrated that both working for rewards and working under threat of punishment reduce intrinsic motivation. An interesting discussion of extrinsic rewards and intrinsic motivation appears in a meta-analytic study (Cameron & Pierce, 1994), three commentary articles (Kohn, 1996; Lepper, Keavney, & Drake, 1996; Ryan & Deci, 1996), and a response paper (Cameron & Pierce, 1996).

As this commentary indicates, the research of Deci and of Lepper and Greene stirred considerable interest among psychologists and educators. If rewards reduce intrinsic motivation, then we must question many educational practices—and certainly many sport and exercise practices. Should we award certificates when students reach physical fitness test standards? Should we give T-shirts to everyone who finishes the 5K run-walk at the Fitness Fair? Such questions do not have simple

Much research has been done on the effects of extrinsic rewards on young children participating in sports.

yes or no answers. Rewards may undermine intrinsic motivation, but they can also modify behaviors and performance in positive, desirable ways.

## Cognitive Evaluation Theory

Deci and Ryan's (1985) cognitive evaluation theory helps sort out the relationships between extrinsic rewards and intrinsic motivation. The theory holds that the critical factor in motivation is not the reward itself, but the person's interpretation of the reward. Deci and Ryan propose two aspects of rewards that affect intrinsic motivation. The *controlling aspect* undermines self-determination. If the controlling aspect of a reward is high, then the individual perceives the reward as controlling. If you run in a race to get a T-shirt or use certain strategies in a tennis match to win the trophy, those rewards have high controlling aspects. On the other hand, if the controlling aspect of the reward is low, then participants do not see the reward as affecting their behavior, and self-determination is high. In Lepper and Greene's study (1975), the expected rewards caused a shift in the children's sense of control (from personal control to the rewards), and the children in this group had no motive to draw when rewards were no longer present. Because the children did not perceive the unexpected rewards as controlling, the rewards did not undermine intrinsic motivation.

### Key Point

The higher the controlling aspect of a reward, the more intrinsic motivation is undermined. If the controlling aspect of the reward is low, then participants do not see the reward as affecting their behavior, and self-determination is high.

Rewards can also affect intrinsic motivation through their *informational aspect.* Whereas the controlling aspect of rewards affects self-determination, the informational aspect affects feelings of competence. A reward with high informational value can provide either positive information about skills, abilities, and behaviors that enhances the individual's feelings of competence, or negative information that detracts from such feelings. For example, receiving a patch for attaining a certain level on a physical fitness test provides positive information and enhances feelings of competence. In most sport and exercise situations, however, rewards are given to a select few, and those who strive for but do not receive rewards may receive negative information that decreases their feelings of competence.

Most rewards have both controlling and informational aspects, but the two aspects vary in salience. Tangible rewards, such as trophies and money, tend to have a highly salient controlling aspect, whereas verbal feedback seems less controlling. Rewards given for specific performance standards have more informational value than rewards distributed on the basis of ambiguous criteria. When the controlling aspect of a reward is salient, the reward is likely to undermine intrinsic motivation. For example, if a basketball coach continually talks about winning the championship trophy and stresses that single goal, the reward is likely to become very controlling and to undermine the players' intrinsic motivation.

When the informational aspect of a reward is salient, the reward may either enhance or detract from intrinsic motivation. For example, if a basketball coach sets clear, specific goals for each player, provides feedback on progress, and verbally praises players who reach their goals, the players may see the feedback and praise as primarily informational. Players who receive positive information may experience increased feelings of competence and enhanced intrinsic motivation. Similarly, players who receive negative feedback may feel incompetent and less intrinsically motivated.

## Key Point

The informational aspect of rewards affects feelings of competence. When the informational aspect of a reward is salient, the reward may either enhance or detract from intrinsic motivation.

Most rewards in physical activity settings can be either highly controlling or highly informational depending on how they are presented and how they are interpreted. Cognitive evaluation theory implies that coaches and instructors should minimize the controlling aspects of rewards, use rewards for informational purposes, and ensure that all participants have a reasonable chance to earn positive feedback.

## Research on Rewards and Intrinsic Motivation in Sport

Several reviews indicate that the undermining effect of rewards is quite robust (Ryan, Vallerand, & Deci, 1984; Weinberg, 1984; Frederick & Ryan, 1995). Not only have many studies in psychology confirmed Deci's (1975) and Lepper and Greene's (1975) original findings, but several show that extrinsic rewards can undermine intrinsic motivation in sport and motor tasks (e.g., Halliwell, 1978; Orlick & Mosher, 1978; Thomas & Tennant, 1978).

## Scholarship Versus Nonscholarship Athletes

In thought-provoking studies, Ryan (1977, 1980) compared the intrinsic motivation of scholarship and nonscholarship athletes. The first study used a questionnaire to assess intrinsic motivation of male athletes. Scores from one of the questions are reported in table 9.1; responses to other questions assessing enjoyment and liking of the sport followed the same pattern. Scholarship athletes reported less intrinsic motivation than nonscholarship athletes, with the difference between the two groups increasing over the four class years. Wagner, Lounsbury, and Fitzgerald (1989) found similar results, with more scholarship athletes perceiving their sport as work.

Ryan (1980) then conducted a similar, larger survey of both male and female athletes in several sports at several schools. The basic finding of the first study was replicated as scholarship football players reported less intrinsic motivation than nonscholarship football players. However, for male wrestlers and female athletes in

**Table 9.1   Intrinsic Motivation of Scholarship and Nonscholarship Athletes**

| | Are college athletics as "much fun" as you had expected? | | | | |
|---|---|---|---|---|---|
| | Freshman | Sophomore | Junior | Senior | Average |
| Scholarship | 3.6 | 4.8 | 4.6 | 4.8 | 4.45 |
| Nonscholarship | 3.7 | 3.6 | 3.8 | 2.8 | 3.48 |

Responses are on a 1 to 7 scale, with 1 indicating much more and 7 indicating much less.

From "Attribution, intrinsic motivation, and athletics" by E.D. Ryan, 1977, in L. Gedvilas and M.E. Kneer (Eds.), Proceedings of the NAPECW/NCPEAM National Conference, 1977, p. 351.

all sports, scholarship athletes showed greater intrinsic motivation than nonscholarship athletes. Ryan suggested two possible reasons for these results. First, if virtually all good football players received scholarships, then the scholarships provided little competence information. However, if only the top wrestlers and top female athletes received scholarships, then the scholarships provided positive information about competence and were more intrinsically motivating. Second, Ryan suggested that football coaches may use scholarships in a more controlling manner than coaches in other sports.

### Coach Feedback and Intrinsic Motivation

As noted by Frederick and Ryan (1995), several studies have examined the influence of coach feedback on participants' self-perceptions (Anshel & Salles, 1990; Brustad, 1988; Chelladurai, Imamura, Yamaguchi, & Oinuma, 1988; Sinclair & Vealey, 1989), but few have addressed the impact on intrinsic motivation. Courneya and McAuley (1991) examined strategies used to increase children's interest in physical activity. Undergraduates were asked to read scenarios depicting children who exhibited high or low interest in an activity and to choose either a low-controlling or high-controlling strategy to maximize the children's interest. For the highly interested children, undergraduates chose low-controlling rewards, and for the children with low interest in the activity, undergraduates were more apt to choose high-controlling rewards. Although we don't know how such reward choices might affect children's motivation, it seems that the undergraduates selected rewards that would not undermine motivation of intrinsically motivated students and attempted to use external rewards (high controlling) when motivation was lacking.

### Competition and Competitive Success

Another issue particularly relevant to sport and exercise is the relationship of competition to intrinsic motivation. Some suggest that competition, and especially a focus on winning, can act as an extrinsic reward to reduce intrinsic motivation. Deci, Betley, Kahle, Abrams, and Porac (1981) compared individuals competing among themselves to those who competed against a standard of excellence. Those in face-to-face competition later exhibited decreased intrinsic motivation in a noncompetitive free-choice period. This effect was especially strong for females.

Weinberg and Ragan (1979) compared individuals in two competition conditions (win, loss) and a no-competition condition. In contrast to the findings of Deci et al., competition enhanced intrinsic motivation for males and had no effect on females. It should be noted that the free-choice activity in Weinberg and Ragan's study involved competition whereas Deci et al. used a noncompetitive free-choice setting, and the question of how competition affects intrinsic motivation is still unsettled.

The effects of competitive success and failure on intrinsic motivation are much clearer. A series of studies by Weinberg and colleagues (Weinberg, 1979; Weinberg & Jackson, 1979; Weinberg & Ragan, 1979) consistently indicated that individuals have greater intrinsic motivation after a win than after a loss. However, in chapter 8 we saw that perceived success and failure are not always synonymous with winning and losing; and perceived success has a more dramatic effect on intrinsic motivation than objective success (McAuley & Tammen, 1989; McAuley, Wraith, & Duncan, 1991; Tammen & Murphy, 1990). For example, Tammen and Murphy (1990) found that although both objective and subjective success affected intrinsic motivation, perceived success had a greater effect than objective success. This influence of success/failure on motivation is logical because of the high informational value of competitive success/failure.

### Positive Information

Similarly, Vallerand (1983) observed that positive comments about performance enhanced youth hockey players' intrinsic motivation, and in a second study Vallerand and Reid (1984) reported that intrinsic motivation increased with positive and decreased with negative feedback. Further analysis revealed that the feedback affected perceived competence, and that perceived competence in turn affected intrinsic motivation—demonstrating clear informational effects that fit with Deci's cognitive evaluation theory.

> **Key Point**
>
> The question of how competition affects intrinsic motivation is still unsettled, though some studies have shown that individuals have greater intrinsic motivation after a win than after a loss. Other studies have shown that intrinsic motivation increases with positive feedback and decreases with negative feedback.

### Perceived Control

The intrinsic motivation literature on the controlling effects of rewards is less consistent, but considerable psychology research indicates that perceived control is a powerful motivating factor. Numerous studies demonstrate that even minor changes giving a bit more choice and control can have strikingly positive effects on motivation and behavior. Women in a fitness program who believed their choices were used to select exercises had higher attendance and greater intrinsic motivation (Thompson & Wankel, 1980). Thus, strategies that allow personal control seem to enhance self-determination, a key component of intrinsic motivation. Thill and Mouanda (1990) examined an additional component in investigating the effects of choice and feedback on intrinsic motivation over time with African handball players. Those who experienced both positive feedback and task choice showed the greatest increases in intrinsic motivation.

### Goal Orientation and Intrinsic Motivation

Williams and Gill (1995), in a study with physical education students, suggested that task orientation offers a sense of internal control leading to greater intrinsic motivation. In contrast, an emphasis on outperforming others, or ego orientation, functions as an external control factor; the authors expected ego orientation to lead to feelings of incompetence, lower intrinsic enjoyment; and decreased effort. The findings supported their expectations about task orientation, but not ego orientation. This study again indicates the importance of perceived competence, further suggesting that feelings of internal control may enhance intrinsic motivation.

## MOTIVATIONAL DIFFERENCES AMONG SPORT AND EXERCISE PARTICIPANTS

Frederick and Ryan (1993) examined motives of participants in sports, including tennis and sailing, and exercise activities including running, aerobics, and weight lifting. Sport participants' motivation centered more on fun, enjoyment, interest, skill development, and challenge, whereas exercisers showed a more extrinsic motivational focus—specifically, exercisers more often reported weight- and appearance-related reasons.

More than 20 years of research on intrinsic motivation have taken us quite far. Whereas psychologists and educators once emphasized extrinsic rewards as primary motivational tools, we now know that we should be cautious in awarding medals and prizes. On the other hand, rewards do not automatically undermine intrinsic motivation any more than they automatically enhance motivation. The practical question, then, is not whether we use rewards and reinforcers, but how we should use them. The individual's interpretation of the reward is critical.

In practice, we should use small rewards that are not too salient or controlling, and we should phase out rewards as intrinsic motivation develops. Rewards cannot undermine intrinsic motivation if no intrinsic motivation exists. Carefully chosen rewards may encourage people to participate in new activities in which they can develop a sense of competence and intrinsic motivation. Rewards may also provide valuable competence information in ongoing activities, especially if given for attaining clearly specified goals that are perceived as within reach of all participants. Coaches and instructors who rely on encouragement and reinforcement, emphasize the process rather than the outcome, and use rewards as symbols of accomplishments rather than to control behavior may find extrinsic rewards useful.

## MEASURES OF INTRINSIC MOTIVATION IN SPORT AND EXERCISE

Most of the studies either measured intrinsic motivation as the amount of free time spent on the task, or used the self-report Intrinsic Motivation Inventory (IMI; Ryan, 1982), which was adapted for the physical domain by McAuley and his colleagues (for example, McAuley & Duncan, 1989; McAuley & Tammen, 1989)

McAuley and colleagues (McAuley & Duncan, 1989; McAuley & Tammen, 1989) examined the psychometrics of the 27-item IMI, which consists of five subscales including interest-enjoyment, perceived competence, effort-importance, pressure-tension, and choice in the sport and exercise setting (see sample questions in table 9.2). Initial psychometric testing indicated adequate reliability and validity for four of the subscales, which all contribute to intrinsic motivation; but the perceived choice (control) dimension demonstrated poor reliability and was dropped by McAuley & Duncan (1989) and McAuley & Tammen (1989), setting a precedent for other researchers using the IMI.

**Table 9.2 IMI Sample Questions**

| | |
|---|---|
| *Interest-enjoyment* | "I enjoy participating in this aerobics class very much." |
| *Pressure-tension* | "I feel very tense while participating in this aerobics class." |
| *Perceived competence* | "I think I am pretty good at aerobics." |
| *Effort-importance* | "I put a lot of effort into this aerobics class." |
| *Choice* | "I participate in this aerobics class because I have no other choice." |

Markland and Hardy (1997) have argued that without a measure of control, the IMI does not accurately reflect the tenets of the cognitive evaluation theory. Additionally, they contend that intrinsic motivation is more complex than conceptualized by McAuley and colleagues (1989, 1991). Markland and Hardy suggest that perceived competence affects intrinsic motivation only when one also has free choice (self-determination), and that interest-enjoyment, effort-importance, and pressure-tension are influenced via perceptions of competence and control.

The IMI and free-choice measures focus solely on intrinsic motivation, ignoring extrinsic motivation. Two new measures of intrinsic motivation, the Sport Motivation Scales (SMS; Pelletier et al., 1995) and the Exercise Motivation Scale (Li, 1997), evolved from the work of Deci and Ryan (1991) and Vallerand and colleagues (1992), suggesting a continuum including amotivation, extrinsic motivation, and intrinsic motivation. *Amotivation* refers to a lack of motivation: an amotivated person sees no link between actions and outcomes, is neither intrinsically nor extrinsically motivated, and has no reason to engage in the given task.

### Key Point

The IMI, SMS, and EMS are measures of intrinsic motivation in sport and exercise.

*Extrinsic motivation,* which refers to behaviors displayed for the purpose of achieving some end, is divided into external regulation, introjection, and identification. *External regulation* refers to behavior controlled by constraints that others impose. Individuals who participate in sport for the school letter, or who run 10Ks for the T-shirt, are motivated by external regulation. When these external sources of motivation (trophies, a T-shirt) have been internalized, we move into *introjection.* At this stage behaviors are reinforced via internal pressures: for example, we might participate in physical activity because we should stay in shape. From introjection we move to *identification,* in which we value the behavior, deem it important, and act out of choice. The behavior, however, is still done for extrinsic reasons. Individuals who work hard to better their personal best are in the identification stage. From this stage we move from extrinsic motivation to intrinsic motivation.

*Intrinsic motivation* refers to behaviors demonstrated voluntarily, in the absence of constraints imposed by others. Three types of intrinsic motivation (IM) have been identified: IM to know, IM toward accomplishments, and IM to experience stimulation. *IM to know* relates to exploration, curiosity, and learning. People who strive to learn training techniques because they like the experience of learning are intrinsically motivated to learn. *IM toward accomplishment* is similar to mastery, efficacy motivation, and task orientation; individuals want to feel competent. Thus, people who strive to learn training techniques to experience personal satisfaction are intrinsically motivated. Lastly, *IM to experience stimulation* refers to the desire to have sensory pleasure, fun, excitement, and aesthetic experiences. The concepts of flow and peak experiences reflect this IM to experience stimulation.

The SMS has four questions for each of the seven subscales of motivation. Individuals indicate the extent to which items correspond to their reasons for participation by responding on a seven-point scale ("Does not correspond at all" = 1; "Corresponds exactly" = 7). Initial psychometric testing has indicated adequate reliability and validity, but further testing is needed. Sample questions for each subscale are given in table 9.3.

## ATTRIBUTIONS AND SPORT

The study of attributions—the perceived causes of events and behaviors—is an active research area in our discipline. Attribution theories focus on people's perceptions and

**Table 9.3    SMS Sample Questions**

| | |
|---|---|
| *Amotivation* | "I used to have good reasons for doing sports, but now I am asking myself if I should continue." |
| *External regulation* | "I engage in sport for the prestige of being an athlete." |
| *Introjection* | "I engage in sport because I should stay in shape." |
| *Identification* | "I engage in sport because I must do sports to feel good about myself." |
| *IM to know* | "I engage in sport for the pleasure it gives me to know more about the sport that I practice." |
| *IM toward accomplishment* | "I engage in sport for the satisfaction I experience while I am perfecting my abilities." |
| *IM to experience stimulation* | "I engage in sport for the excitement I feel while I am really involved in the activity." |

interpretations of the reasons for behaviors. The attributions we make about our successes and failures affect our effort and persistence, as well as our thoughts and feelings about our performance. If you are unable to do the shot put in physical education class, you behave differently depending on why you think you cannot do it. If you think you need practice, you might keep trying. If you think you need instruction, you might ask the teacher for guidance. If you think you are just too weak and uncoordinated, you might give up and try the long jump.

The attributions we make about others also affect our behaviors and interactions. If you go up for a rebound and get elbowed by an opponent, you react differently depending on whether you think the elbowing was intentional or accidental. A teacher who thinks you cannot make the shot because you are not strong enough responds differently than a teacher who thinks you are lazy and not paying attention. Coaches think about the reasons their teams win and lose, and they act on the basis of those attributions in preparing for future contests.

> **Key Point**
>
> Attributions are the perceived causes of events and behaviors. Attribution theories focus on people's perceptions and interpretations of the reasons for behaviors. The attributions we make about ourselves and about others affect our behavior and interactions with others.

## Weiner's Model of Achievement Attributions

Although he was not the first or only person to propose a theoretical model of attributions, Weiner (1974, 1979, 1986; Weiner et al., 1972) has done the most to bring attribution theory to prominence. Using Heider's (1958) original attribution work on the "naive" analysis of behavior and other early cognitive-motivational approaches as a base, Weiner developed an attributional theory of achievement behavior. He suggested that individuals make attributions about their successes and failures and that those attributions affect achievement motivation and behavior—specifically, that the essential difference between high and low achievers is a difference in attributional patterns.

In studying attributional patterns, first we determine the attributions that people actually make. What reasons do people give for success and failure in sport? For example, try the following exercise. Think about the last time you won or performed very successfully in your favorite sport or exercise activity. What was the main reason for your success? Now think about the last time you lost or had a very unsuccessful performance. What was the main reason for your lack of success?

If an individual attributes her lack of success to her unfamiliarity with equipment, she's likely to seek help from an instructor.

According to Weiner, your responses will probably fall into one of four categories:

- Ability
- Effort
- Luck
- Task difficulty

Although other attributions exist, particularly in sport (Roberts & Pascuzzi, 1979), these four categories cover most reasons. *Ability* includes attributions such as "I'm not very good at tennis" or "Our team has the best athletes." *Effort* might include statements such as "We were really up for the game" or "I never gave up when it got tough." *Luck* attributions include random events and also environmental factors (e.g., "We got the breaks" or "They had the ref on their side"). *Task difficulty* includes attributions to the opponent (e.g., "They were a ranked team") and to the task itself (e.g., "The moves were just too complicated").

The four attributions themselves are not the critical consideration. Weiner's original model classified attributions along two dimensions—locus of causality and stability (table 9.4). The locus of causality dimension refers to whether the attribution is to something internal or external to the performer. Ability and effort are internal attributions, whereas luck and task difficulty are external. The stability dimension refers to whether or not the attribution is relatively stable and unlikely to change over time. Ability and task difficulty are stable; your tennis ability does not change much from one match to the next, and the height of the net will not change. On the other hand, effort and luck may change; you might be more up for the next match and try harder, or you might get the breaks on line calls. Natural ability is an internal, stable factor; effort is internal and unstable; task difficulty is external and stable; and luck is external and unstable.

Later, Weiner added a third dimension—controllability—to distinguish between factors that are internal but not very controllable, such as aptitude or natural ability, and those that are internal and controllable such as personal effort. Table 9.5 illustrates this three-way classification. We have all known people who had a natural ability for a particular activity: someone picks up a golf club for the first time and

**Table 9.4    Weiner's 2 × 2 Classification Scheme for Causal Attributions**

|          | Internal | External        |
|----------|----------|-----------------|
| *Stable*   | Ability  | Task difficulty |
| *Unstable* | Effort   | Luck            |

**Table 9.5    Weiner's 2 × 2 × 2 Classification Scheme for Causal Attributions**

|                 | Locus of Causality | | | |
|-----------------|----------|----------|----------|----------|
|                 | Internal | | External | |
| Controllability | Stable | Unstable | Stable | Unstable |
| *Controllable*   | Stable effort | Unstable effort | Other's stable effort | Other's unstable effort |
| *Uncontrollable* | Ability | Mood | Task difficulty | Luck |

swings it as though she has done it all her life. This natural ability is internal, but not something we can control. Personal effort, on the other hand, is an internal quality we can control. Effort is the only controllable attribution; but since we cannot control another's effort, effort can be either an internal or an external attribution.

Now go back to the reasons you gave for your last win and loss and see where your attributions fit in Weiner's classification. Often people make internal attributions for success and external attributions for failure. If you monitor the comments of winning and losing players and coaches for a while, you will notice that external attributions (lucky breaks, officials' calls, weather) almost always come from the losing side. I cannot recall ever hearing a winning coach state that a team won because of a referee's decision. This tendency to attribute success internally and failure externally is usually interpreted as a self-serving bias, meaning that those attributions help us. For example, you probably will feel better about winning the 800-meter run if you think you won because of your own effort than if you think you won because your chief rival had the flu.

According to Weiner, the internal/external dimension relates to feelings of pride and shame. Internal attributions elicit stronger feelings. You take more pride in successes that you earn than in those due to external factors, and feel greater shame when failure is your fault. It does not feel as bad to lose because of poor officiating as it does to lose because you gave up at the end. Thus, attributing success internally and failure externally is self-serving because it maximizes feelings of pride and minimizes feelings of shame. The self-serving bias is one of the most consistent findings in the attribution literature and in sport and exercise psychology research (Bird & Brame, 1978; Gill & Gross, 1979; Iso-Ahola, 1977; Lau & Russell, 1980; McAuley & Duncan, 1989; Roberts, 1978; Scanlan & Passer, 1980; Whitley & Frieze, 1985).

### Key Point

Individuals tend to attribute success internally and failure externally. This tendency is called the self-serving bias because it maximizes feelings of pride and minimizes feelings of shame.

The stability dimension also has implications for achievement behavior. Specifically, stability relates to our expectations. Stable attributions lead us to expect the same outcomes again, whereas unstable attributions allow us to expect different outcomes. If you think your team won the volleyball match because it is the best team in the league, you will expect to keep on winning. If you think you failed to do the high jump because the skill is too complicated for you, you will expect to continue failing. Conversely, if you had to play over your head to win the match, you cannot be confident of future victories; and if you think you were unable to do the high jump because you did not concentrate well, you can change your behavior and maintain hope for future success.

Just as the locus and stability dimensions affect feelings and expectations, the controllability dimension affects behavior. Weiner suggests that controllability affects our moral judgments and reactions to others. We tend to reward and punish people on the basis of controllable attributions. We praise those who give extra effort and criticize those who do not try. We are more apt to criticize a student who slacks off than one who performs poorly because of physical disability.

In general, then, the attributional dimensions affect behavior as follows:

- Locus of causality (internal/external) relates to feelings of pride and shame. We experience stronger feelings with internal attributions than with external attributions.

- Stability relates to future expectations. We expect similar outcomes with stable attributions and changeable outcomes with unstable attributions.

Attributing failure externally—such as blaming an official for making a bad call rather than taking responsibility for a mistake—minimizes feelings of shame or incompetence.

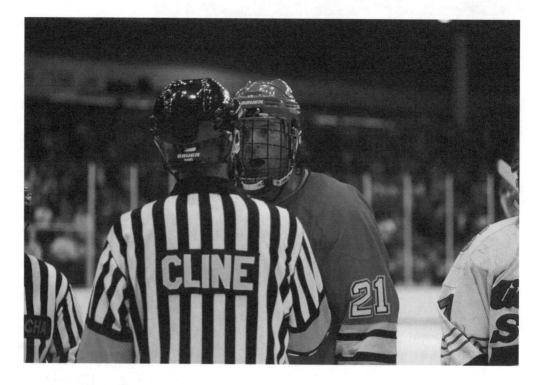

- Controllability relates to our moral judgments and responses to others. We praise people for effort and controllable successes, and we criticize lack of effort and controllable failures.

Weiner's model has been refined and expanded; Weiner himself has made several modifications. Researchers often interpreted the four basic attributions of ability, effort, luck, and task difficulty as the only attributions. But Weiner (1979) pointed out that those were never intended to be the only attributions, and others have found that sport participants gave many attributions that did not fall into the four categories (Bukowski & Moore, 1980; Gill, Ruder, & Gross, 1982; Roberts & Pascuzzi, 1979). Luck and task attributions are rare, and attributions to the team (e.g., teamwork), which are not easily classified, are quite common. In any case, the specific attributions themselves are not of primary importance. As Weiner and several reviewers of the sport and exercise attribution literature have noted (Brawley, 1984; Brawley & Roberts, 1984; Rejeski & Brawley, 1983), the dimensions of attributions are the critical considerations.

## Attribution Research in Sport and Exercise

Results on attributions of winners and losers in sport are equivocal. Some studies have shown that winners make more internal, stable, and controllable attributions than losers (McAuley & Gross, 1983; Watkins, 1986). However, others have shown that winners make more stable and controllable but not more internal attributions (Grove, Hanrahan, & McInman, 1991; Mark, Mutrie, Brooks, & Harris, 1984). As already discussed, it may be that objective success (i.e., win/loss) misrepresents individuals' perceived success and failure.

Spink and Roberts (1980) showed that winners made more internal attributions than losers. However, they found two types of winners: satisfied winners who felt they had earned the win through ability and effort (internal attributions) and dissatisfied winners who felt that the win came easy—that the task was not difficult (external attribution). Likewise, satisfied losers attributed their loss to task difficulty, while dissatisfied losers attributed loss to their low ability. Additionally, McAuley (1985) found perceived success to be a better predictor of internal, stable, controllable attribution than objective success.

## Attributions and Emotions

In addition to the relationship between attributions and achievement behavior, a popular area in both psychology and sport is attributions and emotions. Originally, Weiner et al's (1972) model focused on pride and shame. Later, Weiner (1986) expanded the dimensions to include a greater variety of emotions. In his review, Biddle (1993) notes that emotion consists of physiological, behavioral, and subjective experience components, but most of the research in sport focuses on the subjective experience.

In the early study of attributions and emotional reactions to academic success and failure, Weiner and his colleagues (1972) found outcome-dependent and attribution-dependent emotions. Outcome-dependent emotions are associated with the actual outcome, whereas attribution-dependent emotions are related to the reason for the outcome. It appears that different emotions relate to different attributional dimensions (Biddle & Hill, 1988, 1992; McAuley & Duncan, 1989; Robinson & Howe, 1989).

### Key Point

Outcome-dependent emotions are associated with the actual outcome, while attribution-dependent emotions are related to the reason for the outcome.

As summarized by Biddle (1993), research in sport shows that performance satisfaction, or subjective appraisal, is one of the best predictors of emotion and that attributions play a role. For example, Robinson and Howe (1989), surveying 756 male and female high school students, found that perceived performance consistently predicted emotions, and attributions added to the prediction. Specifically, individuals who perceived themselves as successful made more internal (e.g., ability), stable (e.g., likely to happen again), and controllable (e.g., I can make it happen again) attributions, and experienced emotions that were more positive, than those who perceived themselves as failing. Vlachopoulus, Biddle, and Fox (1996) also found that internal attributions for success emerged as a significant, albeit weak, predictor of positive emotion.

McAuley and Duncan (1989) put an interesting twist on the study of attribution and emotions. Instead of assessing perceptions of success, they manipulated outcomes so that individuals who expected to win lost and those who expected to lose won. Among those who succeeded, feelings of confidence were the strongest for those who made internal attributions. Among those who failed, depression was the greatest for those who attributed the loss to stable and external factors. These results support the concept of self-serving bias. Attributing losses to stable factors also related to more intense feelings of guilt and shame, and attributing losses to external factors also increased feelings of surprise and incompetence. Despite supporting the self-serving bias, this research also suggests that unexpected outcomes result in intense emotions—whether positive or negative.

## Attributions and Health-Related Activities

Most attributional research has been done in sport and physical education, and at this point we can only assume that the findings transfer to exercise and health. Stuart Biddle (1993), reviewing this research, acknowledges efforts of McAuley and his colleagues (McAuley, 1991; McAuley, Poag, Gleason, & Wraith, 1990) that provide evidence on attributional thought processes of participants in health-related activities.

Researchers continue to investigate attributions and to advance beyond Weiner's original model. Other scholars have taken other attributional approaches to the study of motivation. Abramson, Seligman, and Teasdale (1978) discuss learned helplessness in terms of uncontrollable attributions. Specifically, they propose that individuals who perceive outcomes as uncontrollable have motivational, cognitive, and emotional deficits. These individuals are unlikely to initiate responses, are likely to have later difficulty learning that responses do make a difference, and are likely to feel depressed.

## Other Attributional Approaches to Achievement Behavior

As noted earlier, Weiner's attributional theory of achievement behavior, like Atkinson's (1974) theory (chapter 8), considers differences between high and low achievers in choice, effort, and persistence on achievement tasks. Atkinson's theory uses a personality characteristic, the need to achieve, to account for individual differences within a drive framework; in contrast, Weiner adopts a cognitive approach, asserting that high and low achievers differ in their attribution patterns and that those attribution differences account for behavior differences.

Carol Dweck and her colleagues (Burhans & Dweck, 1995; Diener & Dweck, 1978, 1980; Dweck, 1975; Dweck & Leggett, 1988) describe a cognitive model of achievement behavior that combines many ideas we have already discussed about expectations, attributions, and behavior. According to Dweck, initial expectancies (expectations) affect behavior. Higher expectations lead to superior performance and greater persistence on achievement tasks. The performance is evaluated with a score, as a win or loss, or perhaps with verbal feedback from a teacher or coach. The performer then makes an attribution, and that attribution leads to revised expectancies for future performances.

### Learned Helplessness

Dweck is best known for her work on learned helplessness (Burhans & Dweck, 1995; Diener & Dweck, 1978, 1980; Dweck & Leggett, 1988). Learned helplessness is the acquired belief that one has no control over negative events or that failure is inevitable. Learned helplessness is an attributional interpretation of extreme low achievement. According to Dweck, learned-helpless individuals differ from mastery-oriented individuals (high achievers) in their expectancies and attributions in achievement situations, and especially in their failure attributions. Learned-helpless individuals attribute failure to stable, uncontrollable factors—especially lack of ability—and give up after initial failure because they see no hope of future success. In contrast, mastery-oriented individuals tend to see failure as a temporary setback due to unstable, controllable factors. Thus mastery-oriented individuals persist in the wake of failure, often with extra effort; they try and try again.

Earlier in her career, Dweck worked with extremely helpless children in two treatment conditions. Half of the children experienced only successes—a treatment often used with low achievers in which they are given easier tasks that guarantee success. The other half received attribution retraining in which they were successful most of the time but failed on several trials. On the failure trials, the experimenter explicitly attributed the failure to the child's lack of effort. Overall, the attribution retraining was much more effective in changing children's responses to failure and improving performance. Children in the success-only group did not improve performance and did not learn to cope effectively with failure. In general, attributional retraining programs attempt to get people to attribute their successes to their ability (internal, stable, controllable attribution) and their failure to lack of sufficient effort or poor strategy (internal, unstable, controllable attribution) (Dweck, 1975; Foster-ling, 1988).

### Key Point

Attributional training programs attempt to get people to attribute their successes to their ability and their failure to lack of sufficient effort or poor strategy.

### Learned Helplessness in the Physical Domain

Despite an excellent paper on learned helplessness in the physical domain by Robinson in 1990, research in the area is limited. Nonetheless, a few researchers have studied learned-helpless children in physical education and sport settings. Johnson and Biddle (1988) first investigated learned helplessness in the physical domain by examining attributions for success and failure on a balancing task. Individuals who gave up easily were more likely to make negative self-statements, as well as to attribute their failure to the lack of ability and task difficulty, than those who persisted longer. Those who persisted longer made more strategy-related statements. Similar results have been found with middle school physical education students (Martinek & Griffith, 1994; Martinek & Williams, 1997; Walling & Martinek, 1995) and sport participants (Prapavessis & Carron, 1988). Moreover, this recent research has demonstrated a link between individuals' perceptions of success and failure (i.e., goal orientations) and attributions.

Certainly we encounter learned-helpless individuals in sport. The most obvious cases are the children in physical education classes and youth sport programs who "know" they are too slow, uncoordinated, and unathletic to ever do well at sports. Occasionally even highly skilled athletes can become helpless when they suddenly encounter failure after continual success. Dweck's work suggests that we can best help those individuals by encouraging them to attribute their failures to unstable, controllable factors, including not only effort but strategies, practice, techniques, or anything else that could be changed. Of course, we should not tell a 10-year-old girl who has poor balance, flexibility, and strength that she can do a back flip on the balance beam if she only tries harder. But we should encourage her to persist in achieving attainable goals.

### Teacher Feedback and Achievement Behavior

Teachers and coaches can help people develop mastery-oriented achievement cognitions and behaviors. As noted earlier, others' expectations can affect interactions and performance. Within her model, Dweck emphasizes the effect of others on students' achievement cognitions and behaviors. In a provocative study, Dweck (1978) monitored teacher feedback to elementary children, noting differences between feedback to girls and to boys. Considerable research demonstrates gender differences in achievement cognitions. Females report lower expectations of success than males do in most achievement situations (Crandall, 1969; Lenney, 1977). Similarly, females take less responsibility for success and more often attribute failure to lack of ability, whereas males more often make achievement-oriented attributions (Dweck, 1978; Frieze, Parsons, Johnson, Ruble, & Zellman, 1978). Dweck's observations of teacher feedback provide some insight into gender differences in achievement cognitions.

In Dweck's study, teacher feedback was coded as positive or negative and also in terms of whether it was for intellectual or nonintellectual aspects of work (e.g., neatness, conduct). Overall, boys received more negative feedback, but not for their intellectual work. Most negative feedback to boys was for conduct and other nonintellectual aspects of behavior. Almost all negative feedback to girls related directly to their intellectual work. Dweck also recorded the specific attributions made by teachers and observed that failures were attributed to lack of effort eight times more frequently for boys than for girls.

These differences in teacher feedback parallel gender differences in achievement cognitions. Because girls receive negative feedback from teachers for their intellectual work, they interpret such failure feedback to indicate lack of ability. Boys, on the other hand, could easily attribute negative feedback to lack of effort or a generally negative attitude of the teacher. Perhaps the most promising aspect of Dweck's work is a follow-up study in which either the typical "girl" feedback pattern or the typical "boy" feedback pattern was given to both boys and girls. The "girl" pattern elicited more typically female achievement responses from both girls and boys, and the "boy" pattern likewise elicited more achievement-oriented cognitions and behaviors from both girls and boys.

## Summary

Cognitive motivation is one of the most active and prominent areas in sport and exercise psychology. Considerable research indicates that perceptions and interpretations are critical to understanding participation and behavior. Individuals participate in physical activities for intrinsic reasons, and intrinsic motivation is a key influence on sport and exercise behavior. Cognitive constructs, such as attributions, appear to be critical mediators between our teaching and coaching strategies and the participants' behaviors. In general, the collective work on intrinsic motivation and attributions suggests that we should help participants to set challenging, realistic goals and should encourage performers to stress effort and personal control. With the use of these approaches, participants' accomplishments will elicit feelings of competence, personal control, and the desire to continue pursuing sport and exercise activities.

## Review Questions

1.  State the key to explaining motivation and behavior.
2.  Explain the role of extrinsic and intrinsic rewards in terms of the reasons that individuals participate in physical activities.
3.  Explain the controlling aspect and the informational aspect of rewards, and how they each affect intrinsic motivation.
4.  Trace the research findings relating intrinsic motivation to competition, winning or losing, positive feedback, and perceived control.
5.  Contrast sport participants' motivation with exercise participants' motivation.
6.  Explain and summarize the research regarding the appropriate use of rewards.
7.  Identify measures of intrinsic motivation in sport and exercise.
8.  Discuss attributions and attribution theories.
9.  Explain the relationships among internal attributions, external attributions, success, and failure.
10. Contrast outcome-dependent emotions and attribution-dependent emotions.
11. Explain the purpose of attributional retraining programs.

## Recommended Reading

★ Deci, E.L., & Ryan, R.M. (1985). *Intrinsic motivation and self-determination in human behavior.* New York: Plenum Press.

> Deci and Ryan have been leading scholars on intrinsic motivation and cognitive evaluation theory for some time. This source is one of the best overviews of their model and related research. You may also want to read the Pelletier et al. (1995) article on the Sport Motivation Scale, which assesses Deci and Ryan's motivational categories with a sport-specific measure.

★ Biddle, S. (1993). Attribution research and sport psychology. In R.N. Singer, M. Murphey, & L.K. Tennant (Eds.), *Handbook on research on sport psychology* (pp. 437-464). New York: Macmillan.

> Biddle has done considerable work on social cognitive approaches, and in this chapter he provides an excellent overview of attribution theory and research. Biddle is one of several Europeans who have been active sport and exercise psychology scholars for some time, and this chapter may help you begin to recognize some of the extensive work outside of North America.

★ Burhans, K.K., & Dweck, C.S. (1995). Helplessness in early childhood: The role of contingent worth. *Childhood Development, 66,* 1719-1738.

> Dweck is a leading scholar on the development of mastery and helpless orientations. This article presents some of her more recent work, which investigates the influence of an emphasis on competence and effort in the development of children's motivation, persistence, and enjoyment.

## chapter 10

# Emotions and Stress

## CHAPTER OBJECTIVES

After studying this chapter, you should be able to

- explain the major theoretical perspectives and research on emotion that come from psychology,
- understand the sport and exercise psychology work on exercise and emotions, including the application of emotion and stress models to issues such as burnout and injuries, and
- discuss the research on positive emotions in sport and exercise settings.

In the ABC's of psychology, emotion is the "A," or affect component, encompassing all the feelings, emotions, or moods that are part of human behavior. In recent times, psychology has devoted much attention to the "B" and "C" components—behavior and cognition—and left the messier emotions for the poets and philosophers. Of course, emotion is prominent in the real world of sport and exercise. We recognize the thrill of victory and the agony of defeat in Olympic competitors and in 10-year-olds. We might feel exhilarated after a daily run, or embarrassed when we look in the mirror at the fitness center. Emotions abounding in sport and exercise reflect all the complexities of psychology and behavior. That is, emotions truly combine the biological, psychological, and social in a complex, dynamic mix that adds to life, but frustrates traditional scientists and scholars.

Scholars cannot ignore such a pervasive and powerful aspect of behavior as emotion, and we find theories and research on the subject throughout the psychology literature. William James, who provided early insights on most psychology topics, discussed emotion; and 20th century psychologists have offered theories and empirical observations from varied perspectives. Specific issues within the general category of emotion, and particularly anxiety, have been prominent in sport and exercise psychology, but few have tackled the larger issues related to emotion. Behaviorism and social-cognitive movements relegated emotion to the back burners for some time, but recently interest has revived, and exciting new findings and insights appear throughout psychology. Sport and exercise psychologists are just beginning to notice these trends, and likely will expand beyond competitive anxiety to make emotion a major topic in our literature.

Competitive anxiety is such a prominent topic that we will consider the related research separately in the next chapter. Here we will look at the broader area of emotions and stress (including anxiety within that broader framework) and review the major theoretical perspectives and research on emotion that come from psychology. Then we will focus on the sport and exercise work on exercise and emotions, application of emotion and stress models to such issues as burnout and injuries, and some exciting and joyful work on positive emotions in sport and exercise settings.

# EMOTION CONCEPTS AND DEFINITIONS

*Emotion* is a messy research topic, and the related terminology matches. Different scholars define and measure emotion in different ways; moreover, we use several related terms to refer to emotions or aspects of emotions. Here we will use Kleinginna and Kleinginna's (1981) all-embracing definition:

> *Emotion is a complex set of interactions among subjective and objective factors, mediated by neural/hormonal systems, which can (a) give rise to affective experiences such as feelings of arousal, pleasure/displeasure; (b) generate cognitive processes; (c) activate widespread physiological adjustments to the arousing conditions; and (d) lead to behavior that is often, but not always, expressive, goal-directed, and adaptive. (p. 58)*

This definition fits the views of most psychologists who consider emotion a general term. Most psychologists also recognize both physiological and psychological components of emotion and consider emotion a process rather than a static state. Of course, psychologists differ greatly in the details of the process and the relative roles of physiological and social-cognitive processes.

*Arousal,* another term associated with emotion, is prominent in sport psychology work on competitive anxiety. As we noted in part II, motivation includes both intensity and direction of behavior. Other chapters concentrated on the direction component. Here, as we turn to emotion, we incorporate intensity. Arousal is associated with the intensity dimension of behavior, defined as a general state of activation ranging on a continuum from deep sleep to extreme excitement. Arousal per se is neither positive or negative; it increases as we look forward to exciting events as well as when we worry about threats. Arousal and the associated physiological activation are critical for emotion; but without direction and related cognition, arousal is not emotion. Only when thinking of the physiological arousal in combination with direction do we speak of emotion, or more correctly emotions. For example, anxiety, one of the most studied emotions, is typically defined as arousal with a negative (avoidance) direction—we might worry about making an error (and want to avoid it) as our heart races, our hands sweat, and we breathe heavily.

## Key Point

*Arousal* is defined as a general state of activation ranging on a continuum from deep sleep to extreme excitement. *Anxiety* is defined as arousal with a negative (avoidance) direction.

# EMOTION AND STRESS MODELS IN SPORT

With all the physiological and cognitive aspects of emotion, we have a complex phenomenon. Accordingly, the explanations of emotion are multidimensional and complex. In the next section we will review the major historical perspectives on emotion in psychology and then focus on Lazarus's model, which seems especially applicable to sport and exercise psychology.

## Early Models of Emotion and Stress

William James proposed his influential theory in his 1884 essay, "What is an Emotion?" James received training in medicine and taught anatomy and physiology before becoming a philosophy professor, and that background (which now seems impossibly interdisciplinary) certainly gave him a multidimensional perspective on emotion. Danish scientist Lange (1885) presented similar views, and the theory is known as the James-Lange theory. For James, emotion begins with the perception of physiological disturbance (arousal). The physical reactions are the key; "feelings" do not cause emotions. Rather, bodily sensations stem directly from perceptions, and our awareness of the physiological changes is emotion. Walter Cannon (1929) challenged this focus on physiology, and researchers began to look at other systems and central processes.

The most notable counter to the physiologically oriented James-Lange theory is the cognitive approach of Schachter and Singer (1962), who incorporated physiological arousal but emphasized the cognitive component and labeling of emotion. In their classic experiments, subjects received injections of epinephrine, creating physiological arousal, or a placebo. Then, through manipulation of circumstances, some subjects found the emotions appropriate but others had no obvious label. Without a ready explanation, subjects used situational cues to label their emotion. Thus, Schachter and Singer proposed an interaction of cognitive factors with physiological state.

### Key Point

According to the James-Lange theory, bodily sensations stem directly from perceptions, and our awareness of the physiological changes is emotion. Schachter and Singer, on the other hand, proposed an interaction of cognitive factors with physiological state.

Psychologists continue to debate the relative roles of physiology and cognition; and given the complexity of emotion, the lack of agreement on a simple model is not surprising. Moreover, the debates are not limited to simple physiological mechanisms, simple cognitions, and linear models. Models and explanations have become increasingly complex and dynamic. Discussions of complex interactions and multidimensional processes are common, and current work typically incorporates a social or cultural dimension. For example, a book on emotion and culture (Kitayama & Markus, 1994) not only incorporates a social dimension, but presents the argument that emotion is fully social. Lazarus's model, which stems from many years of research, provides an encompassing model that approaches emotion as far-reaching and multidimensional, and moreover as a dynamic process rather than an easily identified state. Lazarus's model reflects current scholarship on emotion and provides a guiding framework for related sport and exercise psychology work.

## Lazarus's Model of Emotion

Richard Lazarus's model has not guided the existing sport and exercise psychology work on stress and emotion, but his framework ties that work together and can serve as a basis for further research and practical applications from a more social dynamics perspective. In his early writing on stress (the precursor to his current emotion model) Lazarus (1966), like Spielberger and others, emphasized cognitive appraisal. That is, actual events, such as waiting for the serve in a close tennis match, pose a potential threat. But only when we think about it, during cognitive appraisal, do we actually perceive a threat. That cognitive appraisal then leads to an emotional response, such as anxiety. Lazarus has maintained this cognitive emphasis but in his more recent work has also expanded the model greatly. It is not easy to illustrate the complex dynamics of the model, but the following list from one review summarizes the major themes (Lazarus, 1986).

- *Stress is best regarded as a rubric or system of interdependent variables.* Stress is a complex system or process rather than a unidimensional variable. You cannot define stress as any one part of that system.

- *The stress process refers to a relationship between a person with certain characteristics and an environment with certain characteristics.* Appraisal is the key; the person's appraisal defines the relationship; the person and environment affect each other; the relationship is more than the sum of its parts. The level of analysis should be the relationship: stress is not in the person or in the environment, but in the relationship. Lazarus's model is sometimes called *transactional*, reflecting this emphasis.

- *The system is recursive in that each variable and process can affect the others, dependent on where in the flow of behavior we look.* We do not have one independent variable and one dependent variable: all variables can be both.

- *Emotion and stress are overlapping constructs.* And emotion is more encompassing and informative. From his early work (e.g., Lazarus, 1966) to the present (e.g., Lazarus, 1993; Smith & Lazarus, 1990), Lazarus has been moving toward an emphasis on emotion, but sport and exercise psychologists have not adopted this aspect of his work. According to Lazarus, studying the intensities, qualities, antecedents, and processes of emotions will give more information on what is important to people and how they think than will continuing to focus on unidimensional stressors.

- *Stress and emotion are best understood as processes rather than static events.* The stress process changes over time. Multiple variables do not a system make! The space between antecedents and consequences is the heart of the process, and we must look at how variables change. Complex analyses will not tell us about process until we actually assess process and change.

- *Not all stressful encounters, severity notwithstanding, have the same significance for mental and physical health.* Some events or hassles are more equal than others. Lazarus made this point in reference to life stressors and health, but it also seems relevant to other sport and exercise concerns (e.g., performance, enjoyment). Some events are more central to the person than others; just summing events misses the process, and individual diagnosis is important.

## Key Point

Lazarus's model provides an encompassing model that approaches emotion as far-reaching and multidimensional, and moreover as a dynamic process rather than an easily identified state.

During 30 years of stress research, Lazarus has moved to a more social dynamic model with emphasis on recursive relationships, dynamic process, and social context. Although Lazarus became more social and dynamic, sport and exercise psychology lags behind. The story of stress in sport and exercise psychology begins with simpler models. The work on anxiety and performance in sport, covered in chapter 11, starts with early anxiety-performance models, progresses to cognitive approaches emphasizing perceptions (similar to the appraisal aspect of Lazarus's model), and now is moving to more dynamic multidimensional approaches that could fit within the Lazarus framework.

Other lines of research and guiding models share features with the Lazarus model and suggest that the framework is appropriate for research and practice related to stress and emotion in sport and exercise. These models all incorporate key features of Lazarus's model: they highlight cognitive appraisal in a multidimensional system of interrelated psychobiological variables, and the complexity of the model highlights the importance of individualizing applications. Given the almost limitless possibilities, the stress process is different for every individual, even with the same situation. This is one of the most important practical implications of the stress research. The complexity of the model makes universal principles or predictions virtually impossible. Stress is individual, coping is individual, and sport and exercise psychologists should focus on individual characteristics and preferences rather than applying universal strategies to all. The importance of individualizing training and intervention is a key element of applied sport psychology programs and a theme of part IV of this text.

## Stress Management Models

Ron Smith (1980) applied a cognitive stress model to stress management for sport. The basic model (figure 10.1) matches Lazarus's; it highlights cognitive appraisal and includes multiple interrelated variables, and the process moves over time. External events, specifically demands and resources in the actual situation, may trigger stress, but individual appraisal is the key. Similarly, the response has physiological, psychological, and behavioral correlates and consequences. Cognitive appraisal of the situation and coping ability interact with physiological responses within the central stress appraisal process, which then leads to resulting behaviors, particularly task and coping behaviors. Smith developed a stress management program with an integrated coping response, involving both cognitive and behavioral strategies, as the key skill. With an integrated set of coping skills and possible strategies, the individual can tailor coping responses to the situation and individual preferences. Others have developed similar interventions, and the model provides a framework for stress management in sport (discussed in more detail in chapter 13).

### Key Point

Smith (1980) developed a stress management program with an integrated coping response, involving both cognitive and behavioral strategies, as the key skill. With an integrated set of coping skills and possible strategies, the individual can tailor coping responses to the situation and individual preferences.

## Stress and Burnout Models

Smith (1986) subsequently adapted the stress model to fit burnout in sport. The burnout model parallels the stress model; indeed, burnout is defined as a form of stress. Smith's burnout model, as well as most related work in sport psychology, follows the approach of Maslach and Jackson (1986), who developed the major model and measure of burnout. Here burnout is a multidimensional syndrome, particularly relevant to those in helping professions including teachers and coaches. Burnout is a consequence of prolonged stress that may result in (a) emotional exhaustion, (b) depersonalization—distancing oneself from others, and (c) reduced sense of meaning or personal accomplishments. The three dimensions are assessed with Maslach and Jackson's (1986) Burnout Inventory. As in Smith's (1986) model, the burnout process

**Figure 10.1**
Mediational model of stress underlying the cognitive-affective stress management program together with the major intervention techniques utilized in development of the integrated coping response.

Reprinted, by permission, from R.E. Smith, 1980, A cognitive-affective approach to stress management training for athletes. In *Psychology of motor behavior and sport*, edited by A. Nadeau (Champaign, IL: Human Kinetics), 54-72.

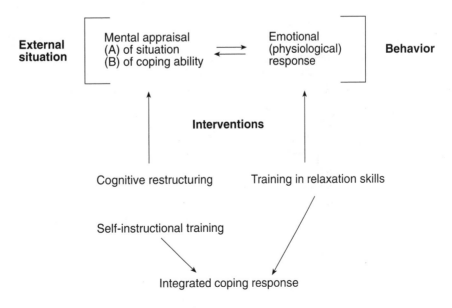

begins with a situation involving high or conflicting demands, low social support, low autonomy, and low reward. Then appraisal is the key, as the person perceives overload, helplessness, or lack of accomplishments. The appraisal interacts with physical symptoms, including tension, depression, or fatigue. The final result is the multidimensional burnout syndrome.

Vealey, Udry, Zimmerman, and Soliday (1992) used Smith's model as a framework and supported the mediating role of cognitive appraisal in coach burnout. Kelly and Gill (1993) also used Smith's framework and supported the main relationships of the model. Specifically, satisfaction with social support, low experience, and gender (being female) were related to stress appraisal and perceived stress, which in turn predicted burnout. Kelly (1994) extended that work to examine the influence of social support, hardiness, gender, and win/loss on stress appraisal and burnout. Other health and stress research suggests that social support is a key social factor; and hardiness, a multidimensional personality construct consisting of control, commitment, and challenge (Kobasa, 1988; Kobasa, Maddi, & Courington, 1981), is a key individual variable in the stress process. Kelly found some support in that both male and female coaches who were lower in hardiness, and male coaches who were lower in social support, had greater perceived stress. Again, stress appraisal predicted all burnout components.

## Stress and Injury Models

Jean Williams and colleagues (Anderson & Williams, 1988; Williams & Roepke, 1993) have adapted the stress model to sport injuries and rehabilitation. As with the other models, the process begins with a potentially stressful situation, but the key to the stress process (and injury) is the interaction of the cognitive appraisal and physiological/attentional processes. As with the stress and burnout models, the stress response is influenced by personal (e.g., hardiness, trait anxiety) and situational (e.g., history of stressors, social support) factors.

Udry (1997) has also used the stress model with its emphasis on cognitive appraisal to investigate the role of coping and support in athletic injury and recovery after knee surgery. During recovery athletes most frequently used instrumental coping, which is problem-focused and uses activities to alleviate stress; and instrumental coping predicted adherence to the rehabilitation program. Although the limits within the rehabilitation situation precluded strong conclusions, Udry provides some initial information and suggests that stress and emotion models offer a framework to guide research and practice on sport injury and rehabilitation.

> ### Key Point
>
> *Burnout* is a consequence of prolonged stress that may result in emotional exhaustion, depersonalization, and a reduced sense of meaning or personal accomplishments. In several research studies, stress appraisal predicted all burnout components, and when Williams and colleagues (1988, 1993) adapted the stress and burnout models to sport injuries, they found that the stress response was influenced by personal as well as situational factors.

# PHYSICAL ACTIVITY AND EMOTION

Most sport and exercise psychology work on stress and emotion focuses on anxiety and performance; we review that work in the next chapter. A few scholars have investigated other aspects of stress and emotion, mostly moving away from competitive sport and into exercise settings. These lines of research often take cues from the growing health psychology literature rather than the experimental, social psychology models that guided the anxiety-performance research. Many health psychology topics (e.g., adherence, stress management, coping, and quality of life) have obvious connections to sport and exercise. Also, health psychology uses a multidimensional, biopsychosocial approach that could provide a nice parallel framework for sport and exercise psychology.

Considerable health psychology work involves the link between stress and health, or more broadly, between emotion and health. Health psychology research links stress with cardiovascular disease and immune function. Alternative approaches to medicine and health, which emphasize the mind-body connection and health psychology themes, enjoy unprecedented popularity with the public and increasingly with the traditional medical community. For example, Bill Moyers's PBS series and subsequent book (Moyers, 1993) on healing and the mind illustrated the prominence and acceptance of this work within medical and research communities. That work is relevant to sport and exercise psychology when we add physical activity to the equation—a triad of stress (emotion), health, and physical activity. Moreover, the medical and health community recognizes the role of physical activity, and researchers as well as practitioners typically welcome contributions of exercise and sport scholars.

## Models and Measures of Emotion in Physical Activity

Physical activity or exercise fits into the health psychology models in several ways, and researchers have begun to investigate some links. One active research line involves physical activity as a mediator between stress and illness (or health). For example, do people who are more fit have less response to stress or recover more quickly? The answer from the early research is yes; but that research is just beginning, and we know little about the processes, mechanisms, and variations involved (e.g., Crews & Landers, 1987). Such a summary of exercise and stress reactivity research is typical of all the work in the larger area of physical activity and emotions. Overall, the growing research in this area confirms popular beliefs in the benefits of physical activity: exercise is associated with more positive emotions. However, specific relationships have not been delineated, and we know little about the exact processes and the many variations.

Gauvin and Brawley (1993) advocate that we clarify our models and measures to better understand the relationships between exercise and emotion or affect. Despite the consistently reported emotional benefits of exercise, the research is not at all consistent. Most research cited as supporting benefits of exercise is narrowly focused on negative emotions, specifically anxiety. Gauvin and Brawley (1993) suggest conceptual models that are more encompassing. Russell's (1978, 1980) circumplex model of affect represents affect along two dimensions: hedonic tone (pleasure-displeasure) and activation (arousal-sleepiness). Russell and colleagues (Russell, Weiss, & Mendelsohn, 1989) have developed a one-item measure called the Affect Grid to match their conceptual model; respondents mark a square on a 9 × 9 grid to indicate affect state. The Affect Grid could be used easily in exercise and sport settings.

To date, exercise and sport psychologists have ignored the Affect Grid, but a few studies followed a similar two-dimensional approach. Hardy and Rejeski (1989) used the Feeling Scale (Rejeski, Best, Griffith, & Kenney, 1987), a bipolar scale reflecting how good-bad one feels during exercise, which parallels hedonic tone. In their study of exercise effects, Hardy and Rejeski also used the rating of perceived exertion (RPE), which might be considered similar to activation. Increased exercise intensities related to decreases on the Feeling Scale and increases in RPE. The Feeling Scale is among the few measures of emotion developed for exercise psychology research, and such measures are critical for extending our understanding of exercise and emotion.

The RPE, developed in the 1960s by Borg (1973, 1982, 1998) and widely used in exercise physiology research, was not designed as a measure of emotion, or indeed for use within any psychological framework. A comprehensive review (Robertson & Noble, 1997) indicates the use of several forms of RPE, most commonly the 15-

© Heartland Images

Health-related quality of life—such as the positive psychological and physical effects of maintaining physical activity levels throughout adulthood—has not been clearly conceptualized and measured within sport and exercise psychology research.

category scale (from 6 = no exertion at all to 20 = maximal exertion) developed by Borg in 1962. As a physiologist, Borg took a psychophysical perspective, and the RPE scales correspond to heart rate increases with exercise-intensity increases. Although most work with RPE is from a physiological base, some have examined psychological correlates. Situational and psychological factors affect our perceptions (RPE) (Robertson & Noble, 1997; Morgan, 1994). Morgan (1994) summarized research demonstrating that anxiety, depression, neuroticism, and extroversion influence RPE during exercise. Morgan's review focuses on one side of the emotion-exercise relationship—how emotion influences exercise and performance. That relationship has not been widely investigated, and certainly not with measures derived from conceptual models as advocated by Gauvin and Brawley (1993).

Most researchers on emotion and exercise examine the reverse relationship, that is, how exercise influences emotion; and some are beginning to use conceptually based models and measures. Specifically, Watson and Tellegen's (1985) two-factor model of affect, and the related Positive Affect Negative Affect Schedule (PANAS; Watson, Clark, & Tellegen, 1988), appear increasingly in the literature. The 20-item PANAS includes two 10-item scales, one for positive affect and one for negative affect. The PANAS has been used in several studies in physical activity settings (e.g., Crocker & Graham, 1995), and Crocker (1997) recently reported confirmatory factor analysis results supporting its validity in youth sport settings.

Although the PANAS may be useful in sport and exercise psychology, it is a general measure. As discussed in earlier chapters on personality and motivation, sport-specific measures and approaches—and more attention to the unique properties of physical activity—may enhance methods and research related to emotion. McAuley and Courneya (1994) suggested that the PANAS may be limited for exercise settings, citing the role of physiological cues in exercise and in our emotional responses within exercise settings. They also pointed out that conclusions from existing research on physical activity and affect are limited by the emphasis on negative emotions. For example, our most popular emotion measure, the Profile of Mood States (McNair, Lorr, & Droppleman, 1971), assesses five negative moods (tension, depression, anger, fatigue, confusion) and only one positive mood (vigor). Most other studies have measured specific negative emotions such as depression or anxiety. As McAuley and Courneya note, psychological health comprises both positive and negative emotion, and we typically dichotomize these states as psychological distress (e.g., anxiety, depression, stress-related emotions) and psychological well-being (e.g., positive affect).

Reviewing the literature on physical activity and health-related quality of life, Rejeski, Brawley, and Shumaker (1996) similarly noted that quality of life, although a key concern in medical and health-related research and practice, has not been clearly conceptualized and measured. Instead, studies have used various measures, typically focusing on negative emotions or the absence of pathologies. Rejeski et al. (1996) conceptualize health-related quality of life (HRQOL) along six dimensions. First they cite global indices of HRQOL and then list physical function, physical symptoms/states, emotional function, social function, and cognitive function. Again, emotional function, the main concern in this chapter, includes both positive and negative subareas. In line with other reviewers, Rejeski et al. (1996) conclude that physical activity is associated with improved HRQOL but that the research largely deals with anxiety, depression, and negative aspects of HRQOL.

McAuley and Courneya (1994) addressed some limits of existing models and measures by developing the Subjective Exercise Experiences Scale (SEES). The three-factor SEES includes positive and negative factors corresponding to psychological well-being and psychological distress, as well as a third factor representing subjective indicants of fatigue. The initial work provided evidence for the validity of the SEES subscales with young and middle-aged adults in exercise settings. The SEES, easily used in such settings, should be useful for investigating questions about emotion and physical activity.

## Effects of Exercise on Negative Emotion

Research on exercise and emotion, mood, or affect is not new (for reviews, see Folkins & Sime, 1981; Hughes, 1984; Morgan & Goldston, 1987). However, as just suggested, most such work has emphasized negative emotion. In their review on the affective benefits of aerobic exercise, Tuson and Sinyor (1993) note that research follows two basic approaches: one approach focuses on chronic effects (those associated with extended training or long-term participation), and the other on acute effects (those of a single exercise session). The authors conclude that acute exercise may be associated with reduced anxiety but does not appear to influence other affective states. They also report that although many explanations and mechanisms have been suggested, none have been supported.

*Key Point*

In studying the effects of exercise on negative emotion, researchers have taken two basic approaches: one focusing on chronic effects and the other on acute effects.

Boutcher (1993) reaches similar conclusions, reporting empirical support for the popular view that we "feel better" after exercise. Several studies and meta-analyses (North, McCullagh, & Tran, 1990; Petruzzello, Landers, Hatfield, Kubitz, & Salazar, 1991) confirm that exercise is associated with reductions in anxiety and depression. Most studies involve running, walking, or cycling, although Berger and Owen (1983) also reported more positive moods in swimmers. Boutcher noted that although vigorous exercise typically results in lower anxiety, light exercise has little effect.

One exception to the general enhanced mood with exercise is the overtraining effect. After reviewing the research, Morgan, Brown, Raglin, O'Connor, and Ellickson (1987) concluded that athletes who overtrain at prolonged intense levels exhibit not only performance decrements and physiological changes, but also more negative mood profiles.

Boutcher (1993) categorized explanations for the benefits of exercise into the physiological and psychological mechanisms listed in table 10.1. Like Tuson and Sinyor (1993), Boutcher concluded that no proposed mechanism had convincing support. He suggested that several physiological and psychological factors might be involved and that the process may vary with the individual. Most people who exercise cite multiple reasons and benefits that fit into different categories. Continuing research may well lead to a complex mix of multidimensional processes rather than one mechanism.

Boutcher concluded by proposing an integrated model, combining Solomon's (Solomon, 1980; Solomon & Corbitt, 1974) opponent process theory with self-efficacy and attribution models. According to opponent process theory repeated exposure to a stimulus (exercise) leads to a rebound pattern; the initial negative emotional response during exercise gradually becomes less aversive and the positive emotion following exercise becomes stronger. Boutcher suggested that individuals in aerobic

**Table 10.1   Benefits of Exercise: Physiological and Psychological Mechanisms**

*Physiological*

*Hyperthermic change:*   increases in body temperature lead to changes in the brain, particularly the hypothalamus, leading to relaxation and feeling better.

*Visceral feedback:*   rhythmic feedback from exercise may dampen brain activity leading to relaxation and positive affect.

*Neurotransmitter changes:*   exercise increases neurotransmitters that are depleted with stress (norephinephrine, dopamine, serotonin) leading to greater psychological well-being.

*Endorphins:*   exercise increases levels of endorphins, which offset pain and induce euphoria, leading to positive emotional state.

*Autonomic rebound:*   sympathetic activity dominates during exercise, but after stopping homeostasis restores parasympathetic influence, and the parasympathetic "rebound" is associated with relaxation and restoration.

*Psychological*

*Self-esteem:*   as discussed in chapter 6, exercise typically leads to enhanced physical self-esteem.

*Mastery:*   successful completion of an activity or exercise bout increases the sense of mastery and related positive emotion.

*Social factors:*   developing and maintaining friendships and social contact enhances positive emotion.

*Time-out:*   exercise is a distraction or escape from stress-inducing activities.

---

exercise programs undergo three stages of physiological adaption (adoption, maintenance, and habituation) in line with Solomon's model. Boutcher added that accompanying these phases are psychological changes, with attribution and self-efficacy prominent during adoption, and behavioral conditioning and opponent process more influential during maintenance and habituation. Although Boutcher's model is speculative and untested, integration of physiological and cognitive processes matches the complexity of emotion and probably provides a better guide than simpler mechanistic explanations.

Other reviews confirm emotional benefits of chronic exercise. Crews and Landers's (1987) meta-analysis indicated that exercise leads to less stress reactivity and faster recovery from stress responses. In a meta-analysis, Long and van Stavel (1995) examined exercise training as stress management. They concluded that exercise training had low to moderate positive effects on anxiety reduction, and that adults with more stressful lifestyles benefited more from exercise training.

Holmes (1993), reviewing research on aerobic fitness and psychological stress, concluded that (a) fitness is associated with lower cardiovascular arousal during and following stress; (b) exercise training can reduce arousal during stress; (c) exercise training can reduce depression following prolonged life stress; (d) exercise training can improve cardiovascular and psychological functioning of cardiac patients; and (e) fitness is associated with less physical illness following prolonged life stress.

In an intriguing line of research related to Holmes's final conclusion, some have examined physical activity as a coping mechanism in recovery and rehabilitation (e.g., physical activity programs with cancer or acquired immunodeficiency syndrome [AIDS] patients). LaPerriere and colleagues (LaPerriere et al., 1990, 1991), in extensive research using exercise programs with human immunodeficiency virus (HIV) and AIDS patients, reported that exercise reduced depression. Lox, McAuley, and Tucker (1995), following LaPerriere's lead, examined the influence of an exercise intervention on psychological well-being with an HIV-1 population: both aerobic and weight-training exercise enhanced physical self-efficacy, positive and negative mood (assessed with PANAS), and life satisfaction. These research programs and related practical applications do not simply look at biological medical outcomes, but consider the "whole" person. Psychological well-being is a key part of health and medical research, and many programs are examining connections between psychology and health in innovative ways.

# POSITIVE EMOTIONS IN SPORT AND EXERCISE

So far we have concentrated on negative emotion because of the research emphasis. But to understand emotion in sport and exercise we must give equal attention to positive emotion. In fact, we could easily argue that positive emotion is even more important in sport and exercise than stress and anxiety. Earlier sections highlighted the growing interest in exercise for alleviating anxiety and depression. But in general, researchers have neglected the role of exercise in enhancing positive emotion and psychological well-being (McAuley & Courneya, 1994; Rejeski et al., 1996). Most people do not participate in exercise and sport to reduce stress, but because they feel better and because physical activity is fun!

## Enjoyment in Sport

Within our discipline, one of the most notable lines of research on positive emotions is that of Tara Scanlan and colleagues (Scanlan & Simons, 1992) on enjoyment in sport. Scanlan's work is partially based on Csikszentmihalyi's (1975, 1990) long-term work on flow and intrinsic motivation, which has inspired sport and exercise psychology researchers to examine flow and fun.

Partly because research on enjoyment is relatively new, and perhaps partly because of the nature of enjoyment, the early work lacks clear structure and definitions. Kimiecik and Harris (1996) have attempted to provide a framework and encourage further work on the positive emotions in physical activity. As they note, several scholars, including Brustad (1988), Scanlan and colleagues (Scanlan & Lewthwaite, 1986; Scanlan, Carpenter, Lobel, & Simons, 1993; Scanlan & Simons, 1992), and Wankel (1993; Wankel & Kreisel, 1985; Wankel & Sefton, 1989), have moved beyond the early participation motivation work to explore enjoyment in physical activity. However, enjoyment has not been conceptualized or measured consistently. Wankel (1993) defined enjoyment as a positive emotion or positive affect state. Scanlan and Simons (1992) referred to enjoyment in similar broad, exploratory terms as a positive affective response to the sport experience that reflects feelings and/or perceptions such as pleasure, liking, and fun.

Measures of enjoyment are more inconsistent than the conceptual definitions. As discussed earlier, the general models of emotion now include positive dimensions; but comparable measures, such as PANAS, are relatively new and not thoroughly validated for sport and exercise settings. We do not have measures of positive affect to match the carefully developed and validated (and often sport specific) measures of anxiety and stress. Several studies of enjoyment have used open-ended measures with content analyses in a more qualititative approach (e.g., Scanlan, Stein, & Ravizza, 1989), and such approaches are helpful. Others have used simple measures developed for specific studies. For example, Brustad (1988) used two items to measure enjoyment; Wankel and Sefton (1989) simply asked "How much fun did you have in the game today?"; and Scanlan, Simons, Carpenter, Schmidt, and Keeler (1993) used a four-item measure of enjoyment. Kendzierski and DeCarlo (1991) developed an 18-item Physical Activity Enjoyment Scale (PACES) and provided some initial evidence for its reliability and validity with college students. Crocker, Bouffard, and Gessaroli (1995) subsequently used confirmatory factor analysis with PACES in youth sport settings and failed to support its unidimensional structure. Crocker et al. (1995) suggested that PACES seems to tap different constructs and may represent both antecedents and perceptions of enjoyment rather than one enjoyment construct.

Kimiecik and Harris (1996) advocated Csikszentmihalyi's work as a conceptual framework for enjoyment. As they noted, Csikszentmihalyi referred to enjoyment in his early (1975) writings on flow, and he has continued (1990) to discuss enjoyment and flow as an optimal experience that is intrinsically rewarding and autotelic (i.e., doing the activity is the reward). Kimiecik and Harris (1996) propose the following adaptation of Csikszentmihalyi's definition of enjoyment as *an optimal psychological state that leads to performing an activity primarily for its own sake and is associated with positive feeling states. (p. 256)*

Defining enjoyment as flow may set the stage for more in-depth research on the links between optimal psychological states and positive affective responses in sport and exercise (Kimiecik & Harris, 1996).

## Flow in Sport

Not only has Csikszentmihalyi's flow construct contributed to work on enjoyment, but several researchers have more specifically explored flow states with sport and exercise participants. Flow occurs when the performer is totally connected to the performance, in a situation in which skills equal challenges (Csikszentmihalyi, 1975, 1990, 1993). Most elite athletes, and even most participants, can relate to flow. Athletes may recall a peak experience—a time when everything just came together and they were totally immersed in the activity. Flow is perhaps the ultimate positive state. Csikszentmihalyi used innovative experience-sampling and in-depth methods to develop his conceptualization of the optimal flow experience and its antecedents. Sue Jackson uses Csikszentmihalyi's model as a starting point for her investigations of flow with athletes. Jackson (1995; Jackson & Marsh, 1996) has employed in-depth interviews and more typical survey approaches to identify characteristics and antecedents of flow.

Elite athletes like Tiger Woods can typically relate to the flow experience—when everything seems to come together and we become totally immersed in the task at hand.

© Brian Ormiston

Flow occurs when the performer is totally connected to the performance, in a situation in which skills equal challenges (Csikszentmihalyi, 1975, 1990, 1993). Most elite athletes, and even most participants, can relate to flow. Athletes may recall a peak experience—a time when everything just came together and they were totally immersed in the activity. Flow is perhaps the ultimate positive state.

Jackson and Marsh (1996) used previous research, Csikszentmihalyi's model, and both qualitative and quantitative analyses to develop the Flow State Scale (FSS). The nine scales of the 36-item FSS represent the dimensions of flow identified by Csikszentmihalyi, and Jackson and Marsh provided good psychometric evidence for the scales and the FSS. All scales are internally consistent, and confirmatory factor analyses supported a hierarchical model with one global, higher-order factor explaining correlations among the nine first-order FSS factors. These are the nine dimensions of flow, from both Csikszentmihalyi's work and Jackson's work with athletes:

- *Challenge-skill balance:* The person perceives a balance between the challenges of a situation and his or her skills, with both at a high level.

- *Action-awareness merging:* Involvement is so deep that it becomes spontaneous or automatic.

- *Clear goals:* Clearly defined goals give the person a strong sense of knowing what to do.

- *Unambiguous feedback:* The person receives immediate and clear feedback, usually from the activity itself.

- *Concentration on task at hand:* Total concentration on the task occurs.

- *Sense of control:* The person experiences a sense of exercising control but without actively trying to exert control.

- *Loss of self-consciousness:* Concern for the self disappears as the person becomes one with the activity.

- *Transformation of time:* Time alters perceptibly, either slowing down or speeding up.

- *Autotelic experience:* An autotelic experience is intrinsically rewarding, done for its own sake.

Many athletes can relate to the flow experience, and the work of Jackson and others provides direction and measures for the continuing exploration of flow and enjoyment in sport and exercise.

## Summary

Emotion pervades all sport and exercise activities, and explanations of sport and exercise behavior that omit the emotional component are incomplete and rather dull. Emotion is a complex biopsychosocial process that challenges researchers. Sport and exercise psychology research focuses on the negative emotions, more specifically on anxiety. The expanding research on physical activity and emotion consistently confirms the benefits of physical activity, but that work is limited and typically involves the effects of aerobic exercise on anxiety reduction. With measures such as the FSS and the SEES, and with models that encompass positive as well as negative emotions, sport and exercise psychology researchers may more fully explore emotion.

More encompassing approaches such as Lazarus's model may provide guidance. Sport and exercise psychologists recognize some aspects of Lazarus's model—

cognitive appraisal, the interactive roles of person and environment, and the importance of individualization. Our methodology has not kept up with these conceptual advances and has not incorporated other aspects of Lazarus's model. We discuss the dynamic, recursive nature of the stress process; but models generally assume one-dimensional predictions, and no methods adequately probe the ongoing process over time.

Sport and exercise psychologists are just beginning to incorporate the social aspect and to recognize emotion as a biopsychosocial process. Social context affects both person and environment, determines both sources and appraisals of stress and emotion, and further influences psychophysiological responses and consequences of stress, as well as coping processes. Perhaps most important, sport and exercise psychologists have not yet followed Lazarus's lead and recognized that while stress and emotion overlap, emotion is the more encompassing and richer concept. For example, although we typically look at anxiety in competition, people might also respond with hope, anger, or sadness or find themselves in a flow state. If we consider the broader emotional response possibilities within a dynamic system of interrelationships, we may better understand sport and exercise behavior.

## Review Questions

1. Define emotion, arousal, and anxiety.

2. Explain the major historical perspectives on emotion in sport and exercise psychology, such as James-Lange theory, Schachter and Singer's cognitive approach, and Lazarus's model of emotion.

3. Explain the relationship between Smith's (1980) stress management model and Lazarus's model of emotion.

4. Define burnout and discuss how stress appraisal relates to most burnout models and stress and injury models.

5. Discuss how measures like the PANAS, POMS, HRQOL, and SEES may help explain how exercise influences emotion.

6. Summarize the two basic approaches researchers have taken in studying the effects of exercise on negative emotion.

7. Compare and contrast the varying definitions of enjoyment in physical activity.

8. Define flow, and explain the nine dimensions of flow from Csikszentmihalyi's work and Jackson's work with athletes.

## Recommended Reading

★ Lazarus, R.S. (1993). From psychological stress to the emotions:
A history of changing outlooks. *Annual Review of Psychology, 44,*
1-21.

> Lazarus has been a leading scholar on stress and coping since the 1960s. More recently, he has taken on the broader complexities of emotion. This review presents some of his many insights in moving from stress to emotions.

★ Rejeski, W.J., Brawley, L.R., & Shumaker, S.A. (1996). Physical
activity and health-related quality of life. *Exercise and Sport
Sciences Reviews, 24,* 71-108.

> Rejeski and his colleagues have often integrated health psychology with sport and exercise psychology. This chapter provides an excellent review of research and thought on health-related quality of life (QOL). QOL is a key construct in health research and practice, and this chapter reviews QOL models and measures, identifies gaps in the research, and provides directions for sport and exercise psychology.

★ Csikszentmihalyi, M. (1990). *Flow: The psychology of optimal experience.* New York: Harper & Row.

Csikszentmihalyi is widely cited for his innovative work on intrinsic motivation and the popular "flow" state. Many sport and exercise psychology scholars and students are drawn to his work, with good reason—they find new ideas and directions. Perhaps you will also get caught up in the flow as you read his work.

# chapter 11

# Competitive Anxiety

## CHAPTER OBJECTIVES

After studying this chapter, you should be able to

- understand the anxiety-performance relationship in sport and exercise and
- explain the importance of individual differences in competitive anxiety in sport and exercise psychology research.

As discussed in chapter 10, emotion has always figured in sport and exercise psychology—and stress has played a leading role. Specifically, we have focused on competitive anxiety and the anxiety-performance relationship (for reviews see Gill, 1994; or Gould & Krane, 1992). Researchers and practitioners are familiar with the stress of competition; we've seen athletes rise to the challenge and athletes choke under stress. Until recently, sport and exercise psychology research on anxiety and performance did not incorporate cognitive appraisal or fit with emotion models discussed in chapter 10. Instead, anxiety was typically conceptualized and measured more narrowly, as arousal.

## AROUSAL CONSTRUCTS AND MEASURES

Arousal, as the intensity dimension of behavior, is the general state of activation ranging on a continuum from deep sleep to extreme excitement. We all recognize the physiological symptoms of increased arousal. Hans Selye (1956) referred to bodily reactions to stress as the General Adaptation Syndrome—the "fight-or-flight" response of the autonomic nervous system that we all experience in stressful situations. You know you are anxious when you breathe rapidly, your heart pounds, your hands sweat, your stomach does flips, your knees turn to jelly, and your mouth tastes like cotton.

In sport and exercise psychology, arousal has little meaning unless we consider the context, the cognitive appraisal, and the larger emotional process; and arousal typically implies psychological as well as physiological responses. A softball player experiencing the physiological symptoms of arousal may also think about the mistakes made last game, worry about everyone watching, and be aware of feeling anxious. Thus, arousal, which we usually discuss as anxiety, is a multidimensional state with both a physiological or somatic component and a psychological or cognitive component.

The cognitive component of anxiety typically involves worrying about performance evaluation or possible failure. Much physical activity involves competition, and by definition, competition involves performance evaluation. Even noncompetitive activities may create some arousal and worry. A child in an elementary physical education class wants to please the teacher and not be the last one through the obstacle course; an adult in a corporate fitness program does not want to appear out of shape in front of colleagues. In sport and exercise activities, individuals typically experience a combination of physiological arousal and cognitive worry, which is state anxiety. However, the early research, which did not incorporate the cognitive component, is more appropriately labeled arousal-performance research.

## Key Point

The cognitive component of anxiety typically involves worrying about performance evaluation or possible failure. Common physiological measures of anxiety are heart rate, respiration rate, blood pressure, and galvanic skin response. Behavioral measures typically take the form of self-report measures, such as the state anxiety inventory of the State-Trait Anxiety Inventory.

If anxiety gets too high during a game, an athlete might "choke" in a situation like this one.

Because arousal has various manifestations, even if cognitive appraisal is not considered, there are various ways to measure it. Common physiological measures include heart rate, respiration rate, blood pressure, and galvanic skin response. Behavioral observations have been used occasionally, but the most common nonphysiological measures are self-report measures, such as the state anxiety inventory of the State-Trait Anxiety Inventory (Spielberger, Gorsuch, & Lushene, 1970) and Thayer's (1967) activation-deactivation checklist.

The various arousal measures are not highly related to each other. Physiological measures do not correlate with self-report measures and often do not even correlate with each other. Individuals apparently have idiosyncratic arousal responses. For example, my face flushes and my muscles tighten, but my hands do not get sweaty. Someone else becomes nauseous but notices no changes in breathing or heart rate. Still another might feel very worried but show no dramatic physiological symptoms. Because anxiety is multidimensional and because individuals manifest anxiety differently, current models emphasize a multidimensional approach with both physiological and psychological measures.

Some self-report anxiety scales assess physiological (somatic) anxiety and cognitive worry on separate dimensions. The Worry-Emotionality Inventory (Liebert & Morris, 1967; Morris, Davis, & Hutchings, 1981), a state anxiety scale, and the Cognitive-Somatic Anxiety Questionnaire (Schwartz, Davidson, & Goleman, 1978), a trait anxiety scale, both assess cognitive and somatic anxiety on separate dimensions. Martens and his colleagues (Martens, Vealey, & Burton, 1990) built upon that work to develop a sport-specific, multidimensional measure of competitive state anxiety, the Competitive State Anxiety Inventory-2 (CSAI-2), which assesses cognitive worry and somatic anxiety on separate scales. We will cover the development of the CSAI-2 and related research in more detail later.

# ANXIETY-PERFORMANCE RELATIONSHIPS: EARLY MODELS AND RESEARCH

The anxiety-performance relationship is a prominent research issue and a practical concern for sport participants. Typical pregame rituals and pep talks aim to increase arousal or get players "psyched up" for competition. Those who use psych-up strategies must believe that such tactics enhance performance. Are they correct? Most of us can recall times when a pep talk seemed to help, or when an athlete responded to the big game with the best performance of the season. The Olympic Games certainly induce high arousal, and the pressure and excitement of the games seem to elicit a large share of record-breaking performances and personal bests.

But the Olympic Games reflect only one side of the picture. You can probably recall other times when performers have choked under pressure. I once coached a team of seventh-grade girls who demonstrated modest basketball skills in practices and intramural games. When faced with competition against a seventh-grade team from another school, those same players completely missed the basket on shots, dribbled off their feet, threw passes into the bleachers, and managed to go through the game without scoring a basket. Clearly, a "win one for the Gipper" speech would have only made the situation worse.

Coaches who hold the image of a stirring Knute Rockne pep talk as the key to mental preparation might be surprised to learn what Rockne actually said about such tactics. Coleman Griffith, a contemporary of Rockne, heard that Rockne did not "key up" the Notre Dame team but instead focused on playing the game "joyously." In December 1924, Griffith wrote to Rockne to ask about his motivational tactics. Rockne replied as follows (from the Coleman Griffith Collection, University Archives, University of Illinois at Urbana-Champaign):

> *Dear Mr. Griffith:*
>
> *I feel very grateful to you for having written me, although I do not know a great deal about psychology.*
>
> *I do try to pick men who like the game of football and who get a lot of fun out of playing. I never try to make football hard work. I do think our team plays good football because they like to play and I do not make any effort to key them up, except on rare, exceptional occasions. I keyed them up for the Nebraska game this year, which was a mistake, as we had a reaction the following Saturday against Northwestern. I try to make our boys take the game less seriously than, I presume, some others do, and we try to make the spirit of the game one of exhilaration and we never allow hatred to enter into it, no matter whom we are playing.*
>
> *Thanking you for your kindness, I am*
>
> *Yours cordially,*
>
> *Knute Rockne*

People have done many strange things in the cause of psyching up athletes even though such tactics often psych them out. As Rockne recognized, performers can be too keyed up. Many beginning coaches turn to psych-up approaches at the very times they are least likely to help—when the situation has already raised arousal beyond optimal levels. Sometimes strategies that increase arousal do improve performance. Clearly, increases in arousal do not always help or always hinder performance.

We look first to the early theories and research on anxiety and performance in psychology. In the beginning, the dominant models were drive theory, which holds that increased arousal increases performance of the dominant response, and the inverted-U hypothesis, which predicts that performance is best at a moderate optimal level and progressively worse with either increases or decreases in arousal.

Both theories were based on experimental psychology research, often on lab studies with animals.

## Drive Theory

Drive theory, an early, influential theory of motivation in psychology, has had a place in sport and exercise psychology research. As developed by Hull (1943) and modified by Spence (1956), drive theory is complex; but we'll consider a simple version and express the arousal-performance relationship as

$$P = f(H \times D).$$

Performance (P) is a function of habit (H) times drive (D). Within the Hull-Spence model, drive is essentially arousal, or the intensity dimension of behavior. The other main component, habit, refers to learned responses or behaviors. The more a response has been reinforced, the greater its habit strength and the more likely it will occur.

Essentially, drive theory proposes that as drive increases (as when one is facing competition), learned responses are more likely to occur. The basic relationship is linear; as arousal increases, performance increases. But performance predictions of drive theory are not that simple. Overall performance does not necessarily improve; what improves is performance of the individual's dominant response. Performance improves only if the dominant and most likely response is correct performance. Until we become proficient at a skill, the dominant response probably is not correct performance, and we are more likely to make mistakes than to do everything right.

### Key Point

Drive theory proposes that as drive increases (as when one is facing competition), learned responses are more likely to occur. The basic relationship is linear; as arousal increases, performance increases.

For example, a golf swing can include many incorrect responses. For the perfect swing the golfer must have proper body alignment; shift weight correctly; keep the body and club in proper alignment throughout the swing; and perform the backswing, forward swing, and follow-through with the correct length, in the correct plane, and at an optimal speed. Unless I am an accomplished golfer with a "grooved" swing, my dominant response is not likely to be the correct swing. As arousal increases, such as in a club match, I am likely to revert to my dominant, error-ridden swing even more than usual; perhaps I will swing too fast, swing out too much, and slice more than usual.

In contrast, a professional golfer has performed each shot so often that the correct swing is the dominant response. When we speak of "grooving" the swing or having automatic skills, we are essentially saying that the correct response is dominant. In that case, as with the pro golfer, increased arousal should improve performance. We can summarize drive theory predictions for sport and motor performance as follows:

- Increased arousal or drive increases the likelihood that the dominant response will occur.
- If a skill is relatively simple or is well learned, the dominant response is the correct response, and increased arousal will improve performance.
- If a skill is complex (as most sport skills are) and not well learned, the dominant response is an incorrect response, and increased arousal will impair performance.

## The Inverted-U Theory

An alternative explanation of the arousal-performance relationship, which has generally displaced drive theory, is the inverted-U theory. The inverted-U (figure 11.1) proposes that performance is optimal at a moderate level of arousal and that performance declines as arousal increases or decreases from that moderate, optimal level. The inverted-U model makes sense and fits our observations. Individuals need some arousal to perform at their best: those who are too mellow give subpar performances; and with too much arousal, performers may be tense and prone to errors.

---

### Key Point

The inverted-U theory proposes that performance is optimal at a moderate level of arousal and that performance declines as arousal increases or decreases from that moderate, optimal level.

---

Although the inverted-U makes intuitive sense, controlled tests of the curvilinear relationship are difficult, and empirical support is limited. In the original inverted-U research of Yerkes and Dodson (1908), mice learned a choice-discrimination task under weak, moderate, and strong arousal, with shock used to manipulate arousal. Learning was best under moderate stimulus levels and demonstrated the inverted-U phenomenon, which is sometimes referred to as the Yerkes-Dodson law.

Martens and Landers (1970) tested the inverted-U theory with motor performance by having junior high school boys perform a tracking task in a controlled experimental setting with low-, moderate-, and high-stress conditions. The three stress conditions yielded three arousal levels, confirmed with both physiological and self-report measures; and performance scores formed an inverted-U pattern with best performances in the moderate stress condition.

Subsequently, Sonstroem and Bernardo (1982) confirmed the inverted-U pattern in a field study with female university basketball players. Comparison of each athlete's lowest, median, and highest pregame state anxiety scores with her composite performance scores for those three games showed an inverted-U relationship. The best performances were associated with moderate state anxiety, and the poorest performances with high state anxiety.

Sonstroem and Bernardo also found that the inverted-U was more pronounced for high competitive trait anxious athletes, illustrating individual differences. Given the same situation, such as an intrasquad tennis match to determine team rankings, one player might be below optimal arousal and need to psych up a bit, whereas

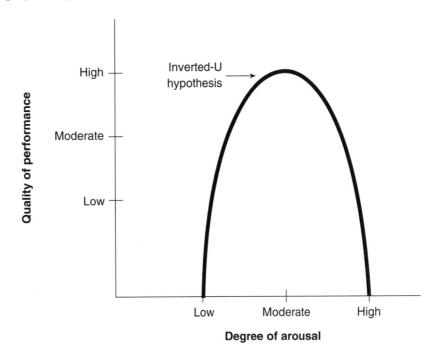

**Figure 11.1**
The arousal/ performance relationship according to the inverted-U hypothesis.

another player might be overaroused and need to calm down to play in top form.

As well as differing between individuals, optimal levels may vary across tasks and skills. For example, putting in golf has a low optimal arousal level; golfers perform best with low arousal, and even slight increases may disrupt their concentration and performance. Weight lifting has a higher optimal arousal level. Oxendine (1970, p. 25) offered the following guidelines for determining the optimal arousal levels of various sport tasks:

- A high level of arousal is essential for optimal performance in gross motor activities involving strength, endurance, or speed.

- A high level of arousal interferes with performances involving complex skills, such as fine muscle movements, coordination, steadiness, and general concentration.

- A slightly above average level of arousal is preferable to a normal or subnormal arousal state for all motor tasks.

As Landers (1978) noted, Oxendine's guidelines may have some practical use, but have little research support. Research does not document that above-average arousal enhances performance on any sport or motor task. Also, most sport tasks requiring speed or strength also involve focusing attention or coordination; for example, a sprinter must get out of the blocks and avoid distraction. Thus, sport tasks are not easily classified. We can conclude that performance is optimal at a moderate level of arousal, and we can qualify that relationship by recognizing that optimal levels vary across tasks and individuals; but we cannot predict precise optimal arousal levels for each performer in each task. Practically, we might better direct our efforts at helping performers recognize their own individual optimal states in varying situations.

Sport and exercise psychologists adopted and tested these theories, and Martens and Landers (1970) published one of the key supporting studies for the inverted-U. Debate on drive versus inverted-U was considerable. Inverted-U won, perhaps as much because of its intuitive appeal as any research support. Drive theory did not really "lose," and was cited in some work (e.g., audience effects on performance). Moreover, the inverted-U did not really "win" and is no longer promoted in sport and exercise psychology. Both drive and inverted-U theories miss one key element of a psychological perspective—thought or cognitive appraisal. Neither drive theory nor the inverted-U hypothesis includes a cognitive step, and neither is prominent today.

## Key Point

Both drive and inverted-U theories miss one key element of a psychological perspective—thought or cognitive appraisal. Neither drive theory nor the inverted-U hypothesis includes a cognitive step, and neither is prominent today.

## Hanin's Zones of Optimal Functioning

Russian sport psychologist Yuri Hanin (1989, 1995) has proposed an alternative that relates to the inverted-U model but emphasizes individual differences. Hanin proposes that athletes have a zone of optimal functioning (ZOF); he suggests that the ZOF is unique to the individual and can be identified through retrospective analyses and systematic multiple observations of athletes' state anxiety and performance levels. Hanin developed his model in the former Soviet system with its emphasis on applied work with elite athletes. Thus, the ZOF model has practical appeal, as well as some empirical support. Recently Hanin and Syrja (1996) extended the ZOF model beyond anxiety to patterns of emotions, moving closer to current emotion models, discussed in chapter 10.

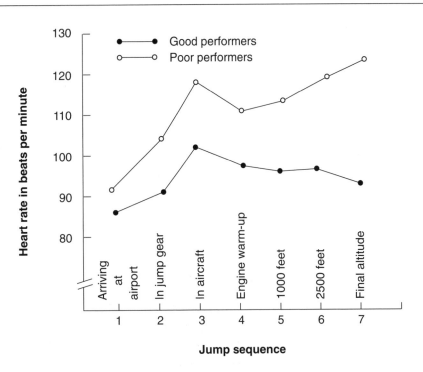

**Figure 11.2**

Continuous recordings of heart rate during a jump sequence of parachutists with good and poor performance.

Reprinted from *Journal of Psychomatic Research*, 18, W.D. Fenz and G.B. Jones, "Cardiac conditioning in a reaction time task and heart rate control during real life stress," 201, copyright 1974, with permission from Elsevier Science.

## ANXIETY PATTERNS AND SPORT PERFORMANCE

Psychologist and parachutist Walter Fenz (1975, 1988) added important insights with his innovative studies of arousal patterns of parachute jumpers. Fenz went out into the field, or into the air, to study an activity that clearly elicits anxiety. Rather than simply taking one measure of arousal, Fenz recorded anxiety changes and patterns over time. Over several years of research he used varied designs and both physiological and self-report measures, but the findings were consistent. Good performers and experienced jumpers did not differ from poorly skilled or novice jumpers in absolute arousal levels. Instead, they differed in anxiety patterns (figure 11.2).

As the figure shows, arousal levels of poor performers (measured by heart rate) continually increase from arrival at the airport to the time of the jump. Good performers increase in arousal at first, but peak earlier and gradually decrease in arousal so that they are at moderate levels at the time of the jump. Fenz confirmed these differences in anxiety patterns across several studies using varied measures and procedures. His work suggests that the difference between better and poorer performers is not a difference in absolute levels, but a difference in the ability to control anxiety. Good performers seem to bring anxiety under control so that they are experiencing moderate levels of arousal at the time of performance.

Additional studies suggest that anxiety control can be disrupted even in experienced, skilled performers. Fenz (1975) reported that one experienced jumper broke an ankle on a jump. Upon returning, this jumper reverted to the novice's pattern of continual increases in arousal up to the jump. Athletes in other sports returning to competition after injury might well exhibit similar patterns.

Fenz also studied whether the arousal pattern of an experienced jumper could be altered by an unusual, threatening situation. After three control jumps, the jumper was told his chute could malfunction during any of the next 10 jumps. Although the jumper had an emergency chute and knew emergency procedures, the perceived threat (cognitive appraisal) of malfunction added to anxiety. Records revealed that the arousal patterns for those 10 jumps were similar to the arousal patterns of novices, with continual increases to a peak at the time of the jump.

In one particularly encouraging training study, Fenz (1988) taught anxiety control techniques to novice jumpers before their first jump. Even in their first jumps, the trained group demonstrated the controlled arousal pattern of the experienced jumpers. Although he did not take specific performance measures, Fenz reported that the experimental jumpers had more fun during their training, and several progressed to become experienced skydivers. These findings provided early support for psychological skills training and suggest that anxiety control training may benefit even novice athletes.

As part of their study of qualifiers and nonqualifiers for the 1976 Olympic gymnastics team, Mahoney and Avener (1977) followed Fenz's approach and examined anxiety patterns over time. Retrospective reports of perceived anxiety revealed that the qualifiers' anxiety levels were just as high as, or higher than, those of nonqualifiers prior to performance; but qualifiers reported lower anxiety than nonqualifiers during performance. As with the parachutists, the better performers seemed to bring anxiety under control at the right time.

Mahoney (1979) suggested that differences in cognitive patterns, specifically precompetition thoughts, accompany the reported differences in anxiety patterns. The qualifiers seemed to approach competition with a task orientation and to focus their energy and attention on the task. In contrast, nonqualifiers worried more about being anxious. Two quotes from the gymnasts illustrate this difference. During an interview, one nonqualifier described his precompetition thoughts as follows:

> When I start chalking up, I feel all queasy and I think to myself, "Oh s—, am I scared! Six thousand people watching! What if I make a mistake? What if I fall off?" I hear myself talking like that and I know I'm not ready. (Mahoney, 1979, p. 436)

In contrast, one Olympic qualifier described similar high anxiety, but then shifted his thoughts from the worry to the performance:

> I get out there and they're waiting for me and all I can think is how scared I am. Twelve years I've worked to lay my life on the line for 30 seconds. Then I try to concentrate—"O.K., this is it; it's now or never. Let's pay attention to your tuck, stay strong on the press-out, and be ready for that dismount." I just start coaching myself. (Mahoney, 1979, p. 436)

Although Fenz did not report the thoughts of parachute jumpers, he observed that experienced jumpers were more task oriented whereas novices were more likely to ruminate on their own fears.

**Key Point**

In general, the early anxiety-performance literature suggests that performance is best at a moderate level of arousal, although that precise optimal level varies across individuals, tasks, and situations. The ability to control anxiety is key in separating better and poorer performers.

## SPORT-SPECIFIC APPROACHES

As psychology became more cognitive, sport and exercise psychology adopted more cognitive approaches. In particular, some anxiety measures developed within the research on achievement motivation, and later motivational orientation, discussed in chapter 8 followed cognitive approaches. Atkinson (1974) included the motive to approach success and the motive to avoid failure. Competitiveness reflects the motive to approach success in competitive sport, as discussed in chapter 8. Similarly, in achievement research, anxiety is the typical measure of the motive to avoid failure. Thus, competitive anxiety may be considered the sport-specific counterpart of the motive to avoid failure, or the tendency to become anxious about failure in sport competition.

Although individual differences had no place in the early arousal-performance research, they are obvious in competitive anxiety. Some people, including highly skilled competitors, become physically ill worrying about an upcoming contest, whereas others remain calm and controlled. Individual differences have clear implications for athletes, and competitive anxiety may have implications for other settings. For example, the director of a cardiac rehabilitation program might take special precautions with a highly competitive-anxious participant, even if the program does not emphasize competition, to ensure appropriate levels of exertion and goal setting.

Individual differences in competitive anxiety and the ability to control anxiety are major concerns in competitive sport programs. Many sport psychology consultants spend considerable time helping participants learn to control anxiety. Given the psychology base and the pervasive practical concerns, the extensive research on competitive anxiety and the implications of individual differences for performance is not surprising. Most of that research stems from Martens's (1977) competitive anxiety model and the Sport Competition Anxiety Test.

## Martens's Model of Competitive Anxiety

Competitive anxiety has been a key sport and exercise psychology issue for some time. Competition creates some anxiety in nearly everyone, and intense anxiety keeps some from performing well or enjoying the activity. Most athletes must deal with intense anxiety at some time, and competitors may experience anxiety states ranging from relative calm to utter panic. Martens began with these real-world observations and then built upon existing psychological work and the following four major guidelines:

1. *Interaction approach.* Competitive anxiety illustrates the importance of an interaction approach. Individual differences in competitive anxiety are easy to see, and situational factors play a role. Close, important games create more anxiety than less important contests. Even the calmest athletes may become anxious under some conditions; a family problem, upcoming exam, or the presence of professional scouts might elicit atypically high anxiety. To understand competitive anxiety, we must consider the person, the situation, and the ongoing interactive process.

2. *State-trait anxiety distinction.* Spielberger (1966) set a model for competitive anxiety by distinguishing the relatively stable personality characteristic of trait anxiety from the immediate, changeable feelings associated with state anxiety. *Trait anxiety* is the tendency to become anxious in stressful situations (a personality disposition). *State anxiety* is the actual state of apprehension and tension at any given moment (an emotional response). Spielberger's (1966) approach matches Lazarus's early stress model in that trait anxiety is a personality variable influencing perceived threat (cognitive appraisal). Perceived threat then elicits state anxiety, which is the immediate emotional response (the fight-or-flight reaction and related responses). A high-trait-anxious person might see an upcoming tennis match as a threat and respond with high state anxiety, while another might perceive it as a challenge and remain relatively calm.

3. *General versus specific anxiety.* Although high-trait-anxious persons tend to become anxious in stressful situations, they may not become equally anxious in all situations. One person may become overly anxious in competitive sport, but remain calm in academic exams. Another might never become anxious in competition, but panic in social settings. Before Martens began his work, psychology researchers had demonstrated that situation-specific trait anxiety measures predict state anxiety more accurately than more general anxiety measures. For example, Mandler and Sarason (1952) reported that test-anxiety measures better identified students who became overly anxious in academic situations. Following that line of thought, Martens proposed a sport-specific trait anxiety measure for predicting state anxiety in competitive sports. He proposed the personality construct of *competitive trait anxiety*, defined as "a tendency to perceive competitive situations as threatening and to respond to these situations with feelings of apprehension or tension" (1977, p. 23).

4. *Competition process.* The final step in Martens's theoretical framework was to place competitive anxiety within the context of the competition process described in chapter 8. As figure 11.3 shows, the objective competitive situation represents the situation, and the primary situational source of anxiety in competition is the threat of evaluation. We want to do well and we worry about performing poorly. But everyone does not worry to the same extent. Competitive trait anxiety affects our perceptions of threat and subsequent anxiety through the subjective competitive situation, which is the cognitive appraisal process that is so central to all emotion.

> **Key Point**
>
> Martens's model of competitive anxiety built on the following four major guidelines: (1) interaction approach, (2) state-trait anxiety distinction, (3) general versus specific anxiety, and (4) competition process.

## The Sport Competition Anxiety Test: A Measure of Competitive Anxiety

To investigate competitive anxiety, Martens developed the Sport Competition Anxiety Test (SCAT), a self-report measure. To determine your competitive anxiety, take the SCAT (reproduced in appendix A) and score your test. If you score high (e.g., above the 75th percentile), you probably tend to be quite nervous and tense in competition; if you have a low score you probably control anxiety well and seldom choke in competition.

The items on SCAT are simple and straightforward. You might think Martens could have developed this test in one afternoon, but he didn't. The items are simple and straightforward because extensive psychometric testing indicated that those items best identified high- and low-anxious competitors. The development of SCAT took about five years and involved testing over 4000 people. Details on the development of SCAT with reliability and validity data are published elsewhere (Martens, 1977; Martens et al., 1990). In brief, the SCAT meets and usually exceeds all generally accepted standards for psychological tests. The SCAT is reliable, and considerable lab and field research demonstrates that it predicts state anxiety in sport competition.

To illustrate, we'll consider one field study with high school girls' basketball teams. All players on nine teams completed the SCAT at a practice session, along with a self-report measure of state anxiety. Later, players completed that same state anxiety measure immediately before a game. If SCAT identifies those who become anxious in competition, SCAT should predict these precompetition state anxiety scores. Indeed, high correlations ($r = .64$) between SCAT and precompetition state

**Figure 11.3**

The relationship of competitive anxiety to the competition process.

From R. Martens, 1977, *Sport Competition Anxiety Test* (Champaign, IL: Human Kinetics), 33. Copyright 1977 by Rainer Martens. Adapted by permission.

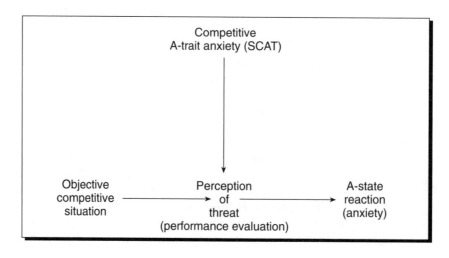

The best performers can control arousal and cognitive worry when they know they must perform.

anxiety confirmed the validity of SCAT. The same basketball players also completed the Trait Anxiety Inventory (TAI; Spielberger et al., 1970), a general trait anxiety measure. If, as Martens proposed, a sport-specific measure of competitive trait anxiety (SCAT) is better than a general measure, then SCAT should be better than the TAI at predicting precompetition state anxiety. It was. The correlation of the TAI and precompetitive state anxiety ($r = .30$) was considerably lower than the correlation for SCAT ($r = .64$). The SCAT is not designed to predict anxiety in other stressful situations, and the correlation of SCAT and state anxiety in the noncompetitive practice setting was considerably lower.

Extensive research with SCAT by Martens and colleagues (for a summary see Martens et al., 1990) consistently demonstrates the validity of SCAT as a predictor of precompetitive state anxiety. The SCAT quickly became one of the few useful personality measures in sport and exercise psychology, and Martens's extensive research and high standards set a model that others have followed to develop sport-specific measures.

The SCAT, a valuable research tool, also has practical value in identifying competitors who might benefit from anxiety management training. As good as SCAT is, though, it is still a personality measure that should not be used without considering the situation. Also, as competitive anxiety research has progressed, we have moved beyond SCAT. As we will discuss later in this chapter, multidimensional models dominate today's research. In fact, Smith, Smoll, and Schutz (1990), who have contributed to sport and exercise psychology in many ways, have developed a multidimensional measure of competitive trait anxiety, the Sport Anxiety Scale, that better fits current models. Moreover, the interaction models that guided Martens and other early work on competitive anxiety fail to capture the dynamic processes and changes in anxiety, other emotional responses, and behaviors in sport and exercise settings.

## MULTIDIMENSIONAL COMPETITIVE ANXIETY MEASURES

Martens's work with SCAT advanced sport and exercise psychology research on anxiety, initiated the shift to sport-specific constructs and measures, and reflects the trends of that time in moving to field research and an interaction perspective considering both the person (competitive trait anxiety) and the situation (competition/noncompetition). Martens and colleagues (Martens et al., 1990) later used a similar approach with state anxiety, and took another important step by looking at anxiety as multidimensional. Psychologists (Borkovec, 1976; Davidson & Schwartz, 1976; Morris et al., 1981) had begun to emphasize multidimensional approaches, with the primary distinction between cognitive and somatic anxiety.

### Sport Anxiety Scale

Before turning to the work on multidimensional state anxiety and advances in the anxiety-performance literature, we will note one important application of the multidimensional approach to competitive trait anxiety. Smith et al. (1990) used the multidimensional anxiety model to develop a sport-specific measure of cognitive and somatic trait anxiety, the Sport Anxiety Scale (SAS). The SAS includes two cognitive anxiety scales—worry and concentration disruption—as well as a somatic anxiety scale. Exploratory and confirmatory factor analyses supported these three factors with several athlete samples. As well as providing good psychometric evidence for the SAS, Smith et al. (1990) reported that the concentration disruption scale was negatively related to college football players' performance. That finding suggests that multidimensional approaches may provide insights into the anxiety-performance relationship; the expanding literature following a multidimensional approach, discussed next, confirms the suggestion.

## Competitive State Anxiety Inventory-2

Just as Smith et al. (1990) adapted multidimensional approaches to anxiety to develop the SAS trait measure, Martens and colleagues (Martens et al., 1990) moved to the development of the multidimensional CSAI-2. The CSAI-2, a sport-specific measure of state anxiety, assesses the separate dimensions of cognitive worry and somatic anxiety. Through the development of the CSAI-2, a third dimension also emerged; that third dimension, labeled self-confidence, appeared to be a cognitive component that was the opposite of cognitive worry. Although Martens et al. (1990) conducted extensive testing and analyses and provided sound evidence for the reliability and validity of the CSAI-2, the self-confidence dimension lacks the conceptual base of the cognitive and somatic dimensions, and its validity for competitive anxiety research is questionable. In fact, many competitive anxiety researchers use only the cognitive and somatic scores.

### Key Point

The SAS includes two cognitive anxiety scales—worry and concentration disruption—as well as a somatic anxiety scale. The CSAI-2, a sport-specific measure of trait anxiety, assesses the separate dimensions of cognitive worry and somatic anxiety.

Research during the development of the CSAI-2, and considerable subsequent work, provide insights into competitive anxiety and anxiety-performance relationships. Although the anxiety subscales are theoretically independent, they are interrelated in most situations. Typically, cognitive and somatic anxiety are moderately related to each other, and both are moderately negatively related to self-confidence. Relationships are interesting, but the differences are more enlightening. In particular, cognitive worry and somatic anxiety show different patterns of change over time. On the basis of existing psychology work, Martens et al. (1990) expected somatic anxiety to rise rapidly and peak immediately before competition—almost an automatic reaction. They expected cognitive worry, which in contrast depends on situational factors, to remain relatively constant before competition and then to increase or decrease depending on the events during competition. In two studies with gymnasts and wrestlers, Martens et al. (1990) confirmed these predictions: cognitive anxiety and self-confidence remained relatively stable before competition while somatic anxiety rapidly increased as time to competition neared. Gould, Petlichkoff, and Weinberg (1984) substantiated these trends with high school volleyball players who completed the CSAI-2 one week, 48 hours, 24 hours, 2 hours, and 20 minutes before competition. As predicted, only somatic anxiety increased over time. These results add to Fenz's (1975) work on arousal patterns, and multidimensional anxiety measures permit further advances in our understanding of anxiety-performance patterns over time.

### Multidimensional Anxiety and Effects on Performance

The CSAI-2 may be most important for having increased our understanding of anxiety and performance. On the basis of multidimensional anxiety theory, Martens et al. (1990) predicted that cognitive anxiety and self-confidence would be stronger predictors of performance than would somatic anxiety, because somatic anxiety dissipates at the onset of competition. In their study with golfers, however, CSAI-2 scores did not predict performance (Martens et al., 1990). Later, Burton (1988) used the CSAI-2 and more precise performance measures with intercollegiate swimmers over the season. Burton predicted an inverted-U relationship between somatic anxiety and performance but a negative linear relationship between cognitive anxiety and performance (and a positive linear relationship between self-confidence and performance). The results confirmed those predictions and supported the application of multidimensional anxiety theory to competitive sport. Gould, Petlichkoff, Simons, and Vevera (1987) used a similar intraindividual approach to compare CSAI-2 scores and shooting performance at a police training institute. The results supported the inverted-U relationship of somatic anxiety and performance but did not show a relationship between cognitive anxiety and performance. As Martens et al. (1990) noted in their comprehensive review of the CSAI-2 research, other studies failed to find anxiety-performance relationships, and we cannot draw definitive conclusions. This inconsistency has prompted consideration of other multidimensional approaches and more elaborate models of the anxiety-performance relationship.

# CURRENT ANXIETY-PERFORMANCE MODELS

Rather than consider multiple dimensions separately, the most recent models have addressed interactions. As an example of one simple interaction, if cognitive anxiety is positive (confidence, no worry), then somatic anxiety or physiological arousal is positively related to performance; but if cognitive anxiety is negative (high worry), then somatic anxiety and performance are negatively related. Although this is not a theory, reversal theory as proposed by Kerr (1990) and Martens's (1987a) discussion of psychic energy in his coaching psychology book, express similar views.

## Reversal Theory

Reversal theory, first advanced as a general framework for arousal and emotional affect (Apter, 1984), holds that the relationship between arousal and affect depends on one's cognitive interpretation of arousal (again, cognitive appraisal is the key). High arousal may be interpreted in positive terms as excitement, or negatively as anxiety. Similarly, low arousal may be interpreted as relaxation (positive) or boredom (negative). Both arousal and interpretive affect vary on a continuum, and reversal theory also adds that a person may switch from one curve to the other—a reversal. Kerr (1985, 1990) has adapted reversal theory to competitive anxiety with arousal and stress (cognitive) dimensions that yield four quadrants: overstimulation (anxiety), understimulation (boredom/fatigue), sleep, and excitement. Perhaps the most important guidelines from reversal theory are that arousal may be either positive or negative and that cognitive interpretation makes all the difference in the anxiety-performance relationship.

### Key Point

Reversal theory holds that the relationship between arousal and affect depends on one's cognitive interpretation of arousal. High arousal may be interpreted positively—excitement—or negatively—anxiety. Low arousal may be interpreted positively—relaxation—or negatively—boredom.

## Catastrophe Model of Anxiety

One intriguing interactive model that has gained attention is catastrophe theory, which several sport psychologists in Great Britain, particularly Lew Hardy (1990, 1996), have promoted. Notably, the catastrophe model includes an interaction similar to the example cited in the first paragraph of this section on current models; but it's much more complex, with three-dimensional, nonlinear relationships. Performance changes depend on the interaction of physiological arousal and cognitive anxiety, but the relationships are not simple. Catastrophe theory suggests that as arousal increases, performance increases up to a point (as in the inverted-U), but as arousal gets beyond the optimal level, performance drops abruptly as the athlete goes over the edge—a catastrophe. Moreover, the athlete who has gone over the edge and tries to regain control, to return to an optimal level, cannot simply go back on the same path. Instead, he or she must go back to much lower anxiety levels to get on track and then gradually build up again. These statements seem reasonable, but showing the process on the model and demonstrating it empirically are a challenge, to say the least. The mathematics are complex, and testing the relationships requires multiple, precise, consistent, and valid measures of both anxiety and performance—and that is easier said than done.

## Key Point

Catastrophe theory suggests that as arousal increases, performance increases up to a point (as in the inverted-U), but as arousal gets beyond the optimal level, performance drops abruptly as the athlete goes over the edge—a catastrophe. Moreover, the athlete who has gone over the edge and tries to regain control, to return to an optimal level, cannot simply go back on the same path. Instead, he or she must go back to much lower anxiety levels to get on track and then gradually build up again.

Hardy (1996) recently clarified the catastrophe model, offered methodological suggestions for testing its predictions, and discussed more practical applications. Hardy's interpretation, informed by his extensive research with the model and with competitive anxiety, provides a helpful guide for researchers who wish to apply catastrophe theory.

First, as Hardy (1996) emphasizes, the catastrophe model is a model, not a theory. It presents testable predictions, but not explanations. The cusp catastrophe model originally proposed by Hardy and Fazey (1987) was developed from catastrophe theory, which had been developed by mathematician Rene Thom (1975) and later extended to the behavioral sciences (Guastello, 1987). Hardy and Fazey saw the catastrophe model as a way to advance from the multidimensional anxiety model, and specifically to incorporate the interaction of anxiety components. Multidimensional anxiety theory (Martens et al., 1990; Burton, 1988) proposes different anxiety-performance relationships for cognitive and somatic anxiety, but does not consider any interactive influences. As well as incorporating an interaction of cognitive anxiety and arousal, the catastrophe model clearly defines physiological arousal as one key dimension, rather than perceived somatic anxiety as assessed with the CSAI-2. The specific model, relationships, and predictions can easily overwhelm researchers; but three key predictions, as explained next, provide guidance (Hardy, 1996).

### Interactive Effects

First, the model describes combined, interactive effects of cognitive anxiety and physiological arousal on performance. As first explained by Hardy and Fazey (1987), the model proposes that high cognitive anxiety will lead to enhanced performance when physiological arousal is low (e.g., days before competition) but to impaired performance when physiological arousal is high (e.g., on game day). The interaction becomes more complex, and the model must be modified to account for varied situational and individual variables. Edwards and Hardy (1996) provided some support for interactive effects in a study of netball players using a modified CSAI-2 with a directional scale assessing the facilitative or debilitative interpretation of anxiety. They found the predicted interaction, with the combination of low physiological arousal and high cognitive anxiety leading to better performance than low physiological arousal and low cognitive anxiety. However, the combination of high physiological arousal and high cognitive anxiety led to worse performance than that of high physiological arousal and low cognitive anxiety.

### Facilitative Versus Debilitative Effects

Hardy emphasizes—in contrast to most views that cognitive worry is always debilitating—that cognitive anxiety can sometimes enhance performance. Specifically, the model predicts that performers' best performances should be better, and their worst performances worse, when they perform under high cognitive anxiety than under low cognitive anxiety. Edwards and Hardy did not find any directional facilitative effects in their study, but earlier work (Hardy & Parfitt, 1991; Hardy, Parfitt, & Pates, 1994) supported this hypothesis.

### Hysteresis Effects

The third feature, hysteresis, is particularly intriguing. Hysteresis is a mathematical term, and in terms of the model, it implies that the graph of performance against physiological arousal follows a different path when arousal is increasing than when arousal is decreasing. Performance increases as arousal increases until arousal hits that peak when performance suddenly drops off sharply. As the athlete tries to gain control and decrease arousal, performance does not jump back up, but stays low and only begins to rise gradually as arousal returns to much lower levels. Hysteresis explains the sudden drop-off or choking phenomenon, and the differing paths have implications for practical issues related to control and recovery.

In discussing practical applications of the catastrophe model, Hardy (1996) first highlights the notion that cognitive anxiety is not necessarily detrimental to performance. This may be the most contentious aspect of the model. Hardy suggests that cognitive anxiety is most likely to be beneficial when performers have low physiological arousal and interpret their anxiety as beneficial; in the real world, those conditions may be difficult to achieve.

Second, Hardy notes that if cognitively anxious performers become too physiologically aroused they will reach that "choke" point, and performance will drop suddenly and dramatically. Recovery will be faster if cognitive anxiety and physiological arousal are addressed simultaneously. Hardy proposes a multimodal stress management approach, advising coaches and sport psychologists to use psyching-up strategies with great caution. Although cognitive anxiety and physiological arousal can be beneficial, there's a fine line between peak performance and disaster.

## Summary

Anxiety is one of the most prevalent topics in sport and exercise psychology. We have drawn upon several anxiety-performance models and made progress with sport-specific models and measures. Early work based on drive and inverted-U models led to general guidelines, but few conclusions. Generally, performance is best at an optimal level of physiological arousal. However, that optimal level varies with the individual, activity, and situation. Further probing of the anxiety-performance relationship, examining anxiety patterns over time, reveals that the ability to control anxiety is key in separating better and poorer performers. Better performers can control arousal and cognitive worry when they must perform, and initial work suggests that cognitive or thought patterns may play a central role in controlling anxiety.

The work of Martens and his colleagues, particularly the development of the sport-specific SCAT, helped us better understand individual differences in competitive anxiety and initiated the move to sport-specific measures. Subsequent work with multidimensional approaches considering the cognitive worry and physiological arousal or somatic anxiety dimensions, including the development of the CSAI-2 state measure, has produced further insights but also more questions and variations. Specifically, cognitive and somatic anxiety seem to have different antecedents, different relationships to performance, and different implications for practice (e.g., stress management). Generally, somatic anxiety seems to rise early, peak immediately before competition, and dissipate thereafter. Cognitive worry, in contrast, is relatively stable prior to competition and then varies depending on events during competition. Multidimensional anxiety-performance predictions are more complex, and research results are inconsistent. Some approaches, such as multidimensional anxiety theory (e.g., Martens et al., 1990), suggest that cognitive worry is always debilitating; but others (e.g., Hardy, 1990, 1996) suggest more complex interactions.

Multidimensional approaches including cognitive and physiological arousal dimensions have advanced beyond earlier models. The cognitive dimension fits the cognitive appraisal role of current emotion models. Physiological arousal appears idiosyncratic, and cognitive and physiological components interact in complex ways—also as implied in current emotion models. Research examining anxiety patterns over time provides more insight than do isolated one-time measures on anxiety and the anxiety-performance relationship—and begins to get at the dynamic nature of anxiety in sport and exercise settings. We have moved closer to the emotion models as we have advanced the research on competitive anxiety, and we may progress further if we move beyond the focus on anxiety to consider multiple emotional processes in sport and exercise.

## Review Questions

1. Discuss the cognitive, physiological, and behavioral measures of anxiety.
2. Compare and contrast drive theory and the inverted-U hypothesis, and identify the element missing from each theory.
3. Explain how Fenz's (1975, 1988) work supports the idea that anxiety control training may benefit athletes.
4. Describe the general findings of the early anxiety-performance literature.
5. Explain the four major guidelines of Martens's model of competitive anxiety.
6. Explain how the SCAT works.
7. Compare the measures of the SAS and the CSAI-2.
8. Define the following current anxiety-performance models: reversal theory and the catastrophe model.

## Recommended Reading

★ Martens, R., Vealey, R.S., & Burton, D. (1990). *Competitive anxiety in sport*. Champaign, IL: Human Kinetics.

> Martens and colleagues began the move toward sport-specific constructs and measures with the development of the Sport Competition Anxiety Test (SCAT) in the 1970s. They followed with the development of multidimensional sport-specific state anxiety measure in the 1980s. This book presents the background literature, theoretical models, related research, and information on both the SCAT and CSAI-2 measures.

★ Smith, R.E., Smoll, F.L., & Schutz, R.W. (1990). Measurement and correlates of sport-specific cognitive and somatic trait anxiety: The Sport Anxiety Scale. *Anxiety Research, 2,* 263-280.

> Smith and colleagues followed up Martens's work with a multidimensional sport-specific measure, the Sport Anxiety Scale, which matches current theory better than the SCAT. This article includes background information as well as information on the development of the SAS.

★ Hardy, L. (1996). Testing the predictions of the cusp catastrophe
model of anxiety and performance. *The Sport Psychologist, 10,*
140-156.

Hardy is a leader in applying catastrophe theory to anxiety and sport performance. Although catastrophe theory is mathematically and theoretically complex, this article is one of the most readable and understandable presentations. If you are interested in anxiety and performance, you would do well to read this article, even if you do not specifically test catastrophe theory.

# Psychological Interventions for Indidivuals

So far in this book we have emphasized research and theories. Now, in part IV, we'll shift to practice. Specifically, we'll draw from the chapters on emotion and competitive anxiety, as well as work on individual differences and motivation, and see how that work applies to psychological interventions for individuals in sport and exercise settings.

Psychological skills training with athletes has expanded tremendously over the last 10 years, and the expansion includes related applied research. This section does not provide a detailed guide to sport and exercise psychology practice; readers might see several applied sport psychology texts for further information (e.g., Murphy, 1995; Van Raalte & Brewer, 1996; Williams, 1998). Indeed, this section borrows liberally from those sources to provide an overview of psychological interventions.

In chapter 12 we'll focus on widely used cognitive interventions, specifically goal setting, attention and thought control, and imagery. In chapter 13 we'll look at specific physical relaxation techniques and move into more comprehensive stress management programs. Finally, in chapter 14, we'll cover comprehensive psychological interventions and psychological skills training, as well as issues that arise when applied sport and exercise psychology extends beyond performance enhancement.

# chapter 12

# Cognitive Interventions

## CHAPTER OBJECTIVES

After studying this chapter, you should be able to

- understand the importance of goal setting in sport and exercise settings,
- explain several attentional control and concentration techniques, and
- explain the use of imagery in psychological skills training.

As discussed in several chapters, cognition or thoughts are the key to many sport and exercise behaviors. Self-efficacy (chapter 6) often predicts performance more strongly than does actual physical ability. Perceptions are keys to understanding participation, persistence, and achievement and are central to emotional processes. Thus, psychological interventions aimed at controlling thoughts are often effective at helping individuals control behavior and enhance their sport and exercise experiences.

This chapter will cover three specific cognitive interventions, starting with goal setting. One of the first things most individuals do when beginning an activity is to set goals, and goal setting is typically the first step in sport and exercise psychology consultation. After considering research and guidelines on goal setting, we'll turn to attention and thought control strategies. Finally, we'll consider imagery, one of the most popular sport and exercise psychology techniques.

## GOAL SETTING

Goals are so common that they are almost unavoidable. Participants usually hold multiple goals, and even if they do not form goals, teachers, coaches, exercise instructors, family, or friends will often set goals for them. Common as they are, though, goals are not automatically effective. Researchers and practitioners quickly learn that it is much easier to set goals than to make them work effectively (Burton, 1993).

A goal is that which an individual is trying to accomplish, a standard of excellence. Additionally, a goal typically refers to a specific level of proficiency on a task, usually within a time limit (Locke, Shaw, Saari, & Latham, 1981). For example, we might set a goal to cut three strokes off our golf game, to lose 10 pounds, or to run a personal best in a 10K event. As Weinberg (1996) notes, these typical goals are "objective" goals, but we might also hold "subjective" goals, such as having fun or trying our best.

Not only are goals common, but goals work! Goal setting has been a popular research topic since the 1960s, when Locke began his influential studies. Locke and colleagues, and many others, have examined goal setting, primarily in industrial and organizational environments. The extensive literature reviewed by Locke et al. in 1981 indicated consistent benefits of goal setting for performance. The literature has continued to accumulate, and updated reviews (Locke & Latham, 1990; Mento, Steel, & Karren, 1987; Tubbs, 1986) add detail but continue to confirm the benefits.

Locke and Latham (1985) proposed that the goal-setting model should work even better for sport, with its easily measured objective performance standards. Several sport and exercise psychologists have investigated goal setting and specifically applied Locke's model; readers should consult reviews by Weinberg (1994, 1996), Burton (1993), or Gould (1993) for more details on these studies.

## Locke and Latham's Theory of Goal Setting

Locke and Latham (1990) developed a theoretical framework for goal setting. First, they concluded that goal setting is effective. Of over 200 studies reviewed, more than 90% confirmed their primary prediction that specific, difficult goals enhance performance more than vague, easy ("do your best") goals or no goals. Then Locke and Latham proposed a mechanism by which goal setting enhances performance, including four components:

1. Directing attention
2. Mobilizing effort
3. Enhancing persistence
4. Developing new learning strategies

Burton (1993) applied the Locke and Latham model to goal setting in sport, listing four major attributes that influence goal effectiveness:

1. **Goal difficulty.** Locke and Latham propose a linear relationship, arguing that more difficult goals lead to better performance, and reviews and meta-analyses consistently confirm this prediction (Mento et al., 1987; Tubbs, 1986; Wood et al., 1987) and suggest moderate effect sizes.

2. **Goal specificity.** Goal difficulty is the cornerstone, but Locke and Latham argue that specific difficult goals are even better. Specific easy goals do not enhance performance.

3. **Goal temporality.** Temporality refers to short-term and long-term goals. Some (e.g., Bandura, 1986) argue that short-term goals are more effective, permitting more frequent evaluation that helps to develop confidence and sense of accomplishment. Burton (1989) holds that short-term goals are more flexible and controllable. However, others caution that short-term goals with overly frequent evaluation can foster a loss of control and detract from intrinsic motivation (e.g., Kirschenbaum, 1985).

4. **Goal collectivity.** Group goals enhance performance just as individual goals do (Locke & Latham, 1990).

Locke and Latham's model includes four moderator variables as well as the four main attributes. Specifically, goal effectiveness may depend on the following:

- **Ability.** Locke and Latham suggest an interaction with goal difficulty. If difficult goals are impossible for a low-ability individual, the person soon reaches a plateau, and goals are ineffective. Therefore, difficult goals are more effective for high-ability people.

- **Commitment.** Highly committed people match their goals, whether goals are difficult or easy. Therefore, high commitment helps only with difficult goals.

- **Feedback.** Both goals and feedback are necessary for performance enhancement. Feedback may enhance efficacy and perceived ability, or may allow for the adjustment of task strategies.

- **Task complexity.** Locke and Latham suggest that task complexity is a moderator, but the exact mechanisms are not clear. More complex tasks may require developing new task strategies before motivational effects can make new strategies work.

## Goal Setting in Sport

Although sport and exercise psychology researchers have examined the Locke and Latham goal-setting model, the results have not been as consistent as in organizational psychology; they are equivocal and do not support all predictions (Burton, 1993; Weinberg, 1994, 1996). Goal setting is effective in sport, but not consistently so. Burton and Weinberg both conclude that specific, difficult, challenging goals improve performance more than "do-your-best" or no goals, although they cite inconsistent results. Kyllo and Landers (1995) used meta-analysis techniques to synthesize the research on goal setting in sport. They concluded that overall, setting goals improves performance by .34 of a standard deviation and that moderate, absolute, and combined short- and long-term goals are associated with the greatest effects. Despite the popularity of goal setting in sport, the research is limited (Burton, 1993). Weinberg (1994) argued that some inconsistency may be due to differing methodologies and moderators in sport (e.g., spontaneous goal setting in control conditions, subject motivation and commitment, task characteristics, and competition) and to the fact that motivation and performance conditions for athletes and exercisers differ from those of other subjects.

Weinberg (1996) classifies Locke and Latham's theory as "mechanistic," in contrast with "cognitive" explanations that emphasize psychological states such as anxiety, confidence, or goal orientations. Burton (1993) proposed a goal-setting model that incorporates motivational orientation (as discussed in chapter 8) and suggests that individual orientation and perceived ability, as well as Locke and Latham's attributes, influence goal setting in sport. Burton (1989) conducted a five-month goal-setting program emphasizing performance goals (improvement) over outcome goals (winning) with swimmers. Athletes who were better at performance goals were less anxious and performed better, demonstrating that goal-setting skills can be learned and developed through practice.

We are interested in goal setting in the real world of athletes or exercisers. "Real-world" settings differ from the environments of most goal-setting research and involve more complex, dynamic relationships. Still, goal setting is popular, and some research supports the process. Gould, Tammen, Murphy, and May (1989) reported that goal setting was the psychological intervention most often used by sport psychologists working with U.S. Olympic athletes. Similarly, Orlick and Partington (1988) reported extensive goal-setting by Canadian Olympic athletes. In addition to Burton's, a study by Weinberg, Stitcher, and Richardson (1994) showed that goal setting was effective over a season with lacrosse players.

Many goal-setting studies in sport and exercise psychology tested Locke's predictions with typical research designs rather than real-world interventions. Using an alternative design, Weinberg, Burton, Yukelson, and Weigand (1993) surveyed athletes at three universities to determine actual goal-setting practices and views. Virtually all the athletes set goals, and most considered goal setting moderately to highly effective. Athletes rated overall performance goals as most important, followed by winning, fun, and skill development; they rated conditioning, psychological skills development, social affiliation, and strategy goals as less important. Among several group differences, females used goal setting more frequently and found it more effective than did male athletes.

Burton (1993) noted that (a) athletes set more goals for competition than for practice; (b) athletes set performance, outcome, and skill-development goals more often than strategy, psychological skills, motivation, and confidence goals; (c) outcome goals were sometimes more important than performance goals; and (d) athletes sometimes set goals that were too difficult, creating stress. Burton suggested interventions that include educating athletes about the role of performance goals, about the use of goal setting for psychological skills and strategies, and about setting practice as well as competition goals.

## Goal-Setting Principles

The extensive research on goal setting, the more limited sport and exercise psychology research, and the reports of those who have conducted goal-setting interventions have led to guidelines for using goal setting effectively. The following list, from Weinberg (1996), is representative:

- **Set specific goals.** One of the most consistent research findings, and a cornerstone of key theories, is that specific goals enhance performance more than "do-your-best" or no goals. Rather than setting the goal of improving free throw shooting or walking more regularly, set specific goals such as improving from 70% to 85% on free throws or walking one mile three days each week.
- **Set realistic but challenging goals.** Goals should be challenging but attainable. The secret is finding a balance between setting oneself up for failure and pushing oneself too hard (Weinberg, 1996). In the middle ground reside challenging, realistic, attainable goals.
- **Set both short- and long-term goals.** Athletes and exercisers typically have long-term goals, which provide a destination. However, short-term goals are important for providing feedback about the long-term goal progress, adjusting goals, setting attainable smaller increments, and generally giving more behavioral direction.
- **Set goals for both practice and competition.** Although competition goals are appropriate, practice goals should not be forgotten with an overemphasis on outcomes. Practice goals can help focus attention and effort, help one develop strategies, and create a more "real" and motivating situation.
- **"Ink it, don't think it."** Many authors advocate writing down and recording goals. Moreover, the goals should be placed where they will be visible and salient.
- **Develop goal-achievement strategies.** Developing strategies is a key mechanism in Locke's model. As well as setting goals, individuals should identify strategies for reaching them. For example, how can one achieve the goal of improving free throw percentage?—perhaps by changing technique or through specific practice drills.
- **Set performance goals.** Goals should focus on individual performance rather than outcomes.
- **Set individual and team goals.** Individual goals have a place in team activities, as long as they do not conflict with team goals but rather focus on the individual's contribution to the team.
- **Provide support for goals.** Social support plays a role in goal attainment; showing a genuine concern for athletes, students, or exercisers provides goal support.
- **Evaluate goals.** It is important that people receive feedback on goal effectiveness as well as on actual performance.

From R. Weinberg, 1996, Goal setting in sport and exercise. In *Exploring sport and exercise psychology,* edited by J.L. Van Raalte and B.W. Brewer (Washington, DC: American Psychological Association), 3-24. Copyright © 1996 by the American Psychological Association. Reprinted with permission.

## Common Goal-Setting Problems

Of course, no intervention is perfect. Some common problems in goal setting, again from Weinberg (1996), are the following:

- **Failure to monitor goal progress and readjust goals.** People often start off strong and set lots of goals, but then lose track of them. Reevaluation can help keep people motivated and on track.

- **Failure to recognize individual differences.** Goal setting should differ among individuals. Giannini, Weinberg, and Jackson (1988) found goal effectiveness maximized when goal orientations matched goals. That is, task-oriented individuals are more motivated by self-improvement goals, whereas ego-oriented individuals are more motivated by outcome goals.

- **Failure to set specific, measurable goals.** People often set general goals (e.g., improving my serve, or my fitness); consultants can help identify more specific goals.

- **Setting too many goals.** Individuals often set too many goals and have difficulty monitoring and tracking them. Consultants can help people focus on priorities and set only a few initial goals.

From R. Weinberg, 1996, Goal setting in sport and exercise. In *Exploring sport and exercise psychology*, edited by J.L. Van Raalte and B.W. Brewer (Washington, DC: American Psychological Association), 3-24. Copyright © 1996 by the American Psychological Association. Reprinted with permission.

# COGNITIVE CONTROL STRATEGIES

In chapter 5 we discussed attention, including Nideffer's (1976a) classification of attentional styles. Nideffer's work is the basis for some popular attention control interventions, and Nideffer himself was among the first to use cognitive interventions in sport psychology consultation. In this section, we will consider attentional control and concentration strategies, including Nideffer's (1993) Attentional Control Training as well as self-talk and cognitive restructuring techniques.

## Attentional Control and Concentration

Concentration is a key psychological skill, and we often tell participants to "keep your eye on the ball" or "focus on the feelings." As with most psychological skills, it is much easier to tell someone (or ourselves) to concentrate than to convey how to do it. Concentration implies control of attention. As discussed in chapter 5, Nideffer proposed a model of attentional style with direction (internal-external) and width (broad-narrow) dimensions. According to Nideffer, although preferred styles differ, individuals can improve their use of various styles as well as their ability to shift styles. Nideffer (1993) developed Attentional Control Training (ACT) according to those principles.

Attentional Control Training is more than a simple cognitive technique, and it moves into relaxation approaches discussed in the next chapter. The main technique in ACT is centering, which involves relaxing muscles, breathing deeply, and focusing on feelings with exhalation. Attentional Control Training (Nideffer, 1993) also involves assessing individual attentional strengths and weaknesses (with the Test of Attentional and Interpersonal Style), assessing the attentional demands of the sport, assessing the situation and/or personal characteristics that affect arousal and/or dictate behavior under pressure, identifying situation-specific problem areas, and developing an intervention program. For more information, see Nideffer's (1993) case examples of ACT with athletes.

> **Key Point**
>
> Nideffer's Attentional Control Training includes the technique of centering, as well as several assessments of situation-specific and personal characteristics. The aim of the training is to develop a personalized intervention program to target an individual's specific problem areas.

Schmid and Peper (1998) list several strategies for developing concentration skills that most sport and exercise participants could easily use. These strategies are either external, focusing on avoiding distractions, or internal, emphasizing staying centered.

### External Strategies to Keep Concentration

External strategies for developing concentration entail various kinds of rehearsal (Schmid & Peper, 1993):

1. *Dress rehearsal.* Dress rehearsal—with such elements as music, uniforms, announcements, and lights matching competition conditions—is particularly effective for sports such as gymnastics, diving, and figure skating.

2. *Rehearsal of simulated competition experiences.* As with dress rehearsal, athletes practice concentrating and dissociating from disruptive stimuli. Simulated competition might involve tapes of competition sounds or crowd noises.

3. *Mental rehearsal.* Mental rehearsal, visualization, or imagery is one of the most widely used and useful cognitive strategies; we will cover imagery in more detail in the next section. One use of imagery is for controlling attention and practicing concentration.

### Internal Strategies to Stay Centered

Internal centering strategies can help train the mind to stay on track (Schmid & Peper, 1993):

1. *Attentional cues and triggers.* Many athletes use verbal or kinesthetic cues to focus concentration or retrigger lost concentration. For example, a free throw shooter may focus on the rim, or a swimmer might focus on the feel of the hand pulling through the water.

2. *Turning failure into success.* With this strategy, one mentally rehearses a successful performance immediately after a failure. After a disastrous free exercise routine, a gymnast might immediately visualize the great routine of last week's meet.

3. *Use of electrodermal feedback.* Electrodermal feedback may be used to show how thoughts affect the body, to monitor relaxation, to identify stressful points during imagery, and to facilitate concentration training. Biofeedback companies sell equipment that measures skin conductance, which indicates arousal. Such devices might be used while an athlete is thinking of an anxiety-provoking situation to illustrate the effects of thoughts on the body.

4. *Increasing focusing and refocusing skills.* Focus training involves bringing attention back when it starts to wander, as in meditation. Schmid and Peper suggest four techniques. First, using *mindfulness,* the person sits quietly and sees how long he or she can stay focused on a single thought. With *one pointing,* the individual looks at an action photo or an object (e.g., a tennis ball) and keeps the focus on that point.

The simple *grid exercise* is used in several psychological skills programs (Harris & Harris, 1984). The grid (see example in figure 12.1) is a $10 \times 10$ block of numbers from 00 to 99 in random locations. The task is to mark off consecutive numbers from 00 to as high as possible, usually within a time such as 2 minutes. The exercise can take various forms. For example, people might try the exercise once as just described and then with background distracting sounds. Athletes may also use different grids and try variations (e.g., going backward). The point is to practice the attentional skills of scanning and focusing (e.g., in soccer one scans the field of play and then focuses on the pass). However, as with most concentration exercises, the value of the grid exercise in generalizing to practice and competition conditions is questionable.

Schmid and Peper (1993) also suggest *video games* as a fourth technique for focusing and refocusing, and we might easily modify that to suggest computerized concentration exercises. As with other focusing exercises, the transition from the computer lab to the playing field can be a big leap. Exercises that incorporate some of these focusing techniques in the actual sport or exercise setting are likely to be more effective than exercises that do not have transitional steps to tie the skills to the activity.

5. *Developing performing protocols.* Schmid and Peper (1993) suggest that athletes might tune in to their ideal performance by associating concentration with certain

**Figure 12.1**
Grid concentration exercise.

Reprinted, by permission, from D.V. Harris and B.L. Harris, 1984, *The athlete's guide to sports psychology* (New York: Leisure Press), 189.

**Directions:** Beginning with 00, put a slash through each number in the proper sequence.

| 84 | 27 | 51 | 78 | 59 | 52 | 13 | 85 | 61 | 55 |
|----|----|----|----|----|----|----|----|----|----|
| 28 | 60 | 92 | 04 | 97 | 90 | 31 | 57 | 29 | 33 |
| 32 | 96 | 65 | 39 | 80 | 77 | 49 | 86 | 18 | 70 |
| 76 | 87 | 71 | 95 | 98 | 81 | 01 | 46 | 88 | 00 |
| 48 | 82 | 89 | 47 | 35 | 17 | 10 | 42 | 62 | 34 |
| 44 | 67 | 93 | 11 | 07 | 43 | 72 | 94 | 69 | 56 |
| 53 | 79 | 05 | 22 | 54 | 74 | 58 | 14 | 91 | 02 |
| 06 | 68 | 99 | 75 | 26 | 15 | 41 | 66 | 20 | 40 |
| 50 | 09 | 64 | 08 | 38 | 30 | 36 | 45 | 83 | 24 |
| 03 | 73 | 21 | 23 | 16 | 37 | 25 | 19 | 12 | 63 |

Comments:

performance rituals. Other sport psychologists refer to preperformance routines, suggesting that consistently practiced protocols will automatically trigger focused attention that leads to good performance. For example, Boutcher and Crews (1987) demonstrated that the use of a preshot concentration routine improved putting performance.

Most top athletes have developed their own mental strategies for concentration (Schmid & Peper, 1993). Concentration is not an innate ability, but a skill acquired through training and practice.

## Self-Talk

Self-talk is the key to cognitive control, according to some (Zinsser, Bunker, & Williams, 1998; Williams & Leffingwell, 1996). Self-talk occurs whenever an individual thinks—whether the "talk" is spoken aloud or silent—and makes perceptions and beliefs conscious. Nearly all athletes use self-talk, but we have little research or advice on the technique.

Early research on psychological skills (see chapter 4), such as Mahoney and Avener's (1987) study of Olympic gymnasts, indicated that elite athletes use considerable self-talk, often as self-coaching. As discussed in chapter 5, verbal persuasion is one source of self-efficacy. Self-talk (e.g., "I can do it; keep your head down") can be as effective as verbal persuasion from others. Highlen and Bennett (1983) reported that divers who qualified for the Pan-American Games used more positive self-instruction and less praising self-talk than nonqualifiers. Orlick and Partington (1988) found that Olympic athletes often used positive self-statements as part of a precompetition plan, and Gould, Eklund, & Jackson (1992) reported that self-talk was a common technique for fostering positive expectations and focusing attention of Olympic wrestlers.

Other largely descriptive studies suggest that self-talk is common and has many uses. Van Raalte, Brewer, Rivera, and Petitpas (1994), using observation and behavioral assessments with junior tennis players, found that negative self-talk was associated with losing. Rushall, Hall, Roux, Sasseville, and Rushall (1988) investigated three types of positive self-talk (task-relevant statements, mood words, and positive self-statements) with cross-country skiers and reported positive performance effects for all three. Overall, these studies indicate that positive self-talk helps athletes.

### Uses of Self-Talk

Self-talk has many uses in sport and exercise settings; Williams and Leffingwell (1996) offer the following list:

- **Correcting bad habits.** Self-coaching or self-instruction (e.g., "Keep your eye on the ball, follow through") can help athletes correct bad habits that have become automatic.

Athletes may use self-talk during competition to help correct bad habits, focus their attention, or maintain the behaviors that have been effective.

- **Focusing attention.** Cue words or statements such as "be here" and "track the ball" can help focus and maintain attention.

- **Modifying activation.** Self-talk (e.g., "easy," "get pumped") can help the athlete modify activation or arousal to reach an optimal emotional state.

- **Building self-confidence.** As discussed in chapter 6, self-confidence is a psychological key to excellence. As in the story "The Little Engine That Could," if we keep repeating "I think I can," eventually we will.

- **Increasing efficacy and maintaining exercise behavior.** Although most sport and exercise literature on psychological skills and self-talk focuses on athletes, self-talk is equally applicable to exercise. As noted in chapter 6, self-efficacy is central in exercise adoption and adherence, and self-talk that builds confidence should work for exercisers and potential exercisers. Gauvin (1990) indicates that persistent exercisers use positive and motivational self-talk while dropouts and sedentaries use self-defeating negative self-talk.

### Characteristics of Self-Talk

For self-talk to be effective, the user first must be aware of the self-talk and its effects and then see whether it needs to be modified. Williams and Leffingwell (1993) listed the following techniques for identifying self-talk:

- **Retrospection.** The individual reflects back on exceptionally good and poor performances and then tries to recall the preceding and subsequent thoughts and feelings (the self-talk). Retrospection is more effective soon after performance, before events are forgotten. Videotapes of performance, or prompts from a consultant, may facilitate recall.

- **Imagery.** Imagery, which seems to have limitless uses, may help identify self-talk. Athletes proficient at imagery can recreate performances to recall thoughts and feelings.

- **Observation.** A sport psychology consultant or other observer can record self-talk while an athlete goes through self-talk out loud.

- **Self-talk logs.** Daily records of self-talk, perhaps including details of the situation and the performance, can increase awareness. A tape recorder may sometimes be helpful.

After identifying effective and ineffective self-talk patterns, one can modify them. Bunker et al. (1993) and Williams and Leffingwell (1996) offer similar lists of commonly used self-talk modification techniques:

- **Thought stopping.** The person uses a cue to interrupt unwanted thoughts as they occur. A common technique is to quickly and clearly say (or yell), "Stop!" as soon as that unwanted thought comes into your mind. Some people use visual cues (e.g., visualizing a red stoplight) or physical cues (e.g., snapping the fingers). Thought stopping is a great wake-up call, but you must then substitute a positive thought.

- **Changing negative to positive thoughts.** Switch from the negative thought to a constructive one: for example, "I always hit into the lake on this hole"—STOP! "But when I take a smooth, easy backswing, I have a solid, straight drive." When we are standing at the tee, we cannot always think of those positive substitute thoughts. Many consultants suggest listing the typical negative thoughts and writing a positive substitute next to each one. This may make it easier to retrieve the replacement thoughts in stressful situations.

- **Countering.** Changing negative to positive thoughts is not very effective if the athlete still believes the negative thought. Countering is an internal debate, using reason to directly challenge self-defeating thoughts. For example, when the heart pounds and muscles tighten, saying "I am calm" is not likely to be

Positive self-talk tends to have positive effects on performance whereas negative self-talk interferes with performance.

effective. To counter the negative self-talk, the athlete might say, "This happens to everyone; when I breathe easily and focus on my shot, I do fine."

- **Reframing.** People often view the world in narrow, rigid terms; reframing changes that perspective. For example, the freshman who starts off with a less-than-stellar season after a glorious high school record might reframe the situation as one in which to learn new skills and develop strategies for the higher-level play.

- **Cognitive restructuring.** Many relatively simple techniques for modifying self-talk and developing concentration relate to cognitive restructuring. Several cognitive techniques come out of cognitive-behavioral therapy, particularly from Beck (1970), Ellis (1982; Ellis & Dryden, 1987), and Meichenbaum (1977). All these programs focus on cognitive restructuring.

### Negative Self-Talk

According to Ellis (1982), among others, the many "irrational" or distorted thoughts that we all hold are debilitating. In therapeutic settings, irrational thinking might be the basis of depression or other clinical disorders. In sport and exercise, such thinking can interfere with performance and detract from the overall experience. Gauron (1984) cited the following list of distorted thoughts common to athletes:

- **Perfection is essential.** Many athletes think they must be perfect all the time. No one is perfect. Such thoughts are irrational and may lead to excessive fear of failure.

- **Catastrophizing.** Catastrophizing often accompanies perfectionism, as the athlete turns any little error into a disaster. Moreover, the catastrophizing athlete gives a lot of thought to "what ifs" (e.g., "What if I strike out?").

- **Worth depends on achievement.** Many athletes think their worth depends on their athletic achievements ("I'm nothing if I don't win this tournament").
- **Personalization.** Personal worth may be linked to the self-defeating tendency to personalize everything (if some spectators laugh, they're laughing at you).
- **Fallacy of fairness.** Fair, in this context, means ideal, and the athlete thinks everything must be ideal or it isn't "fair."
- **Blaming.** Any perceived unfair treatment leads to blaming—making excuses or assigning fault to others. Abdicating personal responsibility is nonproductive and works against the key principle of taking control.
- **Polarized thinking.** Polarized thinking is viewing things in absolutes—in all-or-none terms. It may lead to *labeling*—identifying someone or something with a word or phrase (e.g., "My heart is racing, I'm a choker"). A coach or instructor might "label" an athlete (e.g., "You dropped that ball—butter-fingers").
- **One-trial generalizations.** One-trial generalizations are cognitive distortions that may be superstitions. Athletes link a single incident with inevitable outcome ("I can't play well if it's raining").

The obvious answer is to get rid of debilitating irrational thoughts. But if cognitive restructuring were simple, we would not all recognize so many of these distorted thoughts. In cognitive restructuring, athletes recognize that such thoughts are irrational, identify constructive thoughts to replace them, and practice rational self-statements.

Bunker et al. (1993) suggest constructing *affirmations*, which reflect positive attitudes or thoughts ("I've got a smooth backswing; I fly down the stretch"). Athletes might develop lists of affirmations for different situations and practice those statements. Many write affirmations on cards and post them in lockers. A consultant might have an athlete write out all the typical precompetition thoughts, then identify the irrational thoughts on the list, and finally restructure that list by substituting affirmations.

Another strategy is to develop coping and mastery self-talk tapes, which essentially are programs of affirmations and restructured thoughts (Bunker et al., 1993). For a mastery tape, the athlete might imagine the ideal performance or recall a previous great performance, and then write out the "script" of all the positive thoughts. Bunker et al. (1993) note that the tape should be as long as the actual performance, unless the performance is so long that's not feasible (e.g., a marathon, an entire game). For longer events, the mastery tape might include descriptions of key moments before, during, and after the competition. After the script is reviewed and modified, an audiotape program can be made. The tape might include music that elicits appropriate emotions, and the pace of the text should permit visualizing the scenes. A coping tape is similar but is designed to help the athlete deal with anxiety or get through a difficult part of the event.

# IMAGERY

As discussed in chapter 5, imagery involves using all the senses to create or recreate an experience mentally. As we have already seen, imagery can be effective for practicing other psychological skills such as modifying self-talk, practicing concentration, and building confidence. In the next chapter we will consider imagery for stress management. Most of all, imagery is effective for developing and maintaining physical skills and strategies.

Chapter 5 included information on individual differences in imagery abilities, as well as on imagery as mental practice for physical skills. In this chapter we will incorporate that work along with the advice of sport and exercise psychologists who have used imagery in psychological skills training. Gould and Damarjian (1996) and

Vealey and Greenleaf (1998) reviewed the literature and drew upon their experiences to provide guidelines and exercises for imagery training; readers might consult those sources for more detailed information.

## Guidelines for Using Imagery Effectively

For effective use of imagery, Gould and Damarjian (1996) suggest the following:

- *Practice imagery regularly.* Like other psychological skills, imagery is developed through training and continued practice.

- *Use all senses to enhance image vividness.* As we noted in chapter 5, imagery is more than vision, and is more effective when the image recreates all the sensations. Kinesthetic sense or "feel" is particularly relevant for physical activities.

- *Develop imagery control.* Control is the key to psychological skills; it is important to practice controlling images.

- *Use both internal and external perspectives.* When Mahoney and Avener (1977) reported that elite gymnasts used more internal (perspective of the performer) imagery than external (observer's perspective) imagery, many consultants advised athletes always to use an internal perspective. Most now recognize that the research is inconclusive and that advice varies with the individual, the activity, and the situation.

- *Facilitate imagery through relaxation.* Research (e.g., Weinberg, Seabourne, & Jackson, 1981) suggests that imagery combined with relaxation is more effective than imagery alone.

- *Develop coping strategies through imagery.* Generally, positive imagery is preferable, but negative imagery can be helpful. As discussed in other chapters, the ability to deal with failure often is the key to motivation and success. Athletes can use imagery to develop coping strategies and skills (e.g., come back after striking out the first time at bat).

- *Use imagery in practice as well as competition.* As noted in the section on goal setting, athletes are more likely to use cognitive techniques for competition than in practices. However, practice is the place to practice, and athletes may need some psychological skills more in practice than in game situations.

- *Use video- or audiotapes to enhance imagery skills.* Tapes may be helpful and may add novelty to practices.

- *Use triggers or cues to facilitate imagery quality.* Words, phrases, or objects may aid imagery, just as cues may aid concentration.

- *Emphasize dynamic kinesthetic imagery.* Dynamic imagery focusing on kinesthetic feel of the movements may help athletes recreate the physical experience.

- *Imagine in real time.* Slowing down or speeding up may have a place in imagery training, but most imagery should match the real time and speed at which athletes perform.

- *Use imagery logs.* Logs can help individuals monitor progress, remember cues, or stay with a training program.

These guidelines may help anyone develop more effective imagery strategies, whether in extensive training or in occasional sport and exercise activities.

From D. Gould and N. Damarjian, 1996, Imagery training for peak performance. In *Exploring sport and exercise psychology*, edited by J.L. Van Raalte and B.W. Brewer (Washington, DC: American Psychological Association), 25-50. Copyright © 1996 by the American Psychological Association. Reprinted with permission.

For consultants helping athletes develop an imagery training program, Gould and Damarjian (1996) suggest a four-phase model (keep in mind that any training must be adjusted for the individual and the situation).

- **Phase 1: Awareness, Realistic Expectations, and Basic Education.** Reports of imagery use by Jack Nicklaus, Greg Louganis, or Chris Evert might suggest that imagery is the answer. Imagery—no quick and easy road to success—requires practice. It is not a substitute for physical practice, but a way to enhance practice.

- **Phase 2: Imagery Skill Evaluation and Development.** Individuals vary in their imagery skills and styles. Even without training, some people may have good imagery skills or develop imagery strategies more quickly than others. Consultants might use an inventory, such as the Sport Imagery Questionnaire (see Vealey & Walter, 1993), to help determine whether a person's images are vivid and controllable, whether the person is using all the senses and internal and external perspectives, and whether images are in color. Such assessment will increase awareness of skills and help the consultant work with the person to develop appropriate training strategies. Those training strategies typically follow Martens's (1987a) recommendations and include three steps. *Sensory training* helps you become more aware of all sensations (sounds, smells, feelings) so you can use them in imagery. *Vividness training* might start with simple exercises, such as imaging the bedroom you had as a child, to develop clearer, more vivid images. With *controllability training*, you learn to regulate images—for example, to imagine speeding up and slowing down while running.

- **Phase 3: Using Imagery.** Once imagery skills are developed, they can be used for many purposes, including practicing physical skills or routines or strategies, correcting errors, practicing emotional control, and developing confidence.

- **Phase 4: Imagery Evaluation, Adjustment, and Refinement.** The final step is evaluation to determine whether imagery training has met its goals and whether refinements and adjustments are needed. It is best to evaluate and consider modifications throughout the program.

No two imagery training programs are alike, and we should expect individual variations and adjustments (Gould & Damarjian, 1996). Moreover, imagery does not automatically work, even with the best of intentions and adherence to guidelines. Some common obstacles to successful imagery training are unrealistic expectations,

*Sensory training* focuses on sensations, such as smell, taste, and sound. *Vividness training* helps athletes focus on clear images, say of a childhood toy. *Controllability training* helps athletes regulate images, such as proper form or speeding up or slowing down while running.

lack of commitment to practicing imagery skills, and lack of coach support and follow-up.

## Summary

Cognitions are keys to behavior, and taking control of cognitions is one of the most effective strategies in sport and exercise. Although many cognitive strategies are simple, using them effectively is not so simple. Goal setting is effective, and the literature indicates that specific, challenging goals are more effective than "do-your-best" goals. Sport and exercise psychologists consistently argue the importance of control of attention and thoughts, and people in sport settings use techniques such as thought stopping and cognitive restructuring successfully. Imagery is probably the most widely used technique. Descriptive and experiential reports offer guidance, but the research is limited. Most authors advocate guidelines based on available evidence but recognize the limits of the research. Also, individual differences are keys to effective practice, and most authors advise individual assessments, evaluation, and modifications throughout any cognitive intervention program.

## Review Questions

1. Discuss Locke and Latham's Theory of Goal Setting.
2. List the four major attributes that influence goal effectiveness, according to Burton (1993).
3. Discuss Weinberg's (1996) goal-setting principles.
4. Describe Nideffer's (1993) Attentional Control Training technique.
5. Name several external and internal strategies for maintaining concentration.
6. Describe self-talk, its uses, and its modification techniques.
7. Identify common guidelines for using imagery effectively.
8. Describe the four-phase model suggested by Gould and Damarjian for consultants helping athletes develop an imagery training program.

## Recommended Reading

★ Weinberg, R. (1996). Goal setting in sport and exercise: Research to practice. In J.L. Van Raalte and B.W. Brewer (Eds.), *Exploring sport and exercise psychology* (pp. 3-24). Washington, DC: American Psychological Association.

> Weinberg is a leading researcher on goal setting in sport, and he presents applied information in an understandable manner. This chapter provides ideas and guidelines on goal setting for both research and practice.

★ Zinsser, N., Bunker, L., & Williams, J.M. (1998). Cognitive techniques for building confidence and enhancing performance. In J.M. Williams (Ed.), *Applied sport psychology: Personal growth to peak performance* (3rd ed., pp. 270-295). Mountain View, CA: Mayfield.

> This chapter presents an up-to-date overview of cognitive strategies, such as self-talk, that can be used to build confidence, optimism, and self-efficacy, along with helpful suggestions for practice.

★ Gould, D., & Damarjian, N. (1996). Imagery training for peak performance. In J.L. Van Raalte & B.W. Brewer (Eds.), *Exploring sport and exercise psychology* (pp. 25-50). Washington, DC: American Psychological Association.

> Dan Gould is a leading scientist-practitioner, with considerable experience in both research and practice. This chapter includes a good balance of background research and scholarship along with excellent suggestions for applied work.

# Stress Management

*c h a p t e r* 13

## CHAPTER OBJECTIVES

After studying this chapter, you should be able to

- understand several stress management techniques, including relaxation exercises and progressive relaxation, and
- explain several cognitive-behavioral approaches to stress management.

Stress is common in sport and exercise settings, as we saw in chapters 10 and 11. Researchers and practitioners have focused on competitive anxiety, and in chapter 11 we covered related theories and empirical work. Here we will focus on the practical issues and consider stress management strategies for sport and exercise.

As discussed in chapter 11, anxiety is multidimensional, with both a physiological and a cognitive component. Thus stress management or emotional control strategies may address either or both components. The early anxiety-performance literature suggests that performance is best at a moderate level of arousal, although the precise optimal level varies across individuals, tasks, and situations. But the key factor for performance is the ability to control anxiety. Fenz's (1975, 1988) work with parachutists and Mahoney's (1979) with gymnasts suggest that good performers do become anxious but are able to control arousal and cognitive worry.

Some people easily control their emotions with simple techniques and have few problems. Others, including some professional athletes, have difficulty controlling anxiety and may seek professional help. Many of the cognitive interventions discussed in the previous chapter apply to stress management. Other techniques zero in on the physiological or somatic component of stress and emotion, and the more comprehensive intervention programs combine cognitive strategies with physiological relaxation techniques.

Research on stress management in sport and exercise is limited, but expanding. We cannot say with certainty which techniques are most effective for specific individuals in specific situations or identify the best way to develop emotional control skills. However, the research literature, combined with information from sport psychology consultants, provides guidance and a place to start.

## THE IMPORTANCE OF STRESS MANAGEMENT

As discussed in chapter 11, we need some level of physiological arousal to mobilize our energies and perform physical activities. An individual might be below an optimal arousal level during a practice session, in a repetitive exercise workout, or in a match against a much weaker opponent. In most sport and exercise settings,

187

participants reach an optimal arousal level quickly. Competition or any performance evaluation increases anxiety in nearly everyone, and typical warm-up activities increase physiological activity. When anxiety increases beyond the optimal level, anxiety control skills are needed. Anxiety control generally implies reducing physiological arousal, and most stress management strategies involve relaxation or calming down.

As we have seen, physiological arousal typically is accompanied by cognitive worry. Although a moderate increase in physiological arousal may be useful, increased cognitive worry has little value. In fact, increased worry is associated with lower self-confidence and poorer performance. Arousal-increasing tactics may be useful in nonstressful teaching and practice situations, but even then, those strategies need not have anxiety-provoking connotations that increase cognitive worry.

Even when one considers only physiological arousal, the potential benefits are limited. No research demonstrates that arousal-increasing techniques enhance performance. The autonomic stress responses of increased heart rate, respiration rate, blood pressure, and palmar sweating have no apparent functional value for most physical activities. In fact, increased autonomic activity can be detrimental. Increased palmar sweating can make handling equipment difficult, and stressing the cardiovascular system more than necessary can induce early fatigue and decrease endurance. Increased muscle tension can create special problems for performers.

In a unique early investigation of anxiety effects on motor performance, Weinberg (1977) used electromyographic recordings to examine muscular activity of high- and low-anxious individuals (identified with the Sport Competition Anxiety Test). High-anxious performers exhibited more unnecessary muscular activity and wasted energy before, during, and after the movement. Furthermore, they exhibited simultaneous contraction of the agonist and antagonist muscles, which interferes with coordinated muscle action and creates the feelings of paralysis that most performers can identify. Low-anxious individuals exhibited the more efficient sequential pattern—one muscle contracting as the opposing muscle relaxes.

With increased arousal, some athletes experience a narrowing of the visual field. For baseball players like Mark McGwire, the right amount of narrowing can help block out distracting stimuli, such as roaring crowds or camera flashes.

© Ron Vesely

Physiological arousal is not independent of, but interacts with, cognitions. If I notice my heart beating faster or my knees shaking, I am likely to become more worried. Arousal may be distracting; if I am thinking about my rapid breathing or upset stomach, I cannot be thinking about running the play or performing the routine. In addition, arousal may narrow the attentional field and cause the person to miss peripheral cues.

The narrowing of the visual field with increased arousal is well documented in psychology, particularly in Easterbrook's (1959) cue utilization theory. As arousal increases, the visual field progressively narrows, eliminating more and more peripheral cues. This visual narrowing has implications for performance (Landers, 1978). For sport and exercise tasks requiring a narrow attentional focus, such as putting in golf or batting in baseball, some narrowing of the visual field may help block out distracting stimuli. As the visual field narrows further, however, relevant and important cues may be eliminated. For example, a basketball player leading a fast break may not see a teammate cutting along the sideline. Clearly, high arousal and visual narrowing can create problems for activities requiring a broad attentional span, such as leading the play in soccer or quarterbacking in football. Conversely, tasks requir-

**Figure 13.1**
A negative cycle is created by worry and increases in arousal, and is accompanied by a decrease in performance.

Worry

Increase in arousal

Decrease in performance

ing more concentrated attention, such as bowling or weight lifting, may be performed effectively with higher arousal and a narrower attentional field.

The relationship between arousal and attentional narrowing may explain the inverted-U relationship between physiological arousal and performance. As arousal increases and attention narrows, irrelevant peripheral stimuli are eliminated and performance improves; when arousal increases beyond the optimal level to a point where relevant stimuli are also eliminated, performance is impaired. Nideffer's Attentional Control Training (1993; discussed in chapter 12) is classified as a cognitive technique, but Nideffer highlights arousal and arousal control because of the arousal-attention relationships. Of course, increasing arousal is not the only way, and not the preferred way, to control attention.

Besides the detrimental effects of above-optimal arousal already noted, initial increases in either physiological arousal or cognitive worry may quickly create a negative thought-anxiety cycle, as described by Ziegler (1978; see figure 13.1). In a stressful situation such as athletic competition, evaluation in physical education, or the presence of spectators in the exercise class, an initial increase in cognitive anxiety occurs, accompanied by the physiological changes associated with the stress response. And even slight changes, such as increased muscle tension, may interfere with coordination. Perhaps you are playing shortstop and bobble the first ball hit to you because you are a bit tight or are thinking about the last time this batter hit one by you. Making that error increases cognitive worry and further heightens physiological arousal, decreasing your concentration and increasing the probability of more errors. Unless you can break out of the negative cycle by controlling your worry and physiological arousal, you are in for a long afternoon. Effective stress management skills are the key to breaking the negative cycle.

## Key Point

There are several reasons stress management methods can be beneficial: increased worry often leads to lower self-confidence and poorer performance; increased autonomic activity, such as palmar sweating or muscle tension, can be detrimental to coordination and sport performance; and physiological arousal has been shown to actually narrow the visual field, which can lead to an individual missing peripheral cues he or she may have otherwise seen under non-anxious circumstances.

## EDUCATIONAL STRESS MANAGEMENT TECHNIQUES

One simple but effective stress management technique is learning about anxiety and its impact on performance. Many performers mistakenly believe that high arousal is necessary and that they should prepare by "psyching up." The optimal state for most sport and exercise activities is one of relaxed concentration. Carl Lewis, whose remarkable four gold medal performance at the 1984 Olympics demonstrated peak performance under pressure, described his running as follows:

> When I run like Carl Lewis, relaxed, smooth, easy, I can run races that seem effortless to me and to those watching. (Callahan, 1984a, p. 52)

Of course Carl Lewis put in tremendous effort and worked hard to develop his skills. But at the time of competition, he reduced his physiological arousal to achieve a relaxed state. Athletes and exercisers must be alert and attentive, but they should also be free of excess muscle tension and worry. In short, they should be in control. Most stress management techniques aim to achieve this controlled, relaxed state.

Sometimes simply telling an athlete about the importance of relaxation and control is enough to eliminate ineffective approaches. For example, a baseball player may try to deal with a batting slump by increasing tension and arousal, or a well-intentioned coach might put extra pressure on such an athlete, thereby aggravating a negative thought-anxiety cycle. Information about negative effects of muscle tension and overarousal and about the importance of relaxed concentration may make participants aware of the desired psychological state and encourage alternative tactics.

# COGNITIVE STRESS MANAGEMENT TECHNIQUES

Simple cognitive techniques often are effective. Mahoney (1979) and Fenz (1975, 1988) both reported that successful performers able to control anxiety were more task oriented. Helping an individual shift from negative thoughts to focus on specific actions might well enhance performance. Many of the cognitive interventions discussed in the previous chapter, such as thought stopping, can be applied to control anxiety. When recognizing a negative thought such as "My feet are rooted to the floor," the individual might "STOP" the negative thought and substitute a positive statement, such as "I'm ready to move."

Similarly, attentional control strategies might help an anxious person direct attention away from worry and onto something else. For example, a basketball substitute waiting to enter the game might focus on the movement of an opposing forward along the baseline.

As discussed in the previous chapter, many athletes use imagery to mentally practice moves or routines, and imagery can also serve as a relaxation technique. Simply imaging a calm, peaceful scene may allow a person to transcend a stressful situation mentally and gain control. As in the process of counterconditioning, in which one response is substituted for another, it is impossible to be both relaxed and anxious at the same time.

# RELAXATION EXERCISES

The most widely recognized stress management techniques work directly on physiological arousal. Relaxation techniques include simple breathing exercises, meditation, progressive relaxation, and many variations of these.

## Breathing Exercises

One of the simplest but most effective relaxation techniques is slow, deep breathing. Increased respiration rate is part of the autonomic stress response, and respiration is one of the physiological responses most easy to control. You would have much more difficulty controlling your heart rate or body temperature than controlling your breathing. Fenz (1975) reported that respiration rate tended to come under control earlier in the jump sequence, whereas other physiological responses, including heart rate and palmar sweating, remained at high levels longer. This suggests that controlling breathing might be an effective way to initiate relaxation.

Breathing techniques emphasize slow, deep breathing. One technique is to breathe in slowly and deeply while counting ("1—2—3—4"), then hold the breath for four counts, and then exhale slowly ("1—2—3—4"). A consultant might help by starting the exercise and counting aloud. Many other relaxation techniques incorporate similar deep breathing. Both progressive relaxation and meditation include attention to slow, deep breathing.

## Progressive Relaxation

Progressive relaxation, originally developed by Jacobson (1938), is one of the most popular relaxation techniques used today. Although relatively simple, it requires practice. The technique involves the progressive tensing and relaxing of various muscle groups. An example is included in appendix B.

**Key Point**

Progressive relaxation involves the progressive tensing and relaxing of various muscle groups.

Sport psychology consultants use progressive relaxation extensively. Typically a consultant conducts several sessions, giving cues to tense and then relax specific muscle groups. The first sessions may take 45 minutes to an hour; but as individuals become more proficient, sessions become shorter, as muscle groups are combined and as the tension phase is gradually reduced and finally omitted. The goal is for the individual to learn to recognize subtle levels of muscle tension and to relax those muscles at will. For example, the batter in the on-deck circle, noticing tightness in the neck and shoulders, can then focus attention on those muscles, relax them, and refocus on the task.

People can learn and practice progressive relaxation with the aid of initial instructions, handouts, or tapes. Many athletes and exercisers already use versions of progressive relaxation. The 10K runner who "shakes out" the muscles just before the event, and the basketball player who tightens the shoulders and lets them drop while preparing for a free throw, are using a form of progressive relaxation. Readers who wish to know more about progressive relaxation might read Bernstein and Borkovec's (1973) *Progressive Relaxation: A Manual for the Helping Professions,* an excellent source of background information and practical advice, or might refer to applied sport psychology work on the subject (e.g., Harris & Harris, 1984; Williams & Harris 1998).

## Meditation

As a stress management technique, progressive relaxation involves relaxing the muscles and letting the mind follow. Meditation techniques work the other way, relaxing the mind and letting the body follow. Meditation generally involves a relaxed, passive focusing of attention and an avoidance of tension and strain. Often the meditator simply focuses on breathing with no analytic thought or special effort.

### Key Point

As a stress management technique, progressive relaxation involves relaxing the muscles and letting the mind follow. Meditation techniques work the other way, relaxing the mind and letting the body follow.

Benson's (1976) relaxation response is an easy and popular technique. To use the Benson method, you first find a quiet setting without distractions. Then you attend to your breathing. Benson suggests silently repeating the word "one" or any other nonstimulating word with each exhalation to help maintain attention. Williams and Harris (1998) note that the word "one" often is stimulating to achievement-oriented athletes, suggesting that "calm" or "warm" might be a better choice. Meditation involves passive attention. Neither the mind nor the body is active; you simply attend to breathing, and when attention wanders, bring the focus back to breathing without straining or worrying about it. Harris and Williams (1993) offer these directions for a meditation exercise:

*Sit quietly in a comfortable position.*

*Close your eyes.*

*Deeply relax all your muscles, beginning at your feet and progressing up to your face. Keep them relaxed.*

*Breathe through your nose. Concentrate on your breathing. As you breathe out, say the word "calm" or "warm" silently to yourself. For example, breathe IN . . . OUT, "calm"; IN . . . OUT, "calm"; and so forth. Breathe easily and naturally.*

*Continue for 10 to 20 minutes. You may open your eyes to check the time, but do not use an alarm. When you finish, sit quietly for several minutes, at first with your eyes closed, and later with your eyes open. Do not stand up for a few minutes.*

*Do not worry about whether you are successful in achieving a deep level of relaxation. Practice the technique once or twice daily, but not within two hours after any meal, because the digestive processes seem to interfere with the elicitation of the relaxation response. (p.230)*

## Autogenic Training

Autogenic training, developed in the 1930s by Johannes Schultz in Germany (Williams & Harris, 1998), is similar to meditation and also to hypnosis. In fact, autogenic training is a form of autohypnosis or self-hypnosis. In autogenic training, the person focuses on and tries to induce sensations of warmth and heaviness. As in meditation, attention is passive and one "lets" the feelings happen. Autogenic training takes several months and proceeds through the following six stages:

**Stage 1:** Heaviness. *My right arm is heavy. My left arm is heavy. Both arms are heavy. My right leg is heavy. My left leg is heavy. Both legs are heavy. My arms and legs are very heavy.*

**Stage 2:** Warmth (same as Stage 1).

**Stage 3:** Heart rate. *My heartbeat is regular and calm.*

**Stage 4:** Breathing rate. *My breathing is low, calm, and relaxed: "It breathes me."*

**Stage 5:** Warmth in the solar plexus. *My solar plexus is warm (hand placed on upper abdominal area).*

**Stage 6:** Coolness of the forehead. *My forehead is cool.* (pp. 231-232)

Given the extensive time demands of autogenic training and its lack of direct connection to sport and exercise activities, it has not been the relaxation technique of choice very often. Popular in Europe, it may fit the needs and preferences of some athletes. For people who like the idea of hypnosis, autogenic training with its focus on physical sensations may be particularly appealing.

# COGNITIVE-BEHAVIORAL STRESS MANAGEMENT

The cognitive and relaxation techniques we have covered are all relatively simple techniques that require no special training. More elaborate and comprehensive stress management may be appropriate, especially when a consultant or counselor works with an individual athlete over a longer time period. Some athletes have used hypnosis or biofeedback for stress management; these both require special training and extended time to be effective. The most popular stress management programs in educational and clinical sport psychology work with athletes are cognitive-behavioral programs combining relaxation exercises with cognitive interventions.

## Suinn's Visuo-Motor Behavioral Rehearsal Technique

For example, Suinn (1976, 1983, 1993) uses a combination of progressive relaxation and imagery in his Visuo-Motor Behavioral Rehearsal (VMBR) technique. As described by Suinn (1976, 1993), VMBR is a covert activity whereby a person experiences sensory-motor sensations that reintegrate reality experiences and that include neuromuscular, physiological, and emotional involvement. It involves two steps: relaxation training and imagery rehearsal. In VMBR, unlike mental practice, relaxation is an essential step that always precedes imagery. The VMBR technique seeks a full-dimensional reexperiencing of an event so that the person actually feels as though he or she is in the situation, performing the activity. The content is not random; in VMBR the images that are produced and the actions that occur are subject to control.

In his 1993 review, Suinn cites several case examples and research studies illustrating the effectiveness of VMBR with athletes. He notes that VMBR is a training tool that must be applied in accordance with known principles of skill acquisition, skill building, and skill enhancement. Suinn's use of VMBR with Olympic skiers was among the first and most widely cited psychological skills programs. The combination of relaxation and cognitive intervention as used by Suinn is still the dominant model for current psychological skills training.

## Smith's Cognitive-Affective Stress Management Model

As discussed in chapter 10, Ron Smith's (1980) stress model provides a guide for stress management programs in sport and exercise. Recall that in the model, the stress process begins with an external situation and individual characteristics and then adds cognitive appraisal and physiological components that interact to influence responses and behavior. Stress management may work on any part of the model, including the initial conditions. For example, youth sport programs that provide guidelines for parents, or actually ban spectators, aim to reduce situational stressors. Specific cognitive interventions, such as thought stopping or imagery, work on the cognitive component, whereas relaxation techniques focus on the physiological component. Cognitive-behavioral programs, such as VMBR and Smith's cognitive-affective stress management program, include both cognitive and relaxation skills in more comprehensive or integrated programs. Smith's program incorporates progressive relaxation, along with an emphasis on breathing cues as the relaxation technique, and uses either cognitive restructuring or self-talk as the cognitive component. The key skill in Smith's program is the "integrated coping response," which combines relaxation with cognitive restructuring.

Smith's stress management program is based on earlier work, particularly Wolpe's (1958, 1961) systematic desensitization and Meichenbaum's (1977) stress inoculation training. Systematic desensitization is based on behavioral counter-conditioning principles. In step 1 the therapist teaches a response that is incompatible with anxiety (a relaxation response). Step 2 involves developing a hierarchy of stressful situations, which are then presented while the client is relaxed in step 3.

For many athletes, performing in front of family and friends creates feelings of nervousness, anxiety, and stress, all of which can have a negative impact on performance.

Meichenbaum's (1977, 1985) stress inoculation training adds a more cognitive component and provides a model for much cognitive-behavioral therapy and educational practice. Step 1, an educational phase, gives the client a conceptual framework for the training. As mentioned earlier, education is often effective by itself; and with a training program, this educational phase also serves to gain the client's commitment and active involvement. The next step in stress inoculation training is the rehearsal phase with development of coping skills. Meichenbaum incorporates varied techniques and emphasizes breathing along with relaxation exercises. Cognitive coping emphasizes self-statements such as assessing the real situation, controlling negative thoughts, relabeling and using arousal, coping with fear, and reinforcing effort. In the next step, application training, the client practices these coping skills in stressful situations. Typically the stressful situations gradually progress from less stressful to the main problem situation.

Smith's cognitive-affective stress management training follows the stress inoculation model with some variations, and Smith (1980) has specifically applied the model with athletes. Smith's program typically uses these steps:

1. *Pretreatment assessment.* Before any training, the first step is to assess the situation and individual characteristics. For example, what specific situations bring out excessive anxiety? What physiological symptoms dominate? Some of the measures discussed in chapter 11 (e.g., Competitive State Anxiety Inventory-2, Sport Anxiety Scale) might be used as well as the athlete's and others' reports or observations.

2. *Treatment rationale.* The consultant and athlete develop a plan, and the consultant presents the rationale. This is the education phase, giving the athlete information and an explanation for the training. Most sport and exercise psychology consultants, like most clinicians (Smith is an experienced clinical psychologist), emphasize that the athlete or client must believe in the training and commit to the training if it is to be effective.

3. *Skill acquisition.* During skill acquisition, which continues over several sessions, the individual learns the integrated coping response. Specifically, the person learns relaxation and cognitive coping techniques and combines them into the integrated coping response. Smith uses progressive relaxation exercises, and like Meichenbaum, emphasizes breathing as a relaxation cue. Cognitive coping emphasizes cognitive restructuring and includes self-statements similar to those in stress inoculation training. Smith notes that for some people, particularly young athletes, simple self-instruction statements may be more effective than cognitive restructuring, and the cognitive skills might involve either of those strategies.

4. *Skill rehearsal.* As with the application training step of stress inoculation, the person practices coping skills in stressful situations. However, here Smith departs from the stress inoculation model in advocating practicing in situations that are more stressful than the problem situation. Smith aims to induce affect (hence the term cognitive-affective) that is greater than the person will deal with in actuality. For example, he might have the person image the worst possible scenario, develop all the affect (worry and physiological arousal) that accompanies that situation, and then use the integrated coping skills to control the affect. Training as a clinical psychologist is essential for these procedures. A typical psychological skills training consultant would not attempt to induce extreme anxiety and affect.

5. *Evaluation.* Finally, no effective program stops at training. Smith recognizes the role of evaluation in applied work. Evaluation is important in order for the client to determine whether training is effective, to make modifications and adjustments, and to maintain skills. Evaluation is also important in order for the sport psychologist to develop and refine skills and programs, and in order for the overall field of sport and exercise psychology to build the knowledge base and provide guidance for others.

> ### Key Point
>
> Suinn's VMBR technique combines progressive relaxation and imagery, while Smith's cognitive-affective stress management model combines cognitive and relaxation skills. Both approaches combine some sort of relaxation exercise with cognitive skills.

## Summary

Stress is common in sport and exercise, and stress management techniques are key psychological skills in many interventions. Because anxiety is multidimensional, with cognitive and physiological components, stress management encompasses both cognitive and physical relaxation techniques. Cognitive interventions discussed in the previous chapter, such as imagery and cognitive restructuring, are effective stress management techniques. Physical relaxation techniques include breathing exercises, progressive relaxation, and meditation. Sport and exercise psychology consultants working with individual athletes or exercisers often use more comprehensive stress management programs, such as Smith's cognitive-affective stress management training. These cognitive-behavioral programs typically include both cognitive and relaxation techniques within a training program that progresses from initial assessment and education through skill-development and practice sessions, application of the skills in sport and exercise settings, and evaluation of the stress management program.

## Review Questions

1. Identify various reasons stress management (or anxiety controlling) methods are beneficial in exercise and sport settings.

2. Compare educational stress management techniques, cognitive stress management techniques, and relaxation exercises.

3. Describe progressive relaxation.

4. Contrast progressive relaxation and meditation.

5. Describe the elements of Suinn's VMBR technique (1976, 1983, 1993) and Smith's model (1980) that qualify them as cognitive-behavioral programs.

## Recommended Reading

★ Williams, J.M., & Harris, D.V. (1998). Relaxation and energizing techniques for regulation of arousal. In J.M. Williams (Ed.), *Applied sport psychology: Personal growth to peak performance* (3rd ed., pp. 219-236). Mountain View, CA: Mayfield.

> This chapter provides a good overview of stress management techniques that can be used in many sport and exercise settings, including several muscle-to-mind and mind-to-muscle techniques.

★ Smith, R.E. (1980). A cognitive-affective approach to stress management training for athletes. In C.H. Nadeau, W.R. Halliwell, K.M. Newell, & G.C. Roberts (Eds.), *Psychology of motor behavior and sport—1979* (pp. 54-72). Champaign, IL: Human Kinetics.

> This article is over 20 years old, but this early presentation of Smith's cognitive-affective stress management model and his professional practice approach still is a model for sport and exercise psychologists who want to be effective practitioners.

# Educational Sport Psychology and Psychological Skills Training

## CHAPTER OBJECTIVES

After studying this chapter, you should be able to

- understand the focus and scope of educational sport psychology,
- identify the steps necessary in setting up a psychological skills training plan,
- explain the boundaries between educational psychology and clinical psychology.

In the preceding two chapters we considered several psychological skills—the cognitive techniques of goal setting and attentional control, as well as relaxation techniques and stress management programs. All these are typical components of more elaborate psychological skills training (PST) programs that many consultants use in educational sport psychology practice. Some PST programs consist of a few short sessions with a few simple interventions, and a coach or instructor might suggest these strategies to an individual athlete or exerciser without any formal training program.

Psychological skills training typically is more comprehensive. Like the stress management programs discussed in the previous chapter, PST usually integrates cognitive and relaxation techniques. Moreover, PST is a more encompassing approach to mental training and a complement to physical training. Generally PST integrates multidimensional psychological skills, which the individual acquires over time in progressing through initial learning, development, and skill-maintenance phases. Individualization is a hallmark of most PST programs.

> ### Key Point
>
> Generally PST integrates multidimensional psychological skills, which the individual acquires over time in progressing through initial learning, development, and skill-maintenance phases. Individualization is a hallmark of most PST programs.

Most often, PST is used with athletes and conducted by an "educational" sport psychology consultant with training in exercise and sport science and specialized work in sport psychology, or by a sport psychologist with clinical training and experience. Even clinically trained sport psychologists using PST take an "educational" rather than a "clinical" sport psychology approach. That is, the aim is not to deal with clinical issues or to practice therapy but to educate and develop skills. Sport psychology consultants using PST may confront issues that call for clinical intervention or therapeutic approaches. Such issues are best dealt with outside of and separate from the PST setting, usually through referrals to clinical or counseling services.

# EDUCATIONAL SPORT PSYCHOLOGY

The educational approach of most PST programs highlights individualization and emphasizes the individual's control. Typically a consultant presents several psychological skills, matching the skills to the individual and activity and providing flexibility for varied situations. The consultant organizes and conducts sessions for the practice, development, and maintenance of skills; suggests modifications and progressions; and helps the person integrate cognitive and relaxation skills into a psychological "game" to complement the physical game and, in many cases, incorporate PST into other aspects of life.

## Who Uses Psychological Skills Training

Psychological skills training is not only for Olympic and intercollegiate athletes, who have received publicity for using sport psychology. It may be even more important for younger athletes. Psychological skills training may help individuals progress to "higher" levels, but it is equally useful for gaining optimal benefits of sport and exercise regardless of ambitions. Developing a sense of control, accomplishment, and enjoyment in the activity is the overall goal of most participants, and matching PST to individual interests and needs can help fulfill that goal. Certainly elite athletes can benefit from PST. Just as highly physically skilled athletes continue to practice basic moves and routines, athletes with good mental skills can use PST. Most athletes have not given much time or effort to psychological skills, and PST may be an innovative approach even for elite athletes.

## When Psychological Skills Training Is Used

Psychological skills training is not a technique to start just before the big tournament or when a disaster occurs; it should be part of all training from the earliest developing stages. PST programs are most effective in off-season, practices, or early training stages. An exercise class might include attention cues and relaxation instructions from the beginning. Simple cognitive and relaxation skills incorporated into elementary physical education classes provide variety, may appeal especially to less athletically inclined students, and help develop lifestyle approaches to physical activity.

## Who Conducts Psychological Skills Training

Many psychological skills can be self-taught, but an instructor or consultant can provide additional information and guidance in setting up a program. The instructor can observe, monitor, make suggestions, and evaluate but eventually fades out so that the individual is in control. People get information on their own, and some athletes and exercisers have specific training (e.g., a college course) in sport and exercise psychology. Increasingly, physical education teachers, coaches, and exercise instructors have some training in sport and exercise psychology. For professionals without formal training, psychology information is available in athletic and exercise publications and through workshops.

Finally, those with specialized training in educational sport psychology, usually PhD training in exercise and sport science or in psychology with specialized work in sport and exercise psychology, can provide expertise in PST programs. These professionals are at Olympic training centers, in some intercollegiate athletic departments, or in private practice. Few consultants, whether educational or clinical sport psychologists, work exclusively with PST. Many consultants are academic faculty with a specialization in sport and exercise psychology, and others are practicing psychologists or counselors who devote some of that practice to work with athletes.

## How Psychological Skills Training Professionals Are Certified

People seeking help with PST may have difficulty finding a qualified, competent educational sport psychology consultant. Sport and exercise psychology is not a licensed specialty, as is clinical psychology; and it is not immediately obvious where one could find information on or listings of qualified consultants. Many people might claim to be a sport psychologist, and some might claim great success and make great promises. Perhaps the best advice is the standard, "If it seems too good to be true, it probably is." Competent sport and exercise psychology consultants will not profess to solve all problems or turn you into the next Olympic medalist. Instead, they might emphasize your responsibility and point out that psychological skills require just as much time and effort as physical skills.

Sport and exercise psychology organizations are concerned about maintaining standards and credibility amid the growing popularity of the specialty. Most notably, the Association for the Advancement of Applied Sport Psychology (AAASP), which since its beginning in the late 1980s has focused on application, including professional practice, published certification guidelines in 1989. Members of AAASP may apply for certification, and a committee reviews their credentials (see the box on page 200). Generally, the guidelines require graduate work in both exercise and sport science and psychology as well as supervised practical experience. Certification is not a license, but indicates that the individual has met competency standards. For background information and a more thorough discussion of certification in relation to professional practice and licensing issues, see Zaichowski and Perna (1996).

The U.S. Olympic Committee (USOC) has maintained a registry of sport psychology consultants since 1983 and recently added AAASP certification as a requirement. The USOC also requires membership in the American Psychological Association (which includes Division 47—Exercise and Sport Psychology), the primary professional organization for clinical and other psychology specializations. The APA certifies clinical and counseling psychology programs, and licensing as a clinical psychologist follows APA standards. This organization also has long had ethical standards for psychology training and professional practice. Although clinical psychology licensing is not required for educational sport psychology practice or AAASP certification, APA standards provide a model for training and professional practice that sport and exercise psychology has adopted.

### Key Point

AAASP certification indicates that an individual has met competency standards. The APA certifies clinical and counseling psychology programs, and licensing as a clinical psychologist follows APA standards.

Recently AAASP adopted an ethical code to accompany its certification guidelines. The introduction to the code begins:

> AAASP is dedicated to the development and professionalization of the field of sport psychology. As we establish ourselves as a profession, we must attend to both the privileges and responsibilities of a profession. Privileges derive from society's agreement to accept our designation as a group of trained individuals possessing specialized knowledge and, therefore, the power implicit in this knowledge. Our responsibilities in turn, result from society's trust that the profession will regulate itself to do no harm, and to govern itself to ensure the dignity and welfare of individuals we serve and the public.

The AAASP certification guidelines represent one step toward professionalization in that they establish criteria for designating qualified individuals. The ethics code

1. Completion of a doctoral degree from an institution of higher education accredited by one of the regional accrediting bodies recognized by the Council of Postsecondary Accreditation; in Canada, an institution of higher education must be recognized as a member in good standing of the Association of Universities and Colleges of Canada. Programs leading to a doctoral degree must include the equivalent of three full-time academic years of graduate study, 2 years of which are at the institution from which the doctoral degree is granted, and 1 year of which is in full-time residence at the institution from which the doctoral degree is granted.

2. Knowledge of scientific and professional ethics and standards. This requirement can be met by taking one course on these topics or by taking several courses in which these topics compose parts of the courses or by taking part in other comparable experiences.

3. Knowledge of the sport psychology subdisciplines of intervention-performance enhancement, health-exercise psychology, and social psychology as evidenced by three courses or two courses and one independent study in sport psychology (two of these courses must be taken at the graduate level).

4. Knowledge of the biomechanical and physiological bases of sport (e.g., kinesiology, biomechanics, exercise physiology).

5. Knowledge of the historical, philosophical, social, or motor behavior bases of sport (e.g., motor learning-control, motor development, issues in sport-physical education, sociology of sport, history and philosophy of sport-physical education).

6. Knowledge of psychopathology and its assessment (e.g., abnormal psychology, psychopathology).

7. Training designed to foster basic skills in counseling; (e.g., course work on basic intervention techniques in counseling; supervised practicums in counseling, clinical, or industrial-organizational psychology).*

8. Supervised experience with a qualified person (i.e., one who has an appropriate background in applied sport psychology), during which the individual receives training in the use of sport psychology principles and techniques (e.g., supervised practicums in applied sport psychology in which the recipients of the assessments and interventions are participants in physical activity, exercise, or sport).*

9. Knowledge of skills and techniques within sport or exercise (e.g., supervised practicums in applied sport psychology in which the recipients of the assessments and interventions are participants in physical activity, exercise, or sport).

10. Knowledge and skills in research design, statistics, and psychological assessment.*

At least two of the following four criteria must be met through educational experiences that focus on general psychological principles (rather than sport-specific ones):

11. Knowledge of the biological bases of behavior (e.g., biomechanics-kinesiology, comparative psychology, exercise physiology, neuropsychology, physiological psychology, psychopharmacology, sensation).

12. Knowledge of the cognitive-affective bases of behavior (e.g., cognition, emotion, learning, memory, motivation, motor development, motor learning-control, perception, thinking).

13. Knowledge of the social bases of behavior (e.g., cultural, ethnic, and group processes; gender roles in sport; organizational and systems theory; social psychology; sociology of sport).

14. Knowledge of individual behavior (e.g., developmental psychology, exercise behavior, health psychology, individual differences, personality theory).

*Graduate level only.

is an important step toward taking professional responsibility. Whelan, Meyers, and Elkin (1996) provide an excellent discussion of ethics in professional practice, as well as background on the events leading up to the development of the AAASP ethics code. In 1995, AAASP Fellows passed the ethical principles and in 1996 unanimously accepted the completed *Ethical Principles and Standards of the Association for the Advancement of Applied Sport Psychology*, which includes an Introduction and Preamble, six general principles, and 25 standards more precisely specifying the boundaries of ethical conduct. The six general ethical principles, in summary form, are shown below.

## AAASP General Ethical Principles

The following is reprinted, by permission, from the Ethics Code of the Association for the Advancement of Applied Sport Psychology, in M.L. Sachs, K.C. Burke, S. Gomer (Eds.), 1998, *Directory of Graduate Programs in Applied Sport Psychology*, 5th ed. (Morgantown, WV: Fitness Information Technology, Inc.).

- *Principle A: Competence.* AAASP members maintain the highest standards of competence in their work. They recognize the boundaries of their professional competencies and the limitations of their expertise.

- *Principle B: Integrity.* AAASP members promote integrity in the science, teaching, and practice of their profession . . . they do not make statements that are false, misleading, or deceptive. . . . AAASP members avoid improper and potentially harmful dual relationships.

- *Principle C: Professional and Scientific Responsibility.* AAASP members are responsible for safeguarding the public and AAASP from members who are deficient in ethical conduct.

- *Principle D: Respect for People's Rights and Dignity.* AAASP members accord appropriate respect to the fundamental rights, dignity, and worth of all people. They respect the rights of individuals to privacy, confidentiality, self-determination, and autonomy. . . . AAASP members are aware of cultural, individual, and role differences . . . and they do not knowingly participate in or condone unfair discriminatory practices.

- *Principle E: Concern for Others' Welfare.* AAASP members seek to contribute to the welfare of those with whom they interact professionally. . . . They do not exploit or mislead other people during or after professional relationships.

- *Principle F: Social Responsibility.* AAASP members are aware of their professional and scientific responsibilities to the community and the society in which they work and live. . . . AAASP members try to avoid misuse of their work and they comply with the law.

The certification guidelines provide a framework for identifying professional competencies, and the ethics code contains general guidelines for professional practice. The more specific guidelines for conducting educational sport psychology practice and PST may be found in several of the applied texts and articles. (e.g. Williams, 1998; Van Raalte & Brewer, 1996). As all those sources emphasize, there is no one right way to conduct PST, and any psychological intervention or training program is individualized from the beginning and continually modified to match the dynamics of the process.

# IMPLEMENTATION OF PSYCHOLOGICAL SKILLS TRAINING

Weinberg and Williams (1998) provide an excellent guide to implementing PST that includes three general phases: setting up a mental skills training program, determining what skills to include and how to sequence them, and evaluating program effectiveness.

## Setting Up a Psychological Skills Training Program

The first step is to discuss the approach with the participant to dispel myths, provide a rationale, explain what sport psychology is and can do, explain educational versus clinical approaches, and focus on personal development. In setting up PST, the consultant should emphasize the importance of mental training, pointing out that even elite athletes practice and use mental skills.

The setup phase includes assessment of psychological strengths and weaknesses. Assessment might include inventories that we have discussed in other chapters, such as psychological skills inventories (e.g., Psychological Skills Inventory for Sports, Athletic Coping Skills Inventory), the Profile of Mood States mood measure, or anxiety measures (e.g., Competitive State Anxiety Inventory-2, Sport Anxiety Scale). Inventories give only limited information, and assessments typically include observations, interviews, and analysis of physical demands, conditioning, strategies, and equipment related to the activity. Weinberg and Williams (1993) suggest that a typical interview might include questions about the person's involvement in the sport, psychological strengths and weaknesses, and specific psychological problems and relationships with the coach. Weinberg and Williams also suggest giving written feedback to the athlete and letting the athlete respond to the feedback in a second interview.

## Determining What Skills to Include and How to Sequence Them

The next step is to develop a PST plan based on the assessment and the individual's overall training and lifestyle. Since in most PST settings it is not possible to do everything, one needs to prioritize and emphasize a small number of skills initially. Vealey (1988) classified typical components of PST into a structure that should help consultants develop a plan. First, Vealey differentiated psychological skills and methods. *Skills* are qualities to be obtained, and *methods* are the techniques used to develop those skills. For example, emotional control and focused attention are skills, and progressive relaxation and imagery are methods for developing those skills. Vealey further divided psychological skills and methods as shown in table 14.1.

Methods for developing psychological skills, listed at the top of table 14.1, include foundation methods and psychological skills methods. Psychological skills methods

### Table 14.1   Psychological Skills and Methods

Methods for developing psychological skills

| Foundation methods | Psychological skills methods |
| --- | --- |
| Physical practice | Goal setting |
| Education | Imagery |
| | Physical relaxation |
| | Thought/attention control |

Psychological skills developed in PST programs

| Foundation skills | Performance skills | Facilitative skills |
| --- | --- | --- |
| Volition | Optimal physical arousal | Interpersonal skills |
| Self-awareness | Optimal mental arousal | Lifestyle management |
| Self-esteem | Optimal attention | |
| Self-confidence | | |

Adapted, by permission, from R.S. Vealey, 1988, "Future directions in psychological skills training," *The Sport Psychologist* (2): 318-336.

## Key Point

The three general phases of psychological skills training are setting up a mental skills training program, determining what skills to include and how to sequence them, and evaluating program effectiveness.

are the typical interventions of goal setting, imagery, relaxation, and thought control. Vealey also lists the foundational skills of physical practice and education because productive practice and a basic understanding of mental processes foster skill development.

Vealey (1988) suggests several psychological skills that can be developed using these methods: foundation, performance, and facilitative skills (table 14.1, bottom). Foundation skills are the basics. The first two, volition and self-awareness, imply that the individual is internally motivated and committed to PST and also understands his or her psychological responses. With sufficient motivation and awareness, the person can develop self-esteem and confidence. Performance skills are aimed at the optimal psychological state, specifically optimal physiological arousal, mental (cognitive) arousal, and attention. Facilitative skills are seldom included in basic and more traditional PST, but they are becoming more common as consultants work with the "whole" person in the life setting. The facilitative skills of interpersonal skills and lifestyle management may not directly influence performance or performance states, but they may facilitate behavior in sport or exercise, as well as in other areas of life.

## Practical Pointers for Psychological Skills Training

Williams provides an excellent list of practical pointers for those who wish to use PST. (From *Applied Sport Psychology: Personal Growth to Peak Performance*, 3rd ed., by Jean M. Williams. Copyright © 1998 by Mayfield Publishing Company. Reprinted by permission of the publisher.)

1. *Provide the what, why, when, and how of training.* Psychological skills training works only if the individual consciously and continually uses psychological skills. Individuals who receive this information are more likely to understand the rationale, to make the commitment, and to follow through.

2. *Stress personal responsibility.* Optimal performance is not luck. Athletes can learn to use psychological skills and techniques to take control; assume responsibility for their thoughts, feelings, and actions; and achieve optimal performances more consistently.

3. *Be flexible and individualized.* All individuals do not learn skills the same way at the same pace. A variety is far preferable to forcing everyone into one program.

4. *Use goal setting and journal assignments.* Journals can help people monitor their progress, identify states or responses they might not have noticed otherwise, and provide incentives.

5. *Encourage a passive state of mind versus a forcing attitude.* A passive state of mind implies "letting" things happen, and this is a key to several techniques discussed in previous chapters. Many athletes have difficulty with a passive state, as they are used to trying hard and may equate passive approaches with lack of motivation. Education and continued explanations with specific techniques can help encourage the passive state.

6. *Form precompetition and competition plans.* Plans or routines make preparation more systematic and foster consistency. The most effective readying procedure is individual; the specific plans and protocols vary greatly among individuals.

7. *Stress application to other life pursuits.* The psychological skills developed through PST apply to other areas of life and yield benefits far beyond the playing field and long after the competitive season.

8. *Practice it before teaching it.* Practice helps the coach or consultant develop teaching skills and anticipate others' reactions; the professional may also gain the benefits of psychological skills in other areas of life.

9. *Teach by example.* The coach who is overly anxious and prone to outbursts typically has athletes who react to competition the same way. A coach or consultant leading PST who appears calm and in control may serve as a model.

10. *Observe practices and competitions whenever possible.* A firsthand view adds much to the assessment and monitoring of PST and may help build trust between the consultant and athlete.

11. *Emphasize strengths as competition nears.* Near the time of competition, reassurance and compliments become more important. At the time of performance, high self-confidence is more important than work on weaknesses.

12. *Monitor your behavior.* Monitoring can help the consultant develop skills and communicate more effectively. Observations by someone else, such as a supervisor or colleague, can provide even more information, especially if the observer has experience with PST.

## Evaluating Program Effectiveness

Formal evaluation at the end of the PST program is essential, but should also be ongoing throughout the program. Evaluation is important for tailoring the PST program to the individual, for use by the consultant in continually updating knowledge, and for the larger field in developing a knowledge base for professional practice. Evaluation might include individual or team discussions, written evaluations, objective performance data, and reassessments of psychological skills. Weinberg and Williams (1993) note that it is important to determine how much athletes actually practice the skills and whether they follow their plans, as well as to obtain their evaluations of the program's strengths and weaknesses.

Psychological skills training cannot provide all the answers or turn every potential athlete into a superstar, but it has many potential benefits for participants in all types of activities. Programs planned and developed according to the best available guidelines, and carefully individualized, may not only improve mental skills and the overall sport and exercise experience, but also foster growth and development in other areas of life.

# BETWEEN EDUCATIONAL AND CLINICAL PSYCHOLOGY

The ethics code and certification guidelines of AAASP emphasize competencies and boundaries, which are especially important when consultants doing PST encounter issues that cross over into clinical areas. This text focuses on the scholarly base of sport and exercise psychology, and the intent here is to provide a brief overview of educational sport psychology practice. We will not cover clinical areas, but anyone engaging in applied sport and exercise psychology should understand the boundary issues.

As noted earlier, PST almost always takes place within an educational sport psychology context. Clinical sport psychology practice is the province of those with clinical training (e.g., licensed clinical psychologists and counseling psychologists) who extend that practice to work with sport and exercise participants. Although educational sport psychologists are not trained and generally do not intend to deal with clinical issues (e.g., psychopathology, depression, substance abuse), such issues may well arise during PST.

For educational sport psychologists, the important issues concern knowing the boundaries of their competencies and knowing when to refer individuals for

Though eating disorders are much more common in females than in males, sports such as wrestling and distance running may impose pressure about weight loss on male athletes as well.

counseling or psychotherapy. Van Raalte and Anderson (1996) discuss the referral process in sport and exercise psychology, and Steve Heyman (1993; Heyman & Andersen, 1998), a trained clinical psychologist as well as colleague and contributor to sport and exercise psychology literature and organizations, provides guidelines for the educational sport psychologist or PST instructor. Recognizing that it is not easy to differentiate performance enhancement from more problematic issues that would call for referral, Heyman offers three guidelines. First, the duration of a problem and its place in the person's life are important. For example, an athlete who becomes anxious and lacks confidence in close, important contests probably does not require referral. On the other hand, if competition is an all-or-nothing battle for a sense of self, and if severe anxiety, depression, or substance abuse affects outcomes, referral may be in order.

Second, unusual emotional reactions are a consideration. Severe, prolonged depression after a loss, or excessive anger and abusive behavior, might be signs of underlying issues. Third, it is important to consider the effectiveness of PST. If performance-enhancing techniques such as anxiety management or self-talk do not work as expected, then undisclosed, deeper issues could be involved. Of course, PST techniques could be ineffective for many reasons, but one should consider unusual responses and ineffectiveness within the overall picture in a referral decision. Although one refers typically for psychological disorders, Van Raalte and Anderson (1996) note that physical issues may call for referral to coaches or sports medicine personnel.

Heyman (1993) lists several specific issues that may call for referral.

• *Identity issues.* Most readers can cite examples of athletes whose whole life revolves around their role as athlete. They live for their sport, and they have no life apart from that sport. Identity issues may be especially problematic at career termination (e.g., retirement from pros, graduation from high school or college, getting cut from a team, career-ending injury).

• *Negative identity.* Although we usually think of athletes and exercisers in positive terms, Heyman notes that a negative identity is also possible (e.g., "dumb jock").

• *Sexual orientation and gender role issues.* As Heyman notes, sexual orientation and gender may pose particular problems for athletes. As discussed in chapter 18 on diversity, people typically associate sport and exercise with masculinity and with male heterosexuality. Coaches may chide an athlete for "playing like a girl," and sexual exploits of male athletes typically are discussed in admiring tones. The images present clear issues for female athletes and also pose problems for males who might suppress nurturing, expressive "feminine" characteristics or engage in overly aggressive stereotypical masculine behaviors.

• *Sexuality and human immunodeficiency virus (HIV).* Recent disclosures by prominent athletes (e.g., Magic Johnson, Greg Louganis) of HIV status have brought issues of sexuality and HIV to light within athletics. Moreover, for athletes, acquired immunodeficiency syndrome (AIDS) concerns not only people who are gay, but may involve drug use and heterosexual transmission. Male athletes, in particular, have opportunities for anonymous sexual encounters; and steroid use is part of many athletic and exercise settings. In the age of AIDS, athletes and exercisers may well have fears and concerns that call for referrals.

• *Eating disorders.* Anorexia and bulimia, as well as less severe but problematic disordered eating behaviors, may be an issue. Eating disorders are much more common in females than in males; females are diagnosed with clinical eating disorders about nine times as often as males. Also, eating disorders are more prevalent in younger women. Female athletes, especially high school and college athletes, fall into the high-risk category, and athletics confers no special protection. Moreover, certain sports and activities that emphasize weight and lean appearance (e.g., gymnastics, figure skating, distance running) may impose added pressure. Even male athletes in sports (i.e., wrestling, distance running) are at risk for disordered eating behaviors. Although the exact prevalence rates for diagnosed eating disorders vary among studies and reports (Brewer & Petrie, 1996), the rates for athletes are at least as high as in the comparable nonathlete population. Moreover, although the rates vary and are derived from limited research, researchers and reviewers (e.g., Black & Burckes-Miller, 1988; Petrie & Stoever, 1993; Taub & Benson, 1992) consistently report high incidence of disordered eating and weight-control behaviors among female athletes. Severe cases clearly call for referral, and even suspected eating disorders call for some action. Eating disorders are multifaceted, and with true diagnosed eating disorders, several professionals might be involved, including physicians and nutritionists as well as clinical psychologists and counselors. Even if athletes or exercisers are not diagnosed as anorectic or bulimic, referral for counseling on proper nutrition, information on body composition and weight, or body image and self-esteem issues might be important. Also, educational sport psychologists encountering eating disorder issues might consider educating coaches or instructors who might be communicating the wrong messages and inadvertently encouraging unhealthy behaviors. Swoap and Murphy (1995), recognizing the multidimensional issues, proposed that sport educational programs on eating disorders focus on (a) fitness ideals (as opposed to weight ideals), (b) nutritional information provided by a qualified nutritionist, and (c) improvements in sensitivities of athletic personnel (e.g., coaches) to weight and dieting issues. Sport psychology consultants might consult Swoap and Murphy (1995) or Thompson and Sherman (1993), who discuss many complex practical and professional considerations.

• *Alcohol and substance abuse.* Just as athletes are among the segment of the population prone to eating disorders, the majority are adolescents and young adults, groups for whom concerns about alcohol and substance abuse arise. Substance abuse may be associated with risk taking or sensation-seeking (Zuckerman, 1979), and certain sports may disproportionately attract sensation-seekers. As alluded to earlier, steroid use and identity issues may also relate to alcohol and substance abuse problems.

• *Anger and aggression control.* Many sports encourage being tough and seeing the opponent as an enemy to be defeated, and sanction physical aggression. Although most athletes can control anger and aggressive behavior on and off the field, not all do. Alcohol and substance abuse or identity issues may also contribute to problems with aggressive behavior.

• *Relationship issues.* Athletics (or excessive exercise) takes time and energy away from relationships and may add pressure to relationship issues. Celebrity status also poses problems for some professional or even high school athletes.

As Heyman (1993) indicates, it is not only difficult to know when to refer; it may be just as difficult to make the referral. Identifying the appropriate clinical professional is not easy, and athletes may be reluctant to accept a referral.

Van Raalte and Anderson (1996) caution that there is no one way to make the perfect referral. They offer a list of do's and dont's for the consultant in a referral situation. First, prepare the athlete for referral, and discuss the possibility of referral at the very first meeting. If referral is needed, explain the reason for it. Describe what is generally involved in working with the other practitioner. Be sensitive to the athlete's concerns and fears, and get the athlete's written permission to share information with the other practitioner. Facilitate follow-through on referral, and finally, assess the effectiveness of the referral. On the other hand, complexities and cautions with referrals call for some dont's. Don't oversimplify the situation, and don't disguise the expertise or function of the other practitioner. Don't use referral follow-through as a condition for a favorable report to the coach or as a prerequisite to avoid negative consequences. Don't violate confidentiality. Finally, don't undermine the treatment of the other practitioner.

# Summary

Psychological skills training involves the science and art of educational sport psychology. Both research and professional practice in PST have grown tremendously in recent years. We do not yet have precise answers, but we have guidelines derived from the research and the experience of practitioners. The most effective programs include a variety of skills and techniques, such as those discussed in the chapters on cognitive interventions and stress management, and are matched to the individual and the situation.

Psychological skills training and most applied sport and exercise psychology interventions are conducted within an educational model. That is, the professional presents skills, and individuals practice and develop skills to control their own reactions and behaviors in sport and exercise settings. Although PST training emphasizes performance enhancement, personal issues that cross into clinical areas may arise. Educational sport psychologists or others engaged in PST should be alert to such potential issues (e.g., eating disorders, identity issues), recognize the boundaries of their competencies, and be ready to refer to other professionals.

# Review Questions

1. Define PST, including who uses it, who administers it, and when it is used.

2. Explain the roles of the APA and the AAASP in educational sport psychology training and certification.

3. Identify the three general phases of implementing a PST program.

4. Discuss Weinberg and Williams's (1993) list of practical pointers for those who wish to use PST.

5. Identify issues that may call for PST instructors to refer athletes to counselors, psychotherapists, or sports medicine personnel.

# Recommended Reading

★ Weinberg, R.S., & Williams, J.M. (1998). In J.M. Williams (Ed.), *Applied sport psychology: Personal growth to peak performance* (3rd ed., pp. 329-358). Mountain View, CA: Mayfield.

> These two authors both have extensive experience and they effectively communicate in this overview of psychological skills training. Readers will find good practical advice and helpful guidelines based on current research and practice.

★ Zaichkowsky, L., & Perna, F. (1996). In J.L. Van Raalte and B.W. Brewer (Eds.), *Exploring sport and exercise psychology* (pp. 133-158). Washington, DC: American Psychological Association.

> This chapter provides an overview of the AAASP certification guidelines, including important background information on the development of the guidelines, the role of certification, and continuing issues in sport psychology practice.

★ Whelan, J.P., Meyers, A.W., & Elkin, T.D. (1996). In J.L. Van Raalte and B.W. Brewer (Eds.), *Exploring sport and exercise psychology* (pp. 431-447). Washington, DC: American Psychological Association.

> Whelan and his colleagues discuss ethics in sport and exercise psychology, including the AAASP code and its relationship to the APA code, background information, and the reasons for ethics codes. Anyone who intends to practice in any setting (research, teaching, consultation) must understand and follow professional ethical standards, and this chapter is a good place to start.

# part V

# Social Processes

In earlier chapters we focused on the individual and internal or intrinsic influences on the individual's behavior in sport and exercise settings. Now, in part V, we'll look at the bigger picture and view the individual in relation to others. Specifically, we will consider how others such as instructors and coaches, family, and friends, as well as the larger social context, influence individual behavior; we will also look at interpersonal interactions and group processes.

Chapter 15 addresses behavioral approaches, especially the role of teachers and coaches in modifying individual behavior. We will expand our perspective of the social context and take a more developmental view in chapters 16 and 17 as we consider social development and focus on aggression and moral behavior in physical activity settings. In the last four chapters we will move even further from the individual to social context and interpersonal processes. We'll consider social diversity, emphasizing gender relations, and extend the gender scholarship to other social diversity issues. In chapter 19 we'll review early work on social influence on motor performance and more recent studies on spectators and social support. The final two chapters address group dynamics and interpersonal processes in sport and exercise psychology.

# Behavioral Approaches

## CHAPTER OBJECTIVES

After studying this chapter, you should be able to

- explain basic behavior terminology and
- understand the roles that parents, coaches, and peers can play in helping athletes develop skills, strategies, and other desired behavior patterns.

Although psychology emphasizes individual behavior, most sport and exercise behavior takes place in a social setting. Both the immediate social context and the larger sociocultural background powerfully influence behavior. We will first consider the immediate environment, specifically the direct influence of an instructor or coach on individual participants. Most sport and exercise activities involve such interaction, with one person—coach, trainer, teacher, or consultant—attempting to influence the behavior and enrich the experience of another. In this chapter we will concentrate on the behavioral approaches such instructors or coaches might use to help individuals develop skills, strategies, and desired behavior patterns.

## BEHAVIORAL BASICS

Behavioral theories and reinforcement constructs are among the most widely researched and accepted principles of modern psychology. Behavioral approaches emphasize the environment, and behavioral theories assume that behavior is determined by its consequences. That is, behaviors are strengthened when rewarded and are weakened when punished or ignored.

Behaviors are learned and maintained through two behavioral processes, classical conditioning and operant conditioning. *Classical conditioning* involves learning by association with existing involuntary, reflective responses, whereas *operant conditioning* involves learning new skills and behaviors. Operant conditioning is by far the more relevant process for sport and exercise behavior, and most of this chapter will deal with operant techniques. Before discussing these, let's clarify the conditioning processes.

### Key Point

*Classical conditioning* involves learning by association with existing involuntary, reflective responses, whereas *operant conditioning* involves learning new skills and behaviors.

Classical conditioning is widely known through Pavlov's classic research. Pavlov, a Russian physiologist and Nobel Prize recipient for his physiology work, made his

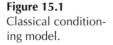

**Figure 15.1**
Classical condition-
ing model.

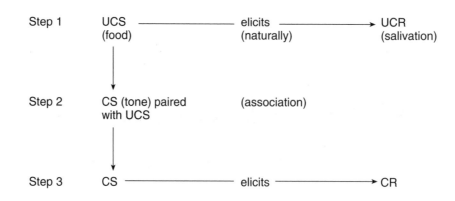

name in psychology somewhat serendipitously after noticing that his dogs began to salivate at the sound of an assistant approaching with food. Pavlov then set up his classical-conditioning experiment. Classical conditioning (see figure 15.1) begins with an existing stimulus-response connection. In this case, the dog naturally salivates to food; conditioning has not yet occurred. Food is the unconditioned stimulus (UCS) and salivation is the unconditioned response (UCR). To begin classical conditioning, Pavlov sounded a tone immediately before presenting the food. After several trials the dog began to salivate at the tone, whether or not the food followed. We now have a conditioned stimulus-response connection, developed by the association of the conditioned stimulus with the unconditioned stimulus. The tone is the conditioned stimulus (CS) and the salivation response to the tone is the conditioned response (CR).

Classical conditioning is seldom used intentionally as an instructional strategy, but it certainly occurs in sport and exercise, as in everyday life. No doubt many sport and exercise participants develop superstitious practices through classical conditioning, and advertisers make wide use of associations to market products.

Operant conditioning involves voluntary behaviors rather than involuntary responses. In most sport and exercise settings we focus on voluntary behaviors. In operant conditioning, one presents reinforcement and punishment to increase desired voluntary behaviors and decrease undesirable voluntary behaviors.

If we look into a physical education class, an exercise session in a cardiac rehab program, or a youth soccer practice, we probably will see instructors using reinforcement and punishment to influence behavior. Teachers and coaches spend much time keeping score, evaluating performance, providing feedback, and generally reinforcing behaviors. But most instructors are not very systematic, and consequently not very effective, at using operant conditioning and reinforcement techniques.

One can apply these reinforcement techniques systematically and effectively by managing behavioral contingencies to improve athletic productivity (Siedentop, 1978). B.F. Skinner (1968), widely recognized as the behavior theorist, took the extreme position that teaching consists entirely of contingency management:

> *Teaching is the arrangement of contingencies of reinforcement under which students learn. They learn without teaching in their natural environments, but teachers arrange special contingencies which expedite learning, hastening the appearance of behavior which would otherwise be acquired slowly or making sure of the appearance of behavior which might otherwise never occur. (pp. 64-65)*

To use reinforcement effectively, instructors must understand the basic principles of contingency management. Some authors (e.g., Dickinson, 1977; Rushall & Siedentop, 1972) emphasize behavioral techniques to the exclusion of other methods, but even sport and exercise psychologists with social-cognitive orientations recognize the power of behavioral contingencies.

The results with effective use of reinforcers can be striking. Skinner demonstrated some remarkable effects in his work with laboratory rats and pigeons. He trained pigeons to identify defective drug capsules on an assembly line and to monitor and correct missile flight paths during World War II. In 1979, newspapers reported that the Coast Guard had trained pigeons to spot orange life rafts and signal a helicopter pilot. Moreover, the pigeons were at least as accurate as humans at locating survivors of maritime disasters. Of particular interest for us, Skinner used reinforcement techniques to teach his pigeons to play a passable version of ping-pong. Many introductory psychology students have seen the filmed evidence of these ping-ponging pigeons, and experimental psychology students have trained rats at similar athletic pursuits with Cheerios or traditional M & M's.

Of course, in sport and exercise we are more concerned about behavioral approaches with humans. Much research documents the effectiveness of behavioral techniques in various institutional settings, health-promotion programs, and standard teaching settings.

## Reinforcement Terminology

To understand behavioral approaches, we need to establish basic terminology. First, the key to behavior modification is *reinforcement*. Reinforcement is any operation that increases the likelihood or strength of the behavior that it immediately follows. Common reinforcers include tangible rewards such as trophies, certificates, T-shirts, and scholarships, as well as nontangible rewards like praise from an instructor, cheers from the crowd, or peer comments on your fit and healthy look. Successful performance itself is a common reinforcer; seeing the ball go through the basket, serving an ace, and jogging that extra mile may reinforce specific behaviors.

In these examples, behaviors are reinforced through provision of something positive such as praise or awards; this is termed *positive reinforcement*. Behaviors also can be strengthened by eliminating something negative or aversive; this is termed *negative reinforcement*. For example, in some experiments, the floor of the Skinner box was a grid that emitted continual shocks unless the rat pushed a bar. Stopping the shock acted as a negative reinforcer and strengthened the behavior of pushing the bar.

Negative reinforcement is less obvious than positive reinforcement, but it does occur. If you learned to dive into the water the way most beginners do, you probably took some painful belly flops. When you finally did the dive correctly, you did not feel the usual pain. Removal of the pain negatively reinforced the correct diving technique. People may find negative reinforcement confusing because we often use terms incorrectly, saying "negative reinforcement" when we mean "punishment." Remember, negative reinforcement is reinforcement—an operation that strengthens behavior.

### Key Point

*Reinforcement* is any operation that increases the likelihood or strength of the behavior that it immediately follows. *Positive reinforcement* occurs when behaviors are reinforced through provision of something positive such as praise or awards. *Negative reinforcement* occurs when behaviors are strengthened by eliminating something negative or aversive.

## Punishment Terminology

*Punishment* is any operation that decreases the strength of a behavior. Punishment can occur through presentation of something negative or aversive or through withdrawal of something positive. Critical comments for poor play, penalties for improper behavior, and being faked out by an opponent may punish the preceding behaviors. Parents often withdraw privileges, such as use of the car. Similarly, coaches might take away a starting role by benching a player for breaking training rules.

**Figure 15.2**
Reinforcement and
punishment opera-
tions.

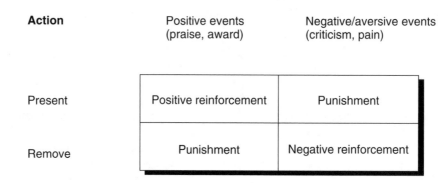

| Action | Positive events (praise, award) | Negative/aversive events (criticism, pain) |
|---|---|---|
| Present | Positive reinforcement | Punishment |
| Remove | Punishment | Negative reinforcement |

As shown in figure 15.2, the two basic behavioral operations are reinforcement and punishment, and either may occur through presenting or removing something. Reinforcement entails presenting something positive (positive reinforcement) or taking away something negative (negative reinforcement). Similarly, punishment entails presenting something negative or taking away something positive.

> **Key Point**
>
> *Punishment* is any operation that decreases the strength of a behavior. Punishment can occur through presentation of something negative or aversive or through withdrawal of something positive.

## BEHAVIOR MANAGEMENT STRATEGIES

Even if we do not take Skinner's extreme position that teaching is entirely contingency management, we recognize that effective application of reinforcement and punishment is a critical component of successful teaching. Like most behavioral scholars, Kauss (1980) advocates that teachers and coaches use positive reinforcement extensively.

Positive reinforcement is more than standing by and saying "nice work." Reinforcement is effective only when applied immediately and consistently, and only when both the teacher and student know what specific behaviors are being reinforced. Kauss lists the following guidelines for effective reinforcement (reprinted, by permission, from D.R. Kauss, 1980, *Peak Performance* [Englewood Cliffs, NJ: Prentice-Hall], 99-101):

• *Reinforce immediately.* The more immediate the reinforcement, the stronger its effect. Do not wait for the next break or the next class, or until after several others have performed.

• *Maintain consistency.* Try to reinforce correct behaviors every time they occur, especially when teaching new skills. Performers often change tactics until something is reinforced. If instructors do not reinforce desired behaviors, students may turn to easier moves or ones that attract attention.

• *Respond to effort and behavior, not to performance outcome alone.* Beginners seldom perform a totally correct skill. Instructors should not wait for the perfect complete skill, but should reinforce efforts and behaviors that move toward the desired performance. Responding to behavior rather than performance outcome is critical. Most sport skills have specific desirable outcomes such as making the putt, scoring a goal, or stopping an opponent. Successful outcomes are powerful reinforcers. For example, a tennis player learning the slice serve may have control problems and resort to a flat serve that allows more accuracy. Instructors can help students focus on proper technique by reinforcing correct moves even when the outcome is not perfect.

• *Remember that learning is not entirely cumulative; it has its ups and downs.* Neither performers nor instructors should panic at occasional mistakes or performance slumps. Unless a performer has slipped into an incorrect pattern, instructors should continue to reinforce correct skills without putting undue pressure on the individual. As noted in earlier chapters, extra pressure may increase anxiety and further aggravate performance difficulties.

• *Use reinforcement to maintain desired behaviors once they are learned.* Frequent and consistent reinforcement is critical during early learning, and reinforcement remains important even after a skill has been well learned. Instructors need not praise every performance, but occasional or *intermittent* reinforcement helps to maintain desired behaviors. Failure to reinforce correct behaviors may lead to their *extinction.* Teachers and coaches often focus on incorrect skills and behaviors and ignore students who create no problems or performers who do not make obvious mistakes. Those students may change their behaviors, resulting in the deterioration of desirable skills and behaviors. Teachers who rely on positive reinforcement likely will have fewer problems maintaining desirable behaviors.

## Shaping: Reinforce Progressive Steps

Of course, behaviors that do not occur cannot be reinforced. If you wait for a beginning high jumper to do the Fosbury flop correctly before giving reinforcing comments, you will wait a long time. Skinner did not wait for the pigeons to walk onto the table and rally back and forth before providing a reward. He used *shaping,* or the reinforcement of successive approximations of the final desired performance. Perhaps he first reinforced the pigeon for going toward the ball, then after that behavior was established rewarded the pigeon for hitting the ball, and eventually rewarded it for hitting the ball over the net.

Shaping is a key technique for sport and exercise settings because most physical skills, plays, and routines develop gradually through progressive steps. Effective teachers and coaches are masters at recognizing successive steps and reinforcing performers as they move toward the correct performance. To develop your own shaping technique, consider a specific skill or routine. Write down the steps that an individual might go through from the beginning stage to the final performance, including as many steps and details as possible. When you work with learners, determine their present level and provide instructions to move them to the next step without overloading them with information about skills beyond their present capabilities. Then, reinforce any efforts or behaviors that move closer to the next step. Humans learn faster than pigeons, but shaping is a gradual process. Learners will not move through all steps like clockwork, and some progress faster than others. If several students are stuck at the same stage, you might reconsider your plans and incorporate additional intermediate steps.

## Punishment: Use With Caution

You may wonder why I am emphasizing reinforcement and ignoring punishment (perhaps I'm using contingency management). If reinforcement enhances learning, will adding punishment double the rate of learning? No. Punishment has a limited role in teaching and coaching. Most experts are cautious about the use of punishment because of its undesirable and often unintended effects.

Kauss (1980) suggests the diagram in figure 15.3 as a guide for effective reinforcement. The diagram assumes that individuals perform correctly about half the time. Reinforce those desirable behaviors as often as possible (all 50% in the diagram). In contrast, ignore bad behaviors most of the time. Punishment should be applied only to behaviors that are intolerable, such as those that are dangerous or disruptive to the group.

In principle, punishing undesirable behaviors should reduce those behaviors. In practice, punishment seldom works as intended and can create problems. We have all witnessed incidents in which intended punishment actually reinforced an undesirable behavior. Perhaps criticism is the only attention an athlete receives from a

**Figure 15.3**

Suggested distribution of reinforcement and punishment for effective teaching and coaching.

From D.R. Kauss, 1980, *Peak performance* (Englewood Cliffs, NJ: Prentice-Hall), 99. Copyright 1980 by David R. Kauss. Reprinted by permission.

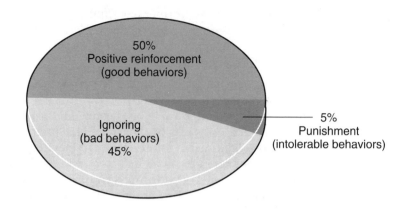

coach, or perhaps singling out the student who disrupts a skill demonstration enhances the student's reputation with classmates.

Even when punishment does not reinforce undesirable behaviors, it may create other problems. A teacher might point out errors by stating, "Don't try to throw before you catch the ball; you're picking your head up too soon." Such statements, although intended to punish undesirable behavior, do not provide alternatives. The individual who wants to avoid the error thinks about the error, and the attention increases the likelihood of picking up the head again. Instead of negative statements directing attention to errors, instructors should use positive, action-oriented statements telling the individual what to do, such as "Look the ball into your glove."

## Key Point

In principle, punishing undesirable behaviors should reduce those behaviors. In practice, punishment seldom works as intended and can create problems.

If undesirable behaviors are not replaced by desirable behaviors, those undesirable behaviors may be suppressed only when the threat of punishment is present. The class clown may be restrained when the teacher is watching but create a disturbance as soon as the teacher turns away. Often we do not teach students alternative behaviors, but teach them to avoid punishment. For example, if a student is embarrassed when the instructor draws attention to poor skill with critical comments, the student may learn to avoid punishment by staying at the back of the line rather than trying to improve. In most sport and exercise settings, people learn skills faster and exhibit more desirable behaviors if positive behaviors are reinforced as often as possible and all but absolutely intolerable behaviors are ignored.

When punishment is necessary, many psychologists recommend a *time-out* procedure. A time-out takes the individual out of the situation and away from all potential reinforcers. The time-out includes no negative events, but it must not offer any potential rewards. Sometimes benching an athlete or sending a student to a quiet area away from everyone else will eliminate attention and potential reinforcers.

## Guidelines for Effective Behavior Modification

In summary, to use behavioral techniques effectively, consider the following guidelines:

- First, and most importantly, positively reinforce correct skills and desirable behaviors as often as possible.
- Make sure participants know which specific behaviors are being reinforced, and provide reinforcers immediately and consistently.

- Ignore most incorrect skills and undesirable behaviors. Do not call attention to errors, but use positive instructions telling the individual what to do.

- Use punishment as a last resort for behaviors that must be stopped immediately. Punishment must be swift, sure, and specific to the undesirable behavior, not a source of attention or reinforcement. Also, when using punishment, be sure to provide an alternative desirable behavior.

## RESEARCH ON BEHAVIORAL MODIFICATION IN SPORT AND EXERCISE

In theory, behavior modification should be a powerful instructional approach, and reinforcement techniques have been successful in nonsport settings. The limited research suggests that behavior modification is effective in some sport and exercise settings with some behaviors.

Rushall and Siedentop (1972) discussed the application of behavior modification in sport at length, and Donahue, Gillis, and King (1980) subsequently reviewed the research. Donahue and colleagues concluded that behavioral strategies could be used effectively to develop, maintain, or change target behaviors in sport and physical education, but they cautioned that the existing research was limited. Furthermore, many of the studies reviewed were unpublished or were methodologically weak.

Some of the strongest effects were reported for nonskill behaviors. For example, McKenzie and Rushall (1974) used public records and token rewards to increase attendance, reduce tardiness, and increase work output at swimming practices. Siedentop (1978) and Donahue et al. (1980) cited use of behavioral techniques to modify attendance, disruptive practice behaviors, interpersonal communication within teams, and athletes' academic behaviors. Donahue et al. (1980) cited a few studies that demonstrated effective modification of jogging and exercise rates, baseball batting performance, sport behaviors at a basketball camp, swimming practice times, and running performances in a basketball preseason conditioning

Coaches and instructors use behavioral techniques to help youngsters develop sport skills, and also to modify nonskill behaviors, such as attendance and disruptive practice behaviors.

© iPhotoNews.com

program. The following sections review selected studies on behavioral approaches to sport performance, to teaching and coaching, and to exercisers.

## Behavior Modification in Sport Settings

Komaki and Barnett (1977) used a multiple-baseline design to examine the effect of a behavioral intervention with a Pop Warner football team. Three specific plays were broken down into five stages, and the correct behavior for each of five players at each stage was specified clearly. Observers used a checklist to record correct execution.

The intervention was introduced after baseline observations of 10 days for Play A, 14 days for Play B, and 18 days for Play C. The intervention included explanation and demonstration of the correct behaviors for each player at each stage, as well as immediate feedback and recognition for correct performance of each stage after each play in practices and games. Performance for Play A improved from 61.7% at baseline to 81.5% after the intervention, Play B improved from 54.4% to 82%, and Play C improved from 65.5% to 79.8%. Performance improved dramatically for each play only after the intervention was introduced for that play.

Behavioral approaches have also been taught to teachers and coaches to use with students. Rushall and Smith (1979), for example, used self-monitoring to increase reward and feedback behaviors of a swimming coach. Allison and Ayllon (1980) developed a behavioral approach to coaching including systematic use of (a) verbal instructions and feedback, (b) positive and negative reinforcement, (c) positive practice, and (d) time-out. The coaches easily applied the method, effectively increasing correct skills and reducing errors in tennis, football, and gymnastics.

Rush and Ayllon (1984) used the same behavioral method in youth soccer with a highly skilled team member who served as peer coach and used behavioral coaching with nine boys whose skills were deficient. All nine players improved in specific soccer skills with behavioral coaching but not with standard coaching. The authors noted that behavioral coaching did not work with one skill, the throw-in. So they introduced shaping, starting with a shorter distance and gradually increasing to the target distance of 20 feet. Shaping improved performances, confirming the importance of successive steps and progressive reinforcement.

Most research on behavioral modification does not tell us much about how and when behavioral techniques affect skill performance and behaviors. Most behavioral techniques used thus far are complex programs involving much more than standard reinforcement. Komaki and Barnett (1977), for example, singled out key players and included a skill breakdown, detailed individual instructions, demonstration, and checklists, as well as positive reinforcement. Any one component of the overall program could be the critical factor affecting performance.

## Behavioral Approaches to Exercise Adherence

Behavioral approaches may help improve exercise adherence in health-oriented exercise programs (discussed in chapter 7). Martin and Dubbert (1984), whose research has documented the effectiveness of behavioral control of exercise behaviors (Martin et al., 1984), provide a useful framework for applying behavioral management strategies to improve health and fitness.

First, Martin and Dubbert (1984) separate exercise behavior into two stages: *acquisition* and *maintenance*. Like Marcus, in her more elaborate stages of change model (Marcus, et al. [1996], discussed in chapter 7), Martin and Dubbert suggest that different strategies are more effective at different stages. They suggest the following behavioral strategies during acquisition:

• *Shaping*. As in teaching sport skills, shaping is probably the most important strategy for establishing a long-term exercise habit. With previously sedentary adults, establishing the habit is more important than building training effects, and gradual progression with reinforcement for small steps is more effective than exercise goals that people cannot reach within a reasonable time.

- *Reinforcement control.* Frequent reinforcement is important during acquisition. Social support and praise during sessions are effective for many beginning exercisers; other specific reinforcers include token reinforcers and lotteries, as well as attention and specific feedback.

- *Stimulus control.* Stimulus control, involving the use of cues, is helpful during acquisition. Many morning exercisers put their gym bags out the night before as a prompt, and organized programs typically use cues in their advertising and in the sessions themselves.

- *Behavioral contracts.* Contracts, often in writing, may be effective. Contracts are a form of goal setting that can provide direction and incentive for exercise behavior.

- *Cognitive strategies.* Martin and Dubbert suggest several of the cognitive strategies described in chapter 12, such as goal setting, positive self-talk, and association-dissociation (distraction), as part of a more cognitive-behavioral approach during acquisition.

After an exerciser has developed the habit, behavioral strategies should change. Martin and Dubbert (1984) suggest behavioral strategies to help the person move from a structured program to more individual and continuing exercise maintenance.

- *Generalization training.* Generalizing involves the gradual fading of the program as the person makes the difficult transition from a structured to an unstructured setting. Some organized programs incorporate home exercise to aid the transition. Generalization training might involve others, such as family or friends.

- *Reinforcement fading.* Gradually reinforcement fades in frequency and intensity as the person transfers to "natural" reinforcers such as positive comments of others, increased feelings of control, and increased energy.

- *Self-control procedures.* As we discussed in the chapters on motivation, a sense of control is a key to intrinsic motivation, and intrinsic motivation is essential for exercise maintenance. Self-monitoring, the most common procedure, actually should begin in the earlier phase. Self-evaluation and reward may also be included, often in a contracting procedure.

- *Relapse-prevention training.* Most exercisers, even the most faithful program adherents, eventually slip out of their exercise pattern (relapse). Thus, most professionals advocate some type of relapse-prevention training (discussed in chapter 7). Exercisers learn to view exercise as a continuum, to recognize and avoid risk situations, and sometimes to try a planned relapse.

Many exercise programs and personal trainers adopt some of the behavioral strategies suggested by Martin and Dubbert. As in sport settings, most practitioners use various strategies and incorporate cognitive as well as behavioral approaches. The evidence does not point to any particular behavioral technique as the best approach, and a limited approach would not accommodate individual differences and changing circumstances. Still, effective use of behavioral strategies can improve teaching and professional practice and enhance participants' sport and exercise experience.

## Tharp and Gallimore's Research on Coaching Style

One of the first attempts to assess coaching behavior was Tharp and Gallimore's (1976) observational study of John Wooden. As you probably know, Wooden was one of the most successful coaches in college basketball—probably the most successful. Before retiring in 1975, Wooden coached UCLA men's basketball teams to 10 national championships in 12 years, a record no one else has approached. Tharp and Gallimore's coding system incorporated standard teaching behavior categories such as reward,

**Table 15.1    Distribution of John Wooden's Coaching Behaviors**

| Code | Category | Description | Percent of total communications |
|------|----------|-------------|---------------------------------|
| I | Instructions | Verbal statements about what to do or how to do it | 50.3 |
| H | Hustles | Verbal statements to activate or intensify previously instructed behavior | 12.7 |
| M+ | Modeling-positive | A demonstration of how to perform | 2.8 |
| M– | Modeling-negative | A demonstration of how *not* to perform | 1.6 |
| V+ | Praises | Verbal compliments, encouragements | 6.9 |
| V– | Scolds | Verbal statements of displeasure | 6.6 |
| NV+ | Nonverbal reward | Nonverbal compliments or encouragements (smiles, pats, jokes) | 1.2 |
| NV– | Nonverbal punishment | This infrequent category included only scowls, gestures of despair, and temporary removal of a player from scrimmage, usually to shoot free throws by himself | Trace |
| W | Scold/reinstruction | A combination category: a single verbal behavior which refers to a specific act, contains a clear scold, and reasserts a previously instructed behavior; e.g., "How many times do I have to tell you to follow through with your head when shooting?" | 8.0 |
| O | Other | Any behavior not falling into the above categories | 2.4 |
| X | Uncodable | The behavior could not be clearly heard or seen | 6.6 |

From "What a coach can teach a teacher" by R.G. Tharp and R. Gallimore, 1976 (January), *Psychology Today*, **9**(8), p. 76. Reprinted with permission from *Psychology Today Magazine*, copyright © 1976 (Sussex Publishers, Inc.).

punishment, and modeling—and a few categories created for Wooden's behavior, such as "hustles." The authors observed 2326 teaching behaviors over 30 hours of practice in the 1974-75 season. The percentage of behavioral acts falling into each category is listed in table 15.1.

The most striking finding was the predominance of instruction. Despite the UCLA team's experience and high skill level, more than 50% of Wooden's behaviors were specific instructions to players. Counting other informational acts, such as modeling and scold/reinstruction, about 75% of Wooden's behaviors provided instruction, and most of the instruction involved basic basketball skills.

The authors found that Wooden seldom used praise. And as the table shows, scolds and nonverbal punishment were only a small portion of his behaviors. Keep in mind that the UCLA basketball players received tremendous praise and public acclaim, and certainly their many successes were rewarding. Most students and athletes do not have this history of success and rewards, and we should not assume that limiting praise is an effective coaching technique. In fact, the most extensive, systematic research on coaching behavior indicates that effective coaches give considerable praise and encouragement and rarely use punitive behaviors (Smith & Smoll, 1997; Smoll & Smith, 1984).

**Key Point**

The most extensive, systematic research on coaching behavior indicates that effective coaches give considerable praise and encouragement and rarely use punitive behaviors (Smith & Smoll, 1997; Smoll & Smith, 1984).

# PUTTING COACHING BEHAVIOR RESEARCH INTO PRACTICE

This chapter has concerned behavioral techniques, and in earlier chapters we discussed cognitive approaches. Teachers and coaches do not use positive reinforcement, goal setting, feedback, or demonstrations in isolation; rather they use various techniques as part of an overall coaching or instructional style, and research suggests that coaching style has considerable influence on participants.

Ron Smith and Frank Smoll's continuing work with youth sport coaches stands out in sport and exercise psychology as a model of systematic research culminating in effective applied training programs. Prior to Smoll and Smith's work, many people talked about youth sports and criticized coaches, but researchers seldom investigated such nebulous topics.

## Coaching Behavior Assessment System

Smith and Smoll took the first step toward understanding the coaching process by developing an observational system, the Coaching Behavior Assessment System (CBAS), to quantify coaching behaviors (Smith, Smoll, & Hunt, 1977). After observing and analyzing the behaviors of coaches in several sports, Smith et al. generated the 12 categories of coaching behaviors listed in table 15.2.

Coaching behaviors fall into two major categories: *reactive behaviors*, which respond to players' behaviors, and *spontaneous behaviors*, which the coach initiates. To use CBAS, observers check the appropriate category for each observed behavior. The proportions of behaviors in the 12 categories are used as the measure of coaching style. Smith et al. (1977) demonstrated that the CBAS is easy to use, includes most coaching behaviors, has good reliability, and shows individual differences among coaches. In general, coaches use considerable reinforcement and instruction; but styles differ, most

### Table 15.2   Response Categories of the CBAS

| Classification | Definition |
| --- | --- |
| *Class I.   Reactive behaviors* | |
| *Responses to desirable performance* | |
| Reinforcement | A positive, rewarding reaction, verbal or nonverbal, to a good play or good effort |
| Nonreinforcement | Failure to respond to a good performance |
| *Responses to mistakes* | |
| Mistake-contingent encouragement | Encouragement given to a player following a mistake |
| Mistake-contingent technical instruction | Instructing or demonstrating to a player how to correct a mistake |
| Punishment | A negative reaction, verbal or nonverbal, following a mistake |
| Punitive technical instruction | Technical instruction that is given in a punitive or hostile manner following a mistake |
| Ignoring mistakes | Failure to respond to a player mistake |
| *Response to misbehavior* | |
| Keeping control | Reactions intended to restore or maintain order among team members |
| *Class II.   Spontaneous behaviors* | |
| *Game related* | |
| General technical instruction | Spontaneous instruction in the techniques and strategies of the sport (not following a mistake) |
| General encouragement | Spontaneous encouragement which does not follow a mistake |
| Organization | Administrative behavior that sets the stage for play by assigning duties, responsibilities, positions, etc. |
| *Game irrelevant* | |
| General communication | Interactions with players unrelated to the game |

Reprinted, by permission, from F. Smell and R. Smith, 1984, Leadership research in youth sports. In *Psychological foundations of sport*, edited by J.M. Silva and R.S. Weinberg (Champaign, IL: Human Kinetics), 375.

Coaching behaviors that combine instruction and encouragement have been shown to positively affect children's enjoyment of sport.

notably in the amounts of instruction and relative proportions of positive behaviors and punitive behaviors.

The CBAS enabled researchers to investigate more intriguing practical questions, such as "Do differences in coaching behaviors affect players?"—and if they do, "Can coaches be trained to use effective behaviors?" In their research program, Smith and Smoll and colleagues addressed these issues. Initially they used the CBAS to assess behaviors of Little League coaches and compared those behaviors to players' attitudes, enjoyment, and self-esteem (Smith, Smoll, & Curtis, 1978). Researchers recorded behaviors with the CBAS; asked coaches to recall their behaviors; asked players to recall coaches' behaviors; and interviewed players to assess their liking for the coach, activity, and teammates, as well as their self-esteem.

In general, the coaches took a positive approach, using a great deal of reinforcement, technical instruction, and general encouragement. The players perceived coaching behaviors accurately, but the coaches' perceptions of their own behaviors were not accurate; coaches did not know which behaviors they used most often. The low correlations between CBAS results and coaches' perceptions imply that the first step in a coach training program should be to make coaches aware of their actual behaviors. That knowledge alone may be sufficient to positively modify the behaviors of many well-intentioned coaches who do not realize how much reinforcement or instruction they actually provide.

Before advocating specific coaching behaviors, let's consider whether those behaviors affect the players. The findings of Smith et al. (1978) confirmed that coaching behaviors do indeed relate to player attitudes. As you might expect, coaches who used more reinforcement and encouragement and fewer punitive behaviors were better liked. Contrary to the belief that children just want to have fun and don't care about skill development, coaches who used more instruction also were better liked. A positive approach combining instruction with encouragement related not only to participants' liking for the coach, but also to their liking for the activity and teammates and to a greater increase in self-esteem over the season.

Perhaps you are wondering if coaching behaviors affected win/loss records. Perhaps coaches who used the positive approach won more games, and success led to more positive player attitudes. In fact, coaching behaviors did not relate to win/ loss records, and players did not like winning coaches any better than losing coaches. The best-liked coaches actually had a slightly poorer win percentage (.422) than the least-liked coaches (.545), but the difference was not significant. Although win/loss records were not related to players' liking for the coach or activity, players on winning teams, in comparison to players on losing teams, thought that the coach liked them more and that their parents liked the coach more. As Smoll and Smith (1984) commented, winning apparently made little difference to the children, but they knew it was important to the adults.

## Coach Effectiveness Training

From their findings, Smoll and Smith developed a behavioral intervention program for youth sport coaches known as Coach Effectiveness Training (CET; Smith, Smoll, & Curtis, 1979). Smith and Smoll (1997) summarized CET guidelines in the following five core principles:

- *Developmental model.* Emphasize the important differences between the professional sport model, in which winning and financial gain are the bottom line, and a developmental model, which focuses on providing a positive developmental context. Winning is defined in terms of giving maximum effort and improving. The explicit, primary focus of a youth sport program is on having fun, deriving satisfaction from being on the team, learning sport skills, increasing self-esteem, and reducing fear of failure.

- *Positive approach.* The positive approach includes liberal use of positive reinforcement, encouragement, and sound technical instruction. Punitive or hostile responses are discouraged. The positive approach should be applied not only to skill development, but also to desirable responses such as teamwork and sportsmanship. One effective way to implement the positive approach is the three-step sandwich approach: sandwich a positive, action-oriented instruction between two encouraging statements. For example, after your shortstop has bobbled a grounder, immediately give a sincere, encouraging statement: "Nice try; you got into position well." Then, give a corrective instruction: "Next time, put your glove on the ground and look the ball into it." Finally, finish off with another encouraging statement: "Hang in there; you'll get it."

- *Mutual support.* Establish norms that emphasize athletes' mutual obligations to help and support one another. When coaches are supportive models and reinforce behaviors that promote team unity, they are likely to develop a "We're in this together" norm.

- *Involve the athletes.* Involving athletes in decisions and reinforcing compliance are more effective for achieving compliance with team roles and responsibilities than is punishing noncompliance.

- *Self-monitoring.* Coaches in CET are urged to obtain behavioral feedback and to engage in self-monitoring to increase awareness and encourage compliance with the guidelines.

A typical CET workshop lasts 3 hours and includes verbal presentation and a manual (Smoll & Smith, 1997), specific suggestions, modeling and role-playing, and a brief self-monitoring form coaches can complete after practices.

Smith et al. (1979) did an intervention study to evaluate whether CET training would modify behaviors and affect player attitudes. The program, which followed the CET guidelines, included discussion of the research results and a follow-up two-week observation period with self-monitoring and feedback to coaches.

Differences in coaching behavior and player attitudes between CET coaches and control coaches paralleled the earlier research findings. Trained coaches used more reinforcement and encouragement than control coaches, and players perceived the trained coaches as using more positive behaviors. Children who played for the trained coaches reported more positive attitudes, liking for the coach, perception of the coach as knowledgeable, liking for teammates, enjoyment of the activity, and self-esteem. Overall, CET was effective in increasing positive supportive behaviors. Those behaviors in turn elicited more positive player attitudes.

Smith and Smoll have continued their research and CET programs with consistent results for 20 years. More than 13,000 youth sport coaches have participated in CET workshops, and CET has been applied at high school, college, and professional levels (Smith & Smoll, 1997). And this research has influenced others. Many youth sport programs have adopted the research-generated guidelines and positive approach. The CBAS is a valuable research tool for studying the relationship of coaching behaviors to other factors. Horn (1984), for example, used the CBAS to investigate teacher expectancies and sport behaviors. Most of all, Smith and Smoll's work provides a model that begins with a systematic research program, progresses to application of empirical findings in an intervention program, and continues with ongoing evaluation of both the practical intervention and related research.

## Summary

Behavioral techniques, which emphasize the role of the environment and behavioral contingencies, are the basics of behavior management. Operant conditioning and related behavior modification techniques can be highly effective with specific sport skills and targeted behaviors. But teachers, coaches, and consultants seldom have the luxury of focusing on selected target behaviors in a controlled context similar to a Skinner box. The most effective behavioral approaches in sport and exercise psychology, such as Smith and Smoll's CET and exercise behavior management programs, are more comprehensive cognitive-behavioral programs with considerable variation, modification, and individualization over time. Behavioral techniques are the basics of effective practice, needed by every teacher, coach, and consultant. But no practitioner can be effective in a dynamic, multifaceted sport or exercise setting with only the basics. Behavioral basics are adapted, modified, and used in conjunction with other approaches that accommodate individuals in a dynamic social context.

## Review Questions

1. Define classical conditioning and operational conditioning.

2. Explain the relationship between behavior management and teaching or coaching.

3. Define reinforcement and identify common tangible and nontangible reinforcers.

4. Contrast positive and negative reinforcement.

5. Define punishment.

6. Discuss Kauss's (1980) guidelines for using reinforcement effectively.

7. Define and give sport-specific examples of shaping.

8. Explain why experts are cautious about the use of punishment.

9. Summarize the findings of behavior modification research in sport and exercise settings.

10. Explain the findings of Martin and Dubbert (1984) with regard to behavior approaches in improving exercise adherence.

11. Explain how Smith, Smoll, and Curtis (1978) used the CBAS to quantify and explain the behaviors of youth sport coaches.

12. Discuss Smith and Smoll's (1997) findings about Coach Effectiveness Training (CET).

## Recommended Readings

★ Rush, D.B., & Ayllon, T. (1984). Peer behavioral coaching: Soccer. *Journal of Sport Psychology, 6*, 325-334.

> This article includes several examples of applied behavioral techniques in sport (specifically, behavioral coaching for youth soccer skills), and also provides a good example of the methods and presentation of behavioral research.

★ Martin, J.E. & Dubbert, P.M. (1984). Behavioral management strategies for improving health and fitness. *Journal of Cardiac Rehabilitation, 4*, 200-208.

> This article provides an overview of behavioral approaches that can be used in exercise settings, such as cardiac rehabilitation. The authors provide an outline of techniques for different settings and for participants at different stages of exercise adoption and maintenance. The suggestions are based on several research studies, and you can check Martin et al. (1984) for the details on the research.

★ Smith, R.E. & Smoll, F.L. (1997). Coaching the coaches: Youth
  sports as a scientific and applied behavioral setting. *Current
  Directions in Psychological Science, 6,* 16-21.

> Smith and Smoll's extensive research and related coach development training is a model of sport and exercise psychology research and practice. They have combined research on coaching behaviors with training programs from their beginning work in the 1970s, and they continue to provide new ideas and inspiration. This article summarizes their extensive work and provides an overview of their coach effectiveness training program.

chapter *16*

# Social Development and Sport

**Lavon Williams, PhD**
*Northern Illinois University*

## CHAPTER OBJECTIVES

After studying this chapter, you should be able to

- explain the different types of reinforcement, and how they can be used to improve performance and motivation in sport and exercise settings and
- understand the concept of modeling, and how "significant others" can have an impact on sport and exercise behavior.

Participation in physical activity involves social interaction with parents, coaches, teachers, trainers, officials, teammates, and opponents. Through these interactions, individuals adopt attitudes about physical activity, and they behave in accordance with these attitudes. That is, through relationships with others we are socialized into who we are as we develop physically, socially, and psychologically. Socialization is commonly defined as a process whereby individuals learn attitudes, values, and behaviors associated with a given social role (McPherson & Brown, 1988).

Two primary means by which the social learning process occurs are reinforcement and modeling. For example, John is raised in a family that loves ice hockey, and he often plays hockey with his older brother, who shows him how to do things (modeling). In the evenings around the dinner table, John talks about going out for the team, and Dad encourages him (reinforcement). In this social environment it is not surprising that John ends up on a hockey team.

In the first part of this chapter we will examine modeling (and reinforcement) as a social process influencing individual development. Then we will take another tack and look at the people—the significant others—whose influence constitutes a social process in itself.

## MODELING: THE DEMONSTRATION PROCESS

Modeling is most prominent in sport and exercise in observational learning. As instructors, we teach by modeling and instruct students to "watch how I do it." The pervasiveness of observational learning raises many questions. Does modeling provide information or motivation to change motor performance? When and how often should we demonstrate skills? Who should demonstrate skills? Should we demonstrate parts of complex skills and common errors or only complete, correct skills? Sport and exercise psychologists and other motor behavior researchers continue to search for the answers.

According to Bandura's (1986) social-cognitive theory, when we observe others we form a cognitive representation of the action that serves as a reference of

227

**Figure 16.1**
Component processes
in Bandura's social
learning analysis of
observational learning.

From *Social Learning
Theory* by Bandura, ©
1977. Reprinted by
permission of Prentice-
Hall, Inc., Upper Saddle
River, N.J.

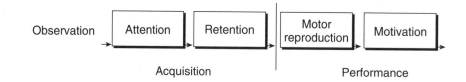

Observation → Attention → Retention | Motor reproduction → Motivation

Acquisition | Performance

correctness. Specifically, modeling affects behaviors through the four-component process illustrated in figure 16.1. The first two processes, attention and retention, relate to learning or acquisition of the skill. The motor-reproduction and motivation processes determine actual performance of the acquired skill.

## Attentional Processes

To learn any skill through modeling, people must first pay attention to the model—specifically, attend to and accurately perceive the significant features of the modeled behavior. If your tennis instructor demonstrates a backhand return but you are watching the ball, you may not pick up the key elements of the stance, swing, and follow-through. Many factors, including characteristics of the model, the observer, and the skill, can affect attentional processes. For instance, young athletes attend to and imitate their favorite professional players. A youngster not only imitates an effective technique, but also may pick up an awkward stance or learn to yell at umpires. Models usually present more information than an observer, especially a beginner, can process effectively. Thus observational learning can be enhanced by channeling attention to critical features of the demonstrated skill (Minas, 1980). Generally, students and athletes are attentive because they like their instructors and coaches, trust their instructor's knowledge, and want to improve their skills. Thus the instructor may use cues or techniques to direct the learner's attention to key elements of the skill.

## Retention Processes

People must not only attend to the model; they must remember the modeled behavior. Retention involves the development of symbolic representations of the skill that serve as internal models for later action. Activities that aid retention, particularly imagery and verbal or symbolic coding, can improve observational learning (Bandura &

Young athletes tend to imitate their favorite players—including effective techniques as well as less positive behaviors, such as yelling at umpires or fighting on the ice.

Jeffery, 1973). For example, mentally rehearsing the serve immediately after a demonstration may strengthen the performer's image of the skill. Good instructors are masters at giving just the right cues or phrases to help performers code the skill in memory. For example, we usually remember dance steps with phrases such as "step-together-step."

## Motor-Reproduction Processes

After attending to and retaining a modeled skill, performers must match their actions to the internal representation of correct performance—which is not easy. I can watch Michael Jordan slam-dunk and can retain a clear image of how to perform that skill, but I will never do the slam dunk. Of course, we usually do not demonstrate skills unless we believe observers could do them. On the other hand, even a capable student does not immediately imitate a complex golf swing or complicated gymnastics move. After modeling sets up an internal image of the skill, the performer—through practice with an instructor's feedback and self-correction—can gradually match actual performance to that image. Physical capabilities, the ability to retain appropriate responses, and accurate feedback are important considerations in the motor-reproduction phase.

## Motivational Processes

The final component in Bandura's model is motivation. We do not imitate everything we learn through observation. External reinforcement (reinforcement to the performer), vicarious reinforcement (reinforcement to the model), and self-reinforcement all help determine which behaviors we will imitate. When you see a teammate elude a defender with a particular dribbling move, you have incentive to imitate that move. Likewise, if your instructor praises you for "getting the idea" of the demonstrated serve you will probably keep trying to do it.

# MODELING AND MOTOR PERFORMANCE

Generally, the quality of a motor skill is determined by the movement form and outcome, and both of these aspects can be influenced by modeling. Most research has assessed modeling effects with outcome measures (McCullagh, 1983); however, more studies are including form measures (Carroll & Bandura, 1985, 1990; Feltz, 1982; Little & McCullagh, 1989; McCullagh, 1987; Weiss, Ebbeck, & Rose, 1992; Wiese-Bjornstal & Weiss, 1992). Some research has demonstrated the value of assessing both form and performance outcome for studying modeling effectiveness (Feltz, 1982; Martens, Burwitz, & Zuckerman, 1976; McCullagh, 1987).

Earlier research showed that modeling provides information about how to perform motor skills (Feltz, 1982; Feltz & Landers, 1977; Gould, 1978; Martens et al., 1976). For example, Gould (1978), comparing the effectiveness of modeling across several motor tasks, reported that modeling was more helpful for a complex task with several steps than for relatively simple tasks.

Research by Weiss and colleagues (McCullagh, Stiehl, & Weiss, 1990; Weiss, 1983; Weiss & Klint, 1987) suggests that age or developmental level also influences the effectiveness of modeling. For example, older children (ages 7-8) performed equally well after observing either a silent or a verbal model, but younger children (ages 4-5) improved only through observing the verbal model (Weiss, 1983). Interestingly, Weiss and Klint (1987) found no age differences as children ranging in age from 5 to 10 years all experienced the performance-enhancing effects of verbal rehearsal. In a subsequent study, McCullagh and colleagues (1990) discovered that the effectiveness of the model depended, in part, on whether the performance outcome or movement form was assessed. Viewing a model resulted in higher form scores irrespective of verbal rehearsal. Interestingly, individuals who received verbal instructions with no modeling were better able to recall the order of tasks. Collectively, these results suggest that one needs to consider developmental factors, particularly verbal-cognitive abilities, when examining the observational learning process.

The characteristics of the model may also have motivational effects. For example, Gould (1978) observed that the sex of the model affected observational learning, and Gould and Weiss (1981) found that models similar to the observer elicited greater endurance performance than did dissimilar models.

In an early study of model characteristics, Landers and Landers (1973) compared the effectiveness of teacher and peer models who were skilled or unskilled on the Bachman ladder task, a novel balancing task. The authors reasoned that modeling would facilitate the performance of fifth- and sixth-grade girls and that skilled models and teacher models would be more effective than unskilled and peer models. Modeling facilitated performance in all groups, but model characteristics did not influence performance as expected. The skilled-teacher model elicited better performance than all the others; but surprisingly, students who observed the unskilled peer performed better than those who saw either the skilled peer or the unskilled teacher.

Lirgg and Feltz (1991) replicated and extended the work of Landers and Landers (1973) by using unfamiliar and videotaped models and assessing both performance outcome and movement form. Viewing skilled models facilitated performance, but there was no model-by-skill interaction. Although skilled models can enhance performance, unskilled models may be appropriate in some cases, particularly if learners receive information they can use to improve their performance (McCullagh, 1993).

## MODELING OF NONPERFORMANCE BEHAVIORS

Although the influence of modeling on performance is our main concern, models also influence nonperformance behaviors. As discussed in chapter 6, vicarious experiences are a major source of self-efficacy. Modeling can enhance self-efficacy and reduce anxiety on fear-provoking sport tasks as well as facilitate performance (Feltz, Landers, & Raeder, 1979; McAuley, 1985). Lirgg and Feltz (1991) found that individuals who watched a skilled model were more efficacious than those viewing either no model or unskilled models.

One of the most notable roles of modeling is in the development of aggressive and prosocial behaviors. Bandura is widely recognized for his "Bobo doll" experiments demonstrating the influence of models on the learning and performance of aggressive behaviors. As we will discuss in more detail in chapter 17, modeling probably plays a major role in violent or aggressive behaviors in sport. In fact, research (Bryan, 1969; Bryan & Walbek, 1970) implies that our actions speak louder than our words when communicating social behaviors.

Bryan (1969) compared the relative importance of words and deeds on the generosity behaviors of elementary school children. After playing a miniature bowling game, the children received certificates that they could either redeem for prizes or donate "to the poor." The model in the study either acted generously and donated the certificates or acted greedily and kept them. At the same time, the model either preached generosity by extolling the values of charity or preached greed by pointing out that the certificates were earned and need not be donated.

Bryan's findings confirmed that actions spoke louder than words. Children did as the model did regardless of what the model said. Hypocrisy had no effect on their decisions. Children were just as generous when the model preached greed but donated the certificates as when the model both preached and practiced generosity, and the findings were analogous when the model kept the certificates. Bryan did suggest that words might provoke thoughts and have long-term effects on behavior even if they did not affect immediate actions. Nevertheless, his findings imply that out-of-shape instructors advocating fitness exercises, and coaches who talk about being a good sport while storming up and down the sidelines, may be wasting their breath.

Bryan's findings confirmed that actions spoke louder than words. Children did as the model did regardless of what the model said.

## SIGNIFICANT OTHERS AS SOCIAL INFLUENCES

In chapter 15 and also here, we have considered social processes, including modeling, in which instructors, coaches, and other significant individuals try to influence the individual's behavioral, psychological, and social development. In Harter's (1978, 1981b) theory of competence motivation, significant others provide feedback and reinforcement that in turn impact the child's self-perceptions and motivation. When we think of significant others in the lives of athletes we think of coaches, but they are not the only ones who impact the development of sport participants.

The significant others who receive the most attention as influences in the psychosocial development of young athletes are parents, peers, and coaches. These three socializing agents can influence physical activity-related cognitions, affect, and behaviors and overall self-concept throughout life. Literature provides evidence that parental influence is particularly strong in childhood, with peers and coaches becoming more influential as one approaches adolescence (Coakley, 1993; Greendorfer, 1977; Greendorfer, Lewko, & Rosengren, 1996; Horn & Weiss, 1991; Weiss & Frazer, 1995). Research has also shown that athletes use parents, peers, and coaches as competence information sources. Most research involves coaches, but we are gaining knowledge on the role of parents and beginning to consider the role of peers. In this section we will examine the literature dealing with parents, peers, and coaches.

There are three socializing agents that can influence physical activity-related cognitions, affect, and behaviors, as well as overall self-concept throughout life: parents, peers, and coaches.

### Parents

Although many theories explain motivation, Eccles and Harrold's (1991) expectancy-value model is particularly useful for understanding the socializing role of parents. The model proposes that parents communicate their value for a given area of achievement (e.g., sport, academics, exercise) and their belief about their child's likelihood of success in a given endeavor (e.g., trying out for a sport team or band). These parental behaviors influence the child's thoughts and behavior. For example, physically active parents tend to have more physically active children than less physically active parents (Freedson & Evenson, 1991). Eccles and Harrold (1991) suggest that parental influence is expressed in two ways. First, parents who value a given activity and hold high expectations are more likely to seek out that type of activity for their child. Additionally, parents help their children interpret information about their ability; parental influence gives children reason to want to do well and to believe they can do well (Brustad, 1993, 1996; Dempsey, Kimiecik, & Horn, 1996; Kimiecik & Horn, 1998; Kimiecik, Horn, & Shurin, 1996).

Brustad (1993, 1996) has focused on the child's psychological outcomes and argued that we must start with an understanding of parents' expectancies and values, and then explore how these influence the children's psychosocial development, including attraction to physical activity (Brustad, 1998). Brustad (1993, 1996) found that fourth-grade children were more attracted to physical activity when they perceived themselves to be more competent, and that those who perceived themselves as more competent had parents who encouraged them to participate. These encouraging parents enjoyed physical activity more than less encouraging parents. Boys reported receiving more encouragement from their parents than girls, and boys also viewed themselves as more competent than girls—further supporting the relationship between encouragement and perceived competence. Perhaps if parents encouraged their daughters as much as their sons, girls would perceive themselves as more competent and in turn be more attracted to physical activity.

Kimiecik and Horn and colleagues (Dempsey et al., 1996; Kimiecik & Horn, 1998; Kimiecik et al., 1996) have used both Eccles's expectancy perspective and Ford and Lerner's (1992) developmental systems theory to study parental beliefs associated with children's participation in moderate-to-vigorous physical activity (MVPA). Their research demonstrates that (a) parents who perceive their children to be competent in physical activity are more likely to have children who perceive themselves to be competent and who are attracted to MVPA; (b) children who believe they are competent in physical activity are more likely to engage in MVPA; and (c) parents who are more task goal oriented are more likely to have children who engage in MVPA. That is, children are more likely to be physically active when they believe they are capable, and are more likely to believe this if their parents do.

Although these studies generally indicate that parents' beliefs relate to their children's perceptions and activity levels, the results are not totally consistent; further research is needed to clarify the relationships. Still, it is evident that parents play a big role in shaping children's sport and exercise behaviors. Children's peers also play a role in shaping attitudes, cognitions, and behaviors relative to physical activity.

## Peers

Peer influence in sport and physical activity is well documented (Gill, Gross, & Huddleston, 1983; Gould, 1993; Gould & Petlichkoff, 1988; Raedeke, 1997; Sapp & Haubenstricker, 1978). As discussed in chapter 7, children indicate that being with friends is an important reason for their sport participation, and peer comparison is an important source of competence information (Horn, Glenn, & Wnetzell, 1993; Horn & Weiss, 1991; Weiss, Ebbeck, & Horn, 1997). Research has also shown that conflict resolution via dialogue with peers can positively impact children's moral development (Romance, Weiss, & Bockoven, 1986).

Although peers are important, particularly in youth sports, few studies have examined peer groups, relations, or interactions in sport. Relying heavily on developmental psychology, Weiss and colleagues (Smith, 1997; Weiss & Smith, 1998; Weiss, Smith, & Theeboom, 1996) have begun an in-depth investigation into peer relationships.

As Smith (1997) notes, most research on peer relationships focuses on peer acceptance, which involves status (worthiness) and popularity (likability) within a group (Bukowski & Hoza, 1989). In sport, status is linked to ability (Chase & Drummer, 1992; Evans & Roberts, 1987; Weiss & Duncan, 1992). For example, boys with greater ability became team captain, selected team members, and decided who would play and where (Evans & Roberts, 1987); and athletic prowess is a means to popularity, particularly for boys (Buchanan, Blankenbaker, & Cotten, 1976). Recently, Smith (1997) found that individuals who saw themselves as accepted group members were also more apt to have a sense of pride and confidence in physical activity endeavors.

In his review of the friendship literature in physical activity, Smith (1997) draws three conclusions. First, friendship is context specific (Zarbatany, Ghesquiere, & Mohr, 1992). That is, we may expect our friends to help us when we experience academic troubles, but not when we are opponents in a sporting event. Sport participants expected their best friend to provide reinforcement and encouragement; to display positive personal characteristics; to demonstrate loyalty, guidance, and emotional support; and to spend time with them (Weiss et al., 1996). Second, sport

Some research has shown a relationship between children's interest in, and self-confidence about, physical activity and their parents' physical activity behaviors and attitudes.

presents opportunities for friendship development, but low physical ability limits friendship options (Bigelow, Lewko, & Salhani, 1989). Third, quality of friendships was linked with affect (Duncan, 1993). Specifically, individuals who placed greater value on companionship and esteem support experienced greater affect in physical activity.

Weiss et al. (1996), interviewing 38 athletes 8 to 16 years of age about their best friends in sport, found both positive and negative dimensions of friendship. Children reported that they liked the companionship, having fun while playing, the acceptance and respect of friends (self-esteem enhancement), the help they received, the nice things their best friends did for them (prosocial behavior), the mutual trust and understanding (intimacy), the common interests, and the mutual emotional support.

Several aspects of friendship were also discussed in both positive and negative terms. For instance, children liked their best friends, but recognized their faults. Participants liked the loyalty when their best friends stuck up for them, and not surprisingly did not like to be betrayed. Betrayal included such things as when a best friend "pays more attention to another friend" (Weiss et al., 1996, p. 371). Lastly, participants did not like conflict with their best friends, but did note that conflict was rare and easy to resolve.

After describing friendship among young people in sport-related activities, Weiss and colleagues (Smith, 1997; Weiss & Smith, 1998; Weiss et al., 1996) pursued relationships among peer acceptance, friendship, and various psychosocial and motivational variables. Smith (1997) examined peer influence on physical self-worth, affective responses associated with physical activity, and motivation among 418 middle school students. As already mentioned, his results supported the relationship of peer acceptance to physical self-worth, but close personal friends in sport and physical activities had the major impact. Specifically, adolescents who have close personal friendships within physical activity are more apt to like the activity, to be more motivated to achieve through hard work, and to be active participants. Clearly, peers in youth sport can have a powerful influence—but coaches, who structure the sporting environment, are also highly influential.

## Coaches

Early research focused on coaches' leadership behavior and the influence of feedback patterns on athlete cognitions, affect, and behavior. For example, Chelladurai's (1993) multidimensional model of leadership and related research, discussed in chapter 21, suggests that the more the leader's actual behaviors match the preferences of the group members and the situation requirements, the better the group's performance and the greater the group members' satisfaction.

Research using Chelladurai's (1993) model and Smith and Smoll's (1997) work on coaching effectiveness, discussed in chapter 15, indicates that athletes seem to be satisfied with the leadership of coaches who emphasize training and instruction and positive feedback contingent on good performance.

# INTERVENTIONS FOR SOCIAL AND PSYCHOLOGICAL DEVELOPMENT THROUGH PHYSICAL ACTIVITY

Understanding how significant others influence youth participants can lead to interventions to enhance children's physical activity experiences and social development. Bredemeier and others have applied a structural-developmental perspective in

Some studies have shown that sport and physical activity can have a positive impact on moral growth, such as respect for officials, rules, opponents, and the right of all participants to play.

physical activity settings (discussed in chapter 17) to demonstrate changes in moral development (Ebbeck & Gibbons, 1998; Gibbons, Ebbeck, & Weiss, 1995; Romance et al., 1986).

Gibbons and colleagues (Gibbons et al., 1995) investigated the effects of Fair Play for Kids, an educational program, on moral judgment, reason, intention, and behavior of fourth and sixth graders. The curriculum emphasizes respect for rules, officials, and opponents, the right of all participants to play, and the importance of self-control. Gibbons et al. (1995) assigned classes into (a) control, (b) Fair Play for Kids curriculum in physical education classes only, and (c) Fair Play for Kids curriculum in all classes. After seven months, both treatment groups scored higher than the control groups on moral judgment, reason, intention, and behavior. These results confirm that sport and physical activity can have a positive impact on moral growth—when designed to do so.

Other physical activity programs aimed at teaching personal and social development (see Cheffers, 1997; Colley, 1998; Hellison, Martinek, & Cutforth, 1996) arose from a sense of need to help at-risk children. Today, not only inner city children and adolescents are at risk for social ills such as child neglect and abuse, homelessness, gang violence, and delinquency; according to Hellison (1995), 50% of affluent suburban families living in the Chicago area are dysfunctional.

On the basis of his experience and his commitment to help students, Hellison (1995) developed a teaching model based on responsibility. The model gives students opportunities to feel empowered, purposeful, and connected to others as well as to experience responsible behavior, to persevere, and to acknowledge activities that impinge upon others' rights (Hellison & Templin, 1991). Responsibility is defined via goals or levels; being responsible outside the gymnasium is the ultimate Level V goal. In Hellison's cumulative approach, each higher level encompasses all lower levels. Individuals can, and often do, function at multiple levels. For example, a student may engage in self-directed play and cooperate with others one minute and shout at and blame another player the next minute. Figure 16.2 describes Hellison's levels.

In Hellison's (1995) gym, lessons usually begin with *awareness talks* in which students learn the importance of the levels. During the lesson, students experience the *levels in action.* For example, students may play an inclusion game to stress the notion that everyone has a right to participate. Opportunities for *individual decision*

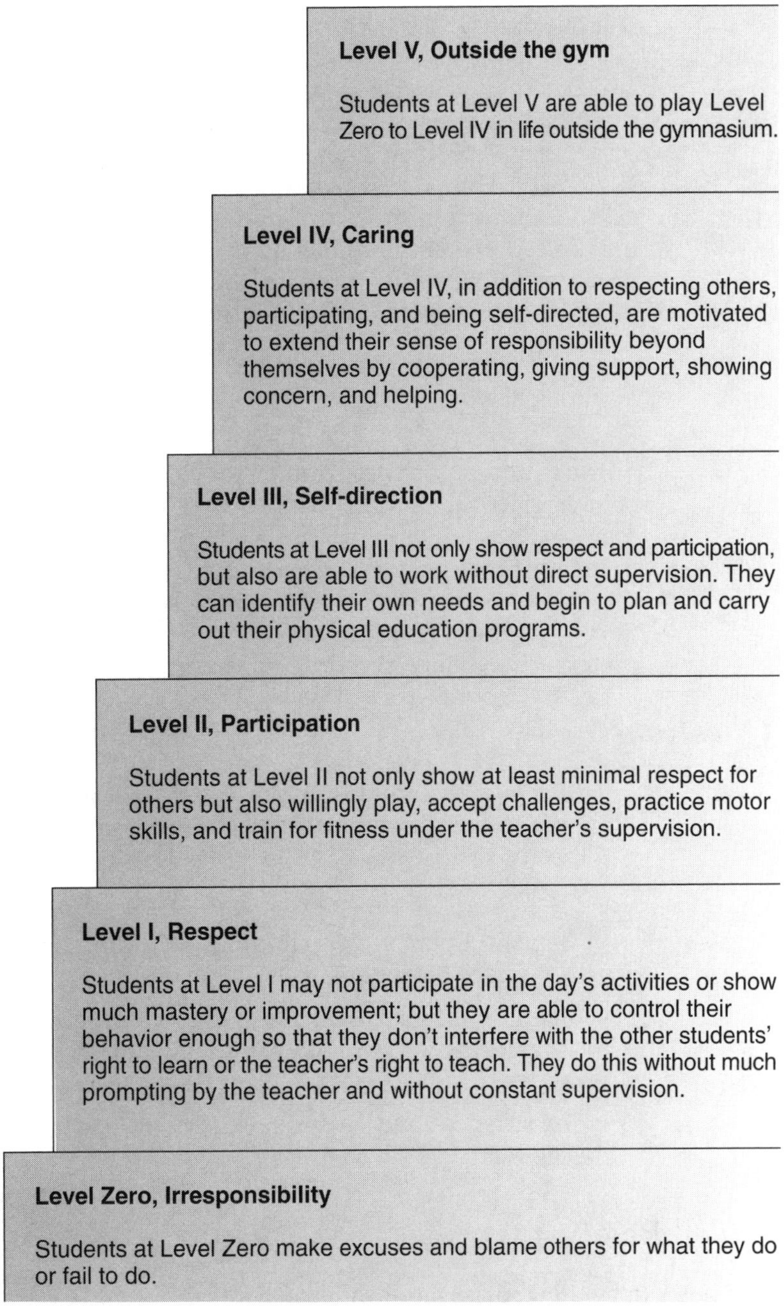

**Figure 16.2**
Hellison's levels presented as a cumulative progression.

Adapted, by permission, from D.R. Hellison, 1995, *Teaching responsibility through physical activity* (Champaign, IL: Human Kinetics), 13.

**Level V, Outside the gym**

Students at Level V are able to play Level Zero to Level IV in life outside the gymnasium.

**Level IV, Caring**

Students at Level IV, in addition to respecting others, participating, and being self-directed, are motivated to extend their sense of responsibility beyond themselves by cooperating, giving support, showing concern, and helping.

**Level III, Self-direction**

Students at Level III not only show respect and participation, but also are able to work without direct supervision. They can identify their own needs and begin to plan and carry out their physical education programs.

**Level II, Participation**

Students at Level II not only show at least minimal respect for others but also willingly play, accept challenges, practice motor skills, and train for fitness under the teacher's supervision.

**Level I, Respect**

Students at Level I may not participate in the day's activities or show much mastery or improvement; but they are able to control their behavior enough so that they don't interfere with the other students' right to learn or the teacher's right to teach. They do this without much prompting by the teacher and without constant supervision.

**Level Zero, Irresponsibility**

Students at Level Zero make excuses and blame others for what they do or fail to do.

*making,* such as choosing activities, are built into instruction. *Group meetings* provide opportunities to share ideas, opinions, and feelings about the program and to practice group decision sharing and decision making. Individual and group decision-making strategies typically come into play in response to a particular incident. The lessons always close with *reflection time* in which students discuss the degree to which they have been respectful of others, involved in the program, self-directed, and helpful to others.

Research on Hellison's Responsibility Model curriculum has been limited, yet encouraging (DeBusk & Hellison, 1989; Puckett & Cutforth, 1996; Williamson & Georgiadis, 1992). For example, DeBusk and Hellison (1989), after conducting pre- and post-six-week responsibility-intervention interviews with 10 fourth-grade boys identified as having behavioral problems, concluded that the intervention helped the students become more aware of self-responsibility concepts and incorporate some of these concepts into their lives. None of the changes were dramatic, and the responsibility lessons learned did not transfer outside the gym.

Despite the lack of strong empirical support, the model has been well received, and others have developed similar programs. The Responsibility Model has been identified as an outstanding curriculum model, an alternative approach to discipline-related problems, and a viable approach for special populations (Hellison, 1995, 1996). Tom Martinek has recently developed a school-based alternative physical education program for underserved youth called Project Effort, which is grounded in the Responsibility Model (Hellison et al., 1996). The continued extension of such programs, along with related research, is both inevitable and welcome as we seek not only to understand, but also to actively promote, social development in real-world activity programs.

## Summary

Through the sport socialization process, individuals learn attitudes, values, and behaviors for sport participation. Most commonly, people learn through reinforcement and observation. We tend to act in a way we will be rewarded for, and attempt to imitate those we wish to learn from. Parents, peers, and coaches are the primary socializing agents in physical activity settings. Both research and practical educational programs have demonstrated that people can learn and practice appropriate prosocial behaviors in sport and physical activity settings.

## Review Questions

1. Explain how modeling affects behavior by relating the concepts of attentional processes, retentional processes, motor-reproduction processes, and motivational processes.

2. Discuss the wide array of research on modeling and motor performance.

3. Explain Bryan's (1969) findings regarding modeling and its effects on nonperformance behaviors.

4. Identify the three socializing agents that can influence physical activity-related cognitions and behaviors in young athletes.

5. Highlight several interventions aimed at enhancing children's physical activity experiences and social development, such as Hellison's Self-Responsibility Model.

## Recommended Reading

★ Brustad, R.J. (1992). Integrating socialization influences into the study of children's motivation in sport. *Journal of Sport & Exercise Psychology, 14,* 59-77.

> Brustad is one of the few sport and exercise psychologists who emphasize social developmental issues, and specifically the influence of coaches, parents, and peers in youth sport settings. In this article he calls for more attention to this important topic, presents background research and models, and suggests directions.

★ Kimiecik, J.C., & Horn, T.S. (1998). Parental beliefs and children's moderate-to-vigorous physical activity. *Research Quarterly for Exercise and Sport, 69,* 163-175.

> The topic of social development is important but difficult to investigate. This article presents results of a study of parental beliefs and children's physical activity.

★ Hellison, D.R. (1995). *Teaching responsibility through physical activity*. Champaign, IL: Human Kinetics.

> Hellison is leading the way in using physical activity programs to promote social development with underserved youth. Many researchers, educators, and social and community program personnel are adopting his approach, and some sport and exercise psychologists have contributed to this exciting work. This source presents the responsibility model that is the basis of much of the ongoing work.

## chapter 17

# Aggression and Prosocial Behavior

**Lavon Williams, PhD**
*Northern Illinois University*
**Diane L. Gill, PhD**
*University of North Carolina–Greensboro*

## CHAPTER OBJECTIVES

After studying this chapter, you should be able to

- explain several concepts and theories of aggression,
- understand the effects of aggression on performance, and
- understand the concept of prosocial behavior, and how it can be encouraged in sport and exercise settings.

Aggressive behavior is obvious in sport and physical activity settings. We may see basketball players "fight" for rebounds, or runners throw elbows and jostle for position in a race. At the more extreme end of the spectrum, we may have read about the rampage of English soccer fans in Brussels before a European Cup match that left 38 people dead and more than 400 injured (Lacayo, 1985), or about how a referee's decision set off a melee, killing 40 and injuring 50, among soccer fans near Johannesburg (Wren, 1991). Closer to home, the "celebration" in Detroit after the Pistons won the 1990 National Basketball Association championship left 8 dead and 127 injured (Dean, 1990). Of course, not all aggressive sport behavior is violent. In fact, many forms of aggressive behavior are accepted and even promoted; often aggression is "part of the game."

Using the term *aggression* to refer to such a wide range of behaviors can cause confusion. We label violent outbursts in sport as aggression but also talk about the "aggressive" player who takes chances in a close contest. Value judgments and emotional connotations further cloud our understanding. We encourage certain aggressive behaviors and praise individuals who use "good" aggressive tactics, but we consider other, "bad" aggressive acts shocking. Most aggressive behaviors in physical activity settings are neither clearly desirable nor clearly undesirable. Instead, they are usually viewed as distasteful by some and as justifiable by others. Although not all researchers will agree (see Mummendey & Mummendey, 1983), we can define and explain aggression more easily if we do not think of aggression as totally positive or negative, desirable or undesirable, but simply as behavior that we want to understand.

In this chapter we will consider concepts and theories of aggression and then look more closely at aggression in sport, including its antecedents and its effects on performance. We will then give some attention to the other side of the coin, which is unfortunately not as widely discussed—prosocial behaviors in sport.

# DEFINING AGGRESSION

Before we discuss explanations of aggression, we need to clarify terms. We could all agree that some behaviors constitute aggression. When Nolan Ryan put a headlock on Robin Ventura and pummeled him with six punches (Wulf, 1993), that was clearly an incident of aggression. Take a minute and write down a definition that you think will clearly delineate behaviors that you consider aggression. Now, let's see how well your definition works as you watch the play-off game between two youth hockey teams, the Blue Bombers and the Red Barons.

1. Mark, one of the Bombers' top players, slams Jeff, a Baron forward, into the boards to keep him away from the puck (a perfectly legal move).

2. Jeff retaliates by swinging his stick and smashing Mark in the ribs (not a perfectly legal move).

3. When the same thing occurs later in the game, Jeff again tries to retaliate by swinging his stick at Mark, but Mark skates away and Jeff misses.

4. Tim, Mark's younger brother and the least-skilled Bomber player, gets into the game for his required ice time in the final minute. Tim is defending the goal as Baron forward Marcia skates toward it to take a shot that could tie the game. Tim tries to take the puck away from Marcia, catches his stick on her skate, and accidentally trips her.

5. Missing her chance to make the tying goal and become the first girl to score a hat trick in a play-off game, Marcia jumps up and yells at Tim that he's a wimp who "should stick to figure skating and eating quiche."

6. Gary, Marcia's father and the Barons' assistant coach, seeing his team's championship hopes end as the time runs out, smashes his clipboard over the bench.

How many of those incidents do you believe are aggression? Does your definition clearly demarcate aggressive from nonaggressive incidents? Do you define legal tactics as aggression? What about accidental injuries? What if someone tries to hit you but misses? Can aggression be verbal? Is throwing a golf club aggression? Everyone may not agree on all these issues. However, most agree that aggression involves the intent to injure: that when Jeff swings his stick at Mark and misses, that is aggression, but Tim's accidental tripping of Marcia is not aggression. Most definitions of aggression include this notion of *intention* to harm.

In *Human Aggression*, Baron and Richardson (1994) offer the following representative definition:

> *Aggression is any form of behavior directed toward the goal of harming or injuring another living being who is motivated to avoid such treatment. (p. 7)*

This definition raises several key points. First, aggression is *behavior.* Aggression is not an attitude, emotion, or motive. Wanting to hurt someone is not aggression; anger is not aggression. Anger and thoughts might play a role in aggressive behavior, but they are not necessary or defining characteristics. Second, aggression is *directed* or *intentional* behavior. Accidental harm is not aggression, but acts that are intended to injure are, whether successful or not. Third, aggression involves *harm* or *injury.* Aggression is not limited to physical assaults but may include verbal and nonverbal acts intended to cause psychological harm, or behaviors that deprive a person of something, such as destroying a teammate's equipment. The fourth criterion is that aggression involves *living beings.* According to Baron and Richardson, kicking your dog is aggression, but kicking a bench is not. Finally, Baron and Richardson limit aggression to incidents in which the victim is motivated to avoid such treatment, eliminating sadomasochistic and suicidal acts from the definition.

Baron and Richardson's definition delineates aggression as we commonly understand it, but many see the need for further clarification. By definition, a defensive back who makes a hard tackle to stop a runner and a football player who gives an opponent an extra punch under the pile are both committing aggression, but most of us look at these two behaviors quite differently. The aggression literature differentiates *instrumental aggression,* or aggressive behavior committed to achieve a nonaggressive goal, from *hostile aggression,* which usually involves anger and has harm or injury as its primary goal. Much aggression in sport is instrumental; participants use aggressive behaviors to get the ball, score points, or stop opponents. Hostile aggression also occurs in sport, and the dividing line between hostile and instrumental aggression is quite fuzzy.

Husman and Silva (1984) also distinguish aggression from *assertive behavior.* Diving into the stands for a basketball and looking for the "kill" shot in volleyball are not aggression, because they do not involve intended harm. Instead, they are purposeful, goal-directed, assertive behaviors. Performers who strive for competitive success or make forceful, decisive plays are not necessarily aggressive; and in this chapter we will restrict the term aggression to behaviors intended to harm or injure others.

### Key Point

*Instrumental aggression* is aggressive behavior committed to achieve a nonaggressive goal. *Hostile aggression* usually involves anger and has harm or injury as its primary goal. *Assertive behavior* is typically distinguished from aggression because assertive behaviors are purposeful and goal-directed, and do not involve intended harm.

## THEORIES OF AGGRESSION

We can now turn to explanations of aggression. The aggression literature, unlike that for many sport and exercise psychology topics, is rich in theory. Because of its prevalence and social implications, people want to know why aggression occurs, what characteristics predispose a person to aggression, what environmental and social factors elicit it, and whether it can be directed or controlled. Explanations of and approaches to aggression fall into three major categories: instinct theories, drive theories, and social learning theories.

### Instinct Theories

Instinct theories propose that aggressiveness is an innate characteristic: we are born with an aggressive instinct that makes aggressive behavior inevitable. The two main categories of instinct theories are psychoanalytic and ethological approaches.

### Key Point

Instinct theories propose that aggressiveness is an innate characteristic: we are born with an aggressive instinct that makes aggressive behavior inevitable.

Psychoanalytic approaches are associated with Freud, who held that human beings have two basic instincts, including *eros,* the energizing life force, and *thanatos,* the death instinct or destructive force. Aggression occurs when the death instinct is turned outward, away from the individual and toward others.

The ethological approach is most familiar through the work of Konrad Lorenz (1966) and other ethologists who assert that the aggressive instinct is an innate fighting instinct developed through evolution. Much of the ethological literature

According to the ethological approach, the aggressive instinct is an innate fighting instinct developed through evolution.

draws comparisons between humans and other species. Ardrey (1966), for example, discusses the instinctive tendency of animals to defend their territory with aggressive behaviors and notes that humans do the same thing. For example, do you feel like throwing out another student who occupies "your" seat in a class? Do you consider it an invasion if another person bypasses all the empty tables in the library to sit right next to you?

According to Lorenz, the fighting instinct spontaneously generates aggressive energy that continues to build up, like steam in a boiler, until it is released through an aggressive act. The more built-up energy there is, the more easily the aggressive behavior is triggered and the more potentially destructive the outburst.

Lorenz suggests that because aggressive energy always accumulates, the best way to prevent destructive violence is to ensure that people release aggressive energy in less destructive ways. Ethologists strongly advocate competitive sport as one of the best ways for people to "let off steam." Lorenz asserted that the greatest value of sport is its provision of an outlet for aggressive energy, and Storr (1968) presented the following view:

> It is obvious that the encouragement of competition in all possible fields is likely to diminish the kind of hostility which leads to war rather than to increase it. . . . Rivalry between nations in sport can do nothing but good. (p. 132)

Many coaches and teachers seem to adhere to an instinct theory of aggression when they make similar statements to promote their competitive sport programs.

Although instinct theories might provide a nice justification for some programs, most researchers do not accept the psychoanalytic or ethological explanations of aggressive behavior. Instinct theories predict that all individuals and cultures have the same innate urges, generate similar levels of aggressive energy, and should exhibit similar levels of aggressive behavior. Cross-cultural comparisons suggest that this is not the case. Instinct theories also imply that the cultures with the greatest number of nondestructive outlets for aggression, or the most aggressive games, will be the least warlike. Again, anthropological evidence suggests otherwise. Are athletes who participate in the most aggressive competitive sports the calmest and least aggressive people off the field? Perhaps some are, but this generalization would probably not hold across many comparisons. Most psychologists do not accept instinct theories, but believe instead that reasoning plays a critical role.

## Drive Theories

Drive theory, the second major theoretical perspective on aggression, has more credibility among psychologists. The most notable drive approach is the frustration-aggression hypothesis of Dollard, Doob, Miller, Mowrer, and Sears (1939). The hypothesis holds that (a) frustration always leads to some form of aggression and (b) aggression always stems from frustration. Actually, frustration does not cause aggression directly. Instead, frustration, which is any blocking of a goal-oriented behavior, induces an *aggressive drive,* which in turn facilitates aggressive behavior.

### Key Point

The frustration-aggression hypothesis of Dollard, Doob, Miller, Mowrer, and Sears (1939) is one of the most notable drive theories. It holds that frustration, which is any blocking of a goal-oriented behavior, induces an *aggressive drive,* which in turn facilitates aggressive behavior.

The proposition that frustration leads to aggression fits with many of our observations in sport. When former Ohio State football coach Woody Hayes slugged the Clemson player who had just intercepted a pass and eliminated any chance of an Ohio State victory, didn't frustration seem like the obvious cause of his aggressive behavior?

On the other hand, I can recall incidents in which obviously frustrated individuals did not commit any aggressive act but took nonaggressive action or simply gave up in despair. Furthermore, many aggressive sport behaviors occur with no evidence of preceding frustration. Thus the frustration-aggression relationship may not be as inevitable as the hypothesis states. Miller, Dollard and colleagues, and others modified their frustration-aggression hypothesis, but most current aggression researchers do not accept the mediating role of aggressive drive as inevitable.

Many aggressive sport behaviors, such as boxing, occur with no evidence of preceding frustration.

© iPhotoNews.com

Although the original frustration-aggression hypothesis is not widely advocated today, one of the most prominent aggression scholars, Leonard Berkowitz (1962, 1965, 1969, 1974, 1993), retains some of its elements in his revision of the frustration-aggression hypothesis. In many ways Berkowitz's views are closer to social learning theory than to drive theory, but he proposes that learning and innate sources of aggression coexist. According to Berkowitz, frustration plays a role by arousing anger and creating a "readiness" for aggressive behavior. Frustration is not a sufficient cause for aggression, however, and readiness for aggression is not a drive that must be released. Instead, learning and situational cues are critical in determining whether or not aggressive behavior actually occurs.

Berkowitz is one of the most productive researchers in aggression. In a typical experiment, a subject was angered or not angered and then given the opportunity to commit aggression against a victim, usually by administering shocks. Within that framework, Berkowitz examined several cues and situational factors. In general, anger arousal influenced aggressive behavior, as subjects who were angered usually gave more shocks. However, situational cues exerted an even greater influence. Watching an aggressive film, the presence of aggressive weapons, and characteristics of the victim that were associated with aggression (such as being a boxer rather than a speech major and having the same name as an aggressive character in a film) all increased aggressive behavior.

## Social Learning Theory

Proponents of the social learning perspective, most notably Albert Bandura (1973), assert that aggression is a learned social behavior and as such is acquired, elicited, and maintained in the same manner as other behaviors. According to Bandura, we learn or acquire aggressive behaviors through direct reinforcement and observational learning. Clearly, many aggressive behaviors are encouraged and reinforced in sport. For example, fans cheer when you slam an opponent into the boards in ice hockey, and giving an opponent a hard elbow under the boards may keep that opponent "off your back" for the rest of a basketball game. Similarly, when you "take out" the shortstop on your slide into second base, you interfere with the throw and allow your softball teammate to reach first base safely.

> **Key Point**
>
> Proponents of the social learning perspective, most notably Albert Bandura (1973), assert that aggression is a learned social behavior and as such is acquired, elicited, and maintained in the same manner as other behaviors. According to Bandura, we learn or acquire aggressive behaviors through direct reinforcement and observational learning.

Sometimes the reinforcement is more subtle. Perhaps the youth soccer coach and league rules punish aggressive acts, but when young Alan gets home his parents tell him he did a great job intimidating the opposing forward with his tough, aggressive play. Perhaps another coach formally abides by the rules against aggressive play but cheers when a player pushes an opponent to get to the ball.

In Bandura's (Bandura, 1965; Bandura, Ross, & Ross, 1963a, 1963b) "Bobo doll" studies on the modeling of aggressive behavior, children watched a model playing with various toys. In one condition, the model threw and punched the Bobo doll while making statements such as "Sock him in the nose" and "Hit him down," whereas another model did not demonstrate aggressive behaviors. Invariably, observing an aggressive model, whether live or on film, increased the children's aggressive behavior. Seeing an aggressive model receive a reward or praise especially elicited aggressive behavior, whereas children who saw an aggressive model punished did not display as much aggressive behavior. When those same children were offered rewards for imitating the aggressive model, however, they displayed just as much aggressive behavior as those who had seen the aggressive model rewarded. The vicarious rewards and punishments to the model influenced the children's actual display of aggressive behaviors, but apparently all of the children learned the behaviors.

Unlike instinct and drive theories, social learning theory does not propose any constant drive toward aggression. Instead, individuals learn aggression through reinforcement and modeling, and commit aggression only under facilitating conditions. Social learning theory is the most optimistic approach to aggression and violence. If people can learn aggressive responses to certain situations and cues, they can also learn nonaggressive responses to those same situations. Whereas instinct and drive theories see aggression as inevitable, social learning theory suggests that aggression is learned and can be controlled.

## AGGRESSION AND SPORT

Sport and exercise psychology research on aggression has taken three main routes. Some have approached aggression in sport as a catharsis that releases aggressive impulses and reduces aggressive behavior in nonsport settings. Others have examined the antecedents and consequences of aggression in sport, and still others have focused on how aggressive behavior affects sport performance.

## Sport as a Catharsis for Aggression

The most debated aggression issue is whether sport, especially highly competitive, contact sport, can act as a catharsis to reduce aggressive behavior in nonsport settings. Will bigger and better Olympic Games reduce the likelihood of war? Will our streets be safer if we start a community basketball program? Proponents often claim that sport can reduce antisocial behaviors in the larger society, and many participants adhere to similar beliefs. For example, former professional football player and coach Mike Ditka once stated:

> There's no question about it. I feel a lot of football players build up a lot of anxieties in the off-season because they have no outlets for them. . . . I'm an overactive person anyway and if I don't get rid of this energy, it just builds up in me and then I blow it off in some other way which is not really the proper way. (Fisher, 1976, pp. 251-252)

Although many contend that sport acts as a catharsis for aggressive behavior, the evidence does not support such claims. As noted earlier, instinct theories support sport as a catharsis, and the original frustration-aggression hypothesis also implies that sport acts as a catharsis by releasing the aggressive drive. Those theories are not major forces in today's aggression literature, however; and neither social learning theory nor the revised frustration-aggression hypothesis provides support for the catharsis phenomenon. In fact, both Bandura and Berkowitz argue that learning and reinforcement of aggressive behavior, which often occur in sport, should *increase* rather than decrease the probability of later aggressive behavior. Indirect support for this comes from Koss and Gaines (1993), who found that participation in sport, particularly revenue-generating sport, was associated with sexual aggression whereas fraternity membership was not.

People may debate whether engaging in aggressive behavior reduces the tendency to engage in subsequent aggressive behavior, but evidence clearly indicates that merely *observing* aggressive behavior has no cathartic effect. As Berkowitz (1970) concludes:

> A decade of laboratory research has virtually demolished the contention that people will lessen their aggressive tendencies by watching other persons beat each other up. (p. 2)

Just as laboratory research refutes the cathartic value of observing aggression, field studies demonstrate that watching aggressive sport increases rather than decreases hostility. In a unique field study, Goldstein and Arms (1971) questioned spectators at a football game and at a gymnastics meet. Spectators at the football game experienced increased feelings of hostility after the game, whereas spectators at the gymnastics meet did not. In a more extensive and controlled replication, individuals who watched aggressive sport contests (wrestling and ice hockey) experienced increased feelings of hostility, but those who watched a swimming meet did not (Arms, Russell, & Sandilands, 1979). The aggression research allows us to conclude that if anything, observing aggressive sports increases the probability of aggressive behavior.

### Key Point

Evidence clearly indicates that merely *observing* aggressive behavior has no cathartic effect. In fact, field studies demonstrate that watching aggressive sport increases rather than decreases hostility.

Even though observing aggression has no cathartic value, participating in vigorous, aggressive activity often seems to help when we are angry. Perhaps performing an aggressive act, even a relatively noninjurious one, lowers arousal and reduces the probability of further aggressive actions.

A few studies (Doob, 1970; Doob & Wood, 1972; Konecni, 1975) indicate that committing aggression directly against the person who annoyed you may reduce aggressive behavior. For example, if you give an extra elbow to an opposing player who has been on your back during most of a game, that act may reduce your anger and make you less likely to commit other aggressive acts. Other studies, however (Berkowitz, 1966; Geen, Stonner, & Shope, 1975), contradict these findings, indicating that even if you do not hit anyone else during that game, the reinforcement may increase the chances that you will commit similar aggressive acts in future games.

The few existing studies on catharsis and physical activity indicate that vigorous activity is not cathartic. Following the Berkowitz paradigm, Ryan (1970) compared the aggressive behaviors of individuals in a control condition to behaviors of those who (a) engaged in vigorous physical activity (pounding a mallet), (b) won in competition, or (c) lost in competition. Ryan found no support for a cathartic effect; the pounding activity did not reduce aggressive behavior.

In another test of the cathartic effect of physical exercise, Zillmann, Katcher, and Milavsky (1972) compared individuals who had been provoked and then performed exercise (on a bicycle ergometer) with individuals who were provoked and then performed a nonarousing task. Not only did the results fail to support catharsis, but the individuals who exercised behaved more aggressively than those who had performed the nonarousing activity. These findings suggest that the arousal created by exercise could actually facilitate aggressive behavior.

A subsequent experiment (Zillmann, Johnson, & Day, 1974) revealed that exercise-induced arousal did not increase aggressive behavior if people knew that their increased arousal was due to exercise. Zillmann et al. reasoned that when heightened arousal clearly stems from exercise, competition, noise, or other sources unrelated to aggression, people do not become more aggressive. But when the source of arousal is not easily identified—as when time has elapsed after exercise—the arousal may be labeled as anger and may increase aggressive behavior. Considering all the catharsis research, Baron (1977) concluded that aggressive acts sometimes reduce arousal, but that even when they do, they may not reduce the probability of later aggression.

## Antecedents of Aggression in Sport

Despite the prevalence of aggressive behavior and the suggestions of Berkowitz and Bandura, very few investigators have attempted to determine antecedents and consequences of aggression in sport. High arousal levels are common in sport and exercise, and provocation is common in sport. As Berkowitz and Bandura propose, whether or not individuals actually behave aggressively depends on the situational cues and on the responses that have been learned and reinforced.

Many aggressive responses are encouraged, reinforced, and expected in sport. Silva (1979b) compared basketball players' guilt reactions to aggressive behavior in sport and in a competitive nonsport setting. As suspected, the players expressed less guilt for aggressive behavior in sport, implying its greater acceptability in that context. Ryan and colleagues (Ryan, Williams, & Wimer, 1990) examined perceived legitimacy of aggressive behaviors, behavioral intentions to commit aggression, and actual aggressive behaviors of female basketball players. Players who accepted aggressive actions as legitimate engaged in a greater number of aggressive behaviors. Interestingly, first-year players exhibited higher acceptance of aggression at the beginning of the season, but their end-of-season legitimacy judgments were similar to those of the more experienced players. It may be that over the season, prosocial behaviors were encouraged, reinforced, and expected.

Michael Smith has written extensively about aggression in sport, particularly the causes of violence in youth ice hockey. Smith (Morra & Smith, 1996; Smith, 1978, 1979, 1988) discounts the instinct and drive theory arguments that speed, contact, intensity, frustration, or a need for catharsis account for the violence in hockey. Referring specifically to youth hockey, Smith takes a social learning perspective and emphatically states that violence is caused by the influence of the professional game. First, the hockey system encourages aggressive behavior as a way to advance to higher levels. Smith reports that the majority of young hockey players agree with the statement, "If you want personal recognition in hockey, it helps to play rough." Additionally, significant others (parents, coaches, teammates) accept and praise aggressive acts. Moreover, the media reward such behavior by focusing on violent incidents. Thus young hockey players learn aggressive behaviors through reinforcement and modeling, just as Bandura would predict.

Smith's work suggests that situational reinforcements and modeling play key roles in sport aggression, but Smith's data are limited, and few controlled studies have examined sources of aggression in sport. For example, some psychology literature suggests gender differences in aggressive behavior, but there is no research on gender differences in sport aggression. Some reviewers (Deaux, 1976; Eagley & Steffen, 1986; Maccoby & Jacklin, 1974) conclude that males exhibit more aggressive behavior than females, but others (Baron, 1977; Frodi, Macauley, & Thome, 1977) disagree. Current work indicates that gender differences in aggression are complex and may be decreasing with societal changes.

Bjorkqvist, Osterman, and Kaukiainen (1992) suggest that females are more likely to use certain types of aggression, specifically indirect (e.g., gossiping, spreading rumors, writing nasty notes) and verbal (e.g., insults, name calling, threats) aggression. In sport and exercise, aggression has been defined in terms of physical behavior. If males and females prefer different forms of aggression, it is not surprising that in the sport setting males tend to be more aggressive than females (Bredemeier, 1994; Brown & Davies, 1978; Duda, Olson, & Templin, 1991; Silva, 1983). Together these studies indicate that males see aggression in sport as more legitimate than females do, and that males are more likely to use violence to solve problems in sport and in daily life.

How athletes define success and how they approach achievement situations relate to their attitudes toward aggression (Duda et al., 1991; Waston, 1986). For example, Waston found that highly anxious low achievers scored higher on aggression than other low achievers and high achievers. In a later study, Duda and her colleagues observed that athletes who placed greater emphasis on skill mastery, improvement, and effort than on outperforming others were less apt to approve of cheating and other unsportspersonlike conduct. Athletes who placed greater emphasis on outperforming others were more likely to view injuring an opponent as a legitimate behavior.

## Aggression and Its Effects on Performance

Just as few researchers have examined antecedents, few have examined the consequences of aggression in sport and exercise. We currently know very little about how aggression affects performance and other behaviors either immediately or over time, how aggression influences our thoughts and feelings, or how participants react to their own or others' aggressive behaviors.

Several investigators have considered the relationship between aggressive behavior and sport performance, but the limited data provide little insight. We often encourage athletes to play tough, hit hard, or intimidate opponents. As mentioned in chapter 4, aggressiveness was identified as a key personality characteristic of successful athletes on the Athletic Motivation Inventory (Tutko, Lyon, & Ogilvie, 1969). But the empirical evidence is not convincing.

McCarthy and Kelly (1978a, 1978b) found a positive correlation between aggressive behavior (penalty minutes) and assists and goals scored in ice hockey, but Wankel (1973) found no difference in the aggressive penalties of winning and losing teams in university hockey. Widmeyer and Birch (1979) reported that all-star university hockey players were either extremely aggressive or extremely nonaggressive, whereas those who were not all-stars were moderately aggressive. Thus, even the data from the limited setting of ice hockey are equivocal. Furthermore, even if penalty minutes did relate positively to success, we could not conclude that aggression causes success; other factors might affect both penalties and success.

Studies on aggression infrequently involve sports other than hockey, but Sachs (1978), in one of the few studies on women, reported that softball success was not related to either hostile or instrumental aggression. In one of the few controlled investigations, Silva (1979b) used confederates to provoke hostile aggression in individuals playing competitive pegboard and three-person basketball. For both tasks, players provoked into hostile aggression exhibited less concentration and poorer performance than individuals in a nonprovoked condition. Silva concluded that hostile aggression may increase arousal, which interferes with concentration and consequently impairs performance.

The existing research, limited as it is, provides no evidence that aggressive behavior improves sport performance. To the contrary, hostile aggression may create anger and arousal that interfere with performance. Results also suggest that the consequences of both hostile and instrumental aggression may extend beyond immediate performance effects. We have far to go before we can discuss the antecedents and consequences of aggressive behavior with any certainty.

## Key Point

The existing research, limited as it is, provides no evidence that aggressive behavior improves sport performance. To the contrary, hostile aggression may create anger and arousal that interfere with performance.

## PROSOCIAL BEHAVIOR IN SPORT

We have explored aggressive behavior at some length. We would like to devote equal time to the other side of the issue—prosocial or helping behavior in sport. Unfortunately, neither theoretical work nor empirical data permit extended discourse. Sport and exercise psychologists have neither documented the existence of helping behaviors nor investigated the factors that elicit and maintain prosocial behaviors or the consequences of such actions for participants.

Sport professionals and the public often discuss "sportsmanship," "sportspersonship," or "sporting behavior." Discussions of sporting behavior, which might be defined as ethical or moral behavior in sport, typically reflect abstract value judgments or opinion rather than theories and evidence. Sport and exercise psychology researchers could contribute a great deal to the discussion but have seldom explored prosocial behaviors.

Kroll (1975), writing on the psychology of sportsmanship, proposed that ethical behaviors develop when the individual must choose between an ethically correct strategy and a success strategy. Many critics decry the emphasis on competition and winning in sport and insist that we can best encourage ethical behavior by eliminating that competitive emphasis. Kroll argued that ethical choices are important only if success is also important. If a participant has nothing to lose by acting in an ethical way, then ethical actions in a sport situation become less significant. Consider the following scenarios:

a. A basketball player refrains from intentionally fouling an opponent and allows the opponent to make an uncontested breakaway-layup when the team has a 20-point lead.

b. A basketball player refrains from making the intentional foul when the score is tied in the last minute.

Which do you consider the more ethical behavior? Avoiding a foul when the score does not matter does not strike us as especially ethical.

Most of the dramatic incidents of ethical behavior you can recall probably involved sacrificing success. Kroll suggests that situations in which the person must choose between an ethical action and a success action are the ones that develop our moral standards and values. We should encourage participants to make ethical choices in such situations. All ethical decisions do not require sacrificing success, but we should not ignore ethical issues as we pursue success. In fact, we should make choices based on relevant ethical criteria.

Although sport and exercise psychologists have seldom investigated ethical decisions and prosocial behaviors, Bredemeier and Shields (Bredemeier & Shields, 1984b; Shields & Bredemeier, 1984) have initiated a systematic investigation of the development of moral behavior in sport using a structural-developmental approach. Bredemeier and her associates conceptualize aggression as a moral issue (Bredemeier & Shields, 1986a; Bredemeier & Shields, 1986b; Weiss & Bredemeier, 1990). They contend that aggression is a social interaction, not simply a behavioral response, and that it represents an evaluation. In their study of the contextual morality of aggression in sport, they advocate Haan's (1991) interactional model of moral processing.

According to Haan (1991), morality in everyday life involves three components: (a) mutually acknowledged moral balance, (b) moral dialogue, and (c) concern for the needs and interests of self and others (Bredemeier & Shields, 1986a). However, the context of sport may promote a morality different from that of everyday life. First, sport is separated from everyday life by specific spatial and temporal boundaries. Second, much of the decision-making power is held by coaches and officials, giving athletes opportunity to negate moral responsibility and accountability for their actions. Third, game rules reduce athletes' need to engage in—and often inhibit—constructive dialogue between teams and opponents. Lastly, shared yet unspoken

*The sport context—such as the spatial and temporal boundaries of this wrestling match—may promote a morality different from that of everyday life.*

moral agreements among athletes encourage a morality distinct from that of everyday life: athletes realize that each player is out for himself or herself and that aggression is often necessary in the pursuit of victory. In these ways, sport releases athletes from the moral requirement of thinking of others. Sport appears to have its own self-centered or egocentric morality, often referred to as "game reasoning" (Bredemeier & Shields, 1986b).

This is not to say that sport is free from moral confines. Sport, although "bracketed" from everyday life, does take place under conditions in which moral imbalance can occur. In sport, moral balance is disrupted when the game turns personal and the athlete's goal is to harm rather than defeat. For example, it is okay for a linebacker to "take out" the quarterback to win the game, but unacceptable if the linebacker was acting out a personal vendetta unrelated to game play. Athletes also view unfair play, as when opponents get away with cheating or take cheap shots, as upsetting the moral balance (Bredemeier & Shields, 1986b).

## Moral Reasoning and Athletic Aggression

Overall, research indicates that athletes with higher levels of moral reasoning are generally less aggressive than athletes with lower levels. In an early study addressing this relationship, Bredemeier and Shields (1984b) found that among female and male intercollegiate basketball players, athletes with less mature moral reasoning were described by their coaches as more likely to engage in aggressive behaviors than were athletes more mature in their moral reasoning.

The relationship between moral reasoning and athletic aggression has also been investigated in young (ages 9-13) children (Bredemeier, Weiss, Shields, & Cooper, 1986; Bredemeier, 1994). Using hypothetical moral dilemmas, the authors found that (a) assertive behaviors were associated with more mature levels of moral reasoning and (b) aggressive behaviors were associated with less mature moral reasoning.

It appears that the reasoning used to determine what constitutes moral behavior depends on the situation (Bredemeier & Shields, 1984a; Bredemeier & Shields, 1986a; Bredemeier, 1994). When Bredemeier and Shields (1984a, 1986a) asked high school and collegiate basketball players, swimmers, and nonathletes to respond to hypothetical dilemmas in sport and daily life, they found that the athletes used lower levels of moral reasoning in sport. Interestingly, in sport, the moral reasoning used by females was more mature than that used by males, but there were no gender differences in the daily life context. The authors suggest that (a) females may emphasize human connection over individuation and may not develop egocentric sport reasoning; and (b) gender role socialization combined with less experience in competitive sport may explain why females' sport reasoning was higher than that of males.

Our understanding of the moral reasoning used by athletes and nonathletes is not very clear. For example, in one study, Bredemeier and Shields (1986c) found no moral reasoning differences between high school basketball players and nonathletes; but in another study (1984b), they found that basketball players employed less mature moral reasoning about sport than both swimmers and nonathletes (who did not differ).

Bredemeier and Shields (1984b) suggested two possible reasons for the similarity between swimmers' and nonathletes' moral reasoning in sport situations. First, the hypothetical dilemmas involved contact team sports and not swimming. Second, the authors reasoned that as an individualistic competitive activity, swimming may require less adaptation of moral reasoning than interactive team sports involving contact. That is, swimmers are less apt to be in a position requiring them to reason at lower levels of morality. Although we have far to go in understanding moral reasoning in sport and exercise, the existing work suggests some conclusions.

Though sport professionals and the public often discuss "good sportspersonship" or "good sporting behavior," little research has been done on such prosocial behaviors.

## Research Conclusions

Overall, the moral reasoning and athletic aggression literature reveals the following:

a. The more mature one's moral reasoning, the less apt one is to engage in aggressive behaviors.

b. Males are more apt to engage in physically aggressive behaviors than females are.

c. Females tend to use higher levels of moral reasoning than do males in sport contexts.

d. Noncontact athletes, who have less opportunity to commit aggression than contact sport athletes, use a higher level of moral reasoning in sport situations than do contact sport athletes.

e. The ability to use different levels of moral reasoning depends on the situation.

Does the sport dictate that participants use lower levels of moral reasoning? The findings may lead you to believe so, but that's not the complete picture. Remember the swimmers who reasoned more like the nonathletes than like the basketball players? The level of moral reasoning depends on the context. Sport environments designed to enhance moral development can have beneficial effects (Bredemeier, Weiss, Shields, & Shewchuk, 1986; Romance, Weiss, & Bockoven, 1986). However, when the environment is ignored, it appears that sport teaches self-interest at the expense of others. Interestingly, athletes who function at less mature levels of moral reasoning and who legitimize aggression on the field appear to function at higher levels off the field. On the other hand, research also indicates that the aggression athletes learn on the field can transfer off the field (Koss & Gaines, 1993). We have much to discover about what people can and do learn about aggression and moral behavior in sport and exercise.

# Summary

Many have written about aggression in sport, but few have conducted systematic research on the topic. The strongest theoretical work suggests that aggression is learned through the modeling and reinforcement of aggressive behaviors. Research does not support the popular notion that sport acts a catharsis to release aggressive urges. Instead, it is likely that the modeling and reinforcement of aggression in sport increase the probability of aggressive behaviors in both sport and nonsport settings. As with aggression, the topic of prosocial or moral behavior abounds with issues and questions, but we have few answers. Sport and exercise psychologists could build upon the work of Berkowitz and Bandura, or explore developmental models of moral reasoning within the unique context of sport and exercise, to clarify the role of aggressive and prosocial behaviors and the characteristics and factors that interact with such behaviors in these settings.

# Review Questions

1. Define aggression as the term is used in this text.
2. Compare and contrast instrumental aggression, hostile aggression, and assertive behavior.
3. Describe the characteristics of instinct theories of aggression.
4. Describe the characteristics of drive theories of aggression, as well as Berkowitz's related theory.
5. Describe the characteristics of social learning theories of aggression.
6. Contrast instinct, drive, and social learning theories of aggression.
7. Explain what researchers have found regarding the idea that sports can act as a catharsis for aggression.
8. Using youth ice hockey as an example, explain how situational cues can contribute to the prevalence of violence in a particular sport setting.
9. Explain the effects of aggression on sport performance.
10. Define prosocial behavior.
11. Identify and contrast the components of morality in everyday life and the morality that exists within a sport context.
12. Describe the relationship between moral reasoning and athletic aggression.

# Recommended Reading

★ Berkowitz, L. (1993). *Aggression: Its causes, consequences, and control*. Philadelphia: Temple University Press.

> Berkowitz has been a leading scholar on aggression throughout his distinguished career, and his research and ideas have shaped our current theories. This recent source presents current thought with extensive background information.

★ Morra, N., & Smith, M.D. (1996). Interpersonal sources of violence in hockey: The influence of the media, parents, coaches, and game officials. In F.L. Smoll & R.E. Smith (Eds.), *Children and youth in sport: A biopsychosocial perspective* (pp. 142-155). Madison, WI: Brown & Benchmark.

> Smith focuses attention on the role of social factors in violence in hockey. This chapter provides an overview of the influence of media, parents, and officials on violence.

★ Weiss, M.R., & Bredemeier, B.J.L. (1990). Moral development in sport. In K.B. Pandolf & J.O. Holloszy (Eds.), *Exercise and Sport Sciences Reviews* (Vol. 18, pp. 331-378). Baltimore: Williams & Wilkins.

Most current views suggest that if aggression depends on social influences, we can also use social influence to promote prosocial behavior and moral development in sport. Bredemeier has done considerable research and writing on this issue. In this chapter, she collaborates with Weiss, a leading developmental sport psychology scholar, to review the research and theory on moral development in sport.

# chapter 18

# Gender and Social Diversity

## CHAPTER OBJECTIVES

After studying this chapter, you should be able to

- understand the concept of social context and
- identify ways in which a person's sport and exercise experience can be affected by gender, race, and cultural stereotypes and discrimination.

Gender and social diversity are relatively recent topics within sport and exercise psychology. Until the 1970s when an identifiable sport psychology emerged, athlete meant male athlete, and male athletes were anything but culturally diverse. Some women engaged in physical activity much earlier, as sport historians note (e.g., Spears, 1978), but females entered the modern athletic world in significant numbers only with the passage of Title IX and the related social changes of the early 1970s. Despite the tremendous influx of females into sport and exercise activities since then, we have little research on gender issues and almost no scholarship on other social diversity issues such as race and ethnicity, sexual orientation, age, and physical abilities. This chapter focuses on gender, but from the gender scholarship I will draw parallels to other diversity issues. Indeed, much emerging work on cultural diversity stems from feminist work on gender. My emphasis on social diversity, with no reference to biology, is intentional. Although gender clearly has a biological dimension (as do other diversity issues), the biological markers are not keys to the behaviors of interest in our discipline.

My emphasis on social context reflects current perspectives on human diversity in psychology. In his introduction to an excellent book on human diversity (Trickett, Watts, & Birman, 1994), Stanley Sue (1994) expresses my thoughts:

> We must understand the cultural blinders that we wear and begin to truly appreciate diversity. . . . Diversity should not be embraced because it helps the oppressed; instead, we will all be served by affirming diversity. Cultural diversity is part of the nature of human beings, and it should be part of the nature of our science and practice in the social sciences. (p. 4)

Diversity has challenged the foundations of psychology by suggesting that traditional psychology is particularistic rather than universal and that its theories reflect the views, limits, and social contexts of their creators (Trickett et al., 1994). Recommending that we find new ways of thinking about diversity, Trickett et al. advocate moving from the dominant psychology view—which emphasizes biology, basic processes, experimental designs, and a critical-realist philosophy of science—to an emphasis on people in context. Their framework for diversity extends beyond

255

cultural or ethnic groups to include age, gender, physical abilities, and sexual orientation, as well as the so-called dominant culture; it deals with both similarities and differences and conveys a positive focus on culture, resilience, and strength as well as consequences of oppression.

By definition, psychology focuses on individual behavior, but as Trickett et al. suggest, we cannot fully understand the individual without considering the larger world—people in context. Sport and exercise psychology is context dependent, and the context extends far beyond competitive athletics to encompass diverse participants in all forms of physical activities in varied settings.

The theme of this chapter is that gender and diversity in sport are much as in other domains, and that social context is the key. We cannot isolate individuals from their gender, and gender makes a difference. Similarly, "Race matters" (to borrow the title of Cornel West's 1993 book), and we must consider people in context to understand their behavior.

# THE GENDERED CONTEXT OF SPORT AND EXERCISE

First, let's consider gender in the sport and exercise context today. In a recent television advertisement, several young women argued that they would be better physically (e.g., less risk of cancer and heart disease), mentally (less depression), and socially (better grades, less teenage pregnancy, greater career success) "if you let me play sports." The company drew upon literature demonstrating the many benefits of sport participation for women. Indeed, female athletic participation has exploded in the last generation. Still, the numbers of female and male participants are not equal. More important, female athletes are not the same as male athletes. Gender makes a difference, but to understand gender issues we must look beyond biological sex and simple dichotomous sex differences to the psychosocial context.

Sport and exercise are physical activities. *Citius, Altius, Fortius*—the Olympic motto—translates as "swifter, higher, stronger," underscoring the physical but also implying that sport is competitive and hierarchical. The average male may be higher, faster, and stronger than the average female, but sport does not have to be higher, faster, stronger—sport might consist of *fun, flair, friendship.* I will note my biases: I am not high, fast, or strong, and I am not competitive.

Although biological sex is part of the gender mix, biology does not explain the mix; all the meanings, social roles, and expectations, as well as the standards of appropriate behavior, beauty, power, and status, are constructed in the sport and exercise culture. We are not born to wear high heels or high-top sneakers.

Before considering the literature on gender and sport, let's see if gender does make a difference in sport and exercise settings. Elsewhere (Gill, 1995) I have used the following cases to help readers think about gender. Consider how gender affects interpretations of and possible approaches to the following athletes:

- A soccer player lacks control and is prone to angry outbursts on the field, and explains by stating, "I really get 'up' for the game, and sometimes I just lose it."

- A basketball player plays tentatively and lacks confidence, and explains "I'm just not a leader and I can't play the way the coach wants."

- The coach thinks a 16-year-old figure skater may have an eating disorder, but the skater explains, "I'm working to keep that 'line,' make it to nationals, and get endorsements."

Imagine each case first with a female athlete and then with a male athlete. Does gender influence your responses to these cases? Do you think a coach, consultant, or parent would behave the same with a female and a male athlete? If you try to be nonsexist, treat everyone the same, and assume that gender does not matter, you will probably have difficulty. Gender does matter, but it's not biological gender that makes the big difference. Trying to treat everyone the same does a disservice to the athletes.

From birth, our world is shaped by gender. Parents, teachers, peers, and coaches react to us as girls or boys. The influence of gender is so pervasive that it's impossible to pinpoint. This is as true in sport as anywhere else, but true in unique ways in the sport world.

# THE HISTORICAL CONTEXT OF SPORT AND EXERCISE

To understand gender in sport and exercise, we must first understand the social and historical context. As discussed in chapter 2, sport and exercise psychology has roots in both psychology and physical education. We find women in both histories, but the histories are quite different. In psychology, women pioneers faced discriminatory practices but made a place in the academic discipline, much as they have in other scholarly fields. In physical education, strong women leaders developed women's physical education as an alternative, separate from men's. These two roots of sport and exercise psychology seldom converged. Sport and exercise psychology has always drawn from psychology, but not from the psychology of women; and psychologists (mostly women) working on gender issues have largely ignored sport and physical activity.

## Psychology Roots

Women's early contributions to psychology have been rediscovered recently; and women's issues, such as violence toward women, have become prominent. Denmark and Fernandez (1993) cite two neglected works particularly relevant to sport and exercise psychology: Mary Putnam Jacobi's (1877) book arguing that women need not refrain from physical activity during menstruation, and Mary Bissell's arguments against women's "fragility" and her advocacy of physical development for women. Several women who did psychology work around the turn of the century are now recognized as pioneers, and their writings foreshadow more current feminist views.

Psychology of women came on strong in the 1970s. Bardwick's *The Psychology of Women* appeared in 1970, and Sherman's *On the Psychology of Women* in 1971. Although scholars on the psychology of women have not embraced sport or physical activity, some have made important contributions. Researchers on competitive anxiety cite Janet Spence's early work on anxiety, and her research on instrumentality/expressiveness and achievement orientation has influenced sport and exercise psychologists. The woman psychologist who influenced sport and exercise psychology the most is Carolyn Sherif. Sherif's legacy is evident in psychology (e.g., Sherif, 1982) and sport and exercise psychology (e.g., Sherif, 1976). Her early and persistent advocacy of social psychology, as well as women's issues, has had considerable influence on my thoughts and work, as it has on others in our field.

## Physical Education Roots

Women had a highly visible presence in the early days of physical education. Women's colleges, which offered academic homes to women psychologists, typically promoted physical activity as part of women's education and development. Physical education for women was separated from men's physical training, and women specialists were needed to plan and conduct such programs. Women's physical education, organized by and for women, provided a women-oriented environment that promoted women's development and achievement long before the women's movement of the 1970s began to encourage such programs.

The early women physical educators contributed some elements that seem to be models for today's sport and exercise psychologists, and other elements that seem to conflict with practices today. One aspect of early women's physical education that seems at odds with today's sport psychology is the approach to competition. A 1923

Today fewer than half of women's teams are coached by women.

conference of key physical education leaders is a benchmark for this anticompetition movement. The guidelines developed by the conference included putting athletes first, preventing exploitation, downplaying competition while emphasizing enjoyment and sportsmanship, promoting activity for all rather than an elite few, and having women as leaders for girls' and women's sports. In a clarification, the Women's Division of the National Amateur Athletic Federation (1930) asserted that they did believe in competition but disapproved of highly intense, specialized competition. What was evil in competition was the emphasis on winning rather than participation, and the statement concluded with the classic, "A game for every girl and every girl in a game."

Competitive athletics today is vastly different from what we might have experienced in 1925, or even 1975. In 1967 Kathy Switzer created a stir when she defied the rules to sneak into the Boston marathon; now we have a women's Olympic marathon. I played backyard baseball as a young child but had few options when my teammates moved into Little League; now girls star on youth soccer teams. The benchmark for this turnaround was the 1972 passage of Title IX of the Educational Amendments Act.

Title IX, which emerged from the civil rights and women's movements, is a broad ban on sex discrimination in all educational programs. Discrimination persists, and Title IX challenges continue today; but the number of girls in interscholastic athletics and of women in intercollegiate athletics has increased about 6- to 10-fold since pre–Title IX days.

### Key Point

Title IX, which emerged from the civil rights and women's movements, is a broad ban on sex discrimination in all educational programs. Discrimination persists, and Title IX challenges continue today; but the number of girls in interscholastic athletics and of women in intercollegiate athletics has increased about 6- to 10-fold since pre–Title IX days. However, before Title IX (1972), over 90% of women's athletic teams were coached by women and had a woman athletic director. Today less than half of women's teams are coached by women, and only 16% have a woman director (Carpenter & Acosta, 1993; Gill, 1992, 1995; Nelson, 1991; Uhlir, 1987).

About one-third of high school, college, and Olympic athletes in the United States are women. But one-third is not one-half, and in other ways women have lost ground. Women have not become coaches, administrators, sportswriters, or sports medicine personnel in significant numbers. Before Title IX (1972), over 90% of women's athletic teams were coached by women and had a woman athletic director. Today less than half of women's teams are coached by women, and only 16% have a woman director (Carpenter & Acosta, 1993; Gill, 1992, 1995; Nelson, 1991; Uhlir, 1987).

# GENDER SCHOLARSHIP IN SPORT AND EXERCISE PSYCHOLOGY

Gender scholarship in sport and exercise psychology largely follows gender scholarship within psychology. The focus of psychology scholarship has shifted from sex differences, to gender role as personality, to social context and processes.

## Sex Differences

The early sex differences work, exemplified by Maccoby and Jacklin's (1974) review, assumed dichotomous biology-based psychological differences—that is, that male and female are opposites. Today, consensus holds that psychological characteristics associated with females and males are neither dichotomous nor biology based (e.g., Bem, 1993; Deaux, 1984; Eagley, 1987; Gill, 1992, 1995; Hyde & Linn, 1986).

Ashmore (1990), summarizing the research, concluded that sex differences are relatively large for certain physical abilities (i.e., throwing velocity) and body use/ posturing, more modest for other abilities and social behaviors (e.g., math, aggression), and negligible for all other domains (e.g., leadership, attitudes, reaction time). Even the larger sex differences are confounded with nonbiological influences. Ashmore advocates, as do others (Maccoby, 1990; Jacklin, 1989), abandoning sex differences approaches for multifaceted, social approaches. Most biological factors are not dichotomously divided, but normally distributed within both females and males. For example, the average male basketball center is taller than the average female center, but the average female center is taller than most men. For social psychological characteristics such as aggressiveness or confidence, even average differences are elusive, and the evidence does not support biological dichotomous sex-linked connections. With criticisms of the sex differences approach, and its failure to shed light on gender-related behavior, psychologists turned to personality.

## Personality and Gender Role Orientation

Psychologists focused on gender role orientation, particularly Bem's (1974, 1978a) work and the Bem Sex Role Inventory (BSRI). For Bem, personality is not a function of biology; both males and females can have masculine or feminine personalities, and androgyny (a balance of feminine and masculine personalities) is best. Advocates of androgyny argue that we should treat everyone the same and encourage both masculine and feminine personalities. The gender role work has been widely criticized, and even Bem (1993) has progressed to a more encompassing gender perspective. Still, most sport and exercise psychology gender research is based on her early work.

In contrast to earlier approaches, Bem conceived of masculinity and femininity as independent, desirable sets of characteristics rather than opposites. The BSRI contains 20 stereotypically feminine characteristics (e.g., affectionate, sensitive to the needs of others), 20 stereotypically masculine characteristics (e.g., independent, willing to take risks), and 20 fillers (e.g., truthful, happy). The respondent indicates how true of himself or herself each characteristic is. Figure 18.1 shows the rating scale and sample items.

One of Bem's main goals in developing the BSRI was to assess androgyny, which is indicated by high scores on both masculinity and femininity. Bem originally

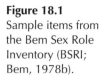

**Figure 18.1**
Sample items from
the Bem Sex Role
Inventory (BSRI;
Bem, 1978b).

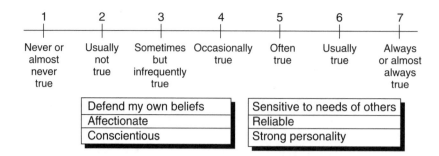

recommended using difference scores to determine androgyny but quickly moved to the four-way classification (see table 18.1), now widely used in gender role research. Individuals (either females or males) who score high on both masculinity and femininity are androgynous; those high on masculinity and low on femininity are masculine; those high on femininity and low on masculinity are feminine; and those low on both are undifferentiated.

Helmreich and Spence (1977) developed their own gender role model and measure (Personality Attributes Questionnaire, PAQ), sampled intercollegiate athletes, and reported that most female athletes were either androgynous or masculine whereas nonathlete college females were most often feminine. Subsequent studies yielded similar findings. Harris and Jennings (1977) found that most surveyed female distance runners were androgynous or masculine. Among many more studies with athletes using the BSRI or PAQ, two showed that most intercollegiate athletes were androgynous or masculine (Del Rey & Sheppard, 1981; Colker & Widom, 1980). Another indicated that most female racquetball players were androgynous whereas most male racquetball players were masculine (Myers & Lips, 1978).

Overall, this research suggests that female athletes possess more masculine personality characteristics than do female nonathletes (Gill, 1992, 1995). This is not particularly enlightening. Sport and physical activity, especially competitive athletics, demands instrumental, assertive (certainly competitive) behaviors. Both the BSRI and PAQ include "competitive" as a masculine item, and the higher masculine scores of female athletes probably reflect an overlap with competitiveness. We can measure competitive orientation directly (e.g., Gill & Deeter, 1988; Gill & Dzewaltowski, 1988), and do not need to invoke more indirect, controversial measures that do not yield additional information.

More important, athlete/nonathlete status is an indirect and nonspecific measure of behavior. If instrumental and expressive personality characteristics predict instrumental and expressive behaviors, we should examine those instrumental and expressive behaviors. Even within highly competitive sports, expressive behaviors may be advantageous. Creative, expressive actions may be the key to success for a gymnast; supportive behaviors of teammates may be critical on a soccer team; and sensitivity to others may help an Olympic coach communicate with athletes. Today, most psychologists recognize the limits of earlier sex differences and gender role approaches and look beyond the dichotomies.

**Table 18.1    Four-Way Classification of Individuals on Masculinity and Femininity**

|  |  | Masculinity | |
|---|---|---|---|
|  |  | Above median | Below median |
| Femininity | Above median | Androgynous | Feminine |
|  | Below median | Masculine | Undifferentiated |

## Gender and Competitive Achievement Orientation

Most sport and exercise activities involve achievement behavior, particularly competitive achievement. In the early achievement work (McClelland, Atkinson, Clark, & Lowell, 1953), researchers simply took male behavior as the norm until Matina Horner's (1972) doctoral work on fear of success focused attention on gender. Horner's work was widely publicized, but quickly dismissed by critics (e.g., Condry & Dyer, 1976; Tresemer, 1977). McElroy and Willis (1979), examining women's achievement conflicts in sport contexts, concluded that no evidence supported a fear of success in female athletes and that female athletes' achievement attitudes are similar to those of male athletes.

We have replaced global achievement motives with multidimensional constructs and an emphasis on achievement cognitions (as discussed in chapters 8 and 9). Spence and Helmreich (1978, 1983) developed a multidimensional measure with separate dimensions of mastery, work, and competitiveness; they found that males scored higher than females on mastery and competitiveness, whereas females scored higher than males on work. Gender differences diminished for athletes, but males remained higher than females on competitiveness. Also, masculinity scores related positively to all three achievement dimensions, whereas femininity scores related slightly positively to work and negatively to competitiveness. Generally, gender influence was strongest and most consistent for competitiveness.

My work (Gill, 1988, 1993) on competitive sport orientation, discussed in chapter 8, also suggests that gender influences vary across dimensions. Using the sport-specific, multidimensional Sport Orientation Questionnaire (SOQ; Gill & Deeter, 1988), we investigated competitive orientation with several samples and usually found gender differences. Overall, males consistently scored higher than females on SOQ competitiveness and win orientation, and also reported more competitive sport activity and experience. However, on SOQ goal orientation and general achievement, females were just as high as males, and sometimes higher. Also, females were just as likely as males to participate in noncompetitive sport and nonsport achievement activities.

Tables 18.2 and 18.3, showing the SOQ competitiveness scores from several of our samples, help put the gender "differences" into perspective. Although generally males are more competitive than females, overlap and similarity are the rule. Moreover, differences between athletes and nonathletes, and within athlete samples, typically are stronger than gender differences.

Table 18.2 depicts our early university and high school samples (for details see Gill, 1988). The gender difference was statistically significant, but less than one standard deviation, suggesting considerable overlap. We have consistently found standard deviations of approximately 10 for SOQ competitiveness in all our samples; this helps put differences in perspective.

Table 18.3 depicts differences (or lack of differences) for several athlete and nonathlete samples (for more details see Gill, 1993). The combined Iowa athletes and nonathletes at the top of the table showed a gender difference, but the difference was not consistent. Female athletes did not differ significantly from male athletes, and the mean for female athletes was higher than that for male nonathletes. The middle of table 18.3 shows competitiveness scores from a study (Kang, Gill, Acevedo, & Deeter,

**Table 18.2   SOQ Competitiveness Scores for Males and Females in University and High School Samples**

| Sample | Males M | Females M | Combined M | (SD) |
|---|---|---|---|---|
| University | 52.8 | 43.7 | 48.3 | (10.9) |
| High school | 52.2 | 43.8 | 47.8 | (11.6) |

**Table 18.3   SOQ Competitiveness Scores for Male and Female Athletes and Nonathletes**

| Iowa | Male | Female |
|------|------|--------|
| Athletes | 59.1 | 57.1 |
| Nonathletes | 49.4 | 43.5 |
| Combined | 54.9 | 49.4 |

| Taiwan | Male | Female |
|--------|------|--------|
| International | 49.9 | 48.2 |
| University | 42.8 | 50.7 |
| Nonathletes | 46.9 | 56.6 |
| Combined | 53.3 | 50.6 |

| Ultramarathoners | Male | Female |
|------------------|------|--------|
|  | 47.5 | 50.3 |

1990) comparing international athletes, university athletes, and nonathletes in Taiwan. Overall, females were slightly (but not significantly) lower than males in competitiveness. Again, athlete-nonathlete differences were much stronger, with a pattern similar to that in the Iowa sample; female international athletes were more competitive than male university athletes, and female university athletes were more competitive than male nonathletes.

Finally, for our unique sample of ultramarathoners (table 18.3, bottom), not only is the gender difference nonsignificant; females are slightly higher on competitiveness than males. Also, note that the ultramarathoners are similar in competitiveness to the nonathlete samples, but much higher than nonathletes and other athlete samples on goal orientation.

Overall, gender differences in competitiveness are limited, and do not seem to reflect either general achievement orientation or interest in sport and exercise activities per se. Instead, competitiveness seems to reflect opportunity and experience in competitive sport, and gender is related to an emphasis on social comparison and winning within sport.

Others report similar gender influences on reactions to competitive sport. When McNally and Orlick (1975) introduced a cooperative broomball game to children in urban Canada and in the northern territories, they found that girls were more receptive to the cooperative rules than were boys. They also noted cultural differences, with northern children more receptive; but the gender influence held in both cultures. Duda (1986a) similarly reported both gender and cultural influences on competitiveness with Anglo and Navajo children in the southwestern United States. Male Anglo children, the most win oriented, placed the most emphasis on athletic ability. Weinberg and Jackson (1979) found that males were more affected by success/failure than were females; and in a related study (Weinberg & Ragan, 1979), males were more interested in a competitive activity whereas females preferred a noncompetitive activity.

Although several lines of research suggest gender influences on competitive sport achievement, no unique gender-related personality construct appears as an explanation. Instead, most investigators are turning to socialization, societal influences, and social-cognitive models for explanations.

Jacquelynne Eccles's (1985, 1987; Eccles et al., 1983) model incorporates such sociocultural factors along with achievement cognitions. Eccles recognizes that both expectations and importance, or value, determine achievement choices and behaviors. Gender differences in expectations are common, and gender also influences the value of achievement. These differences develop over time and are influenced by gender role socialization, stereotyped expectations of others, and sociocultural norms, as well as individual characteristics and experiences. Eccles and Harrold (1991) provided new evidence that Eccles's model holds for sport achievement, that gender influences children's sport achievement perceptions and behaviors at a very young age, and that these gender differences seem to result from gender role socialization.

## Physical Activity and Self-Perceptions

Before moving from personality, let's consider self-perceptions. Females often lack confidence in their sport and exercise capabilities, and physical activity has great potential to enhance women's sense of competence and control. Many women beginning activity programs report enhanced self-esteem and a sense of physical competence that carries over into other aspects of their lives. Some studies support these testimonials, showing that exercise programs, particularly weight and strength training, enhance women's self-concepts (Holloway, Beuter, & Duda, 1988; Brown & Harrison, 1986; Trujillo, 1983).

### Key Point

Some studies support the hypothesis that exercise programs, particularly weight and strength training, enhance women's self-concepts (Holloway, Beuter, & Duda, 1988; Brown & Harrison, 1986; Trujillo, 1983).

Besides developing feelings of physical strength and confidence, sport offers the opportunity to strive for excellence and accomplish goals through effort and training, as well as the psychological challenge of competition. Diana Nyad (1978), the marathon swimmer, expressed this:

> When asked why, I say that marathon swimming is the most difficult physical, intellectual, and emotional battleground I have encountered, and each time I win, each time I reach the other shore, I feel worthy of any other challenge life has to offer. (p. 152)

We should note particularly the work on gender and body image within sport and exercise settings (for reviews see *The Bodywise Woman;* Melpomene Institute, 1996; Rodin, Silberstein, & Striegel-Moore, 1985). Images of the ideal body, particularly the ideal female body, change through history and across social contexts. Most women recognize and strive for today's ideal female body, slender and lean. Males also have body image concerns, but the literature indicates that females are much more negative about their bodies. Moreover, the concerns are gender related. Girls focus on physical beauty and maintaining the ideal thin shape, whereas boys focus more on size, strength, and power. Societal pressure for a body image that is not particularly healthy or attainable for many women likely has a negative influence on self-esteem and psychological well-being, as well as on physical well-being.

Women athletes are just as susceptible as others to societal pressures toward unrealistic, unhealthy thinness and eating disorders. Such pressures are of particular concern in the "thin-body" sports such as gymnastics, dance, and running. Coaches and instructors in such activities should be especially careful in what they communicate about body shape. One athlete reported:

> At age 14 my cycling coach told me I was "fat" in front of my entire team. . . . At 5'5", 124 pounds, I was not fat, but my self-esteem was so low that I simply believed him. After all, he was the coach. (Melpomene Institute, 1996, pp. 71-72)

Pressuring an athlete already under societal pressure to lose weight is not desirable. Most enlightened coaches and instructors follow nutritional guidelines and emphasize healthy eating and exercise behaviors rather than weight standards.

# SOCIAL PERSPECTIVES IN GENDER RESEARCH

In the 1980s, gender research turned from the sex differences and personality approaches to a more social approach emphasizing gender beliefs and stereotypes. How people think males and females differ is more important than how they actually differ. Although actual differences on such characteristics as independence or competitiveness are small and inconsistent, we maintain our stereotypes (e.g., Bem, 1985; Deaux, 1984; Deaux & Kite, 1987, 1993; Deaux & Major, 1987; Spence & Helmreich, 1978). We exaggerate minimal differences into larger perceived differences through social processes, and these perceptions in turn exert a strong influence that may elicit further gender differences. This cycle reflects the pervasive social construction of gender.

Gender stereotypes certainly exist within sport. In her classic analysis of the social acceptability of various sports, Eleanor Metheny (1965) identified gender stereotypes, concluding that it was not considered appropriate for women to engage in contests in which

- the resistance of the opponent is overcome by bodily contact,
- the resistance of a heavy object is overcome by direct application of bodily force, or
- the body is projected into or through space over long distances or for extended periods of time.

According to Metheny, acceptable sports for women (e.g., gymnastics, swimming, tennis) emphasized aesthetic qualities and often were individual activities rather than direct competition and team sports. Although Metheny wrote over 30 years ago, our gender stereotypes have not disappeared with implementation of Title IX. Kane and Snyder (1989) confirmed gender stereotyping of sports as suggested by Metheny and more explicitly identified physicality--emphasizing physical muscularity, strength, and power—as the key feature. Others have confirmed that sports are sex typed (mostly as masculine) (Matteo, 1986, 1988; Csizma, Wittig, & Schurr, 1988). Matteo (1986, 1988) further reported that sex-typed individuals (masculine males, feminine females) did not participate in gender-inappropriate sports.

Research suggests a gender bias in the evaluation of performance. Goldberg (1968) reported a bias in the academic world favoring male authors of scholarly articles. Subsequent studies confirmed a male bias but suggested that the bias varied with information and situational characteristics (e.g., Pheterson, Kiesler, & Goldberg, 1971; Wallston & O'Leary, 1981). Studies using the Goldberg approach to examine gender bias in attitudes toward hypothetical female and male coaches (Parkhouse & Williams, 1986; Weinberg, Reveles, & Jackson, 1984; Williams & Parkhouse, 1988) revealed a bias favoring male coaches. However, Williams and Parkhouse (1988) reported that female basketball players coached by a successful female did not exhibit the male bias, suggesting more complex influences on gender stereotypes and evaluations.

Gender beliefs and stereotypes are everywhere. Parents, teachers, peers, and institutions treat girls and boys differently from birth (e.g., American Association of University Women, 1992; Geis, 1993; Sadker, Sadker, & Klein, 1991; Unger & Crawford, 1992). Overall, differential treatment is consistent with producing independence and efficacy in boys and emotional sensitivity, nurturance, and helplessness in girls.

## Gender Bias in the Media

One prominent source of differential treatment of sport is the media. Coverage of female and male athletes shows several forms of gender bias (e.g., Kane, 1989; Kane

& Parks, 1992; Messner, Duncan, & Jensen, 1993). Females receive little coverage (less than 10%) in terms of television airtime, newspaper space, feature articles, and photographs. Moreover, females and males receive different coverage, reflecting gender hierarchy. Generally, the emphasis is on athletic ability and accomplishments for men, and on femininity and physical attractiveness for women. The 1987-88 Northwest Louisiana State women's basketball media guide showed team members in Playboy bunny ears and tails with the caption, "These girls can Play, boy!" (Kane, 1989).

Gender bias in the sport media is usually more subtle. Eitzen and Baca Zinn (1993) reported that a majority of colleges had sexist nicknames or symbols (e.g., names ending in "elle" or "ette"; "Lady") that gender marked the women athletes as different from and less than the men athletes. In a study of 1989 National Collegiate Athletic Association (NCAA) basketball tournaments and U.S. Open tennis coverage, Messner et al. (1993) noted less stereotyping than in earlier studies, but still found considerable gender marking (e.g., "women's final four" but "final four" for men) and gendered hierarchy of naming (e.g., females referred to as girls, young ladies, or women; men never referred to as boys).

**Key Point**

There are still several forms of gender bias present in media coverage of female sporting events. These biases include less coverage, airtime, newspaper space, and photographs for females; less emphasis on athletic ability in females; use of sexist nicknames or symbols for female sport teams; gender marking ("women's final four" for women, but "final four" for men); and use of gendered language (use of women's first names but men's last names, for example).

Gender marking may be appropriate when symmetrical, as it was for most of the tennis coverage; but dissimilar marking labels females as "other." Gendered language was also apparent in comments about strength and weakness, which were ambivalent for women but clearly about strength for men; and emotional reasons for failure (e.g., nerves, lack of confidence) were cited more often for women. Messner et al. (1993), noting that "dominants" in society typically are referred to by last names and subordinates by first names, found first names used over 50% of the time to refer to females but only 10% of the time for males. Also, the few male athletes referred to by first names were black male basketball players. No race differences were observed for females; gender seemed to be the more powerful feature.

My observations of recent Olympic and NCAA tournaments suggest less stereotyping and trivialization of female athletes; but institutional change is slow, and gendered beliefs seem to persist in sport. Overt discrimination is unlikely, and participants may not recognize gendered beliefs. For example, many sport administrators and participants fail to recognize the gender beliefs operating when athletic programs developed by and for men, stressing male-linked values and characteristics, are opened to females.

## Gender Stereotypes Within the Social Context

The social aspect of gender is more than perceptions and stereotypes; it's part of the whole context. In *The Female World*, Jesse Bernard (1981) proposed that the social worlds for females and males are different even when they appear similar. In earlier times we created separate worlds with segregated physical education and sport programs. Although we now have coed activities, we still have the separate worlds: different social worlds for female and male university basketball players, joggers, and participants in youth soccer games.

Stereotypes are a concern because we act on them, exaggerating minimal gender differences and restricting opportunities for everyone. Gender beliefs keep many women out of sport and restrict the behaviors of all. Both girls and boys can participate in youth gymnastics or baseball, and at early ages physical capabilities are similar. Yet children see female gymnasts and male baseball players as role models; peers gravitate to sex-segregated activities; and most parents, teachers, and coaches support gender-appropriate activities of children.

To illustrate the role of social context, let's consider confidence. Earlier research suggested that females display lower confidence than males across varied settings; Lenney (1977) concluded that the particular social situation was the primary source of the difference. Specifically, gender differences emerged when tasks were masculine, when settings were competitive, and when clear, unambiguous feedback was missing. Several studies within sport and exercise psychology (e.g., Corbin, 1981; Corbin & Nix, 1979; Corbin, Stewart, & Blair, 1981; Corbin, Landers, Feltz, & Senior, 1983) confirmed Lenney's propositions. However, these were experimental studies with novel motor tasks, conducted in lab settings that purposely strip away social context. In the real world we cannot ignore the larger social context. Sport tasks are typically seen as masculine, competition is the norm, and males and females develop confidence along with physical skills through radically different experiences and opportunities.

# GENDER AND SOCIAL DIVERSITY

Although we should consider gender within the wider context of social diversity, sport and exercise psychologists have not done so. Gender is just as prominent in youth sport, recreational settings, and exercise classes as in competitive athletics. Sport is not only male, but white, young, middle-class, heterosexual male; gender is only one of several social identities that affect sport and exercise participants.

## Race and Ethnicity

On race and ethnicity, sport and exercise psychology presents a striking void (Duda & Allison, 1990). Most gender issues have parallels in race and ethnicity. That is, stereotypes are pervasive and multifaceted; racial and ethnic socialization, self-perceptions, and social context influence behavior; and a grounding in sociocultural history would enhance our understanding of race and ethnicity in sport and exercise. Although analogous issues arise, race and class are qualitatively different from gender, and we do not even have limited work on stereotypes and individual characteristics to parallel the gender research. Also, gender likely interacts with other diversity characteristics in many complex ways. For example, the experiences of a black, female tennis player are not simply a combination of the experiences of being female and black. Althea Gibson's (1979) personal account highlights some complex interactions of race and gender, illustrating how social history and the immediate social situation influenced her development as a tennis player and person.

Many athletes are not white and middle class, yet power remains solidly white and middle class. Sport's glass ceiling keeps all but white middle-class athletes clustered at the bottom. The popular media and some scholars have referred to such practices as "stacking" (e.g., African-Americans in positions such as running back or outfielder but not quarterback or pitcher) and to the nearly exclusive white male dominance of coaching and management. To date, few of these reports have included in-depth or critical analysis of race or class within sport.

> **Key Point**
>
> Many athletes are not white and middle class, yet power remains solidly white and middle class. Sport's glass ceiling keeps all but white middle-class athletes clustered at the bottom. The popular media and some scholars have referred to such practices as "stacking" (e.g., African-Americans in positions such as running back or outfielder but not quarterback or pitcher) and to the nearly exclusive white male dominance of coaching and management.

Majors (1990) contributed critical analysis in discussing the "cool pose" (i.e., a set of expressive lifestyle behaviors) used by black males to counter racism. Majors noted that although a few black males escape limits and express pride, power, and control, the emphasis on the cool pose is self-defeating for the majority because it comes at the expense of education and other opportunities. Moreover, the cool pose uses sexist oppression to counter racist oppression rather than encouraging empowering strategies. Majors ties together analyses of race and gender, but few others have done so. Smith's (1992) primary conclusion, after reviewing the literature on women of color in sport and society, was that we have a deafening silence on diverse ethnic women in sport.

Brooks and Althouse (1993) have edited a volume on racism in college athletics, focusing on the African-American athlete. They bring together needed scholarship on race and sport and include a welcome section on gender and race. Corbett and Johnson (1993) in their chapter draw upon the limited research and their own insights on African-American women in college sport. African-American women have a social-historical context of sexual exploitation, low wages, and substandard education and are stereotyped as independent, loud, and dominating. The authors also debunk our popular myth that African-American women gravitate to track. African-American women have had more opportunities in track than in some other activities, and talented athletes from Wilma Rudolph to Jackie Joyner-Kersee are famous; but survey data indicate that track is not a particularly popular activity for African-American students, and social stereotypes and constraints probably limit opportunities. In another chapter, Tina Sloan Green (1993) optimistically discusses such opportunities as girls' clubs, YWCA, the PGM Golf Clinic, and the NCAA's national Youth Sport Program as strategies to encourage more young African-American women to develop their potential in sport and athletics.

## Gender and Sexuality

Although sport is stereotypically masculine, scholars recognize that gender beliefs affect men. As discussed by Messner (1992), sport powerfully socializes boys and men into a restricted masculine identity. For Messner, the major forces in sport are a competitive hierarchical structure with conditional self-worth that enforces the "must win" style, and homophobia. Messner, who describes the extent of homophobia in sport as staggering, states that homophobia leads all boys and men (gay or straight) to conform to a narrow definition of masculinity. Real men compete, and above all avoid anything feminine that might lead to being branded as a sissy. One successful elite athlete told Messner that as a child he had been interested in dance but instead threw himself into athletics; looking back he felt he had wanted the macho image of the athlete. Messner ties this masculine identity to sport violence; notably, female athletes are less comfortable with aggression in sport. Messner further notes that homophobia in athletics is closely linked with misogyny; in sport there is a bonding among men as superior to women.

Messner's linking of homophobia and misogyny reflects Lenskyj's (1987, 1991) analysis citing compulsory heterosexuality as the root of sexist sport practices, as well as Bem's (1993) contention that sexism, heterosexism, and homophobia are related consequences of the same gender lenses in society. We expect to see men dominate women, and we are uncomfortable with bigger, stronger women who take active, dominant roles expected of athletes.

Homophobia in sport has been discussed most often as a problem for lesbians, with good reason. In her chapter, "A Silence So Loud, It Screams," Nelson (1991) illustrates barriers by describing one Ladies' Professional Golf Association tour player who remained closeted to protect her status with friends, family, sponsors, tour personnel, and the public (prior to Muffin Spencer-Devlin's relatively accepted public coming-out statement in 1997). Not surprisingly, people in women's athletics often make great effort to avoid any hint of lesbianism. Pat Griffin, who has written and conducted workshops on homophobia in sport and physical education, de-

Homophobia is a
significant problem
in women's sports—
a "huge lavender
elephant sleeping
in the locker room"
(Griffin, 1987).

scribes the women's sports world as a giant closet with everyone "tip-toeing around
the huge lavender elephant sleeping in the locker room" (1987, p. 3). As Griffin notes
(1987, 1992), lesbians are not the problem; homophobia is. Homophobia manifests
itself in women's sports as

- silence,
- denial,
- apology,
- promotion of a heterosexy image,
- attacks on lesbians, and
- preference for male coaches.

We stereotypically assume that sport attracts lesbians (of course not gay men), but
sexual orientation and sport have no inherent relationship. Homophobia has doubt-
less kept more heterosexual women than lesbians out of sport and restricts the
behavior of all women in sport. Moreover, as the analyses of Messner (1992) and
Ponger (1990) suggest, homophobia probably restricts men in sport even more.

Recognition of gender and diversity is critical to effective sport and exercise
psychology practice. In trying to take a more social perspective in my work, I have
developed a stronger commitment to putting research into practice, and I'll indulge
that bias in the following section.

## TOWARD FEMINIST PRACTICE IN SPORT AND EXERCISE PSYCHOLOGY

Following Kurt Lewin's lead, as discussed in chapter 3, I have the goal of "practical
theory." Although translating scholarship on gender and diversity into practice is a
challenge, the expanding literature on feminist practice in psychology provides some
guidance.

First, we must avoid sexist assumptions, standards, and practices. Then, we
might follow the lead of psychologists who have moved to more actively feminist
approaches. Feminist practice (Worell & Remer, 1992) incorporates gender scholarship, emphasizes neglected experiences of women, and takes a more nonhierarchical,
empowering, process-oriented approach that shifts emphasis from personal change
to social change. For example, feminist approaches might provide insights on such
issues as aggression and competition, eating disorders, and sexual harassment.

### Key Point

Feminist practice (Worell & Remer, 1992) incorporates gender scholarship, emphasizes neglected
experiences of women, and takes a more nonhierarchical, empowering, process-oriented approach that
shifts emphasis from personal change to social change. For example, feminist approaches might provide
insights on such issues as aggression and competition, eating disorders, and sexual harassment.

An aggressive soccer player could be male or female, but a male soccer player is more likely to grow up in a world that reinforces aggressive behavior and to continue to have such behaviors reinforced. Even talented, competitive female athletes are socialized to keep quiet, be good, and let others take the lead. Moreover, most female athletes not only have a male coach, trainer, athletic director, and male professors, but also deal with males in most other power positions.

Overly aggressive, uncontrolled behavior is not exclusively male; tentative styles are not exclusively female. Still, we will work more effectively if we recognize gender influences. Anger control or confidence building has a different context, and likely requires different strategies, for females and males. For example, how does sport fit into the player's life? How do others (coach, teammates, family, spectators, friends) react to the player? Behavior is not just within the athlete, but within a particular sport context and larger social context, both of which are gender related.

Consider a figure skater with a potential eating disorder. Gender influences psychological disorders and diagnoses (e.g., Russo & Green, 1993; Travis, 1988). For example, women are more likely to present major depression and simple phobias, whereas men are more likely to present antisocial personality disorder or alcohol abuse. In the United States, the largest gender gap, by far, is for eating disorders; females are nine times as likely as males to exhibit anorexia or bulimia. The figure skater is much more likely to be female than male (as well as white, middle-upper class, and adolescent), and body image plays a major role (e.g., Rodin et al., 1985).

Females in certain sports may have exaggerated body image concerns related to appearance and performance. Judges look for a "line," and appearance affects endorsements. An educational approach emphasizing proper nutrition and training, without discounting the athlete's concerns, might be effective. Feminist practitioners might move still further to social action—educate others and try to change the system that leads athletes to pursue an unhealthy body image.

Our discipline has neglected sexual harassment, an issue that is prevalent and likely to emerge in practice. In psychology, work on violence toward women has expanded greatly. Given the prevalence of sexual harassment and assault, especially for college women, female athletes are much more likely to present problems related to these issues than eating disorders or any other potentially clinical issue. Yet I have seen virtually nothing in the applied sport psychology research or professional literature on this topic.

Recently, both academic and popular literature has demonstrated the prevalence of sexual harassment and assault (for reviews see Matlin, 1993; or Unger & Crawford, 1992). About one-third of college women report having been sexually harassed, and when discriminatory remarks are included, the number rises to more than 50%. Koss's (1990; Koss, Gidycz, & Wisniewiski, 1987) research indicates that 38 of 1000 college women experience rape or attempted rape in one year, that 85% of sexual assaults are by acquaintances, and that men and women define and interpret sexual situations and behaviors differently. All women are at risk, and no particular psychological pattern characterizes victims, although college students are at particular risk and alcohol is often involved. Given that most sport and exercise psychology consultants work with college athletes, we should be familiar with this information (Koss, 1990).

Although I do not know of sport and exercise psychology research on this topic, some have started to discuss the issues. Nelson (1991) in her chapter, "Running Scared," notes that harassment is almost routine for women runners. Women cannot run any time, any place. Lenskyj (1992) recently discussed sexual harassment in sport and pointed out some concerns unique to female athletes: sport (as a nonfeminine activity) may elicit derisive comments; the clothes are revealing; male coaches are often fit and conventionally attractive; female athletes may have spent much time training and less in general social activity; coaches are authoritarian and rule much of athletes' lives; and for some sports, merit is equated with heterosexual attractiveness.

Sexual harassment can occur with same-sex athletes and coaches. Fears of lesbian harassment are often invoked, but reality is otherwise. Overwhelmingly, sexual harassment is by males of females. As Lenskyj (1992) notes, and earlier discussion of homophobia suggests, lesbians and gay men are more likely to be targets than perpetrators of sexual harassment. Allegations of lesbianism may deter female athletes (regardless of sexual orientation) from rejecting male advances or complaining about harassment (Lenskyj, 1992). A student in my class on women and sport interviewed female coaches about lesbianism, and to her surprise, found the married coach more open and willing to discuss issues than single coaches (lesbian or heterosexual). Given the sport climate, we should not be surprised that female coaches are so worried about charges of lesbianism that they refrain from complaining about harassment or seeking equity for their programs. Sexual harassment (heterosexual or homophobic) intimidates women and maintains traditional power structures.

Sexual harassment and assault as a concern for male athletes have recently come to public attention. Some accounts (e.g., Neimark, 1993) suggest that male athletes are particularly prone to committing sexual assault. These reports in the popular media, as well as more theoretical work (e.g., Lenskyj, 1992; Messner, 1992), suggest that male bonding, the privileged status of athletes, and the macho image of sport are contributing factors.

Sexual harassment and assault probably occur much more often than we recognize. Consultants aware of sport and gender dynamics might be quicker to recognize such issues and help athletes with them. Because athletes often train in isolated locations and at odd hours, and frequently travel, they may be in vulnerable situations more often than others, and female athletes must be aware of sexual harassment and assault. Most universities have policies as well as counseling and educational programs on these issues. Consultants can use these resources (e.g. refer victims, incorporate workshops) or develop programs targeted to athletes.

> **Key Point**
>
> Reports in the popular media, as well as more theoretical work (e.g., Lenskyj, 1992; Messner, 1992), suggest that male bonding, the privileged status of athletes, and the macho image of sport are factors that may contribute to male athletes' proneness to committing sexual assault.

Male athletes must also be aware of the issues, and male administrators can support educational efforts. Several rape-prevention programs have been designed for male athletes, with support of coaches and administrators, that aim to prevent aggression on the field from affecting personal lives (Guernsey, 1993). Sport and exercise psychologists might use relevant resources to educate female and male athletes, coaches, and others. Again, to take a more feminist approach, we could attempt to change the social situation as well as educate individuals—perhaps by demanding safe lighting, secure facilities, and clear, enforceable policies.

## Summary

Gender makes a difference, race matters, and human diversity characterizes all of us in all we do. Gender is a pervasive force that is particularly ingrained in our sport and exercise structure and practice. We cannot simply treat everyone the same. However, we cannot assume that males and females are dichotomous opposites and treat all males one way and all females another way. Biology is part of the mix, but biology is not destiny. Gender is a dynamic, social influence that varies with the individual, situation, and time. Our research and practice are just beginning to consider gender within the dynamic social context of sport and exercise. We can move on to the greater challenge and embrace human diversity to advance our understanding and enrich our practice.

# *Review Questions*

1. Explain Trickett et al.'s (1994) emphasis on people in context.
2. Trace women's early contributions to the disciplines of psychology and physical education.
3. Explain Title IX, its impact on girls' and women's sport participation rates, and its impact on the prevalence of women in coaching and administration positions.
4. Discuss the scholarship relating to sex differences.
5. Discuss the scholarship relating to gender role orientation.
6. Describe the relationship between self-perception and gender in sport and exercise settings.
7. Identify several forms of gender bias in media coverage of female athletes.
8. Define the racist practice of "stacking," and explain its effect on power.
9. Explain the relationships among sexism, heterosexism, and homophobia in sport settings.
10. Describe the "feminist practice" movement in psychology and its implications for sport and exercise psychology.
11. Discuss sexual harassment and identify specific issues for the research on female athletes.

# *Recommended Reading*

★ Eccles, J.S., & Harrold, R.D. (1991). Gender differences in sport involvement: Applying the Eccles' expectancy-value model. *Journal of Applied Sport Psychology, 3,* 7-35.

> Eccles has done extensive research on the development of achievement expectations, values, and behaviors, and she always incorporates gender issues. She is one of the few psychology scholars who specifically addresses physical activity as well as academic activities, and this article summarizes her research, guiding model, and specific applications to physical activity.

★ Messner, M.A. (1992). *Power at play: Sports and the problem of masculinity.* Boston: Beacon Press.

> Most of the work on gender issues in sport relates to women in sport. Messner has written extensively, and his work makes it clear that gender is an issue for men in sport. This book presents his insightful analyses and illustrates how masculinity and our gender constraints limit men, as well as women, in sport.

★ Smith, Y.R. (1992). Women of color in society and sport. *Quest, 44,* 228-250.

> We live in a multicultural society, and physical activity participants and issues reflect that society. But, our research and professional practice have not yet embraced many areas of social diversity. Smith's article describes some of the issues for women of color in sport, and also points out the striking gap in our literature. Perhaps reading her article will inspire you to seek more information or to explore issues yourself; sport and exercise psychology will be richer if you do that.

# Social Influence

## CHAPTER OBJECTIVES

After studying this chapter, you should be able to

- identify ways in which the presence of others can influence sport and exercise performance and
- explain the influence of evaluative comments, competition, and social support on performance.

Social influence, central in the research of the 1960s and 1970s, remains prominent because virtually all sport and exercise activity is social. Much sport activity involves competition, which is social by definition. Even noncompetitive sport and exercise activities such as physical education classes, fitness programs, and recreational sports usually involve social interaction. Similarly, exercise instructors and sport leaders exert social influence when they give directions, watch us perform, and tell us how we're doing. We often win or lose in front of family, friends, and the general public. Classmates see whether we can do the handstand, and colleagues in the noon aerobic exercise group notice if we're out of shape.

In this chapter we will consider the major types of social influence that sport and exercise psychology research has addressed. We will focus on *social facilitation* (the influence of the presence of others on performance) and also the more active influence of social reinforcement (evaluative comments and actions) and of competition. We considered social influence in the chapters on behavioral approaches and social development. Our interest here is in the specific social influence processes that dominated early research as well as in the contemporary approaches, which address social support.

## SOCIAL FACILITATION

Social facilitation, which refers to the influence of the presence of others on performance, includes audience effects and coaction effects. In the social facilitation literature, audience refers to passive spectators who simply observe, such as students

> **Key Point**
>
> *Social facilitation* refers to the influence of the presence of others on performance, including audience effects and coaction effects.

in a golf class standing back to watch another student practice a shot. Coaction refers to other people doing the same thing at the same time, for instance, students lined up together practicing the shot.

## Early Social Facilitation Research

Social facilitation is one of the oldest research topics in social psychology. As we noted in chapter 2, the first social psychology experiment was Triplett's (1898) investigation of social facilitation and motor performance. Competitive cycling was popular then, and Triplett was a cycling enthusiast as well as a psychologist. Using cycling records, Triplett found that paced times were faster (by about 35 seconds per mile) than unpaced times and that competitive times were fastest of all. In a controlled experiment to test his observations, Triplett found that children performed the task of winding a fishing reel faster in pairs than when alone. Triplett proposed the principle of *dynamogeny*, asserting that the presence of others arouses competitive drive, releases energy, and increases speed of performance.

Subsequent social facilitation research expanded on Triplett's work. Allport (1924) conducted several experiments and coined the term *social facilitation* to refer to performance improvements due to the presence of others. However, the widening research revealed that the presence of others did not always improve performance. Some studies confirmed Triplett's findings, showing that people performed better with an audience or coactors on certain tasks (the pursuit rotor, monitoring of a light panel, and multiplication problems). Investigators observed that chickens ate more in the presence of other chickens and that ants exhibited more nest-building activity when other ants were nearby. On the other hand, some researchers reported that people were less accurate, made more errors, and had more trouble learning nonsense syllables or following a finger maze when others were present. Reviews by Landers and McCullagh (1976) and Wankel (1984) provide more details on the early social facilitation research.

## Zajonc's Interpretation of Social Facilitation

Social facilitation research appeared to be stalled by the contradictory findings when Zajonc (1965) rejuvenated the topic. Zajonc proposed that drive theory (discussed in chapter 11) could explain the equivocal findings. Specifically, Zajonc proposed the following:

- The presence of others, either as an audience or as coactors, creates arousal or drive.

- Increased arousal increases the likelihood that the individual's dominant response will occur.

- If the skill is simple or well learned, the dominant response is the correct response and performance improves (facilitation).

- If the skill is complex and not well learned, the dominant response is an incorrect response and performance is impaired.

These proposals inspired considerable research, much of which confirmed his explanation. Of most interest here, Martens (1969) tested Zajonc's predictions with a motor task. Martens's study included separate learning and performance phases, with male college students performing a coincident-timing task either alone or in the presence of 10 other students. The audience condition elicited more arousal than the alone condition during both the learning and performance phases. During learning, individuals performed better when alone. During the performance phase when the task was well learned, the audience condition still elicited more arousal, but performance was better than in the alone condition.

Martens's findings confirmed Zajonc's predictions: the presence of an audience created arousal, which impaired learning but facilitated performance after the task was well learned. Subsequent sport and exercise psychology studies added further support. For example, coactors elicited faster running times (Obermeier, Landers, & Ester, 1977) and better performance on a muscular endurance task (Martens & Landers, 1969), but worsened performance on more complex tasks (Burwitz & Newell, 1972; Martens & Landers, 1972).

## Alternative Explanations of Social Facilitation

According to Zajonc (1965), the mere presence of others creates arousal that in turn affects performance. Cottrell (1968) challenged this, pointing out that the presence of others is sometimes calming. Cottrell maintained that the presence of others creates arousal only when the others can evaluate performance. Thus, it is *evaluation apprehension*—the perception that others can judge one's performance—that creates arousal. Cottrell's own research, as well as later studies with motor tasks (Burwitz & Newell, 1972; Martens & Landers, 1972), supports the role of evaluation apprehension in social facilitation.

> ### Key Point
>
> Cottrell maintained that the presence of others creates arousal only when the others can evaluate performance. Thus, it is *evaluation apprehension*—the perception that others can judge one's performance—that creates arousal.

Subsequently some, suggesting that the drive theory explanation of social facilitation effects is limiting, proposed cognitive explanations. In a review, Geen and Gange (1977) concluded that drive theory was the best explanation for social facilitation yet, but argued for more attention to cognitive processes. Baron, Moore, and Sanders (1978) suggested that distraction, rather than the mere presence of others or evaluation apprehension, accounts for performance changes. Landers (1980) advocated a focus on attentional processes for social facilitation research in sport. In any event, neither drive theory nor evaluation apprehension has stirred much interest in the last 20 years, and sport and exercise psychologists have turned to more cognitive approaches, such as self-presentation, and to a wider investigation of social interaction processes.

# AUDIENCE EFFECTS IN THE REAL WORLD

Perhaps the main reason sport and exercise psychologists abandoned social facilitation research was the failure to demonstrate any effects in the real world. Many of the experiments were trivial, and the results of the few field studies were disappointing. Paulus and colleagues, for example, examined audience effects on gymnastics and on batting performance in professional baseball (Paulus & Cornelius, 1974; Paulus, Judd, & Bernstein, 1977). Crowd size was not related to batting performance, and contrary to predictions, better gymnasts were less facilitated by an audience than were poorer gymnasts.

In a critique and replication of Martens's audience study, Landers, Bauer, and Feltz (1978) pointed out several problems with the social facilitation research. Landers et al., and also Martens (1979) in his reply, acknowledged that even though some laboratory experiments supported Zajonc's predictions, the findings had not been generalized to actual sport settings and that the research had limited practical value.

## Home Advantage

One practical issue involving social influence is the widely held belief in the "home advantage." Schwartz and Barsky (1977) documented the home advantage with professional baseball, football, and hockey teams and college basketball and football teams. Teams won games more often at home than away for all sports; the home advantage was greatest for the indoor sports, hockey and basketball. Further analyses revealed that the home advantage held for offensive play (e.g., hits, goals, shots, points), but defensive statistics (e.g., errors, saves, fouls) did not differ for home and away games.

In a further investigation with basketball teams, Varca (1980) observed that home and away teams did not differ on field goal percentage, free throw percentage, or turnovers. Instead, the home team demonstrated more "functionally aggressive behavior" (steals, blocked shots, rebounds), whereas the away team demonstrated more "dysfunctionally aggressive behavior" (fouls). Although all these studies document a home advantage, the research is largely descriptive and suggestive; we do not know the extent of the home advantage or its underlying processes.

In fact, some work (Baumeister, 1984; Baumeister & Steinhilber, 1984) documents a home disadvantage. Baumeister proposed that directing attention internally, or increased self-consciousness, can disrupt the performance of well-learned, automatic skills. Professional athletes perform skills automatically with minimal conscious attention. Baumeister reasoned that the opportunity to win a championship in front of the home crowd would increase self-consciousness and disrupt skilled performance. Data from World Series baseball and professional basketball confirmed Baumeister's views; home teams tended to choke in the final, decisive game. However, Baumeister's data were limited, and subsequent studies did not support the final-game "choke."

Courneya and Carron (1992), reviewing over 30 studies, concluded that the research documented the home advantage with a home winning percentage ranging from 52.5 (effect size = .07) for baseball to 69 (effect size = .38) for soccer. They noted that these largely descriptive studies did not address possible reasons for a home advantage. They found no support for travel, crowd size, or aggression as an explanation. At this time, the literature supports a home advantage, but offers no insights or explanations.

## Basking in Reflected Glory

Before moving from audience effects to other social effects, let's consider one interesting line of research that reverses social facilitation to examine how performers affect the audience. Cialdini and his colleagues (Cialdini, et al. 1976; Cialdini & Richardson, 1980) investigated the common observation that many spectators identify with sport teams. Cialdini suggested that spectators identify with teams to share in the glory as a form of self-presentation or impression management: one's image is more positive if one is associated with a successful team than with an unsuccessful team. In an initial study (Cialdini et al., 1976), observers monitored students in classes the day after football games at several major universities to see whether they were wearing school-identifying apparel. As expected, students (who were not necessarily football fans) were more likely to wear apparel identifying the university after a win than after a loss. The students were "basking in reflected glory" even though they personally had no role in the success. In a second study (Cialdini, et al. 1976), investigators randomly telephoned students and as part of an "opinion survey" asked them to describe the outcome of a recent football game. Analysis of the students' language showed that they tended to claim "we" won and "they" lost, again supporting the phenomenon of basking in reflected glory (BIRG).

### Key Point

"Basking in reflected glory" refers to a phenomenon in which spectators identify with teams to share in the glory as a form of self-representation; that is, one's own self-image is more positive if one is associated with a successful team than with an unsuccessful team.

Studies have shown that students are more likely to wear apparel identifying their university after a win than after a loss. These students are "basking in reflected glory" as a form of self-representation.

Zillmann and Paulus (1993) used the dispositional theory of sport spectatorship (Zillmann, Bryant, & Sopolsky, 1989) to extend the description of BIRG. Zillmann et al. focused on affective consequences when spectators form tacit alliances with teams and performers. We may have either positive or negative dispositions toward teams. For example, I grew up as a Yankee fan, but I knew others whose favorite team was "anyone who's playing the Yankees." Zillmann et al. offered two predictions:

- Enjoyment derived from witnessing the success and victory of athletic competitors (a) increases with positive affective dispositions and (b) decreases with negative affective dispositions toward these competitors.

- Enjoyment derived from witnessing the failure and defeat of athletic competitors (a) increases with negative affective dispositions and (b) decreases with positive affective disposition toward these competitors.

## Summary Perspective on Performance Influences

Zillmann and Paulus (1993) summarized social influence on motor performance in a model based on the cognitive-motivational model of Paulus (1983). Characteristics of the spectator situation, such as the number of spectators, evaluative characteristics, and expectations, determine the pressure performers feel. Increased pressure may affect motivation or effort, anxiety or drive, and distraction or task-irrelevant cognitive processes. Increased pressure and resultant increased effort and arousal may improve performance on simple tasks, and distraction should not be much of a problem. With complex tasks, effort is typically high anyway, and arousal and distraction likely have detrimental effects. Zillmann and Paulus added that when spectators are supportive, pressure should be reduced, which reduces arousal and distraction but increases effort. Thus, supportive spectators (home audience) should be beneficial, although Baumeister's (1984) home disadvantage—

and the possible reduced effort with an unconditionally supportive audience—could be detrimental.

# SOCIAL REINFORCEMENT AND MOTOR PERFORMANCE

Like social facilitation, social reinforcement was prominent in the early research. In fact, the social reinforcement work followed the same designs and is a variation on the research on social influence and motor performance. Social facilitation involves a passive audience, but in social reinforcement, audience members have an active (although limited) role. Social reinforcement consists of positive or negative evaluative comments and actions, such as verbal praise and criticism or body language (smiles, frowns, gestures). Most audiences in sport and exercise settings—including home/away audiences and most instructors and coparticipants—provide social reinforcement; it was logical to extend social influence to include this evaluative component.

A series of studies, mainly by Martens and colleagues, followed the experimental social psychology model of the social facilitation research. The tasks were novel complex motor tasks, and the experimental manipulations consisted of positive and negative comments. In experiments with college males performing a coincident-timing task (Roberts & Martens, 1970) and with preschool children rolling a ball up a ramp to a target (Martens, 1970), none of the social reinforcement conditions improved performance. In two subsequent studies examining internal-external control (Martens, 1971) and socioeconomic status (Martens, 1972), results again revealed no social reinforcement effects.

Martens offered some explanations for lack of effects with motor performance in light of extensive social reinforcement effects in the psychology literature. Performers received better, more specific information from the task itself than from social reinforcement, which provided only redundant information that did not help improve performance.

Even if social reinforcement provides no information, we might expect motivational effects. However, most sport and exercise tasks, and even the motor tasks of these experiments, already have a clear goal and intrinsic interest. Most individuals want to perform well, and unless they have been doing the task to the point of boredom, social reinforcement will not add much to an already high level of intrinsic motivation. And until a complex task is mastered, individuals cannot control and modify their performance at will, even if highly motivated.

Harney and Parker (1972) proposed that social reinforcement must be frequent and intense to affect performance. When they administered positive and negative social reinforcement "enthusiastically" after every trial, performance was better than in a control condition. Two other studies (Wankel, 1975; Martens, Burwitz, & Newell, 1972) addressed the influence of social reinforcement during later performance stages, when individuals could be bored and less motivated; and both provided some indications that social reinforcement has motivational effects.

In my (long-ago and almost forgotten) master's thesis work (Gill & Martens, 1975), I created four conditions: (1) social reinforcement with praise for good scores and negative comments for poor scores, (2) knowledge of results with precise error scores, (3) social reinforcement combined with knowledge of results, and (4) control with neither social reinforcement nor knowledge of results. Both social reinforcement and knowledge of results improved performance, and the group receiving both performed best. Surprisingly, the group with only social reinforcement performed better than the group with only knowledge of results, suggesting that social reinforcement information was sufficient for performance improvement and possibly had a motivational effect.

Overall, these studies suggest that social reinforcement may have an informational effect when other information sources are absent, and may have a motivational effect when the activity is not intrinsically motivating. However, no observed effects were very dramatic, and most experimental situations were quite artificial. Most performers have information that is clearer and more precise than social reinforcement. Thus, the social reinforcement effects on motor performance are limited at best.

The limited extent of this influence does not imply that social reinforcement is undesirable, though. None of these studies, or any other research I know of, has shown detrimental effects on performance, and social reinforcement has other beneficial effects. It is a key component of teaching and coaching behavior and of communication and interpersonal style. The work on coaching behaviors, discussed in chapter 15, indicates that the relative use of positive, reinforcing behaviors versus punitive behaviors strongly influences players' attitudes toward the coach and the activity.

Communication styles and the use of social reinforcement are part of more current work on social support. Sport and exercise psychology has moved well past the controlled lab experiments of the early research to real sport and exercise settings and more complex social interactions. The current work on social support moves from isolated social influence effects on performance to more complex social influence processes.

# COMPETITION AND MOTOR PERFORMANCE

Competition involves the presence of others, but like social reinforcement, it involves more. Competition entails a more direct social evaluation process than the standard audience situation. Because the social evaluation is so clear and intense, competition should increase arousal and affect performance just as the presence of others does— or even more so. Although research on competition is more limited than research on audience effects, the findings show parallels.

Generally, competition improves performance on simple or well-learned skills and on speed, strength, and endurance tasks. Competition improved performance on a dynamometer task (Berridge, 1935), elicited faster reaction times (Church, 1962; Gaebelein & Taylor, 1971), and facilitated endurance performance on a bicycle ergometer (Wilmore, 1968). Gill (1978) reported that competition improved performance on a well-learned motor maze task; Wankel (1972) found that competition improved performance of high-ability individuals, whereas low-ability individuals performed better under noncompetitive conditions. Research showing detrimental effects of competition is sparse, but some early studies revealed that competition impaired accuracy while facilitating speed (Church, 1968; Dashiell, 1935; Whittemore, 1924).

## Key Point

Generally, competition improves performance on simple or well-learned skills and on speed, strength, and endurance tasks.

Gross and Gill's (1982) results suggest that the influence of competition is more complex. We varied instructions on a dart-throwing task across five conditions ranging from complete emphasis on speed, to equal emphasis on speed and accuracy, to complete emphasis on accuracy. Competition improved speed, but only when the instructions emphasized speed. When the instructions emphasized accuracy, performers were slower in competition. However, competition did not affect accuracy, even when the instructions emphasized accuracy.

## Competition and Arousal

Starkes and Allard (1983) investigated competition effects using a signal-detection paradigm to see how quickly and accurately individuals could detect a volleyball in slides flashed rapidly on a screen. Volleyball players and nonplayers attempted the task under competitive and noncompetitive conditions. Overall, players were faster than nonplayers, but the more important finding here is that competition increased arousal (assessed as increases in heart rate) and elicited faster times in both players and nonplayers, with a much greater increase in speed for nonplayers. Competition also decreased accuracy on the detection task, but Starkes and Allard asserted that the increased speed was more striking than the decreased accuracy and that volleyball players may purposely choose to sacrifice a small degree of accuracy for a very fast response. The results from Starkes and Allard and Gross and Gill imply that performers can adopt varying speed-accuracy strategies depending on the task demands, and that competition may further modify the speed-accuracy components of performance.

## Competition and Winning or Losing

The social influence of competition on performance may be complex, and to complicate matters even further, we must consider winning and losing or success and failure. Success/failure affects competitors' emotions, satisfaction, and perceived ability (e.g., Gill, 1977) and likely affects performance in competition.

In a controlled experiment, Martens and White (1975) systematically varied the win/loss ratio and reported that individuals performed better when the win/loss ratio was 50/50 than when it was higher or lower. This finding fits with the achievement motivation literature discussed in chapter 8, as achievement situations with a 50% chance of success represent maximum challenge and elicit the strongest achievement efforts.

## Cooperation Within Competition

Studies of volleyball players have shown that competition increases arousal and reaction time.

In sport and exercise psychology we often assume that competition is the model—that cooperation is a different world. A moment's reflection should counter that view. Most sport and exercise activity, even highly competitive athletics, involves considerable cooperation. Within the classic reward definition framework (Deutsch, 1949), competition is a zero-sum game: what one wins, the other loses. In a cooperative situation, all work for the same goal and share in the rewards. We can also add the typical third situation—the individual structure—in which what one person achieves has no effect on anyone else.

Triplett's (1898) early research set the stage for the common assumption that competition leads to better performance than cooperation or individual structures. Despite the firmly held belief in competition, considerable evidence indicates that, in fact, cooperation leads to greater achievement as well as greater social and psychological benefits in most areas of society, including sport and exercise. Cooperation even aids in bicycle racing. Albert (1991) used ethnographic and interview approaches to investigate the subculture of bicycle racing, and his data clearly counter the conventional view of unambiguous conflict or competition among racers. Instead, cooperative efforts between opponents were central to the social order, with strong sanctions for noncompliance. Albert further noted that media coverage, which ignores cooperative efforts, creates and perpetuates erroneous stereotypes.

Several educational psychologists have researched cooperative learning environments (for reviews of various lines of research on cooperative groups, see Hertz-Lazarowitz & Miller, 1992), and the conclusions are uniform—cooperative learning environments lead to greater achievement, better learning, and enhanced social and psychological development. Johnson and Johnson (1992), who have extended this work to sport and exercise settings, have summarized their own research (more than 80 studies over 20 years) as well as over 500 other studies comparing cooperative, competitive, and individualistic structures. In terms of achievement or productivity, cooperation clearly was most effective, with an advantage over both competitive (effect size = .67) and individualistic (effect size = .66) structures. Stanne's (1993) dissertation at Minnesota (Johnson and Johnson's institution) was a meta-analysis of social interdependence (cooperation) and motor performance—the particular interest of sport and exercise psychology. Stanne found similar cooperative advantages over competition (effect size = .82) and individualist structures (effect size = .66). In their review chapter, Johnson and Johnson (1992) offered three general conclusions:

1. Under a broad range of conditions, cooperative efforts resulted in higher achievements and greater productivity than did competitive or individualistic efforts.

2. Generally, cooperative efforts resulted in greater interpersonal attraction and more social support than did competitive or individualistic efforts.

3. Generally, cooperative efforts resulted in higher self-esteem and greater psychological health than did competitive or individualistic efforts.

The evidence is convincing. But we should not view this as a contest between competition and cooperation. Competition is a social process, and even competitive sport activities typically involve cooperation or social interdependence. We would do a great service as researchers and practitioners if we devoted more attention to developing and maintaining effective social interdependence in sport and exercise settings—whether we work with intercollegiate athletes, children in a community sport program, or adults in a cardiac rehabilitation clinic.

## SOCIAL SUPPORT

Sport and exercise psychologists seldom study or apply the social influence models of the early work on social facilitation and social reinforcement. Social influence remains prominent, but current work approaches social influence as a process and emphasizes ongoing social interaction, specifically social support. For example, Carron, Hausenblas, and Mack (1996), in a meta-analysis on social influence and exercise, defined social influence as including family, important others, class leaders, and group cohesion as well as more traditional social facilitation (coexercisers). They concluded that social influence has a small to moderate positive effect (effect size from .20 to .50) on exercise behaviors, cognitions, and affect. However, the larger effects did not involve traditional audience influences. Moderate to large effects were found for family support and attitudes, task cohesion and adherence, important others and attitudes, and family support and compliance behavior.

Similarly, Turner, Rejeski, and Brawley (1997) looked at the influence of the social environment (leader behavior) on feeling states and self-efficacy following a physical activity session. The exercise leader engaged in either "bland" or "socially enriched" interactions. Participants in the socially enriched environment were more positive on revitalization and positive engagement and showed a greater increase in self-efficacy, suggesting a social influence on psychological benefits of activity. Their socially enriched environment involved much more than mere presence (social facilitation) or social reinforcement, although contingent praise and encouragement were part of the manipulation. Exercise leaders followed a positive approach similar to Smith and Smoll's positive coaching model (discussed in chapter 15), provided frequent individual attention, and engaged in general conversation.

These studies reflect the current work on social influence in real-world settings. Social influence is complex and multidimensional. Early social influence work with drive models and isolated variables was neither multidimensional nor process oriented, and it focused on limited performance responses rather than the full range of cognitions, feelings, and behaviors. The current research does not provide clear answers, but represents the complexities of social influence in sport and exercise. Much of the current work has focused on social support, which is conceptually similar to social influence.

## Social Support Definitions

Social support is a familiar term, referring to the support of others; but for research and practice, we must be more specific. Social support has been studied largely within the health area and thus has been defined and understood in terms of health benefits. Researchers often cite Durkheim (1951) for his initial empirical work on social support. In examining suicide rates, Durkheim reported that the loss of social ties, or anomie, negatively affected psychological well-being. Researchers have often operationally defined social support as the number of friends, relatives, or social involvements; conceptually social support has typically denoted a vague sense of belongingness or acceptance. With progress in research and conceptual models, we have come to see social support as multidimensional, and consensus suggests that quality of support is more important than quantity of social contacts. Here, we'll use Shumaker and Brownell's (1984) definition of social support as

> an exchange of resources between at least two individuals perceived by the provider or the recipient to be intended to enhance the well-being of the recipient. (p. 13)

## A Model of the Social Support Process

Shumaker and Brownell's definition, which is consistent with most current research and major models, suggests that social support is a process with both provider and recipient. Rosenfeld and Richman's (1997) model (see figure 19.1) depicts that process and includes the commonly accepted dimensions of social support.

The figure shows three broad types of social support: *tangible* (e.g., assisting someone with a task), *informational* (e.g., telling team members they have mutual responsibilities), and *emotional* (e.g., comforting someone). Providers communicate these types of support through behaviors, and we typically view social support from the recipient's perspective (Rosenfeld & Richman, 1997). Behaviors constitute social support when the recipient perceives them as enhancing well-being. Sarason, Sarason, and Pierce (1990) argue that perceived social support, more than actual received support, is the key contributor to health and well-being.

The perceived communicated behaviors, which take eight forms in the model, are based on several studies (Hardy & Crace, 1993; Pines, Aronson, & Kafry, 1981; Richman, Rosenfeld, & Hardy, 1993; Weiss, 1974):

- **Listening support.** Others listen to you without giving advice or being judgmental.

- **Emotional support.** Others comfort and care for you and indicate they are on your side.

- **Emotional challenge.** Others challenge you to evaluate your attitudes, values, and feelings.

- **Task appreciation.** Others acknowledge your efforts and express appreciation for the work you do.

**Provider**
**(team, coaches, support personnel, friends, family)**

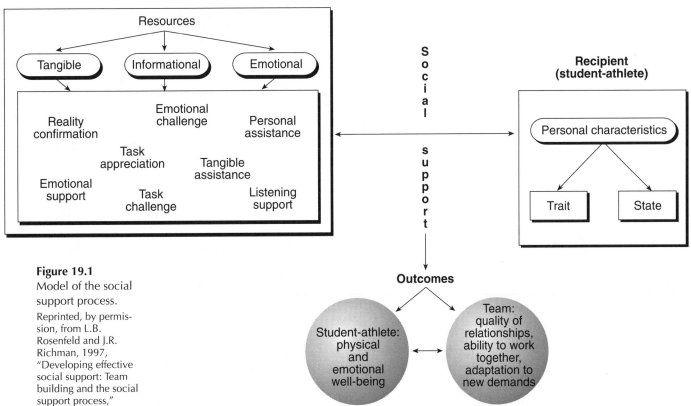

**Figure 19.1**
Model of the social support process.

Reprinted, by permission, from L.B. Rosenfeld and J.R. Richman, 1997, "Developing effective social support: Team building and the social support process," *Journal of Applied Sport Psychology, 9*, 133-53.

- **Task challenge.** Others challenge your way of thinking about your work in order to stretch you, motivate you, and lead you to greater creativity, excitement, and involvement.

- **Reality confirmation.** Others are similar to you, see things the way you do, and help you confirm your perception of the world.

- **Tangible assistance.** Others provide you with financial assistance, products, or gifts.

- **Personal assistance.** Others provide services or help, such as running errands or offering expertise, to help you accomplish your tasks.

Other investigators have listed different dimensions or specific forms of social support, but all suggest similar main dimensions. Most agree that social support benefits are based on direct assistance (tangible support), advice (informational support), or encouragement (emotional support). Weiss (1974), an early investigator, proposed a theory of social relations with six functions obtained from social relationships: *attachment* (emotional support), *social integration* (network support), *reassurance of worth* (esteem support), *reliable alliance* (tangible aid), *guidance* (informational support), and *opportunity for nurturance* (bolstering sense of self-worth by assisting others).

## Social Support Measures

Social support measures, developed in conjunction with models, reflect similar dimensions. Measuring social interaction is not easy, and measures often lack solid reliability and validity. Commonly used measures in the health and sport psychology areas are the Social Support Questionnaire (SSQ; Sarason, Levine, Basham, & Sarason, 1983), the Social Support Inventory (SSI; Brown, Alpert, Lent, Hunt, & Brady, 1988;

Social support can come in many forms: the tangible support a coach provides as an athlete masters a task, the emotional support a parent provides an athlete, or the task challenge a teammate provides during practice.

Brown, Brady, Lent, Wolfert, & Hall, 1987), the Social Provisions Scale (Cutrona & Russell, 1987), and the Social Support Survey (Richman et al., 1993).

The SSQ, based on Sarason's work, assesses the number of others who provide support and the degree of satisfaction with that support. The SSQ is widely used and has psychometric strength, but it is unidimensional and seems to best reflect emotional support. The SSI assesses five factors: acceptance and belonging, appraisal and coping assistance, behavioral and cognitive guidance, tangible assistance and material aid, and modeling. The Social Provisions Scale was developed to assess Weiss's six relational provisions, and Duncan and McAuley's (1993) confirmatory factor analysis confirmed these six dimensions with use of the measure in an exercise sample.

Several social support measures have been used or adapted for research in sport and exercise settings. As just noted, Duncan and McAuley used the Social Provisions Scale to investigate whether self-efficacy cognitions mediate the relationship between social support and health-promoting behaviors. Specifically, they assessed social support, self-efficacy, and exercise behaviors with sedentary, middle-aged men and women. Social support did not directly influence exercise behavior but had an indirect effect through self-efficacy. The results suggest that social support may help promote self-efficacy for exercise and thus health-related exercise behavior. Duncan and McAuley cautioned that in practice, exercise leaders or others in support positions may have difficulty matching support to needs, and that it is important to monitor perceived support in relation to intentions and program goals. Also, with the mediating role of self-efficacy, supportive interventions should aim at fostering self-reliance and avoiding dependency.

Sarason et al. (1990) summarized much social support research using the SSQ, and Kelley and Gill (1993) used the SSQ to investigate the role of social support in stress and burnout with collegiate coaches. Using Smith's (1983) stress and burnout model as a framework, they found that satisfaction with social support related to perceived stress and that perceived stress in turn predicted burnout.

Rosenfeld and Richman (1977), noting that considerable work has been done within their model on the role of social support for individual athletes, proposed extensions to a team-building model. Rosenfeld, Richman, and Hardy (1989) found that student-athletes' social support networks consisted of coaches and teammates who provided mostly task challenge support, friends who provided mostly listening support, and parents who provided mostly task appreciation support.

Social support is particularly applicable to sport injury and rehabilitation processes (Hardy & Crace, 1993). Literature in health psychology and related areas (e.g., Cohen, 1988; Cohen & Wills, 1985; Shumaker & Brownell, 1984; Wallston, Alagna, DeVellis, & DeVellis, 1983) indicates that social support has a role in stress reduction and health promotion. Several sport and exercise psychologists suggest that social support may have a similar role in sport injury and rehabilitation (e.g., Rotella & Heyman, 1986; Silva & Hardy, 1991; Weiss & Troxel, 1986; Wiese & Weiss, 1987).

## Guidelines for Providing Social Support to Injured Athletes

On the basis of the literature, Hardy and Crace (1993) offer guidelines to sport psychology consultants and other sports medicine professionals for providing social support to injured athletes:

### Providing Emotional Support

- **Listen carefully.** Be an active listener and focus on the what and how of communication. Use supportive and confirming behaviors while listening, and be patient.
- **Know thyself.** Be aware of your needs as well as your reactions to others.
- **Switch hats occasionally.** Be ready to use different forms of support, and find a form that is natural for you.
- **Involve the natural helping network.** Have regular informal contact with coaches, teammates, trainers, family, and important others.
- **Create an open environment.** Create an open and accepting environment.

### Providing Informational Support

- **Develop your injury knowledge base.** You must have content expertise to provide task support.
- **Deliver effective instructional feedback.** Feedback should affirm task mastery and effort and should be sincere.
- **Use technical modalities.** Use physiological, biomechanical, or psychological tools as appropriate. Modern computer and interactive technology has much to offer.
- **Don't be afraid to challenge and confront.** Deal with injured athletes in a straightforward, honest manner.
- **Provide reality touchstones.** This might involve meetings with other injured athletes or support groups.

### Providing Tangible Support

- **Beware of boundaries.** Consider National Collegiate Athletic Association regulations; check with coaches, administrators, or trainers.
- **Define your boundaries.** Develop your philosophy in relation to regulations, your qualifications, and options. Communicate your boundaries to athletes.
- **Deliver on time.** Tangible support is best received at the time it is requested. But while timeliness is important, some injured athletes may require long-term tangible support, and use of a supportive network may help avoid depletion of resources or burnout.
- **Offer tangible support interest-free.** Do not put the recipient in a state of indebtedness to you, especially psychologically. Give support freely and unconditionally.

Hardy and Crace (1993) also offer general advice for effective support with injured athletes. Athletes should list potential supporters and describe what they would like these people to do. Then athletes should develop a plan—list steps for requesting support, a time frame, and some alternative or back-up plans. Athletes should maintain regular contact with their support network and monitor the support process. They need to find ways to show that the support provider is appreciated and valued. Also, athletes must realize that they can use their own resources as a support system for themselves and others. As with most psychological skills and strategies, the goal is self-control, mastery, and the development of a self-support system.

At this time, sport and exercise psychologists have incorporated social support primarily in relation to injuries and rehabilitation. This work is promising, not only for sport injury but also for wider application. Social support has obvious ties to such group dynamics topics as communication and cohesion, and Rosenfeld and Richman (1997) offer a social support perspective on team building.

## Summary

Social influence is prominent in sport and exercise activities, but we have abandoned the limited approaches of the early social facilitation research and moved to more process-oriented and multifaceted approaches. Audiences and instructors are not passive evaluators or simply providers of reinforcement. Today we see coaching and teaching behavior as a set of behaviors, or a style, and social support is part of that mix. Competition is not a simple stimulus, but an interactive process involving cooperative behavior. Social support has attracted attention in sport and exercise psychology, especially in relation to injured athletes. Social support has many potential applications across the widest range of sport and exercise settings, with the widest range of participants. It is one of the most promising variations on social influence, and effective social influence processes can enhance physical activity for all participants.

## Review Questions

1. Define social facilitation.
2. Explain the relationship between drive theory and social facilitation.
3. Describe evaluation apprehension and its role in social facilitation.
4. Trace the research documenting evidence of "home advantage" or "home disadvantage."
5. Describe the phenomenon of "basking in reflected glory."
6. Contrast social facilitation and social reinforcement.
7. Describe competition's effects on performance.
8. Describe the influence of cooperation on achievement, interpersonal attraction, social support, and self-esteem.
9. Define social support, and contrast the results of actual social support and perceived social support.
10. Compare and contrast tangible support, informational support, and emotional support.
11. Give examples of appropriate ways to give emotional, tangible, and informational support to injured or rehabilitating athletes.

## *Recommended Reading*

★ Zillmann, D. & Paulus, P.B. (1993). Spectators: Reactions to sports events and effects on athletic performance. In R.N. Singer, M. Murphey & L.K. Tennant (Eds.), *Handbook of research on sport psychology* (pp. 600-619). New York: Macmillan.

> Spectators are one of the clearest examples of social influence in sport, and spectator influence is one of our earliest research topics. Zillman and Paulus review that literature and provide a guiding framework in this chapter.

★ Carron, A.V., Hausenblas, H.A., & Mack, D. (1996). Social influence: A meta-analysis. *Journal of Sport & Exercise Psychology, 18,* 1-16.

> This article presents a meta-analysis of the social influence literature. The article summarizes a long-time research topic and provides interpretations that may help take research in more productive directions.

★ Rosenfeld, L.B. & Richman, J.R. (1997). Developing effective social support: Team building and the social support process. *Journal of Applied Social Psychology, 9,* 133-153.

> Social support has gained popularity in sport and exercise psychology, and appears to have more promise for our research and practice than the limited studies of spectator influence. In this article, two scholars who have done considerable work on social support apply their model and research to sport and the team-building process.

# Group Processes and Performance

## CHAPTER OBJECTIVES

After studying this chapter, you should be able to

- explain group dynamics models as they relate to sport and exercise settings and
- understand the relationship between motivation and group performance.

Most sport and exercise activities, including so-called individual sports, involve groups or teams. We learn motor skills in physical education classes, play volleyball with friends, join racquetball clubs, and participate in exercise groups. But group dynamics research is noticeably rare in sport and exercise psychology.

The reluctance of sport and exercise psychologists to take on group-research topics may be attributed, in part, to the complexity of group dynamics. On sport teams, as with other groups, several individuals with varying relationships to each other interact through various processes over time and in changing environmental conditions. Groups by definition involve interaction; and the dynamic nature of group processes makes it difficult to identify researchable questions, let alone reach conclusions and draw implications for practice. Even if we limit attention to team performance, one of the more identifiable and easily measured group constructs, we must consider many factors and relationships.

## GROUP DYNAMICS MODELS

First, we should define *group*. Certainly a professional basketball team, a youth soccer team, and the noon exercise club at a local business are groups. But what about several people jogging on the same route, or the crowd at a football game? Most who have written about groups (e.g., McGrath, 1984; Shaw, 1976) agree that a collection of individuals does not make a group. *Interaction* is the defining feature. Group members must be aware of each other, relate to each other in some way, and be able to interact with each other through group processes.

"Groups are those social aggregates that involve mutual awareness and potential interaction" (McGrath, 1984, p. 7). When I jog I meet walkers, in-line skaters, and other joggers. We may exchange greetings, but we do not relate to each other, do not interact, and are not a group. McGrath also excludes crowds and organizations that are too large for mutual awareness and interaction. Groups must be small enough to allow interdependence and continuity over time. McGrath acknowledges that the dividing line between groups and nongroups is vague, and defines groups as "fuzzy sets."

Carron and Dennis (1998), referring to sport groups, also focus on dynamic mutual interdependence, listing the following defining features of a group:

- A collective identity
- A sense of shared purpose
- Structured patterns of interaction
- Structured methods of communication
- Personal and task interdependence
- Interpersonal attraction
- A shared common fate
- A perception of the unit as a group

For our purposes, most sport teams, exercise groups, and physical skill classes meet these criteria, and application of a group dynamics framework may help us understand sport and exercise groups.

## McGrath's Conceptual Framework for Groups

McGrath's (1984) conceptual framework for the group dynamics process (figure 20.1) is not a theory, but a model that might encompass several theories. The model may serve as a guide for investigating and understanding the interactive relationships and processes within group dynamics. With a complex problem such as group dynamics, you cannot study everything at once; the model helps you find a manageable chunk and see how that chunk fits into the overall problem.

Group interaction, the defining characteristic of a group, is the model's central element. The rest of the model specifies factors and relationships that both influence and are influenced by the interactive processes. Individual characteristics influence group structures and patterns; environmental properties affect the group task and situation; and those factors collectively influence the behavioral setting under which group interaction takes place. Group interaction is influenced by all those components, as well as by forces within the interaction process itself. Furthermore, the interaction process may in turn lead to changes in the group's members, the environment, and the relationships in the group.

### Key Point

According to McGrath's conceptual framework for groups, individual characteristics influence group structures and patterns; environmental properties affect the group task and situation; and those factors collectively influence the behavioral setting under which group interaction takes place. Group interaction is influenced by all those components, as well as by forces within the interaction process itself.

To help make the model more meaningful, let's consider a soccer team. Individual players have varying individual characteristics including physical characteristics, specific soccer skills, and psychological and social characteristics (e.g., goals and motivational orientation, cognitive skills, competitive experience). Those individual characteristics affect group structures and patterns, such as starting positions, leadership roles, and offensive and defensive plays. Environmental properties also influence the task and situation. For example, the opponent, field conditions, or weather might influence positioning and strategies. The ongoing interaction and game progress influence the environment, individuals, and relationships. These may lead to modification of strategies, and the player who is having a great day may get the ball more often and play with enhanced confidence.

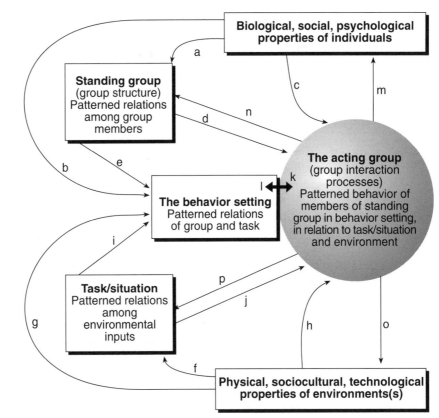

**Figure 20.1**
McGrath's framework for the study of groups.

From *Groups: Interaction and Performance*, by McGrath, © 1991. Reprinted by permission of Prentice-Hall, Inc., Upper Saddle River, NJ.

| Arrow in the model | Relations implied |
| --- | --- |
| a | Member composition of focal group. |
| b and c | Extramember effects of individuals on behavior setting and on group interaction process. |
| d and e | Effects of standing group (group structure) on behavior setting and on group interaction process. |
| f | Environmental factors as they structure the task/situation. |
| g and h | Extratask effects of environment on behavior setting and on group interaction process. |
| i and j | Effects of task/situation on behavior setting and on group interaction process. |
| k and l | The dynamic relation between the behavior setting and group interaction process. |
| m and n | Effects of group interaction process on members and on the standing group. |
| o and p | Effects of group interaction process on task/situation and on the environment. |

## Sport and Exercise Group Dynamics Models

From the McGrath model we can move to simpler models in the sport and exercise psychology literature. Widmeyer, Brawley, and Carron (1992), who have done much of the group dynamics research in sport and exercise psychology, offer as a framework a linear model (figure 20.2) that includes components and relationships similar to those in McGrath's model. Like McGrath, Widmeyer et al. include individual attributes and the environment as starting input components. These influence group structure, which influences group cohesion, which then influences group processes. Finally, group processes influence group and individual outputs. Group cohesion stands out in this framework, reflecting the prominence of group cohesion in the sport and exercise psychology literature. Cohesion, as we will discuss in more detail in the

**Figure 20.2**
A conceptual
framework for
examining the sport
team as a group.

Adapted, by permission,
from A.V. Carron and
H.A. Hausenblas, 1998,
*Group dynamics in
sport*, 2nd ed.
(Morgantown, WV:
Fitness Information
Technology, Inc.), 20.

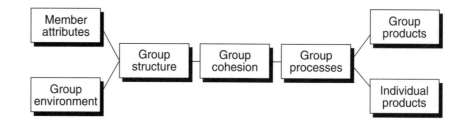

next chapter, involves dynamic interrelationships among group members, and might better fit within the central interaction processes of the McGrath model than as a step in Widmeyer et al.'s linear model.

In current work on team building, Carron and colleagues (Carron & Spink, 1993; Carron, Spink, & Prapavessis, 1997) have moved cohesion to the output side of the model. Sport and exercise psychologists have begun to adapt team-building approaches developed largely in industrial and organizational psychology. Team building is becoming prominent in psychological skills training and applied programs with sport teams—and may well be the impetus that revitalizes group dynamics research in sport and exercise psychology. We may find new ways to incorporate and modify earlier group dynamics research, and McGrath's framework may help researchers and practitioners put it all together.

The framework for team building involves an inputs-to-throughputs-to-outputs model. Reviewing the literature for their introduction to a special issue of *Journal of Applied Sport Psychology* on team building, Hardy and Crace (1997) noted that most models (e.g., that of Tannenbaum, Beard, & Salas [1992]) focus on enhancing team effectiveness by improving team processes. Teams are groups, teams have shared objectives, and members have specific roles. In team-building models, inputs include individual and team characteristics, task characteristics, and work structure. Throughputs are processes, and outputs are changes in individuals and teams as well as team performance.

Team performance is the output we typically focus on, but in Carron and Spink's (1993) team-building framework (figure 20.3), cohesion is the target output. Here, inputs include group environment (distinctiveness) and group structure (i.e., group norms and positions). Throughput is the group process—interaction, communication, and sacrifices in the study. Cohesion, the output component, is typically measured as the four dimensions of the Group Environment Questionnaire.

**Figure 20.3**
Conceptual frame-
work used as a basis
for the implementa-
tion of a team-
building program in
fitness classes.

From Carron, A.V., &
Spink, K.S. (1993). Team
building in an exercise
setting. *The Sport
Psychologist, 7*, 8-18.

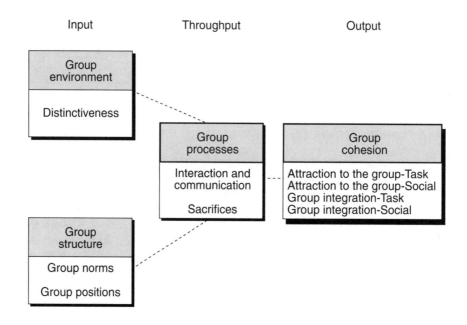

Although the three-stage team-building model is simpler than McGrath's (1984) model, all the components are part of McGrath's framework. Moreover, McGrath's model with its dynamic interrelationships more accurately reflects the complexities of real-world group dynamics. Processes at one time may change individuals, the group, or the environment so that inputs are different the next time.

Given the complexities of the model, it is not surprising that researchers have not delineated the factors and processes that affect sport and exercise groups. This text will not unravel all the mysteries, but we will examine the existing literature for insights into group performance, a primary concern for sport and exercise groups. In the next chapter we will turn to cohesion. There we will also return to the team-building models and the overall group dynamics framework to look at the big picture of sport and exercise group dynamics.

# GROUP PERFORMANCE IN SPORT AND EXERCISE

Group performance is a pressing practical issue in sport and exercise psychology. Those who work with sport teams devote prodigious effort to maximizing group performance. Perhaps the maxim most accepted by researchers and practitioners is that the best individuals make the best team. In general, this rule undoubtedly holds; five intercollegiate basketball players will defeat five intramural players consistently. But the relationship between individual abilities and group performance is far from perfect. You probably can recall instances when teams with all the talent to win the championship did not, or times when teams without individual stars performed exceptionally well as teams. Simply summing the abilities of individual group members does not accurately describe group performance; we must also consider the group process—interaction.

## Steiner's Model of Individual-Group Performance

Steiner (1972) proposed a theoretical model that helps clarify the individual-group performance relationship. The essence of Steiner's model is expressed in the equation:

Actual productivity = Potential productivity – Losses due to faulty process

*Potential productivity* is the group's best possible performance given its resources and task demands. The group's *resources* comprise all the relevant knowledge and skills of individual members, including the overall level and distribution of talents.

Individual ability, demonstrated by individual performance, is the most important resource of most sport groups. According to Steiner's model, greater resources increase potential productivity, and, as in the maxim, the best individuals make the best team. But Steiner's model goes beyond the maxim.

To contribute to potential performance, resources must be relevant to the task. Height is a relevant resource for volleyball, but not for track. *Task demands*—the rules and requirements the task imposes—determine which resources are relevant to performance. When a group effectively uses its available resources to meet task demands, its actual productivity or performance approaches its potential.

In Steiner's model, a group's actual performance falls short of its potential (we're never perfect) because of faulty process. *Process* includes all individual and interactive actions by which a group transforms its resources into a collective product or performance—"putting it all together." Process losses comprise two general categories. *Coordination losses* occur when poor timing or ineffective strategies detract from the group's potential, such as when a basketball team fails to get the ball to the top scorer; *motivational losses* occur when group members slack off or give less than their best effort.

These process losses are critical considerations in work with sport and exercise groups. Coaches have some influence on group resources when they recruit individual talent or provide instruction to improve individual skills, but resources and task demands are relatively stable. The main task of a coach or instructor working with a team is to reduce process losses by (a) developing organizational strategies that reduce coordination losses and (b) maintaining optimal motivation levels.

Process losses and the strategies for reducing them vary with the task. Activities requiring considerable interaction or cooperation, such as basketball, are more susceptible to coordination losses than are activities demanding less interaction, such as softball or swimming. Consequently, the basketball coach emphasizes developing strategies and drills to achieve precise timing and team movement patterns. The softball coach spends some time working on interactive skills, such as double plays, but emphasizes developing individual batting and fielding skills. The swimming coach may try to develop efficient transitions among relay members, but spends little time on interactive skills.

## Research on Individual-Group Motor Performance

Comrey (1953), using a pegboard task, and Wiest, Porter, and Ghiselli (1961), using puzzles, had subjects perform a series of individual trials followed by a series of group trials. In all cases the individual scores of both partners were positively related to group performance, and combining the two individual scores in a multiple correlation yielded a moderate positive relationship with group performance.

In a study with sport teams, Jones (1974) compared team performance (rankings or final win/loss records) to individual statistics (i.e., singles rankings in tennis; points for and against in football; runs batted in and earned run averages in baseball; and points, assists, and rebounds in basketball) for professional teams. Group effectiveness was positively related to individual effectiveness in all cases. The relationship was weakest for basketball, the sport with the greatest interaction, suggesting that interaction requirements may reduce the individual-group performance relationship.

These studies indicate a positive individual-group performance relationship, but do not suggest that we can predict team performance from individual performance. In a more controlled experiment, I (Gill, 1979) formed two-person teams matched on individual performance on a motor maze task. The teams, representing a range of average ability levels and discrepancies between partners, then performed the group task in a separate session. Multiple regression analyses revealed a moderate positive correlation between group performance and the combination of average ability and ability discrepancy in both experiments. Average ability was the primary predictor, but ability discrepancy (a large difference between partners) negatively affected cooperative performance.

### Key Point

Jones's (1974) studies indicate a positive individual-group performance relationship, but do not suggest that we can predict team performance from individual performance.

In the second experiment, designed to check the reliability of individual performance, a control group of individuals performed by themselves in both sessions. Individual performance was not very reliable from session to session and almost totally unreliable from trial to trial. Sport performance, which is subject to numerous influences that were controlled in the lab, likely is even less reliable. For example, a baseball batter often goes 3-for-4 in one game and 1-for-4 in the next. Individual abilities relate to group performance, but in light of the variability of both individual and group performance, more than a moderate prediction of team performance is unrealistic.

# GROUP PROCESSES AND GROUP PERFORMANCE

Most research on sport groups has not considered group process. An exception is a line of research addressing individual performance in relation to group size—and eventually zeroing in on motivation.

## The Ringelmann Effect

Research on group process in sport originates in an obscure, unpublished study of individual and group performance on a rope-pulling task. Over 100 years ago, a French agricultural engineer named Ringelmann observed individuals and groups of various sizes pulling on a rope (cited in Ingham, Levinger, Graves, & Peckham, 1974; Kravitz & Martin, 1986). Groups pulled with more force than individuals, but not with as much force as would be predicted by adding individual scores. Eight-person groups pulled only four times as hard as individuals. The average individual force exerted by members of two-person groups was 93% of the average individual force in solo performance, that for three-person groups was 85%, and that for eight-person groups was 49%. This phenomenon—of average individual performance decreasing with increases in group size—is known as the *Ringelmann effect.*

No one actually demonstrated the Ringelmann effect until Ingham et al. (1974) resurrected the original Ringelmann paradigm with updated controls. Ingham et al. first replicated Ringelmann's work using individuals and groups of two, three, four, five, and six persons. Experiment 1 partially replicated the Ringelmann effect; the average performance of individuals in two-person groups was 91% of the average solo performance, and that for three-person groups was 83%. Groups of four, five, and six did not exhibit further decreases but leveled off, with the average performance in six-person groups at 78% of the average solo performance. (See figure 20.4 for a comparison of the Ingham et al. and Ringelmann findings.)

By eliminating the coordination requirements of the group task, Ingham et al. extended their investigation to see whether the Ringelmann effect was attributable to coordination losses or motivation losses. In Experiment 2, only one subject actually pulled on the rope, but through use of blindfolds and trained confederates who pretended to pull, subjects were led to believe they were performing in groups of one to six members. The results were virtually identical to those of Experiment 1. Average performance dropped to 85% in three-person groups, and there were no further drops. Ingham et al. concluded that the decreases in average performance were due to motivational losses within groups, which led to further research on motivation in this context.

## Social Loafing in Groups

In the 1970s Latane and colleagues undertook a systematic investigation of group performance, and in light of the Ingham et al. findings dubbed the motivational losses in groups "social loafing." A first study (Latane, Williams, & Harkins, 1979) included two experiments using clapping and shouting as group tasks. Experiment 1 confirmed the Ringelmann effect as the average sound produced per person decreased from the solo performance to 71% in two-person groups, 51% in four-person groups, and 40% in six-person groups.

> **Key Point**
>
> The phenomenon of average individual performance decreasing with increases in group size is known as the *Ringelmann effect.* Latane and colleagues dubbed such motivational losses in groups *social loafing.*

Experiment 2 included pseudogroups as well as actual groups. In the pseudogroups, instructions and background noise played through earphones led

**Figure 20.4**
Individual rope-pulling scores as a function of group size.

"The Ringelmann Effect: Studies of Group Size and Group performance" by A. Ingham, G. Levinger, J. Graves, and V. Peckham, 1974, *Journal of Experimental Social Psychology*, 10, p. 377, copyright © 1974 by Academic Press, reprinted by permission.

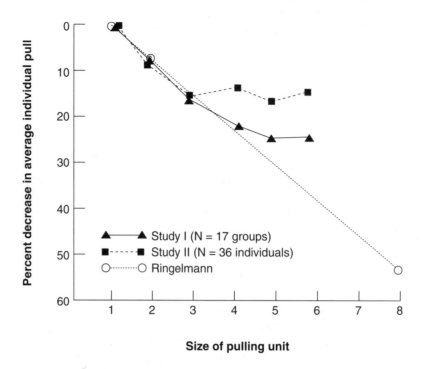

subjects to believe they were clapping or shouting in groups when in fact they were performing alone. Actual groups in Experiment 2 replicated Experiment 1 results, with the average sound produced in two- and six-person groups at 66% and 36% of the average solo performance. Pseudogroups also exhibited social loafing, with the average sound dropping to 82% in two-person groups and 74% in six-person groups. Because coordination losses (e.g., interfering sound waves) were eliminated in the pseudogroups, Latane et al. concluded that the performance drop was due to motivation losses or social loafing. The greater performance drop for actual groups represented a combination of coordination losses and motivation losses.

After confirming the motivation losses, Latane and colleagues pursued explanations of social loafing. They proposed that *identifiability* of individual performance is critical (Williams, Harkins, & Latane, 1981). When individual efforts are "lost in the crowd," performance decreases. In two experiments, Williams et al. demonstrated that when group members believed their individual outputs were identifiable (i.e., known to others), social loafing was eliminated.

Introducing identifiability reconciles the apparently conflicting coaction effects in the social facilitation literature (discussed in the previous chapter) and the social loafing phenomenon in the group dynamics literature. In typical coaction situations, evaluation potential increases with more coactors. In typical social loafing situations, evaluation potential decreases as group size increases. When identifiability remains high in group performance situations, evaluation potential does not decrease, and the Williams et al. findings indicate that performance does not decrease. In "Social Loafing and Social Facilitation: New Wine in Old Bottles," Harkins and Szymanski (1987) suggest that social loafing and social facilitation are complementary phenomena.

## Social Incentives in Sport Groups

If monitoring individual performance can eliminate social loafing, perhaps other tactics can provide social incentives to increase individual efforts in groups. Sport teams seem to provide social incentives in the form of social support and peer pressure. Latane, Harkins, and Williams (1980), noting the common belief that athletes perform better when in a relay or group than when alone, examined social loafing and identifiability in a sport setting.

Latane and colleagues first checked individual and relay times at the 1977 Big Ten intercollegiate swim meet. A comparison of swimmers who swam both individual and relay events with the same stroke revealed no social loafing. Instead, relay times were faster than individual times. Faster starts in relays could account for the difference, and Latane et al. designed an experiment to test their observations (Williams, Nida, Baca, & Latane, 1989).

In an experimental competition, 16 members of an intercollegiate team swam their stroke both as individuals and as one member of a relay team. The starts were standardized by having all swimmers use the faster relay starts, and identifiability was manipulated by announcing or not announcing individuals' lap times. An interaction between identifiability and individual relay was found for performance times. Under low identifiability, individual times (61.34 sec) were faster than relay times (61.66), implying social loafing. Under high identifiability, individual times (60.95) were slower than relay times (60.18). Not only was social loafing eliminated, but the group seemed to provide a social incentive. Time differences were small, but such small differences often determine places in competitive events.

Everett, Smith, and Williams (1992) tried to replicate the identifiability effect in a similar study with both men's and women's swim teams. Everett et al. also added cohesion to their design to see whether cohesion would moderate social loafing. They failed to replicate the identifiability effects found by Latane et al., perhaps due to a small sample and limitations of the study. However, they did find a negative relationship between cohesion and loafing for the women, suggesting that cohesion may provide a social incentive.

---

Social loafing is one of few group dynamics research lines that have continued into the 1990s. Karau and Williams (1993, 1995), who have conducted much of that research, reviewed over 80 studies on social loafing, formally defined as "a reduction in motivation and effort when individuals work collectively compared to when they work individually or coactively." Their meta-analysis yielded a moderate effect size of 0.44, indicating that individuals "loaf" when working collectively. Moreover, they found social loafing consistently across a wide variety of tasks (e.g., physical, cognitive, creative tasks) and across most subject populations.

Karau and Williams also reviewed the major theories of social loafing and proposed an integrated model as a conceptual framework for continuing work. Four theories have guided most social loafing research:

• **Social impact theory.** Social impact theory (Latane, 1981) focuses on social influence and suggests that when individuals work collectively, social influence is diffused across group members. Social influence is a function of the strength, immediacy, and number of sources of influence and targets (recipients of influence) present; and each additional group member has less influence as group size increases.

• **Arousal reduction.** Arousal reduction (Jackson & Williams, 1985) follows a drive model, as discussed in relation to social facilitation (chapter 19). Arousal enhances drive and facilitates the dominant response. Working collectively reduces arousal, thereby reducing performance on simple tasks but enhancing performance on complex tasks.

• **Evaluation approaches.** Evaluation interpretations (e.g., Harkins, 1987) suggest that working collectively makes individual group members' inputs difficult to identify and evaluate. Evaluation may eliminate social loafing if (a) the participants' inputs are identifiable and (b) there is a standard with which these inputs can be compared.

• **Dispensability of effort.** Dispensability views (Kerr, 1983) suggest that working collectively reduces effort because people feel their inputs are not essential to a high-quality group product.

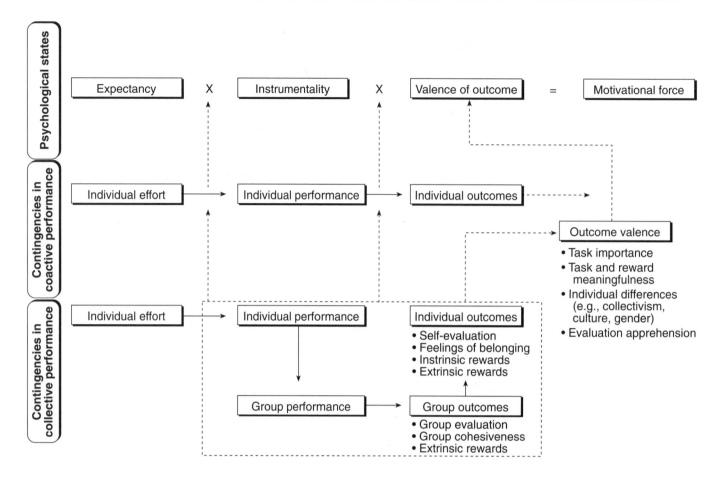

**Figure 20.5**
The collective effort model. The top two rows depict the psychological states and
performance contingencies, relevant to coactive tasks, that are specified by
traditional expectancy-value models. The bottom row depicts additional performance contingencies relevant to collective tasks. The bulleted items in the bottom
row highlight factors relevant to self-evaluation processes in group settings.
Vertical arrows highlight common contingencies between coactive and collective
performance and indicate how those contingencies map onto psychological
states.

Reprinted, by permission, from S.J. Karau and K.D. Williams, 1993, "Social loafing:
Research findings, implications, and future directions, *Psychological Science* 4(5): 134–139.

All four views have limitations (Karau & Williams, 1995). All apply only within
restricted domains, and none specify underlying psychological processes. As an
integrative framework, Karau and Williams (1993) offer the Collective Effort Model
(CEM), which combines traditional expectancy-value models of effort with self-
evaluation processes in groups. The CEM (figure 20.5) proposes that individuals will
exert effort on a collective task only to the degree that they expect their efforts to help
them obtain personally valued outcomes—that is, outcomes that are important,
meaningful, or intrinsically satisfying. For individuals to work hard on a collective
task, several factors must be present: (1) individual effort must relate to individual
performance (link 1 in figure 20.5); (2) individual performance in turn must be related
to group performance (link 2); (3) group performance must lead to a favorable group
outcome (link 3), which is related to a favorable individual outcome (link 4); and (4)
the individual must attach personal value to this outcome (link 5).

Karau and Williams (1995) point to implications of the CEM that we can apply to
sport and exercise settings. First, collective work settings are quite susceptible to
social loafing, and many sport and exercise activities are collective, with little direct

## Key Point

Karau and Williams's (1993) Collective Effort Model (CEM) combines traditional expectancy-value models of effort with self-evaluation processes in groups. The CEM proposes that individuals will exert effort on a collective task only to the degree that they expect their efforts to help them obtain personally valued outcomes—that is, outcomes that are important, meaningful, or intrinsically satisfying.

connection between individual effort and outcomes. Karau and Williams suggest that social loafing is reduced in the following situations:

1. **When individuals believe that others can evaluate their collective performance.** Sport teams' collective performances are evaluated in competition. In noncompetitive activities in which group outcomes are valued, coaches, instructors, and leaders might make special effort to evaluate group outcomes.

2. **When people work in smaller groups.** This suggests the usefulness of small-group activities (or partners), rather than one large group, in practice and instruction or recreational settings.

3. **When people perceive their contributions to the collective product as unique.** Everyone has his or her own role or position, and each contributes uniquely. Coaches and instructors can use varied tactics to recognize individual contributions. Such recognition is especially important with team sports or group activities that obscure individuals. For example, Latane et al. (1980) noted that effective football coaches used several techniques to increase the identifiability and recognition of individual linemen. When basketball coach Lute Olson was at Iowa, he developed and publicized a "total performance chart" to rate each player's performance in each game.

4. **When people have a standard with which to compare their group's performance.** Standards typically are clear with team sports, but clarifying group standards for an elementary activity class or exercise group could be a greater challenge. Still, if group outcomes (performance or nonperformance) are valued, standards are important.

5. **When people work on tasks that are intrinsically interesting, meaningful, important to others, or high in personal involvement.** Although physical activities usually are intrinsically interesting to participants, this may not hold for all sport and exercise settings. Even highly competitive athletes who thrive on their sport may find practice or training activities less than thrilling and "loaf."

6. **When individuals work with people they respect or in a situation that activates a salient group identity.** Sport teams at all levels typically have a salient identity, but the particular mix of people is constantly changing, posing challenges. Group identity is unlikely to be present in most exercise settings without special effort, but the effort is worthwhile if it's important for the group to work together.

7. **When individuals expect their coworkers to perform poorly.** If group members want to do well and believe others will have difficulty, they may put in extra effort to compensate.

8. **When people have a dispositional tendency to view favorable collective outcomes as valuable and important.** Some athletes and group members are more "team players" than others.

Interestingly, Karau and Williams (1993, 1995) found gender and culture also moderated social loafing effects: the effects were smaller for women than for men, and for individuals from Eastern cultures than for those from Western cultures.

We have far to go to fully understand social loafing and collective efforts (Karau & Williams, 1995). Most studies have been lab experiments that do not reflect groups in the real world. Moreover, in focusing on social loafing, the research is one-sided;

we might also devote attention to social incentives with collective groups. Recent initiatives related to team building (discussed in the following chapter) may help us move in that direction.

## Summary

Group dynamics is complex; we cannot understand everything about sport and exercise groups, or even the performance of one team. McGrath's framework and the team-building approaches help us focus on relevant relationships, and research following these approaches provides some guidelines for working with sport and exercise groups—as well as more questions. First, the group dynamics literature confirms our common belief that the best individuals make the best team. Selecting the best individuals is not easy; group performance may require skills not evident in individual performances. For example, a track relay involves skills of passing the baton as well as individual speed. Sports requiring greater interaction impose many skill requirements such as timing passes, coordinating double plays, and playing zone defenses. Identifying persons with interactive as well as performance skills could reduce coordination losses and enhance group performance. Also, coaches, instructors, and leaders might direct efforts toward developing team members' interactive skills to reduce coordination losses.

Even with minimized coordination losses, motivation losses or "social loafing" may affect group performance. The social loafing research suggests many strategies to reduce loafing, and the most promising work suggests that social incentives may actually enhance individual efforts in groups. Research on incentive properties of groups offers more questions than answers, and the complexities of group process make simple answers unlikely. Still, the existing research is promising and offers guidelines. Specifically, most work suggests that social loafing is reduced and individual effort enhanced when individual contributions to the group are clearly identified and recognized. Team coaches and group leaders need to (a) identify individual behaviors that contribute to desired group performance and nonperformance outcomes, especially easily overlooked interactive behaviors; and (b) make sure those individual behaviors are recognized and encouraged.

## Review Questions

1. Define "group" as the term is used in sport and exercise research.
2. Explain McGrath's conceptual framework for groups, and compare it to Widmeyer et al.'s (1992) linear model.
3. Describe Carron and Spink's (1993) team-building framework.
4. Discuss Steiner's model of individual-group performance.
5. Describe the results of research comparing team performance to individual performance.
6. Define the Ringelmann effect, and its related term, "social loafing."
7. Describe the four theories guiding most social loafing research.
8. Explain Karau and Williams (1993) Collective Effort Model.
9. Identify situations in which social loafing is reduced.

# *Recommended Reading*

★ Carron, A.V., & Dennis, P.W. (1998). The sport team as an effective group. In J.M. Williams, *Applied sport psychology: Personal growth to peak performance* (3rd ed.). Mountain View, CA: Mayfield.

> This chapter provides an overview of the sport team as an effective group, including definitions and models of group processes, the role of cohesion, leadership, and team building in effective groups.

★ Karau, S.J. & Williams, K.D. (1993). Social loafing: A meta-analytic review and theoretical integration. *Journal of Personality and Social Psychology, 65,* 681-706.

★ Karau, S.J., & Williams, K.D. (1995). Social loafing: Research findings, implications, and future directions. *Psychological Science, 4* (5), 134-139.

> "Social loafing," which refers to individuals giving less effort in groups, is a popular topic in group dynamics that has relevance to sport teams. In the 1995 article, Karau and Williams provide an excellent overview of that research with implications and future directions. For more details, go to the 1993 article, which presents the results of a meta-analysis and a more complete discussion of their theoretical integration.

# Interpersonal Relationships and Cohesion

## CHAPTER OBJECTIVES

After studying this chapter, you should be able to

- explain several leadership models in sport and exercise psychology,
- understand the relationship between group cohesiveness and group performance, and
- explain team-building models and research related to sport and exercise settings.

As the previous chapter illustrates, understanding the dynamics of sport and exercise groups is no simple task. Even if we focus on the apparently straightforward relationship of individual abilities to group performance, we quickly find that we must consider the social context and interpersonal relationships within group interaction processes. Recent team-building research indicates that even those who work with highly competitive, task-oriented teams often seek to improve group communication or cohesion. In recreational sport activities and exercise programs we may even be more concerned with interpersonal relationships than with performance outcomes.

Sport and exercise psychologists might pose many questions about interpersonal relationships and processes. For instance, why do certain group members have more influence than others? How does turnover of team members affect team goals, relationships, and performance? How do communication patterns develop in recreational groups? Does group culture affect adherence to exercise programs? Answers are few; sport and exercise psychologists have given interpersonal relationships scant attention. The traditional social psychology literature on groups typically involves decision making and problem solving rather than physical activity, and the formal organizational models are far removed from the unique relationships of sport teams. Most research within sport and exercise psychology focuses on cohesion, and to a lesser extent, leadership. But even that work is limited: the leadership research stresses the coach, and the cohesion literature stresses the relationship between cohesion and team performance. In this chapter, we will review the literature on leadership and the larger literature on cohesion. Then we'll return to the "big picture" and consider the overall group dynamics model as we look at the emerging work on team building.

# LEADERSHIP MODELS IN SPORT AND EXERCISE GROUPS

Leadership is a traditional group dynamics topic, and sport and exercise psychology has adapted some of that work. Although we often think of the team coach, class instructor, or exercise director as the leader, leadership is not simply a characteristic of a single person. Instead, leadership is a complex social relationship, defined by Barrow (1977) as "the behavioral process of influencing individuals and groups toward set goals" (p. 232). Thus defined, leadership involves the situation and all group members as well as an identified "leader."

Early research on leadership followed a trait approach. Often the aim was to identify common characteristics of great leaders—to examine what is often called the "great man theory of leadership" (indeed it was a theory of great men—no women were included). Like the early trait personality research, the leadership trait work yielded few conclusive findings. Gradually leadership research shifted to an interactive model considering leadership styles and behaviors in varying group situations.

## Fiedler's Contingency Model

Fiedler's (1967) contingency model of leadership effectiveness, which guided much of the early work, classifies leaders as *task oriented* (primarily focused on performance) or *person oriented* (primarily concerned with interpersonal relationships). Leader effectiveness depends on situation favorableness, which is the product of (1) leader-member relations, (2) task structure, and (3) the leader's position power or authority. The situation is most favorable with warm, positive leader-member relations, a clearly and highly defined task structure, and strong position power (and is least favorable accordingly). Combinations of these elements lead to varying degrees of favorableness. According to Fiedler, task-oriented leaders are more effective in both the most favorable and least favorable situations, whereas person-oriented leaders are more effective in moderately favorable situations.

### Key Point

Leader effectiveness depends on situation favorableness, which is the product of (1) leader-member relations, (2) task structure, and (3) the leader's position power or authority. The situation is most favorable with warm, positive leader-member relations, a clearly and highly defined task structure, and strong position power (and is least favorable accordingly).

Fielder's model was the "leader" in the 1970s. A few sport psychologists used it (e.g., Bird, 1977), but findings were inconclusive. Although the model is appealing, the variables are difficult to assess. The model may not represent all combinations of sport and exercise situations, and its appropriateness for sport and exercise groups is questionable.

## Grusky's Group Structure Model

Another line of research that caught on in the 1970s took a situational approach by examining group structure and leadership. In 1963 Grusky, applying a model of group structure and organizational leadership to professional baseball, proposed that players in more central playing positions perform more dependent, coordinative tasks and interact more with players in other positions. Those high interactors then develop leadership skills and become managers more often than low interactors. As you could guess, the high interactors in baseball are infielders and catchers. Pitchers and outfielders are low interactors. Grusky's examination of baseball records confirmed his theory: catchers and infielders did become managers more often than pitchers and outfielders did.

Subsequent studies supported Grusky's model (for a review see Loy, Curtis, & Sage, 1979). Research with high school baseball teams (Loy & Sage, 1970) and intercollegiate softball teams (Gill & Perry, 1979) confirmed that infielders and catchers were selected as captains or were rated higher on leadership than pitchers and outfielders. Tropp and Landers (1979) observed that goalies were rated high on leadership despite being low interactors in peripheral positions. The authors suggested that performing independent, critical tasks may be more important to leadership than spatial location in a highly dynamic, interactive sport such as field hockey.

Grusky's model and related research did not extend far beyond his original propositions. Approaches that consider both individual characteristics and situational factors offer more promise for understanding leadership in sport and exercise.

## Chelladurai's Multidimensional Model of Leadership

Chelladurai and colleagues conducted one of the few systematic investigations of leadership in sport and exercise. Chelladurai's model (Chelladurai, 1984b; Chelladurai & Carron, 1978), pictured in figure 21.1, considers the influence of situational, leader, and member characteristics on leader behaviors and subsequent influence of leader behaviors on group performance and satisfaction. The major proposition is that the degree of congruence among the three components of leadership behavior is positively related to performance and satisfaction. In other words, the more the leader's actual behaviors match the preferences of group members and situation requirements, the better the group's performance and the greater the group members' satisfaction.

As an initial step in their leadership research, Chelladurai and Saleh (1980) developed the Leadership Scale for Sports (LSS). Psychometric testing revealed good internal consistency and test-retest reliability, and factor analysis yielded five dimensions of leader behaviors in sport: training/instruction, democratic, autocratic, social support, and positive feedback behaviors (see table 21.1).

Using the multidimensional model, Chelladurai and Saleh (1978) examined gender differences in preferred leader behaviors, and observed that males preferred more autocratic and social support behaviors than did females. Other studies of gender and personality differences have yielded inconsistent findings, and Chelladurai and Carron (1983) failed to find the expected relationships between athletic experience and preferred leader behaviors.

In a test of the congruence prediction, Chelladurai (1984a) reported that the discrepancy between preferred and actual leader behavior was related to satisfac-

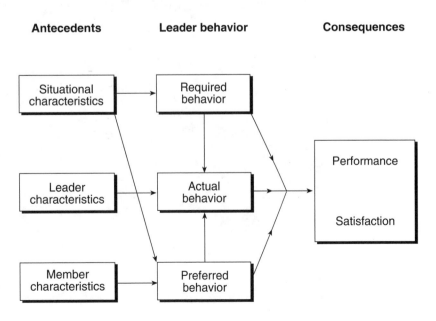

**Figure 21.1**
Chelladurai's multidimensional model of leadership.

Reprinted, by permission, from P. Chelladurai, 1984, Leadership in sports. In *Psychological foundations of sport*, edited by J.M. Silva and R.S. Weinberg (Champaign, IL: Human Kinetics), 338.

**Table 21.1    Dimensions of the LSS**

| Dimension | Description |
| --- | --- |
| *Training and instruction behavior* | Behavior aimed at improving athletes' performance by emphasizing and facilitating hard and strenuous training; instructing them in the skills, techniques, and tactics of the sport; clarifying the relationship among the members; and structuring and coordinating the members' activities. |
| *Democratic behavior* | Behavior that allows greater participation by the athletes in decisions pertaining to group goals, practice methods, and game tactics and strategies. |
| *Autocratic behavior* | Behavior that involves independent decision making and stresses personal authority. |
| *Social support behavior* | Behavior characterized by a concern for the welfare of individual athletes, positive group atmosphere, and warm interpersonal relations with members. |
| *Positive feedback* | Behavior that reinforces an athlete by recognizing and rewarding good performance. |

Reprinted, by permission, from P. Chelladurai, 1984, Leadership in sports. In *Psychological foundations of sport,* edited by J.M. Silva and R.S. Weinberg (Champaign, IL: Human Kinetics), 332.

tion. Athletes in wrestling, basketball, and track and field preferred an emphasis on training and instruction, and the more the coach matched those preferences, the greater the athletes' satisfaction. Basketball players were more satisfied when positive feedback met or exceeded their preferences, but athletes in wrestling and track were not. These findings may reflect Smoll and Smith's (1984) observation (discussed in chapter 15) that youth sport coaches who provided more instruction and encouragement were better liked and had players who were more satisfied with the sport experience.

## Chelladurai's Research on Coaches' Decision-Making Styles

More recently Chelladurai (e.g., Chelladurai & Doherty, 1998) has adapted the leader behavior dimensions of the LSS to investigate decision-making styles of coaches. With the LSS dimensions, training/instruction and positive feedback relate to task

According to Chelladurai (1984a), wrestlers preferred their coaches to emphasize training instruction.

and performance; social support relates to athletes' personal needs; and the remaining two dimensions—autocratic and democratic behavior—refer to decision making. Earlier leadership research suggested that an autocratic style was incompatible with social support, but Chelladurai and Doherty (1998) note that athletes' preferences for autocratic styles do not negate their desire for social support.

Democratic styles, which many advocate, imply participative decision making. As Chelladurai and Doherty (1998) point out, participatory decision making has advantages: more information is available; members feel decisions are their own, increasing acceptance; and participation contributes to personal growth. On the other hand, participative decision making is time consuming, less effective for complex problems, and heavily dependent on the degree of group integration. Moreover, the situation may constrain participation.

Chelladurai and Haggerty (1978) proposed a normative model of decision-making style in coaching that involves seven problem attributes (situational considerations) along with the decision styles. The problem attributes relevant to the athletic context are (1) time pressure; (2) decision quality required (e.g., one optimal decision or several acceptable alternatives); (3) information location (do athletes have the relevant information?); (4) problem complexity; (5) group acceptance; (6) coaches' power; and (7) group integration.

The normative model specified three decision styles:

1. **Autocratic style.** The coach makes the decision. In later research this style was divided into an autocratic style in which the coach simply makes the decision with available information, and a second autocratic style in which the coach makes the decision, but has obtained information from players.

2. **Participative style.** The coach is a member of the group, and the group makes the decision. This has sometimes been labeled a "group" style.

3. **Delegative style.** The coach delegates decision making to one or more team members and does not participate in the decision.

Several studies have used the normative model; most addressed only selected problem attributes or situational factors. Also, the decision-making styles have been modified to represent actual coaching style variations and player preferences. Most notably, a consultative style has been separated out:

• **Consultative style.** The coach consults with players and then makes the decision, which may or may not reflect players' influence. Some studies further divide the consultative style according to whether the coach consults players individually or as a group.

In early studies (Chelladurai & Arnott, 1985), the delegative style was rejected and thus was not included in later research. Two subsequent studies with basketball teams (Chelladurai, Haggerty, & Baxter, 1989; Chelladurai & Quek, 1995) used five decision styles (autocratic I and II, consultative I and II, and group) to examine coaches' styles and athletes' preferences. Although the style choices varied among groups (male and female players, coaches) and across situations, overall preferences were consistent. Autocratic styles were the first choice; and between the two autocratic styles, preference was for the coach making the decision alone. The second choice was the consultative style on a group basis; the participative group style was chosen less than 20% of the time by all groups.

Chelladurai and Doherty (1998) noted that choices varied with the problem situation, suggesting that it would be appropriate to refer to the situation as democratic or autocratic rather than labeling coaches as democratic or autocratic. Notably the autocratic choice was quite acceptable, despite its reputation as a tool of dictators and undesirable elements. The authors stressed that contrasting decision styles do not concern values—that an autocratic style can reflect humanism and concern for team members' welfare. They also suggested that coaches and other leaders need to select a decision style appropriate to the situation rather than assume that participatory decisions are always best.

# COHESIVENESS IN SPORT AND EXERCISE GROUPS

For over 30 years, investigators have examined the relationship between cohesiveness and sport team performance. Unfortunately, the evidence does not consistently support the intuitively appealing assumption that cohesive teams win more games. Some studies have yielded positive relationships, but others have not, and some have even shown a negative relationship. Although we do not have clear answers, we can find some patterns and consistencies. We will next consider the conceptual models, definitions, and measures of cohesiveness and then review research on the cohesiveness-performance relationship in sport teams. Finally, we'll look at a more encompassing group dynamics framework and turn to the team-building work in sport and exercise psychology.

## Definition of Cohesiveness

Before discussing the research, we should clarify terms. First, we will use the terms cohesion and cohesiveness interchangeably, as is the case in the literature. Then, what do we mean by cohesiveness? There are nearly as many definitions as researchers. Concepts of cohesiveness are elusive in general; Mudrack (1989a) noted that cohesiveness is "a construct that does not lend itself readily to precise definition, consistent measurement, or standard experimentation" (p. 38).

To the intuitive mind, defining cohesion may seem a trivial exercise. We all know what cohesiveness is (sticking together, team unity, etc.), and we can all cite examples of cohesive and noncohesive teams. But intuitive definitions are not adequate, and our intuitive definitions often are retrospective: we tend to look at a successful team and say, "That's a cohesive team." Such retrospection yields a vague, loosely applied construct and circular explanations. Instead, we must start with a shared conceptual definition.

The literature gives the impression of a common understanding, as virtually every article cites the classic definition of cohesiveness as "the total field of forces which act on members to remain in a group" (Festinger, Schachter, & Back, 1950, p. 164). Many other definitions are variations of this one, including such phrases as "resultant forces," "fields of forces," "attraction-to-group," or "sense of we-ness." Unfortunately, these characterizations are nearly impossible to operationalize, and they emphasize individuals at the expense of "group" cohesiveness.

Within sport and exercise psychology, the most systematic research has been conducted by the Canadian trio of Bert Carron, Neil Widmeyer, and Larry Brawley. Carron (1982) laid the groundwork by developing a conceptual framework and defining cohesiveness as "a dynamic process which is reflected in the tendency for a group to stick together and remain united in the pursuit of its goals and objectives" (p. 124). Carron's definition provides a starting point and incorporates some features particularly relevant to sport and exercise psychology (Carron & Dennis, 1998).

First, cohesion is *multidimensional,* resulting from many factors that may differ among even apparently similar groups. Second, cohesion is *dynamic:* it can change over time, and its sources and consequences can change through the dynamic group processes. Third, cohesion is *instrumental:* group members cohere for instrumental reasons, whether to be part of a university basketball team or to maintain an exercise program. Fourth, cohesion has an *affective* dimension; even in highly task-oriented groups such as sport teams, social cohesion generally develops as a result of members' instrumental and social interactions and communications. Finally, because the goals of all groups are *complex* and varied, cohesion is perceived differently by different groups and members. Carron and colleagues (e.g., Carron, Widmeyer, & Brawley, 1985) proposed a multidimensional model (discussed in the section on measures) that is the basis for most current sport and exercise psychology work on cohesion.

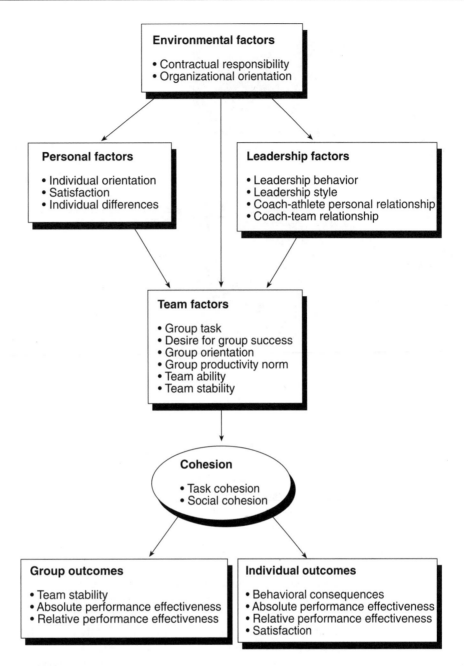

**Figure 21.2**
Carron's conceptual system for cohesiveness in sport teams.

From A.V. Carron, 1982, "Cohesiveness in sport groups: Interpretations and considerations," *Journal of Sport Psychology, 4*, 131. Copyright 1984 by Human Kinetics Publishers, Inc. Reprinted by permission.

## Carron's Conceptual Model of Cohesion

Carron's (1982; see figure 21.2) framework for cohesiveness in sport teams continues to guide the research. The model includes situational, personal, leadership, and team factors that contribute to multidimensional cohesion. These cohesion sources parallel the environmental, individual, and group factors of the group dynamics models presented in the preceding chapter.

*Situational factors* include physical *proximity*, as individuals who are physically closer to each other tend to bond together, as do team members who live near each other or travel together. *Distinctiveness* from other groups also increases feelings of unity, contributing to cohesion. Special privileges, club T-shirts, or group rituals might all enhance distinctiveness. Widmeyer, Brawley, and Carron (1990) suggest an inverted-U relationship between group *size* and social cohesion in intramural basketball, with moderate-sized groups showing greatest cohesiveness. However, Williams and Widmeyer (1991) found no relationship between group size and social cohesion with golf teams, and we cannot draw strong conclusions about size and cohesion.

Some research has shown that performance success increases team cohesion.

*Personal factors* reflect individual abilities, attitudes, and commitment. *Similarity* of personal factors seems related to cohesion, but evidence is sparse. Carron and Dennis (1998) suggest that the most important personal factor is *satisfaction*, also listing *commitment* to the team as a personal source of cohesion.

*Leadership factors* reflect interrelationships with the coach; the research on leadership and decision-making styles is relevant here. Generally, a more democratic *decision style* is better for cohesiveness than an autocratic style, and *compatibility* between coaches and athletes is also related to cohesiveness.

*Team factors* relate to the four elements of group structure: position, status, roles, and norms. Group *positions* refer to consistently occupied space; *roles* are sets of behaviors expected of occupants of specific positions. For example, a coach has a clear position and expectations, such as planning strategies and instructing athletes. Roles may be formal (e.g., team captain, forward) or informal (team enforcer, class clown). Research suggests that when individuals understand their roles (role clarity), accept their roles (role acceptance), and carry out their roles (role performance), groups are more effective, and as Carron and Dennis (1998) note, more cohesive. Group *norms*, which are standards or expectations, are another relevant factor: establishing group goals and rewards influences task cohesiveness, suggesting that coaches should emphasize group goals while downplaying individual rewards (Carron & Dennis, 1998). *Communication* is associated with cohesiveness in a circular way: increased communication on task and social issues increases cohesion, and more cohesive groups have increased communication. Finally, *performance success* increases cohesiveness (Carron & Dennis, 1998); we'll discuss this in more detail when reviewing the research.

## Measures of Cohesiveness

Most definitions and measures of cohesiveness are multidimensional, and usually cohesiveness is divided into interpersonal attraction (assessed in individual terms with friendship choices or other sociometric items) and a more direct attraction-to-group dimension (assessed with group-related items). Most early work used simple measures developed for each study. For example, among 23 studies conducted between 1975 and 1985, no two measured cohesiveness in the same way (Mudrack, 1989b). Initially, attraction-to-group was the most common measure, but the various measures were not consistent, lacked established reliability or validity, and probably did not all tap the same thing.

The first instrument developed to measure cohesiveness in sport was the Sport Cohesiveness Questionnaire (SCQ: Martens, Landers, & Loy, 1972). Items assess attraction among group members, attraction to the whole group, and perception of the entire group. The SCQ was the only sport-specific measure before 1984, but researchers questioned its validity (Widmeyer, Brawley, & Carron, 1993), and it is seldom used today.

Carron's (1982) conceptual model prompted two sport-specific instruments. The Multidimensional Sport Cohesion Instrument (MSCI; Yukelson, Weinberg, & Jackson, 1984) assessed both task and social aspects of group cohesiveness. Initial studies with the MSCI indicated that cohesiveness includes attraction to the group, unity of purpose, quality of teamwork, and valued roles. The MSCI was not developed from a conceptual model, and items were specific to basketball. Reliability and validity were not established, and the MSCI has not been used subsequently.

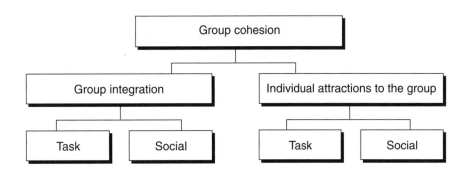

**Figure 21.3**
Conceptual model of group cohesion.

Reprinted, by permission, from A.V. Carron, W.N. Widmeyer, and L.R. Brawley, 1985, "The measurement of cohesion in sport teams," *Journal of Sport Psychology* 3(7): 244-264.

The most important contributions to group cohesiveness in sport have been made by Brawley, Carron, and Widmeyer. Working together (cohesively, no doubt), they developed the most widely accepted instrument for measuring cohesiveness in sport and exercise groups. Using Carron's (1982) definition, they developed a model as well as a measure. The model (figure 21.3; for detailed discussion see Widmeyer, Brawley, & Carron, 1992; Widmeyer et al., 1993) assumes that each group member develops perceptions of group cohesiveness, which can be classified into two general categories: (1) *group integration* (perceptions of the group as a whole) and (2) *individual attractions to the group* (personal attractions to the group). Each of these has task and social aspects, and the resulting model includes four related dimensions of cohesiveness:

Group integration—Task

Group integration—Social

Individual attractions to the group—Task

Individual attractions to the group—Social

These four factors contribute to cohesiveness dynamically and collectively; as the cohesiveness of a team changes over time, so do the members' perceptions of cohesiveness. To measure the four dimensions, the authors developed the Group Environment Questionnaire (GEQ; Brawley, Carron, & Widmeyer, 1987, 1988; Carron et al., 1985, 1988; Widmeyer, Brawley, & Carron, 1985). This 18-item, four-scale measure has good internal consistency and is applicable to a variety of sport and exercise groups.

---

**Key Point**

Researchers have taken four approaches to measuring cohesiveness: (1) attraction-to-group; (2) the Martens, Landers, & Loy Sport Cohesiveness Questionnaire; (3) the Yukelson, Weinberg, & Jackson Multidimensional Sport Cohesion Instrument; and (4) the Widmeyer, Brawley, & Carron Group Environment Questionnaire.

---

## RESEARCH ON THE COHESIVENESS-PERFORMANCE RELATIONSHIP IN SPORT

Martens and Peterson's studies involving over 1200 male intramural basketball players on 144 teams are an early benchmark in sport cohesiveness research, providing some of the strongest support for a positive cohesiveness-performance relationship. The first study (Martens & Peterson, 1971), examining preseason cohesiveness as a determinant of team success, showed that high-cohesive teams won more games than low-cohesive teams. The second study (Peterson & Martens, 1972), investigating the influence of team success on postseason cohesiveness, showed that successful teams were more cohesive than less successful teams.

A number of studies (Arnold & Straub, 1972; Carron & Chelladurai, 1979; Landers, Wilkinson, Hatfield, & Barber, 1982; Klein & Christiansen, 1969; Nixon, 1977; Shangi & Carron, 1987; Vander Velden, 1971; Widmeyer et al., 1990; Widmeyer & Martens, 1978) confirmed the positive relationship between cohesiveness and success with basketball teams. Others compared cohesiveness and team performance (generally the season win/loss ratio) in other activities. There were positive relationships for intercollegiate football (Stogdill, 1963), high school baseball (Landers & Crum, 1971), intercollegiate and high school ice hockey (Ball & Carron, 1976; Carron & Ball, 1977), volleyball (Bird, 1977; Ruder & Gill, 1982), wrestling (Carron & Chelladurai, 1981), field hockey (Williams & Hacker, 1982), and golf (Williams & Widmeyer, 1991).

The number and variety of these studies seem to make a strong case, but some convincing evidence argues otherwise. Melnick and Chemers (1974), for example, used Martens and Peterson's (1971) measure and followed similar procedures, but found no relationship between cohesiveness and success. Additionally, studies have shown negative relationships for high school basketball (Fiedler, 1954; Grace, 1954), intramural bowling (Landers & Lueschen, 1974), rifle teams (McGrath, 1962), and world-class rowing teams (Lenk, 1969, 1977). The case for a positive relationship is further weakened when one notes that many of the reported positive relationships actually represent mixed results, with positive relationships holding only for selected measures or certain times within the overall design.

The lack of consistent support for a positive cohesion-performance relationship does not imply that we should disregard our intuitive notions and observations. We might first try to dismiss the negative findings on methodological grounds. The cohesiveness research includes a number of questionable measures, poor sampling procedures, and inappropriate statistical analyses. Well-designed and well-conducted studies are the exception, especially before the development of the GEQ. However, methodological deficiencies are not confined to studies with negative relationships and do not account for the equivocal findings.

## Causality in the Cohesiveness-Performance Relationship

With updated models and measures, sport and exercise psychologists examined the direction of causality in the cohesiveness-performance relationship. Historically, sport psychologists have been amazingly cavalier in their consideration of causality. Many researchers have not even specified whether cohesiveness measures were taken before, during, or after performance. Others have noted the time sequence but interpreted data as though time made no difference. In fact, time of measurement makes a great deal of difference.

A common way of inferring causality is to examine how preseason cohesiveness relates to subsequent team performance (usually win/loss ratio). Several studies using this approach all showed mixed results (Martens & Peterson, 1971; Arnold & Straub, 1972; Ball & Carron, 1976; Widmeyer & Martens, 1978). Research on the reverse relationship (i.e., how season performance relates to postseason cohesiveness) has yielded stronger and more consistent positive relationships (Arnold & Straub, 1972; Landers & Crum, 1971; Peterson & Martens, 1972; Nixon, 1977).

A more direct test of causality is provided by the cross-lagged panel design first applied to cohesiveness and performance by Bakeman and Helmreich (1975). This study of aquanaut teams assessed both cohesiveness and performance at two separate times. Correlations and partial correlations indicated that first-segment performance was highly related to second-segment cohesiveness, whereas first-segment cohesiveness was not related to second-segment performance. Bakeman and Helmreich concluded that cohesiveness was not an important determinant of performance, but that good performance may well have been a cause of cohesiveness. Carron and Ball (1977) applied the cross-lagged panel design with ice hockey teams. Their results also suggested an effect of performance on cohesiveness—indicated by a positive correlation between midseason performance and postseason cohesiveness—but showed no support for the influence of cohesiveness on later performance success.

Others have likewise reported a stronger influence of performance success on cohesiveness than vice versa. Peterson and Martens's (1972) study of performance success and postseason cohesiveness yielded much stronger relationships than the study (Martens & Peterson, 1971) of preseason cohesiveness and performance success. Myers (1962) and McGrath (1962) used the same sample of Reserve Officers' Training Corps rifle teams. Myers observed that success led to greater esteem for teammates, whereas McGrath reported a negative relationship between positive interpersonal relations and later performance success. Thus, the cohesiveness literature suggests that causality flows from performance success to cohesiveness; evidence in the other direction is weak at best.

These findings may be disconcerting to those who believe cohesiveness determines success. But we cannot conclude that cohesiveness does not influence team performance. If cohesiveness is assessed at preseason, before members have interacted as a group, responses are likely to be rather random and unreliable. Although most teams have a limited history of interaction, it would be surprising if preseason cohesiveness were reliably related to anything. With postseason measures, the team members have had an opportunity to interact and develop some level of cohesiveness, but retrospective postseason measures pose problems also. These may reflect the "glow of success" as team members look back and think, "We won; we must have been cohesive."

More studies taking account of time and causality, using reliable, valid cohesiveness measures, may establish a causal relationship. Most likely, the cohesiveness-performance relationship is more dynamic and complex than our observations and the early research findings suggest.

## Mediators and Moderators of the Cohesiveness-Performance Relationship

Even using common measures and considering causal direction, the literature on the cohesiveness-performance relationship is not consistent. Widmeyer et al. (1993) identified several variables that may have an impact, dividing these into moderating and mediating variables.

Moderator variables affect the conditions under which cohesion and performance are related; among these, *task characteristics* may be the most important for sport. Landers (1974), applying Steiner's (1972) model, noted that positive relationships had generally been reported for divisible tasks (tasks divided into subtasks, such as basketball and football), whereas negative relationships had generally been observed with unitary tasks (tasks that do not involve mutual assistance, such as bowling, rowing, and rifling). A positive cohesiveness-performance relationship, then, seems to hold for activities that require cooperation and interaction. With sports requiring little interaction, cohesiveness is not positively related to team success and may have a negative influence.

Zander (1971) suggested that cohesiveness leads to greater motivation and commitment to team goals—termed "group drive" by Widmeyer et al. (1993). If team performance depends on team goals, cohesiveness should have a positive influence; but if individual performance is the primary concern, commitment to team goals may be irrelevant. In fact, if emphasizing team goals detracts from individual goals, cohesiveness may negatively influence individual performance. In sports in which individual performance is critical and team members do not interact during events (e.g., gymnastics, wrestling, golf, swimming), perhaps individual goals should be emphasized. Support and encouragement from teammates may help, but such support can be directed toward individual performance rather than team victory. If cohesiveness enhances commitment to team goals, and if team goals emphasize important individual contributions, then cohesiveness should enhance performance for noninteractive as well as interactive sports. Indeed, a recent study with golf teams (Williams & Widmeyer, 1991) supports a positive relationship between team task cohesion and performance.

Another moderating variable, *group norms,* received more attention in the early social psychology literature. In a classic lab experiment, Schachter, Ellerton, McBride, and Gregory (1951) observed that members of high-cohesive groups complied with the group norm whether the norm was for greater or lesser productivity. Subsequent studies (Berkowitz, 1954, 1956; Mikalachki, 1969; Seashore, 1954) confirmed that highly cohesive groups outperformed less cohesive groups only if the group norms called for better performance.

Despite the consistent evidence, the moderating role of group norms may not be critical for sport teams. A sport team adhering to a group norm that contradicts performance success is difficult to imagine. Rather than specific performance norms, we might consider the unique norms of sport and exercise groups. Sport teams are highly task-oriented groups, but most studies of cohesiveness involve informal social groups. Anderson (1975) demonstrated that value similarity (typically associated with interpersonal attraction) was associated with cohesiveness in informal social groups, but goal-path clarity (agreement on group task procedures) was more related to cohesiveness in task-oriented groups. With task-oriented sport teams, cohesiveness is more likely related to commitment to team task goals, agreement on task roles and strategies, and other task-related team norms than to interpersonal attraction. As noted earlier, interpersonal attraction is generally not related to team performance. Anderson suggests that there is no reason why it should be, as interpersonal attraction does not represent cohesiveness in a task-oriented group.

To fully understand the cohesiveness-performance relationship in sport, we should also consider mediating variables, that is, how and why cohesiveness influences performance (Widmeyer et al., 1993). Widmeyer et al. propose team stability, role clarity, and role acceptance as likely mediators. Investigators have tended to ignore the transitory nature of many sport and exercise groups, but variations in team stability could profoundly influence the development and maintenance of cohesion, and subsequently the cohesion-performance relationship. As noted earlier, role acceptance, role clarity, communication skills, satisfaction, and goal acceptance are further possible mediators.

Sport and exercise psychologists have spent much time conceptualizing and measuring cohesiveness but have virtually ignored moderating and mediating variables. As defined by Carron (1982), cohesiveness is dynamic; we must move beyond our starting definitions and incorporate moderator and mediator variables in our research in this area.

## Conclusions About the Cohesiveness-Performance Relationship in Sport

Although not totally consistent, the literature indicates that cohesiveness, defined and measured as a direct group component of a multidimensional construct, is positively related to team success for interactive sports. Success is more likely to lead to cohesiveness than vice versa. Task characteristics and group norms are important considerations in the relationship, and other factors might be equally important.

Even if the cohesiveness-performance relationship is weak and limited, the practical value of team cohesiveness is not necessarily so limited. Teamwork is only one potential consequence of cohesiveness, which may affect teams and individuals in ways unrelated to performance. Perhaps sport and exercise psychologists could investigate the influence of cohesiveness on interpersonal and cooperative skills. Do team members really develop team spirit or learn to value and work for team goals? Do these values transfer to areas outside sport? Regardless of the team's performance, cohesiveness could influence team members' satisfaction with the team experience, liking for the activity, and later participation in sport.

We know little about how cohesiveness is developed and maintained in sport and exercise groups. The key likely lies somewhere in the complexities of group process. The recent work on team building may well help us move to a fuller understanding of cohesion and the dynamics of sport and exercise groups.

# PUTTING GROUP DYNAMICS INTO PRACTICE THROUGH TEAM BUILDING

In the previous chapter we noted that recent team-building work puts group dynamics models and research into practice in sport and exercise settings. Now we will consider the team-building work in more detail. That approach moves beyond the limited focus of the earlier work on cohesiveness and performance to a more encompassing group dynamics framework. Also, Carron and colleagues have specifically applied their team-building approach in both sport and exercise settings.

## Team-Building Objectives

Carron and colleagues (Carron & Spink, 1993; Carron, Spink, & Prapavessis, 1997) adopt Newman's (1984) view that the aim of team-building interventions is to increase group effectiveness by enhancing group cohesiveness. Sport and exercise settings differ from the organizational settings of most team-building work in that the team-building interventions are more indirect (Carron et al., 1997). That is, most interventions are filtered through a coach or leader. Thus, Carron and colleagues work with the coach or leader a great deal. Others who have used team building, such as Yukelson (1997), have worked more directly with team members.

> **Key Point**
>
> The aim of team-building interventions in sport and exercise settings is to increase group effectiveness by enhancing group cohesiveness.

## Team-Building Model

The guiding model for the team-building efforts of Carron and colleagues involves four stages. The first three stages typically occur in a workshop with coaches or leaders; in the fourth stage, the coach or leader applies team-building strategies with the team members. The *introductory stage* and the *conceptual stage* give the coach or leader an overview of the benefits of cohesion and a frame of reference. The conceptual model (figure 20.3 in the previous chapter) identifies factors within each category that contribute to the development of cohesiveness. In the *practical stage*, coaches brainstorm to identify specific strategies to use for team building with their group. Finally, in the *intervention stage*, the coaches or leaders introduce and maintain the team-building protocols in the group setting.

Carron and colleagues (Carron & Spink, 1993; Carron et al., 1997) have used their intervention successfully with fitness classes and sport teams. With university aerobics classes (Carron & Spink, 1993), specific interventions addressed group environment, group structure, and group processes. Distinctiveness, the target group environment intervention, included such strategies as group names and T-shirts. Group structure included both individual position (e.g., pick spots) and group norm (e.g., establish partner goals) interventions. Group process interventions included sacrifices (regulars helping new people) and interaction and communication (taking turns in partner activities). The eight-week intervention led to an increase in group task cohesion, which was consistent with the intervention. Carron et al. (1997) report continuing research and team-building interventions with other groups and teams, and all the initial results are promising.

Other sport and exercise psychologists have developed team-building interventions. Crace and Hardy (1997) take a values-based approach and emphasize awareness of individual and team values, identification of interfering factors, and development of interventions to improve mutual respect and cohesion. Yukelson (1997) focuses on developing an effective team culture with ongoing open communication. The following suggestions, which Yukelson offers coaches, might easily be adapted for other sport and exercise groups:

- **Get to know your athletes as unique individuals.** Find out something personal and special about each athlete; show genuine interest in athletes' lives outside sport.

- **Develop pride in group membership and a sense of team identity.** Some ways to develop team identity include goal boards, mission statements, team covenants, and team credos.

- **Develop team goals and team commitment.** Have a comprehensive goal-setting program; clarify how team standards facilitate effectiveness.

- **Provide for goal evaluations.** Periodically evaluate and adjust goals, and chart progress; communication, ongoing evaluation, and feedback are essential.

- **Make roles clear.** Clarify role expectations and help each individual feel valued; have teammates get to know each other's responsibilities to help build mutual understanding.

- **Have periodic team meetings to discuss how things are progressing.** Set aside a designated time to talk openly and honestly.

- **Use player counsel.** Yukelson has used player counsel effectively at Penn State, through regularly scheduled breakfast or lunch meetings with team leaders or representatives from classes or subgroups, to keep coaches informed of attitudes and feelings in the group.

## Summary

Interpersonal relationships and ongoing processes are keys to understanding group dynamics. At the same time, the complex dynamics of these interrelationships and processes makes it difficult to draw firm conclusions and offer specific guidelines. Individual characteristics, the environment, and group structure interact in complex ways to influence group processes and outcomes. Moreover, the cycle continues, with outcomes such as performance or cohesion influencing the input variables and group processes.

The sport and exercise psychology literature on leadership and decision-making styles suggests that the effectiveness of a style varies with the situation. Participatory styles are often promoted, but they may be ineffective—and are seldom preferred by coaches and athletes on competitive teams. On the other hand, participatory styles might enhance cohesion and adherence in an exercise program.

Research on sport teams indicates that cohesiveness is positively related to team success, but the relationship is not simple. The influence of success on cohesion is stronger than vice versa, and many mediators and moderators influence the cohesion-performance relationship.

Most important, the focus on the cohesion-performance relationship in sport and exercise psychology research is limiting. To understand complex, dynamic processes and provide empirical results to guide practice, we must consider multidimensional relationships and dynamic processes. The team-building work clearly calls for this approach, and Brawley and Paskevich (1997) provide some suggestions to guide team-building research. Researchers cannot look at everything at once, but, by keeping an overall group dynamics framework in mind, can provide useful information and guidelines.

## Review Questions

1. Define leadership.
2. Identify the three variables influencing leader effectiveness, according to Fiedler's contingency model.
3. Describe group structure factors that influence leadership development.
4. Explain Chelladurai's Multidimensional Model of Leadership.
5. Summarize Chelladurai's research on coaches' decision-making styles.
6. Identify the five features of Carron's (1982) definition of cohesiveness.
7. Describe Carron's conceptual model of cohesion.
8. Identify four approaches to measuring cohesiveness.
9. Trace the findings of research on the cohesiveness-performance relationship in sport.
10. Discuss the direction of causality evidenced in cohesiveness-performance research.
11. Identify several moderating and mediating variables that may have an impact on the cohesiveness-performance relationship.
12. Identify the aim of team-building interventions in sport and exercise settings.
13. Explain the four stages of Carron et al.'s (1997) team-building model.

## Recommended Reading

★ Chelladurai, P., & Doherty, A.J. (1998). Styles of decision making in coaching. In J.M. Williams (Ed.), *Applied sport psychology: Personal growth to peak performance* (3rd ed.). Mountain View, CA: Mayfield.

> This chapter provides an overview of Chelladurai's leadership model, along with recent related research and implications for coaching.

★ Carron, A.V., Widmeyer, W.N., & Brawley, L.R. (1985). The development of an instrument to assess cohesion in sport teams: The Group Environment Questionnaire. *Journal of Sport Psychology, 7,* 244-266.

> This Canadian trio has conducted much of the scholarly work on sport group dynamics. This article describes the development of the Group Environment Questionnaire, their multidimensional cohesion measure that has been widely used in sport and exercise psychology.

★ Carron, A.V., Spink, K.S., & Prapavessis, H. (1997). Team building and cohesiveness in the sport and exercise setting: Use of indirect interventions. *Journal of Applied Sport Psychology, 9,* 61-72.

> Team building has recently become a prominent topic in sport group dynamics, and team building is particularly relevant to sport psychology practice. In this article the authors present their model of team building and sport group cohesion, and they offer suggestions for both research and intervention.

We now conclude our review and discussion of sport and exercise psychology. Most likely you have read this text for a course, and you have discussed the material in class or with colleagues. Perhaps you focused on a specific topic, gathered further material, and developed a review paper or research study. Perhaps you used the techniques and guidelines to develop psychological skills training interventions, to improve your teaching or coaching, or to control your "mental game" in your daily activities.

We have covered a lot of material, including personality and individual differences, motivation, psychological skills training, emotions, behavioral strategies, social development, diversity, and group dynamics. Moreover, nearly every topic and issue is multifaceted, and can be addressed from several perspectives. Human behavior in sport and exercise is complex and dynamic, and our answers to our many questions are also complex and dynamic.

If you return to the questions posed at the beginning of chapter 1, you may find that you can now answer them easily with your sport and exercise psychology knowledge. But, you have also developed new insights into the complexities of behavior, and as you reflect, you will likely find that the answers are not so easy.

Answering the questions in chapter 1, or on a course exam, is *not* the true test of your understanding of sport and exercise psychology. The truer test will come in your professional practice as you draw upon the knowledge and practical theories of sport and exercise psychology and integrate that knowledge with your professional insights. Perhaps you will use sport and exercise psychology when you are coaching a youth soccer team, consulting with an intercollegiate athlete, developing a program for a cardiac rehabilitation client, working with a community youth development program, or trying to maintain a healthy lifestyle in your hectic daily schedule. Perhaps you will remember intrinsic motivation theories as you consider the rewards in your soccer program, or use your knowledge of PST to help a client develop stress management skills. I hope you will remember the many interacting influences, including social diversity and interpersonal relations, as you work with individuals in complex, changing settings. Guidelines and practical theories will help, but the mix is different for every individual in every situation.

In writing this book I have shared my knowledge and views of sport and exercise psychology. I now invite you to do the same. I would like to hear your reactions to the book—let me know what you found useful; what sections might be deleted, added, or revised; and any suggestions for the next revisions. Also, let me know your thoughts on sport and exercise psychology research and practice. Sport and exercise psychology continues to expand and move in new directions, and you can help us advance our understanding of sport and exercise behavior.

# Sport Competition Anxiety Test for Adults

*Directions:* Below are some statements about how persons feel when they compete in sports and games. Read each statement and decide if you HARDLY EVER, or SOMETIMES, or OFTEN feel this way when you compete in sports and games. If your choice is HARDLY EVER, blacken the square labeled A; if your choice is SOMETIMES, blacken the square labeled B; and if your choice is OFTEN, blacken the square labeled C. There are no right or wrong answers. Do not spend too much time on any one question. Remember to choose the word that describes how you *usually* feel when competing in *sports and games*.

| | Hardly ever | Sometimes | Often |
|---|---|---|---|
| 1. Competing against others is socially enjoyable. | A ❑ | B ❑ | C ❑ |
| 2. Before I compete I feel uneasy. | A ❑ | B ❑ | C ❑ |
| 3. Before I compete I worry about not performing well. | A ❑ | B ❑ | C ❑ |
| 4. I am a good sportsman when I compete. | A ❑ | B ❑ | C ❑ |
| 5. When I compete I worry about making mistakes. | A ❑ | B ❑ | C ❑ |
| 6. Before I compete I am calm. | A ❑ | B ❑ | C ❑ |
| 7. Setting a goal is important when competing. | A ❑ | B ❑ | C ❑ |
| 8. Before I compete I get a queasy feeling in my stomach. | A ❑ | B ❑ | C ❑ |
| 9. Just before competing I notice my heart beats faster than usual. | A ❑ | B ❑ | C ❑ |
| 10. I like to compete in games that demand considerable physical energy. | A ❑ | B ❑ | C ❑ |
| 11. Before I compete I feel relaxed. | A ❑ | B ❑ | C ❑ |
| 12. Before I compete I am nervous. | A ❑ | B ❑ | C ❑ |
| 13. Team sports are more exciting than individual sports. | A ❑ | B ❑ | C ❑ |
| 14. I get nervous wanting to start the game. | A ❑ | B ❑ | C ❑ |
| 15. Before I compete I usually get uptight. | A ❑ | B ❑ | C ❑ |

## Instructions for Scoring SCAT for Adults

For each item three responses are possible: (a) Hardly ever, (b) Sometimes, and (c) Often. The 10 test items are 2, 3, 5, 6, 8, 9, 11, 12, 14, and 15. The spurious items (1, 4, 7, 10, and 13) are *not* scored. Items 2, 3, 5, 8, 9, 12, 14, and 15 are worded so that they are scored according to the following key:

1 = Hardly ever

2 = Sometimes

3 = Often

Items 6 and 11 are scored according to the following key:

1 = Often

2 = Sometimes

3 = Hardly ever

The range of scores on SCAT is from 10 (low competitive A-trait) to 30 (high competitive A-trait).

If a person deletes 1 of the 10 test items, a prorated full-scale score can be obtained by computing the mean score for the 9 items answered, multiplying this value by 10, and rounding the product to the next whole number. When two or more items are omitted, the respondent's questionnaire should be invalidated.

Select raw scores and corresponding percentile norms for college-age adults are included in the following section. A more detailed discussion of SCAT scores and additional norms are included in Martens' (1977) SCAT monograph.

### SCAT-A Norms for Normal College-Age Adults

| Raw score | Male percentile | Female percentile |
|-----------|-----------------|-------------------|
| 30 | 99 | 99 |
| 28 | 97 | 88 |
| 26 | 89 | 75 |
| 24 | 82 | 59 |
| 22 | 74 | 47 |
| 20 | 61 | 35 |
| 18 | 40 | 22 |
| 16 | 24 | 10 |
| 14 | 14 | 6 |
| 12 | 7 | 3 |
| 10 | 1 | 1 |

*Note.* Instructions and norms modified from *Sport Competition Anxiety Test* (pp. 91 & 99). By R. Martens, 1977, Champaign, IL: Human Kinetics. Copyright 1977 by Rainer Martens. Reprinted by permission.

# Progressive Relaxation Exercise

This exercise is adapted from *Progressive Relaxation: A Manual for the Helping Professions* by D.A. Bernstein and T.D. Borkovec, 1973, Champaign, IL: Research Press. Copyright 1973 by the authors. Reprinted by permission.

## INTRODUCTION

As the name implies, progressive relaxation involves the progressive tensing and relaxing of various muscle groups. Although the exercise is a relaxation technique, we start with tension because most individuals find it easier to go from a tensed state to a relaxed state than to simply relax muscles. Progressing from a tensed state to relaxation also helps to develop the ability to recognize and differentiate the feelings of tension and relaxation in the muscles. The first session of progressive relaxation training might take 30 to 45 minutes. As training continues, however, the sessions become shorter; muscle groups can be combined and the tension phase can be omitted. The goal of progressive relaxation training is self-control. With practice an individual can learn to recognize subtle levels of muscle tension and immediately relax those muscles.

## GENERAL INSTRUCTIONS

As we proceed through this exercise, various muscle groups will be tensed for a short time and then relaxed on the following cues: *NOW* for tension and the word *RELAX* for relaxation. On the word *NOW*, you should tense the muscles and hold the tension until the word *RELAX*, and then you should let all the tension go at once, not gradually.

As we go through tension and relaxation, I will ask you to pay attention to the feelings of tension and relaxation. This is in part a concentration exercise; try to focus attention on the feelings in your muscles. Today try to remain awake and pay attention to the feelings in your muscles. Later you can also use this exercise as a sleep aid.

Once a muscle group has been relaxed, try not to move it except to be comfortable; try to tense only the particular muscle group that we are working on.

Do not talk during the exercise; ignore distracting sounds and activities; and keep your attention on the feelings in your muscles.

We will go through each of 16 muscle groups twice. Each time I will remind you about the tension methods, give you the signal to tense (the word *NOW*), then the signal to *RELAX*. We will go through the tension and relaxation a second time, and then we will go on to the next muscle group.

The 16 muscle groups that we will go through and the general instruction for tensing those muscles include the following:

1. Dominant (right) hand and lower arm: Make a fist.

2. Dominant biceps and upper arm: push elbow down and pull back, without moving the lower arm.

3. Nondominant (left) hand and lower arm: Same as 1.

4. Nondominant biceps and upper arm: Same as 2.

5. Forehead (upper face): Lift eyebrows as high as possible and wrinkle forehead.

6. Central face: Squint and wrinkle nose.

7. Lower face and jaw: Clench teeth and pull back corners of mouth.

8. Neck: Pull chin forward and neck back.

9. Chest, back, and shoulders: Pull shoulder blades together and take a deep breath; continue to take a deep breath while tensing and release with slow, easy breathing as you are relaxing.

10. Stomach/abdomen: Make stomach hard.

11. Dominant (right) upper leg: Counterpose top and bottom thigh muscles.

12. Dominant calf and lower leg: Pull toes toward head.

13. Dominant foot: Curl toes and foot inward (do not hold too long to avoid foot cramps).

14. Nondominant upper leg: Same as 11.

15. Nondominant calf and lower leg: Same as 12.

16. Nondominant foot: Same as 13.

For a shorter session, the muscle groups may be combined as follows:

1. Dominant hand and arm (hand, lower arm, upper arm).

2. Nondominant hand and arm.

3. Face (upper, central, and lower face muscles).

4. Neck.

5. Trunk area (chest, back, shoulders, stomach, abdomen).

6. Dominant leg and foot (upper leg, lower leg, foot).

7. Nondominant leg and foot.

## Specific Instructions

Make yourself comfortable; remove any constraining items that might get in your way such as watches, glasses, or shoes. Close your eyes and take three deep, relaxed breaths. Breathe in slowly and completely, and breathe out slowly and relaxed.

Focus your attention on the muscles of your dominant (right) lower arm and hand. When I give the signal, make a fist and tense the muscles of your dominant lower arm and hand. Ready . . . *NOW.*

## Tension Talk

Feel the tension. . . . Focus on the tension. . . . Feel the muscles pull. . . . Notice the tightness. . . . Hold the tension. . . . Put tension in the muscle. . . . Hold it. . . . (5-7 seconds) and—*RELAX.*

## Relaxation Talk

Let all the tension go. . . . Let the muscles get more and more relaxed. . . . Let go. . . . Notice how you feel as relaxation takes place. . . . Notice the feelings of relaxation. . . . Relax deeper and deeper. . . . Just let the muscles go. . . . more and more completely. . . . Notice the pleasant feelings of relaxation. . . . Continue letting the muscles relax. . . . Keep relaxing. . . . Let yourself relax. . . . Feel the relaxation through the muscles. . . . Continue letting go. . . . Let the muscles keep relaxing. . . . Nothing to do but let the muscles relax. . . . Feel the relaxation come into the muscles. . . . Pay attention to the feelings of relaxation as the muscles relax more and more . . . more and more completely . . . deeply relaxed. . . . Let the muscles loosen up and smooth out. . . . Relax. . . . Notice how you feel as the muscles relax. . . . Let the tension go away. . . . Feel calm, peaceful relaxation. . . . Let the tension go as you breathe slow and easy. . . . Feel calm, rested. . . . With each breath the muscles relax more and more. . . . Notice the difference between tension and relaxation. . . . See if the muscles of the arm feel as relaxed as those of the hand. . . . Just let the muscles continue to relax. . . . Relax. . . . Relax. . . . (30-40 seconds).

We're going to repeat the tension/relaxation sequence again for the dominant hand and lower arm. All right, I'd like you to again make a fist and tense the muscles of the dominant hand and lower arm. Ready, *NOW*. (Repeat tension phase 5-7 seconds.) And *RELAX*. (Repeat relaxation phase 45-60 seconds.)

All right. NOW I'd like you to shift your attention to the muscles of the upper arm and biceps of your dominant arm. Ignore the lower arm and focus only on the upper arm throughout the exercise. (Continue to go through each of the 16 muscle groups twice following the same tension and relaxation phases as for the dominant hand and lower arm.)

## General Relaxation Talk

Notice the relaxation in all the muscles. . . . Complete and deep relaxation. . . . Check the muscles in your dominant hand; let those muscles keep relaxing. . . . Check your other muscles. . . . If you notice tension, just let the muscle keep relaxing. . . . Let the tension go. . . . Let the face muscles relax. . . . Let your shoulders relax. . . . Breathe slowly and easily. . . . With each breath, the muscles relax more and more. . . . Enjoy the feelings of relaxation. . . . (45-60 seconds).

## End of Exercise

In a moment I will count backwards from four to one. On the count of four, you should move your legs and feet; on three, move your arms and hands; on two, move your head and neck; and on one you can open your eyes and get up slowly. All right. *Four:* Move your legs and feet; stretch out. *Three:* Move your hands and arms. *Two:* Move your head and neck. *One:* Open your eyes, get up, and move around when you're ready. You may feel a little dizzy, so move slowly as you become more alert.

# references

Abernethy, B. (1993). Attention. In R.N. Singer, M. Murphey, & L.K. Tennant (Eds.), *Handbook of research on sport psychology* (pp. 127-170). New York: Macmillan.

Abernethy, B., & Russell, D.G. (1987). Expert-novice differences in an applied selective attention task. *Journal of S`orshPsychology, 9,* 326-345.

Abramson, L.Y., Seligman, M.E.P., & Teasdale, J.D. (1978). Learned helplessness in humans: Critique and reformulation. *Journal of Abnormal Psychology, 87,* 49-74.

Acevedo, E., Gill, D.L., & Dzewaltowski, D. (1987, September). *Sport-specific psychological characteristics of ultramarathoners.* Paper presented at the Association for the Advancement of Applied Sport Psychology Conference, Newport Beach, CA.

Adame, D.D., Johnson, T.C., Cole, S.P., Matthiasson, H., & Abbas, M.A. (1990). Physical fitness in relation to amount of physical exercise, body image, and locus of control among college men and women. *Perceptual and Motor Skills, 70,* 1347-1350.

Ahsen, A. (1984). ISM: The triple code model for imagery and psychophysiology. *Journal of Mental Imagery, 8,* 15-42.

Ajzen, I. (1985). From intentions to actions: A theory of focus on these important subgroups. In J. Kuhl & J. Reckman (Eds.), *Action-control: From cognition to behavior* (pp. 11-39). Heidelberg: Springer.

Albert, E. (1991). Riding a line: Competition and cooperation in the sport of bicycle racing. *Sociology of Sport Journal, 8,* 341-361.

Albinson, J.G. (1974). Life style of physically active and physically inactive college males. *International Journal of Sport Psychology, 5,* 93-101.

Albrecht, R.R., & Feltz, D.L. (1985, May). *Relationships among a sport-specific measure of attentional style, anxiety, and performance of collegiate baseball and softball batters.* Paper presented at the North American Society for the Psychology of Sport and Physical Activity Conference, Gulfpark, MS.

Allard, F., & Burnett, N. (1985). Skill in sport. *Canadian Journal of Psychology, 39,* 294-312.

Allard, F., Graham, S., & Paarsalu, M.T. (1980). Perception in sport: Basketball. *Journal of Sport Psychology, 2,* 14-21.

Allard, F., & Starkes, J.L. (1980). Perception in sport: Volleyball. *Journal of Sport Psychology, 2,* 22-33.

Allison, M.G., & Ayllon, T. (1980). Behavioral coaching in the development of skills in football, gymnastics, and tennis. *Journal of Applied Behavior Analysis, 13,* 297-314.

Allport, F.H. (1924). *Social psychology.* Boston: Houghton Mifflin.

American Association of University Women. (1992). *The AAUW report: How schools shortchange girls. Executive summary.* Washington, DC: American Association of University Women Educational Foundation.

American College of Sports Medicine (1990). Position statement on the recommended quantity and quality of exercise for developing and maintaining cardiorespiratory and muscular fitness in healthy adults. *Medicine and Science in Sports and Exercise, 22,* 265-274.

Ames, C. (1984). Conceptions of motivation within competitive and noncompetitive goal structures. In R. Schwarzer (Ed.), *Self-related cognitions in anxiety and motivation* (pp. 205-241). Hillsdale, NJ: Erlbaum.

Ames, C. (1992). Achievement goals, motivational climate, and motivational processes. In G.C. Roberts (Ed.), *Motivation in sport and exercise* (pp. 161-176). Champaign, IL: Human Kinetics.

Ames, C., & Ames, R. (1981). Competitive versus individualistic goal structures: The salience of past performance information for causal attributions and affect. *Journal of Educational Psychology, 73,* 411-418.

Ames, C., & Archer, J. (1988). Achievement goals in the classroom: Students' learning strategies and motivation processes. *Journal of Educational Psychology, 80,* 260-267.

Anderson, A.B. (1975). Combined effects of interpersonal attraction and goal-path clarity on the cohesiveness of task oriented groups. *Journal of Personality and Social Psychology, 31,* 68-75.

Anderson, M., & Williams, J. (1988). A model of stress and athletic injury: Prediction and prevention. *Journal of Sport and Exercise Psychology, 10,* 294-306.

Apter, M.J. (1984). Reversal theory and personality: A review. *Journal of Research in Personality, 18,* 265-288.

Ardrey, R. (1966). *The territorial imperative.* New York: Atheneum.

Arms, R.L., Russell, G.W., & Sandilands, M.L. (1979). Effects of viewing aggressive sports on the hostility of spectators. *Social Psychology Quarterly, 42,* 275-279.

Arnold, G.E., & Straub, W.F. (1972). Personality and group cohesiveness as determinants of success among interscholastic basketball teams. *Proceedings: Fourth Canadian Symposium on Psychomotor Learning and Sport Psychology.* Ottawa: Health and Welfare Canada.

Ashmore, R.D. (1990). Sex, gender, and the individual. In L.A. Pervin (Ed.), *Handbook of personality theory and research* (pp. 486-526). New York: Guilford.

Association for the Advancement of Applied Sport Psychology (1986, Winter). Nags Head meeting launches AAASP. *AAASP Newsletter, 1*(1).

Atkinson, J.W. (1964). *An introduction to motivation.* Princeton, NJ: Van Nostrand.

Atkinson, J.W. (1974). The mainsprings of achievement-oriented activity. In J.W. Atkinson & J.O. Raynor (Eds.), *Motivation and achievement* (pp. 13-41). New York: Halstead.

Baillie, P.H.F., & Danish, S.J. (1992). Understanding the career transition of athletes. *The Sport Psychologist, 6,* 77-98.

Bakeman, R., & Helmreich, R. (1975). Cohesiveness and performance: Covariation and causality in an undersea environment. *Journal of Experimental Social Psychology, 11,* 478-489.

Ball, J.R., & Carron, A.V. (1976). The influence of team cohesion and participation motivation upon performance success in intercollegiate ice hockey. *Canadian Journal of Applied Sport Sciences, 1,* 271-275.

Bandura, A. (1965). Influence of models' reinforcement contingencies on the acquisition of imitative responses. *Journal of Personality and Social Psychology, 1,* 589-595.

Bandura, A. (1973). *Aggression: A social learning analysis.* Englewood Cliffs, NJ: Prentice-Hall.

Bandura, A. (1977a). Self-efficacy: Toward a unifying theory of behavioral change. *Psychological Review, 84,* 191-215.

Bandura, A. (1977b). *Social learning theory.* Englewood Cliffs, NJ: Prentice-Hall.

Bandura, A. (1982). Self-efficacy mechanism in human agency. *American Psychologist, 37,* 122-147.

Bandura, A. (1986). *Social foundations of thought and action: A social cognitive theory.* Englewood Cliffs, NJ: Prentice-Hall.

Bandura, A., & Jeffery, R.W. (1973). Role of symbolic coding and rehearsal processes in observational learning. *Journal of Personality and Social Psychology, 37,* 122-130.

Bandura, A., Ross, D., & Ross, S.A. (1963a). Imitation of film-mediated aggressive models. *Journal of Abnormal and Social Psychology, 66*, 3-11.

Bandura, A., Ross, D., & Ross, S.A. (1963b). Vicarious reinforcement and imitative learning. *Journal of Abnormal and Social Psychology, 67*, 601-607.

Bardwick, J. (1970). *The psychology of women: A study of bio-cultural conflicts.* New York: Harper & Row.

Baron, R., Moore, D., & Sanders, G.S. (1978). Distraction as a source of drive in social facilitation research. *Journal of Personality and Social Psychology, 36*, 816-824.

Baron, R.A. (1977). *Human aggression.* New York: Plenum Press.

Baron, R.A., & Richardson, D.R. (1994). *Human aggression.* New York: Plenum Press.

Barrow, J.C. (1977). The variables of leadership: A review and conceptual framework. *Academy of Management Review, 74*, 231-251.

Baumeister, R.F. (1984). Choking under pressure: Self-consciousness and paradoxical effects of incentives on skillful performance. *Journal of Personality and Social Psychology, 47*, 85-93.

Baumeister, R.F. (1986). *Public self and private self.* New York: Springer-Verlag.

Baumeister, R.F. & Steinhilber, A. (1984). Paradoxical effects of supportive audiences on performance under pressure: The home field disadvantage in sports championships. *Journal of Personality and Social Psychology, 47*, 85-93.

Beck, A.T. (1970). Cognitive therapy. *Behavior Modification, 1*, 184-200.

Bem, D.J. (1967). Self-perception: An alternative interpretation of cognitive dissonance phenomena. *Psychological Review, 74*, 183-200.

Bem, S.L. (1974). The measurement of psychological androgyny. *Journal of Consulting and Clinical Psychology, 42*, 155-162.

Bem, S.L. (1978a). Beyond androgyny: Some presumptuous prescriptions for a liberated sexual identity. In J. Sherman & F. Denmark (Eds.), *Psychology of women: Future directions for research* (pp. 1-23). New York: Psychological Dimensions.

Bem, S.L. (1978b). *The short Bem Sex-Role Inventory.* Palo Alto, CA: Consulting Psychologists Press.

Bem, S.L. (1985). Androgyny and gender schema theory: A conceptual and empirical integration. In T.B. Sonderegger (Ed.), *Nebraska Symposium on Motivation, 1984: Psychology and gender* (pp. 179-226). Lincoln, NE: University of Nebraska Press.

Bem, S.L. (1993). *The lenses of gender.* New Haven, CT: Yale University Press.

Benson, H. (1976). *The relaxation response.* New York: William Morrow.

Berger, B.G. (1994). Coping with stress: The effectiveness of exercise. *Quest, 46*, 100-119.

Berger, B.G., & McInman, A. (1993). Exercise and the quality of life. In R.N. Singer, M. Murphey, & L.K. Tennant (Eds.), *Handbook of research on sport psychology* (pp. 729-760). New York: Macmillan.

Berger, B.G., & Owen, D.R. (1983). Mood alterations with swimming—swimmers really do feel better. *Psychosomatic Medicine, 45*, 425-433.

Berglas, S., & Jones, E.E. (1978). Drug choice as an externalization strategy in response to noncontingent success. *Journal of Personality and Social Psychology, 36*, 405-417.

Berkowitz, L. (1954). Group standards, cohesiveness, and productivity. *Human Relations, 7*, 509-519.

Berkowitz, L. (1956). Group norms among bomber crews: Patterns of perceived crew attitudes, "active" crew attitudes, and crew liking related to air crew effectiveness in Far Eastern combat. *Sociometry, 19*, 141-153.

Berkowitz, L. (1962). *Aggression: A social psychological analysis.* New York: McGraw-Hill.

Berkowitz, L. (1965). The concept of aggressive drive: Some additional considerations. In L. Berkowitz (Ed.), *Advances in experimental social psychology* (Vol. 2, pp. 301-329). New York: Academic Press.

Berkowitz, L. (1966). On not being able to aggress. *British Journal of Social and Clinical Psychology, 5*, 130-139.

Berkowitz, L. (1969). *Roots of aggression.* New York: Atherton Press.

Berkowitz, L. (1970). Experimental investigations of hostility catharsis. *Journal of Consulting and Clinical Psychology, 35*, 1-7.

Berkowitz, L. (1974). Some determinants of impulsive aggression: The role of mediated associations with reinforcements for aggression. *Psychological Review, 81*, 165-176.

Berkowitz, L. (1993). *Aggression: Its causes, consequences, and control.* Philadelphia: Temple University Press.

Bernard, J. (1981). *The female world.* New York: Free Press.

Bernstein, D.A., & Borkovec, T.D. (1973). *Progressive relaxation: A manual for the helping professions.* Champaign, IL: Research Press.

Berridge, H. (1935). An experiment in the psychology of competition. *Research Quarterly, 6*, 37-42.

Betts, G.H. (1909). *The distribution and functions of mental imagery.* New York: Columbia University, Teachers College.

Biddle, S. (1993). Attribution research and sport psychology. In R.N. Singer, M. Murphey, & L.K. Tennant (Eds.), *Handbook on research on sport psychology* (pp. 437-464). New York: Macmillan.

Biddle, S., & Hill, A.B. (1988). Causal attributions and emotional reactions to outcome in a sporting contest. *Personality and Individual Differences, 9*, 213-223.

Biddle, S., & Hill, A.B. (1992). Relationships between attributions and emotions in a laboratory-based sporting contest. *Journal of Sport Sciences, 10*, 65-75.

Bigelow, B.J., Lewko, J.H., & Salhani, L. (1989). Sport-involved children's friendship expectations. *Journal of Sport & Exercise Psychology, 11*, 152-160.

Bird, A.M. (1977). Development of a model for predicting team performance. *Research Quarterly, 48*, 24-32.

Bird, A.M., & Brame, J.M. (1978). Self versus team attributions: A test of the "I'm OK, but the team's so-so" phenomenon. *Research Quarterly for Exercise and Sport, 49*, 260-268.

Bjorkqvist, K., Osterman, K., & Kaukiainen, A. (1992). The development of direct and indirect aggressive strategies in males and females. In K. Bjorkqvist & P. Niemela (Eds.), *Of mice and women: Aspects of female aggression* (pp. 51-64). New York: Academic Press.

Black, D., & Burckes-Miller, M. (1988). Male and female college athletes: Use of anorexia nervosa and bulimia nervosa weight loss methods. *Research Quarterly for Exercise and Sport, 59*, 252-256.

Blair, S.N., Powell, K.E., Bazzarre, T.L., Early, J.L., Epstein, L.H., Green, L.W., Harris, S.S., Haskell, W.L., King, A.C., Kaplan, J., Marcus, B., Paffenbarger, R.S., & Yeager, K.C. (1993). Physical inactivity, Workshop V. *Circulation, 88*, 1402-1405.

Blann, F.W. (1985). Intercollegiate athletic competition and students' educational and career plans. *Journal of College Student Personnel, 26*, 115-116.

Blinde, E.M., & Greendorfer, S.L. (1985). A reconceptualization of the process of leaving the role of competitive athlete. *International Review for the Sociology of Sport, 20*, 87-93.

Blumenthal, J.A., O'Toole, L.C., & Chang, J.L. (1984). Is running an analogue of anorexia nervosa? *Journal of the American Medical Association, 252* (4), 520-523.

Blumenthal, J.A., Rose, S., & Chang, J.L. (1985). Anorexia nervosa and exercise: Implications from recent findings. *Sports Medicine, 2*, 237-247.

Borg, G. (1973). Psychophysical basis of perceived exertion. *Medicine and Science in Sports and Exercise, 14*, 377-81.

Borg, G. (1982). Perceived exertion: A note on "history" and methods. *Medicine and Science in Sports and Exercise, 5*, 90-93.

Borg, G. (1998). *Borg's perceived exertion and pain scales.* Champaign, IL: Human Kinetics.

Borkovec, T.D. (1976). Physiological and cognitive processes in the regulation of anxiety. In G. Schwartz & D. Shapiro (Eds.), *Consciousness and self-regulation: Advances in research* (Vol. 1, pp. 261-312). New York: Plenum Press.

Boutcher, S. (1993). Emotion and aerobic exercise. In R.N. Singer, M. Murphey, & L.K. Tennant (Eds.), *Handbook of research on sport psychology* (pp. 799-814). New York: Macmillan.

Boutcher, S.H., & Crews, D.J. (1987). The effect of a preshot attentional routine on a well-learned skill. *International Journal of Sport Psychology, 18,* 30-39.

Boutcher, S., & Zinsser, N.W. (1990). Cardiac deceleration of elite and beginning golfers during putting. *Journal of Sport & Exercise Psychology, 12,* 37-47.

Boyer, E.L. (1990). *Scholarship reconsidered.* Princeton, NJ: The Carnegie Foundation for the Advancement of Teaching.

Brawley, L.R. (1984). Attributions as social cognitions: Contemporary perspectives in sport. In W.F. Straub & J.M. Williams (Eds.), *Cognitive sport psychology* (pp. 212-230). Lansing, NY: Sport Science Associates.

Brawley, L.R., Carron, A.V., & Widmeyer, W.N. (1987). Assessing cohesion of teams: Validity of the Group Environment Questionnaire. *Journal of Sport Psychology, 9,* 275-294.

Brawley, L.R., Carron, A.V., & Widmeyer, W.N. (1988). Exploring the relationship between cohesion and group resistance to disruption. *Journal of Sport & Exercise Psychology, 10,* 199-213.

Brawley, L.R., & Paskevich, D.M. (1997). Conducting team building research in the context of sport and exercise. *Journal of Applied Sport Psychology, 9,* 11-40.

Brawley, L.R., & Roberts, G.C. (1984). Attributions in sport: Research foundations, characteristics, and limitations. In J.M. Silva & R.S. Weinberg (Eds.), *Psychological foundations of sport* (pp. 197-213). Champaign, IL: Human Kinetics.

Brawley, L.R., & Rodgers, W.M. (1992). Social psychological aspects of fitness promotion. In P. Seraganian (Ed.), *Exercise psychology.* New York: Wiley.

Bredemeier, B.J.L. (1994). Children's moral reasoning and their assertive, aggressive, and submissive tendencies in sport and daily life. *Journal of Sport & Exercise Psychology, 16,* 1-14.

Bredemeier, B.J., & Shields, D. (1984a). Divergence in moral reasoning about sport and every day life. *Sociology of Sport Journal, 1,* 348-357.

Bredemeier, B.J., & Shields, D.L. (1984b). The utility of moral stage analysis in the investigation of athletic aggression. *Sociology of Sport Journal, 1,* 138-149.

Bredemeier, B.J., & Shields, D.L. (1986a). Athletic aggression: An issue of contextual morality. *Sociology of Sport Journal, 3,* 152-28.

Bredemeier, B.J., & Shields, D.L. (1986b). Game reasoning and interactional morality. *Journal of Genetic Psychology, 147,* 257-275.

Bredemeier, B.J., & Shields, D.L. (1986c). Moral growth among athletes and nonathletes: A comparative analysis. *Journal of Genetic Psychology, 147,* 7-18.

Bredemeier, B.J., Weiss, M.R., Shields, D.L., & Cooper, B.A.B. (1986). The relationship of sport involvement with children's moral reasoning and aggression tendencies. *Journal of Sport Psychology, 8,* 304-318.

Bredemeier, B.J., Weiss, M.R., Shields, D.L., & Shewchuk, R.M. (1986). Promoting moral growth in a summer sport camp: The implementation of theoretically grounded instructional strategies. *Journal of Moral Education, 15,* 212-220.

Brewer, B.W., & Petrie, T.A. (1996). In J.L. Van Raalte & B.W. Brewer (Eds.), *Exploring sport and exercise psychology* (pp. 257-274). Washington, DC: American Psychological Association.

Brewer, B.W., Van Raalte, J.L., & Linder, D.W. (1993). Athletic identity: Hercules' muscles or Achilles heel? *International Journal of Sport Psychology, 24,* 237-254.

Brodkin, P., & Weiss, M.R. (1990). Developmental differences in motivation for participation in competitive swimming. *Journal of Sport & Exercise Psychology, 12,* 248-263.

Brone, R., & Reznikoff, M. (1989). Strength gains, locus of control, and self-description of college football players. *Perceptual and Motor Skills, 69,* 483-493.

Brooks, D., & Althouse, R. (1993). *Racism in college athletics: The African-American athlete's experience.* Morgantown, WV: Fitness Information Technology.

Brown, J.M., & Davies, N. (1978). Attitudes towards violence among college athletes. *Journal of Sport Behavior, 1,* 61-70.

Brown, R.D., & Harrison, J.M. (1986). The effects of a strength training program on the strength and self-concept of two female age groups. *Research Quarterly for Exercise and Sport, 57,* 315-320.

Brownell, K.D. (1989). *The LEARN program for weight control.* Dallas: Brownell & Hager.

Brownell, K.D., Marlatt, G.A., Lichtenstein, E., & Wilson, G.T. (1986). Understanding and preventing relapse. *American Psychologist, 41,* 765-782.

Brustad, R.J. (1988). Affective outcomes in competitive youth sport: The influence of intrapersonal and socialization factors. *Journal of Sport & Exercise Psychology, 10,* 307-321.

Brustad, R.J. (1992). Integrating socialization influences into the study of children's motivation in sport. *Journal of Sport & Exercise Psychology, 14,* 59-77.

Brustad, R.J. (1993). Who will go out and play? Parental and psychological influences on children's attraction to physical activity. *Pediatric Exercise Science, 5,* 210-223.

Brustad, R.J. (1996). Attraction to physical activity in urban schoolchildren: Parental socialization and gender influences. *Research Quarterly for Exercise and Sport, 67,* 316-323.

Brustad, R.J. (1998, June). *Parental influence on youth motivation in physical activity.* Paper presented at the annual meeting of the North American Society for the Psychology of Sport and Physical Activity, St. Charles, IL.

Bryan, J.H. (1969, December). How adults teach hypocrisy. *Psychology Today, 3,* 50-52, 65.

Bryan, J.H., & Walbek, N.H. (1970). Preaching and practicing generosity: Some determinants of sharing in children. *Child Development, 41,* 329-354.

Buchanan, H.T., Blankenbaker, J., & Cotten, D. (1976). Academic and athletic ability as popularity factors in elementary school children. *Research Quarterly, 47,* 320-325.

Bukowski, W.M., & Hoza, B. (1989). Popularity and friendship: Issues in theory, measurement, and outcome. In T.J. Berndt & G.W. Ladd (Eds.), *Peer relationships in child development* (pp. 15-45). New York: Wiley.

Bukowski, W.M., & Moore, D. (1980). Winners' and losers' attributions for success and failure in a series of athletic events. *Journal of Sport Psychology, 2,* 195-210.

Buonamano, R., Cei, A., & Mussino, A. (1995). Participation motivation in Italian youth sport. *The Sport Psychologist, 9,* 265-281.

Burhans, K.K., & Dweck, C.S. (1995). Helplessness in early childhood: The role of contingent worth. *Childhood Development, 66,* 1719-1738.

Burton, D. (1988). Do anxious swimmers swim slower? Reexamining the elusive anxiety-performance relationship. *Journal of Sport & Exercise Psychology, 10,* 26-37.

Burton, D. (1989). Winning isn't everything: Examining the impact of performance goals on collegiate swimmers' cognitions and performance. *The Sport Psychologist, 2,* 105-132.

Burton, D. (1993). Goal setting in sport. In R.N. Singer, M. Murphey, & L.K. Tennant (Eds.), *Handbook of research on sport psychology* (pp. 467-491). New York: Macmillan.

Burwitz, L., & Newell, K.M. (1972). The effects of the mere presence of co-actors on learning a motor skill. *Journal of Motor Behavior, 4,* 99-102.

Butt, D.S. (1995). On the measurement of competence motivation. In P.E. Shrout & S.T. Fiske (Eds.), *Personality research, methods, and theory: A Festschrift honoring Donald W. Fiske* (pp. 313-331). Hillsdale, NJ: Erlbaum.

Callahan, T. (1984a, July 30). No limit to what he can do. *Time,* pp. 52-59.

Callahan, T. (1984b, July 30). Star-spangled home team. *Time,* pp. 60-63.

Cameron, J., & Pierce, W.D. (1994). Reinforcement, reward, and intrinsic motivation: A meta-analysis. *Review of Educational Research, 64,* 363-423.

Cameron, J., & Pierce, W.D. (1996). The debate about rewards and intrinsic motivation: Protests and accusations do not alter the results. *Review of Educational Research, 66,* 39-51.

Cannon, W.B. (1929). *Bodily changes in pain, hunger, fear and rage* (2nd ed.). New York: Appleton-Century-Crofts.

Carpenter, L.J., & Acosta, R.V. (1993). Back to the future: Reform with a woman's voice. In D.S. Eitzen (Ed.), *Sport in contemporary society: An anthology* (4th ed., pp. 388-398). New York: St. Martin's Press.

Carroll, L. (1992). *Alice's adventures in wonderland and through the looking glass*. New York: Dell Books.

Carroll, W.R., & Bandura, A. (1985). Role of timing visual monitoring and motor rehearsal in observational learning of action patterns. *Journal of Motor Behavior, 19*, 269-281.

Carroll, W.R., & Bandura, A. (1990). Representational guidance of action production in observational learning: A causal analysis. *Journal of Motor Behavior, 22*, 85-97.

Carron, A.V. (1982). Cohesiveness in sport groups: Interpretations and considerations. *Journal of Sport Psychology, 4*, 123-138.

Carron, A.V. (1988). *Group dynamics in sport: Theoretical and practical issues*. London, Ontario: Spodym.

Carron, A.V., & Ball, J.R. (1977). Cause-effect characteristics of cohesiveness and participation motivation in intercollegiate hockey. *International Review of Sport Sociology, 12*, 49-60.

Carron, A.V., & Chelladurai, P. (1979). Cohesiveness as a factor in sport performance. *International Review of Sport Sociology, 16*, 244-266.

Carron, A.V., & Chelladurai, P. (1981). Cohesion as a factor in sport performance. *International Review of Sport Sociology, 16*, 21-41.

Carron, A.V., & Dennis, P.W. (1998). The sport team as an effective group. In J.M. Williams, *Applied sport psychology: Personal growth to peak performance* (3rd ed.). Mountain View, CA: Mayfield.

Carron, A.V., Hausenblas, H.A., & Mack, D. (1996). Social influence: A meta-analysis. *Journal of Sport & Exercise Psychology, 18*, 1-16.

Carron, A.V., & Spink, K.S. (1993). Team building in an exercise setting. *The Sport Psychologist, 7*, 8-18.

Carron, A.V., Spink, K.S., & Prapavessis, H. (1997). Team building and cohesiveness in the sport and exercise setting: Use of indirect interventions. *Journal of Applied Sport Psychology, 9*, 61-72.

Carron, A.V., Widmeyer, W.N., & Brawley, L.R. (1985). The development of an instrument to assess cohesion in sport teams: The Group Environment Questionnaire. *Journal of Sport Psychology, 7*, 244-266.

Carron, A.V., Widmeyer, W.N., & Brawley, L.R. (1988). Group cohesion and individual adherence to physical activity. *Journal of Sport & Exercise Psychology, 10*, 119-126.

Carver, C.S., & Scheier, M.F. (1990). Origins and functions of positive and negative affect: A control process view. *Psychological Review, 97*, 19-35.

Caspersen, C.J., & DiPietro, L. (1991). National estimates of physical activity among older adults [Abstract]. *Medicine and Science in Sports and Exercise, 23* (Suppl.), S106.

Caspersen, C.J., Merritt, R.K., Heath, G.W., & Yeager, K.K. (1990). Physical activity patterns of adults aged 60 years and older. *Medicine and Science in Sports and Exercise, 22* (Suppl.), S79.

Chartrand, J., Jowdy, D.P., & Danish, S.J. (1992). The Psychological Skills Inventory for Sports: Psychometric characteristics and applied implications. *Journal of Sport & Exercise Psychology, 14*, 405-413.

Chase, M.A., & Drummer, G.M. (1992). The role of sports as a social status determinant for children. *Research Quarterly for Exercise and Sport, 63*, 418-424.

Chase, W.G., & Simon, H.A. (1973). Perception in chess. *Cognitive Psychology, 4*, 55-81.

Cheffers, J. (1997). Tuesdays and Thursdays with Boston's inner-city youth. *Quest, 49*, 50-66.

Chelladurai, P. (1984a). Discrepancy between preferences and perceptions of leadership behavior and satisfaction of athletes in varying sports. *Journal of Sport Psychology, 6*, 26-41.

Chelladurai, P. (1984b). Leadership in sports. In J.M. Silva & R.S. Weinberg (Eds.), *Psychological foundations of sport* (pp. 329-339). Champaign, IL: Human Kinetics.

Chelladurai, P. (1993). Leadership. In R.N. Singer, M. Murphey, & L.K. Tennant (Eds.), *Handbook of research on sport psychology*. New York: Macmillan.

Chelladurai, P., & Arnott, M. (1985). Decision styles in coaching: Preferences of basketball players. *Research Quarterly for Exercise and Sport, 56* (1), 15-24.

Chelladurai, P., & Carron, A.V. (1978). *Leadership* [Monograph]. Ottawa: Canadian Association for Health, Physical Education, and Recreation.

Chelladurai, P., & Carron, A.V. (1983). Athletic maturity and preferred leadership. *Journal of Sport Psychology, 5*, 371-380.

Chelladurai, P., & Doherty, A.J. (1998). Styles of decision making in coaching. In J.M. Williams (Ed.), *Applied sport psychology: Personal growth to peak performance* (3rd ed.). Mountain View, CA: Mayfield.

Chelladurai, P., & Haggerty, T. (1978). A normative model of decision-making styles in coaching. *Athletic Administration, 13*, 6-9.

Chelladurai, P., Haggerty, T.R., & Baxter, P.R. (1989). Decision style choices of university basketball coaches and players. *Journal of Sport & Exercise Psychology, 11*, 201-215.

Chelladurai, P., Imamura, I., Yamaguchi, Y., & Oinuma, Y. (1988). Sport leadership in a cross-national setting: The case of Japanese and Canadian university athletes. *Journal of Sport & Exercise Psychology, 10*, 374-389.

Chelladurai, P., & Quek, C.B. (1995). Decision style choices of high school coaches: The effects of situational and coach characteristics. *Journal of Sport Behavior, 18* (2), 91-108.

Chelladurai, P. & Saleh, S. (1978). Preferred leadership in sports. *Canadian Journal of Applied Sport Sciences, 3*, 85-92.

Chelladurai, P., & Saleh, S.D. (1980). Dimensions of leader behavior in sports: Development of a leadership scale. *Journal of Sport Psychology, 2*, 34-45.

Church, R.M. (1962). The effects of competition on reaction time and palmar skin conductance. *Journal of Abnormal and Social Psychology, 65*, 32-40.

Church, R.M. (1968). Applications of behavior theory to social psychology: Imitation and competition. In E.C. Simmer, R.A. Hope, & G.A. Milton (Eds.), *Social facilitation and imitative behavior* (pp. 135-168). Boston: Allyn & Bacon.

Cialdini, R.B., Borden, R.J., Thorne, A., Walker, M.R., Freeman, S., & Sloan, L.R. (1976). Basking in reflected glory: Three (football) field studies. *Journal of Personality and Social Psychology, 34*, 366-375.

Cialdini, R.B., & Richardson, K.D. (1980). Two indirect tactics of image management: Basking and blasting. *Journal of Personality and Social Psychology, 39*, 406-415.

Coakley, J. (1993). Social determinants of intensive training and participation in youth sports. In B.R. Cahill & A.J. Pearl (Eds.), *Intensive participation in children's sports* (pp. 77-94). Champaign, IL: Human Kinetics.

Cohen, S. (1988). Psychosocial models of the role of social support in the etiology of physical disease. *Health Psychology, 7* (3), 269-297.

Cohen, S., & Wills, T.A. (1985). Stress, social support, and the buffering hypothesis. *Psychological Bulletin, 98*, 310-357.

Colker, R., & Widom, C.S. (1980). Correlates of female athletic participation. *Sex Roles, 6*, 47-53.

Colley, J.A. (1998). Risky business: Innovative at-risk youth programming. *Journal of Physical Education, Recreation, and Dance, 69*, 39-43.

Comrey, A.L. (1953). Group performance in a manual dexterity task. *Journal of Applied Psychology, 37*, 207-210.

Condry, J., & Dyer, S. (1976). Fear of success: Attribution of cause to the victim. *Journal of Social Issues, 32*, 63-83.

Cooley, C.H. (1902). *Human nature and the social order*. New York: Scribner.

Coopersmith, S. (1967). *The antecedents of self-esteem*. San Francisco: Freeman.

Corbett, D., & Johnson W. (1993). The African-American female in collegiate sport: Sexism and racism. In D. Brooks & R. Althouse (Eds.), *Racism in college athletics: The African-American athlete's experience* (pp. 179-204). Morgantown, WV: Fitness Information Technology.

Corbin, C.B. (1972). Mental practice. In W.P. Morgan (Ed.), *Ergogenic aids and muscular performance* (pp. 93-118). New York: Academic Press.

Corbin, C.B. (1981). Sex of subject, sex of opponent, and opponent ability as factors affecting self-confidence in a competitive situation. *Journal of Sport Psychology, 3,* 265-270.

Corbin, C.B., Landers, D.M., Feltz, D.L., & Senior, K. (1983). Sex differences in performance estimates: Female lack of confidence vs. male boastfulness. *Research Quarterly for Exercise and Sport, 54,* 407-410.

Corbin, C.B., & Nix, C. (1979). Sex-typing of physical activities and success predictions of children before and after cross-sex competition. *Journal of Sport Psychology, 1,* 43-52.

Corbin, C.B., Stewart, M.J., & Blair, W.O. (1981). Self-confidence and motor performance of preadolescent boys and girls in different feedback situations. *Journal of Sport Psychology, 3,* 30-34.

Costa, P.T. Jr., & McCrae, R.R. (1985). *The NEO Personality Inventory manual.* Odessa, FL: Psychological Assessment Resources.

Cottrell, N.B. (1968). Performance in the presence of other human beings: Mere presence, audience, and affiliation effects. In E.C. Simmer, R.A. Hope, & G.A. Milton (Eds.), *Social facilitation and imitative behavior* (pp. 91-110). Boston: Allyn & Bacon.

Courneya, K.S., & Carron, A.V. (1992). The home advantage in sport competitions: A literature review. *Journal of Sport & Exercise Psychology, 14,* 13-27.

Courneya, K.S., & McAuley, E. (1991). Perceived effectiveness of motivational strategies to enhance children's intrinsic interest in sport and physical activity. *Journal of Social Behavior and Personality, 6,* 125-136.

Crace, R.K., & Hardy, C.J. (1997). Individual values and the team building process. *Journal of Applied Sport Psychology, 9,* 41-60.

Crandall, V.C. (1969). Sex differences in expectancy of intellectual and academic reinforcement. In C.P. Smith (Ed.), *Achievement-related motives in children* (pp. 11-45). New York: Russell Sage Foundation.

Cratty, B.J. (1964). *Movement behavior and motor learning.* Philadelphia: Lea & Febiger.

Cratty, B.J. (1967). *Psychology and physical activity.* Englewood Cliffs, NJ: Prentice Hall.

Crews, D.J., & Landers, D.M. (1987). A meta-analytic review of aerobic fitness and reactivity to psychosocial stressors. *Medicine and Science in Sports and Exercise, 19,* S114-S120.

Crews, D.J., & Landers, D.M. (1991). *Cardiac pattern as an indicator of attention: A test of two hypotheses.* Manuscript submitted for publication.

Crocker, P.R.E. (1997). A confirmatory factor analysis of the Positive Affect Negative Affect Schedule (PANAS) with a youth sport sample. *Journal of Sport & Exercise Psychology, 19,* 91-97.

Crocker, P.R.E., Bouffard, M., & Gessaroli, M.E. (1995). Measuring enjoyment in youth sport settings: A confirmatory factor analysis of the Physical Activity Enjoyment Scale. *Journal of Sport & Exercise Psychology, 17,* 200-205.

Crocker, P.R.E., & Graham, T.R. (1995). Coping by competitive athletes with performance stress: Gender differences and relationships with affect. *The Sport Psychologist, 9,* 325-338.

Csikszentmihalyi, M. (1975). *Beyond boredom and anxiety.* San Francisco: Jossey-Bass.

Csikszentmihalyi, M. (1990). *Flow: The psychology of optimal experience.* New York: Harper & Row.

Csikszentmihalyi, M. (1993). *The evolving self.* New York: Harper Collins.

Csizma, K.A., Wittig, A.F., & Schurr, K.T. (1988). Sport stereotypes and gender. *Journal of Sport & Exercise Psychology, 10,* 62-74.

Cutrona, C.E. & Russell, D.W. (1987). The provisions of social relationships and adaptation to stress. In W.H. Jones and D. Perlman (Eds.), *Advances in personal relationships* (Vol. 1, pp. 37-67). Greenwich, CT: JAI Press.

Dashiell, J.F. (1935). Experimental studies of the influence of social situations on the behavior of individual human adults. In C. Murchison (Ed.), *A handbook of social psychology* (pp. 1097-1158). Worcester, MA: Clark University Press.

Davidson, R.J. & Schwartz, G.E. (1976). The psychobiology of relaxation and related states: A multi-process theory. In D.I. Mostofsky (Ed.), *Behavior control and modification of physiological activity* (pp. 399-442). Englewood Cliffs, NJ: Prentice Hall.

Dean, P. (1990, October 15). Bloody Sunday: Experts try to find reasons for increasing fan violence around the world. *Los Angeles Times,* p. E1.

Deaux, K. (1976). *The behavior of men and women.* Monterey, CA: Brooks/Cole.

Deaux, K. (1984). From individual differences to social categories: Analysis of a decade's research on gender. *American Psychologist, 39,* 105-116.

Deaux, K., & Kite, M.E. (1987). Thinking about gender. In B.B. Hess & M.M. Ferree (Eds.), *Analyzing gender* (pp. 92-117). Beverly Hills, CA: Sage.

Deaux, K., & Major, B. (1987). Putting gender into context: An interactive model of gender-related behavior. *Psychological Review, 94,* 369-389.

DeBusk, M., & Hellison, D.R. (1989). Implementing a physical education self-responsibility model for delinquency-prone youth. *Journal of Teaching Physical Education, 8,* 104-112.

Deci, E.L. (1975). *Intrinsic motivation.* New York: Plenum Press.

Deci, E.L., Betley, G., Kahle, J., Abrams, L., & Porac, J. (1981). When trying to win: Competition and intrinsic motivation. *Personality and Social Psychology Bulletin, 7,* 79-83.

Deci, E.L., & Ryan, R.M. (1985). *Intrinsic motivation and self-determination in human behavior.* New York: Plenum Press.

Deeter, T.E. (1989). Development of a model of achievement behavior for physical activity. *Journal of Sport & Exercise Psychology, 11,* 13-25.

Del Rey, P., & Sheppard, S. (1981). Relationship of psychological androgyny in female athletes to self-esteem. *International Journal of Sport Psychology, 12,* 165-175.

Dempsey, J.M., Kimiecik, J.C., & Horn, T.S. (1996). Parental influence on children's moderate to vigorous physical activity participation: An expectancy-value approach. *Pediatric and Exercise Science, 5,* 151-167.

Denmark, F.L., & Fernandez, L.C. (1993). Historical development of the psychology of women. In F.L. Denmark & M.A. Paludi (Eds.), *Psychology of women: A handbook of issues and theories* (pp. 3-22). Westport, CT: Greenwood Press.

Denzin, N.K., & Lincoln, Y.S. (1994). *Handbook on qualitative research.* Thousand Oaks, CA: Sage.

Deutsch, M. (1949). A theory of cooperation and competition. *Human Relations, 2,* 129-152.

Dewar, A., & Horn, T.S. (1992). A critical analysis of knowledge construction in sport psychology (pp. 13-22). In T.S. Horn (Ed.), *Advances in sport psychology.* Champaign, IL: Human Kinetics.

Dewey, D., Brawley, L.R., & Allard, F. (1989). Do the TAIS attentional-style scales predict how visual information is processed? *Journal of Sport & Exercise Psychology, 11,* 171-186.

Dickinson, J. (1977). *A behavioral analysis of sport.* Princeton, NJ: Princeton Books.

Diener, C.I., & Dweck, C.S. (1978). Analysis of learned helplessness: Continuous changes in performance, strategy, and achievement cognitions following failure. *Journal of Personality and Social Psychology, 36,* 451-462.

Diener, C.I., & Dweck, C.S. (1980). An analysis of learned helplessness II: The processing of success. *Journal of Personality and Social Psychology, 39,* 940-952.

Dishman, R.K. (1982). Contemporary sport psychology. In R.L. Terjung (Ed.), *Exercise and Sport Sciences Reviews* (Vol. 10, pp. 120-159). Philadelphia: Franklin Institute Press.

Dishman, R.K. (1984). Motivation and exercise adherence. In J.M. Silva & R.S. Weinberg (Eds.), *Psychological foundations of sport* (pp. 420-434). Champaign, IL: Human Kinetics.

Dishman, R.K. (1986). Exercise compliance: A new view for public health. *Physician and Sportsmedicine, 14,* 127-145.

Dishman, R.K. (1990). Determinants of participation in physical activity. In C. Bouchard, R.J. Shephard, T. Stephens, J.R. Sutton,

& B.D. McPherson (Eds.), *Exercise, fitness, and health* (75-102). Champaign, IL: Human Kinetics.

Dollard, J., Dobb, J., Miller, N., Mower, O., & Sears, R. (1939). *Frustration and aggression*. New Haven, CT: Yale University Press.

Donahue, J.A., Gillis, J.H., & King, K. (1980). Behavior modification in sport and physical education. *Journal of Sport Psychology, 2,* 311-328.

Doob, A.N. (1970). Catharsis and aggression: The effect of hurting one's enemy. *Journal of Experimental Research in Personality, 4,* 291-296.

Doob, A.N., & Wood, L. (1972). Catharsis and aggression: The effects of annoyance and retaliation on aggressive behavior. *Journal of Personality and Social Psychology, 22,* 156-162.

Duda, J.L. (1981). Achievement motivation among Navaho students: A conceptual analysis with preliminary data. In G.C. Roberts & D.M. Landers (Eds.), *Psychology of motor behavior and sport—1980.* Champaign, IL: Human Kinetics.

Duda, J.L. (1985). Goals and achievement orientations of Anglo and Mexican-American adolescents in sport and the classroom. *International Journal of Intercultural Relations, 9,* 131-155.

Duda, J.L. (1986a). A cross-cultural analysis of achievement motivation in sport and the classroom. In L. VanderVelden and J. Humphrey (Eds.), *Psychology and sociology in sport: Current selected research* (Vol. I, pp. 115-134). New York: AMS Press.

Duda, J.L. (1986b). Perceptions of sport success and failure among white, black, and Hispanic adolescents. In J. Watkins, T. Reilly, & L. Burwitz (Eds.), *Sport science* (pp. 214-222). London: Spon.

Duda, J.L. (1988). The relationship between goal perspectives and persistence and intensity among recreational sport participants. *Leisure Sciences, 10,* 95-106.

Duda, J.L. (1989a). Goal perspectives and behavior in sport and exercise settings. In C. Amers & M. Maehr (Eds.), *Advances in motivation and achievement* (Vol. VI, pp. 81-115). Greenwich, CT: JAI Press.

Duda, J.L. (1992). Motivation in sport settings: A goal perspective approach. In G.C. Roberts (Ed.), *Motivation in sport and exercise* (pp. 57-91). Champaign, IL: Human Kinetics.

Duda, J.L. & Allison, M.T. (1990). Cross-cultural analysis in exercise and sport psychology: A void in the field. *Journal of Sport & Exercise Psychology, 12,* 114-131.

Duda, J.L., Chi, L., Newton, M., Walling, M.D., & Catley, D. (1995). Task and ego orientation and intrinsic motivation in sport. *International Journal of Sport Psychology, 26,* 40-63.

Duda, J.L., Fox, K.R., Biddle, S.J.H., & Armstrong, N. (1992). Children's achievement goals and beliefs about success in sport. *British Journal of Educational Psychology, 62,* 313-323.

Duda, J.L., & Hom, H.L. (1993). Interdependencies between the perceived and self-reported goal orientations of young athletes and their parents. *Pediatric Exercise Science, 5,* 234-241.

Duda, J.L., Newton, M., & Chi, L. (1990, May). *The relationship of task and ego orientation and expectations to multidimensional state anxiety.* Paper presented at the annual meeting of the North American Society for the Psychology of Sport and Physical Activity, University of Houston, TX.

Duda, J.L., & Nicholls, J.G. (1992). Dimensions of achievement motivation in schoolwork and sport. *Journal of Educational Sport Psychology, 84,* 1-10.

Duda, J.L., Olson, L.K., & Templin, T.J. (1991). The relationship of task and ego orientation to sportsmanship attitudes and perceived legitimacy of injurious acts. *Research Quarterly for Exercise and Sport, 62,* 79-87.

Duda, J.L., & Tappe, M.K. (1988). Predictors of personal investment in physical activity among middle-aged and older adults. *Perceptual and Motor Skills, 66,* 3543-3549.

Duda, J.L., & Tappe, M.K. (1989). The Personal Incentives for Exercise Questionnaire: Preliminary development. *Perceptual and Motor Skills, 68,* 1122.

Duncan, S.C. (1993). The role of cognitive appraisal and friendship provisions in adolescents' affect and motivation toward activ-

ity in physical education. *Research Quarterly for Exercise and Sport, 64,* 314-323.

Duncan, T.E., & McAuley, E. (1993). Social support and efficacy cognitions in exercise adherence: A latent growth curve analysis. *Journal of Behavioral Medicine, 16* (2), 199-218.

Durkheim, E. (1951). *Suicide: A study in sociology.* Glencoe, IL: Free Press.

Duval, S., & Wicklund, R.A. (1972). *A theory of objective self-awareness.* New York: Academic Press.

Dweck, C.S. (1975). The role of expectations and attributions in the alleviation of learned helplessness. *Journal of Personality and Social Psychology, 31,* 674-685.

Dweck, C.S. (1978). Achievement. In M.E. Lamb (Ed.), *Social and personality development* (pp. 114-130). New York: Holt, Reinhart & Winston.

Dweck, C.S. (1986). Motivational processes affecting learning. *American Psychologist, 41,* 1040-1048.

Dweck, C.S., & Elliott, E.S. (1983). Achievement motivation. In E.M. Hetherington (Ed.), *Handbook of child psychology: Socialization, personality, and social development* (3rd ed., pp. 643-691). New York: Wiley.

Dweck, C.S., & Leggett, E.L. (1988). A social-cognitive approach to motivation and personality. *Psychological Review, 95,* 256-269.

Dwyer, J.J.M. (1992). Informal structure of participation motivation questionnaire completed by undergraduates. *Psychological Reports, 70,* 283-290.

Dzewaltowski, D.A. (1989). Toward a model of exercise motivation. *Journal of Sport & Exercise Psychology, 11,* 251-269.

Dzewaltowski, D.A. (1997). The ecology of physical activity and sport: Merging science and practice. *Journal of Applied Sport Psychology, 9* (2), 254-276.

Dzewaltowski, D.A., Noble, J.M., & Shaw, J.M. (1990). Physical activity participation: Social cognitive theory versus the theories of reasoned action and planned behavior. *Journal of Sport & Exercise Psychology, 12,* 388-405.

Eagley, A.H. (1987). *Sex differences in social behavior: A social-role interpretation.* Hillsdale, NJ: Erlbaum.

Eagley, A.H., & Steffen, V.J. (1986). Gender and aggressive behavior: A meta-analytical review of the social psychological literature. *Psychological Bulletin, 100,* 309-330.

Easterbrook, J.A. (1959). The effect of emotion on cue utilization and the organization of behavior. *Psychological Review, 66,* 183-201.

Ebbeck, V., & Becker, S.L. (1994). Psychosocial predictors of goal orientations in youth soccer. *Research Quarterly for Exercise and Sport, 65,* 355-362.

Ebbeck, V., & Gibbons, S.L. (1998). The effect of a team building program on the self-conceptions of grade 6 and 7 physical education students. *Journal of Sport & Exercise Psychology, 20,* 300-310.

Eccles, J.S. (1985). Sex differences in achievement patterns. In T. Sonderegger (Ed.), *Nebraska Symposium on Motivation, 1984: Psychology and gender* (pp. 97-132). Lincoln, NE: University of Nebraska Press.

Eccles, J.S. (1987). Gender roles and women's achievement-related decisions. *Psychology of Women Quarterly, 11,* 135-172.

Eccles, J.S., Adler, T.F., Futterman, R., Goff, S.B., Kaczala, C.M., Meece, J.L., & Midgley, C. (1983). Expectations, values and academic behaviors. In J. Spence (Ed.), *Achievement and achievement motives* (pp. 75-146). San Francisco: Freeman.

Eccles, J.S., & Harrold, R.D. (1991). Gender differences in sport involvement: Applying the Eccles' expectancy-value model. *Journal of Applied Sport Psychology, 3,* 7-35.

Edwards, T., & Hardy, L. (1996). The interactive effects of intensity and direction of cognitive and somatic anxiety and self-confidence upon performance. *Journal of Sport & Exercise Psychology, 18,* 296-312.

Ehrenreich, B. (1996, July). The real swimsuit issue. *Time,* p. 68.

Eitzen, D.S., & Baca Zinn, M. (1993). The de-athleticization of women: The naming and gender marking of collegiate sports teams. In D.S. Eitzen (Ed.), *Sport in contemporary society: An anthology* (4th ed., pp. 396-405). New York: St. Martin's Press.

Ellis, A. (1982). Self-direction in sport and life. *Rational Living, 17,* 27-33.

Ellis, A. & Dryden, W. (1987). *The practice of rational emotive therapy.* New York: Springer.

Erikson, E.H. (1968). *Identity: Youth and crisis.* New York: Norton.

Evans, J., & Roberts, G.C. (1987). Physical competence and the development of children's peer relations. *Quest, 39,* 23-35.

Everett, J.J., Smith, R.E., & Williams, K.D. (1992). Effects of team cohesion and identifiability on social loafing in relay swimming performance. *International Journal of Sport Psychology, 23,* 311-324.

Ewart, C.K., Stewart, K.J., Gillian, R.E., Keleman, M.H., Valenti, S.A., Manley, J.D., & Kaleman, M.D. (1986). Usefulness of self-efficacy in predicting overexertion during programmed exercise in coronary artery disease. *American Journal of Cardiology, 57,* 557-561.

Ewart, C.K., Taylor, C.B., Reese, L.B., & DeBusk, R.F. (1983). Effects of early post myocardial infarction exercise testing on self-perception and subsequent physical activity. *American Journal of Cardiology, 51,* 1076-1080.

Eysenck, H.J. (1991). Dimensions of personality: 16, 5, or 3?—Criteria for a taxonomic paradigm. *Personality and Individual Differences, 12,* 773-790.

Feltz, D.L. (1982). The effects of age and number of demonstrations on modeling of form and performance. *Research Quarterly for Exercise and Sport, 53,* 291-296.

Feltz, D.L. (1984a). Path analysis of the causal elements in Bandura's theory of self-efficacy and an anxiety-based model of avoidance behavior. *Journal of Personality and Social Psychology, 42,* 764-781.

Feltz, D.L. (1984b). Self-efficacy as a cognitive mediator of athletic performance. In W.F. Straub & J.M. Williams (Eds.), *Cognitive sport psychology* (pp. 191-198). Lansing, NY: Sport Science Associates.

Feltz, D.L. (1988). Self-confidence and sports performance. In K.B. Pandolf (Ed.), *Exercise and Sport Sciences Reviews* (pp. 423-457) vol. 16. New York: Macmillan.

Feltz, D.L., Landers, D.L., & Raeder, U. (1979). Enhancing self-efficacy in high avoidance motor tasks: A comparison of modeling techniques. *Journal of Sport Psychology, 1,* 112-122.

Feltz, D.L., & Landers, D.M. (1977). Informational-motivational components of a model's demonstration. *Research Quarterly for Exercise and Sport, 48,* 525-533.

Feltz, D.L., & Landers, D.M. (1983). The effects of mental practice on motor skill learning and performance: A meta-analysis. *Journal of Sport Psychology, 5,* 25-57.

Feltz, D.L., & Mugno, D.A. (1983). A replication of the path analysis of the causal elements in Bandura's theory of self-efficacy and the influence of autonomic perception. *Journal of Sport Psychology, 5,* 262-277.

Fenz, W.D. (1975). Coping mechanisms and performance under stress. In D.M. Landers, R.W. Christina, & D.V. Harris (Eds.), *Psychology of sport and motor behavior-II* (pp. 3-24). University Park, PA: Pennsylvania State University.

Fenz, W.D. (1988). Learning to anticipate stressful events. *Journal of Sport & Exercise Psychology, 10,* 223-228.

Fenz, W.D., & Jones, G.B. (1974). Cardiac conditioning in a reaction time task and heart rate control during real life stress. *Journal of Psychosomatic Research, 18,* 199-203.

Festinger, L., Schachter, S., & Back, K. (1950). *Social pressures in informal groups.* New York: Harper & Row.

Fiedler, F.E. (1954). Assumed similarity measures as predictors of team effectiveness. *Journal of Abnormal and Social Psychology, 49,* 381-388.

Fiedler, F.E. (1967). *A theory of leadership effectiveness.* New York: McGraw-Hill.

Fishbein, M., & Ajzen, I. (1974). Attitudes toward objects as predictors of single and multiple behavioral criteria. *Psychological Review, 81,* 59-74.

Fisher, A.C. (1976). *Psychology of sport.* Palo Alto, CA: Mayfield.

Fisher, A.C., Ryan, E.D., & Martens, R. (1976). Current status and future directions of personality research related to motor be-

havior and sport: Three panelists' views. In A.C. Fisher (Ed.), *Psychology of sport* (pp. 400-431). Palo Alto, CA: Mayfield.

Folkins, C.H., & Sime, W.E. (1981). Physical fitness training and mental health. *American Psychologist, 36,* 373-389.

Ford, D., & Lerner, R. (1992). *Developmental systems theory.* Newbury Park, CA: Sage.

Forscher, B.K. (1963). Chaos in the brickyard. *Science, 142,* 3590.

Forsterling, F. (1988). *Attribution theory in clinical psychology.* Chichester, England: Wiley.

Fox, K.H. (1990). *The Physical Self-Perception Profile manual.* DeKalb, IL: Northern Illinois University, Office for Health Promotion.

Fox, K.R., & Corbin, C.B. (1989). The Physical Self-Perception Profile: Development and preliminary validation. *Journal of Sport & Exercise Psychology, 11,* 408-430.

Franzoi, S.L., & Shields, S.A. (1984). The Body Esteem Scale: Multi-dimensional structure and sex differences in a college population. *Journal of Personality Assessment, 48,* 173-178.

Frederick, C.M., & Ryan, R.M. (1993). Differences in motivation for sport and exercise and their relations with participation and mental health. *Journal of Sport Behavior, 16* (3), 124-146.

Frederick, C.M., & Ryan, R.M. (1995). Self-determination in sport: A review using Cognitive Evaluation Theory. *International Journal of Sport Psychology, 26,* 5-23.

Freedson, P.S., & Evenson, S. (1991). Familial aggregation in physical activity. *Research Quarterly for Exercise and Sport, 62,* 384-389.

Frieze, I.H., Parsons, J.E., Johnson, P.B., Ruble, D.N., & Zellman, G.L. (1978). *Women and sex roles: A social psychological perspective.* New York: Norton.

Frodi, A., Macauley, J., & Thome, P.R. (1977). Are women always less aggressive than men? A review of the experimental literature. *Psychological Bulletin, 84,* 638-660.

Gaebelein, J., & Taylor, S. (1971). The effects of competition and attack on physical aggression. *Psychonomic Science, 24,* 65-67.

Galton, F. (1883). *Inquiries into human faculty and its development.* London: Macmillan.

Garner, D.M. (1984). *Eating Disorder Inventory-2 professional manual.* Odessa, FL: Psychological Assessment Resources.

Gartside, P.S., Khoury, P., & Glueck, C.J. (1984). Determinants of high-density lipo-protein cholesterol in blacks and whites: The second National Health and Nutrition Examination Survey. *American Heart Journal, 108,* 641.

Gauron, E.F. (1984). *Mental training for peak performance.* Lansing, NY: Sport Science Associates.

Gauvin, L. (1990). An experiential perspective on the motivational features of exercise and lifestyle. *Canadian Journal of Sport Sciences, 15,* 51-58.

Gauvin, L., & Brawley, L.R. (1993). Alternative psychological models and methodologies for the study of exercise and affect. In P. Seraganian (Ed.), *Exercise psychology: The influence of physical exercise on psychological processes* (pp. 146-171). New York: Wiley.

Gayton, W.F., Matthews, G.R., & Burchstead, G.N. (1986). An investigation of the validity of the physical self-efficacy scale in predicting marathon performance. *Perceptual and Motor Skills, 63,* 752-754.

Gedvilas, L.I., & Kneer, M.E. (Eds.). 1977. *Proceedings of the NAPECW/NCPEAM National Conference, 1977.* Chicago: University of Illinois at Chicago Circle, Office of Publications Services.

Geen, R.G., & Gange, J.G. (1977). Drive theory of social facilitation: Twelve years of theory and research. *Psychological Bulletin, 84,* 1267-1288.

Geen, R.G., Stonner, D., & Shope, G.L. (1975). The facilitation of aggression by aggression: Evidence against the catharsis hypothesis. *Journal of Personality and Social Psychology, 31,* 721-726.

Geis, F.L. (1993). Self-fulfilling prophecies: A social psychological view of gender. In A.E. Beall & R.J. Sternberg (Eds.), *The psychology of gender* (pp. 9-54). New York: Guilford.

Giannini, J., Weinberg, R.S., & Jackson, A. (1988). The effects of master, competitive and cooperative goals on the performance of simple and complex basketball skills. *Journal of Sport & Exercise Psychology, 10,* 408-417.

Gibbons, S.L., Ebbeck, V., & Weiss, M.R. (1995). Fair play for kids: Effects on the moral development of children in physical education. *Research Quarterly for Exercise and Sport, 66,* 247-255.

Gibson, A. (1979). I always wanted to be somebody. In S.L. Twin (Ed.), *Out of the bleachers* (pp. 130-142). Old Westbury, NY: Feminist Press.

Gill, D.L. (1977). The influence of group success-failure and relative ability on intrapersonal variables. *Research Quarterly, 48,* 685-694.

Gill, D.L. (1978). The influence of competition on individual and group motor performance. *Journal of Human Movement Studies, 4,* 36-43.

Gill, D.L. (1979). The prediction of group motor performance from individual member abilities. *Journal of Motor Behavior, 11,* 113-122.

Gill, D.L. (1986). *Psychological dynamics of sport.* Champaign, IL: Human Kinetics.

Gill, D.L. (1988). Gender differences in competitive orientation and sport participation. *International Journal of Sport Psychology, 19,* 145-159.

Gill, D.L. (1992). Gender and sport behavior. In T.S. Horn (Ed.), *Advances in sport psychology* (pp. 143-160). Champaign, IL: Human Kinetics.

Gill, D.L. (1993). Competitiveness and competitive orientation in sport. In R.A. Singer, M. Murphey, & L.K. Tennant (Eds.), *Handbook of research on sport psychology* (pp. 314-327). New York: Macmillan.

Gill, D.L. (1994). A sport and exercise psychology perspective on stress. *Quest, 46,* 20-27.

Gill, D.L. (1995). Gender issues: A social-educational perspective. In S.M. Murphy (Ed.), *Sport psychology interventions* (pp. 205-234). Champaign, IL: Human Kinetics.

Gill, D.L. (1997). Sport and exercise psychology. In J. Massengale & R. Swanson (Eds.), *History of exercise and sport science* (pp. 293-320). Champaign, IL: Human Kinetics.

Gill, D.L., & Deeter, T.E. (1988). Development of the Sport Orientation Questionnaire. *Research Quarterly for Exercise and Sport, 59,* 191-202.

Gill, D.L., Dowd, D.A., Williams, L., Beaudoin, C.M., & Martin, J.J. (1996). Competitive orientation and motives of adult sport and exercise participants. *Journal of Sport Behavior, 19,* 307-318.

Gill, D.L., & Dzewaltowski, D.A. (1988). Competitive orientations among intercollegiate athletes: Is winning the only thing? *The Sport Psychologist, 2,* 212-221.

Gill, D.L., & Gross, J.B. (1979). The influences of group success-failure on selected intrapersonal variables. In G.C. Roberts & K.M. Newell (Eds.), *Psychology of motor behavior and sport—1978* (pp. 61-71). Champaign, IL: Human Kinetics.

Gill, D.L., Gross, J.B., & Huddleston, S. (1983). Participation motivation in youth sports. *International Journal of Sport Psychology, 14,* 1-14.

Gill, D.L., & Martens, R. (1975). The informational and motivational influence of social reinforcement on motor performance. *Journal of Motor Behavior, 7,* 171-182.

Gill, D.L., & Perry, J.L. (1979). A case study of leadership in women's intercollegiate softball. *International Review of Sport Sociology, 14,* 83-91.

Gill, D.L., Ruder, M.K., & Gross, J.B. (1982). Open-ended attributions in team competition. *Journal of Sport Psychology, 4,* 159-169.

Gill, D.L., & Strom, E.H. (1985). The effect of attentional focus on performance of an endurance task. *International Journal of Sport Psychology, 16,* 217-223.

Glasser, W. (1976). *Positive addiction.* New York: Harper & Row.

Godin, G. (1993). The theories of reasoned action and planned behavior: Overview of findings, emerging research problems, and usefulness for exercise promotion. *Journal of Applied Sport Psychology, 5,* 141-157.

Goldberg, L.R. (1993). The structure of phenotypic personality traits. *American Psychologist, 48,* 26-34.

Goldberg, P. (1968). Are women prejudiced against women. *Transaction, 5,* 28-30.

Goldstein, J., & Arms, R. (1971). Effects of observing athletic contests on hostility. *Sociometry, 54,* 83-91.

Gordon, R. (1949). An investigation into some of the factors that favour the formation of stereotyped images. *British Journal of Psychology, 39,* 156-167.

Gould, D. (1978). *The influence of motor task types on model effectiveness.* Unpublished doctoral dissertation, University of Illinois at Urbana-Champaign.

Gould, D. (1982). Sport psychology in the 1980's: Status, direction and challenge in youth sports research. *Journal of Sport Psychology, 4,* 203-218.

Gould, D. (1993). Intensive sports participation and the prepubescent athlete: Competitive stress and burnout effects. In B. Cahill (Ed.), *Intensive training and participation in youth sports* (pp. 19-36). Champaign, IL: Human Kinetics.

Gould, D., & Damarjian, N. (1996). Imagery training for peak performance. In J.L. Van Raalte & B.W. Brewer (Eds.), *Exploring sport and exercise psychology* (pp. 25-50). Washington, DC: American Psychological Association.

Gould, D., Eklund, R.C., & Jackson, S.A. (1992). 1988 U.S. Olympic wrestling excellence: I. Mental preparation, precompetitive cognition, and affect. *The Sport Psychologist, 6,* 358-382.

Gould, D., Feltz, D., Horn, T., & Weiss, M. (1982). Reasons for attrition in competitive youth swimming. *Journal of Sport Behavior, 5,* 155-165.

Gould, D., Feltz, D., & Weiss, M. (1985). Motives for participating in competitive youth swimming. *International Journal of Sport Psychology, 6,* 126-140.

Gould, D., & Krane, V. (1992). The arousal-athletic performance relationship: Current status and future directions. In T. Horn (Ed.), *Advances in sport psychology* (pp. 119-141). Champaign, IL: Human Kinetics.

Gould, D., & Petlichkoff, L. (1988). Participation motivation and attrition in young athletes. In F.L. Smoll, R.J. Magill, & M.J. Ash (Eds.), *Children in sport* (3rd ed., pp. 161-178). Champaign, IL: Human Kinetics.

Gould, D., Petlichkoff, L., Simons, J., & Vevera, M. (1987). Relationship between Competitive State Anxiety-2 subscale scores and pistol shooting performance. *Journal of Sport Psychology, 9,* 33-42.

Gould, D., Petlichkoff, L., & Weinberg, R.S. (1984). Antecedents of, temporal changes in, and relationships between CSAI-2 subcomponents. *Journal of Sport Psychology, 6,* 289-304.

Gould, D., & Pick, S. (1995). Sport psychology: The Griffith era, 1920-1940. *The Sport Psychologist, 9,* 391-405.

Gould, D., Tammen, V., Murphy, S., & May, J. (1989). An examination of U.S. Olympic sport psychology consultants and the services they provide. *The Sport Psychologist, 3,* 300-312.

Gould, D., & Weiss, M.R. (1981). The effects of model similarity and model talk on self-efficacy and muscular endurance. *Journal of Sport Psychology, 3,* 17-29.

Gould, D., Weiss, M., & Weinberg, R. (1981). Psychological characteristics of successful and nonsuccessful Big Ten wrestlers. *Journal of Sport Psychology, 3,* 69-81.

Grace, H. (1954). Conformance and performance. *Journal of Social Psychology, 40,* 233-237.

Green, T.S. (1993). The future of African-American female athletes. In D. Brooks & R. Althouse (Eds.), *Racism in college athletics: The African-American athlete's experience.* Morgantown, WV: Fitness Information Technology.

Greendorfer, S. (1977). Role of socializing agents in female sport involvement. *Research Quarterly for Exercise and Sport, 48,* 305-310.

Greendorfer, S.L., & Blinde, E.M. (1985). "Retirement" from intercollegiate sport: Theoretical and empirical considerations. *Sociology of Sport Journal, 2,* 101-110.

Greendorfer, S.L., Lewko, J.H., & Rosengren, K.S. (1996). Family and gender-based influences in sport socialization of children and adolescents. In F.L. Smoll & R.E. Smith (Eds.), *Children and youth in sport: A biopsychosocial perspective.* Madison, WI: Brown & Benchmark.

Greene, D., & Lepper, M.R. (1974). Effects of extrinsic rewards on children's subsequent intrinsic interest. *Child Development, 45,* 1141-1145.

Griffin, P. (1992). Changing the game: Homophobia, sexism, and lesbians in sport. *Quest, 44,* 251-265.

Griffin, P.S. (1987, August). *Homophobia, lesbians, and women's sports: An exploratory analysis.* Paper presented at the American Psychological Association convention, New York.

Griffith, C.R. (1925). Psychology and its relation to athletic competition. *American Physical Education Review, 30,* 193-198.

Griffith, C.R. (1926). *Psychology of coaching.* New York: Scribners.

Griffith, C.R. (1928). *Psychology and athletics.* New York: Scribners.

Gross, J.B., & Gill, D.L. (1982). Competition and instructional set effects on the speed and accuracy of a throwing task. *Research Quarterly for Exercise and Sport, 53,* 125-132.

Grove, J.R., Hanrahan, S.J., & McInman, A. (1991). Success/failure bias in attributions across involvement categories in sport. *Personality and Social Psychology Bulletin, 17,* 93-97.

Grusky, O. (1963). The effects of formal structure on managerial recruitment: A study of baseball organization. *Sociometry, 26,* 345-353.

Guastello, S.J. (1987). A butterfly catastrophe model of motivation in organizations: Academic performance. *Journal of Applied Psychology, 72,* 161-182.

Guernsey, L. (1993, February 10). More campuses offer rape-prevention programs for male athletes. *Chronicle of Higher Education,* pp. A35, A37.

Haan, N. (1991). Moral development and action from a social constructivist perspective. In W.M. Kurtines & J.L. Gerwitz (Eds.), *Handbook of moral behavior and development: Vol. 1. Theory.* Hillsdale, NJ: Erlbaum.

Hall, C.R., Pongrac, J., & Buckolz, E. (1985). The measurement of imagery ability. *Human Movement Science, 4,* 107-118.

Hall, C.R., Rodgers, W.M., & Barr, K.A. (1990). The use of imagery by athletes in selected sports. *The Sport Psychologist, 4,* 1-10.

Hall, G.S. (1908). Physical education in colleges. *Report of the National Educaiton Association.* Chicago: University of Chicago Press.

Halliwell, W.R. (1978). The effect of cognitive development on children's perceptions of intrinsically motivated behavior. In D.M. Landers & R.W. Christina (Eds.), *Psychology of motor behavior and sport—1977* (pp. 403-419). Champaign, IL: Human Kinetics.

Hanin, Y. (1989). Interpersonal and intragroup anxiety in sports. In D. Hackfort & C.D. Spielberger (Eds.), *Anxiety in sports: An international perspective* (pp. 19-28). Washington, DC: Hemisphere.

Hanin, Y. (1995). Individual zones of optimal functioning (IZOF) model: An idiographic approach to anxiety. In K. Henschen & W. Straub (Eds.), *Sport psychology: An analysis of athlete behavior* (pp. 103-119). Longmeadow, MA: Mouvement.

Hanin, Y., & Syrja, P. (1996). Predicted, actual, and recalled affect in Olympic-level soccer players: Idiographic assessments on individualized scales. *Journal of Sport & Exercise Psychology, 18,* 325-335.

Hardy, C.J., & Crace, R.K. (1993). The dimensions of social support when dealing with sport injuries. In D. Pargman (Ed.), *Psychological bases of sport injuries* (pp. 121-144). Morgantown, WV: Fitness Technology.

Hardy, C.J., & Crace, R.K. (1997). Foundations of team building: Introduction to the team building primer. *Journal of Applied Sport Psychology, 9,* 1-10.

Hardy, C.J., & Rejeski, W.J. (1989). Not what, but how one feels: The measurement of affect during exercise. *Journal of Sport & Exercise Psychology, 11,* 304-317.

Hardy, L. (1990). A catastrophe model of performance in sport. In J.G. Jones & L. Hardy (Eds.), *Stress and performance in sport* (pp. 81-106). Chichester, England: Wiley.

Hardy, L. (1996). Testing the predictions of the cusp catastrophe model of anxiety and performance. *The Sport Psychologist, 10,* 140-156.

Hardy, L., & Fazey, J. (1987, June). *The inverted-U hypothesis: A catastrophe for sport psychology.* Paper presented at the meeting of the North American Society for the Psychology of Sport and Physical Activity, Vancouver, BC.

Hardy, L., & Parfitt, C.G. (1991). A catastrophe model of anxiety and performance. *British Journal of Psychology, 82,* 163-178.

Hardy, L., Parfitt, C.G., & Pates, J. (1994). Performance catastrophes in sport. *Journal of Sport Sciences, 12,* 327-334.

Harkins, S.G. (1987). Social loafing and social facilitation. *Experimental Social Psychology, 23,* 1-18.

Harkins, S.G. & Szymanski, K. (1987). Social loafing and social facilitation: New wine in old bottles. In C. Hendrick (Ed.), *Group processes and intergroup relations* (pp. 167-188). Newburg Park, CA: Sage.

Harney, D.M., & Parker, R. (1972). Effects of social reinforcement, subject sex, and experimenter sex on children's motor performance. *Research Quarterly, 43,* 187-196.

Harris, D.V., & Harris, B.L. (1984). *The athlete's guide to sports psychology: Mental skills for physical people.* New York: Leisure Press.

Harris, D.V., & Jennings, S.E. (1977). Self-perceptions of female distance runners. *Annals of the New York Academy of Sciences, 301,* 808-815.

Hart, E.A., Leary, M.R., & Rejeski, W.J. (1989). The measurement of social physique anxiety. *Journal of Sport & Exercise Psychology, 11,* 94-104.

Harter, S. (1978). Effacance motivation reconsidered. *Human Development, 21,* 34-64.

Harter, S. (1981a). The development of competence motivation in the mastery of cognitive and physical skills: Is there still a place for joy? In G.C. Roberts & D.M. Landers (Eds.), *Psychology of motor behavior and sport—1980* (pp. 3-29). Champaign, IL: Human Kinetics.

Harter, S. (1981b). A model of intrinsic mastery motivation in children: Individual differences and developmental change. In W. A. Collins (Ed.), *Minnesota Symposium on Child Psychology* (pp. 215-255). Hillsdale, NJ: Erlbaum.

Harter, S. (1983). Developmental perspectives on the self-system. In E.M. Hetherington (Ed.), *Handbook of child psychology: Social and personality development* (Vol. 4, pp. 275-385). New York: Wiley.

Harter, S. (1985). *Manual for the Self-Perception Profile for Children.* Denver: University of Denver.

Harter, S. (1990). Causes, correlates and the functional role of global self-worth: A life-span perspective. In R.J. Sternberg & J. Kolligan (Eds.), *Competence considered* (pp. 67-97). New Haven, CT: Yale University Press.

Hatfield, B.D., Landers, D.M., & Ray, W.J. (1984). Cognitive processes during self-paced motor performance: An electroencephalographic profile of skilled marksmen. *Journal of Sport Psychology, 6,* 42-59.

Haywood, K.M. (1993). *Life span motor development* (2nd ed.). Champaign, IL: Human Kinetics.

Heider, F. (1958). *The psychology of interpersonal relations.* New York: Wiley.

Heil, J., & Henschen, K. (1996). Assessment in sport and exercise psychology. In J.L. Van Raalte & B.W. Brewer (Eds.), *Exploring sport and exercise psychology* (pp. 229-255). Washington, DC: American Psychological Association.

Heinzelmann, F., & Bagley, R.W. (1970). Response to physical activity programs and their effects on health behavior. *Public Health Report, 85,* 905-911.

Hellison, D.R. (1995). *Teaching responsibility through physical activity.* Champaign, IL: Human Kinetics.

Hellison, D.R. (1996). Teaching personal and social responsibility in physical education. In S.J. Silverman & E.D. Ennis (Eds.), *Student learning in physical education: Applying research to enhance instruction* (pp. 269-286). Champaign, IL: Human Kinetics.

Hellison, D.R., Martinek, T.J., & Cutforth, N.J. (1996). Beyond violence prevention in inner-city physical activity programs. *Peace and Conflict: Journal of Peace Psychology, 2,* 321-337.

Hellison, D.R., & Templin, T.J. (1991). *A reflective approach to teaching physical education.* Champaign, IL: Human Kinetics.

Helmreich, R.L., & Spence, J.T. (1977). Sex roles and achievement. In R.W. Christina & D.M. Landers (Eds.), *Psychology of motor behavior and sport—1976* (Vol. 2, pp. 33-46). Champaign, IL: Human Kinetics.

Hertz-Lazarowitz, R., & Miller, N. (Eds.). (1992). *Interaction in cooperative groups.* New York: Cambridge University Press.

Heyman, S.R. (1993). When to refer athletes for counseling or psychotherapy. In J.M. Williams (Ed.) *Applied sport psychology: Personal growth to peak performance* (2nd ed., pp. 299-308). Mountain View, CA: Mayfield.

Heyman, S.R., & Andersen, M.B. (1998). When to refer athletes for counseling or psychotherapy. In J.M. Williams (Ed.), *Applied sport psychology: Personal growth to peak performance* (3rd ed., pp. 359-371). Mountain View, CA: Mayfield.

Highlen, P.S., & Bennett, B.B. (1979). Psychological characteristics of successful and nonsuccessful elite wrestlers: An exploratory study. *Journal of Sport Psychology, 1,* 123-137.

Highlen, P.S., & Bennett, B.B. (1983). Elite divers and wrestlers: A comparison between open- and closed-skill athletes. *Journal of Sport Psychology, 5,* 390-409.

Holloway, J.B., Beuter, A., & Duda, J.L. (1988). Self-efficacy and training for strength in adolescent girls. *Journal of Applied Social Psychology, 18,* 699-719.

Holmes, D.S. (1993). Aerobic fitness and the response to psychological stress. In P. Seraganian (Ed.), *Exercise psychology: The influence of physical exercise on psychological processes* (pp. 39-63). New York: Wiley.

Horn, T.S. (1984). Expectancy effects in the interscholastic setting: Methodological considerations. *Journal of Sport Psychology, 6,* 60-76.

Horn, T.S., Glenn, S.D., & Wnetzell, A.M. (1993). Sources of information underlying personal ability judgments of high school athletes. *Pediatric Exercise Science, 5,* 263-274.

Horn, T.S., & Weiss, M.R. (1991). A developmental analysis of children's self-ability judgments in the physical domain. *Pediatric Exercise Science, 3,* 310-326.

Horner, M.S. (1972). Toward an understanding of achievement-related conflicts in women. *Journal of Social Issues, 28,* 157-176.

Horney, K. (1950). *Neurosis and human growth.* New York: Norton.

Hovland, C.I., Janis, I.L., & Kelley, H.H. (1953). *Communication and persuasion.* New Ha2ven, CT: Yale University Press.

Hughes, J.R. (1984). Psychological effects of habitual aerobic exercise: A critical review. *Preventive Medicine, 13,* 66-78.

Hull, C.L. (1943). *Principles of behavior.* New York: Appleton-Century-Crofts.

Husman, B.F., & Silva, J.M. (1984). Aggression in sport: Definitional and theoretical considerations. In J.M. Silva & R.S. Weinberg (Eds.), *Psychological foundations of sport* (pp. 246-260). Champaign, IL: Human Kinetics.

Hyde, J.S., & Linn, M.C. (Eds.). (1986). *The psychology of gender: Advances through meta-analysis.* Baltimore: Johns Hopkins University Press.

Ingham, A.G., Levinger, G., Graves, J., & Peckham, V. (1974). The Ringelmann effect: Studies of group size and group performance. *Journal of Experimental Social Psychology, 10,* 371-384.

Iso-Ahola, S. (1977). Effects of team outcome on children's self-perception: Little league baseball. *Scandinavian Journal of Psychology, 18,* 38-42.

Jacklin, C.N. (1989). Female and male: Issues of gender. *American Psychologist, 44,* 127-133.

Jackson, J.M., & Williams, K.D. (1985). Social loafing on difficult tasks: Working collectively can improve performance. *Journal of Personality and Social Psychology, 49,* 937-942.

Jackson, S.A. (1995). Factors influencing the occurrence of flow state in elite athletes. *Journal of Applied Sport Psychology, 7,* 138-166.

Jackson, S.A., & Marsh, H.W. (1996). Development and validation of a scale to measure optimal experience: The flow state scale. *Journal of Sport & Exercise Psychology, 18,* 17-35.

Jacobi, M.P. (1877). *The question of rest for women during menstruation.* New York: Putnam.

Jacobson, E. (1931). Electrical measurements of neuromuscular states during mental activities. *American Journal of Physiology, 96.*

Jacobson, E. (1938). *Progressive relaxation.* Chicago: University of Chicago Press.

James, W. (1884). What is an emotion? *Mind, 9,* 188-204.

James, W. (1890). *The principles of psychology* (Vol. 1). New York: Holt.

James, W. (1892). *Psychology: Briefer course.* New York: Holt.

Janis, I.L., & Mann, L. (1977). *Decision making: A psychological analysis of conflict, choice and commitment.* New York: Free Press.

Janz, N.K., & Becker, M.H. (1984). The health belief model: A decade later. *Health Education Quarterly, 11* (1), 1-47.

John, O.P. (1990). The "Big Five" factor taxonomy: Dimensions of personality in the natural language and in questionnaires. In L.A. Pervin (Ed.), *Handbook of personality: Theory and research* (pp. 66-100). New York: Guilford.

Johnson, D.W., & Johnson, R.T. (1992). Positive interdependence: Key to effective cooperation. In R. Hertz-Lazarowitz & N. Miller (Eds.), *Interaction in cooperative groups* (pp. 174-199). New York: Cambridge University Press.

Johnson, L., & Biddle, S.J.H. (1988). Persistence after failure: An exploratory look at "learned helplessness" in motor performance. *British Journal of Physical Education Research Supplement, 5,* 7-10.

Johnson, W.R. (1949). A study of emotion revealed in two types of athletic sport contests. *Research Quarterly, 20,* 72-79.

Jones, E.E. (1964). *Ingratiation.* New York: Appleton-Century-Crofts.

Jones, M.B. (1974). Regressing group on individual effectiveness. *Organizational Behavior and Human Performance, 11,* 426-451.

Joseph, P., & Robbins, J.M. (1981). Worker or runner? The impact of commitment to running and work on self-identification. In M. Sacks & M. Sachs (Eds.), *Psychology of running* (pp. 131-149). Champaign, IL: Human Kinetics.

Kagan, D.M., & Squires, R.L. (1985). Addictive aspects of physical exercise. *Journal of Sports Medicine, 25,* 227-237.

Kagan, J. (1995). *Galen's prophecy: Temperament in human nature.* New York: Basic Books.

Kahneman, D. (1973). *Attention and effort.* Englewood Cliffs, NJ: Prentice-Hall.

Kane, M.J. (1989). The post Title IX female athlete in the media. *Journal of Physical Education, Recreation, and Dance, 60,* 58-62.

Kane, M.J., & Parks, J.B. (1992). The social construction of gender difference and hierarchy in sport journalism—few new twists on very old themes. *Women in Sport and Physical Activity Journal, 1,* 49-83.

Kane, M.J., & Snyder, E. (1989). Sport "typing": The social "containment" of women. *Arena Review, 13,* 77-96.

Kang, L., Gill, D.L., Acevedo, E.D., & Deeter, T.E. (1990). Competitive orientations among athletes and nonathletes in Taiwan. *International Journal of Sport Psychology, 21,* 146-152.

Kann, L., Kinchen S.A., Williams, B.I., Ross, J.G., Loury, R., Hill, C.V., et al. 1998. Youth Risk Behavior Surveillance—United States, 1997. In CDC Surveillance Summaries, August 14, 1998. *Morbidity and Mortality Weekly Report* 47 (No. 55-3): 1-89.

Karau, S.J. & Williams, K.D. (1993). Social loafing: A meta-analytic review and theoretical integration. *Journal of Personality and Social Psychology, 65,* 681-706.

Karau, S.J., & Williams, K.D. (1995). Social loafing: Research findings, implications, and future directions. *Psychological Science, 4* (5), 134-139.

Kauss, D.R. (1980). *Peak performance.* Englewood Cliffs, NJ: Prentice-Hall.

Keele, S.W. (1973). *Attention and human performance.* Pacific Palisades, CA: Goodyear.

Kelley, B.C. (1994). A model of stress and burnout in collegiate coaches: Effects of gender and time of season. *Research Quarterly for Exercise and Sport, 65,* 48-58.

Kelley, B.C., & Gill, D.L. (1993). An examination of personal/situational variable, stress appraisal, and burnout in collegiate teacher-coaches. *Research Quarterly for Exercise and Sport, 64,* 94-102.

Kelly, R.B., Zyzanski, S.J., & Alemagno, S.A. (1991). Prediction of motivation and behavior change following health promotion:

Role of health beliefs, social support, and self-efficacy. *Social Science and Medicine, 32*, 311-320.

Kendzierski, D. (1994). Schema theory: An information processing focus. In R.K. Dishman (Ed.), *Advances in exercise adherence* (pp. 137-159). Champaign, IL: Human Kinetics.

Kendzierski, D., & DeCarlo, K.J. (1991). Physical activity enjoyment scale: Two validation studies. *Journal of Sport & Exercise Psychology, 13*, 50-64.

Kennedy, S.R., & Dimick, K.M. (1987). Career maturity and professional sports expectations of college football and basketball players. *Journal of College Student Personnel, 28*, 293-297.

Kenyon, G.S., & Grogg, T.M. (1970). *Contemporary psychology of sport.* Chicago: Athletic Institute.

Kerr, J. (1990). Stress and sport: Reversal theory. In J.G. Jones & L. Hardy (Eds.), *Stress and performance in sport* (pp. 107-131). Chichester: Wiley.

Kerr, J.H. (1985). The experience of arousal: A new basis for studying arousal effects in sport. *Journal of Sport Sciences, 3*, 169-179.

Kerr, N.L. (1983). Motivation losses in small groups: A social dilemma analysis. *Journal of Personality and Social Psychology, 45*, 819-828.

Kimiecik, J.C., Allison, M.T., & Duda, J.L. (1986). Performance satisfaction, perceived competence and game outcome: The competitive experience of boys' club youth. *International Journal of Sport Psychology, 17*, 255-268.

Kimiecik, J.C., & Harris, A.T. (1996). What is enjoyment? A conceptual/definitional analysis with implications for sport and exercise psychology. *Journal of Sport & Exercise Psychology, 18*, 247-263.

Kimiecik, J.C., & Horn, T.S. (1998). Parental beliefs and children's moderate-to-vigorous physical activity. *Research Quarterly for Exercise and Sport, 69*, 163-175.

Kimiecik, J.C., Horn, T.S., & Shurin, C.S. (1996). Relationships among children's beliefs, perceptions of their parent's beliefs, and their moderate-to-vigorous physical activity. *Research Quarterly for Exercise and Sport, 67*, 324-336.

Kirschenbaum, D.S. (1985). Proximity and specifity of planning: A position paper. *Cognitive Therapy and Research, 9*, 489-506.

Kitayama, S., & Markus, H.R. (Eds.) (1994). *Emotion and culture.* Washington, DC: American Psychological Association.

Klein, M., & Christiansen, G. (1969). Group composition, group structure and group effectiveness of basketball teams. In J.W. Loy & G.S. Kenyon (Eds.), *Sport, culture, and society* (pp. 397-408). New York: Macmillan.

Kleinginna, P.R., & Kleinginna, A.M. (1981). A categorized list of emotional definitions, with suggestions for a consensual definition. *Motivation and Emotion, 5*, 345-379.

Klint, K.A., & Weiss, M.R. (1986). Dropping in and dropping out: Participation motives of current and former youth gymnasts. *Canadian Journal of Applied Sport Sciences, 11*, 106-114.

Klint, K.A., & Weiss, M.R. (1987). Perceived competence and motives for participating in youth sports: A test of Harter's competence motivation theory. *Journal of Sport Psychology, 9*, 55-65.

Knight, P.O., Schocken, D.D., Powers, P.S., Feld, S., & Smith, J.T. (1987). Gender comparison in anorexia nervosa and obligate running. *Medicine and Science in Sports and Exercise, 19*, S66.

Kobasa, S.C. (1988). *The Hardiness Test* (3rd ed.). New York: Hardiness Institute.

Kobasa, S.C., Maddi, S.R., & Courington, S. (1981). Personality and constitution as mediators in the stress-illness relationship. *Journal of Health and Social Behavior, 22*, 368-378.

Kohn, A. (1996). By all available means: Cameron and Pierce's defense of extrinsic motivators. *Review of Educational Research, 66*, 5-32.

Komaki, J., & Barnett, F. (1977). A behavioral approach to coaching football: Improving the play execution of the offensive backfield on a youth football team. *Journal of Applied Behavior Analysis, 10*, 657-664.

Konecni, V.J. (1975). Annoyance, type, and duration of postannoyance activity, and aggression: The "cathartic" effect. *Journal of Experimental Psychology: General, 104*, 76-102.

Koss, M.P. (1990). The women's mental health research agenda. *American Psychologist, 45*, 374-380.

Koss, M.P., & Gaines, J.A. (1993). The prediction of sexual aggression by alcohol use, athletic participation, and fraternity affiliation. *Journal of Interpersonal Violence, 8*, 84-108.

Kosslyn, S.M. (1983). *Ghosts in the mind's machine: Creating and using images in the brain.* New York: Norton.

Kravitz, D.A., & Martin, B. (1986). Ringelmann rediscovered: The original article. *Journal of Personality and Social Psychology, 50*, 936-941.

Kroll, W. (1975, March). *Psychology of sportsmanship.* Paper presented at the American Association of Health, Physical Education, and Recreation Convention, Atlantic City, NJ.

Kroll, W., & Lewis, G. (1970). America's first sport psychologist. *Quest, 13*, 1-4.

Kubler-Ross, E. (1969). *On death and dying.* New York: Macmillan.

Kyllo, L.B., & Landers, D.M. (1995). Goal setting in sport and exercise: A research synthesis to resolve the controversy. *Journal of Sport & Exercise Psychology, 17*, 117-137.

Lacayo, R. (1985, June 10). Blood in the stands. *Time*, 38-41.

Lan, L.Y., & Gill, D.L. (1984). The relationships among self-efficacy, stress responses, and a cognitive feedback manipulation. *Journal of Sport Psychology, 6*, 227-238.

Landers, D.M. (1974). Taxonomic considerations in measuring group performance and the analysis of selected group motor performance tasks. In M.G. Wade & R. Martens (Eds.), *Psychology of motor behavior and sport.* Champaign, Illinois: Human Kinetics.

Landers, D.M. (1978). Motivation and performance: The role of arousal and attentional factors. In W.F. Straub (Ed.), *Sport psychology: An analysis of athlete behavior* (pp. 91-103). Ithaca, NY: Mouvement.

Landers, D.M. (1980). The arousal/performance relationship revisited. *Research Quarterly for Exercise and Sport, 51*, 77-90.

Landers, D.M. (1981). Arousal, attention and skilled performance: Further considerations. *Quest, 33*, 271-283.

Landers, D.M. (1983). Whatever happened to theory testing in sport psychology? *Journal of Sport Psychology, 5*, 135-151.

Landers, D.M. (1985, May). *Beyond the TAIS: Alternative behavioral and psychophysiological measures for determining an internal vs. external focus of attention.* Paper presented at the North American Society for the Psychology of Sport and Physical Activity Conference, Gulfpark, MS.

Landers, D.M., Bauer, R.S., & Feltz, D.L. (1978). Social facilitation during the initial stage of motor learning: A re-examination of Martens' audience study. *Journal of Motor Behavior, 10*, 325-337.

Landers, D.M., Christina, B.D., Hatfield, L.A., Doyle, L.A., & Daniels, F.S. (1980). Moving competitive shooting into the scientists' lab. *American Rifleman, 128*, 36-37, 76-77.

Landers, D.M., & Courtet, P. (1979, May). *Peripheral narrowing among experienced and inexperienced rifle shooters under low and high stress conditions.* Paper presented at the North American Society for the Psychology of Sport and Physical Activity Conference, Trois Rivieres, Canada.

Landers, D.M., & Crum, T. (1971). The effects of team success and formal structure on interpersonal relationships and cohesiveness of baseball teams. *International Journal of Sport Psychology, 2*, 88-96.

Landers, D.M., Harris, D.V., & Christina, R.W. (1975). *Psychology of sport and motor behavior II.* University Park, PA: Pennsylvania State University Press.

Landers, D.M., & Landers, D.M. (1973). Teacher versus peer models: Effects of model's presence and performance level on motor behavior. *Journal of Sport Psychology, 5*, 129-139.

Landers, D.M., & Lueschen, G. (1974). Team performance outcome and the cohesiveness of competitive coacting groups. *International Review of Sport Sociology, 9*, 57-71.

Landers, D.M., & McCullagh, P.D. (1976). Social facilitation of motor performance. In J. Keough & R.S. Hutton (Eds.), *Exercise and Sport Sciences Reviews* (Vol. 4, pp. 125-162). Santa Barbara, CA: Journal Publishing Affiliates.

Landers, D.M., Wilkinson, M.O., Hatfield, B.D., & Barber, H. (1982). Causality and the cohesion-performance relationship. *Journal of Sport Psychology, 4,* 170-183.

Lang, P.J. (1977). Imagery in therapy: An information processing analysis of fear. *Behavior Therapy, 8,* 862-886.

Lang, P.J. (1979). A bio-informational theory of emotional imagery. *Psychophysiology, 16,* 495-512.

Lange, C.G. (1885). *Om sindsbevaegelser. et psyko. fysidog. studie.* Copenhagen: Kronar.

LaPerriere, A.R., Antoni, M.H., Schneiderman, N., Ironson, G., Klimas, N., Caralis, P., & Fletcher, M.A. (1990). Exercise intervention attenuates emotional distress and natural killer cell decrements following notification of positive serologic status for HIV-1. *Biofeedback and Self-Regulation, 15,* 229-242.

LaPerriere, A.R., Fletcher, M.A., Antoni, M.H., Klimas, N.G., Ironson, G., & Schneiderman, N. (1991). Aerobic exercise training in an AIDS risk group. *International Journal of Sports Medicine, 12,* S53-S57.

Latane, B. (1981). The psychology of social impact. *American Psychologist, 36,* 343-356.

Latane, B., Harkins, S.G., & Williams, K.D. (1980). *Many hands make light the work: Social loafing as a social disease.* Unpublished manuscript, Ohio State University, Columbus.

Latane, B., Williams, K.D., & Harkins, S.G. (1979). Many hands make light the work: The causes and consequences of social loafing. *Journal of Personality and Social Psychology, 37,* 823-832.

Lau, R.R., & Russell, D. (1980). Attributions in the sport pages. *Journal of Personality and Social Psychology, 39,* 29-38.

Lawther, J.D. (1951). *The psychology of coaching.* Englewood Cliffs, NJ: Prentice Hall.

Lazarus, R.S. (1966). *Psychological stress and the coping process.* New York: McGraw-Hill.

Lazarus, R.S. (1986). Stress: Appraisal and coping capacities. In A. Eichler, M.M. Silverman, & D.M. Pratt (Eds.), *How to define and research stress* (pp. 5-12). Washington, DC: American Psychiatric Press.

Lazarus, R.S. (1993). From psychological stress to the emotions: A history of changing outlooks. *Annual Review of Psychology, 44,* 1-21.

Lazarus, R.S., & Monat, A. (1979). *Personality* (3rd ed.). Englewood Cliffs, NJ: Prentice-Hall.

Leary, M.R. (1992). Self-presentational processes in exercise and sport. *Journal of Sport & Exercise Psychology, 14,* 339-351.

Lenk, H. (1969). Top performance despite internal conflict: An antithesis to a functionalistic proposition. In J.W. Loy & G.S. Kenyon (Eds.), *Sport, culture, and society* (pp. 393-397). New York: Macmillan.

Lenk, H. (1977). *Team dynamics.* Champaign, IL: Human Kinetics.

Lenney, E. (1977). Women's self-confidence in achievement situations. *Psychological Bulletin, 84,* 1-13.

Lenskyj, H. (1987). *Out of bounds: Women, sport and sexuality.* Toronto: Women's Press.

Lenskyj, H. (1991). Combatting homophobia in sport and physical education. *Sociology of Sport Journal, 8,* 61-69.

Lenskyj, H. (1992). Unsafe at home base: Women's experiences of sexual harassment in university sport and physical education. *Women in Sport & Physical Activity Journal, 1,* 19-33.

Leo, J. (1984a, July 30). Leading the invasion. *Time,* pp. 64-67.

Lepper, M.R., & Greene, D. (1975). Turning play into work: Effects of adult surveillance and extrinsic rewards on children's intrinsic motivation. *Journal of Personality and Social Psychology, 31,* 479-486.

Lepper, M.R., Greene, D., & Nisbett, R.E. (1973). Undermining children's intrinsic interest with extrinsic rewards: A test of the overjustification hypothesis. *Journal of Personality and Social Psychology, 28,* 129-137.

Lepper, M.R., Keavney, M., & Drake, M. (1996). Intrinsic motivation and extrinsic rewards: A commentary on Cameron and Pierce's meta-analysis. *Review of Educational Research, 66,* 5-32.

Lewin, K. (1935). *A dynamic theory of personality.* New York: McGraw-Hill.

Lewin, K. (1948). *Resolving social conflicts.* New York: Harper & Row.

Lewin, K. (1951). *Field theory in social science.* New York: Harper & Brothers.

Lewin, K. (1997). *Resolving social conflicts; and, Field theory in social science.* Washington, D.C.: American Psychological Association.

Li, F. (1997). *The exercise motivation scale: Its multifaceted structure and construct validity.* Microform Publications, International Institute for Sport and Human Performance, University of Oregon, Eugene.

Liebert, R.M., & Morris, L.W. (1967). Cognitive and emotional components of test anxiety: A distinction and some initial data. *Psychological Reports, 20,* 975-978.

Lirgg, C.D., & Feltz, D.L. (1991). Teacher versus peer models revisited: Effects on motor performance and self-efficacy. *Research Quarterly for Exercise and Sport, 62,* 217-224.

Little, W.S., & McCullagh, P. (1989). Motivational orientation and modeled instruction strategies: The effects on form and accuracy. *Journal of Sport & Exercise Psychology, 11,* 41-53.

Lochbaum, M.R., & Roberts, G.C. (1993). Goal orientations and perceptions of the sport experience. *Journal of Sport & Exercise Psychology, 15,* 160-171.

Locke, E.A., & Latham, G.P. (1990). *A theory of goal setting and task performance.* Englewood Cliffs, NJ: Prentice Hall.

Locke, E.A., Saari, L.M., Shaw, K.N., & Latham, G.P. (1981). Goal setting and task performance: 1969-1980. *Psychological Bulletin, 90,* 125-152.

Long, B.C., & van Stavel, R. (1995). Effects of exercise training on anxiety: A meta-analysis. *Journal of Applied Sport Psychology, 7,* 167-189.

Longhurst, K., & Spink, K.S. (1987). Participation motivation of Australian children involved in organized sport. *Canadian Journal of Sport Sciences, 12,* 24-30.

Lorenz, K. (1966). *On aggression.* New York: Harcourt, Brace, & World.

Lox, C.L., McAuley, E., & Tucker, R.S. (1995). Exercise as an intervention for enhancing subjective well-being in an HIV-1 population. *Journal of Sport & Exercise Psychology, 17,* 345-362.

Loy, J.W. (1974). A brief history of the North American Society for the Psychology of Sport and Physical Activity. In M.G. Wade & R. Martens (Eds.), *Psychology of motor behavior and sport* (pp. 2-11). Champaign, IL: Human Kinetics.

Loy, J.W., Curtis, J.E., & Sage, J.N. (1979). Relative centrality of playing position and leadership recruitment in team sports. In R.S. Hutton (Ed.), *Exercise and Sport Sciences Reviews* (Vol. 6, pp. 257-284). Santa Barbara, CA: Journal Publishing Affiliates.

Loy, J.W., & Sage, J.N. (1970). The effects of formal structure on organizational leadership: An investigation of interscholastic baseball teams. In G.S. Kenyon & T.M Grogg (Eds.), *Contemporary psychology of sport* (pp. 363-373). Chicago: Athletic Institute.

Maccoby, E.E. (1990). Gender and relationships. *American Psychologist, 45,* 513-520.

Maccoby, E., & Jacklin, C. (1974). *The psychology of sex differences.* Stanford, CA: Stanford University Press.

Maddux, J.E. (1993). Social cognitive models of health and exercise behavior: An introduction and review of conceptual issues. *Journal of Applied Sport Psychology, 5,* 116-140.

Maehr, M.L. (1984). Meaning and motivation. In R. Ames & C. Ames (Eds.), *Research on motivation in education* (Vol. I, pp. 38-61). New York: Academic Press.

Maehr, M.L., & Braskamp, L. (1986). *The motivation factor: A theory of personal investment.* Lexington, MA: Heath.

Maehr, M.L., & Nicholls, J.G. (1980). Culture and achievement motivation: A second look. In N. Warren (Ed.), *Studies in cross-cultural psychology* (Vol. 3, pp. 221-267). New York: Academic Press.

Mahoney, M.J. (1979). Cognitive skills and athletic performance. In P.C. Kendall & S.D. Hollon (Eds.), *Cognitive-behavioral intervention: Theory, research, and procedures* (pp. 423-443). New York: Academic Press.

Mahoney, M.J. (1991). *Human change processes: The scientific foundations of psychotherapy.* New York: Basic Books.

Mahoney, M.J., & Avener, M. (1977). Psychology of the elite athlete: An exploratory study. *Cognitive Therapy and Research, 1,* 135-141.

Mahoney, M.J., Gabriel, T.J., & Perkins, T.S. (1987). Psychological skills and exceptional athletic performance. *The Sport Psychologist, 1,* 181-199.

Majors, R. (1990). Cool pose: Black masculinity and sports. In M.A. Messner & D.F. Sabo (Eds.), *Sport, men, and the gender order* (pp. 109-114). Champaign, IL: Human Kinetics.

Mandler, G., & Sarason, S.B. (1952). A study of anxiety and learning. *Journal of Abnormal and Social Psychology, 47,* 166-173.

Marcus, B.H., Bock, B.C., Pinto, B.M., & Clark, M.M. (1996). Exercise initiation, adoption, and maintenance. In J.L. Van Raalte & B.W. Brewer (Eds.), *Exploring sport and exercise psychology* (pp. 133-158). Washington, DC: American Psychological Association.

Marcus, B.H., Eaton, C.A., Rossi, J.S., & Harlow, L.L. (1994). Self-efficacy, decision making and stages of change: An integrative model of physical exercise. *Journal of Applied Social Psychology, 24,* 489-508.

Marcus, B.H., Emmons, K.M., Simkin, L.R., Taylor, E.R., Linnan, L., Rossi, J.S., & Abrams, D.B. (1994). Comparison of stage-matched versus standard care physical activity interventions at the workplace. *Annals of Behavioral Medicine, 16,* S035.

Marcus, B.H., & Owen, N. (1992). Motivational readiness, self-efficacy and decision-making for exercise. *Journal of Applied Social Psychology, 22,* 3-16.

Marcus, B.H., Pinto, B.M., Simkin, L.R., Audrain, J.E., & Taylor, E.R. (1994). Application of theoretical models to exercise behavior among employed women. *American Journal of Health Promotion, 9,* 49-55.

Marcus, B.H., Rakowski, W., & Rossi, J.S. (1992). Assessing motivational readiness and decision-making for exercise. *Health Psychology, 11,* 257-261.

Marcus, B.H., Rossi, J.S., Selby, V.C., Niaura, R.S., & Abrams, D.B. (1992). The stages and processes of exercise adoption and maintenance in a worksite sample. *Health Psychology, 11,* 386-395.

Marcus, B.H., Selby, V.C., Niaura, R.S., & Rossi, J.S. (1992). Self-efficacy and the stages of exercise behavior change. *Research Quarterly for Exercise and Sport, 63,* 60-66.

Marcus, B.H., & Stanton, A.L. (1993). Evaluation of relapse prevention and reinforcement interventions to promote exercise adherence in sedentary females. *Research Quarterly for Exercise and Sport, 64,* 447-452.

Mark, M.M., Mutrie, N., Brooks, D.R., & Harris, D.V. (1984). Causal attributions of winners and losers in individual competitive sports: Toward a reformulation of the self-serving bias. *Journal of Sport Psychology, 6,* 184-196.

Markland, D., & Hardy, L. (1997). On the factorial and construct validity of the Intrinsic Motivation Inventory: Conceptual and operational concerns. *Research Quarterly for Exercise and Sport, 68,* 20-32.

Marks, D.F. (1973). Visual imagery differences in the recall of patterns. *British Journal of Psychology, 64,* 17-24.

Marks, D.F. (1977). Imagery and consciousness: A theoretical review from an individual differences perspective. *Journal of Mental Imagery, 2,* 275-290.

Markus, H. (1977). Self-schemata and processing information about the self. *Journal of Personality and Social Psychology, 35,* 63-78.

Markus, H., & Wurf, E. (1987). The dynamic self-concept: A social psychological perspective. *Annual Review of Psychology, 38,* 299-337.

Marlatt, G.A., & Gordon, J.R. (1985). *Relapse prevention: Maintenance strategies in addictive behavior change.* New York: Guilford.

Marsh, H.W. (1990). A multidimensional, hierarchical self-concept: Theoretical and empirical justification. *Educational Psychology Review, 2,* 77-172.

Marsh, H.W. (1992). *Self-Description Questionnaire II: Manual.* Campbelltown, Australia: University of Western Sydney, Macarthur, Publication Unit, Faculty of Education.

Marsh, H.W. (1993). Academic self-concept: Theory measurement and research. In J. Suls (Ed.), *Psychological perspectives on the self* (Vol. 4, pp. 59-98). Hillsdale, NJ: Erlbaum.

Marsh, H.W. (1996). Construct validity of physical self-description questionnaire responses: Relations to external criteria. *Journal of Sport & Exercise Psychology, 18,* 111-113.

Marsh, H.W., Richards, G.E., & Barnes, J. (1986a). Multidimensional self-concepts: The effect of participation in an outward bound program. *Journal of Personality and Social Psychology, 50,* 195-204.

Marsh, H.W., Richards, G.E., & Barnes, J. (1986b). Multidimensional self-concepts: A long-term follow-up of the effect of participation in an outward bound program. *Personality and Social Psychology Bulletin, 12,* 475-492.

Marsh, H.W., Richards, G.E., Johnson, S., Roche, L., & Tremayne, P. (1994). Physical Self-Description Questionnaire: Psychometric properties and multitrait-multimethod analysis of relations to existing instruments. *Journal of Sport & Exercise Psychology, 16,* 270-305.

Martens, R. (1969). Effect of an audience on learning and performance of a complex motor skill. *Journal of Personality and Social Psychology, 12,* 252-260.

Martens, R. (1970). A social psychology of physical activity. *Quest, 14,* 8-17.

Martens, R. (1971). Internal-external control and social reinforcement effects on motor performance. *Research Quarterly, 42,* 107-113.

Martens, R. (1972). Social reinforcement effects on motor performance as a function of socio-economic status. *Perceptual and Motor Skills, 35,* 215-218.

Martens, R. (1975a). *Social psychology and physical activity.* New York: Harper & Row.

Martens, R. (1975b). *Sport Competition Anxiety Test.* Champaign, IL: Human Kinetics.

Martens, R. (1976b). *Competitiveness and sport.* Paper presented at the International Congress of Physical Activity, Science, Quebec City.

Martens, R. (1977). *Sport Competition Anxiety Test.* Champaign, IL: Human Kinetics.

Martens, R. (1979). From smocks to jocks. *Journal of Sport Psychology, 1,* 94-99.

Martens, R. (1987a). *Coaches guide to sport psychology.* Champaign, IL: Human Kinetics.

Martens, R. (1987b). Science, knowledge and sport psychology. *The Sport Psychologist, 1,* 29-55.

Martens, R., Burwitz, L., & Newell, K.M. (1972). Money and praise: Do they improve motor learning and performance? *Research Quarterly, 47,* 429-442.

Martens, R., Burwitz, L., & Zuckerman, J. (1976). Modeling effects on motor performance. *Research Quarterly for Exercise and Sport, 47,* 277-291.

Martens, R., & Landers, D.M. (1969). Coaction effects on a muscular endurance task. *Research Quarterly, 40,* 733-737.

Martens, R., & Landers, D.M. (1970). Motor performance under stress: A test of the inverted-U hypothesis. *Journal of Personality and Social Psychology, 16,* 29-37.

Martens, R., & Landers, D.M. (1972). Evaluation potential as a determinant of coaction effects. *Journal of Experimental Social Psychology, 8,* 347-359.

Martens, R., Landers, D.M., & Loy, J.W. (1972). *Sport cohesiveness questionnaire.* Unpublished report, University of Illinois at Urbana-Champaign.

Martens, R., & Peterson, J.A. (1971). Group cohesiveness as a determinant of success and member satisfaction in team performance. *International Review of Sport Sociology, 6,* 49-61.

Martens, R., Vealey, R.S., & Burton, D. (1990). *Competitive anxiety in sport.* Champaign, IL: Human Kinetics.

Martens, R., & White, V. (1975). Influence of win-loss ratio on performance, satisfaction and preference for opponents. *Journal of Experimental Social Psychology, 11,* 343-362.

Martin, J.E. & Dubbert, P.M. (1984). Behavioral management strategies for improving health and fitness. *Journal of Cardiac Rehabilitation, 4,* 200-208.

Martin, J.E., Dubbert, P.M., Katell, A.D., Thompson, J.K., Raczynski, J.R., Lake, M., Smith, P.O., Webster, J.S., Sikora, T., & Cohen, R.E. (1984). Behavioral control of exercise in sedentary adults: Studies 1 through 6. *Journal of Consulting and Clinical Psychology, 52,* 795-811.

Martin, J.J., Adams-Mushett, C., & Smith, K.L. (1995). Athletic identity and sport orientation of adolescent swimmers with disabilities. *Adapted Physical Activity Quarterly, 12,* 113-123.

Martinek, T., & Griffith, J.B. (1994). Learned helplessness in physical education: A developmental study of causal attributions and task persistence. *Journal of Teaching in Physical Education, 13,* 108-122.

Martinek, T., & Williams, L. (1997). Goal orientation and task persistence in learned helplessness and mastery oriented students in middle school physical education classes. *International Sports Journal, 1,* 63-76.

Maslach, C., & Jackson, S.E. (1986). *Maslach Burnout Inventory manual* (6th ed.). Palo Alto, CA: Consulting Psychologists Press.

Maslow, A.H. (1954). *Motivation and personality.* New York: Harper.

Matteo, S. (1986). The effect of sex and gender-schematic processing on sport participation. *Sex Roles, 15,* 417-432.

Matteo, S. (1988). The effect of gender-schematic processing on decisions about sex-inappropriate sport behavior. *Sex Roles, 18,* 41-58.

McAuley, E. (1985). Modeling status as a determinant of attention in observational learning and performance. *Journal of Sport Psychology, 7,* 283-295.

McAuley, E. (1991). Efficacy, attributional, and affective responses to exercise participation. *Journal of Sport & Exercise Psychology, 13,* 382-393.

McAuley, E. (1992b). Self-referent thought in sport and physical activity. In T.S. Horn (Ed.), *Advances in sport psychology* (pp. 101-118). Champaign, IL: Human Kinetics.

McAuley, E. (1992c). Understanding exercise behavior: A self-efficacy perspective. In G.C. Roberts (Ed.), *Motivation in sport and exercise* (pp. 107-127). Champaign, IL: Human Kinetics.

McAuley, E. (1993). Self-referent thought in sport and physical activity. In T.S. Horn (Ed.), *Advances in sport psychology* (pp. 101-118). Champaign, IL: Human Kinetics.

McAuley, E., & Courneya, K.S. (1993). Adherence to exercise and physical activity as health-promoting behaviors: Attitudinal and self-efficacy influences. *Applied & Preventive Psychology, 2,* 65-77.

McAuley, E., & Courneya, K.S. (1994). The subjective exercise experience scale (SEES): Development and preliminary validation. *Journal of Sport & Exercise Psychology, 16,* 163-177.

McAuley, E., & Duncan, T. E. (1989). Causal attributions and affective reactions to disconfirming outcomes in motor performance. *Journal of Sport & Exercise Psychology, 11,* 187-200.

McAuley, E., & Gill, D.L. (1983). Reliability and validity of the physical self-efficacy scale in a competitive sport setting. *Journal of Sport Psychology, 5,* 410-418.

McAuley, E., & Gross, J.B. (1983). Perceptions of causality in sport: An application of the Causal Dimension Scale. *Journal of Sport & Exercise Psychology, 5,* 72-76.

McAuley, E., Poag, K., Gleason, A., & Wraith, S. (1990). Attrition from exercise programs: Attributional and affective perspectives. *Journal of Social Behavior and Personality, 5,* 591-602.

McAuley, E., & Tammen, V.V. (1989). The effects of subjective and objective competitive outcomes on intrinsic motivation. *Journal of Sport & Exercise Psychology, 11,* 84-93.

McAuley, E., Wraith, S., & Duncan, T.E. (1991). Self-efficacy, perceptions of success, and intrinsic motivation for exercise. *Journal of Applied Social Psychology, 21,* 139-155.

McCarthy, J.F., & Kelly, B.R. (1978a). Aggression, performance variables, and anger self-report in ice hockey players. *Journal of Psychology, 99,* 97-101.

McCarthy, J.F., & Kelly, B.R. (1978b). Aggressive behaviors and its effect on performance over time in ice hockey athletes: An archival study. *International Journal of Sport Psychology, 9,* 90-96.

McClelland, D.C., Atkinson, J.W., Clark, R.A., & Lowell, E.C. (1953). *The achievement motive.* New York: Appleton-Century-Crofts.

McCrae, R.R., & Costa, P.T. Jr. (1987). Validation of the five-factor model of personality across instruments and observers. *Journal of Personality and Social Psychology, 52,* 81-90.

McCrae, R.R., & Costa, P.T. Jr. (1989). The structure of interpersonal traits: Wiggins' circumplex and the five-factor model. *Journal of Personality and Social Psychology, 56,* 586-595.

McCullagh, P. (1987). Model similarity effects on motor performance. *Journal of Sport Psychology, 9,* 249-260.

McCullagh, P. (1993). Modeling: Learning, developmental, and social psychological considerations. In R.N. Singer, M. Murphey, & L.K. Tennant (Eds.), *Handbook of research on sport psychology* (pp. 106-126). New York: Macmillan.

McCullagh, P., Stiehl, J., & Weiss, M.R. (1990). Developmental modeling effects on the quantitative and qualitative aspects of motor performance. *Research Quarterly for Exercise and Sport, 61,* 344-350.

McElroy, M.A., & Willis, J.D. (1979). Women and the achievement conflict in sport: A preliminary study. *Journal of Sport Psychology, 1,* 241-247.

McGrath, J.E. (1962). The influence of positive interpersonal relations on adjustment and effectiveness in rifle teams. *Journal of Abnormal and Social Psychology, 65,* 365-375.

McGrath, J.E. (1984). *Groups: Interaction and performance.* Englewood Cliffs, NJ: Prentice-Hall.

McKenzie, T., & Rushall, B. (1974). Effects of self-recording on attendance and performance in a competitive swimming training environment. *Journal of Applied Behavior Analysis, 7,* 199-206.

McCloy, C.H. (1930). Character building through physical education. *Research Quarterly, 1,* 41-61.

McNair, D.M., Lorr, M., & Droppleman, L.F. (1971). *Manual for the profile of mood states.* San Diego: Educational and Industrial Testing Service.

McNally, J., & Orlick, T. (1975). Cooperative sport structures: A preliminary analysis. *Mouvement, 7,* 267-271.

McPherson, B.D., & Brown, B.A. (1988). The structure, processes, and consequences of sport for children. In F.L. Smoll, R.A. Magill, & M.J. Ash (Eds.), *Children in sport* (3rd ed., pp. 287-300). Champaign, IL: Human Kinetics.

Meichenbaum, D. (1977). *Cognitive-behavior modification.* New York: Plenum.

Meichenbaum, D. (!985). *Stress inoculation training.* New York: Pergamon Press.

Melnick, M.J., & Chemers, M.M. (1974). Effects of group structure on the success of basketball teams. *Research Quarterly, 45,* 1-8.

Melpomene Institute (1996). *The bodywise woman* (2nd ed.). Champaign, IL: Human Kinetics.

Mento, A.J., Steel, R.P., & Karren, R.J. (1987). A meta-analytic study of the effects of goal setting on task performance: 1966-1984. *Organizational Behavior and Human Decision Processes, 39,* 52-83.

Messner, M.A. (1992). *Power at play: Sports and the problem of masculinity.* Boston: Beacon Press.

Messner, M.A., Duncan, M.C., & Jensen, K. (1993). Separating the men from the girls: The gendered language of televised sports. In D.S. Eitzen (Ed.), *Sport in contemporary society: An anthology* (4th ed., pp. 219-233). New York: St. Martin's Press.

Metheny, E. (1965). Symbolic forms of movement: The feminine image in sports. In E. Metheny, *Connotations of movement in sport and dance* (pp. 43-56). Dubuque, IA: Brown.

Meyers, A.W., Cooke, C.J., Cullen, J., & Liles, L. (1979). Psychological aspects of athletic competitors: A replication across sports. *Cognitive Therapy and Research, 3,* 361-366.

Mikalachki, A. (1969). *Group cohesion reconsidered.* London, Ontario: University of Western Ontario, School of Business Administration.

Miles, W.R. (1928). Studies in physical exertion: I. A multiple chronograph for measuring groups of men. *American Physical Education Review, 33,* 379-387.

Miles, W.R. (1931). Studies in physical exertion: II. Individual and group reaction time in football charging. *Research Quarterly, 2,* 14-31.

Minas, S.C. (1980). Acquisition of a motor skill following guided mental and physical practice. *Journal of Human Movement Studies, 6,* 127-141.

Mischel, W. (1968). *Personality and adjustment.* New York: Wiley.

Mischel, W. (1973). Toward a cognitive social learning reconceptualization of personality. *Psychological Review, 80,* 252-283.

Morgan, W.P. (1978). Sport personology: The credulous-skeptical argument in perspective. In W.F. Straub (Ed.), *Sport psychology: An analysis of athlete behavior* (pp. 330-339). Ithaca, NY: Mouvement.

Morgan, W.P. (1979). Negative addiction in runners. *Physician and Sportsmedicine, 7* (2), 57-70.

Morgan, W.P. (1980). The trait psychology controversy. *Research Quarterly for Exercise and Sport, 51,* 50-76.

Morgan, W.P. (1981a). Psychological benefits of physical activity. In F.J. Nagle & H.J. Montoye (Eds.), *Exercise in health and disease* (pp. 299-315). Springfield, IL: Charles C Thomas.

Morgan, W.P. (1981b). Psychophysiology of self-awareness during vigorous physical activity. *Research Quarterly for Exercise and Sport, 52,* 385-427.

Morgan, W.P. (1985). Affective beneficence of vigorous physical activity. *Medicine and Science in Sports and Exercise, 17,* 94-100.

Morgan, W.P. (1994). Psychological components of effort sense. *Medicine and Science in Sports and Exercise, 26,* 1071-1077.

Morgan, W.P., Brown, D.R., Raglin, J.S., O'Connor, P.J., & Ellickson, K.A. (1987). Psychological monitoring of overtraining and staleness. *British Journal of Sports Medicine, 21,* 107-114.

Morgan, W.P., & Goldston, S.E. (1987). *Exercise and mental health.* Washington, DC: Hemisphere.

Morgan, W.P., Horstman, D.H., Cymerman, A., & Stokes, J. (1983). Facilitation of physical performance by means of a cognitive strategy. *Cognitive Therapy and Research, 7,* 251-264.

Morgan, W.P., & Pollock, M.L. (1977). Psychologic characterization of the elite distance runner. *Annals of the New York Academy of Sciences, 301,* 382-403.

Morra, N., & Smith, M.D. (1996). Interpersonal sources of violence in hockey: The influence of the media, parents, coaches, and game officials. In F.L. Smoll & R.E. Smith (Eds.), *Children and youth in sport: A biopsychosocial perspective* (pp. 142-155). Madison, WI: Brown & Benchmark.

Morris, L.W., Davis, M.A., & Hutchings, C.H. (1981). Cognitive and emotional components of anxiety: Literature review and a revised worry-emotionality scale. *Journal of Educational Psychology, 73,* 541-555.

Moyer, K.E. (1973, July). The physiology of violence. *Psychology Today, 7,* 35-38.

Moyers, B. (1993). *Healing and the mind.* New York: Doubleday.

Mudrack, P.E. (1989a). Defining group cohesiveness: A legacy of confusion. *Small Group Behavior, 20,* 37-49.

Mudrack, P.E. (1989b). Group cohesiveness and productivity: A closer look. *Human Relations, 42,* 771-785.

Mummendey, A., & Mummendey, H.D. (1983). Aggressive behavior of soccer players as social interaction. In J.H. Goldstein (Ed.), *Sports violence.* New York: Springer-Verlag.

Murphy, S.M. (1995). Introduction to sport psychology interventions. In S.M. Murphy (Ed.), *Sport psychology interventions* (pp. 1-15). Champaign, IL: Human Kinetics.

Murray, H.A. (1938). *Explorations in personality.* New York: Oxford University Press.

Myers, A.E. (1962). Team competition, success, and adjustment of group members. *Journal of Abnormal and Social Psychology, 65,* 325-332.

Myers, A.E., & Lips, H.M. (1978). Participation in competitive amateur sports as a function of psychological androgyny. *Sex Roles, 4,* 571-578.

National Amateur Athletic Federation, Women's Division (1930). *Women and athletics. Compiled and edited by the Women's Division, National Amateur Athletic Federation.* New York: Barnes.

Neimark, J. (1993). Out of bounds: The truth about athletes and rape. In D.S. Eitzen (Ed.), *Sport in contemporary society: An anthology* (4th ed.) (pp. 130-137). New York: St. Martin's Press.

Nelson, M.B. (1991). *Are we winning yet? How women are changing sports and sports are changing women.* New York: Random House.

Ness, R.G., & Patton, R.W. (1979). The effects of beliefs on maximum weight-lifting performance. *Cognitive Therapy and Research, 3,* 205-211.

Newman, B. (1984). Expediency as benefactor: How team building saves time and gets the job done. *Training and Development Journal, 38,* 26-30.

Newton, M., & Duda, J.L. (1992, April). *The relationship between dispositional goal perspectives and effort, interest, involvement, and trait anxiety in adolescent tennis players.* Paper presented at the American Alliance for Health, Physical Education, Recreation and Dance, Indianapolis.

Nicholls, J. (1984). Conceptions of ability and achievement motivation. In R. Ames & C. Ames (Eds.), *Research on motivation in education: Student motivation* (Vol. I, pp. 39-73). New York: Academic Press.

Nicholls, J.G. (1989). *The competitive ethos and democratic education.* Cambridge, MA: Harvard University Press.

Nicholls, J.G. (1992). The general and the specific in the development and expression of achievement motivation. In G. Roberts (Ed.), *Motivation in sport and exercise* (pp. 31-56). Champaign, IL: Human Kinetics.

Nicholls, J.G., & Miller, A.T. (1984). Development and its discontents: The differentiation of the concept of ability. In J.G. Nicholls (Ed.), *Advances in motivation and achievement* (Vol. III, pp. 185-218). London: JAI Press.

Nicholls, J.G., Patashnick, M., & Nolen, S.B. (1985). Adolescents' theories of education. *Journal of Educational Psychology, 77,* 683-692.

Nideffer, R.M. (1976a). *The inner athlete.* New York: Crowell.

Nideffer, R.M.S. (1976b). Test of attentional and interpersonal style. *Journal of Personality and Social Psychology, 34,* 394-404.

Nideffer, R.M. (1985). *Athlete's guide to mental training.* Champaign, IL: Human Kinetics.

Nideffer, R.M. (1993). Concentration and attention control training. In J.M. Williams (Ed.), *Applied sport psychology: Personal growth to peak performance,* (2nd ed., pp. 243-261). Mountain View, CA: Mayfield.

Nixon, H.L. (1977). "Cohesiveness" and team success: A theoretical reformulation. *Review of Sport and Leisure, 2,* 36-57.

North, T.S., McCullagh, P., & Tran, Z.V. (1990). Effects of exercise on depression. *Exercise and Sport Sciences Reviews, 18,* 379-415.

Nyad, D. (1978). *Other shores.* New York: Random House.

Obermeier, G.E., Landers, D.M., & Ester, M.A. (1977). Social facilitation of speed events: The coaction effect in racing dogs and trackmen. In R.W. Christina & D.M. Landers (Eds.), *Psychology of motor behavior and sport—1976* (Vol. 2, pp. 9-23). Champaign, IL: Human Kinetics.

Ogilvie, B.C. (1968). Psychological consistencies within the personality of high-level competitors. *Journal of the American Medical Association, 205,* 156-162.

Ogilvie, B.C., & Tutko, T.A. (1966). *Problem athletes and how to handle them.* London: Pelham Books.

O'Leary, A. (1985). Self-efficacy and health. *Behavior and Research Therapy, 23,* 437-451.

Orlick, T.D. (1974, November/December). The athletic drop-out: A high price for inefficiency. *Canadian Association for Health, Physical Education, and Recreation Journal,* pp. 21-27.

Orlick, T. (1980). *In pursuit of excellence.* Champaign, IL: Human Kinetics.

Orlick, T. (1990). *In pursuit of excellence* (2nd ed.). Champaign, IL: Leisure Press.

Orlick, T.D., & Mosher, R. (1978). Extrinsic rewards and participant motivation in a sport-related task. *International Journal of Sport Psychology, 9,* 27-39.

Orlick, T., & Partington, J. (1988). Mental links to excellence. *The Sport Psychologist, 2,* 105-130.

Ostrow, A.C. (Ed.). (1990). *Directory of psychological tests in the sport and exercise sciences.* Morgantown, WV: Fitness Information Technology.

Ostrow, A.C. (1996). *Directory of psychological tests in the sport and exercise sciences* (2nd ed.). Morgantown, WV: Fitness Information Technology.

Oxendine, J.B. (1970). Emotional arousal and motor performance. *Quest, 13*, 23-32.

Paivio, A. (1971). *Imagery and verbal processes.* New York: Holt, Reinhart & Winston.

Pargman, D. (1993). Individual differences: Cognitive and perceptual styles. In R.N. Singer, M. Murphey, & L.K. Tennant (Eds.), *Handbook of research on sport psychology* (pp. 379-401). New York: Macmillan.

Parkhouse, B.L., & Williams, J.M. (1986). Differential effects of sex and status on evaluation of coaching ability. *Research Quarterly for Exercise and Sport, 57,* 53-59.

Passer, M.W. (1988). Determinants and consequences of children's competitive stress. In F. Smoll, R. Magill, & M. Ash (Eds.), *Children in sport* (3rd ed., pp. 203-228). Champaign, IL: Human Kinetics.

Pate, R.R., Pratt, M., Blair, S.N., Haskell, W.L., Macera, C.A., Bouchard, C., Buchner, D., Caspersen, C.J., Ettinger, W., Heath, G.W., King, A.C., Kriska, A., Leon, A.S., Marcus, B.H., Morris, J., Paffenbarger, R.S., Patrick, K., Pollock, M.L., Rippe, J.M., Sallis, J., & Wilmore, J.H. (1995). Physical activity and public health: A recommendation from the Centers for Disease Control and Prevention and the American College of Sports Medicine. *Journal of the American Medical Association, 273,* 402-407.

Patrick, G.T.W. (1903). The psychology of football. *American Journal of Psychology, 14,* 104-117.

Paulus, P.B. (1983). Group influence on individual task performance. In P.B. Paulus (Ed.), *Basic group processes* (pp. 97-120). New York: Springer-Verlag.

Paulus, P.B., & Cornelius, W.L. (1974). An analysis of gymnastic performance under conditions of practice and spectator observation. *Research Quarterly, 45,* 56-63.

Paulus, P.B., Judd, B.B., & Bernstein, I.H. (1977). Social facilitation in sports. In R.W. Christina & D.M. Landers (Eds.), *Psychology of motor behavior and sport—1976* (Vol. 2, pp. 2-8). Champaign, IL: Human Kinetics.

Pelletier, L.G., Fortier, M.S., Vallerand, R.J., Tuson, K.M., Briere, N.M., & Blais, M.R. (1995). Toward a new measure of intrinsic motivation, extrinsic motivation, and amotivation in sports: The sport motivation scale (SMS). *Journal of Sport & Exercise Psychology, 17,* 335-353.

Pennebaker, J.W., & Lightner, J.M. (1980). Competition of internal and external information in an exercise setting. *Journal of Personality and Social Psychology, 39,* 165-174.

Peterson, J.A., & Martens, R. (1972). Success and residential affiliation as determinants of team cohesiveness. *Research Quarterly, 43,* 62-76.

Petrie, T., & Stoever, S. (1993). The incidence of bulimia nervosa and pathogenic weight control behaviors in female collegiate gymnasts. *Research Quarterly for Exercise and Sport, 64,* 238-241.

Petruzzello, S., Landers, D.M., Hatfield, B.D., Kubitz, K.A., & Salazar, W. (1991). A meta-analysis on the anxiety-reducing effects of acute and chronic exercise: Outcomes and mechanisms. *Sports Medicine, 11,* 143-182.

Pheterson, G.I., Kiesler, S.B., & Goldberg, P.A. (1971). Evaluation of the performance of women as a function of their sex, achievement, and personal history. *Journal of Personality and Social Psychology, 19,* 114-118.

Pines, A.M., Aronson, E., & Kafry, D. (1981). *Burnout.* New York: Free Press.

Platt, J.R. (1964). Strong inference. *Science, 146* (3642), 347-352.

Ponger, B. (1990). Gay jocks: A phenomenology of gay men in athletics. In M.A. Messner & D.F. Sabo (Eds.), *Sport, men, and the gender order* (pp. 141-152). Champaign, IL: Human Kinetics.

Prapavessis, H., & Carron, A.V. (1988). Learned helplessness in sport. *The Sport Psychologist, 2,* 189-201.

Prochaska, J.O., Velicer, W.F., Rossi, J.S., Goldstein, M.G., Marcus, B.H., Rakowski, W., Fiore, C., Harlow, L.L., Redding, C.A., Rosenbloom, D., & Rossi, S.R. (1994). Stages of change and decisional balance for twelve problem behaviors. *Health Psychology, 13,* 39-46.

Puckett, K., & Cutforth, N.J. (1996). *A qualitative evaluation of an urban cross-age teaching program.* Paper presented at the Annual Allied Health Forum, College of Associated Health Professions, University of Illinois at Chicago.

Raedeke, T.D. (1997). Is athlete burnout more than just stress? A sport commitment perspective. *Journal of Sport & Exercise Psychology, 19,* 396-417.

Raglin, J.S. (1993). Overtraining and staleness: Psychometric monitoring of endurance athletes. In R.B. Singer, M. Murphey, & L.K. Tennant (Eds.), *Handbook of research on sports psychology* (pp. 840-850). New York: Macmillan.

Reel, J.J., & Gill, D.L. (1996). Psychosocial factors related to eating disorders among high school and college female cheerleaders. *The Sport Psychologist, 10,* 195-206.

Rejeski, W.J. (1996, May). *Quality of life in the elderly: Application to physical activity.* Tutorial lecture at the American College of Sports Medicine Convention, Cincinnati.

Rejeski, W.J., Best, D.L., Griffith, P., & Kenney, E. (1987). Sex-role orientation and the responses of men to exercise stress. *Research Quarterly for Exercise and Sport, 58,* 260-264.

Rejeski, W.J., & Brawley, L.R. (1983). Attribution theory in sport: Current status and new perspectives. *Journal of Sport Psychology, 5,* 77-99.

Rejeski, W.J., Brawley, L.R., & Shumaker, S.A. (1996). Physical activity and health-related quality of life. *Exercise and Sport Sciences Reviews, 24,* 71-108.

Richardson, A. (1967a). Mental practice: A review and discussion. Part I. *Research Quarterly, 38,* 95-107.

Richardson, A. (1967b). Mental practice: A review and discussion. Part II. *Research Quarterly, 38,* 263-273.

Richardson, A. (1977). Verbalizer-visualizer: A cognitive style dimension. *Journal of Mental Imagery, 1,* 109-126.

Richman, J.M. & Rosenfeld, L.B. & Hardy, C.J. (1993). The social support survey: An initial evaluation of a clinical measure and practice model of the social support process. *Research on Social Work Practice, 3,* 288-311.

Robbins, J.M., & Joseph, P. (1985). Experiencing exercise withdrawal: Possible consequences of therapeutic and mastery running. *Journal of Sport Psychology, 7,* 23-39.

Roberts, G.C. (1978). Children's assignment of responsibility for winning and losing. In F.L. Smoll & R.E. Smith (Eds.), *Psychological perspectives in youth sports* (pp. 145-171). Washington, DC: Hemisphere.

Roberts, G.C. (1992). Motivation in sport and exercise: Conceptual constraints and convergence. In G.C. Roberts (Ed.), *Motivation in sport and exercise.* Champaign, IL: Human Kinetics.

Roberts, G.C., & Duda, J.L. (1984). Motivation in sport: The mediating role of perceived ability. *Journal of Sport Psychology, 6,* 312-324.

Roberts, G.C., & Martens, R. (1970). Social reinforcement and complex motor performance. *Research Quarterly, 41,* 175-181.

Roberts, G.C., & Pascuzzi, D. (1979). Causal attributions in sport: Some theoretical implications. *Journal of Sport Psychology, 1,* 203-211.

Robertson, R.J., & Noble, B.J. (1997). Perception of physical exertion: Methods, mediators, and applications. *Exercise and Sport Sciences Reviews, 25,* 407-452.

Robinson, D.W. (1990). An attributional analysis of student demoralization in physical education settings. *Quest, 42,* 27-39.

Robinson, D.W., & Howe, B.L. (1989). Appraisal variable/affect relationships in youth sport: A test of Weiner's attributional model. *Journal of Sport & Exercise Psychology, 11,* 431-443.

Rodin, J., & Larson, L. (1992). Social factors and the ideal body shape. In K.D. Brownell, J. Rodin, & J.H. Wilmore (Eds.), *Eating, body weight, and performance in athletes* (pp. 146-158). Philadelphia: Lea & Febiger.

Rodin, J., Silberstein, L., & Streigel-Moore, R. (1985). Women and weight: A normative discontent. In T.B. Sonderegger (Ed.), *Nebraska Symposium on Motivation, 1984: Psychology and gender* (Vol. 32, pp. 267-307). Lincoln, NE: University of Nebraska Press.

Rogers, C.R. (1951). *Client-centered therapy: Its current practice, implications, and theory.* Boston: Houghton Mifflin.

Romance, T.J., Weiss, M.R., & Bockoven, J. (1986). A program to promote moral development through elementary school physical education. *Journal of Teaching in Physical Education, 5,* 126-136.

Rosen, G.M., & Ross, A.O. (1968). Relationship of body image to self-concept. *Journal of Consulting and Clinical Psychology, 32,* 100.

Rosenberg, M. (1979). *Conceiving the self.* New York: Basic Books.

Rosenfeld, L.B., Richman, J.M., & Hardy, C.J. (1989). An examination of social support networks among athletes: Description and relationship to stress. *The Sport Psychologist, 3,* 23-33.

Rosenfeld, L.B. & Richman, J.R. (1997). Developing effective social support: Team building and the social support process. *Journal of Applied Social Psychology, 9,* 133-153.

Rosenstock, I.M. (1966). Historical origins of the health belief model. *Health Education Monographs, 2,* 328-335.

Rosenstock, I.M., Strecher, V.J., & Becker, M.H. (1988). Social learning theory and the health belief model. *Health Education Quarterly, 15,* 175-183.

Rotella, R.J., & Heyman, S.R. (1986). Stress, injury, and the psychological rehabilitation of athletes. In J.M. Williams (Ed.), *Applied sport psychology: Personal growth to peak performance* (pp. 343-364). Mountain View, CA: Mayfield.

Rotter, J.B. (1966). Generalized expectancies for internal versus external control of reinforcement. *Psychological Monographs, 80* (1, No. 609).

Rowley, A.J., Landers, D., Kyllo, L.B., & Etnier, J.L. (1995). Does the Iceberg Profile discriminate between successful and less successful athletes? A meta analysis. *Journal of Sport & Exercise Psychology, 17* (2), 185-199.

Ruder, M.D., & Gill, D.L. (1982). Immediate effects of win-loss on perceptions of cohesion in intramural volleyball teams. *Journal of Sport Psychology, 4,* 227-234.

Rush, D.B., & Ayllon, T. (1984). Peer behavioral coaching: Soccer. *Journal of Sport Psychology, 6,* 325-334.

Rushall, B.S., Hall, M., Roux, L., Sasseville, J., & Rushall, A.C. (1988). Effects of three types of thought content instructions on skiing performance. *The Sport Psychologist, 2,* 283-297.

Rushall, B.S., & Siedentop, D. (1972). *The development and control of behavior in sport and physical education.* Philadelphia: Lea & Febiger.

Rushall, B.S., & Smith, K.C. (1979). The modification of the quality and quantity of behavior categories in a swimming coach. *Journal of Sport Psychology, 1,* 138-150.

Russell, J.A. (1978). Evidence of convergent validity on the dimensions of affect. *Journal of Personality and Social Psychology, 36,* 1152-1168.

Russell, J.A. (1980). A circumplex model of affect. *Journal of Personality and Social Psychology, 57,* 491-502.

Russell, J.A., Weiss, A., & Mendelsohn, G.A. (1989). Affect grid: A single item scale of pleasure and arousal. *Journal of Personality and Social Psychology, 39,* 1161-1178.

Russo, N.F., & Green, B.L. (1993). Women and mental health. In F.L. Denmark & M.A. Paludi (Eds.), *Psychology of women: A handbook of issues and theories* (pp. 379-436). Westport, CT: Greenwood Press.

Ryan, E.D. (1968). Reaction to "sport and personality dynamics". In the Proceedings of the National College Physical Education Association for Men (pp. 70-75).

Ryan, E.D. (1970). The cathartic effect of vigorous motor activity on aggressive behavior. *Research Quarterly, 41,* 542-551.

Ryan, E.D. (1977). Attribution, intrinsic motivation, and athletics. In L.I. Gedvilas & M.E. Kneer (Eds.), *Proceedings of the NAPECW/ NCPEAM National Conference, 1977* (pp. 346-353). Chicago: University of Illinois at Chicago Circle, Office of Publications Services.

Ryan, E.D. (1980). Attribution, intrinsic motivation, and athletics: A replication and extension. In C.H. Nadeau, W.R. Halliwell, K.M. Newell, & G.C. Roberts (Eds.), *Psychology of motor behavior and sport—1979* (pp. 19-26). Champaign, IL: Human Kinetics.

Ryan, E.D. (1981). The emergence of psychological research as related to performance in physical activity. In G. Brooks (Ed.), *Perspective on the academic discipline of physical education* (pp. 327-341). Champaign, IL: Human Kinetics.

Ryan, K.R., Williams, J.M., & Wimer, B. (1990). Athletic aggression: Perceived legitimacy and behavioral intentions in girl's high school basketball. *Journal of Sport & Exercise Psychology, 12,* 48-55.

Ryan, R.M. (1982). Control and information in the intrapersonal sphere: An extension of cognitive evaluation theory. *Journal of Personality and Social Psychology, 45,* 435-449.

Ryan, R.M., & Deci, E.L. (1996). When paradigms clash: Comments on Cameron and Pierce's claim that rewards do not undermine intrinsic motivation. *Review of Educational Research, 66,* 33-38.

Ryan, R.M., Vallerand, R.J., & Deci, E.L. (1984). Intrinsic motivation in sport: A cognitive evaluation theory interpretation. In W.F. Straub & J.M. Williams (Eds.), *Cognitive sport psychology* (pp. 231-242). Lansing, NY: Sport Science Associates.

Ryckman, R.M., Robbins, M.A., Thornton, B., & Cantrell, P. (1982). Development and validation of a physical self-efficacy scale. *Journal of Personality and Social Psychology, 42,* 891-900.

Sachs, M.L. (1978). An analysis of aggression in female softball players. *Review of Sport and Leisure, 3,* 85-97.

Sachs, M.L. (1981). Running addiction. In M. Sacks & M. Sachs (Eds.), *Psychology of running* (pp. 116-127). Champaign, IL: Human Kinetics.

Sadker, M., Sadker, D., & Klein, S. (1991). The issue of gender in elementary and secondary education. In *Review of research in education* (pp. 269-334). Washington, DC: American Educational Research Association.

Sallis, J.F., Haskell, W.L., Fortmann, S.P., Vranizan, K.M., Taylor, C.B., & Solomon, D.S. (1986). Predictors of adoption and maintenance of physical activity in a community sample. *Preventive Medicine, 15,* 331-341.

Sallis, J.F., Hovell, M.F., Hofstetter, C.R., Elder, J.P., Faucher, P., Spry, V.M., Barrington, E., & Hackley, M. (1990). Lifetime history of relapse from exercise. *Addictive Behaviors, 15,* 573-579.

Sapp, M., & Haubenstricker, J. (1978, April). *Motivation for joining and reasons for not continuing in youth sport programs in Michigan.* Paper presented at the meeting of the American Alliance for Health, Physical Education, Recreation and Dance, Kansas City, MO.

Sarason, I.G., Levine, H., Basham, R., & Sarason, B. (1983). Concomitants of social support: The social support questionnaire. *Journal of Personality and Social Psychology, 44,* 127-139.

Sarason, I.G., Sarason, B.R., & Pierce, G.R. (1990). Social support, personality and performance. *Journal of Applied Sport Psychology, 2,* 117-127.

Scanlan, T.K. (1978). Antecedent of competitiveness. In R.A. Magill, M.J. Ash, & F.L. Smoll (Eds.), *Children in sport: A contemporary anthology* (pp. 53-75). Champaign, IL: Human Kinetics.

Scanlan, T.K. (1988). Social evaluation and the competitive process. In F.L. Smoll, R.A. Magill, & M.J. Ash (Eds.), *Children in sport.* Champaign, IL: Human Kinetics.

Scanlan, T.K., Carpenter, P.J., Lobel, M., & Simons, J.P. (1993). Sources of enjoyment for youth sport athletes. *Pediatric Exercise Science, 5,* 275-285.

Scanlan, T.K., Carpenter, P.J., Schmidt, G.W., Simons, J.P., & Keeler, B. (1993). An introduction to the Sport Commitment Model. *Journal of Sport & Exercise Psychology, 15,* 1-15.

Scanlan, T.K., & Lewthwaite, R. (1986). Social psychological aspects of competitive sport experience for male youth sport participants: IV. Predictors of enjoyment. *Journal of Sport Psychology, 8,* 25-35.

Scanlan, T.K., & Passer, M.W. (1980). Self-serving biases in the competitive sport setting: An attributional dilemma. *Journal of Sport Psychology, 2,* 124-136.

Scanlan, T.K., & Simons, J.P. (1992). The construct of sport enjoyment. In G. Roberts (Ed.), *Motivation in sport and exercise* (pp. 199-215). Champaign, IL: Human Kinetics.

Scanlan, T.K., Simons, J.P., Carpenter, P.J., Schmidt, G.W., & Keeler, B. (1993). The Sport Commitment Model: Measurement development for the youth-sport domain. *Journal of Sport & Exercise Psychology, 15*, 16-38.

Scanlan, T.K., Stein, G.L., & Ravizza, K. (1989). An in-depth study of former elite figure skaters: 2. Sources of enjoyment. *Journal of Sport & Exercise Psychology, 11*, 65-83.

Schachter, S., Ellerton, N., McBride, D., & Gregory, D. (1951). An experimental study of cohesiveness and productivity. *Human Relations, 4*, 229-238.

Schachter, S., & Singer, J. (1962). Cognitive, social and physiological determinants of emotional state. *Psychological Review, 69*, 378-399.

Schmid, A., & Peper, E. (1998). Strategies for training concentration. In J.M. Williams (Ed.), *Appled Sport Psychology* (3rd ed., pp. 316-328). Mountain View, CA: Mayfield.

Schmidt, R.A. (1988). *Motor control and learning: A behavioral emphasis* (2nd ed.). Champaign, IL: Human Kinetics.

Schmidt, R.A., & Lee, T. (1999). *Motor control and learning* (3rd ed.). Champaign, IL: Human Kinetics.

Schoenborn, C.A. (1986). Health habits of U.S. adults: The "Alameda 7" revisited. *Public Health Reports, 101*, 571-580.

Schomer, H. (1987). Mental strategy training programme for marathon runners. *International Journal of Sport Psychology, 18*, 133-151.

Schutz, R.W. (1993). Methodological issues and measurement problems in sport psychology. In S. Serpa, J. Alves, V. Ferreira, & A. Paulo-Brito (Eds.), *Proceedings of the 8th World Congress of Sport Psychology* (pp. 119-131). Lisbon: International Society of Sport Psychology.

Schutz, R.W., & Gessaroli, M.E. (1993). Use, misuse, and disuse of psychometrics in sport psychology research. In R.N. Singer, M. Murphey, & L.K. Tennant (Eds.), *Handbook of research on sport psychology* (pp. 901-917). New York: Macmillan.

Schwartz, B., & Barsky, S.F. (1977). The home advantage. *Social Forces, 55*, 641-661.

Schwartz, G.E., Davidson, R.J., & Goleman, D.J. (1978). Patterning of cognitive and somatic processes in the self-regulation of anxiety: Effects of meditation versus exercise. *Psychosomatic Medicine, 40*, 321-328.

Seashore, S.E. (1954). *Group cohesiveness in the industrial work group.* Ann Arbor, MI: University of Michigan.

Secord, P.F., & Jourard, S.M. (1953). The appraisal of body cathexis: Body cathexis and the self. *Journal of Consulting Psychology, 17*, 343-347.

Seifriz, J.J., Duda, J.L., & Chi, L. (1991). *The relationship of perceived motivational climate to intrinsic motivation and beliefs about success in basketball.* Manuscript submitted for publication.

Selye, H. (1956). *The stress of life.* New York: McGraw-Hill.

Shangi, G., & Carron, A.V. (1987). Group cohesion and its relationship with performance and satisfaction among high school basketball players. *Canadian Journal of Sport Sciences, 12*, 20.

Shavelson, R.J., Hubner, J.J., & Stanton, G.C. (1976). Self-concept: Validation of construct interpretations. *Review of Educational Research, 46*, 407-441.

Shaw, M.E. (1976). *Group dynamics: The psychology of small group behavior* (2nd ed.). New York: McGraw-Hill.

Sheehan, P.W. (1967). A shortened form of Betts' questionnaire upon mental imagery. *Journal of Clinical Psychology, 23*, 386-389.

Sheehan, P.W., Ashton, R., & White, K. (1983). Assessment of mental imagery. In A.A. Sheikh (Ed.), *Imagery: Current theory, research, and application* (pp. 189-221). New York: Wiley.

Sheldon, W.H., & Stevens, S.S. (1942). *The varieties of temperament: A psychology of constitutional differences.* New York: Harper & Row.

Sherif, C.W. (1976). The social context of competition. In D. Landers (Ed.), *Social problems in athletics* (pp. 18-36). Champaign, IL: Human Kinetics.

Sherif, C.W. (1982). Needed concepts in the study of gender identity. *Psychology of Women Quarterly, 6*, 375-398.

Sherman, J. (1971). *On the psychology of women.* Springfield, IL: Charles C Thomas.

Shields, D.L., & Bredemeier, B.J. (1984). Sport and moral growth: A structural developmental perspective. In W.F. Straub & J.M. Williams (Eds.), *Cognitive sport psychology* (pp. 89-101). Lansing, NY: Sport Science Associates.

Shumaker, S.A., & Brownell, A. (1984). Toward a theory of social support: Closing conceptual gaps. *Journal of Social Issues, 40*, 11-36.

Siedentop, D. (1978). The management of practice behavior. In W.F. Straub (Ed.), *Sport psychology: An analysis of athlete behavior* (pp. 49-55). Ithaca, NY: Mouvement.

Silva, J.M. (1979a). Behavioral and situational factors affecting concentration and skill performance. *Journal of Sport Psychology, 1*, 221-227.

Silva, J.M. (1979b). Changes in the affective state of guilt as a function of exhibiting proactive assertion or hostile aggression. In G.C. Roberts & K.M. Newell (Eds.), *Psychology of motor behavior and sport—1978* (pp. 98-108). Champaign, IL: Human Kinetics.

Silva, J.M. (1983). The perceived legitimacy of rule violating behavior in sport. *Journal of Sport Psychology, 5*, 438-448.

Silva, J.M., & Applebaum, M.S. (1989). Association-dissociation patterns of United States Olympic marathon trial contestants. *Cognition—Therapy and Research, 13*, 185-192.

Silva, J.M., & Hardy, C.J. (1991). The sport psychologist: Psychological aspects of injury in sport. In F.O. Mueller & A. Ryan (Eds.), *The sports medicine team and athlete injury prevention* (pp. 114-132). Philadelphia: Davis.

Sinclair, D.A., & Vealey, R.S. (1989). Effects of coaches' expectations and feedback on the self-perceptions of athletes. *Journal of Sport Behavior, 11* (3), 77-91.

Singer, R.N. (1968). *Motor learning and human performance.* New York: Macmillan.

Skinner, B.F. (1968). *The technology of teaching.* New York: Appleton-Century-Crofts.

Smith, A.L. (1997). *Peer relationships and physical activity participation in early adolescence.* Unpublished doctoral dissertation, University of Oregon, Eugene.

Smith, A.L., Gill, D.L., Crews, D.J., Hopewell, R., & Morgan, D.W. (1995). Attentional strategy use by experienced distance runners: Physiological and psychological effects. *Research Quarterly for Exercise and Sport, 66*, 142-150.

Smith, C.A., & Lazarus, R.S. (1990). Emotion and adaptation. In L.A. Pervin (Ed.), *Handbook of personality theory and research* (pp. 609-637). New York: Guilford.

Smith, M.D. (1978). Hockey violence: Interring some myths. In W.F. Straub (Ed.), *Sport psychology: An analysis of athlete behavior* (pp. 187-192). Ithaca, NY: Mouvement.

Smith, M.D. (1979). Social determinant of violence in ice hockey: A review. *Canadian Journal of Applied Sport Sciences, 4*, 76-82.

Smith, M.D. (1988). Interpersonal sources of violence in hockey: The influence of parents, coaches, and teammates. In F.L. Smoll, R.A. Magill, & M.J. Ash (Eds.), *Children in sport* (3rd ed., pp. 301-313). Champaign, IL: Human Kinetics.

Smith, R.E. (1980). A cognitive-affective approach to stress management training for athletes. In C.H. Nadeau, W.R. Halliwell, K.M. Newell, & G.C. Roberts (Eds.), *Psychology of motor behavior and sport—1979* (pp. 54-72). Champaign, IL: Human Kinetics.

Smith, R.E. (1986). Toward a cognitive-affective model of athletic burnout. *Journal of Sport & Exercise Psychology, 8*, 36-50.

Smith, R.E., Schutz, R.W, Smoll, F.L., & Ptacek, J.T. (1995). Development and validation of a multidimensional measure of sport-specific psychological skills: The Athletic Coping Skills Inventory-28. *Journal of Sport & Exercise Psychology, 17*, 379-398.

Smith, R.E. & Smoll, F.L. (1997). Coaching the coaches: Youth sports as a scientific and applied behavioral setting. *Current Directions in Psychological Science, 6*, 16-21.

Smith, R.E., Smoll, F.L., & Curtis, B. (1978). Coaching behaviors in little league baseball. In F.L. Smoll & R.E. Smith (Eds.), *Psychological perspectives in youth sports* (pp. 173-201). Washington, DC: Hemisphere.

Smith, R.E., Smoll, F.L., & Curtis, B. (1979). Coach effectiveness training: A cognitive-behavioral approach to enhancing relationship skills in youth sport coaches. *Journal of Sport Psychology, 1*, 59-75.

Smith, R.E., Smoll, F.L., & Hunt, E. (1977). A system for the behavioral assessment of athletic coaches. *Research Quarterly, 48,* 401-407.

Smith, R.E., Smoll, F.L., & Schutz, R.W. (1990). Measurement and correlates of sport-specific cognitive and somatic trait anxiety: The Sport Anxiety Scale. *Anxiety Research, 2,* 263-280.

Smith, Y.R. (1992). Women of color in society and sport. *Quest, 44,* 228-250.

Smoll, F.L., & Smith, R.E. (1984). Leadership research in youth sports. In J.M. Silva & R.S. Weinberg (Eds.), *Psychological foundations of sport* (pp. 371-386). Champaign, IL: Human Kinetics.

Smoll, F.L. & Smith, R.E. (1997). *Coaches who never lose: A 30-minute primer for coaching effectiveness.* Portola Valley, CA: Warde Publishers.

Snyder, M. (1987). *Public appearances/private realities: The psychology of self-monitoring.* New York: Freeman.

Solomon, R.L. (1980). The opponent process theory of acquired motivation. *American Psychologist, 35,* 691-712.

Solomon, R.L., & Corbitt, J.D. (1974). An opponent-process theory of motivation: I. Temporal dynamics of affect. *Psychological Review, 81,* 119-145.

Sonstroem, R.J. (1978). Physical Estimation and Attraction Scales: Rationale and research. *Medicine and Science in Sports, 10,* 97-102.

Sonstroem, R.J., & Bernardo, P.B. (1982). Intraindividual pregame state anxiety and basketball performance: A re-examination of the inverted-U curve. *Journal of Sport Psychology, 4,* 235-245.

Sonstroem, R.J., & Morgan, W.P. (1989). Exercise and self-esteem: Rationale and model. *Medicine and Science in Sports and Exercise, 21,* 329-337.

Sonstroem, R.J., Speliotis, E.D., & Fava, J.L. (1992). Perceived physical competence in adults: An examination of the Physical Self-Perception Scale. *Journal of Sport & Exercise Psychology, 10,* 207-221.

Spears, B. (1978). Prologue: The myth. In C. Oglesby (Ed.), *Women in sport: From myth to reality* (pp. 3-15). Philadelphia: Lea & Febiger.

Spence, J.T., & Helmreich, R.L. (1978). *Masculinity and femininity: Their psychological dimensions, correlates, and antecedents.* Austin, TX: University of Texas Press.

Spence, J.T., & Helmreich, R.L. (1983). Achievement-related motives and behaviors. In J.T. Spence (Ed.), *Achievement and achievement motives* (pp. 7-74). San Francisco: Freeman.

Spence, K.W. (1956). *Behavior theory and conditioning.* New Haven, CT: Yale University Press.

Spielberger, C.D. (1966). *Anxiety and behavior.* New York: Academic Press.

Spielberger, C.D., Gorsuch, R.L., & Lushene, R.E. (1970). *Manual for the State-Trait Anxiety Inventory.* Palo Alto, CA: Consulting Psychologists Press.

Spink, K.S. (1990). Group cohesion and collective efficacy of volleyball teams. *Journal of Sport & Exercise Psychology, 12,* 301-311.

Spink, K.S., & Roberts, G.C. (1980). Ambiguity of outcome and causal attributions. *Journal of Sport Psychology, 2,* 237-244.

Stanne, M. (1993). *The impact of social interdependence on motor performance, social, & self acceptance: A meta-analysis.* Unpublished doctoral dissertation, University of Minnesota.

Starkes, J.L. (1987). Skill in field hockey: The nature of the cognitive advantage. *Journal of Sport Psychology, 9,* 146-60.

Starkes, J.L., & Allard, F. (1983). Perception in volleyball: The effects of competitive stress. *Journal of Sport Psychology, 5,* 189-196.

Steiner, I.D. (1972). *Group process and productivity.* New York: Academic Press.

Stogdill, R.M.S. (1963). *Team achievement under high motivation.* Columbus, OH: Ohio State University, Bureau of Business Research.

Storr, A. (1968). *Human aggression.* New York: Atheneum.

Sue, S. (1994). Introduction. In E.J. Trickett, R.J. Watts, & D. Birman (Eds.), *Human diversity: Perspectives on people in context* (pp. 1-4). San Francisco: Jossey-Bass.

Suinn, R.S. (1976, July). Body thinking: Psychology for Olympic champs. *Psychology Today, 10,* 38-43.

Suinn, R.S. (1983). Imagery and sports. In A.A. Sheikh (Ed.), *Imagery: Current theory, research, and application* (pp. 507-534). New York: Wiley.

Suinn, R. (1993). Imagery: In R.N. Singer, M. Murphey, & L.K. Tennant (Eds.), *Handbook of research on sports psychology* (pp. 492-510). New York: Macmillan.

Sullivan, H.S. (1953). *The interpersonal theory of psychiatry.* New York: Norton.

Swoap, R.A. & Murphy, S.M. (1995). Eating disorders and weight management in athletes. In S.M. Murphy (Ed.), *Sport psychology interventions* (pp. 307-329). Champaign, IL: Human Kinetics.

Tammen, V.V., & Murphy, S. (1990). *The effects of four competitive outcomes on elite athletes' intrinsic motivation.* Paper presented at the annual conference of the Association for the Advancement of Applied Sport Psychology, San Antonio.

Tannenbaum, S.I., Beard, R.L., & Salas, E. (1992). Team building and its influence on team effectiveness: An examination of conceptual and empirical developments. In K. Kelley (Ed.), *Issues, theory and research in industrial/organizational psychology* (pp. 117-153). Amsterdam: Elsevier.

Taub, D., & Benson, R. (1992). Weight concerns, weight control techniques, and eating disorders among adolescent competitive swimmers: The effect of gender. *Sociology of Sport Journal, 9,* 76-86.

Taylor, C.B., Bandura, A., Ewart, C.K., Miller, N.H., & DeBusk, R.T. (1985). Exercise testing to enhance wives' confidence in their husbands' cardiac capabilities soon after clinically uncomplicated acute myocardial infarction. *American Journal of Cardiology, 55,* 6335-6638.

Tharp, R.G., & Gallimore, R. (1976, January). What a coach can teach a teacher. *Psychology Today, 9,* 74-78.

Thayer, R.E. (1967). Measurement of activation through self-report. *Psychological Reports, 20,* 663-678.

Thill, E., & Mouanda, J. (1990). Autonomy or control in the sports context. *International Journal of Sport Psychology, 21,* 1-20.

Thom, R. (1975). *Structural stability and morphogenesis* (D.H. Fowler, trans.). New York: Benjamin-Addison-Wesley.

Thomas, J.R., & Nelson, J.K. (1996). *Research methods in physical activity.* Champaign, IL: Human Kinetics.

Thomas, J.R., & Tennant, L.K. (1978). Effects of rewards on children's motivation for an athletic task. In F.L. Smoll & R.E. Smith (Eds.), *Psychological perspectives in youth sports* (pp. 123-144). Washington, DC: Hemisphere.

Thompson, C.E., & Wankel, L.M. (1980). The effects of perceived activity choice upon frequency of exercise behavior. *Journal of Applied Social Psychology, 10,* 436-444.

Thompson, J.K., & Blanton, P. (1987). Energy conservation and exercise dependence: A sympathetic arousal hypothesis. *Medicine and Science in Sports and Exercise, 19,* 91-99.

Thompson, R.A., & Sherman, R. (1993). *Helping athletes with eating disorders.* Champaign, IL: Human Kinetics.

Thurstone, L.L. (1938). Primary mental abilities. *Psychometrika Monographs* (1).

Travis, C.B. (1988). *Women and health psychology: Mental health issues.* Hillsdale, NJ: Erlbaum.

Treasure, D.C., & Roberts, G.C. (1994). Cognitive and affective concomitants of task and ego orientation during middle school years. *Journal of Sport & Exercise Psychology, 16,* 15-28.

Tresemer, D.W. (1977). *Fear of success.* New York: Plenum Press.

Trickett, E.J., Watts, R.J., & Birman, D. (Eds.). (1994). *Human diversity: Perspectives on people in context.* San Francisco: Jossey-Bass.

Triplett, N. (1898). The dynamogenic factors in pacemaking and competition. *American Journal of Psychology, 9,* 507-553.

Tropp, L.J., & Landers, D.M. (1979). Team interaction and the emergence of leadership and interpersonal attraction in field hockey. *Journal of Sport Psychology, 1,* 228-240.

Trujillo, C. (1983). The effect of weight training and running exercise intervention on the self-esteem of college women. *International Journal of Sport Psychology, 14,* 162-173.

Tubbs, M.E. (1986). Goal setting: A meta-analytic examination of the empirical evidence. *Journal of Applied Psychology, 71,* 474-483.

Tucker, L.A. (1983). Effect of weight training on self-concept: A profile of those influenced most. *Research Quarterly for Exercise and Sport, 54,* 389-397.

Tucker, L.A. (1987). Effect of weight training on body attitudes: Who benefits most? *Journal of Sports Medicine and Physical Fitness, 27,* 70-78.

Turner, E.E., Rejeski, W.J., & Brawley (1997). Psychological benefits of physical activity are influenced by the social environment. *Journal of Sport & Exercise Psychology, 19,* 119-130.

Tuson, K.M., & Sinyor, D. (1993). On the affective benefits of aerobic exercise: Taking stock after twenty years of research. In P. Seraganian (Ed.), *Exercise psychology: The influence of physical exercise on psychological processes* (pp. 80-121). New York: Wiley.

Tutko, T.A., Lyon, L.P., & Ogilvie, B.C. (1969). *Athletic Motivation Inventory.* San Jose, CA: Institute for the Study of Athletic Motivation.

Udry, E. (1997). Coping and social support among injured athletes following surgery. *Journal of Sport & Exercise Psychology, 19,* 71-90.

Uhlir, G.A. (1987). Athletics and the university: The post-women's era. *Academe, 73,* 25-29.

Unger, R., & Crawford, M. (1992). *Women and gender: A feminist psychology.* New York: McGraw-Hill.

United States Centers for Disease Control and Prevention (1993). Prevalence of sedentary lifestyle—behavioral risk factor surveillance system, United States, 1991. *Morbidity and Mortality Weekly Report, 42,* 576-579.

Vallerand, R.J. (1983). Effect of differential amounts of positive verbal feedback on the intrinsic motivation of male hockey players. *Journal of Sport Psychology, 5,* 101-107.

Vallerand, R.J., & Reid, G. (1984). On the causal effects of perceived competence on intrinsic motivation: A test of cognitive evaluation theory. *Journal of Sport Psychology, 6,* 94-102.

Vanden Auweele, Y., De Cuyper, B.D., Van Mele, V., & Rzewnicki, R. (1993). Elite performance and personality: From description and prediction to diagnosis and intervention. In R.N. Singer, M. Murphey, & L.K. Tennant (Eds.), *Handbook of research on sport psychology* (pp. 257-289). New York: Macmillan.

Vander Velden, L. (1971). *Relationships among member, team, and situational variables and basketball team success: A social psychological inquiry.* Unpublished doctoral dissertation, University of Wisconsin.

Vanek, M. (1985, Summer). A message from the president of ISSP: Prof. Dr. Miroslav Vanek. *ISSP Newsletter, 1* (1), 1-2.

Vanek, M. (1993). On the inception, development and perspectives of ISSP's image and self-image. In S. Serpa, J. Alves, V. Ferreira, & A. Paula-Brito (Eds.), *Proceedings VIII World Congress of Sport Psychology* (pp. 154-158). Lisbon, Portugal: International Society of Sport Psychology.

Van Raalte, J.L., & Andersen, M.B. (1996). In J.L. Van Raalte and B.W. Brewer (Eds.), *Exploring sport and exercise psychology* (pp. 275-284). Washington, DC: American Psychological Association.

Van Raalte, J.L., & Brewer, B.W. (Eds.) (1996). *Exploring sport and exercise psychology.* Washington, DC: American Psychological Association.

Van Raalte, J.L., Brewer, B.W., Rivera, P.M., & Petitpas, A.J. (1994). The relationship between observable self-talk and competitive junior tennis players' match performance. *Journal of Sport & Exercise Psychology, 16,* 400-415.

Van Schoyck, S.R., & Grasha, A.F. (1981). Attentional style variations and athletic ability: The advantages of a sports-specific test. *Journal of Sport Psychology, 3,* 149-165.

Varca, P.E. (1980). An analysis of home and away game performance of male college basketball teams. *Journal of Sport Psychology, 2,* 245-257.

Vealey, R.S. (1986). Conceptualization of sport-confidence and competitive orientation: Preliminary investigation and instrument development. *Journal of Sport Psychology, 8,* 221-246.

Vealey, R.S. (1988). Future directions in psychological skills training. *The Sport Psychologist, 2,* 318-336.

Vealey, R.S., & Greenleaf, C.A. (1998). Seeing is believing: Understanding and using imagery in sport. In J.M. Williams (Ed.), *Applied sport psychology: Personal growth to peak performance* (3rd ed., pp. 237-269). Mountain View, CA: Mayfield.

Vealey, R.S., Udry, E.M., Zimmerman, V., & Soliday, J. (1992). Intrapersonal and situational predictors of coaching burnout. *Journal of Sport & Exercise Psychology, 14,* 40-58.

Vealey, R., & Walter, S. (1993). Imagery training for performance enhancement. In J.M. Williams (Ed.), *Applied sport psychology: Personal growth to peak performance* (2nd ed., pp. 200-224). Mountain View, CA: Mayfield.

Veroff, J. (1969). Social comparison and the development of achievement motivation. In C. Smith (Ed.), *Achievement related motives in children* (pp. 46-110). New York: Russell Sage Foundation.

Vital statistics. (1996, July/August). *Health, 10*(4), 18.

Vlachopoulos, S., Biddle, S., & Fox, K. (1996). A social-cognitive investigation into the mechanism of affect generation in children's physical activity. *Journal of Sport & Exercise Psychology, 18,* 174-193.

Wade, M.G., & Martens, R. (1974). *Psychology of motor behavior and sport.* Urbana, IL: Human Kinetics.

Wagner, S.L., Lounsbury, J.W., & Fitzgerald, L.G. (1989). Attribute factors associated with work/leisure perception. *Journal of Leisure Research, 21,* 155-166.

Walling, M.D., Duda, J.L., & Chi, L. (1993). The perceived motivational climate in sport questionnaire: Construct and predictive validity. *Journal of Sport & Exercise Psychology, 15,* 172-183.

Walling, M., & Martinek, T. (1995). Learned helplessness: A case study of a middle school student. *Journal of Teaching in Physical Education, 14,* 454-466.

Wallston, B.S., Alagna, S.W., DeVellis, B.M., & DeVellis, R.F. (1983). Social support and health. *Health Psychology, 2,* 367-391.

Wallston, B.S., & O'Leary, V.E. (1981). Sex and gender make a difference: The differential perceptions of women and men. *Review of Personality and Social Psychology, 2,* 9-41.

Wankel, L.M. (1972). Competition in motor performance: An experimental analysis of motivational components. *Journal of Experimental Social Psychology, 8,* 427-437.

Wankel, L.M. (1973). *An examination of illegal aggression in intercollegiate hockey.* Paper presented at the Proceeding of the Fourth Canadian Psychomotor Learning and Sport Psychology Symposium, Waterloo, Ontario.

Wankel, L.M. (1975). The effects of social reinforcement and audience presence upon the motor performance of boys with different levels of initial ability. *Journal of Motor Behavior, 7,* 207-216.

Wankel, L.M. (1984). Decision-making and social support strategies for increasing exercise involvement. *Journal of Cardiac Rehabilitation, 4,* 124-135.

Wankel, L.M. (1993). The importance of enjoyment to adherence and psychological benefits from physical activity. *International Journal of Sport Psychology, 24,* 151-169.

Wankel, L.M., & Kreisel, P.J. (1985). Factors underlying enjoyment of youth sports: Sport and age group comparisons. *Journal of Sport Psychology, 7,* 51-64.

Wankel, L.M., & Sefton, J.M. (1989). A season-long investigation of fun in youth sports. *Journal of Sport & Exercise Psychology, 11,* 355-366.

Waston, G.G. (1986). Approach-avoidance behaviour in team sports: An application to leading Australian national hockey players. *International Journal of Sport Psychology, 17,* 136-155.

Watkins, D. (1986). Attributions in the New Zealand sports pages. *Journal of Social Psychology, 126,* 817-819.

Watson, D., Clark, L.A., & Tellegen, A. (1988). Development and validation of brief measures of positive and negative affect. The PANAS scales. *Journal of Personality and Social Psychology, 54,* 1063-1070.

Watson, D., & Tellegen, A. (1985). Toward a consensual analysis of mood. *Psychological Bulletin, 98,* 219-235.

Weight, L.M., & Noakes, T.D. (1987). Is running an analogue of anorexia? A survey of the incidence of eating disorders in female distance runners. *Medicine and Science in Sports and Exercise, 19* (3), 213-217.

Weinberg, R. (1996). Goal setting in sport and exercise: Research to practice. In J.L. Van Raalte and B.W. Brewer (Eds.), *Exploring sport and exercise psychology* (pp. 3-24). Washington, DC: American Psychological Association.

Weinberg, R., Reveles, M., & Jackson, A. (1984). Attitudes of male and female athletes toward male and female coaches. *Journal of Sport Psychology, 6,* 448-453.

Weinberg, R.S. (1977). Anxiety and motor behavior: A new direction. In R.W. Christina & D.M. Landers (Eds.), *Psychology of motor behavior and sport—1976* (Vol. 2, pp. 132-139). Champaign, IL: Human Kinetics.

Weinberg, R.S. (1979). Intrinsic motivation in a competitive setting. *Medicine and Science in Sport, 11,* 146-149.

Weinberg, R.S. (1984). The relationship between extrinsic rewards and intrinsic motivation. In J.M. Silva & R.S. Weinberg (Eds.), *Psychological foundations of sport* (pp. 177-189). Champaign, IL: Human Kinetics.

Weinberg, R.S. (1994). Goal setting and performance in sport and exercise settings: A synthesis and critique. *Medicine and Science in Sport and Exercise, 26,* 469-477.

Weinberg, R.S., Burton, D., Yukelson, D., & Weigand, D. (1993). Goal setting in competitive sport: An exploratory investigation of practices of collegiate athletes. *The Sport Psychologist, 7,* 275-289.

Weinberg, R.S., Gould, D., & Jackson, A. (1979). Expectations and performance: An empirical test of Bandura's self-efficacy theory. *Journal of Sport Psychology, 1,* 320-331.

Weinberg, R.S., & Jackson, A. (1979). Competition and extrinsic rewards: Effect on intrinsic motivation. *Research Quarterly, 50,* 494-502.

Weinberg, R.S., & Ragan, J. (1979). Effects of competition, success/ failure, and sex on intrinsic motivation. *Research Quarterly for Exercise and Sport, 50,* 503-510.

Weinberg, R.S., Seabourne, T.G., & Jackson, A. (1981). Effects of visuo-motor behavior rehearsal, relaxation, and imagery on karate performance. *Journal of Sport Psychology, 3,* 228-238.

Weinberg, R.S., Stitcher, T., & Richardson, P. (1994). Effects of a seasonal goal setting program on lacrosse performance. *The Sport Psychologist, 8,* 166-175.

Weinberg, R.S., & Williams, J.M. (1998). In J.M. Williams (Ed.), *Applied sport psychology: Personal growth to peak performance* (3rd ed., pp. 329-358). Mountain View, CA: Mayfield.

Weiner, B. (1974). *Achievement motivation and attribution theory.* Morristown, NJ: General Learning Press.

Weiner, B. (1979). A theory of motivation for some classroom experiences. *Journal of Educational Psychology, 71,* 3-25.

Weiner, B. (1986). *An attributional theory of motivation and emotion.* New York: Springer-Verlag.

Weiner, B., Frieze, I., Kukla, A., Reed, L., Rest, S., & Rosenbaum, R.M.S. (1972). Perceiving the causes of success and failure. In E.E. Jones, D.E. Kanouse, H.H. Kelley, R.E. Nisbett, S. Valins, & B. Weiner (Eds.), *Attribution: Perceiving the causes of behavior* (pp. 95-120). Morristown, NJ: General Learning Press.

Weingarten, G., Furst, D., Tenenbaum, G., & Schaefer, U. (1984). Motives of Israeli youth for participation in sport. In J.L. Callaghan (Ed.), *Proceedings of the International Symposium "Children to Champions"* (pp. 145-153). Los Angeles: University of Southern California.

Weiss, M.R. (1974). The provision of social relationships. In Z. Rubin (Ed.), *Doing unto others* (pp. 17-26). Englewood Cliffs, NJ: Prentice-Hall.

Weiss, M.R. (1983). Modeling and motor performance: A developmental perspective. *Research Quarterly for Exercise and Sport, 54,* 190-197.

Weiss, M.R. (1993). Children's participation in physical activity: Are we having fun yet? *Pediatric Exercise Science, 5,* 205-209.

Weiss, M.R., & Bredemeier, B.J.L. (1990). Moral development in sport. In K.B. Pandolf & J.O. Holloszy (Eds.), *Exercise and Sport Sciences Reviews* (Vol. 18, pp. 331-378). Baltimore: Williams & Wilkins.

Weiss, M.R., & Chaumeton, N. (1992). Motivational orientations in sport. In T. Horn (Ed.), *Advances in sport psychology* (pp. 61-99). Champaign, IL: Human Kinetics.

Weiss, M.R., & Duncan, S.C. (1992). The relationship between physical competence and peer acceptance in the context of children's sports participation. *Journal of Sport & Exercise Psychology, 14,* 177-191.

Weiss, M.R., Ebbeck, V., & Horn, T.S. (1997). Children's self-perceptions and sources of physical competence information: A cluster analysis. *Journal of Sport & Exercise Psychology, 19,* 64-83.

Weiss, M.R., Ebbeck, V., & Rose, D.J. (1992). "Show and tell" in the gymnasium revisited: Developmental differences in modeling and verbal rehearsal effects on motor skill learning and performance. *Research Quarterly for Exercise and Sport, 63,* 292-301.

Weiss, M.R., & Frazer, K.M. (1995). Initial, continued, and sustained motivation in adolescent female athletes: A season-long analysis. *Pediatric Exercise Science, 7,* 314-329.

Weiss, M.R., & Klint, K.A. (1987). "Show and tell" in the gymnasium: Developmental differences in modeling and verbal rehearsal effects on motor skill learning and performance. *Research Quarterly for Exercise and Sport, 58,* 234-241.

Weiss, M.R., & Smith, A.L. (1998, June). *Quality of friendships in youth sport: Measurement development and validation.* Paper presented at the annual conference for the North American Society for the Psychology of Sport and Physical Activity, St. Charles, IL.

Weiss, M.R., Smith, A.L., & Theeboom, M. (1996). "That's what friends are for": Children's and teenagers' perceptions of peer relationships in the sport domain. *Journal of Sport & Exercise Psychology, 18,* 347-379.

Weiss, M.R., & Troxel, R.K. (1986). Psychology of the injured athlete. *Athletic Training, 21* (2), 104-109, 154.

Werthner, P., & Orlick, T. (1986). Retirement experiences of successful Olympic athletes. *International Journal of Sport Psychology, 17,* 337-363.

Wheeler, G.C., Wall, S.R., Belcastro, A.N., Conger, P., & Cumming, D.C. (1986). Are anorexic tendencies prevalent in the habitual runner? *British Journal of Sports Medicine, 20* (2), 77-81.

Whelan, J.P., Meyers, A.W., & Elkin, T.D. (1996). In J.L. Van Raalte and B.W. Brewer (Eds.), *Exploring sport and exercise psychology* (pp. 431-447). Washington, DC: American Psychological Association.

White, A., & Coakley, J. (1986). *Making decisions: The response of young people in the Medway towns to the "Ever thought about sport?" campaign.* London: Sports Council.

White, K.D., Ashton, R., & Lewis, S. (1979). Learning a complex skill: Effects of mental practice, physical practice and imagery ability. *International Journal of Sport Psychology, 10,* 71-78.

White, R.W. (1959). Motivation reconsidered: The concept of competence. *Psychological Review, 66,* 297-333.

White, S.A., & Duda, J.L. (1994). The relationship of gender, level of sport involvement, and participation motivation to task and ego orientation. *International Journal of Sport Psychology, 25,* 4-18.

White, S.A., Duda, J.L., & Keller, M.R. (1993). *The relationship between goal orientation and perceived purposes of sport among youth sport participants.* Paper presented at the Association for the Advancement of Applied Sport Psychology Annual Conference, Montreal.

Whitley, B.E., Jr., & Frieze, I.H. (1985). Children's causal attributions for success and failure in achievement settings: A meta-analysis. *Journal of Educational Psychology, 77,* 608-616.

Whittemore, J.C. (1924). Influence of competition on performance: An experimental study. *Journal of Abnormal and Social Psychology, 19,* 236-253.

Wickens, C.D. (1984). *Engineering psychology and human performance.* Columbus, OH: Charles E. Merrill.

Widmeyer, W.N., & Birch, J.S. (1979). The relationship between aggression and performance outcomes in hockey. *Canadian Journal of Applied Sport Sciences, 4,* 91-94.

Widmeyer, W.N., Brawley, L.R., & Carron, A.V. (1985). *The measurement of cohesion in sport teams: The Group Environment Questionnaire.* London, Ontario: Sports Dynamics.

Widmeyer, W.N., Brawley, L.R., & Carron, A.V. (1990). Group size in sport. *Journal of Sport & Exercise Psychology, 12,* 177-190.

Widmeyer, W.N., Brawley, L.R., & Carron, A.V. (1992). Group dynamics in sport. In T.S. Horn (Ed.), *Advances in sport psychology.* Champaign, IL: Human Kinetics.

Widmeyer, W.N., Brawley, L.R., & Carron, A.V. (1993). Group cohesion in sport and exercise. In R.N. Singer, M. Murphy, & L.K. Tennant (Eds.), *Handbook of research on sport psychology* (pp. 672-692). New York: Macmillan.

Widmeyer, W.N., & Martens, R. (1978). When cohesion predicts performance outcome in sport. *Research Quarterly, 49,* 372-380.

Wiese, D.M., & Weiss, M.R. (1987). Psychological rehabilitation and physical injury: Implication for the sports medicine team. *The Sport Psychologist, 1,* 318-330.

Wiese-Bjornstal, D., & Weiss, M.R. (1992). Modeling effects on children's form kinematics, performance outcome, and cognitive recognition of a sport skill: An integrated perspective. *Research Quarterly for Exercise and Sport, 63,* 67-75.

Wiest, W.M., Porter, L.W., & Ghiselli, E.E. (1961). Relationships between individual proficiency and team performance and efficiency. *Journal of Applied Psychology, 45,* 435-440.

Wiggins, D.K. (1984). The history of sport psychology in North America. In J.M. Silva & R.S. Weinberg (Eds.), *Psychological foundations of sport* (pp.9-22). Champaign, IL: Human Kinetics.

Williams, J.M. (Ed.) (1986). *Applied sport psychology: Personal growth to peak performance.* Mountain View, CA: Mayfield.

Williams, J.M. (Ed.) (1998). *Applied sport psychology: Personal growth to peak performance* (3rd ed.). Mountain View, CA: Mayfield.

Williams, J.M., & Hacker, C.M. (1982). Causal relationships among cohesion, satisfaction and performance in women's intercollegiate field hockey teams. *Journal of Sport Psychology, 4,* 324-337.

Williams, J.M., & Harris, D.V. (1998). Relaxation and energizing techniques for regulation of arousal. In J.M. Williams (Ed.), *Applied sport psychology: Personal growth to peak performance* (3rd ed., pp. 219-236). Mountain View, CA: Mayfield.

Williams, J.M. & Leffingwell, T.R. (1996). Cognitive strategies in sport and exercise psychology. In J.L. Van Raalte & B.W. Brewer (Eds.), *Exploring sport and exercise psychology* (pp. 51-73). Washington, DC: American Psychological Association.

Williams, J.M., & Parkhouse, B.L. (1988). Social learning theory as a foundation for examining sex bias in evaluation of coaches. *Journal of Sport & Exercise Psychology, 10,* 322-333.

Williams, J.M., & Roepke, N. (1993). Psychology of injury and injury rehabilitation. In R.N. Singer, M. Murphey, & L.K. Tennant (Eds.), *Handbook of research on sport psychology* (pp. 815-839). New York: Macmillan.

Williams, J.M., & Widmeyer, W.N. (1991). The cohesion-performance outcome relationship in a coacting sport. *Journal of Sport & Exercise Psychology, 13,* 364-371.

Williams, K., Harkins, S., & Latane, B. (1981). Identifiability and social loafing: Two cheering experiments. *Journal of Personality and Social Psychology, 40,* 303-311.

Williams, K.D., Nida, S.A., Baca, L.D., & Latane, B. (1989). Social loafing and swimming: Effects of identifiability on individual and relay performance for intercollegiate swimmers. *Basic and Applied Sport Psychology, 10,* 73-81.

Williams, L. (1994a). Goal orientations and athletes' preferences for competence information sources. *Journal of Sport & Exercise Psychology, 16,* 416-430.

Williams, L. (1994b). *The role of perceived competence in the motivation of physical activity.* Paper presented at the National Conference of the Association for the Advancement of Applied Sport Psychology, Tahoe, NV.

Williams, L. (1998). Contextual influences and goal perspectives among female youth sport participants. *Research Quarterly for Exercise and Sport, 69,* 47-57.

Williams, L., & Gill, D. (1995). The role of perceived competence in the motivation of physical activity. *Journal of Sport & Exercise Psychology, 17,* 363-378.

Williamson, K.M., & Georgiadis, N. (1992). Teaching an inner-city after-school program. *Journal of Physical Education, Recreation, and Dance, 63,* 14-18.

Willis, J.D., & Campbell, L.F. (1992). *Exercise psychology.* Champaign, IL: Human Kinetics.

Wilmore, J.H. (1968). Influence of motivation on physical work capacity and performance. *Journal of Applied Physiology, 24,* 459-463.

Witkin, H.A. (1973). *Field dependence-interdependence and psychological differentiation: A bibliography through 1972 with index.* Princeton, NJ: Educational Testing Service.

Wolpe, J. (1958). *Psychotherapy by reciprocal inhibition.* Stanford, CA: Stanford University Press.

Wolpe, J. (1961). The systematic desensitization treatment of neurosis. *Journal of Nervous and Mental Disease, 132,* 189-203.

Wood, R.E., Mento, A.J., & Locke, E.A. (1987). Task complexity as a moderator of goal effects: A meta-analysis. *Journal of Applied Psychology, 72,* 416-425.

Worell, J., & Remer, P. (1992). *Feminist perspectives in therapy: An empowerment model for women.* Chichester, England: Wiley.

Wren, C.S. (1991, Jan. 14). 40 killed and 50 injured as fans riot at a South African soccer match. *New York Times,* p. A3.

Wulf, S. (1993, August 16). Basebrawl: Nolan Ryan's pummeling of Robin Ventura epitomizes a season marred by bench-clearing incidents. *Sports Illustrated, 79,* 12-17.

Wylie, R. (1979). *The self-concept, Volume 2: Theory and research on selected topics.* Lincoln, NE: University of Nebraska.

Yates, A., Leehey, K., & Shisslak, C.M. (1983). Running—an analogue of anorexia. *New England Journal of Medicine, 308,* 251-255.

Yerkes, R.M., & Dodson, J.D. (1908). The relation of strength of stimulus to rapidity of habit formation. *Journal of Comparative and Neurological Psychology, 18,* 459-482.

Young, M.L. (1985). Estimation of fitness and physical ability, physical performance, and self-concept among adolescent females. *Journal of Sports Medicine and Physical Fitness, 25,* 144-150.

Yukelson, D. (1997). Principles of effective team building intervention in sport: A direct services approach at Penn State University. *Journal of Applied Sport Psychology, 9,* 73-96.

Yukelson, D., Weinberg, R., & Jackson, A. (1984). A multidimensional sport cohesion instrument for intercollegiate basketball teams. *Journal of Sport Psychology, 6,* 103-117.

Zaichkowsky, L., & Perna, F. (1996). In J.L. Van Raalte and B.W. Brewer (Eds.), *Exploring sport and exercise psychology* (pp. 395-411). Washington, DC: American Psychological Association.

Zajonc, R.B. (1965). Social facilitation. *Science, 149,* 269-274.

Zander, A. (1971). *Motives and goals in groups.* New York: Academic Press.

Zarbatany, L., Ghesquiere, K., & Mohr, K. (1992). A context perspective on early adolescents' friendship expectations. *Journal of Early Adolescence, 12,* 111-126.

Ziegler, S.G. (1978). An overview of anxiety management strategies in sport. In W.F. Straub (Ed.), *Sport psychology: An analysis of athlete behavior* (pp. 257-264). Ithaca, NY: Mouvement.

Zillmann, D., Bryant, J., & Sapolsky, B.S. (1989). Enjoyment from sport spectatorship. In J.H. Goldstein (Ed.), *Sports, games, and play: Social and psychological viewpoints* (2nd ed., pp. 241-278). Hillsdale, NJ: Erlbaum.

Zillmann, D., Johnson, R.C., & Day, K.D. (1974). Provoked and unprovoked aggressiveness in athletes. *Journal of Research in Personality, 8,* 139-152.

Zillmann, D., Katcher, A.H., & Milavsky, B. (1972). Excitation transfer from physical exercise to subsequent aggressive behavior. *Journal of Experimental Social Psychology, 8,* 247-259.

Zillmann, D. & Paulus, P.B. (1993). Spectators: Reactions to sports events and effects on athletic performance. In R.N. Singer, M. Murphey & L.K. Tennant (Eds.), *Handbook of research on sport psychology* (pp. 600-619). New York: Macmillan.

Zimmerman, R.S., & Conner, C. (1989). Health promotion in context: The effects of significant others on health behavior change. *Health Education Quarterly, 16,* 57-75.

Zinsser, N., Bunker, L., & Williams, J.M. (1998). Cognitive techniques for building confidence and enhancing performance. In J.M. Williams (Ed.), *Applied sport psychology: Personal growth to peak performance* (3rd ed., pp. 270-295). Mountain View, CA: Mayfield.

Zuckerman, M. (1994). *Behavioral expressions and biosocial bases of sensation seeking.* New York: Cambridge University Press.

Zuckerman, M. (1979). *Sensation-seeking: Beyond the optimal level of arousal.* Hillsdale, NJ: Erlbaum.

*Note:* The italicized *f* and *t* following page numbers refer to figures and tables, respectively.

Diane L. Gill is a professor and former head of the Department of Exercise and Sport Science at the University of North Carolina, Greensboro. She was editor of the *Journal of Sport and Exercise Psychology,* and serves on the editorial boards of several sport and exercise psychology publications. She was president of the North American Society for the Psychology of Sport and Physical Activity (NASPSPA), is a charter member and fellow of the Association for the Advancement of Applied Sport Psychology (AAASP), and is current president of Division 47 (Exercise and Sport) of the American Psychological Association (APA). Her research interests focus on physical activity and psychological well-being across the lifespan, with an emphasis in social psychology.

# Other Books From Human Kinetics

## FOUNDATIONS OF SPORT AND EXERCISE PSYCHOLOGY
*(Second Edition)*

Robert S. Weinberg, PhD, and Daniel Gould, PhD
1999 • Hardback • 560 pp • ISBN 0-88011-824-5
$52.00 ($77.95 Canadian)

The first edition of *Foundations of Sport and Exercise Psychology* set a new standard for introductory textbooks. This new edition builds on that success and raises the standard to a new level. Comprehensive, understandable, and now completely updated, this engaging book captures superbly the intriguing world of sport and exercise psychology. It not only explains the basic concepts and principles in the field, but it also shows how they can be applied to counseling, teaching, coaching, sports medicine, and fitness instruction.

## SPORT HYPNOSIS

Donald R. Liggett
2000 • Paperback • 208 pp • ISBN 0-7360-0214-6
$17.95 ($26.95 Canadian) T

Harness the power of your own mind! Hypnosis can help you sharpen your mental focus, relax your body, visualize success, stimulate healing, and control your emotions during training or when facing important competitions. The positive effects are similar to what sport psychologists, coaches, and athletes refer to when they talk about "getting in the zone." In this state of mental functioning you channel attention and energies fully toward the task at hand. *Sport Hypnosis* is a guide to that special psychological realm and the higher performance athletes aspire to.

## LEARNING EXPERIENCES IN SPORT PSYCHOLOGY
*(Second Edition)*

Glyn C. Roberts, PhD, Kevin S. Spink, PhD, and Cynthia Pemberton, PhD
1999 • Spiral • 200 pp • ISBN 0-88011-932-2
$25.00 ($37.50 Canadian)

The only learning experience book in sport psychology is now completely updated! *Learning Experiences in Sport Psychology* (Second Edition) covers all substantive areas of sport psychology. The book is divided into three parts. **Part I**, Research Methods Experiences, covers the major concepts of conducting research. **Part II**, Understanding Sport Psychological Phenomena, presents the major psychological processes examined in sport psychology. **Part III**, Applying Sport Psychological Phenomena, introduces students to psychological skills and coaching strategies used to deal with stress or optimize performance in the sport setting.

To request more information or to order, U.S. customers call 1-800-747-4457,
e-mail us at **humank@hkusa.com**, or visit our Web site at **www.humankinetics.com**.
Persons outside the U.S. can contact us via our Web site or use the appropriate telephone number,
postal address, or e-mail address shown in the front of this book.

**Human Kinetics**
The Information Leader
in Physical Activity